Erasmus of Europe

The Prince of Humanists
1501–1536

*   *

Frontispiece. Portrait of Erasmus in 1523 by Hans Holbein the Younger, now in The Louvre, Paris.

Erasmus of Europe

The Prince of Humanists
1501–1536

* *

R. J. Schoeck

EDINBURGH UNIVERSITY PRESS

Uxori dilectissimae
decennis laboris consorti patientissimae

© R. J. Schoeck, 1993

Edinburgh University Press Ltd
22 George Square, Edinburgh

Typeset in Linotron Garamond 3
by Koinonia Ltd., Bury, and
printed in Great Britain
by The Alden Press Ltd, Oxford,
and bound by Hunter & Foulis Ltd,
Edinburgh

A CIP record for this book is available from
the British Library

ISBN 0 7486 0384 0

Contents

Preface

In the first volume of this biography we followed Erasmus of Rotterdam from his earliest years in Holland to his maturer years in Paris; and we witnessed the publication in 1500 of his first book, *Adagiorum Collectanea*. That little book of 152 pages may not now seem like a great achievement for an ambitious humanistic scholar of thirty-three, but a good deal of growth can be marked as we moved from the early letters and poems to this stage of his development.[1] Further, while there is some Greek among the 818 adages of the 1500 *Collectanea* it is fundamentally a work of Latin scholarship, drawing from the poets of the Latin canon, dramatists and a range of prose writers. Among the Fathers of the Church use was made especially of Jerome and Augustine. And we found that Erasmus also drew from such 'moderns' as Politian, Hermolaus Barbarus, and Filelfo. Except for a few Romans who were omitted or slighted, perhaps simply because they did not readily yield up adages for Erasmus' net – Ovid and Lucretius notably – Erasmus made use of the major authors of the renaissance canon, and he had established his remarkable familiarity with their texts. That range of authors will be extended much more widely, especially after 1508, to include more Greek writers. Along with Erasmus' rapidly developing style, everywhere remarked upon and everywhere imitated (but rarely with complete success) for its great ease and grace, the 1500 *Collectanea* indeed marked Erasmus' growth as a humanist.

By this time Erasmus was no longer primarily Dutch, and from time to time he referred to himself as German. At Paris he had belonged to the German nation of students, and his world was rapidly widening to include the Rhineland and, quite soon, Switzerland and Italy. He was becoming, in fact, *homo Europaeus*,[2] and very much a cosmopolitan. His home after 1500 would be where his books were, and his friends were no further away than a letter; and the time needed for letters to reach a correspondent in one of the major cities of western Europe could be little more than it is today. Another change can be marked: Erasmus did not want to continue as a teacher of rhetoric (as he had been in Paris from 1496 to 1500), but he was not yet able to know security without patrons, whom he had to seek out and solicit, even beg from. Hence his years of teaching at Cambridge a few years into the new century. But once finished there, he never again committed himself to university, patron, or prince: never before had a man of letters known such independence, such liberty of study, expression and writing.

Above all, Erasmus was a humanist, and he had well-nigh mastered all the tools and arts: first, grammar, rhetoric, and poetics, together with a mastery of the Latin language and style; then Greek, a developing theory of textual criticism and an unrivalled knowledge of the classical world.

If the publication of the *Adagiorum Collectanea* in 1500 marked his maturing as a humanist, the publication in 1503 of his *Enchiridion* would mark his maturing as a Christian humanist and establish his seriousness of purpose as a theologian.

Then the publication of the far more ambitious *Adagiorum Chiliades* in 1508 marked the final maturity of scholarship and the achievement of his unique style. Next, 1516 – by virtue of his New Testament, his Jerome, and his *Querela Pacis* – was an *annus mirabilis*; and throughout Europe he was now recognised as the prince of humanists.

After 1517 Erasmus was plunged into more and more controversy, not only with the Reformers but also with hypercritical Roman Catholic theologians, to justify his New Testament scholarship, to explain his ecclesiological position, to justify his editorial method; and he responded whenever he felt it necessary to correct false accusations against himself or misunderstandings of humanism. All too much energy was given in his remaining years to these polemical writings, yet account must be given of them in this biography, for they were a part of him.

But the scholarship continued in a remarkable flow, not only the ongoing work (revising, correcting until his final months), but also continuing revisions of and additions to the *Adagia* and *Colloquia*, editions of classical and patristic authors, and other educational and literary works.

The leitmotif of Volume 1 was the maturing of a renaissance humanist and the discovery of a vocation as an independent scholar; that of Volume 2 is his unique achievement as a humanist, his fame, his becoming (to borrow the phrase from Craig R. Thompson) a revolution in himself (*Colloquies*, xiii), though he had never been a revolutionary.

Thus there are all of these themes to identify and to view in their contexts, tracing their continuing development after 1500. The centrality of rhetoric in his educational programme, and for himself as a writer, is one striking emphasis. Another is piety, and theology (and no one schooled by the Brethren of the Common Life with its indebtedness to *The Imitation of Christ* would identify the two). Before 1500 Erasmus does not write much of piety, except for elements in the *De Contemptu Mundi*; he does so after that date, as we shall see in this volume – despite the criticisms of men like Lefèvre in 1515, or Luther after that (or of modern scholars like Hyma who write *de parti pris*) to the effect that Erasmus was not interested in piety – or even, unfairly and inaccurately, that he was a failure as a priest, a faulty judgment still being repeated as late as 1988.

For centuries the religion of Erasmus was not understood. To Reformers he was one who could not take the final step and leave the Rome of which he was critical; to Roman Catholics he was one who was almost a fifth columnist in his failure to condemn all Reformers outright. Even today, there is still widespread failure to understand what it was that Erasmus was trying to do; and I cite the 1988 volume in *CWE* in which it is recognised that Erasmus' enterprise was profoundly Christian, and yet the editor speaks of 'Erasmus' own defection from the monastery of Steyn' and asserts, without qualification, that 'he was a failed monk' (*CWE* 66:xxix). The first statement is hardly accurate, for 'defection' implies leaving without consent or permission, desertion even. In fact Erasmus was careful to observe his proper relationship of obedience to the prior of Steyn until 1506, when he obtained a partial dispensation; the later dispensation of 1517 (see appendix C) removed any question of the legality or licitness of Erasmus' way of life. The second statement is only partly correct: he did discover that he lacked a vocation for monasticism, at least in the form of the monastery of Steyn. But what needs to be said is that Erasmus nonetheless believed that he had a calling to be a scholar, a humanist, and a writer while still remaining an Augustinian canon and a priest; and that for the remaining decades of his life (after his first dispensation) he lived up to that vocation which his own conscience had forged for him. At this point one might quote from an unexpected source, namely Schleiermacher, on the sense of vocation that I am urging we recognise in Erasmus:

> The virtuosity (or special calling) of a person is at the same time the melody of the person's life, and it remains a simple, meager series of notes unless religion, with its endlessly rich variety, accompanies it with all notes and raises the simple song to a full-voiced, glorious harmony.[3]

So we may, indeed we must, speak of the profoundly Christian melody of Erasmus, and we shall come to recognise and still more to accept the deep spirituality that was at the core of that melody.

In addition to Valla, whose influence upon Erasmus began in the 1480s and continued with the engendering of a life-commitment to edit and translate the New Testament, there was after 1499 the powerful impact of John Colet; and we may well reflect upon the observation of Dominic Baker-Smith that Colet had a 'radical influence on Erasmus and More'.[4] If we understand this to mean 'arising from or going to a root or source', then Colet did indeed have this kind of radical influence, and the drive *ad fontes* which Erasmus had acquired from Valla and other Italian humanists in the areas of classical studies (the *studia humanitatis*) was now applied to the study of the Bible with profound results. Especially in his scriptural studies Erasmus more and more felt the need to go to the roots of the Biblical texts, and thus he set about learning Greek in order to go further back, and deeper, than the Vulgate. But if 'radical' is taken to mean 'favouring or effecting extreme or revolutionary changes', then, no: this political sense was not Colet's main concern or interest, and Erasmus was never a revolutionary. He was not Thomas Paine. To the influence of Colet after 1499 will be joined that of Vitrier after 1501: two holy and learned men, who excited Erasmus, encouraged and counselled him. His strength of purpose after 1500 owes much to Colet and Vitrier. From an early date Erasmus was a disciple of Valla, and his early letters, as we have seen in Volume 1, defended Valla as a model of learning. With the discovery of Valla's manuscript at the Abbaye du Parc, the *Annotations on the New Testament*, Valla gave Erasmus a methodology for his commentaries on the New Testament. After years of study, the flowering of his Scriptural scholarship would come in Erasmus' commentaries, editing and paraphrases of the New Testament after 1516 and continuing until 1535: truly a lifework.

Erasmus' growing recognition of the need for Greek in his New Testament work is significant for its opening a door into a wider world of literature and thought, as well as for its role in the study of the texts of the New Testament. Still more, there was much in the Greek tradition of the Catholic Church that had been lost to the West for centuries, and Erasmus' role in rediscovering the Greek tradition and attempting to restore its part in the life of the whole Church is a vital one.

The reader will discover a gallery of other men and women of the Renaissance and Reformation: high-ranking ecclesiastics and worldly monarchs side by side in Erasmus' world with humanists who are no longer (for some once were) household names. *Contempo-raries of Erasmus* identifies the more than 1900 people, mentioned in the correspondence and works of Erasmus, who died after 1450; his was a world rich with friends and acquaintances. The index of names will indicate points at which these figures entered into the narrative of Erasmus' life and recross different paths, and further information will be found by pursuing footnotes.

Finally, there is also the flowering of Erasmian irony, begun in the pre-1500 years, as we have seen, but nurtured by the reading of Lucian after 1500 and by his collaboration with Thomas More in the translating of Lucian. The irony that develops is not simply a rhe-torical tool, but becomes a part of a moral and aesthetic vision of man. Thus in the *Praise of Folly* (written 1509, published 1511 and revised in 1514) Erasmus is ready for and capable of rising to a Pauline ecstasy. After the *Praise of Folly* there will come the *Collo-quies*, which began unremarkably as rhetorical formulae and sud-denly, steadily, matured into a unique form, original in its develop-ment of the quattrocento dialogue he had inherited, and distinctive in its urbane and ironic mode.

Much lay ahead of Erasmus as he began the new century – and was, in Acton's words, ready to face prospects of incalculable change – and we shall study his manifold and prodigious work on the Bible and the Church Fathers (editing, paraphrasing, translating from Greek to Latin), his own exploration of literary genres, and his pouring of creative energies into the later *Adages* and *Colloquies*. Increasingly after 1515 there was an immense amount of time and effort spent on his controversial writings, first against Catholic crit-ics and then against the Protestant Reformers: defending, explaining and correcting, justifying. And always the outpouring of letters to his correspondents everywhere in Europe: after July 1514 the in-creasing flow of letters fills ten of the eleven volumes in Allen's magnificent edition. The range and reach of the letters increases:

> Alongside the running comment on personal affairs which still
> continues, the letters to a far greater degree than hitherto con-
> tain illuminating comments, sometimes developed into full-
> scale essays on classical, biblical, and patristic scholarship, on
> contemporary literary criticism, on the reform of education and
> theology through a combination of *bonae litterae* and the
> *philosophia Christi*, on the horrors of war, and on all the problems
> raised by the Lutheran Reformation. At a time when there were
> no learned journals in which scholars could have their articles
> published, letters, whether intended to be printed or merely to
> be circulated in manuscript, served much the same purpose. It

was to a large extent through his correspondence with scholars, many of whom he had never met, that Erasmus gave unity and a common purpose to the movement of Christian humanism in the years before the decisive emergence of Martin Luther.[5]

Thus letters continue to be a vital part of the presentation of Erasmus' activities and thought throughout Volume 2 as in Volume 1.

In this volume we shall study all these developments and themes, and we shall witness both the flowering of Erasmus into the Prince of Humanists and his heroic scholarship in the eye of the reformation hurricane. I have tried to write a biography of the life and achievements of Erasmus that will be both readable by that mythical general reader and at the same time satisfying to the rigorous demands of the scholarly reader. With the first reader in mind I have striven to keep the narrative to a readable length, and some footnotes are intended to enable the general reader to expand the horizons of a particular detail at hand or to serve to call attention to paths that go off from the narrative road at that point – whether the history of a university at which Erasmus is working, or the careers of individuals with whom he is connected. With the scholarly reader in mind I have presented the evidence for the interpretation offered at every step: citations from the letters carry references to both the English translation in *CWE* and the Latin text in Allen, and the evidence is presented for the many statements and conclusions I have written. I echo the hope of Donald M. Frame in his readable and scholarly biography of Montaigne: 'I hope I have not fallen between two stools, and that the nonspecialist may read this book with interest, the scholar with confidence.'

Yet there may well be the criticism that I quote too much, both from Erasmus and from secondary sources. As for the first charge, I have long taken to heart the wisdom of Gilson's dictum that before one can argue about what something says, one must know what it means: and to do that we must have the words of Erasmus himself on crucial issues – hence the practice of giving Erasmus in English translation but indicating at nearly every point the wording as well as the source of the original Latin. Further, I would hope that there will be the cumulative effect of hearing Erasmus' words, of becoming accustomed to his style, so that we can be in tune with his thinking.[6] We want to see him at work as a humanist.

As for the second charge, there are two answers to offer. First, I want to be scrupulous in giving credit to the scholars who have given us their perceptive thoughts, or whose way of perceiving Erasmus had become our accepted way; for that I have thought it desirable to quote their own words as much as possible. In the humanities we are playing the game of Penelope's web, always weaving by day and unweaving by night: that is, in forever trying to capture the essence of an idea, a book, a figure of thought, just a little more precisely, we unweave what has been done before; but we must allow for the critics who follow to insist on their unweaving. Over the years I have accumulated the writings and (I trust) wisdom of many Erasmian scholars, and I feel that I must acknowledge that wisdom even as I respect it, make use of it for understanding the complexities of Erasmus, and try to incorporate it into the structure being built that is called *Erasmus of Europe*.

It is one of the unique characteristics of the humanities (as distinguished from the sciences) that we students of the *studia humanitatis* work with all that has been written in the past. Each idea has its own history, each published work its unique historical milieu, and we do not – we cannot – read in a vacuum or with only the present in view. We must remind our students and our readers that the past is a part of our responsibility as well as the present, and this always includes the history of the question at hand. *Connexa sunt studia humanitatis*, as Salutati rightly declared; that connecting includes our predecessors as well as our contemporaries, and it does not ignore our students and readers. Therefore there are also twentieth-century writers who are brought into the sphere of discussion, for I feel strongly the validity of T. S. Eliot's dictum that 'the whole of the literature of Europe from Homer and within it the whole of the literature of [one's] own country has a simultaneous existence and composes a simultaneous order'.[7] Erasmus would have understood and largely agreed with this formulation, for at nearly every step of his own writing career he related the literature of the past to the present and insisted upon the process by which the 'ideal order' of existing monuments is modified.

In addition to the debts and many courtesies acknowledged in Volume 1, I wish to express thanks to the following: Bibliothèque humaniste (Sélestat), Bodleian Library (Oxford), Stadtsbibliothek and Universitäts Bibliothek (Trier), Universitäts Bibliothek (Göttingen), Staatsbibliothek (Berlin), Gemeentebibliotheek (Rotterdam), Rijks-universiteitbibliotheek (Gent), and the University of Kansas Library (Lawrence). I also wish to thank the Rev. Marcus A. Haworth, SJ for permission to quote from his translations of a number of the later letters of Erasmus.

Finally, two personal acknowledgments need to be repeated, and both with greater warmth than in Volume 1: to Dr Ian D. L. Clark, to whose editing this volume like the first owes much, reminding one of Erasmus' praise of his co-editor and friend Beatus Rhenanus as a friend after Pythagoras' own heart (on which see *Adag.* I.i.2); and again to my wife, Megan, who has made the Dutch humanist welcome far beyond the proverbial three days, and even beyond the Horatian nine years.

R. J. Schoeck
Trier-Lawrence

Notes

1) In the introduction to the forthcoming facsimile edition of the collection, edited by G. C. Kuiper and myself (and to be published by MRTS, Binghamton, New York), I have commented in much greater detail on the context, achievement and importance of this work.

2) The word *eruopaeus* is recorded in the *OCD*, which provides usages by Curtius Rufus and Cornelius Nepos.

3) Friedrich Schleiermacher, *Addresses 2* (q. by Jaroslav Pelikan, *The Melody of Theology* 1988, 167).

4) Made, but without fuller explanation, in *History Today* (August 1986) 5–13.

5) W. K. Ferguson, Introduction to Vol. 1 of *The Correspondence of Erasmus* [= *CWE*] (Toronto, 1974) xii.

6) The principle of quotation and citation at many points is analogous to that of citation in the *OED*, where one wishes to establish the earliest usage of a word in a particular signification or to indicate its currency by a quite recent citation. So too with the 'open questions' (*Quaestiones disputatae*) of scholarship: often one wishes to give credit for the original formulation or expression of an idea – which helps to establish the 'originality' of Erasmus – or one may wish to call attention to its currency or its problematics. I am mindful of the words of Mark Pattison in his *Memoirs*: 'A man who does not know what has been thought by those who have gone before him is sure to set an undue value upon his own ideas' (78; q. by Acton in his lecture on *The Study of History*, London, 1911, 80).

7) Eliot continues: 'the existing monuments form an ideal order among themselves, which is modified by the introduction of the new (the really new) work of art among them …' – 'Tradition and the Individual Talent' (1919), in *Selected Essays*, 3d ed. (London, 1951) 14–15. In a forthcoming essay on Charles Du Bos I shall discuss what I there call 'the Aesthetics of Quotation'.

List of Abbreviations

Allen	P.S. Allen et al., *Opus Epistolarum Des. Roterodami* (Oxford, 1906–58)
ARG	*Archiv für Reformationsgeschichte*
ASD	*Opera Desiderii Erasmi Roterodami* (Amsterdam, 1969–)
BHR	*Bibliothèque d'Humanisme et Renaissance*
BL	British Library (London)
BM	British Museum (London)
BN	Bibliothèque Nationale (Paris)
BR	*Contemporaries of Erasmus – A Biographical Register,* 3 vols, ed. P. Bietenholz et al. (Toronto, 1985–7)
CHLMP	*Cambridge History of Later Medieval Philosophy*, ed. N. Kretzmann et al. (Cambridge, 1982)
CHRP	*Cambridge History of Renaissance Philosophy*, ed. C.B. Schmitt (Cambridge, 1988)
COD	*Conciliorum Oecumenicorum Decreta*, 3rd ed., ed. G. Alberigo et al. (Bologna, 1973)
CWE	*Collected Works of Erasmus* (Toronto, 1974–)
DACL	*Dictionnnaire d'archéologie chrétienne et de liturgie,* ed. F. Cabrol and H. Leclerq (Paris, 1924 ff.)
DHGE	*Dictionnaire d'histoire et de géographie ecclésiastique*, ed. A. Baudrillart et al. (Paris, 1912 ff.)
DSAM	*Dictionnaire de spiritualité ascétique et mystique*, ed. M. Viller (Paris, 1932 ff.)
DTC	*Dictionnaire de théologie catholique,* ed. A. Vacant et al. (Paris, 1930 ff.)
EB	*Encyclopaedia Britannica*
EHR	*English Historical Review*
ELN	*English Language Notes* (Boulder, Colo.)
ERSYB	*Erasmus of Rotterdam Society Yearbook*
Hain	L. Hain, *Repertorium bibliographicum*, 4 vols (Stuttgart & Paris, 1826–38, rptd. 1903); with suppl. by W.A. Copinger, 3 vols (London, 1895–1902).
HumLov	*Humanistica Lovaniensia*
IANLS	International Association for Neo-Latin Studies
JHI	*Journal of the History of Ideas*
JWCI	*Journal of the Warburg and Courtauld Institutes*
LB	*Desiderii Erasmi Roterodami opera omnia*, ed. J. Leclerc (Leiden, 1703–6; rptd. 1961–2)

LThK	*Lexikon für Theologie und Kirche*, 2nd ed., ed. J. Höfer and K. Rahner (Freiburg, 1957)
MedStud	*Mediaeval Studies* (Toronto)
NCE	*New Catholic Encyclopedia*
OCD	*Oxford Classical Dictionary*
Opuscula	*Erasmi Opuscula*, ed. W.K. Ferguson (The Hague, 1933)
PL	*Patrologia Latina*, ed. J.P. Migne, 217 vols (1878–90)
Reedijk	C. Reedijk, ed., *Poems of Erasmus* (Leiden, 1956)
RenQ	*Renaissance Quarterly*
RHE	*Revue d'Histoire Ecclésiastique*
StPhil	*Studies in Philology*
StRen	*Studies in the Renaissance*
STC	A.V. Pollard and G.R. Redgrave, *A short-title catalogue of books printed in England ...* (1926)

Full bibliographical information may be found in the Bibliography.

List of Illustrations

I. Europe in the early sixteenth century.

II. The Low Countries in Erasmus' time.

18

Return from England: The Years in Flanders and Paris, 1501–1502

One who aspires to wisdom should therefore apply himself to
reading, learning, and *meditation.*

John of Salisbury, *Metalogicon,* lib. 1, c.24

All sacred scriptures should be read in the spirit in which they
were written ... If you desire to profit, read with humility,
simplicity, and faith, and have no concern to appear learned.

Thomas à Kempis, *The Imitation of Christ*, 1, 5

The winter of 1500–1501 may well have been one of the worst
periods in the life of the struggling Dutch humanist, for his money
had run out (as narrated in chapter 17), and his chances of patronage
were slim. Hoping to rebuild his shaky finances, Erasmus was ready
to turn away from the *merdas gallicas* of Paris, a biting phrase in a
letter (translated in *CWE* 1:193/13 as 'among French dunghills').
But this phrase occurs in a letter to his Paris jesting companion,
Fausto Andrelini (Epistle 103), and it is a private, not a public,
letter. Yet for a number of reasons, not least the health conditions in
the city, Erasmus did not want to remain in Paris, where he had
returned on 2 February 1500. However, his relationship with his
bishop Hendrik van Bergen was cooling (perhaps, as suggested in
Volume 1, owing to the reports of his enemy Standonck), and in any
event Hendrik accompanied archduke Philip the Handsome of Burgundy and Joanna of Spain on their journey to Spain in 1501.

Erasmus turned his eyes instead towards Flanders, where his
friend Jacob Batt was already helping him from his own personal
resources – and Erasmus kept pressing him for more – and there was
the continuing hope that Batt might intercede for him with Lady
Anne of Veere, a wealthy heiress in her own right. Erasmus tried all
possible sources for financial help, including the abbot of St Bertin,
Antoon van Bergen, brother of his bishop, to whom Erasmus had
written an account of a recent witchcraft trial in Orleans (chapter
17); and he had delicately asked another illegitimate son of Antoon

of Burgundy, Nicholas of Burgundy (who in 1498 had been made provost of St Peter's Church at Utrecht) for influence with Lady Anne, to whom the provost was closely related.

Finally then in this sequence of petitions for support, Erasmus wrote to 'The Most Noble Lady, Anna van Borssele, Princess of Veere' herself (Epistle 145) from Paris, on 27 January 1501. Cleverly Erasmus promised her that (properly supported) his praise of her would make her rank with the other Annas of ancient literature: Anna the sister of Dido; Hanna the wife of Elkanah and mother of Samuel; and lastly Anna the mother of the Blessed Virgin:

> And I would that now my pen too might find skill enough to make posterity aware how devout, how pure, how chaste your soul is, for then it would add you, a fourth Anna, to the former three; which will surely come to pass, if my poor talent should but prove equal to your goodness. (*CWE* 2:13/15–18; Allen 1, 342/12–15)

Throughout 1501 the letters to and from Erasmus are filled with the dreary business of requesting money, some in direct appeal, some more indirectly, as with the above letter to Anna Borssele. Indirect: yet there are some pointed hints in the letter: 'the little money that a scholar's leisure requires can easily be supplied from your wealth' (*CWE* 2:14/79–80). If not the full measure of money that would have taken him to Italy (which remained as distant a dream as the modern hope of winning a lottery), some money was provided for travel and an offer of support in Flanders. Yet Erasmus rather churlishly wrote to Batt in January (Epistle 146 is dated 27 January, the same date as Epistle 145 quoted above) that he 'never wrote anything so much against the grain as the nonsense – indeed the Gnathonisms [a kind of parasitical expression] – I have penned to the Lady, the provost, and the abbot.' (*CWE* 2:19/27–9; Allen 1, 347/25–27).

And the rest of this Epistle 146 is filled with details of the precarious state of his finances, beseeching Batt to get the Lady to give him a sum of two hundred francs and to 'send the rest of the gold pieces by some reliable messenger, and also, if I can prevail upon you, four or five gold pieces of your own, to save me from destitution meantime. You will get them back when the Lady's money arrives. See how my little hoard has melted away... ' (*CWE* 2:21/79–82; Allen 1, 348/70–3).

Erasmus' rosy hopes for patronage from Lady Anne of Veere continued until her remarriage. Her second marriage to Lodewijk van Montfoort (under whose influence she had already come in 1501 [*BR*], although Erasmus seems not to have known or accepted this) occurred in 1502, together with the death of his old friend Jacob

Batt at some date before 2 July 1502.[1] These two events together
ended Erasmus' long-cultivated hopes for patronage in Flanders, and
he therefore moved to Louvain (chapter 19). It had been Batt who
had introduced Erasmus to the Lady Anne and her court, and his
death was a keen personal loss for Erasmus as well as a blow to his
campaign for patronage.

These and other letters indicate how money worries plagued
Erasmus. His anxieties – the more galling because he could not
accept the ready solution of returning to his monastery at Steyn – can
be blamed, in large part, for much of his pettiness and worse during
these trying months; his otherwise inexcusable churlishness expressed over Lady Anne to Batt, and his charging Batt with timidity
in approaching her. Money worries were as much a plague in his soul
as the physical plague that was raging in Paris. Erasmus still lacked a
regular patron, now that the bishop of Cambrai had ceased whatever
support he had given earlier, and being unable or unwilling to call
upon his monastery for support.[2] This searching for patronage surely
explains much of the travelling that Erasmus did in 1500–02, travelling that has led some scholars and biographers to assert that
Erasmus was by nature nomadic. At least one trip out of Paris was
the result of fear of the plague and probably others too. Some of the
travelling, we would say, was job-related; but above all, if he wanted
to achieve independence away from his monastery he had no alterna-
tive: he had to win patronage. One must recognise, however, that
there were what Tracy has perceptively called 'the centrifugal tendencies of Erasmus' nature'[3] – tendencies which had pulled him away
from the monastery, and ambitions which led him into the service of
the bishop of Cambrai and from there to Paris, and now pulled him
again away from Paris.

It is a mark of his motivation and sense of vocation that despite
the searching for money and the need for patronage that he so
despised, Erasmus continued his studying and his scholarly writing.
There was, as we shall see, much reading, and the bringing together
of his notes on Cicero's *De Officiis* published in 1501. The preface to
this work is important for several reasons.[4] A friend for many years –
until their shared year of death, 1536 – Jacob de Voecht (Voogd) was
a young doctor of law at Orleans with whom Erasmus lodged during
the last three moths of 1500.[5] Epistle 152 at Paris (28 December
1501) is the preface for Erasmus' edition of Cicero's *De Officiis*, which
he had intended to dedicate to Adolph de Veere but decided not to
after patronage from that family failed to materialise. The 1501
edition of *De Officiis* was Erasmus' first annotated edition of a classical work – there were to be more of Cicero and many more of other

Latin and Greek authors – and in the prefatory letter to de Voecht Erasmus gives us an introduction to his critical method. He tells us that he aimed at a pocket-sized handbook, easy to be carried about, and he speaks of Cicero's rich work as 'this tiny dagger' (*CWE* 2:31/ 41; Allen 1, 357/33: '*hunc pugiunculum*' – a metaphor that anticipates the dagger image of the *Enchiridion* only two years later). As for the text of Cicero itself: 'I found a great many flaws, as one would expect in such a familiar work; one scribe will throw the order into confusion as he copies, while another will replace a word, which perhaps had eluded him, with an approximation. These flaws are of course not monstrosities, but still they are intolerable in such a great author. I have corrected all of them, partly by collating editions … partly by informed guesswork based on Cicero's style…' (*CWE* 2:31/ 31–8; Allen 1, 356–7/25–31). Here is a work which marks Erasmus' emergence as an editor of a classical text, no small matter for a young humanist. We shall return to the question of Erasmus as an editor of classical texts.

The record of his reading during this period is impressive, and in a later letter (Epistle 1347, ll. 351–3) Erasmus will speak of his constant application to study.

Reading is the English equivalent of the Latin *lectura, lectio* (which produced the modern English *lecture*, which is one kind of reading). We are here concerned with the first of the dictionary significations for the word: 'to examine and grasp the meaning of written or printed characters, words, or sentences', and not so much the second, 'to utter or render aloud'. Even in modern English we move quickly to a further signification: 'to study or make a study of', which is learning by the act of or by virtue of grasping the meaning of words. *Lecture* (from the Middle English, 'a reading') has come to mean the exposition of a subject before an audience or class.

In the medieval scheme of learning, the *lectio* was the centre-pin of the whole system, as the quotation of John of Salisbury (which is the epigraph to this chapter) indicates: 'one who aspires to wisdom should therefore apply himself to *reading, learning,* and *meditation*'. And *lectio* might consist of one or all of the following: a) the *lectio* or magistral reading of the master; b) the *lectio* or discipular reading of the pupil; and c) the *lectio* or personal reading of an individual done in private. Thus reading could mean either the activity of teaching and being taught, or it could refer to the occupation of studying written things by oneself.[6] For Erasmus there were the earlier kinds of *lectio* when he was still an adolescent, followed by the more directed kinds of *lectio* as a novice and canon at Steyn: he listened to readings, he attended directed readings, and he more and more was self-motivated in private reading especially of humanistic texts (see chapter 5). For Erasmus reading had come to be a vital part of his existence, and the fruits of reading are everywhere manifest in his writings, sometimes years after the act of reading and after the kind of learning and meditation that John of Salisbury advised. Still, we cannot speak with complete certainty: we do not know what his most private reading – works of spirituality, especially – may have been during this period. But much is clear.

Under whatever impulses (whether Colet's, Vitrier's, or others') the Dutch humanist deepened his study of Scripture, and during these two years he was working towards a commentary on the Pauline Epistles (Epistle 164, 1. 41–2): 'I have been carefully preparing an interpretation of him for some time,' Erasmus wrote to Johann Poppenruyter, a layman who has been identified with a Johann Poppenruyter who came from Nürnberg and had established a gun foundry at Mechlin before 1510; and this letter forms the introduction to the *Enchiridion* (1503), which Erasmus seems to have written at the earnest request of a pious lady known to both Batt and himself, who felt that her husband was in need of spiritual inspiration and guidance. This immersion in the whole body of Paul's letters provided more than 126 citations from Paul which have been noted in the *Enchiridion*.[7]

In addition to Paul, Erasmus continued his study of the Gospels and the Psalms, of course, and almost equally he continued his reading of Jerome, Ambrose, and Augustine (see chapter 5). While in Saint-Omer he borrowed from Vitrier his copy of the *Homilies* of Origen on Genesis, Exodus and the Song of Songs; and Tracy has particularised the assimilation of Origen and its significance.[8]

Confirming one's sense of Erasmus' continuing piety and his dynamic spirituality, we may note that at about this same time he wrote his brief *Prayer to Jesus* (*Precatio ad Jesum*), first printed in 1503 by Dirk Martens at Antwerp in the *Lucubratiunculae*[9] and reprinted more than a dozen times before his death. He had earlier written two *Prayers to the Virgin* (1499) for Anne of Veere; the *Prayer to Jesus*, written later, as Erasmus later noted (in 1523 to Botzheim, Allen 1, 20/21) was 'more to my own heart'. Less extravagant in language and rhetorical piety than the prayers addressed to the Virgin Mary, it calls upon Christ to redeem sinning mankind and for men to avail themselves of the sacraments. Perhaps Origen provided the inspiration for Erasmus' concept of the 'vital soul, glowing with Your holy breath, immortal, of aethereal seed, sculpted after Your image', by which man was capable of the vision of God (as Tracy has suggested, 87–8).

During this period Erasmus was intensifying his efforts to learn Greek; and in Greek he read Homer, Hesiod, Epictetus (in particular the *Enchiridion*), Euripides, and Isocrates.[10] He spoke of spending money first for Greek books and after that for clothes.[11] He had already used a number of Greek authors for the *Adagiorum* (Epistle 126), and he would widen his nets dramatically by 1508 for the greatly expanded *Adagia* (chapter 24). Plato he doubtless read in the Latin translation of Ficino, because, as Kristeller has pointed out,[12] there was no Greek edition of Plato until 1513. As Erasmus wrote to Willem Hermans in Epistle 172 from Louvain in September/October 1502, 'the study of Greek absorbs me completely, and I have not wholly wasted my efforts, for I have made such good progress that I am capable of expressing my meaning in Greek with reasonable proficiency and, what is more, extempore' (*CWE* 2:59/12–15; Allen 1, 381/9–12). We have already noted his writing of epigrams in Greek by 1502.

But he was reading and working with Latin authors as well. Before the writing of his own *Enchiridion* he had brought together his notes from his reading of Cicero, and the 1501 edition of Cicero's important *De Officiis* was his first annotated edition of a classical work. In the dedicatory letter (Epistle 152) that has already been noted, Erasmus explained his brief notes: 'being that, like little stars, they should conveniently illuminate each obscure passage' (*CWE* 2:30/25–6; Allen 1, 356/22–5). As well as abandoning his idea of dedicating the edition to Adolph of Veere, Erasmus' intention of dedicating the *De Conscribendis Epistolis* and *De Copia* to Adolph was likewise abandoned.[13] The dedication of editions and of his own works was an all-important instrument in gaining the support of patrons.

He read other Latin authors as well as Cicero, of course. His dedicatory letter to Mountjoy prefaced to the 1500 edition of *Adagiorum* speaks of Pliny, Terence, Plautus, Varro, Catullus, Horace, Martial, Ausonius, Aulus Gellius, and others. No less impressive is the number of Neo-Latin authors whom he had been reading, studying, and working with during this period: Valla always (see chapter 9), other grammarians, rhetoricians and poets. In spite of being in part a child of the *Devotio Moderna*, Erasmus shows considerable familiarity with some scholastics, notably St Thomas Aquinas – and how could he not, after his years at the University of Paris, that citadel of scholasticism? (chapter 11) – and it would have been surprising if he had not continued to pursue themes of interest in Ficino and Pico, so much admired by Colet and More (chapter 15).

Before settling in with Jacob Batt – into 'the welcoming arms of

Batt', as Erasmus wrote in Epistle 159 – Erasmus travelled about for
two months in the spring of 1501, when the plague had again
broken out in Paris. He seems to have gone directly to Holland and
visited friends at Steyn (perhaps staying in the monastery) and with
his old friend Willem Hermans at Haarlem. From there Erasmus
went down to Brussels to visit the bishop of Cambrai, and from there
to Antwerp, Veere, and Tournhem. In Epistle 154 dated from
Tournhem on 12 July 1501, Erasmus wrote to Hendrik van Bergen
– who had apparently reproached him with ingratitude (*CWE* 2:34/
4–5). It is noteworthy that Erasmus declared 'To this very day I have
not once said a mass without beseeching immortal God to repay you
with ample interest, since he alone can, for all that you have given
me' (*CWE* 2:34/22–4; Allen 1, 359/19–21) – for not only is this a
direct comment on Erasmus' proclaimed attitude towards his bishop,
but it is also invaluable in informing us that Erasmus was saying
mass with some regularity.[14] The letter closes with some information
concerning plans:

> I have stayed for more than a month with my brethren in
> Holland. They have decided that I ought to spend a year longer
> on my studies; they think it will be discreditable to themselves
> as well as to me if I return after all those years without acquir-
> ing any qualification at all. (*CWE* 2:35/49–52; Allen 1, 360/
> 45–47)

The important thing, it seems clear, is that Erasmus 'wished to
remind the bishop that he was not absent from his monastery without leave, and that the authorities at Steyn were willing to permit
him to continue his studies abroad' *CWE* 2:35n). Would Erasmus
not still be under the jurisdiction of the bishop of Cambrai? The
letter to the bishop is one of several – three that are extant – all
written on the same date, written somewhat hurriedly, doubtless to
catch a messenger leaving that day.

By mid-July Erasmus was in Saint-Omer at St Bertin's Abbey
(only a dozen miles from Tournhem), still keeping one eye on the
remote possibility that the Lady Anne might yet provide some help.
But, he writes to another friend, 'for the present your Erasmus is
living on his own resources and clothing himself in his own feathers'
(*CWE* 2:40/45–6; Allen 1, 363/38). We are struck by the fact that
Erasmus has had to leave his things with different friends: with Batt
(Epistle 163), with Nikolaas Bensrott (Epistle 160), and doubtless
others – a clear sign of his uncertain status. He could not yet claim to
be master of his own fortunes. Small wonder that he writes to de
Voecht of not having made up his mind, 'still waiting in suspense,
with the intention of setting my course whichever way a fair wind

favours me' (Epistle 159, *CWE* 2:45/72–3; Allen 1, 368/65–6). Yet
he also writes that he is spending nearly all his time on studies,
especially Greek.

Here we may take account of the death of Robert Gaguin on 22
May 1501. Gaguin, who at the end of his life was 'cruellement
infirme' (thus Renaudet, 402), had been a valued friend in the
unfriendly milieu of Paris; his death marked the end of the early
Paris humanism and also of a formative period in Erasmus' life.

In midsummer 1501 Erasmus met Jean Vitrier, the warden of the
Franciscan convent at Saint-Omer. Although at first in his relations
with the warden and the abbot Erasmus suspected the motives of the
warden and their first relations were difficult (Epistle 163), a friendship quickly struck fire. Many years later Erasmus joined Vitrier
together with Colet in a loving remembrance: two pious and learned
men who had much in common and who deepened his love for St
Paul (Epistle 1211, which is a 'parallel life' of Colet and Vitrier). In
the final months of his life Erasmus in his *Ecclesiastes* paid tribute to
Vitrier as a model preacher and as one who disregarded the *pro forma*
observance of Church ceremonies (*LB* V, 987C; see also Allen,
Epistle 1211, IV, 509/62n). It is to Vitrier that we must pay tribute
for the quickening of Erasmus' interest in Origen as theologian, and
(borrowing books from Vitrier) Erasmus turned with great
enthusiasm to Origen's commentary on the Epistle to the Romans as
well as to his homilies.

Vitrier followed Colet as a shaping influence upon Erasmus; he
seems in fact to have been even more of an inspiration. That the 1503
Enchiridion is filled with both direct citations of and indirect allusions to Origen is a mark of Vitrier's influence; and one may indeed
see the *Enchiridion* as a flowering of the powerful stirring by Vitrier
of the inner life of Erasmus, so troubled during these difficult
months. Perhaps too the example of Vitrier's battles for the purity of
faith and for a religion founded on the Gospels (as Godin puts it in
BR) served Erasmus as a consolation and cure in his many battles
with scholastic theologians and others too literal of mind and too
small of spirit.[15]

Thus when twenty years later he was asked by his dear friend
Justus Jonas for a life of Colet, Erasmus in Epistle 1211 from
Anderlecht in 1521 wrote a warm recollection of Vitrier's character
and wisdom:

> He was about forty-four when I first knew him, and at once he
> conceived an affection for me, though a man much unlike
> himself. His opinion carried very great weight with those whose
> approval was worth having, and he was most acceptable to

many in high place; he was tall and well built [the same adjectives used to describe Colet], gifted by nature, and with such high standards that nothing could be more civilised. The niceties of Scotist philosophy he had imbibed as a boy, and neither wholly rejected them (for there were clever things in it, he thought, though expressed in inelegant words) nor again did he set much store by them. In any case, once he had the good fortune to sample Ambrose and Cyprian and Jerome, he thought wondrous little of the scholastics compared with them. In sacred studies he admired no one more than Origen; and when I said, not very seriously, that I wondered he could enjoy reading a heretic, he retorted in the most lively way, 'there can be no doubt that the Holy Spirit dwelt in a heart that produced so many books with such learning and such fire' ... The Holy Scriptures, and especially the Pauline Epistles, he had got by heart, and no one knew his own fingers and toes [cf. *Adagia* II, iv, 91] better than he knew every word of Paul his master ... He was absorbed by a kind of incredible passion for bringing men to the true philosophy of Christ [*ad synceram Christi philosophiam*] and from labours of this sort he hoped to win the glory of martyrdom. (*CWE* 8:226/19 ff., 227/49 ff., 228/77 ff.; Allen IV, 508/16 ff., 44–5, 509/71–3)

And then Erasmus tells a revealing little story about his own habits and Vitrier's reasonableness about fasting (for he attached little importance to ceremonies, or to superstition):

I myself was staying at the time [winter 1500–01], with Antoon van Bergen, the abbot of St Bertin's where no one ever dined till after midday, and my stomach could not endure to go so long without food – and it was Lent – especially as I was working very hard; so I used before dinner to fortify my digestion with a small hot drink to enable it to hold out till dinnertime. On this point I consulted with him to know if I was breaking the rules; and after looking round for his companion, who at the time was a layman, for fear he might be shocked, he said: 'On the contrary, you would be doing wrong if you did not do this, and if through the need for some quite unimportant food you had to break off your sacred studies and damage your health' ... (*CWE* 8:230/163–172; Allen IV, 511/149–157)

It is clear not only that Erasmus had the highest respect and admiration for Vitrier, but also that Vitrier had recognised the importance of Erasmus' studies and indeed had accepted and encouraged Erasmus' sense of vocation.

The impact of Vitrier upon Erasmus at this critical time was very great, and the influence lasted until the end of the Dutch humanist's life. Vitrier's advice on ceremony bore fruit in the *Enchiridion*, where Erasmus talks of the greater freedom of men to fulfil the spirit of Christ's law instead of trying to live under a heavy burden of ceremonies that impeded their life of grace.[16] In analysing the influence of that powerful personality of Vitrier, a learned and mystical Franciscan,[17] one perceives the strength of Erasmus' own ever-growing spirituality; and one recognises how much the *Enchiridion* (a key work in this period of Erasmus' life) 'concentrated on the interior dimension of *libertas*, the freedom of a monk (like Jean Voirier [Vitrier]) who did not feel slavishly bound to the rules but observed them nonetheless, lest he scandalise the weaker brethren'.[18]

May one not admire – indeed, must one not admire – the Dutch humanist for his courage in pursuing his own sense of vocation during years of discouragement and deeply troubling worries over money, and may we not also remark on his clarity of vision in being able to write a work like the *Enchiridion* at such a time?[19]

Notes

1) In Ep. 170 to de Voecht (which is dated Saint-Omer, 2 July) we learn of Batt's death. Erasmus wrote feelingly, 'Now Batt is dead, who can doubt that Erasmus has died as well?' (*CWE* 2:58/13). In Ep. 172 to Willem Hermans (written later from Louvain, and questioningly dated by Allen, 1, 381), Erasmus wrote that 'Death – or poison rather – has taken Batt' (*CWE* 2:59/4); but no reason or evidence is given for this surprising statement. Especially during the period from December 1500 to March 1501, Batt had been 'undoubtedly one of Erasmus' most faithful friends' (*BR*). Epp. 95 & 101 indicate that there had been discussion of their living together at Louvain, but these plans were never realised. For Batt's *ex libris* Erasmus had composed a short verse (printed in the *Adagia Epigrammata* of 1506/7, Reedijk, 61); and on his death he composed two epitaphs, the first in Greek (Reedijk, 62–3).

2) While in Spain early in 1502, Hendrik van Bergen quarrelled with François de Busleyden (a brother of Erasmus' later friend Jerome de Busleyden, and after 1490 a councillor of Philip the Handsome and chancellor of Flanders), who in 1501 had just been made a cardinal by pope Alexander VI. Sent home in disgrace, Hendrik died on 7 October 1502, shortly after his return to Cambrai (*BR*). Erasmus composed four epitaphs for him, one in Greek is now missing (see Reedijk, 64–6). In Ep. 178 to Willem Hermans from Louvain on 27 September 1503, Erasmus wrote, 'I have written three Latin epitaphs, and one Greek one, in honour of the bishop of Cambrai; for which they sent me only six florins, so as to keep up in death the character he had in life!' (*CWE* 2:77/54–6; Allen 1, 395/49–51).

3) Tracy spoke in the context of Erasmus' defence to Colet: 'Colet belongs with Nicholas Werner and Robert Gaguin in the sequence of sober and

thoughtful men who showed some understanding for the centrifugal tendencies of Erasmus' nature but at the same time reminded him of his promises
about theology' (*Erasmus*, 84). There can be no question of denying the fact
that Erasmus travelled much, but it must be recognised that a number of
reasons were involved. Even the adjective *centrifugal* still connotes a temporal
centre or axis away from which there is motion: may we not say that for
Erasmus there was the central axis of his humanistic vocation around which
his movements, and everything else, turned? And that there was never any
uncertainty about the end towards which this system was moving, and that
this end was God.

4) This preface was omitted from the edition published by Philippi in 1501
(perhaps, as Allen suggests, it was overlooked because of Erasmus' hurried
departure from Paris in May of 1501, after the edition itself had gone to the
printer). It was first printed in a 1520 edition published by Froben (Allen 1,
355), together with a new preface addressed to de Voecht in Sept. 1519.

5) From 1506 to 1536 de Voecht lived as a pensionary in Antwerp, where
he was a friend of Pieter Gillis; as a result of a mission to London in 1509 he
met Thomas More (*BR*). Early in the prefatory letter Erasmus had spoken of
his friendship with de Voecht and expressed the expectation that it would
last for life (*CWE* 2:30/10); and he decided to bind such good friends
together by something imperishable. 'Now, so far as human affairs are concerned, clearly literature is permanent if anything is' (*CWE* 2:30/15–16;
Allen 1, 356/11–12: 'in rebus autem humanis aut nihil omnino durabile, aut
profecto literae sunt').

6) I have followed M.-D. Chenu in this division of reading (as elsewhere
in medieval studies in philosophy and theology): see his *Towards Understanding St Thomas*, trans. by A.M. Landry & D. Hughes (Chicago, 1964) 81 & n.
While the old monastic term *lectio* 'as found in the 48th chapter of the Rule
of Saint Benedict, thus came to new life in a cultural and academic meaning'
(Chenu writes), the older monastic signification continued in the monasteries, where Erasmus without doubt would have encountered it. In the medieval scheme, lectio prepared for the emendatio, enerratio, and judicium (all
elements in interpretation); and students and teachers added annotations
between the lines (glossa interlinearis) or in the margins (glossa marginalis):
these tell us much of the kind and degree of concentration of the reading. At
the University of Paris in the 13th c. a required text might be read cursorily
(*cursorie*), that is rapidly, or it might be read in the ordinary way *ordinarie*),
with an effort to discover the meaning beyond the letter of the text (Chenu,
84 & n.). The system described by Chenu as the norm in the 13th c. was still
operative in the early 16th century. As a devoted student of Quintilian,
Erasmus would have been familiar as well with Book 1, ch. viii of the
Institutio Oratoria, which deals with reading as part of the training of an orator
and emphasises reading aloud.

7) See Himelick ed., 1963. Plato is the only classical author cited with
marked frequency in the *Enchiridion*. It would have been read in Ficino's
translation, and six dialogues are quoted (Tracy, 85 n. 16).

8) *Erasmus*, 86 & n. On the impact of Origen, see André Godin in *BR* and,
far more fully and persuasively, *Erasme lecteur d'Origène* (Geneva, 1982). In *BR*
Godin has noted references much later in the *Ecclesiastes* to Vitrier as the ideal
preacher and even a resurrected Origen.

9) One must comment on the make-up of the little volume of 1503 called *Lucubratiunculae aliquot* originally, then less apologetically *Lucubrationes*. For this volume is at the very crossroads of Erasmus' literary and spiritual development. It contained the following works: *Enchiridion, Disputatio de Tedio, Exhortatio ad virtutem, Precatio ad Virginis-filium Jesum, Paean Virgini Matri canendus, Obsecratio ad Mariam, Oratio in Laudem pueri Jesu, Enerratio ... in primum psalmum, Carmen de casa natalicia, Carmen Jesu ad mortales, Carmen complura dep. Jes., Carmen de Angeli, Carmen graecanicum BVM*. As well as the *Enchiridion*, whose importance is stressed in this chapter and whose structure and meaning are discussed in ch. 20, there are prayers and poems to the Blessed Virgin (a clear signalling of his emphasis in religious life, along with his dwelling on the child Jesus), a kind of commentary on the first psalm that looks forward to his lifetime of editing and paraphrasing the New Testament, and other poems, for Erasmus still thought of himself as a poet.

10) See Tracy, 85–6. It is difficult to say precisely when his interest in Lucian began; on that question see ch. 22.

11) Ep. 124 (*CWE* 1:252/72–4; Allen 1, 288/63–4). Cf. Ep. 126, the dedicatory preface to *Adagiorum Collectanea*, in which Erasmus writes to Mountjoy that he has given his doctor the slip, 'for he solemnly warned me against having anything at all to do with books' (*CWE* 1:255/14–5): how much of this is sheer play is difficult to say.

12) P.O. Kristeller, *RenQ*, xxiii (1970) 9. Kristeller is patently referring to printed editions: manuscripts of Plato were in circulation, but I do not know of evidence that Erasmus was making use of them. In Kristeller's judgment they were 'hardly accessible to Erasmus' before he reached Venice (9).

13) Renaudet, *Préréforme*, 402–3, sketches the milieu of 1501 in Paris: Gaguin printing a new edition of his *compendium*, Bade annotating the *Ars Poetica* and *Epistles* of Horace, and the *Georgics, Eclogues* and *Aeneid* of Vergil ('mais ses commentaires s'adressaient trop strictement aux petites classes des écoles'); Brant's *Ship of Fools* bringing in a fresh spirit of originality, while Syntheim's edition of the *Doctrinale* brought out a new edition of an older work.

14) Such comments on the saying of Mass are rare indeed. We know that Erasmus heard mass in September 1518 (*CWE* 6:117/74; Allen III, 395/68), and there are one or two much later allusions to his private worship.

15) See André Godin, *Spiritualité franciscaine en Flandre au XVIème siècle: L'Homelaire de Jean Vitrier* (Geneva, 1971) and *Érasme lecteur d'Origène* (Geneva, 1982). The name is variously spelled (Voirier, Vitrarius, Viterius, etc.).

16) *Libertas*, as Tracy has rightly observed, was for Erasmus a freedom *from* obligatory rules of custom and cult in order to be free – 'free *to* fulfil the spirit of Christ's law voluntarily and with alacrity'. And he continues: 'the idea of *humanitas* supplied him with a faith that, once freed of burdensome constraints, men would of their own will be drawn to imitate the life and teaching of Christ' (145, italics are those of Tracy). Later in the *Annotations on the New Testament* (see ch. 33), Erasmus will comment on the important passage in Matt. 11:30 that points to charity as the law of Christ; and Erasmus cites this passage in the *Enchiridion* (see ch. 20 for discussions of the

implications of his theology of grace). 'Minus imperat Evangelica charitas, sed plus impetrat', Erasmus wrote in his *Annotationes:* see Erasmus' *Annotations on the New Testament*, ed. Anne Reeve (London, 1986) 56 (*LB* VI, 63–4).

17) Later Erasmus often criticised Franciscans – along with Dominicans and Carmelites – on various scores (in the *Colloquies* and elsewhere); but his personal indebtedness to this Franciscan remained, and was acknowledged.

18) Tracy, ibid. It does not weaken the force of Tracy's argument that Vitrier as a Franciscan was technically a friar and not a monk, as Erasmus was.

19) Until he was at least 30 years of age, Erasmus thought of himself as a poet, and it was as a poet that he had entered into the intellectual world of Paris (Vol.1,189). With notable exceptions, such as the *Carmen alpestre* and the *Precepts for Christians* (Reedijk, 83 and 94), Erasmus' poems diminished in number and length in his later years. During the 1520s and 1530s the bulk of them were epigraphs and epigrams. One must recognise the range of subjects (liturgical and meditative, humanistic, occasional) as well as the variety of verse forms and changes of style. That he was a versatile poet cannot be questioned, but some scholars may see in the very ranging of which I speak Erasmus' search for his own poetic voice, and the number of early poems which are dialogues or dialogic anticipates his later turning to the dialogue form in his *Colloquies*. There are many elements in the poetry which have great biographical interest (even if they cannot be pursued in this relatively condensed biography). One might here point to the early poem 'In Praise of Gregory the Great' (Reedijk, 17) that recalls the fact that the monastery of Steyn was dedicated to St Gregory. Thus the movement in Erasmus towards a sense of vocation – which came to be (as we shall see) a formulation unique for his age – involved obviously much more than just learning how to write for publication, and there was a redirection of aspirations (including his earlier writing of poems and being recognised as a poet).

The Early Louvain Years, 1502–1504

I have dictated this work instead of writing it, and, in doing so,
I have given my doctor the slip, for he solemnly warned me
against having anything at all to do with books. But I agree with
Pliny that every moment not bestowed upon study is wasted.

> Epistle 126 (preface to *Adagiorum Collectanea*,
> *CWE* 1:255/14–7; Allen 1, 290/10–13)

... I am like the fox in Horace,
   ... terrified
   Because those footprints mostly point to you
   and none point back.[1]

> (*CWE* 1:285/18–21; Allen 1, 312/14–17)

My mind is burning with indescribable eagerness to bring all
my small literary works to their conclusion, and at the same
moment to acquire a certain limited competence in the use of
Greek, and thereby go on to devote myself entirely to sacred
literature...

> Epistle 138 (*CWE* 1:295–6/49–53; Allen 1, 321/44–48)

With the dashing of hopes for patronage from Lady Anne of Veere,
owing to her remarriage in 1502, Erasmus moved to Louvain, where
he settled for two years. It was a city to which he would return later
in life, and it had a university from which would come some of his
bitterest critics. Not least, it was emerging as a centre for printing.
Louvain – to follow the usual Anglo-American form of the name
instead of the Flemish *Leuven* (although, further to complicate matters, the English pronunciation *Louvain* differs from the French) –
was a large and fortified town, with canals serving the needs of the
prosperous merchants, and boasting a number of generous squares
and notable churches, as well as a magnificent city hall. It was a town
to which Erasmus had earlier thought of moving with Jacob Batt.
Now he had come on his own.[2]

In the Middle Ages Louvain had been both the capital of Brabant
and its most important city, being also the residence of the dukes of

Brabant. But the uprising of 1379 by citizens of the city led to the advantage of Brussels and the fleeing of many weavers to Holland and England. In the fourteenth century the population had been perhaps 50,000, with a guild of weavers that numbered 2400 members. The old Cloth Weavers' Hall became the home of the university in the late seventeenth century.

At the end of the fourteenth century, Louvain was the official residence of the powerful dukes of Burgundy, and it was duke (Hertog) Jan IV who obtained the approval of pope Martin V for the establishment of a university at Louvain, in part because of 'the geographically advantageous location of the town', lying between the North and the South of the region, and because of its 'quiet, peaceable surroundings'.

A symbol of the prosperity of the city was the town hall, with its rich pointed Gothic architecture, its lofty roof and graceful towers facing the town square. Among the many churches one must note that of St Peter, constructed by the end of the fifteenth century (but damaged in 1914 and restored); for ecclesiastics from this church figured in the events of Erasmus' stay in Louvain.

Louvain is close to Brussels, and the university had many connexions with the court; in Louvain the politics of the ducal court were in the air. Erasmus' host, though not necessarily the person inviting him to the city, was Jean Desmarez, who had been at court (Epistle 197/6–7). Desmarez was a native of Cassel, near Saint-Omer, and it is possible that Erasmus had met him during his months in the vicinity of Tournhem and Saint-Omer.

But there were others who were doubtless instrumental in welcoming and introducing Erasmus and guiding his steps. Philibert Naturel, a doctor of both civil and canon law, had been named provost of the cathedral chapter of Utrecht – connexions with Utrecht keep cropping up – in 1500; 'he spent most of his life in the diplomatic service of the house of Hapsburg' (*BR*); and in 1503 Erasmus referred to Naturel as his neighbour. Another was Busleyden: Erasmus had met Jerome de Busleyden at Orleans in 1500, where he, a younger brother of Gillis de Busleyden (master of the chambre des comptes of the duke of Burgundy) was studying law. In 1503 Jerome obtained a doctorate of law at Padua, and soon after his return from Italy he became councillor and master of requests in the grand council of Mechlin (*BR*). We shall return to both Jerome and Gillis de Busleyden in tracing the foundation of a Collegium Trilingue at Louvain in 1517 (chapter 33).

Yet another was Nicolas Ruistre, whose importance has been identified in Volume 1 (pp. 136, 144 n. 22). A master of requests in the service of the duke of Burgundy, he became provost of St Peter's in 1487 (succeeded in 1500 by Naturel) and in 1502 he was consecrated bishop of Arras. It seems likely that Ruistre was instrumental in the entrusting to Erasmus of the distinction and responsibility of delivering the oration welcoming Philip the Handsome upon his return from Spain in January 1504. In 1503 Erasmus presented to Ruistre his Latin translations of three declamations by Libanius (Epistle 177); and it was natural that the printed *Panegyricus* carried a prefatory epistle (Epistle 179) to Ruistre (see *BR*).

The name of the Spanish humanist Juan Luis Vives is associated with Louvain – and also with Bruges, Paris and Oxford – but he is almost a generation younger than Erasmus. He did not arrive in the Low Countries until 1512, having left Paris out of dissatisfaction with the Collège de Montaigu and the rigid scholastic curriculum of the university, like Erasmus earlier. But Vives did not meet Erasmus until abut 1516 or 1517 (see chapters 32 and 34).

All the major countries of Europe had their universities: Italy, Spain, Portugal, France, Germany, England, and that part of central Europe that is now Hungary. In the Low Countries during Erasmus' lifetime there was but one university, Louvain; for Leiden was erected only in 1575.[3]

But not all of these universities could be thought of as a 'Studium Generale' which had to have four faculties: the arts faculty for its foundation of the liberal arts, and the theological faculty for its crowning of the hierarchy of learning (see chapter 13); the faculties of law and medicine were professional schools much like those of the twentieth century. Although founded in 1425, Louvain did not possess a theological faculty until 1432:[4] this fourth faculty was canonically erected by pope Eugene IV in 1432, a theological faculty being permitted by the Holy See only after a university had given proof of its eminence (or, more realistically, competence) in the other faculties.

Louvain's university was a recent foundation by comparison with the University of Paris; but by the turn of the century it had become one of the leading universities of Europe and famed especially for its theological faculty, which was known for its orthodoxy. The striking impact of its foundation is that thenceforth students from the Low Countries no longer had to enroll in a university outside their region – generally before 1425 it had been either Paris or Cologne – and a 'native' university must have contributed greatly to pride of *pays* (see chapter 1).[5] Within the university there were colleges that had their own traditions by the beginning of the sixteenth century: the Pork, the Falcon, the Lily, Arras and others. And early in the 1520s there would be the Collège du Pape, Pope's College, founded by Adrian VI.[6]

The model for the new university in the Low Countries in 1425 was Paris, in its structure, its special emphasis on the faculty of theology, and its orthodox scholasticism, in the arts as well as the theological faculty.[7] In matters of ecclesiastical politics the faculty of theology at Louvain opposed conciliar doctrine; this too was part of its deep orthodoxy.[8] Erasmus' decision to settle in Louvain is therefore somewhat surprising; but he did not go there for a degree, and there were individuals in the town and university whose presence he valued. We have spoken of the ecclesiastical figures of prominence at the ducal court and in the town; among the eminent scholars, statesmen and theologians who taught or had studied at Louvain one can single out Adrian of Utrecht (later pope Adrian VI) and, later, Vives, Justus Lipsius, Mercator, Dodoens, Vesalius, Riga.[9] But first let us speak of Adrian of Utrecht.

Nearly a decade older than Erasmus, Adriaan Floriszoon Dedel (1459–1523) was the son of a shipwright, and after attending the Latin school in Utrecht he went to a school of the Brethren of the Common Life, perhaps in Zwolle (*BR*) and thus shared much of the emphasis of the *Devotio Moderna* with Erasmus and so many others among renaissance humanists of their generation. He obtained his doctorate in theology in 1491 and in the same year was ordained. Adrian (to use the form more familiar in English) had just finished a second term as rector of the university when Erasmus arrived in Louvain, some time in the autumn of 1502;[10] and it was Adrian who persuaded the magistracy of the city to offer Erasmus a lectureship in rhetoric. 'Hardly had I reached Louvain', Erasmus wrote to Nicolas Werner, his old friend and now prior at Steyn, in early autumn 1502 (Epistle 171), 'when the town magistrates offered me the responsibility of lecturing publicly – a charge I had neither sought nor expected – and this, too, on a recommendation volunteered by Master Adrian of Utrecht, dean of Louvain' (*CWE* 2:58–9/13–16; Allen 1, 380/10–13). To turn down the security and immediate pay offered by this lectureship took courage, and it tells us much about Erasmus' dedication to the study of Greek and preparation for his lifework on the New Testament.

Among the contemporary theologians of Louvain, key figures during the lifetime of Erasmus, were Latomus, Dorp, Driedo, Dierckx, Baechem and Sichen. The quarrel with Martin van Dorp began somewhat earlier, but his quarrels with the others are all after 1516 (see chapters 32 and 34) and the publication of his edition of the New Testament. There were two theologians who had first studied at Louvain, and these must be noted. The first is the greatly influential figure of Jan Standonck – 'illustrious' to at least one scholar, but 'notorious' to another[11] – who was such a dark influence upon Erasmus at the Collège de Montaigu. In 1499–1500 Standonck founded a college for poor students at Louvain, the Collège du Porc, which was modelled upon Montaigu.[12] Next there was Jacobus Latomus (Masson), a disciple of Standonck at Paris who had been a student of Adrian and obtained his doctorate in theology at Louvain, becoming a most influential figure in the university. Dorp will come into the picture in 1515, and he will be discussed at that time.

The importance of the printing press in the Low Countries can scarcely be overestimated, as has already been declared in chapter 1, and after 1473 Louvain became a major European centre of printing, especially of humanistic texts. One printer with whom Erasmus was long connected must serve as an example, for he printed over fifty books by Erasmus and in other ways theirs was a close relationship.

Dirk Martens (Latinised as Theodoricus Alustensis, and variously spelled in Dutch: Dieryck, Martins, etc.) was born c. 1446–7 in Aalst, a Flemish town between Brussels and Ghent. After an apprenticeship in Italy (apparently with Girardus de Lisa, of Ghent), Martens returned to Aalst and established his first press there by 1473. Again Martens travelled abroad, perhaps to Spain, but by 1486 or 1487 he was back in Aalst, where he produced mainly devotional and scholastic books until 1492. 'In 1491 his edition of Alexander de Villa Dei's *Doctrinale* (Heireman 18) is the first book printed in the Netherlands which includes Greek characters' (thus IJsewijn in *BR*). He may have learned some Greek in Italy, and he was in fact something of a scholar. He moved from Aalst to Antwerp and may have had relations with the court at Brussels – it is tempting to conjecture that there may have been some contact with Erasmus this early, but IJsewijn cautions that there is no evidence. (The correspondence of Erasmus, so rich in so many other respects, is conspicuously silent about some of his closest relationships.) By 1512 Erasmus and Martens were staunch friends, for, with the *Lucubratiunculae* Martens published books by Erasmus as early as 1503.[13]

In 1497 Martens registered at the University of Louvain and opened a press in front of University Hall, working there for four years before returning to Antwerp in 1502. During these years Martens had as corrector the young Pieter Gillis: first acquaintance of Erasmus and Martens can certainly be traced to this period,

whether through Gillis or through the university.[14] What is notable
is that Martens printed his earliest editions of Erasmus' books from
Antwerp, and these included the following: *Lucubratiunculae* (15
February 1503, reprinted in 1509); the *Panegyricus* (1504, reprinted
in 1504 and 1516); the *Moriae Encomium* (January 1512). Other
works by Erasmus included the translations from Lucian in 1512 and
the *De Ratione Studii* in the same year. These will all be discussed in
later chapters, as well as the complex and fascinating printing history of More's *Utopia* in 1516.

An anecdote relating to Dirk Martens must be told. The story is
recounted in a letter from Dorp in 1514 (Epistle 304), who wrote
that the printer had asked him to remember him to Erasmus:

> He wanted very much to see you, and indeed to entertain you in
> a friendly and hospitable fashion, and set off to Antwerp for the
> purpose; when he heard you were not there, but at Louvain, he
> came straight back, and by travelling all night reached Louvain
> the next day about an hour and a half after you had gone. (*CWE*
> 3:23/167–71; Allen II, 16/151–4; *CWE* notes that Erasmus had
> gone from Ghent to Bergen, 23/169)

Such a story speaks volumes about Martens' warm feelings for
Erasmus in the ripeness of their friendship, which endured until
Martens' death in 1534, and it also underscores the difficulties, and
perils, of communication at that time. It is appropriate that Martens'
printer's emblem was an anchor.

It may well have been that the presence of Martens at Louvain was
a strong reason for Erasmus' decision to settle there in 1502, for he
had a number of things in his luggage that he hoped to get into
print, especially the *Enchiridion*, as we infer from the printing of this
work so soon after his arrival in Louvain (chapter 20). Martens was a
stellar figure in the post-incunable world, to use that most useful
term coined by Nijhoff for books printed after 1500 and before
1520.[15]

And so in the autumn or late summer of 1502 Erasmus settled in
Louvain, where he hoped to devote himself to his studies. A host for
part of this first period at Louvain (1502–4) was Jean Desmarez
(called *Paludanus*: a Latin translation of 'Desmarez' or 'of the
marshes'), with whom Erasmus lived for most of his stay in the city.

Desmarez taught Latin in the College of the Falcon and was
professor of eloquence and canon of St Peter's. He introduced
Erasmus to a group of humanists in the College of the Lily, and
apparently it was he who urged Erasmus to publish his *Panegyricus*; it
may have been he who introduced Erasmus to Nicolas Ruistre, the

chancellor of the University of Louvain to whom the *Panegyricus* is dedicated, as others have suggested.[16] But it seems patent from Epistle 180 to Desmarez (February 1504) that not only was it Desmarez who had encouraged Erasmus to undertake the task and the offering of it to Philip the Handsome, but that 'finally it was you again' (he writes to Desmarez) 'who refused to be satisfied until you had persuaded me to publish it' (*CWE* 2:85/194–5, 197–8; Allen I, 403/177 ff.). Such a view still permits us to see Ruistre as the prime mover, perhaps the one responsible for Erasmus' being named the orator for the occasion.[17]

One cannot emphasise too strongly the conventionality of a dedicatory letter. This convention had been firmly established as a kind of writing early in the Quattrocento with the dedicatory letters that presented Guarino's translation of Plutarch's *Lives*, for example. In the convention of the dedicatory letter one finds such formal features as the establishment of the relationship between translator and dedicatee (social status, quality of learning, and the like); and among the themes in the traditional form of the dedicatory letter are *humanitas* as a central concept, a special virtue characteristic of patrons (or potential patrons) of high rank. Often, too, there is a praising of the rewards of rhetoric.[18]

Written during September 1503 (and Erasmus complained of the hard work in writing it), the *Panegyricus ad Philippum Austriae ducem* was delivered before the ducal court at Brussels on 6 January 1504. The following month Martens printed it in Antwerp, and Erasmus' letter to Ruistre (Epistle 179) served as preface.

It was an opportunity to win patronage that Erasmus seized. The occasion was highly charged with politics: it was the welcoming by the Estates of Brabant of Philip in the ducal court at Brussels, and it was the feast of the Epiphany 1504.[19] Ruistre was of course present at the ceremony (as was Thomas de Plaine, the high chancellor of Burgundy), and he and the prince were well pleased that Erasmus justifed Ruistre's choice of him for the oration. It has been doubted whether Philip understood Latin – at least the elegant Latin of Erasmus' oration – and one may also doubt that Erasmus delivered the entire long oration upon 6 January. Rather than speaking of the published form of February 1504 as a revision, then, it would seem more accurate to speak of it as the full text which Erasmus had looked forward to publishing.[20] At the end of the *Panegyricus*, and following the dedicatory Epistle 180, a 101-line poem is printed: 'Illustrissimo principi Philippo feliciter in patriam redeunti gratulatorium carmen Erasmi sub persona patriae' (in Reedijk, 272–6). It must be added that the duke, as Erasmus wrote in Epistle 179, 'promised me the earth if I were willing to come to court as a member of his household' (*CWE* 2:78/19–20; Allen I, 396/15–16). It appears that the duke gave Erasmus a gift of 1 livre 'pour ses peines et labeurs d'un beau livre par lui lors fait et composé à la louange de Monditseigneur touchant son voyaige d'Espaigne, et lequel il lui avoit le ix du mois de janvier xv^ciii présenté en don' (Allen I, 396n.). In the following October he was given an additional 10 livres (Allen I, 403n).

At first reading – and all too often the piece has not had a second reading – the *Panegyricus* is to the modern reader a boring and excessively flattering piece of writing, and in fact some of his friends thought Erasmus had flattered the prince more than the occasion called for.[21] And Erasmus himself recognised this, for in writing to John Colet in 1504 (Epistle 181) he declared:

> I was so reluctant to compose the *Panegyricus* that I do not remember ever doing anything more unwillingly; for I saw that this kind of thing could not be handled without some flattery. However I employed a novel stratagem: I was completely frank while I flattered and also very flattering in my frankness.[22]

Why then – as Otto Herding put it in his introduction to the *ASD* edition of the tract – why did Erasmus not allow his *Panegyricus* to die a quiet death after the demise of Philip in 1506? Instead he revised it for a reprinting by Bade in Paris in 1504, and there were further minor revisions in the editions by Froben, who printed it with the *Institutio Principis Christiani*. That decision by Froben points the way to an answer to the question; for as Betty Radice has made clear, 'this is the first of Erasmus' treatises on the proper use of political power in the hands of a Christian ruler' (*CWE* 27:5), and in it Erasmus argues against flattery in this most flattering of orations. Further, he treats of the duty of the prince to maintain peace at home and abroad: it is the first of Erasmus' treatises on peace, leading to the satire of *Moria* and the later adages on peace, *Dulce bellum inexpertis* most notably, and the still later *Querela pacis*.

Working from the traditional Latin panegyric, and especially that genre of the oration delivered at the funeral of an eminent person in which his virtues (and those of his illustrious ancestors) were praised, and his public achievements (both military and political) singled out for praise, Erasmus from what was on hand developed his exaggerated eulogy. Betty Radice has written on Erasmus' specific citation of Pliny's turgid *Panegyric* as his main model (*CWE* 27: 4), and the result is an oration that demonstrates the expense of *imitatio* in a waste of *adulatio*. Erasmus himself later thought of the work as one of serious moral character, expressing the doctrine of the responsibilities of the

Christian prince, as he did in his more direct *Institutio principis* of
1516 (Tracy, *Politics*, 17).

The political dimensions of the work are significant, but likely to
be important only to a student of the Burgundian court, or of the
brief unhappy reign of Philip; to a modern reader it is doubtless
enough to have read it and perceived its fear of Philip's undertaking
war either against France or Guelders (Tracy, 20). But another dimension calls attention to Erasmus' sense of politics, for the
Panegyricus, as Tracy writes, is also the document of a faction:

> Erasmus' original informants included imperial partisans like
> Philibert Naturel and Floris of Edmond, son of Frederick, Lord
> of Ijselstein. Naturel was Maximilian's candidate (against
> Nicholas Ruistre, who was supported by Philip) to succeed
> Henry of Bergen as Chancellor of the Golden Fleece.[23] The
> Holland branch of the Egmond family had long been faithful to
> the emperor. To his friend Willem Hermans, still in the cloister
> at Steyn, Erasmus boasted of his acquaintance with Floris of
> Ijselstein [near Gouda], scion of a house famous in Holland...
> (Tracy, *Politics*, 20)

To return to the reception of the *Panegyricus:* there was the 1504
Paris printing by Bade, and after 1516 several editions, with some
further revisions, by Froben, who printed it with the *Institutio
Principis Christiani* (*CWE* 27:4). Tracy has usefully summarised the
changes in Erasmus' own opinion of his *Panegyricus* over the years:
'Shortly after publication he professed to be displeased by it, perhaps
because learned friends felt he flattered the prince more than was
necessary. In later years he thought it a work of serious moral
character, expressing, if more guardedly, the same high doctrine of
the Christian prince's responsibilities which is to be found in his
Institutio principis of 1516' (17).

By late 1503 Erasmus had also completed his translation of three
short speeches from the works of Libanius, and on 17 November he
presented a manuscript copy to Nicolas Ruistre, chancellor of the
University of Louvain.[24] Although this work was not actually printed
until 1519, a discussion of it belongs here because it tells us much
about Erasmus' Greek studies and his keen interest in rhetoric generally and *declamatio* in particular.

Libanius was a fourth-century rhetorician who had among his
pupils John Chrysostom and Theodore of Mopsuestia almost certainly, and Basil and Gregory of Naziansus probably (*OCD 2*). Much
of the work of Libanius survives, including speeches dealing with
public affairs, educational and cultural questions, and funeral

ceremonies; the *OCD* notes that there also survive some 1600 letters, fifty-one school declamations, numerous model rhetorical exercises and minor rhetorical works. Despite a difficult style he was esteemed as a model of style in Byzantine times. To explain his choice of Libanius to Ruistre, Erasmus pointed to the rhetorical skills of Libanius, 'to whom the verdict of scholarship awards a leading place among the practitioners of Attic style' (*CWE* 2:73/72–3; Allen I, 392/59–60).

Erasmus' translation has been studied by Erika Rummel, and I here follow her analysis.[25] In the first edition of 1519 there are corrections of several errors and omissions contained in the manuscript version; and in the second edition of 1522 most of the remaining mistakes are eliminated and some improvement is made in a number of passages (22). Even in what Erasmus called his 'apprentice work' there is 'proof of his linguistic skills and his native rhetorical powers'; and Rummel goes on to declare that 'Erasmus succeeded admirably in devising natural and idiomatically correct versions for difficult Greek phrases', and she provides examples (23). To conclude, we may echo Rummel's declaration that 'It is proof of Erasmus' remarkable talent and industry that he could produce a translation of this quality after only four years of study undertaken in difficult circumstances, without a proper supply of texts, without regular professional supervision, and during an unsettling period that saw several changes of residence'(26).

Why was it not published in 1503? The Toronto editors express the view that 'the delay in publication may have been partly due to the fact that it made only a small book of sixteen quarto pages and also to the fact that Martens could not yet print Greek' (*CWE* 2:71n). But this last is only partly true: Martens had already printed some Greek, although not much. One must consider that in 1503 Erasmus was also working on the *Panegyricus,* which was published separately, and that he had just published his *Lucubratiunculae* in February with Martens; but this was a little volume of miscellaneous pieces largely religious or devotional in nature, and the translations from Libanius would not fit into such a collection thematically. After 1504 Erasmus moved from Louvain, and it is possible that he did not carry with him another copy of his *Libanius*, or that he no longer cared deeply enough to have it printed. It had served its purpose, as a work presented to Ruistre and as an effort in his further mastering of Greek.

In the ceremony at the ducal court in Brussels on 6 January 1504, Erasmus 'declaimed' his *Panegyricus* – in the sense of orating it, delivering it orally – but it was not a *declamatio* in the rhetorical sense; and those meanings which Erasmus later thought were latent in the *Panegyricus* were not developed structurally. Erasmus was still learning the potentialities of the form of the *declamatio* and the effort of translating Libanius contributed to that process; and he was still working towards the full reaches of irony.[26] From 1503 to 1509 and the genesis of *Moriae Encomium* is only a space of six years, but Erasmus continued to learn and grow, as we shall see.

At Louvain Erasmus was now back in a Flemish-speaking environment. Although he did not speak of the matter in any letters now available to us, after eight years of living in a French-speaking court and in Paris (interrupted by six months in England), the return to his mother-tongue was certainly an everyday aspect of his settling in Louvain. Perhaps Erasmus' apparent silence on this matter indicates that he no longer clung to his mother-tongue; after all, the academic and learned language everywhere was Latin, and the vernacular was for merchants and servants. Perhaps not: there might not have been the occasion to speak of the matter.

In any case, he did not return to his native Netherlands, because he did not have to go back to Deventer or Den Bosch or Steyn. Only at Steyn was he assured of a long-term place to stay, but the terms were too high to pay.

Notes

1) 'And none point back': Erasmus in his own mind had surely passed the point of no return. He could not return to the monastery at Steyn, although we know he maintained proper communication with the prior and spent some time there as late as 1501 (ch. 18), and he would not return, except for brief visits, to Paris (perhaps he had burned that bridge in his relations with Standonck).

2) There is a gap between Ep. 170, written from Saint-Omer on 2 July 1502, and Ep. 171, written from Louvain in late September or early October of that year, a gap of nearly three months. As Allen notes (1, 379–80), it is possible that 'he returned again [to Paris] in July or August 1502; but if he did so, he must have been frightened away again very quickly by a fresh outbreak of the disease [plague]. He next thought of going to Cologne, but there the ravages of the pestilence were as great as in Paris (Ep. 172 n.6), and he therefore betook himself to Louvain'.

3) *Leuven, Traditie, en toekomst van een universiteit* (Tielt, 1970) 21.

4) For a recent emphasis of this point see J. Sperna Weiland, 'Het verre land Utopia' in *Erasmus – De actualiteit van zijn denken* (Amsterdam, 1986) 77.

5) The prime source is V. Denis, *Catholic University of Louvain, 1425–1958* (Louvain, 1958) and his brief but excellent article in *NCE*. See also *Leuven*. The traditional medieval mobility of *clerici* continued: cf., e.g., Erasmus' friend

Cornelis Gerard (Aurelius), who studied at Cologne, Louvain and Paris: see K. Tilmans, *Aurelius en de Divisiekroniek van 1517 – Historiografie en humanisme in Holland in de tijd van Erasmus* (Hilversum, 1988) 19.

6) The fundamental *instrument de travail* is H. De Jongh, *L'ancienne faculté de théologie de Louvain au premier siècle de son existence, 1432–1540* (Louvain, 1911); for the period under study, see H. de Vocht, *Texts and Studies about Louvain Humanists of the first Half of the XVIth Century* (*HumLov*, 4, Louvain, 1934) and *History of the Foundation and the Rise of the Collegium Trilingue Lovaniense, 1517–1550* (*HumLov*, 10–13, Louvain, 1951–55).

7) See ch. 10 & 11.

8) See Etienne, 95. Perhaps to make clear their independence from Paris, Louvain theologians had little consultation with their Paris colleagues; Farge in his *Orthodoxy and Reform* identifies only three known occasions: 1470, 1519 and 1545 (the last 'to express surprise over Paris' failure to censure certain books', p. 249).

9) *Leuven*, 21.

10) Adrian received many academic and ecclesiastical distinctions: at the time of Ep. 171 he was dean of St Peter's, Louvain, and chancellor of the university. We shall discuss the friendship of Erasmus and Adrian at several points subsequently not least in their serving as councillors to Charles V and at the time of Adrian's election to the papacy. The founding of the Collegium Trilingue at Louvain in 1518, while it owed much to the inspiration of Erasmus, was also indebted to Adrian for counsel (and obviously to the close friend of both Adrian and Erasmus, Jerome de Busleyden, whose endowment made the Collegium possible). In a number of letters Erasmus later congratulated his former friend on his becoming pope, and Adrian offered a benefice, which Erasmus declined (*BR*). Worth noting is the publication of Adrian's *Quaestiones quodlibeticae,* which was edited by Dorp (Rummel, *Erasmus and Cath. Critics*) and cited by Thomas More (*Selected Letters*, 26–7).

11) For the adjective 'illustrious' see Farge, *Orthodoxy and Reform*, 248. For the judgment of 'notorious', see Renaudet, 'Jean Standonck, un reformateur catholique avant la Réforme', *Hum. et Ren*, Travaux 30 (1958) 114–61.

12) The first head of the residence was Latomus (*BR*). I am not aware of any indication of Latomus' response to Erasmus during this first period (1502–4) of Erasmus in Louvain; in 1517 (ch. 34) Latomus was one who gave him a friendly welcome (*BR*). See Etienne, 163–86.

13) Some comment is necessary on the fact that several of Erasmus' early close ties were with men a generation older: Gaguin in Paris, Martens in Louvain, and shortly Aldus Manutius in Venice; Froben in Basel came after those early years. To be sure, three of these four named were printers.

14) On connections between printers and universities, see the most interesting paper by Severin Corsten, 'Universities and early printing', in *Bibliography and the Study of 15th-Century Civilisation, British Library Occasional Papers 5*, ed. Lotte Hellinga and John Goldfinch (British Library, 1987) 83–123. On Erasmus and his printers, the essay by P.S. Allen in *Erasmus* (1934) 109–37 is still a necessary starting-point.

15) See e.g., the discussion of Martens' edition of Erasmus' *Parabolae* of 1515, in *Post Incunabula en Heen Uitgevers in de Lage Landen*, ed. Hendrik D. L. Vervliet (The Hague, 1978) 176–7.

16) Yet Ruistre had served the dukes of Burgundy as secretary and councillor, and it seems unlikely that young Erasmus would not have met him during his service in the household of Hendrik van Bergen (ch. 7). At that time Erasmus was very much an apprentice; however, Ep. 177 may seem to imply that they had not met before Erasmus' coming to Louvain. Still this is a public letter (the dedicatory preface to three declamations of Libanius, published by Martens at Louvain in 1519), and it lacks completeness.

17) Without providing evidence Halkin declares that 'Ruistre charge Erasme du perilleux honneur d'accuellir le fils de Maximilien à Bruxelles' (*Erasme*, 89).

18) See Marianne Pade, 'The Dedicatory Letter as a Genre: The Preface of Guarino Veronese's Translations of Plutarch', in *Acta Conventus Neo-Latini Torontonensis* (Binghamton, NY, 1991) 559–68; and further, Karl Schottenloher, *Die Widmungsrede im Buch des 16. Jahrhunderts* (1953), and, for the tradition earlier among classical writers, Tore Janson, *Latin Prose Prefaces* (Stockholm, 1964).

19) Tracy, 19. Erasmus declaimed the *Panegyricus* (in the sense of orating it) but it was not, properly speaking, a *declamatio*; and those meanings which Erasmus later thought were latent in it were not reinforced structurally by virtue of the *declamatio* as genre. He was still working towards the ironic, which in *Moriae Encomium* suffused the genre.

20) However, in Ep. 180 he wrote to Desmarez in the prefatory letter that he 'stitched in new material at many places, extempore at that' (*CWE* 2: 84/166–7; Allen I, 402/151–2). Erasmus, we must observe, was not always a reliable witness to details of this kind. The adjective *extempore* calls attention to the high value put on the facility of speaking to the moment (cf. Quintilian X. vi. 1ff).

21) Even in the prefatory Epistle 180 to Desmarez he alluded to the hostile criticism: *CWE* 2:80/12 ff., and 27–9.

22) *CWE* 2:87/63–67. The rhetorical play is more clear in the Latin: *Ego tamen novo sum usus artificio, ut et in adulando sim liberrimus et in libertate adulantissimus* (Allen I, 405/57–8). Erasmus is artful even when discounting his artifice.

23) On the Order of the Golden Fleece see ch. 7. Tracy notes (*Politics*, 139 n. 66) that Naturel won the election in November 1504.

24) Ep. 177. The presentation copy of the ms. of both the letter (Ep. 177) and the translation is now at Trinity College, Cambridge (MS R.9.26) – Allen II, xix; and it is in Erasmus' autograph with professional illumination (*CWE* 2:71 n.). In the first sentence of his letter to Ruistre (177/1) Erasmus writes, 'I have recently come into possession of certain Greek declamations': but that ms. does not seem to have been identified, and we have no clues to its provenance.

25) Rummel, *Erasmus as a Translator of the Classics* (Toronto, 1985), ch. 2. Rummel cites the critical Latin text by R.A.B. Mynors (*ASD* 1–1, 181–92) and provides references to it.

26) The three works that Erasmus selected for translation were rhetorical declamations, model speeches on literary themes: Menelaus demanding the return of Helen, Medea contemplating the murder of her children, and Andromache addressing Hector (Rummel, 21) – all splendid models of the

declamatio recommended by Quintilian for speaking on hypothetical cases. (In Book II, ii and ff. of the *Inst.*, Quintilian discusses fully the pedagogical functions of the *declamatio*.) The form of the *declamatio* will be discussed further with respect first to the *Moriae Encomium*, and then more briefly with More's *Utopia*. In a stimulating monograph Marc van der Poel has surveyed the *declamatio* in its humanistic phases, beginning with Salutati: see *De Declamatio bij de Humanisten* (Nieuwkoop, 1987). For useful translations of typical classical declamations, see William A. Edward, *the Suasoriae of the Elder Seneca* (Cambridge, 1927); a most useful survey of the declamation is provided by S.F. Bonner, *Roman Declamation in the Late Republic and Early Empire* (Liverpool, 1949).

The Enchiridion: 'philosophia Christi'

...they are growing old in the letter ...
Enchiridion (CWE 66: 35)

Life flies so fast that we must have a present remedy within our reach ...
   Who can carry the *Secunda secundae* of Aquinas round with him?
Erasmus to Abbot Paul Volz, Epistle 858
(*CWE* 6: 75/55, 67–81; Allen III, 363/59–60)

I have tried to teach a kind of art of piety, as certain others have written the theory of certain sciences.
Erasmus to John Colet, December 1504,
Epistle 181 (Allen I, 405/50–1)

The *Enchiridion* can be read as more than one kind of book, and so readers have done at different times. Most recently Tracy has seen it quite broadly as a charter for a vision of reform, but it has been seen by many as primarily an address to a lay audience beyond the hot-tempered and dissolute-living person to whom it was addressed. Certainly it announces a major shift in writings on devotion, and it embodies (as do all Erasmus' books) awareness of the new potentialities of the printed book. In the context of Erasmus' development it is a landmark, for it represents his first major effort as a pastoral theologian, one writing for the guidance of souls and not for an audience of other speculative theologians. It follows that Erasmus here manifests the deeply formative and lasting influence of the *Devotio Moderna* on his own spiritual formation. The *Enchiridion*, one may summarise, is a mature and powerful work which incorporates his own theological thinking and embodies his own emerging spirituality. With this work it can be said that Erasmus becomes a theologian. Luther echoed it in his letters and sermons, and after 1519 it was quickly translated into nine European languages. The *Enchiridion* demands a chapter devoted entirely to it, and we turn therefore to examine the aspects and questions here indicated.

Before the publication of his *Enchiridion* Erasmus was only a *collector* with his 1500 *Collectanea*, to follow the terminology of St Bonaventure;[1] with his appearance as the author of a printed book – and now in the full medieval sense of the word an *auctor* – he began slowly to accrue the authority bestowed upon one who had written a major book and his authority grew uniquely until a dozen years later, after many works and editions, he became known universally as the prince of humanists.

Like all the works of Erasmus, the *Enchiridion* had roots that were deep: in experiences of the immediate past, in the working with laymen in his Paris years and most enduringly still earlier in his formative years at Steyn where, as discussed in Volume 1, the stress – the implosion, even – of the *Imitatio Christi* upon a young man of burning motivation and aspiring spirituality found a ready disciple, and forged a rigorous inner discipline.

The metaphor of a small dagger (*pugiunculus*) that one can carry always in readiness occurs in the prefatory epistle to his edition of Cicero's *De Officiis* – itself a handbook of private and civic virtues – and in this same letter Erasmus called attention to the Greek word *enchiridion*, noting that it had the double meaning of 'dagger' and 'handbook'. It is evident that the military metaphor[2] had been germinating in his mind during the winter of 1500–01 while he visited in Holland and stayed with Batt in Tournhem.

Still wanting to escape the plague that was raging in Paris, Erasmus during the summer of 1501 found more permanent quarters in the Benedictine monastery of St Bertin at Saint-Omer, a dozen miles from Tournhem. Its abbot, Antony of Bergen, was brother of the bishop of Cambrai. There he found leisure, always a precious commodity for him, and at the Franciscan convent nearby he found Jean Vitrier, who deepened an enthusiasm for St Paul already kindled at Oxford in 1499 and instilled a new enthusiasm for Origen. During the autumn Erasmus moved again, to the castle of Courtebourne thirty miles away (any Dutchman knew the proverb that after three days, guests, like fish, begin to stink and three months was a long time to be a guest). It was Batt who arranged the plan for Erasmus to live 'apud Petrum' – Peter being an old friend of Batt – and there at Courtebourne he took up the plea of an unnamed christian wife to 'shake some religion' into her philandering husband, identified as Johann Poppenruyter of Nürnberg.[3]

At this time Erasmus was working on a commentary upon the Pauline Epistles (Epistles 164/41–2 and 181/36–8), and he had memorised much of the corpus of Paul and could – and did in the *Enchiridion* – quote extensively from memory. From Vitrier he

borrowed the *Homilies* of Origen on Genesis, Exodus, and the Song of
Songs, all echoed in the *Enchiridion*.[4] Other studies are woven as well
into the fabric of this work: Jerome, Ambrose, Augustine, Bernard
and other Church Fathers; but one may well stress the point that
nearly every theme of the *Enchiridion* may be found in the *Imitation of
Christ* as well.

The impact of this vital little book grew only very slowly. First
printed in Antwerp by Martens, it was not reprinted for six years,
again by Martens in 1509, and then again not for another six years,
with the printing by Schürer at Strasbourg in 1515. Thereafter the
work was reprinted nearly every year – and eight times in 1521, and
five times in 1522 – with a total of nearly sixty reprintings during
Erasmus' lifetime. A remarkable record.

In its first appearance the *Enchiridion* was included in a volume
called *Lucubratiunculae* – a diminutive meaning 'night-work' (as in
Aulus Gellius' *Praefatio* to the *Attic Nights* § 14) – along with several
other compositions of a devotional nature, including a brief *Prayer to
Jesus* and *Prayers to the Virgin*. The *Lucubratiunculae* was changed to
the more classical title *Lucubrationes* by Schürer in 1515, and after
1515 the *Enchiridion* was printed independently by Martens in
Louvain. Especially when seen together as the first and subsequent
editions of the *Lucubratiunculae* presented them, these writings show
the importance of prayer in Erasmus' literary programme and spirituality, and this work alone makes ridiculous the ignorance of some
twentieth-century scholars who accuse Erasmus of failing to make
religion central in his life and work.

Although, as we have seen in chapter 19, he used Greek types as
early as 1493, it appears that Marten's Greek font was not extensive,
at least not this early; and when Erasmus wanted to publish something with much more Greek – as with the 1508 *Adagiorum Chiliades*
– he did not take it to Martens. Later, however, and especially after
1517 and the foundation of the Collegium Trilingue, Martens not
only printed classical and humanist authors (and we must note that
it was he who printed More's *Utopia* in 1516), but he also printed
Greek and Hebrew grammars and dictionaries that were badly
needed (see Epistle 795). Printers too had to change.[5]

Editions of the Latin original of the *Enchiridion* were frequent
enough, but the book reached a still wider audience through translations.[6] It was first translated into English by William Tyndale,
perhaps as early as 1520, certainly before he set out for Germany in
1524. This early work, which may well represent Tyndale's 'appren-
tice-work as a translator', was revised for publication by Wynkyn de
Worde and John Byddell in November 1533: 'A book called in

Latyn Enchiridion militis Christiani and in Englysshe The manuell
of the christen knyght...' Much revised in a second edition of 1534,
it received four more editions (1538, 1541, and two in 1544), which
embody terminological revisions to reflect the religious changes of
the times. There were seven further editions or abridgements of the
Enchiridion in English by the 1560s, and throughout the century it
continued to be a popular book in the libraries of Oxford and Cambridge scholars.

The first vernacular language into which the *Enchiridion* was
translated was Czech in 1519, followed by a German translation at
Basel in 1520, and a Low German translation by Fuchs at Cologne in
1525. One Dutch translation was published at Amsterdam in 1523,
and a month later another at Antwerp. The Amsterdam translation,
which is freer than that of Antwerp, was reprinted fourteen times
between 1540 and 1616, a period in which Erasmian influence was
widely diffused.

The influence of Erasmus in Spain has been beautifully studied by
Bataillon; a translation was made in 1525 by an archdeacon of Alcor
who was a famous preacher, Alonso Fernandez de Madrid. Dedicated
to Don Alonso Manrique, who was archbishop of Seville and inquisitor general, the work had a second printing of thousands (Epistles
1742, 1746), and the translator wrote to Erasmus in 1527, 'In the
court of the emperor, in the cities, in the churches, in the convents,
even in the inns and in the streets there is no one without a copy of
Erasmus' *Enchiridion* in Spanish.' Despite – perhaps in part because
of – such great popularity, the treatise generated an opposition that
was well-nigh fanatical and led to inquisitorial proceedings in Spain
against the writings and teachings of Erasmus. The 1525 translation
nonetheless was reprinted a dozen times before 1556, including
editions in Coimbra and Antwerp (*CWE* 66: 4–5).

The story of the French translation of the *Enchiridion*, first published in Antwerp in 1529 and reprinted in 1532 and 1542, has a
particular point of interest. This first French translation (there was
another in 1543 at Antwerp) is attributed to a nobleman named
Louis de Berquin, who was associated with bishop Briçonnet's circle
of humanists at Meaux that included Lefèvre d'Etaples and
Guillaume Farel among others. One of the aims of this group was a
return to the simplicity of the Gospels, and the *Enchiridion* was most
attractive for this reason. But de Berquin's writings, which included
translations of Erasmus' *Encomium Matrimonii* and the *Querela Pacis*,
'had already earned him the condemnation of the Sorbonne and
eventually resulted in his burning at the stake in the Place de Grève
in 1529' (*CWE* 66:5), shortly after the publication of the translation

of Erasmus' *Enchiridion*. The story of the French translation must be considered as part of the history of ongoing controversies with the Sorbonne.

The Italian translation came from the chancellor of Brescia, Emilio de' Migli, and *Una piccola armatura per lo soldato christiania* was published at Brescia in 1531 – without the prefatory letter to Volz, as Erasmus himself had advised for the sake of prudence (Epistle 2165). This translation was reprinted four times at Venice before 1543. In a long letter during the spring of 1535, a young Italian humanist named Giovanni Angelo Odoni, who lived under Martin Bucer's wing in Strasbourg, assured the older humanist that Italians were buying and eagerly reading his book (*CWE* 66:6).

In addition there was a Polish translation of 1558 and a Swedish in 1592: not surprisingly, for Erasmus had correspondents and followers in Poland and Scandinavia; and one finds evidence that many churchmen owned individual copies of Erasmian works.

To such strong bibliographical evidence for the immense popularity of the work everywhere in sixteenth-century Europe, other kinds of testimony must be added. Erasmus himself wrote to Thomas More in 1516 that the bishop of Basel 'carries it round with him everywhere – I have seen all the margins marked in his own hand' (Epistle 412, *CWE* 3:291/26–8; Allen II, 242/25–6) and Adrianus Cornelii Barlandus named the *Enchiridion* first in a list of Erasmus' works made for his brother: 'a small book of pure gold, and of the greatest use to all those who have determined to abandon the pleasures of the body, to gird up their loins for the life of virtue and make their way to Christ' (Epistle 492, *CWE* 4:133/25–8; Allen II, 387/24–6). Albrecht Dürer, who knew Erasmus and many of his writings, may well have been guided, even inspired, by the *Enchiridion* in making his famous woodcut of 'The Knight, Death and the Devil', although other analogues were available to him. More certainly, Luther knew the *Enchiridion* intimately, for there are many echoes in his sermons of 1516 and 1517; and as Smith observes (58), 'Luther's famous work, *The Liberty of a Christian Man*, has a striking resemblance to the *Enchiridion*, both in its leading thought of the distinction between the inner and outer man, and in the idea of the universal priesthood of believers as worked out from the New Testament by Erasmus' (*LB* V, 47D–F). We shall speak in later chapters of the flow of Erasmian concepts of *simplicitas* and *humanitas* into the reform movement.

We turn now to the work itself to examine the structure and ideas, recalling again that *Enchiridion* means both a weapon and a manual or handbook. One may divide the book into two parts. The

first is a series of essays on life, the nature of man, and the reading of
Scriptures, connected by the theme of the armour of the christian
warrior. The second is a series of twenty-two rules of true Christianity. The full title of the work – 'The handbook [or dagger] of the
Christian soldier, replete with most salutary precepts of much efficacy against all the allurements of vice, and a model of true Christianity' – is thereby enlarged and justified. Above all, as Erasmus later
made explicit in the 1518 prefatory letter to abbot Paul Volz, 'we
must take thought all the time for the unlettered multitude, for
whom Christ died'. Here in his first explicitly theological work
Erasmus is vigorously christocentric, and the controlling image of
the work as a whole is the Cross. The main grounding of his personal
piety and thought is to be located in his early schooling by the
Brethren of the Common Life and in a monastery committed, however imperfectly, to the *Devotio Moderna*.

At the heart of the thought of the *Enchiridion* and fundamental for
the entire life of a Christian is baptism, for the christian soldier is
enrolled in the army of Christ through the sacrament of baptism.

> Are you not aware, O Christian soldier, that when you were
> initiated into the mysteries of the life-giving font, you enrolled
> in the army of Christ, your general, to whom you twice owed
> your life, since he both gave it and restored it to you, and to
> whom you owed more than to your very self. (*CWE* 66:26)

So Erasmus writes on the third page of his treatise, and baptism is
the standard by which the christian soldier directs his life. As Kohls
put it, in his stress on baptism in the light of the principal theological concepts of Erasmus,

> The sacrament of baptism ... becomes alpha and omega; and as
> a gift and responsibility it becomes an essential motif of the
> Christian life: 'Baptism is the first expression of Christian
> philosophy which is common to all Christians', as Erasmus later
> defines it in the *Paraclesis*.[7]

In the battle that takes place for the Christian living in a world so
threatened by powers of anti-god, it is God and Christ who support
the christian soldier. 'God is love, and where God is, there is love'
(*CWE* 66:28; *LB* V, 4D). In stressing the following of Christ,
Erasmus is stressing Christ in his human nature. The christology is
simple, and it is clearly presented.

Here, as elsewhere in his religious writings, Erasmus taught that
the study of the sacred Scriptures will guide and develop the imitation of Christ. There is reverence for God's word, and Erasmus
affirms his belief that the Scriptures are divinely inspired: 'All sacred
Scripture is divinely inspired and has proceeded from God, its

author' (*CWE* 66:32). 'Therefore,' he continues, 'if you dedicate yourself entirely to the study of the Scriptures, if you meditate day and night on the law of the Lord, you will have no fear, day or night, but you will be protected against any attack of the enemy' (*CWE* 66:33; *LB* V, 7C).

But the Christian must read actively, not passively. 'Meditation on a single verse will have more savour and nourishment, if you break through the husk and extract the kernel, than the whole Psalter chanted monotonously with regard only for the letter.' The recitation of a great number of psalms each day is not the culmination of piety:

> I think the principal reason why we see that monastic piety is everywhere so cold, languid, and almost extinct is that they are growing old in the letter and never take pains to learn the spiritual sense of the Scriptures. They do not hear Christ crying out in the gospel: 'The flesh is of no profit; it is the spirit that gives life', nor do they hear Paul, who adds to the words of the master: 'The letter kills, it is the spirit that gives life'. (*CWE* 66:35; *LB* 8F–9A)

Even the sacraments are valueless without or apart from the spirit.

Yet these simple and fundamental teachings – to which should be added Erasmus' stress on those precepts binding upon every Christian, at the same time that he distinguishes monasticism as but one way of living, not suitable to all – do not represent the eloquence of his writing. For that we must go to his own prose itself, and two extended paragraphs must serve. The first occurs midway in the very long section on the Sixth Rule: 'be in disaccord with the crowd and have only Christ as the model of piety, and be mindful of the paradoxes of true Christianity' [*veri Christianismi paradoxa*]:

> The Christian should be sincerely well disposed towards all men, pray duly for all, do good to all. He should not harm the deserving or benefit the undeserving. He should rejoice at another's prosperity as if it were his own, and be saddened at another's misfortune as if it were his own. This is surely what the Apostle bids us: 'to weep with those who weep, to rejoice with those who rejoice'. He should bear another's sufferings even more grievously than his own, and be happier at another's good fortune than at his own. It is not fitting for a Christian to entertain thoughts like this: 'What have I to do with this fellow? I don't know whether he is black or white. He is unknown to me, a total stranger. He never did me any favours; he offended me once: one was never of any help to me'. None of this! Recall only for what merit of yours Christ bestowed all his

gifts. It was his wish that the kindness he conferred upon you
would be reciprocated not to himself but to your neighbour.
Consider only what your neighbour's needs are and what you
can do for him. Make this one simple reflection: 'He is my
brother in the Lord, a co-heir in Christ, a member of the same
body, redeemed by the same blood, a partner in the same faith,
called to the same grace and happiness of the future life'...

Weaving an intertextual tapestry of scriptural allusions Erasmus
continued:

Let this one thought pass before your mind and let it suffice.
'He is my flesh; he is my brother in Christ'. Is it not so that
whatever happens to one member has repercussions on the
whole body and therefore on the Head? We are all members one
of the other. Members that adhere to each other constitute a
body; the Head of the body is Jesus Christ; the Head of Christ is
God. Whatever is done to any member, whether it be good or
evil, is done to you, to each individual member, to Christ, to
God. These are all one: God, Christ, the body and the members.
The common saying 'Like is attracted to like' and 'Dissimilarity
is the mother of hatred' have no rightful place among Christians. Of what use are words of dissension where such unity
exists? It does not savour of Christianity that a general animosity should exist between courtier and townsman, countryman
and city dweller, patrician and plebeian, magistrate and private
citizen, rich man and poor man, a man of renown and one of no
notoriety, the powerful and the weak, the Italian and the German, the Frenchman and the Englishman, the Englishman and
the Scot, the grammarian and the theologian, the logician and
the grammarian, the doctor and the lawyer, the learned man
and the illiterate, the eloquent and the inarticulate, the bachelor and the husband, the young man and the old man, the
cleric and the layman, the priest and the monk, the Franciscan
and the Colletine, the Carmelite and the Dominican, and, not
to mention all the divisions, between those who are unlike one
another in trivial matters. (*CWE* 66:93–5; *LB* V, 44E–45D)

The rich interweaving of several themes is self-evident, as is the
richness of the evocation of the Scriptures in Erasmus' quotations and
allusions. Above all, the tone is now distinctive: it has that quality of
directness and intimacy which is a characteristic of all of Erasmus'
mature writing. The *Enchiridion* is therefore important as a discovering by Erasmus of his own mind; as a realisation of the freedom to be
himself; and as a mastering of his own style.

The second passage manifests Erasmus' deep understanding of

Hellenic myth, and it comes, significantly, in his analysis of the two-part nature of man that is analogous to the two-fold nature of Scripture:

> With divinely inspired knowledge of all these things, Plato wrote in the *Timaeus* that the children of the gods had fashioned in man in their own image a soul composed of two parts, one divine and immortal, and the other mortal and subject to various disorders. The first of these is pleasure, the bait of evil, as he said; next is pain, which causes us to flee from good and puts obstacles in its path; then come fear and recklessness, foolish counsellors. To these are added implacable anger as well as delusive hope, together with irrational feelings and love, which stops at nothing. Such are Plato's views almost word for word. It did not escape him, either, that happiness in life consists in repressing such disorders. He writes in this same work that those who subdue these passions will live justly and those who are vanquished by them will live unjustly. And he established the seat of the divine soul, that is, reason, in the brain, as if in the citadel of our city, like a king, in the loftiest part of the body nearest to the heavens. It is the least brutish part of the body since it is made up of very fine bony material, not encumbered by sinews and flesh, but very well protected by internal and external senses, so that through their messages, as it were, no uprisings can take place in the republic without its being fully conscious of them immediately. But the mortal parts of the soul, namely the passions, according as they are either too compliant or too antagonistic to man, he removed from the divine soul. Between the brain and the midriff he placed that part of the soul which partakes of courage and wrath, the latter a passion that is rebellious and must be held in check, but is not entirely bestial. For that reason he placed it midway between the upper and the lower parts, for if it were too close, it would disturb the king's tranquillity, or if corrupted by contact with the base populace, would conspire with them against him. He confined the appetitive instinct, which is attracted to food and drink and by which we are driven to the pleasures of Venus, below the midriff to the region of the liver and the belly, far from the royal seat, so that it might live there in a stall like a wild, untamed animal, because it is in the habit of inciting violent uprisings and is least obedient to the orders of the commander. Proof of the brutish and rebellious nature of this lowest part is that shameful part of the body, where concupiscence most exercises its tyranny, which alone of all

members foments rebellion with obscene movements despite the vain protests of the king. (*CWE* 66:42–3; *LB* V, 13E–14D)

Here too is made evident how deeply Neoplatonism has penetrated the thought of Erasmus, and how naturally Erasmus draws upon that key dialogue of Plato, the *Timaeus*, to make his exposition of the nature of man in a work of christian theology.[8] It admirably exemplifies the special quality of Erasmus' *philosophia Christi*: the teaching that there is a simple christian way of life, and it is to be learned and guided by studying the sacred Scriptures as well as classical thought and letters in order to follow and fulfil one's baptismal vows.

The future of Christendom, Erasmus came more and more to realise, lay with the laity and not with the monastic clergy, although he would not condemn monasticism absolutely, as many of the reformers and iconoclasts would do in the stormy 1520s and 1530s. One can with profit contrast Erasmus' handbook for the lay Christian with a typical handbook for the priest, such as the contemporary *Lavacrum Conscientiae* of Jacobus de Gruytrode (or Gruitroede), a Carthusian who died 1475. His manual on the observance of obligation and rules of the priesthood begins with the priest as exemplary. The thrust of Erasmus' manual is to make the layperson central and exemplary; and in his treatment of the responsibilities of the lay Christian and in his glowing exhortation to the christian soldier with its implications to make use of the resources available, Erasmus indeed provides a conviction of the sharing by the laity with the clergy of the freedom to study Scripture, and one can adduce a sense of the priesthood of all believers as Luther later did explicitly.

It is remarkable that simultaneously Erasmus was composing his *Panegyricus* for a very worldly ruler and studying Greek to the level of translating Libanius and two plays by Euripides, as well as working upon his annotations to the Pauline Epistles and editing the *De Officiis* of Cicero – yet he also wrote the *Enchiridion*. These very different works interrelate and interact in significant ways. Erasmus was always interested in teaching (chapter 14), and the *Panegyricus* is part of a continuing effort to instruct the prince that is evident in many letters and culminates in the *Institutio Principis Christiani*. Cicero's noble writing on the duties and offices of man makes that work more available to contemporary readers. The *Enchiridion* completes a structure in that here for the layman are the guidelines of a lay-oriented piety.

The larger aim, however, is a humanistically nurtured life of reading the Scriptures, a habit of study. For the lay person too has a vocation and the laity constitute the key to reform of the Church and renewal of the christian religion. A growing need was felt by many to study the New Testament in its original language, hence Erasmus' conviction that he had to master Greek in order to have direct access to the Greek text of the New Testament, to read the words of Paul himself.[9] The little book of 1503, the *Enchiridion*, touches all of these needs and aspirations; it mattered greatly to Erasmus.

One can map a number of misreadings of this seemingly simple text, for all texts can be misread and all can be so interpreted as to serve only the needs of a later generation.

First, the *Enchiridion* is not, as some have read it, a professional treatise for theologians. Erasmus more often than not wrote for the layman who possessed no special training in the theology of the schools. This work is (as Erasmus called it) a way of life for the laity, and consequently one may not take it as a full and definitive expression of Erasmus' thought and spirituality. For that one may point to the *Ecclesiastes*, his mature work on preaching published in his last year, as an example of a treatise intended for the clergy; there are others. The *Enchiridion* is a key to the new lay piety, characteristic of so much of the *Devotio Moderna*, and it was conceived as a lay person's guide to Scripture, leading into the simple yet learned, but non-scholastic and non-intellectual, *philosophia Christi*. According to this 'philosophy' – philosophy in the basic sense of 'love of wisdom' – Christ is the model to be followed, and the New Testament provides the 'lex Christi' which informs the conduct of the Christian. Reading Scripture regularly is the key to this new piety for lay people, and the texts of Scripture are to be studied for the spiritual, not literal, meaning.

The phrase *'philosophia Christi'* can be seen, in part, as a 'slogan for a purified Christianity based on the New Testament, above all in the teaching of Jesus embodied in the Sermon on the Mount'. But its roots run very deep, and its full meaning is complex; and its goal is nothing less than the perfecting of human nature. Therefore it is time to speak in greater detail and to attempt greater precision about the *philosophia Christi* of Erasmus. Guided by Agricola's fusion of the teaching of the *Devotio Moderna* with that of his pious Italian masters (on which see *Erasmus Grandescens*, 44–5), there was in Erasmus as in Agricola a basically non-speculative interest in philosophy and theology (both the result of excessive scholastic theorising and a counter-thrust against it), an emphasis upon the practical with a strongly moralistic stress on the essential business of living in this world. The *philosophia Christi* was not easy to proclaim, despite the simplicity of its message of Christ; and it was often (and sometimes wildly) misunderstood. It was strongly moralistic, drawing strength from Stoic teachings as well as Christian; but it was not puritanical, for who relished the joy of living more than Erasmus? Above all, it endorsed classical learning and wisdom, and valued the role of rhetoric, especially Ciceronian and Quintilianesque, in arriving at and in teaching wisdom. Fundamentally then there was in Agricola and Erasmus, as in Colet and Vitrier, a commitment to the study of the christian Scriptures and deep, abiding love of Christ, and a complete acceptance of the fact, the actuality, the presence of Christianity.

Second, many of the generation following drew upon this work, as they did on others by Erasmus. But all the doctrine of those later men and women cannot be traced to or blamed on the Dutch humanist. One example must suffice here in our discussion of the *Enchiridion* and its ideas. It has been argued that more radical reformers in the 1520s built upon Erasmian foundations, and the fact that Balthasar Hubmaier visited Erasmus at Basel in 1522 has been made much of. To be sure, the Dutchman admired the purity in their way of living shown by the Anabaptists, and he admired also their great fortitude under sometimes savage persecution. But as Epistles 1313 and 1369 make clear, Erasmus did not accept the teaching and practice of the Anabaptists on baptism, however much it had been inspired by his emphasis on baptism and by his exhortation to the christian soldier to remember enrolling in the army of Christ, 'your general, to whom you twice owned your life'. Kohls has argued that the spiritual grace given and the moral effort required are reciprocal;[10] this concept of a reciprocal functioning of grace and will is essentially Erasmian and will be studied more fully in chapter 39.

One may speak briefly of those things which are not explicitly treated in this work. Behind the christocentric emphasis are two essential points. It follows that the Old Testament law had a reduced importance for Erasmus: that law in its literal sense no longer holds meaning for Christians, and it is only in the spiritual sense that there is significance and relevance for them. Secondly, while Erasmus in no way questions the Trinity, according to Kohls 'only through God's acts of salvation for man can God be recognised'.[11] The divine economy of salvation as Erasmus presented it in *Enchiridion* (for which one accepts Kohls' summary-statement) 'has Christ as its centre'.

The *Enchiridion*, fundamentally offering an art as well as a theory of piety, is impressively complete and is firmly based in Scripture. It is 'Human will freed by Grace'. It is also an essential text for our understanding of Erasmus' fundamental teaching that the end of a christian life is an interior direction towards the following of Christ; we need no other excuse or argument for speaking of the spirituality of Erasmus. For it is deep and sincere, and it continues to the end of his life.

Notes

1) For Erasmus, the move from *scriptor* (which he had doubtless been in the monastery at Steyn) to *compilator* (which is fundamentally his role in the 1500 *Collectanea*) to *commentator* (in his edition of Cicero in 1501) is notable. The final step to *auctor* was achieved in 1503 with the *Enchiridion*, although he had been struggling in that direction with his early writings like the *Antibarbari* and *De Contemptu Mundi*, works which actually were not published until years later. In the *Panegyricus* he is both *orator* (in the oral delivery of the work at court) and *auctor* (by virtue of the printing of the text). The *locus classicus* for this distinction is in the fourth quaestio of the proem to St Bonaventure's commentary on the *Sentences* of Peter Lombard, in *Opera* (Quaracchi ed., 1882) 1, 14/col.2. Cf. J. A. Burrow, *Medieval Writers and Their Work* (Oxford, 1982) 29–30, and the fruitful discussion of A. J. Minnis in *Medieval Theory of Authorship*, 2d ed. (London, 1988) esp. 95 ff.

2) The complex meanings of the military topos (which still had life in the 19th-c. 'Onward Christian Soldiers') needs further study.

3) O. Schottenloher identified the unnamed husband as Johann Poppenruyter, a cannon-founder of Mechelen: 'Erasmus, Johann Poppenreuter und die Entstehung des *Enchiridion Militis Christiani*', *ARG* 45 (1954) 109–16. There is an irony in a tract employing the metaphor of military weaponry being addressed to a maker of cannons.

4) On the wealth of allusion in the *Enchiridion*, see *CWE* 66:xxv ff.

5) See Allen, 'Erasmus and His Printers'. On the importance of Martens, see J. IJsewijn in *BR*. Martens published the first editions of the following works: *Panegyricus, Opuscula aliquot, Apophthegmata, Isocrates, Institutio Principis Christiani, Epistolae aliquot illustrium virorum, Ausonii apophthegmata, Eucherius, Aliquot declamatiunculae graecae*, and *Libanius* – all in the period from 1504 to 1519. In the year 1516 Erasmus was also occupied with helping to see More's *Utopia* through Martens' press.

6) C. Fantazzi has discussed the translations in *CWE* 66:4–7.

7) Ernst-W. Kohls, 'The Principal Theological Thoughts in the *Enchiridion Militis Christiani*', in *Essays on the Works of Erasmus*, ed. R. L. DeMolen (New Haven, 1978) 62.

8) Plato is the only classical author cited frequently in the *Enchiridion*, read in Ficino's translation. Six dialogues of Plato are quoted (Tracy, 85 n. 16).

9) Bearing in mind the humanists' cry *Ad fontes*, one perceives that the indicated fountains for spiritual nourishment are the Scriptures in their original tongue: in the original Greek and not in the later Latin translation, the accepted and nominally 'official' Vulgate, which came to be seen more and more by humanist scholars as inaccurate and unreliable. See now J. D. Tracy, '*Ad Fontes*: The Humanist Understanding of Scripture as Nourishment for the Soul', in *Christian Spirituality: High Middle Ages and Reformation*, ed. J. Raitt et al. (London, 1988) 252 ff.

10) E.-W Kohls, *Theologie*, 1, 73 ff. & 122 ff.

11) Kohls, in *Essays on Erasmus*, 72.

1504, A Threshold Year

When you are not the man you were, why wish to go on living?
Adagia 1.viii.45

Fortune has had a glorious fling at my expense this year!
Epistle 172 (*CWE* 2: 59/3–4; Allen I, 381/1–2)

Even if Holland despises me, I am at any rate not invariably
despised here, whether among noblemen or clerics or scholars.
Epistle 178 from Louvain (*CWE* 2:76/26–27; Allen I, 394/
23–5)

The opening years of the sixteenth century manifested an eagerness,
a quickening of pace – 'armed for untried experience and ready to
watch with hopefulness a prospect of incalculable change' as Acton
has written – and one mark of the changing atmosphere of the early
years of the first decade of the new century is the strikingly different
awareness of *une jeunesse studieuse*. It is in part an addressing of a new
audience, but it is also a new attitude. From 1501 to 1532 Josse
Bade, who was such a key figure in humanistic printing and whose
shop was a centre for humanistic exchange in Paris, addressed many
of his letter-prefaces to this *jeunesse studieuse*; it is a just observation,
although he also addressed others as well, in his international con-
stituency of readers.[1]

How is this to be explained? These are the years in which the
increasing power and appeal of the printing-press is becoming more
and more evident; Erasmus was among the first to take advantage of
its possibilities. For one thing, more students were buying books
themselves (independently of books required by a university sylla-
bus), rather than reading library copies or making their own books
by dictation; and the falling cost of books (as well, no doubt, as the
increase in income of students from middle-class families) helped to
make this possible. Further, the old textbooks, often those prescribed
in the statutes of the universities, were often centuries old (chapter
10), and there was a crying out for new texts. Erasmus was quick on

the mark to supply new ways of studying rhetoric, of writing letters, of appreciating a copious style, as well as new editions of classical authors, beginning with Cicero in 1501, and works of his own authorship too. No one can deny that a change of dimensions impossible to grasp, and leading towards still further and unimaginable prospects of change, was taking place all around Europe, and Erasmus was eager to have the humanist-printers like Martens, Bade, and later Aldus and Froben, as his friends and partners in new ventures.[2]

But a change in his fortunes had not yet occurred. In Louvain he continued to struggle. Huizinga justly speaks of his 'daring indigence so as to be able to realize his shining ideal of restoring theology'(57). He composed epitaphs for wealthy patrons (Epistle 178; Allen, n.51), which was hack work, to be sure, but it bears comparison with the portraits of wealthy merchants that so many of the painters of the Low Countries increasingly turned to for their living. We note the painfully few and small receipts of this period; he received six florins from Cambrai for his epitaphs for the funeral of Hendrik van Bergen;[3] and in November of 1503 Nicolas Ruistre sent him ten gold pieces through the dean of Mechlin. With difficulty he managed to keep his head above water. Small wonder that when an invitation to travel to England materialised in 1505, Erasmus went, after first going to Paris.[4]

Erasmus chose not to return to Holland, and Huizinga is at his best in commenting on Erasmus and the Dutch:

> There was, however, another psychological influence which acted to alienate him from Holland. After he had seen at Paris the perspectives of his own capacities, he became confirmed in the conviction that Holland failed to appreciate him, that it distrusted and slandered him. Perhaps there was indeed some ground for this conviction. But, partly, it was also a reaction of injured self-love. In Holland people knew too much about him. They had seen him in his smallnesses and feebleness ... (43–4)

Perhaps too his illegitimacy was still remembered in Holland but unknown or forgotten in England.

Writing to Nicolas Werner in late 1502 (Epistle 171), Erasmus had spoken of turning down an offer to lecture publicly at Louvain: 'I have rejected this offer for specific reasons, one of them being that I am so close to these Dutch tongues ['*ab Hollandicis linguis*'], which know how to inflict deep wounds and have never learnt how to be helpful to anybody.' (*CWE* 2:59/16–9; Allen 1, 380/13–5.) It is not clear whether Erasmus is here speaking simply of people in Louvain or whether he means to allude to malicious gossip about and against him at Steyn; he seems to have recognised that his outspoken rejoinders to his Steyn critics probably offended even some old friends there. Werner died on 5 September 1504, and Erasmus lost a prior who was sympathetic to his remaining away from Gouda, unlike his successor Servatius Rogers.

Still, Erasmus maintained his ties with Holland, as we see in Epistles 174–6. In the first, Erasmus is addressed in a letter from Jacob Faber written at Deventer on 9 July 1503, a letter prefatory to Faber's edition of *Alexander Hegii ... Carmina* (printed at Deventer by Richard Pafraet in July 1503). Much of the letter is praising of Hegius, of whom Faber speaks as 'your teacher and mine'; Faber recognises how loyal Erasmus has been to Hegius and Agricola, and he asks for Erasmus' translation of Libanius while sending him the edition of Hegius' poems. This is a public letter, declaring in print something of Erasmus' allegiances to Hegius and Agricola and reminding at least Dutch readers of Erasmus' Dutch roots.

In Epistle 175, the second of this group of letters, written to Robert de Keysere from Louvain in September 1503, and printed in an edition that is now rare of Erasmus' *Concio de puero Jesu a puero in schola Coletica nuper Londini instituta pronuncianda* (probably printed at Ghent in 1511, but written in 1503 and preserved by de Keysere)[5] Erasmus comments on Keysere's difficulties as a schoolmaster at Ghent and declares to him that teaching is 'the noblest of all and most acceptable in the sight of God; that is, to prepare the youth of Ghent for the mastery of the highest forms of learning, by inculcating a pure Latin style' (CWE 2:69/3–5; Allen 1, 389/2–3). Here is yet another indication of Erasmus' high valuation of style and a rationale for that judgment.

The third letter, Epistle 176 to Jacob Mauritszoon, dated 28 September from Louvain, responds to some unknown request by Mauritszoon, which he declines. And as a fourth we may add Epistle 178 to Willem Hermans, his old friend, a little later;[6] for this letter touches base with his faithful correspondent, whom he criticises for not taking more initiative in visiting Louvain or in writing congratulatory poems or letters. Friendship, Erasmus always felt, had to be a two-way street.

The *loci* of these letters are all Dutch: Deventer, Ghent and Gouda. Huizinga has remarked that after 1501 there is no evidence that he ever set foot on Dutch soil and thereafter spoke of Holland and things Dutch with at best irony and at worst a kind of 'apologetic contempt' (44). But in the 1523 colloquy 'The Shipwreck' it is the Hollanders who take in the castaways, and through the character Adolf, Erasmus speaks most charitably of them: 'No people could be more kindly, though they do have savage neighbours' (Thompson, *Colloquies*, 146).

In September 1504 Servatius Rogers was chosen the eighth prior of Steyn upon the death of Nicolas Werner (Claes Warnerszoon). Servatius and Erasmus had been close friends while both were in the monastery (chapter 5), and he had visited Erasmus while he was in the service of the bishop of Cambrai (Epistle 39, chapter 7); but there seems to have been little contact after Erasmus' departure from the monastery (*BR*). That there were letters which are now lost is all but certain;[7] and their friendship foundered on lost letters and, it seems, hurt feelings (for whatever reasons) on the part of Servatius. Epistle 185 to Servatius does not appear to have been written after long silence, and yet it is in this letter that Erasmus first informs Steyn of his trip to England. The disapproval of Servatius (again probably in a letter now lost) would seem to be mirrored in the curt tone of Erasmus' very brief letter from Italy in 1506 (Epistle 200).[8] It may be that this situation was felt by Erasmus to be growing tense or hostile, and that it was the prime reason for seeking a dispensation from certain of his monastic vows (as will be discussed in chapter 22): in January 1506 Erasmus obtained the first of his papal dispensations (see appendix C).

A bright spot in this year was his meeting Pieter Gillis, who then remained one of Erasmus' closest friends. Their meeting was probably in February 1504, when Gillis was a corrector in Martens' press and Erasmus was seeing his *Panegyricus* through the press.[9] In 1510 Gillis became chief secretary of the town of Antwerp, but he continued to work for Martens for several years. In the casting and printing of More's *Utopia*, Gillis and Erasmus come together in a remarkable way, Gillis being one of the speakers in More's dialogue (see chapter 31).[10] Soon after their first meeting Gillis and Erasmus were in correspondence with each other (see Epistle 184), and Erasmus often stayed in the Antwerp house of Gillis (his paternal house 'De Spiegel' or 'In Speculo' on the Oude Beurs [*BR*]). Much of Gillis' own studies was in jurisprudence, which goes far to explain Erasmus' growing interest in a subject he had once thought arid.

Until this date Erasmus was primarily interested in Lorenzo Valla as a philologist or grammarian, and as one who worked mainly on classical texts. In 1504 he discovered the Valla who had revolution-ised the textual criticism of the New Testament, and the greatest number of Erasmus' many references to Valla scattered throughout his works cite Valla's scriptural criticism, usually in agreement but at times in opposition.[11]

The first version of Valla's work on the text of the New Testament had been issued in 1443 as *Collatio Novi Testamenti*; it was the revised 1449 version that Erasmus discovered in the library of the Praemonstratensian Abbaye du Parc, outside Louvain: *Laurentii Vallensis ... In Latinam Novi Testamenti interpretationem ex collatione Graecorum ex-emplarium Adnotationes*. The operative word here is *collatio*: the patient recording of the variant readings of manuscripts (with Valla emphasising the Greek), for no textual scholarship is possible without collation.[12]

It is therefore striking that Erasmus should have discovered a manuscript – one of the dreams of the renaissance humanists, who indeed hunted manuscripts like treasure-trove – and carried it off for printing, and then absorbed that work into his own ambitious programme for scholarship. The story can be quickly told, but we shall then want to dwell upon its effects and implications.

It is patent that Erasmus came upon the manuscript of the *Adnotationes* – by 1504 an all but forgotten work – quite by chance. In Epistle 182 to Christopher Fisher, written in Paris most likely in March of 1505, and repaying Fisher's hospitality by dedicating his edition of Valla to him, we read in Erasmus' own words, 'As I was hunting last summer in an ancient library, for those coverts offer by far the most enjoyable sport, luck brought into my toils a prey of no ordinary importance: Lorenzo Valla's notes on the New Testament.' (*CWE* 2:89/4–6; Allen 1, 407/1–4.) Even the style and language of Erasmus' description – hunting in an old library, and finding prey – were part of a humanist *topos*; but Erasmus, as always, endeavours to make it seem casual and utterly informal.

We have heard much of Erasmus' ambition to present the New Testament to his own age in a more pure text – thus involving the work of a textual scholar in editing the Greek, and of a grammarian in annotating that text, and then of a translator in paraphrasing it in a clear and simple Latin – it was the ambition of a lifetime of work. Almost instantaneously then, the discovery of Valla's *Annotations* became for Erasmus 'the instrument that would make possible a renewal of religious thought itself', as Louis Bouyer has rightly put it; and I shall quote Father Bouyer at greater length to stress the transformation involved:

> there is here something analogous to what probably happened to Aquinas, with respect of the method he inherited from Abelard. To have made of Abelard's dialectical criticism – so vigorously opposed by William of Saint-Thierry and St Bernard – the chief prop of a radically renewed theology which still remained faithful to its own tradition is unquestionably no

more astonishing a feat than Erasmus' own: the turning of
Valla's philological criticism into the point of departure for a
renewal of biblical studies firmly spiritual and evangelical in its
orientation.[13]

To write, as one distinguished reformation scholar has done on the
Annotations, 'They contain nothing especially exciting. They are just
philological notes ... '[14] totally misses their significance. In his
preface to the 1505 edition of Valla, Erasmus made it clear that the
translation of the Bible by St Jerome was in need of emendation, a
conclusion he could not have reached a dozen years earlier in the
Augustinian monastery of Steyn where the text of Jerome was not to
be questioned (chapter 5).

Erasmus might have had Martens print Valla's *Annotations* in
Louvain, but he did not. As others have suggested, perhaps he felt
that Martens' press was not adequate, lacking sufficient Greek in his
case. But quite possibly Martens did not want to print the Valla
because it was by a writer under a cloud of disapproval or even hatred
(chapter 9).

En tout cas, Erasmus returned to Paris with his manuscript and
Bade in fact printed it, for he already knew and valued Valla's
Elegantiae.[15] Bade's letter to Erasmus (Epistle 183, Paris 7 March
1505) is inserted in Erasmus' edition following the dedicatory letter
to Christopher Fisher (Epistle 182). Bade stands firmly with
Erasmus, declaring 'I cannot fail to agree with your authoritative
opinion, frankly expressed, about our Valla: no fair-minded person
could take exception to him, and all students already owe him a
considerable debt of gratitude and goodwill.'

Then, citing Augustine in *De Doctrina Christiana*, 'matters which
are somewhat obscure and unintelligible in one tongue become lu-
minous and explicit when they are compared with a version in
another ... ' Bade closes by picking up the topos of book-hunting
floated by Erasmus, 'for my hope is that your hunting will be as
pleasant as it is welcome to all students of divinity.' (*CWE* 2:97/2–
13; Allen 1, 413/1–11.) It is worth observing that Bade, who was
five years younger than Erasmus, was a native of Brabant and one
who had been educated by the Brethren of the Common Life at their
Ghent school. Afterwards Bade studied in Italy under the younger
Guarino, and among his own writings (other than more than 225
prefatory letters) was a life of Thomas à Kempis.

During his Louvain period from 1502 to 1504 Erasmus often visited
Antwerp, and through Pieter Gillis (with whom he generally stayed)
he probably met a goodly number of people interested in humanism

and printing, the larger number of whom have faded from view. There is a recollection of one conversation he had at Antwerp in the house of Nicolaas of Middelburg, a physician; but this Nicolaas has not been identified (*BR*). It was in his *Responsio adversus febricitantis cujusdam libellum* of 1529, directed against Luis de Carvajal, that Erasmus recalled the conversation, and he thought that it had been about twenty-six years in the past.[16] One can only speculate on their conversation: it might have been about Middelburg, a port near Veere of some importance then (prince Charles was at Middelburg preparing to sail from there to Spain, Epistle 596 in 1517, *CWE* 5:6; and earlier Jan Becker van Borssele had been given a canonry at Middelburg, Epistle 291, *CWE* 2:285 and note). Or Erasmus might have wished to confer with yet another physician.

Our knowledge of Erasmus' personal relationships during the early years is far from complete.

After a visit to Antwerp in February 1504 (and there were doubtless others we do not know of, visits to Martens and to Gillis),[17] Erasmus returned to Louvain and would remain there into the summer. Some time in the late autumn of 1504 (no later than December) Erasmus was back in Paris. There is a long gap from Epistle 180 to Desmarez, which we have already discussed and which is dated February 1504, until Epistle 181 to John Colet, which is from Paris and is to be dated, we think, December 1504.[18] In this letter to Colet, Erasmus writes of 'a small literary gift, consisting of a few of my minor works' (*CWE* 2:87/49–50), which included the *Lucubratiunculae* printed by Martens the year before in February; one of the works in the *Lucubratiunculae* was the *Enchiridion*. More significant than his speaking of the sale of copies of his *Adagia* which had been sent to England at his own expense is his declaring to Colet his desire to 'discharge the commitments I have entered into with respect to secular literature' (*CWE* 2:88/81–2; Allen I, 405/71–4). We cannot be sure of these commitments, or to whom they were made, but Erasmus clearly feels that they have a compelling force. 'So I beseech you to help me as far as you can', Erasmus continues, 'in my burning zeal for sacred studies by releasing me from the kind of literature which has now ceased to give me pleasure' (*CWE* 2: 88/85–7; Allen I, 406/76–9). This echoes the expression earlier in the letter of being eager 'to approach sacred literature full sail, full gallop' (29–30).

That request to Colet seems to have born fruit in an invitation to come to England, a trip Erasmus would make in 1505 (chapter 22). The Dutch humanist continued to work on his Greek studies and on his many projects. To Willem Hermans he wrote in October 1502 that 'the study of Greek absorbs me completely, and I have not wholly wasted my efforts, for I have made such good progress that I am capable of expressing my meaning in Greek with reasonable proficiency and, what is more, extempore' (*CWE* 2:59/12–15; Allen I, 381/9–12). the term *extempore* is significant. As Tracy has rightly observed, whether at Steyn or at Paris Erasmus 'made it a precept that pupils should express themselves "extemporaneously" in letters' (74). For him then to have reached the level of being able to express himself *extempore* in Greek was an exact measure of his achievement.[19]

When Erasmus left Louvain for Paris he carried with him his usual *impedimenta* of unfinished works. But this time he had two manuscripts that would reach the printed page rather quickly: his edition of Valla's *Adnotationes* (published in March 1505), and his translation of Euripides (published by Bade in 1506). In Paris Erasmus also worked on his adages, revising the first edition, which he claimed to regret – at least to Colet, in the letter requesting Colet's help for work on sacred studies[20] – and the second edition was published by Bade in 1506 (Epistle 126 is the prefatory letter to the 1500 edition and it was replaced by Epistle 211, also addressed to Mountjoy, in the greatly enlarged Aldine edition of 1508, the *Adagiorum Chiliades*).

By the end of 1504, then, Erasmus had published or prepared for publication the early texts for the main tracks of his career. The 1500 *Adagiorum Collectanea* had been printed in 1500 and he was at work on the massive *Adagiorum Chiliades*, beginning the ongoing revisions of the adages that would last until his death.[21] In the discovery of Valla's *Adnotationes* and the preparation of the manuscript for a Paris printing Erasmus was announcing the textual theory and the emphasis upon text that was the foundation for his lifelong work on the New Testament. The *Enchiridion* was the first of works of religious teaching, and together with the pieces in the *Lucubratiunculae* it establishes beyond question or cavil the central role of religion in Erasmus' life and the christocentric nature of his theology. And the first of a number of works dealing with humanist and political affairs had appeared with the *Panegyricus*; ideas and themes merely sketched or intimated in this eulogistic *declamatio* for a Burgundian duke were later developed in the *Education of a Christian Prince* (chapter 31).

If he began his Louvain years with the feeling that fortune had had its fling at his expense, and if he could write with some rhetorical understatement that he was not despised in Louvain, at the end of 1504 Erasmus could have considerable confidence that his reputation as a humanist was being strongly forged everywhere.

Notes

1) See Maurice Lebel, ed., *Josse Bade, Dit Badius (1462–1535)*; and for greater detail and wider scope, Renaudet, *Préréforme et Humanisme*. Phillips has remarked on Erasmus' consideration of audience in his prefaces: 'In many of these prefaces we see the enthusiasm for the work of restoration [of texts and of antiquity] linked continually with hopes for the young, with the vision of a new age. "What riches, if only one could be a boy again, *O divitias, si liceat repubescere!*"' 'Erasmus and the Classics' in *Erasmus*, ed. Dorey (London, 1970) 17, q. from Epistle 643 of 1517 (Allen III, 65/27).

2) There was to be sure an overlap of manuscript and print: see the invaluable testimony of Bade in his 225 and more prefaces, and the recent studies (cited above) by Trapp, Hellinga, *et al.*

3) See *CWE* 2:75/9 for an estimation of the value of these coins (and Allen I, 395/51 n., introd. note to Ep. 181).

4) See *CWE* 2:n. to Epistle 185. It is noteworthy that Erasmus here writes to Servatius Rogers, now his prior at Steyn – probably at the end of 1505 – informing him that he has been staying with Mountjoy in London for several months, and he signs the letter 'from the bishop's palace': scarcely a letter intended to endear himself to his prior (although he does begin with the excuse of missing letters), but calculated to impress with the fact of being under the roof of the bishop.

5) Allen thinks it more probable that 'it may be supposed that Caesar [Keyzere] obtained the *Concio* [1511] and the poems from Erasmus in Paris, with which he then had connexions, in the summer of 1511, and that in reprinting them he added, though unconnected, a letter written to himself some years before, which he had doubtless treasured' (1, 388 n.).

6) Allen dated the letter 27 November 1503 (I, 393), but *CWE* dates it 27 September (*CWE* 2:75). It clearly follows the letter to Ruistre, which is 17 November 1503, and no reason is provided in *CWE* for its changed dating.

7) See Epistle 185/1–2, 'a letter which will, I think, have been delivered to you'; and Epistle 189/1–2, 'I have sent you several letters already … '

8) Given that some letters were lost even in 1504–5, is it not likely that Erasmus would not have wanted to keep a letter from Servatius explicitly directing him to return to his monastry?

9) The first letter in their extensive correspondence is Epistle 184. See *CWE* 2:97–8 n., and Allen I, 413 n.; also *BR*.

10) In a striking way the friendship of Erasmus and Gillis – of each with the other, and of both with More – is celebrated in the diptych by Metsys (see chapter 33 and figures 1 and 2). Gillis helped Erasmus greatly in negotiations with printers, and in financial matters (*BR*).

11) See Trinkaus in *BR* and Chomarat, *Grammaire et Rhetorique*, 11, 777 ff.

12) E. J. Kenney, *The Classical Text*, 25 ff: the traditional view by 16th c editors of the editorial task 'was to *improve* the texts by correction: *emendare, corrigere, emaculare*'. Collation has two related significations: a critical examination of mss or editions with a view to ascertaining the correct or better text; and the recorded result of such comparison, various readings obtained by comparing different exemplars.

13) Louis Bouyer in *Cambridge History of the Bible*, 11, 495.

14) To be sure, Bainton goes on to say that Valla's subjecting the New Testament to the same philological scrutiny as any other book 'may well have stimulated Erasmus to undertake his own translation and   annotations' (ibid.). But this *may* takes away the point of Bouyer's emphasis, and it does not redeem what is essentially a misreading.

15) Cf. Lebel on Bade, 8, 15 & passim.

16) Cf. *BR* and Allen IV, xxi–xxii; the allusion is in Erasmus' *Responsio adversus febricitantis libellum* of 1529 (*LB* x, 1681D).

17) It is well to remind ourselves from time to time of the fragmentary nature of the evidence that we are given: chiefly Erasmus' correspondence, much of which has come down to us by accident. We cannot speak as though we knew the whole story, whatever that was.

18) Allen has a long and valuable note on the dating of Erasmus' move-ments in 1504 (I, 403 n.); and in this note Allen details a grant from the archduke Philip that Erasmus receipted on the 21st of October of this year. His letter to Colet was probably written shortly after his arrival in Paris, likely in December; Allen thinks (I, 413 n.) that Erasmus was probably back in Paris only once between the spring of 1501 and the autumn of 1504. Even if there were not the worry of plague, it was a moderately long trip, and expensive for Erasmus at this time.

19) The English translation *extempore* renders the Latin *ex tempore*, meaning *instantaneously* or *on the spur of the moment*, as in Cicero, *De Oratore* III, 50. 194, where he comments on his example: 'how much more easily shall we achieve this in prose, given practice and training' (Loeb trans., 155). This facility mattered greatly to Erasmus. 'Writing swiftly does not teach good writing, but writing well permits one to write swiftly' (see Tracy, 71); and this just observation surely provides the key to Erasmus' well-nigh incredible facility for writing swiftly.

20) To Colet he lamented in 1504 that his *Adagia* of 1500 (which he already referred to as the first edition) 'is so full of printers' errors that it looks as if it had been deliberately spoiled' (*CWE* 2: 88/93-3); and of his translation of Euripides he wrote to Aldus Manutius (in Ep. 207 of October 1507) that 'the whole thing is chock-full of errors' and blamed Bade for not taking proper precautions (*CWE* 2:132/33-4).

21) Related both to the *Adages* and to his other writings, the *Colloquies* - although the concept of the genre was begun in a number of early epistles, and developed by other aspects of his Paris teaching - would not see print until 1519 and later. Still other educational writings that had been begun in the Paris period as well would see publication only later.

Return to England, 1505–1506

I am deeply preoccupied with pondering how I can wholly
devote to religion and to Christ whatever life remains to me.
How much this may be, I do not know. I am conscious how
fleeting and insubstantial is the life of man, even the longest;
and I can see also that my own health is frail, and has been
further weakened to a considerable degree by my laborious
studies, and to some extent also by misfortune. I can see that
those studies have no end, and every day I seem to begin all
over again. Therefore I have made up my mind to be content
with my present undistinguished fortune, especially when I
have acquired as much Greek as I need, and to pay attention to
the contemplation of my death and the state of my soul ...
Erasmus to Servatius Rogers, 1 April 1506
Epistle 189 (*CWE* 2: 111/7–16; Allen I, 421/6–14)

Erasmus' relations with Holland were far from satisfactory at this
time (Huizinga, 59); certainly he was not happy with his failure to
obtain steady patronage from Tournhem or Brussels, and two years
in Louvain had been unsuccessful in securing anything beyond an
offer to lecture. Relations with his monastery continued to be
strained, and it is possible that threats were made by his prior. His
hopes therefore turned to England, and in 1504 he focused his efforts
in a letter to Colet asking for help.[1] Colet's reply is missing, but it is
most likely that Erasmus owed something to Colet for passing on to
Mountjoy his need for help and perhaps also for the king's promise of
a benefice that continued to be dangled before Erasmus. We must
connect the hope of a benefice with Erasmus' seeking a dispensation,
the petition for which was surely set in motion before he left Paris
and the language of which clearly has in view an English benefice.

How long was Erasmus in Paris this time? Long enough to see his
edition of Valla's *Annotations* through the press with Bade, and to
prepare his translation of Euripides into Latin (which was printed in
1506: see *CWE* 2:107n). It is likely that he made use of his time[2]
(other than continuing his Greek) to establish further relations with
other scholars and perhaps other printers than Bade .[3]

In February of 1504 his old enemy Jan Standonck had died at
Paris; the shadow of the enmity haunted Erasmus for the rest of his
life, and there were doubtless others at the Sorbonne not too kindly
disposed towards the sharp-tongued Dutchman who never finished
his Paris doctorate (chapter 13); a leading anti-Erasmian was Noël
Béda. Nonetheless there were friends and fellow-humanists at Paris.

To be sure, Gaguin was dead, having died an old and suffering
man of nearly four-score on 22 May 1501; but others of the humanist
circle were very much active. Josse Clichtove, a Fleming who had
been a pupil of Charles Fernand (chapter 12), was a disciple of
Lefèvre and became his principal collaborator even before Erasmus
left Paris in 1499 (*BR*). Although he was altogether reform-minded,
he and Erasmus were to part ways over the Lutheran question after
1520. The younger Alsatian scholar Beatus Rhenanus was then
studying with Fausto Andrelini (who more than Erasmus was continuing his career as a poet), with Clichtove, Lefèvre, and Georgius
Hieronymus, who taught Greek to Reuchlin, Erasmus, Beatus
Rhenanus, and Budé (*BR*). All were scholars who had some connections with Erasmus – some earlier, as with Fausto in the 1490s, some
later as with Beatus Rhenanus.[4] A larger point is that Erasmus had
many old friends to revisit, and perhaps the most notable figure at
this time was Josse Bade, with whom he was beginning to publish;[5]
Bade had published many of the humanists north of the Alps, and his
printing-shop was a clearing house for scholars and even for their
mail.

Erasmus was never inactive, and we know that his Greek studies
were continuing; but there are few clues to his everyday or even
weekly activities. It was another period of relative silence in his
correspondence, which may not necessarily mean that he was closing
the door to future biographers; it may simply call attention yet once
more to the sometimes accidental nature of the letters as biographical evidence, for so often our main evidence for his life and activities
is in letters not preserved by Erasmus himself, as discussed in chapter
4.[6]

In the early summer of 1506 Erasmus wrote to Thomas Linacre
(Epistle 194) that he had as much affection for his French friends as
for the English ones, and that is a needed reminder lest we think too
exclusively of the Sorbonne in terms of those who opposed him.

In his letter to Servatius written from London at the end of 1505
(Epistle 185), Erasmus declared that 'to explain what had induced
me to go back to England would be tedious' (*CWE* 2:99/5–6; Allen
I, 414/4–5), scarcely the tone for winning the approval of one's
unsympathetic religious superior. But he did inform his prior that he

had solid reasons and good counsel: 'The further success of my enterprise depends on Heaven's good will; but I have come so that scholarship may profit, and not to make my own fortune' (*CWE* 2:99/9–11; Allen I, 414/9–10). Is Erasmus answering a charge making the rounds in the rumour mill that he is greedy, or interested mainly in money? Carefully, one infers, Erasmus informed his prior that Lord Mountjoy had 'pressingly invited' him to come back to England (*CWE* 2:99/13; Allen I, 414/11–12), and that in extending this invitation Mountjoy 'was seconded by the entire scholarly community': a remarkable bit of rhetoric and doubtless something of an exaggeration. And then to Servatius he also added that England had five or six scholars as distinguished ('profoundly versed', '*in utraque lingua exacte docti*') in Latin and Greek as Italy possessed (*CWE* 2:99/ 14–16). The letter closes with a prayerful expression: 'Yet I cannot regard myself as successful unless I have the approval of Christ also: and my true happiness depends upon His verdict'. The failure of Servatius to reply (or so it seems from the evidence on Erasmus' side of the ledger) signals his growing coolness towards Erasmus.

Upon arriving in London Erasmus stayed with Thomas More and his first wife, Jane Colt; for More's house was open to all friends. One must think of the appropriateness of Erasmus' first adage in the *Adagiorum Chiliades*: *amicorum communia omnia* (I.i.I.) – between friends all is common. But with More such generosity was also a manifestation of christian charity. There is no evidence that it was learned from his lawyer-father; it is possible that this habit of mind and heart was acquired while a page in the household of cardinal Morton and confirmed during his years in the London Charterhouse. Except for his apparent dislike of More's second wife (which may have been an exaggeration), Erasmus was always a grateful guest in More's household.

Through Erasmus and his letter we gain a sense of the 'entire scholarly community' in England, and there was indeed a gallery of fine scholars, with some 'profoundly versed in Latin and Greek'. We have already encountered bishop John Fisher in chapter 15. When Erasmus arrived this time, Fisher was about thirty-seven and reaching the peak of his distinguished academic and ecclesiastical career. In 1501 he had been made vice-chancellor of Cambridge University, and in 1503 he was appointed to the new chair of divinity founded by Lady Margaret Tudor. In 1504 he became chancellor of the University, and on 12 April 1505 he was made president of Queens' College, an office he held for three years. In the same year that he became chancellor (1504) he was elevated to the see of Rochester, at the age of thirty-five; re-elected annually to the chancellorship of

Cambridge until 1514, he was then elected for life.[7] Fisher's impressive achievements at Cambridge can be seen by his hand in Lady Margaret Beaufort's foundation of a chair in theology (1503) and two new colleges, Christ's College (1505–6) and St John's (1511). Fisher was a complex ecclesiastic and man, but his humanistic enthusiasms were very real and strong (Bradshaw, 7). The intimacy between Fisher and Erasmus lasted throughout their lives, with Erasmus living only one year beyond the martyrdom of Fisher in 1535. Erasmus' three years at Cambridge (1511–1514), Bradshaw writes, 'represented a major coup – recognised more in the aftermath than at the time, it seems – for the University and particularly for Queens', where Fisher, as former president of the College (1505–8), arranged for Erasmus to stay'(7). It would seem likely that the arranging for the extended stay of Erasmus would have been done in 1506 during Erasmus' second visit to England.

Christopher Fisher (apparently no relative of the bishop) was a doctor of civil and canon law who in 1506 was made (but may not have been installed as) bishop of Elphin in Ireland; from 1508 to 1510 he was in Rome as one of the king's solicitors at the Curia, and in 1510 he was appointed nuncio to England. During the winter of 1504–5 Fisher had been in Paris for some reason, and Erasmus was a guest in his house. Epistle 182 indicates that Fisher had encouraged him in the publication of Valla's *Annotations*, and to Fisher Erasmus dedicated his edition of 1505 (Epistle 182, March 1505, *CWE* 2:89; Allen I, 407). Allen notes that Fisher was praised by Bade as '*vir heroica plane virtuta et Ciceroniana dicendi maiestate praeditus*' (Allen IV, xxii). He died in 1511 or 1512 (*BR*), depriving Erasmus of a valuable friend.

William Warham (c.1456–1532) was favourable to the new humanistic ideas, and Erasmus praised him highly for his patronage after their first meeting in 1506 when Erasmus was brought to Lambeth by William Grocyn and presented the bishop with his translation of Euripides' *Hecuba*.[8] Erasmus repeatedly praised the archbishop for his modesty, wisdom and generosity ('one unrivalled Maecenas'). A canonist, from 1506 until his death he was chancellor of Oxford University and lord chancellor of England from 1503 until his relinquishing the office to Wolsey in 1515. After Warham's death in 1532 Erasmus sang his praises in the preface to the 1533 edition of the *Adagia*, and in *Ecclesiastes* at the end of his own life Erasmus paid one last tribute to his generous benefactor (*LB* V, 810F–812A).[9]

Richard Foxe (c. 1446/7–1528) is the third of the English prelates whom Erasmus knew intimately and whose support and patronage he enjoyed; Wolsley he knew, and his patronage was solicited, but Erasmus never enjoyed his support or confidence. Foxe was a supporter of humanism, as may be seen in the books of the classical revival that he gathered for Corpus Christi College, Oxford.[10] Erasmus and Foxe first met in 1500, when Foxe was bishop of Durham, and the prelate, a doctor of law, was Erasmus' host in London 1505 and certainly his patron at about that time. Later, we may note here as a token of Foxe's strong support, Foxe 'publicly declared Erasmus' translation of the New Testament worth ten commentaries' (*BR*, citing Epistle 502). A range of works dedicated to Foxe speaks both of his generosity and of his own breadth of interests (*BR*).

With Christopher Urswick (c. 1448–1522) we turn to another lawyer, a doctor of canon law from Cambridge in 1482, who held many preferments and became dean of York (1488–94) and of Windsor (1496–1505), but retired about 1512 as rector of Hackney. He was a member of the London-Oxford humanist circle as patron, and was friendly with Colet, Tunstall, More and Polydore Virgil, as well as Erasmus (*BR*). Having met Urswick on his first visit and having renewed the acquaintance during his second stay, Erasmus dedicated to Urswick his translation of Lucian's *Gallus*, printed in 1506 (Epistle 193, which is the dedicatory preface). As we learn from a later letter (Epistle 416 of 1516), Erasmus received a horse from Urswick, which was one he greatly valued for it took him twice on the round trip to Basel from the Low Countries.[11]

The thesis of Seebohm has been well known for more than a century, and the misplaced emphasis upon Oxford in his title has been adjusted by the now-current phrase 'the London-Oxford humanist circle' (for example, Trapp on Urswick and Colet in *BR*). The prime figures were Linacre, Colet, Grocyn and Thomas More.

Colet, already discussed in chapter 15, remained central in Erasmus' life and career until his death in 1519. As we have seen from the correspondence, Erasmus was not hesitant in making clear to Colet that he needed financial help (Epistle 181 especially). Trapp notes that Colet came into his substantial patrimony by the end of 1505, and then adds (with rare unkindness) that 'within three months ... Erasmus was in London' (*BR*).[12] It is quite likely that Erasmus was hopeful of even stronger support from Colet, and he knew that Colet was instrumental with Mountjoy and others in eliciting further patronage. But, as Trapp remarks, 'Colet seems not always to have come up to Erasmus' financial expectations' (*BR*) and had to be reminded of his duty, and of the modes of giving; yet he was in fact helpful to Erasmus and others (*BR*). What is much more vital is their sharing of theological concerns, and in this Colet and Erasmus were very close, only Vitrier came as close (chapter 18); with Colet there was also the sharing of deep educational concerns as well. The same age as Erasmus, Colet was carried off by three attacks of the sweating sickness that eventually caused his death in 1519. Erasmus did not tire of singing his praises, and his encomium in a letter to Justus Jonas (Epistle 1211 of 13 June 1521) is a memorable portrait.

Thomas Linacre (c. 1460–1524) emerges from an early life about which nothing is known. He was elected a fellow of All Souls College, Oxford, in 1484, and in 1487 left for Italy, where he studied for a dozen years, longer than any of Erasmus' English friends had done. In the early years of his Italian period he studied Greek and Latin with Chalcondyles and Poliziano in Florence; and he was a fellow student of Grocyn, Latimer, and Giovanni de Medici, the future Leo X. He took a degree in medicine at Padua in 1496, and during the period 1497–9 he worked closely with Aldus Manutius, chiefly in helping the publication of the *editiones principes* of Aristotle's works in Greek. By August 1499 he had returned to London, and at about the same time he was charged with the education of the young prince. In 1500 Thomas More studied Greek with Linacre. In 1509 he was appointed physician to Henry VIII, and in 1518 he founded the College of Physicians (later the Royal College of Physicians) and remained president until his death. Three letters survive from the earlier years of the friendship between Linacre and Erasmus (Epistles 194 of 1506, 415 of 1516, and 1230 of 1521). Not only did Erasmus consult him as physician and receive prescriptions, but he was interested in Linacre's translations of Greek. Erasmus admired him without qualifications (*BR*).[13]

The oldest of the group of humanist-reformers was William Grocyn, who was probably born in the 1440s, for in 1463 he was a scholar of Winchester College, Oxford, and a full fellow of New College in 1467. In 1488 Grocyn resigned a readership at Magdalen College and went to Italy, spending two years studying under Chalcondyles and Poliziano, in company with Linacre and the younger William Latimer. At some point Grocyn met Aldus Manutius, the Venetian printer (*BR*). When Erasmus made his first trip to England in 1499 he found Grocyn and Colet at the core of the humanist circle that was intensely interested in Greek and humanism; at one time Grocyn had been tutor to William Warham. In 1496 Grocyn was appointed rector of St Lawrence Jewry in London, and thereafter he was increasingly occupied with affairs (including teaching More and Croke) in London. As Colet appears to have left Oxford for London in 1504, the centre for the London-Oxford reformers was now definitely London. Erasmus admired Grocyn among the older humanists in England, and it pleased him that the older scholar approved of his translation of two Euripidean tragedies (Epistles 207, his letter to Aldus of 1507, which also indicates the approval of Linacre, Latimer and Tunstall, 'who are your friends as well as mine'; and Epistle 1479 of 1524 to Haio Hermann). So much a friend was Grocyn that Erasmus tried to excuse his not writing for publication – for only one letter to Aldus appeared in print during his lifetime (see Epistle 534) – by calling attention to his failing eyesight.[14]

The youngest, and in many ways the brightest star, of the group was Thomas More: born in 1478 he was about eleven years younger than Erasmus, which did not seem to matter in 1499 when they first met and More was barely twenty-one (see chapter 15). By the time of Erasmus' second visit to England More had left the Charterhouse and married Jane Colt, had lectured on Augustine at Grocyn's church of St Lawrence Jewry, and had been returned as a member of Parliament. During these years More was also continuing his studies in Greek with Grocyn, and he and Erasmus began their translating of Lucian together. (The later story of More's career and of their friendship will be resumed in later chapters.) What is important is to stress the closeness of their friendship, for 'from this date onwards, the lives and intellectual development of the two friends are closely intertwined'. All More's early humanistic works are the result of a close collaboration with Erasmus[15] – as in the case of the translations from Lucian – or reflect Erasmus' concept of the classics and his programme of study – as do the *Utopia* and *Richard III* (although the latter is a work that Erasmus, for whatever reason, never mentioned). Conversely, a number of Erasmus' writings, among them the *Enchiridion*, bear marks of the influence of More (thus R. J. Schoeck, *BR*). In the friendship of More and Erasmus the differences are as striking as the likenesses, and both are important.[16]

The rhetorician Lucian of Samosata, on whom More and Erasmus worked together, left some eighty pieces, chiefly in dialogue form,[17] and especially in those marked by his 'joking in earnest' (*ridentem dicere verum*) he offered sharp criticism of inept and pretentious language. He created a unique kind of dialogue for which he is celebrated, and it had a long life, cropping up in the eighteenth and nineteenth centuries in the dialogues of the eighteenth century and the imaginary conversations of Landor and the satirical novels of Peacock. In his prefatory letter to the *Gallus* (Epistle 193, addressed

to Urswick from Hammes at the beginning of June 1506) Erasmus
explained why the ancient rhetorician's writings were so attractive:

> Nobody, in my opinion, has succeeded so well at this [mingling
> usefulness with pleasure] as our Lucian. Recalling the out-
> spokenness of the Old Comedy, but lacking its acerbity, he
> satirises everything with inexpressible skill and grace, ridicules
> everything, and submits everything to the chastisement of his
> superb wit ... (*CWE* 2:116/31–4; Allen I, 425/27–31)

> He possesses such grace of style, such felicity of invention, such
> a charming sense of humour, and such pointedness in satire ...
> (ibid., lines 48–50; Allen I, 425/43–5)

During his second visit to England of 1505–6 Erasmus had More to
share his enthusiasm for Lucian, and together the two had a 'friendly
competition' in translating Lucian (Rummel, 49 ff.). Together the
two friends translated a number of the dialogues: in the 1506 edition
five are by Erasmus and four by More, and were first published in
1506 as *Luciani opuscula* ,with Epistle 193 as the prefatory epistle.
Erasmus added further translations of Lucian's dialogues while in
Italy, and these were separately printed by Martens in 1512. By the
year of Erasmus' death there were some three dozen printings of the
translations. The direct influence of Lucian upon the writing of the
Praise of Folly will be discussed in chapter 26, and for More the
influence of Lucian is to be seen in his *Utopia*.

It was thus a remarkable group of humanist scholars that Erasmus
met in Oxford and London, and his first impressions of 1499 were
more than fulfilled in 1505. That enthusiastic portrait he had
painted in December 1499 for Robert Fisher (Epistle 118, quoted
above in chapter 15, p. 223), was borne out in the lives of Colet,
Linacre, Grocyn, and More from 1499 to 1505; and Erasmus' appreciation of them as Greek scholars and as friends continued to deepen.
In the friendly competition with More in the translation of Lucian,
Erasmus' facility in Greek continued to grow.[18]

But he had not been granted the benefice that he so desperately
needed for financial security. He had petitioned for, and permission
was granted, to study for a doctorate in theology, but he gave up this
idea in order to accept the opportunity of travel in Italy.[19] In May of
1506 he accepted an invitation to accompany the two sons of the
Genoese Giambattista Boerio, physician to Henry VII. In June, just
before leaving London, Erasmus dedicated another of his Lucianic
translations, *Timon*, to Thomas Ruthall, secretary to the king
(Epistle 192), and in later letters he tried to gain the support of

Ruthall, who had (as bishop of Durham and secretary to both Henry VII and VIII) some means for dispensing patronage and who had given Erasmus some assurance of goodwill (Epistles 243 and others). But that patronage which he sought in coming to England was still beyond his reach as he left, and with Ruthall he seems to have pressed too hard (*BR*).

The influence of these humanist reformers in England can be seen in McConica's much-cited study of *English Humanists and Reformation Politics*, which relates the humanists and other scholars to their patrons. The influence of the English reformers in Europe has yet to be studied in full (indeed they are scarcely understood as a whole); but a quick sense can be caught by such hints as Erasmus' reference to Linacre, Grocyn, Latimer and Tunstall in his letter to Aldus of 1507, 'who are your friends as well as mine':[20] 'You are aware that these men are too scholarly to be at sea in their judgment ...' (*CWE* 2:132/26–7; Allen I, 438/21–5). One needs a more precise reading of the role of English reformers like Colet and More in the thought of continental humanists like Budé, for the flow of ideas across the Channel was not simply one way.

Leaving England, there was for Erasmus the inevitable Channel crossing that he so dreaded: he was ill for several days on account of the food and seasickness. From Hamme, near Calais, he dispatched his translation of the *Gallus* (Cock) of Lucian to Christopher Urswick (Allen I, 424). Arriving at Paris on 11 June , Erasmus began to put his second visit to England behind him, although he did not forget his friends and supporters; and in Paris he made ready for the trip to Italy that turned out to be a very long one. Among his English friends discussed in this chapter, only Thomas More, the layman, had not been to Italy; and though older now than the young student who had dreamed of studies in Italy, Erasmus was no less eager to see Rome and other centres of learning for himself. He also looked forward to meeting a number of Italian humanists.

Notes

1) See especially the lines 85 ff. in Ep. 181: 'So I beseech you to help me as far as you can in my burning zeal for sacred studies by releasing me from the kind of literature which has now ceased to give me pleasure' (*CWE* 2:88/85–87; Allen I, 406/76–8). Immediately following that *cri de coeur* Erasmus rather cunningly planted with Colet the possibility that Mountjoy could be a means of further support, though Erasmus did not feel he could ask him directly (*CWE* 2:88/87–91; Allen I, 406/78–82).

2) As well as publishing Erasmus' *Valla*, Bade was also at this time

publishing Budé's translation of Plutarch, *De Placitis Philosophorum*; and in Rome during May, Budé dedicated to Julius II his translation of the *De tranquillitate animi* of Plutarch. One has a vision of Erasmus thumbing his way through the shop of Bade to stay au courant with the latest publications, as an American scholar from a provincial university makes use of the shelves in the Warburg and other research libraries. Yet there is no evidence that these two humanists, the most learned of men, ever met in Paris (see *BR*).

3) We have only the following letters written by Erasmus during this brief Paris period: Ep. 181 to Colet (Dec. 1504), Ep. 182 to Christopher Fisher (c. March 1505), Ep. 184 to Gillis (c. March 1505). One clue to his other activities is in the letter to Gillis, where he speaks of an interest in Agricola: 'get together from any source you can', he writes, 'the minor works of Rodolphus Agricola, and bring them with you'. He had earlier purchased a number of Agricola's works (see Epistles 174, 184, and ch. 3).

4) The actual meeting of Beatus and Erasmus did not take place until after both had left Paris (see ch. 30).

5) Bade published 43 books with works by Erasmus, separately or combined with other authors, and 48 works edited or annotated by Erasmus (*BR*). Erasmus kept close touch with Bade for many years, and in fact he was a kind of successor to Gaguin for Erasmus: see Renaudet, 409.

6) It is more likely that there were letters pertaining to Erasmus' dispensation, for as Ferguson observes in his note to Ep. 187A (in *CWE* 2: 103 headnote), 'Erasmus had undoubtedly begun negotiations for such a dispensation at this time because he had hopes of receiving a benefice in England', for the brief from Julius was dated from Rome, 4 January 1506. Yet we have no epistolary evidence of such negotiations before Epistle 187A: but why would Erasmus have wanted to preserve such letters (unless there were other interest in them?)

7) See E. Surtz sj, *The Works and Days of John Fisher, 1469–1535* (Cambridge, Mass., 1967); and *Humanism, Reform and the Reformation – The Career of Bishop John Fisher*, ed. Brendan Bradshaw and Eamon Duffy (Cambridge, 1989).

8) On the way home after visiting Warham at Lambeth, Erasmus indicated to Grocyn that Warham's present of money for the *Hecuba* was only a small sum; and Grocyn smilingly replied that Warham probably thought that Erasmus was in the habit of dedicating the same work to more than one patron (*CWE* 2:107 n. and *BR*). On returning to Paris Erasmus added the *Iphigenia* and dedicated the expanded work to Warham (Ep. 188 and 208). Ep. 208 is an expanded preface in the edition published by Aldus in December 1507 (Allen, 417–8). Cf. H. W. Garrod, 'Erasmus and his English patrons', *The Library* 5th ser., IV (1949–50) 1–13. Praise of Warham is to be found in the preface to the 1533 ed. of the *Adagia*.

9) To the tribute to Warham is joined a final brief commemoration of John Fisher (V, 812A).

10) See *Letters of Richard Fox*, ed. P. S. Allen, xiv. Corpus Christi College was a foundation of 1516, whch saw the chief building completed in 1517 (Trapp in *BR*): the college is a lovely connecting link between Foxe in the 16th c. and Allen and Mynors in the 20th.

11) 'Your horse has brought me great good fortune. Twice has he carried

me safely to Basel and back again, although the journey was most perilous as well as long ...' (*CWE* 3:298/2–4; Allen II, 247–8/1 ff.).

12) Trapp's account of Colet in *BR* is admirably lucid, and I am much indebted to it. See further his collected studies in *Essays on the Renaissance and the Classical Tradition* (London, 1990).

13) The standard work on Linacre is now *Linacre Studies: Essays on the Life and Work of Thomas Linacre*, ed. F. Maddison, M. Pelling, and C. Webster (Oxford, 1977), with its detailed bibliography.

14) See J. K. McConica, *English Humanists and Reformation Politics*, 14; 'William Grocyn ... is justly seen as the first great native product of the new traditions of learning'. On Grocyn's not writing for publication see Ep. 540 and *Ciceronianus* (*CWE* 28:422–3; *LB* I, 1012D).

15) More's translation of the life of Giovanni Pico della Mirandola was not published until 1509 or 1510, but it was most likely written about 1504 and reflects More's arriving at the decision to leave the Charterhouse: to become a lay scholar in the world and to marry, a double decision which was very Erasmian and reflects (or parallels) much of the teaching of the *Enchiridion*.

16) On the friendship of More and Erasmus, see my essay 'Telling More from Erasmus: An *Essai* in Renaissance Humanism', *Moreana* xxiii 91–2 (Nov. 1986) 11–19. The likenesses and differences matter.

17) See *Oxford Classical Dictionary*,[2] (1970) 621. Erasmus' translations from Lucian are discussed by Rummel in *Erasmus as a Translator of the Classics*, 49–69; see also her introd. to 'Erasmus and the Greek Classics' in *CWE* 29: *Literary and Educational Writings* 7 (1989) xxx–xxxi.

18) See Rummel, *Erasmus as Translator*, for a comparison of the translations by More and Erasmus.

19) Smith, *Erasmus*, 65; *Grace Book, containing the records of the University of Cambridge, 1501–42*, ed. W. G. Searle (1908) p. 46.

20) Cuthbert Tunstall (1474–1559) has not yet come into our picure, for he returned to England only in 1506, having taken a doctorate in law at Padua. He soon became the chancellor of Warham in 1508, and later proved to be a generous patron and supporter of Erasmus (*CWE* 2:132/125). In Italy he had become a friend of Jerome de Busleyden and Lefèvre d'Etaples as well as Aldus (BR). Later bishop of London (consecrated 19 October 1522 by Warham, Wolsey and Fisher) Tunstall played a significant role in relations of Thomas More with the Reformation in England.

Italy, 1506–1509

Vidimus Ausoniae semieruta moenia Romae,
hic, ubi cum sacris venditur ipse deus ...
> Ulrich von Hutten, *Epigrammata ex urbe missa*
> *ad Crotum Rubianum de stato Romano*

Nouveau venu, qui cherches Rome en Rome
Et rien de Rome en Rome n'apperçois,
Ces vieux palais, ces vieux arcz que tu vois,
Et ces vieux murs, c'est ce que Rome on nomme.
> Joachim du Bellay, *Les Antiquitez de Rome*

Par tibi, Roma, nihil, cum sis prope tota ruina;
Quam magni fueris integra fracta doces.
> Hildebert of Lavardin (1055–1133), quoted by C. H.
> Haskins (*The Renaissance of the Twelfth Century*, 1927)

Throughout the western Middle Ages the Eternal City was thought of as the centre of the ancient world and the heart of Christendom.[1] Other northern humanists, together with artists and students in various fields, were moved to travel to Italy: Colet and others of the London-Oxford circle to study Greek, philosophy, and medicine; Copernicus to study canon law and, as an adjunct, astronomy; Dürer and others, painting; Martens, printing. Erasmus had come of age having as role models Agricola, even Hendrik van Bergen, and what must have seemed like so many others, who had studied in Italy. Their motives must have been diverse, and the reactions and returns varied greatly. Later, in a letter that is a defence of his life and work, Erasmus wrote to a compatriot from the Low Countries, Marcus Lauwerijns (Laurinus) in Epistle 809 that 'To Italy alone I have journeyed of my own free will, partly to pay at least one visit to her holy places, partly to profit from the libraries of that part of the world and make the acquaintance of its men of learning.' (5 April 1518, *CWE* 5:365/142–5; Allen III, 267/124–5.)

In August 1506 Erasmus and his group crossed the Alps, travelling through Savoy and by way of the Mont Cenis. On this journey by horseback along twisting Alpine roads Erasmus wrote an ode that he called *Carmen equestre vel potius alpestre*, and it is perhaps (as Huizinga characterises it)[2] Erasmus' most important poem. It won the praise of Johannes Secundus and many others. Erasmus was nearing forty, and for many men this is a time for reflecting on the events of one's past life and thinking himself on the threshold of old age. The poem is therefore sometimes called *Carmen de senectute*. Even the dedication of the poem to Guillaume Cop (c. 1466–1532; Kopp, Latin *coppus*) reflects the concern of the poem with failing health, for Cop was a physician, a student from Basel, where he graduated MA in 1483, studied medicine at Paris and became a doctor of medicine in 1496 (*BR*). One of the new humanist-physicians, he studied Greek with Lascaris and Aleandro (who dedicated his edition of a Ciceronian work, *De Divinatione*, to him); he attended Lefèvre and worked closely with Budé; and it was he who attended Erasmus during bouts of fever in Paris.[3]

A few months earlier Erasmus had sketched the main themes of this poem in his Epistle 189 to Servatius (April 1506), already discussed. 'For myself', the Augustinian canon wrote to his prior,

> I am deeply preoccupied with pondering how I can wholly devote to religion and to Christ whatever life remains to me. How much this may be, I do not know. I am conscious how fleeting and insubstantial is the life of man, even the longest; and I can see also that my own health is frail, and has been further weakened to a considerable degree by my laborious studies, and to some extent also by misfortune. I can see that those studies have no end, and every day I seem to begin all over again ... (*CWE* 2:111/7–13; Allen I, 421/6–12)

We must agree that Erasmus felt obliged to justify his continuing absence to Servatius, and that 'he made Servatius know where he was and why'. Huizinga has his doubts about the sincerity of this letter; but, with Tracy we may feel that, 'there is no reason to doubt that he was sufficiently struck by the relentlessness of time to feel himself "senex" at the age of 36'.[4] There is, in short, nothing insincere or artificially literary in Erasmus' feelings about ageing.[5]

What gives vibrancy to this poem written against the Alpine landscape is first the striking of the note of malady evoked by the address to the famous physician:

> *cedit fugitque morbi*
> *Ingenio genus omne tuo* (lines 6–7)

'every kind of malady flees and surrenders to your genius, except for old age, for which there is no cure.' The poet looks back on his life: his playing as a child, his eagerness for study as a boy, and his interest in poetry, the ways of philosophy and the colours of rhetoric as a young man (painting too, a young interest). His study of Greek and his aspirations to the fame of scholarship are surveyed; but in the midst of it all, old age has come quite suddenly. What remains? It is time to renounce the world and to devote himself to Christ, as he had just a few months earlier written Servatius. He concludes with the affirmation that the decision has been taken to consecrate himself to Christ:

> *Pectore jam soli toto penitusque dicato*
> *Certum est vacare Christo* (lines 229–30)

It is an important poem, perhaps Erasmus' finest achievement as a poet, and it expresses both his fear of ageing and the imminence of death, and also his dedication to Christ. It is, *pace* Huizinga, not 'a stray element of his soul' (61); it is the voicing of that strength of impulse that gave directness and fullness to his life.

The party of the Italian physician Boerio and his two sons, another tutor named Clifton, and Erasmus, together with servants, had set out from Paris on the road through Lyon. One stopover at a country inn is recorded with what must have been irony on the part of Erasmus; the account is given in one of the Colloquies, 'Inns':

> No one's treated better in his own home than in a public house in Lyons ... At the table some woman would always be standing by to enliven the meal with jokes and pleasantries (and the women there are awfully good-looking, too). First the hostess would come and welcome us, bidding us be merry and accept with good grace whatever was served ... [the food was] really sumptuous; so sumptuous I wonder they can take guests for so low a price ... (Thompson, *Colloquies*, 148)

Thompson remarks that 'as an inveterate traveller but fastidious guest, Erasmus often had occasion to grumble about the dangers of the road and the inconveniences of inns' (147). The inn at Lyon may have been the paragon that Erasmus describes only a dozen and a half years later (the 'Inns' having been first printed in the edition of 1523), but there is such extravagant praise that one suspects irony.

At Turin, the seat of the dukedom of Savoy, on 4 September 1506, Erasmus received the degrees of master and doctor in theology; and, in writing to friends (Epistles 200 & 201) allowed the interpretation that he had received his doctorate at the far more prestigious University of Bologna.[6]

Mail-order kind of degree or not, it was a doctorate in theology from a recognised university, and it gave him a certain status, or at least it disarmed some of the criticism of him for presuming to write on theological matters.

From Turin the party descended the Po to Pavia, where he viewed the splendid cathedral, completed in Gothic style only in 1465, with the cloister and transepts having been built only that year. In his Colloquy called 'The Godly Feast' (1522) Erasmus describes the expenses of the churches, rather than their beauty, and berates the rich men who 'covet a monument for themselves in churches where formerly there was not room for saints' (*Colloquies*, 70).

The travellers had planned go on to Bologna, but were compelled instead to go to Florence because of the papal armies that were then besieging Bologna. In Florence Erasmus never spoke of the churches and other splendid buildings, nor did he ever mention works of art individually. But he did praise Dante and Petrarch (though he thought Petrarch's Latin style was barbarous in the *Ciceronianus, LB* I, 1008E), and he spoke of having read Poggio, Filelfo, and Aretino. While in Florence he translated more dialogues of Lucian. Again in the *Ciceronianus* he observed that the humanists' libraries at Rome were filled with pagan, not Christian, art.[7] But it is well to bear in mind how little there is of Erasmus' correspondence during the Italian years.

The party of travellers reached Bologna in time to witness the triumphal entry of Julius II on 22 November 1506. First there were the soldiers, then the papal officers and Julius in his chair of state, followed by bishops, generals of the orders, and the papal guard. An immense crowd greeted the entry of Julius (Smith, 105), and Erasmus thought it shocking to see the Vicar of Christ entering like a triumphant Roman general and celebrating bloody victories (see his *Apologia ad Stunicam, LB* IX, 361DE). Earlier the Dutch humanist had given indications of pacifist views in his *Panegyricus* and other writings; now he was scandalised and deeply shocked. After the death of Julius (21 February 1513) a dialogue appeared that satirised the warlike pope; first published in 1517, it was at once attributed to Erasmus (chapter 33).

Erasmus had contracted to serve as tutor to the young Boerio boys for one year, and most of that time was spent in Bologna. For Erasmus himself it was a year spent in study, although there is no evidence that he advanced his Greek significantly, and he was disappointed that there was only one person in Bologna at home in Greek. This was Paulo Bombasio (Bombace, or Bombasius), one of several good friends among scholars there, at that time a professor in rhetoric and poetry (with a chair in Greek added in 1506); later he was secretary to cardinal Pucci and then to Clement VII. Bombasio welcomed Erasmus warmly and offered him lodgings and help with Greek (*BR*). In later letters of 1533 (Epistles 2874 and 3032 of

1535) Erasmus named Bombasio as one of the purest minds he had met in Italy or elsewhere.

In public a man of prudence generally and not less so in Italy, Erasmus was scrupulously correct in his dress until he experienced a threat of violence. Hitherto he had worn the usual black gown of an Augustinian canon, with a black mantle (or capuce) and a white hood carried over his arm like a scarf. At this time, however, physicians in Bologna who were attending plague victims dressed very similarly, and a mob took him for such a physician until a kind lady explained to the crowd that this was an ecclesiastic.[8] Therefore he adopted the dress of the secular priest during his remaining months in Italy. In his letter to Servatius Rogers of 8 July 1514 (Epistle 296), Erasmus took up the problem of dress, and in his 1516 letter to Grunnius, at the time of his requesting a fuller dispensation from the pope, he alluded to dress, expressing his dismay over 'some foolish people who think that the whole sum and substance of religion consists in the dress'.[9] Yet it was no small matter, and it could not be ignored in replying to his prior in 1514; but then Erasmus argued that he had dispensed with his canonical habit only when there was a real need. One differs from Margaret Mann Phillips reluctantly, but her statement that 'surely the fundamental reason for adopting the ordinary dress of a secular cleric was his profound distaste for all that pertained to the monastic life' needs to be examined.[10] DeMolen's response is surely a more sound one: the argument of Phillips would be tenable if Erasmus associated the religious life with the religious habit; but he did not, and instead he clearly distinguished between them (195). The permission to wear a simple priest's dress once granted by the pope, Erasmus kept that dress for the remainder of his life.

In mid-November 1506 Erasmus wrote to the prince Henry in England, but the letter is lost except for a fragment. Yet it produced a reply from the prince, written from Richmond on 17 January 1507, and it expressed in graceful Latin his praises of Erasmus: 'Still, why do I go about to praise the eloquence of a man like you whose learning is world-famous? I cannot invent anything in your praise which could be truly worthy of your consummate scholarship ...' (Epistles 204, 206; *CWE* 2:129/12–15; Allen I, 436/7–11). Some hesitation has been expressed on the question of young Henry's authorship of so creditable a letter, and Ammonio may indeed have had a hand in vetting it (Allen I, 436 n). But Henry had been well schooled by Mountjoy; and Pace for one testified that he had heard Henry speak Latin with ease and readiness.

Thereafter there is a long gap in the correspondence: no letters from January to October 1507. Even allowing for the fact that the correspondence for the years 1506 and 1507 was very thin, some notice must be taken of this. (There will be another, even longer, interruption after his return to England in the summer of 1509 until April 1511.) Erasmus did not save his letters at this time (see chapter 25).

Having completed his contracted year with the Boerio family, Erasmus was making plans to move on from Bologna. On 28 October 1507 he wrote to Aldus Manutius, enclosing his translations of two Greek tragedies, and this led immediately to the edition of Euripides published by Aldus in December 1507, for which a dedicatory epistle to Warham (Epistle 208) was included.[11] Aldus answered favourably, and Erasmus went to Venice in November 1507. He spent about a year there, about eight months of which he lived with Aldus.

Aldus had brought together a number of learned scholars, two of them Greek (Marcus Musurus and John Lascaris), who worked with and for his press. It was a household that numbered more than thirty scholars and printers working together, and some of them at least spoke Greek among themselves. Erasmus shared a room with Girolamo Aleandro, a young man still in his twenties who possessed an enviable knowledge of Hebrew and Greek; when he left for Paris in 1508 Aleandro had letters of introduction from Erasmus to open doors there for him. Later, in 1521, Aleandro was a papal nuncio at the Diet of Worms, and Erasmus engendered a violent suspicion of his motives and actions (chapter 34).

Many years later in one of the late Colloquies – 'Sordid Wealth' or 'Penny-Pinching' (*Opulentia sordida*), first printed in 1531 – Erasmus gave a picture of the so-called New Academy living in the household of Aldus; but the writing of that colloquy is distanced not only by years but also by quarrels that cropped up after the death of Aldus in 1515. The comico-satirical picture paints smokey rooms from the burning of roots for fuel, the keeping of women apart from the men, the adding of water to the dregs of long-standing wine, and the nuisance of fleas and bedbugs in the summer. Moreover, there was penny-pinching in the providing of food: the bread was as hard as rocks, and no breakfast was served. The soup was indigestible and all but indescribable. Erasmus blamed his kidney stones on the miserable old wine that was served. And the dialogue ends with the speaker declaring that he is off 'to a good old French tavern, to make up for lost time!' (*Colloquies*, 499).

But work he did, and the massive volume of *Adagiorum Chiliades* (literally, thousands of adages, see chapter 24) – was the main but not the only achievement of his months in the household of Aldo and with the support of Aldus' New Academy. His later work on the pronunciation of Greek (*Dialogus de recta latini graecique sermonis pronuntiatione*, first printed in 1528) came out of the daily conversations in and about Greek.[12] Deno J. Geanakoplos has demonstrated that Erasmus owed much to his contacts with the Greek colony in Venice and has argued that he derived from those scholars much of his knowledge of classical Greek writings that were not yet available in the rest of Europe. Although once or twice in later life he decried his improvement in Greek during his Venetian sojourn, there can be little question that he gained immensely in Greek learning, thanks chiefly to Musurus and Lascaris. Further, Kristeller has shown that a passage in the *Moriae Encomium* is indebted to Ficino, whom he is unlikely to have read before going to Italy.[13]

In late October or early November of 1508, Erasmus left Venice for the university town of Padua; and there he became tutor to Alexander Stewart, the illegitimate son of James IV of Scotland. Alexander arrived in Padua in 1508, having already been chosen to succeed his uncle as the archbishop of St Andrews (*BR*), and in Padua Alexander and his brother James Stewart, earl of Moray, were instructed in Latin and rhetoric by Erasmus. At Paris Alexander appears to have been registered to study canon law (*BR*). They left Padua out of fear of war.

In December of 1508 the party of Erasmus and his charges went to Ferrara, the celebrated seat of the house of Este; and there Erasmus met a well-known scholar, Celio Calcagnini, who in fact welcomed him with an oration. A friend of Copernicus, with whom he had studied canon law at Ferrara, Calcagnini had written a treatise on the Copernican theory, *That the sky stands still and the earth moves (BR)*. More than a dozen years later Calcagnini wrote a treatise on Free Will, and in it he praised Erasmus' work on the subject (see Epistle 2869, 17 September 1533, Allen X, 303–4, and *BR*).

After a short stop of only a few days, the party moved on to Siena, and there during carnival time in February 1509 they witnessed a curious bullfight in which a wooden animal was moved by men hidden inside (*LB* IX, 516C: *Cujusmodi pugnae simulacrum vidimus quondam in urbem Senensi*); and it was the contrast between pagan and christian that caught Erasmus' attention and offended him. In Siena he met Richard Pace, a student at Padua and quickly a friend (Smith, 111). Strikingly, Erasmus met an ambassador from Hungary to Julius II, one Jacobus Piso,[14] who found a manuscript collection of Erasmus' epistles at a bookseller's (so such things circulated then), which he purchased and gave to Erasmus; and Erasmus, having no thoughts of publishing his own correspondence at that time, burned the manuscript (Epistle 216; cf. *LB* Epistle 507). And recovering from illness, he wrote a declamation on death, his popular *De Morte Declamatio* (first printed in Basel by Froben in December 1517, and reprinted more than twenty times, first in English by Berthelet in 1553).

From Siena Erasmus went to Rome in the spring of 1509. At that time Rome paled by comparison with the more prosperous cities of Florence (with its 100,000 inhabitants), or Venice (167,000), or, *a fortiori*, with Paris,[15] for other than the Curia, Rome was scarcely more than a town, with but 40,000. The ancient ruins were still there, but the bulk of modern archaeological work had still to be done, and there were chiefly such monuments as the baths, temples, and Colosseum. In 1509 the new St Peter's had not yet begun to appear, and Michelangelo was still working on the Sistine Chapel. But the Curia was a colourful court, and the cardinals lived in splendid palaces, like princes of the world. Erasmus, we know, met several. Domenico Grimani was a wealthy cardinal, and writing in 1515 Erasmus recalled his courtesy, eloquence and learning (*BR*). During their meeting in 1509 (as Erasmus recalled in 1531, Epistle 2465), Grimani invited him to join his household and become tutor of his nephew. Erasmus also met Raphael Riario, cardinal of St George (Epistles 333, 334); and cardinal de'Medici, later Clement VII.

While in Rome for several months he saw more than enough of the blasphemies, venalities, simony and inflated rhetoric of the Papal Court. Of one sermon at a Good Friday service – an oration, really, in praise of Julius as Jupiter Optimus Maximus – he wrote: 'But what has all this to do with the Julius who is the head of the Christian religion, the vice regent of Christ, the successor of Peter and Paul? What could be more utterly frigid and banal?' (in the *Ciceronianus, LB* I 993C).

There were inducements to remain in Rome, and he was tempted, perhaps as much from the fact that he was received with courtesy and warmth, especially after the appearance of the *Adagiorum* in 1508. In Epistle 253 of 8 February 1512 written to a Robert Guibé, a Breton residing in Rome (having been made cardinal in 1505 and bishop of Nantes in 1507, but at the time of Erasmus' writing – having had to resign his bishopric owing to a quarrel between Louis XII and Julius – he was appointed legate at Avignon and bishop-administrator of Vannes) he admits:

> I should have to look for a new river of Lethe if I wished to forget that city [Rome], and to be no more racked with longing

for it; for I cannot without anguish recall the climate, the green places, the libraries, the colonnades, and the honeyed talks with scholars – the lights of the world, the position, the prospects, that I put from me so readily (*CWE* 2:214/7–11; Allen I, 499/ 4–9)

Clearly intending to go to England then, Erasmus made one final excursion in Italy. About April of 1509 he visited Naples, and we have his description of the Grotto on the road from Naples to Cumae (in the *Adages*, *LB* II, no. 4120). In Naples he may have met Giovanni Pietro Caraffa, founder of the Theatine Order, and later pope Paul IV (see Epistles 377 and 640; Allen I, 550). He learned of the death of Henry VII and the accession of Henry VIII to the English throne on 22 May 1509; and Mountjoy, announcing the event to him, spoke of a golden age of learning about to dawn (Epistle 215). Calling on Bombasio in Bologna before September – but not spending much time in visiting, for travellers had to think of the threats of snow in the high mountains – Erasmus continued northwards to the Splügen Pass, and, stopping at Chur in Switzerland, he went on to Constance and Strasbourg, and then down the Rhine to Antwerp. Making a short visit to Louvain (Allen I, 62), he moved on to England, which he had left in June 1506, more than three years earlier.

Before departing from Italy for Scotland, Alexander Stewart gave Erasmus a gold ring encasing an antique gem, showing a bust that Erasmus took to be the god Terminus, whence he derived his motto 'Concedo nulli' (*BR*). Characteristically Erasmus some time later saw in the ring and its motto a warning that the end of his life was near. In 1519 he had Metsys place the figure of Terminus on the reverse of a medal-portrait of Erasmus himself; and Holbein made use of the motif in at least two drawings, including the woodcut of 1535.[16]

Following so closely upon the *Carmen alpestre* with its preoccupation with ageing and death, one does not find the Terminus motif surprising. Besides, in 1509 Erasmus was forty-one or forty-two: a climacteric year in itself, and only seven years from the most dangerous climacteric of forty-nine, it being the square of seven.[17] Yet, finally, one is led to accept the iconographic interpretation of W. S. Heckscher, one that sees in the Terminus motto an assertion of Erasmus' resolution in the midst of war and controversy surrounding him: 'the theme is the Stoic *tranquillitas* of one in harmony both with self and the world, and so protected against the whims of *Fortuna*'.[18] The Stoic motto '*Faber est suae quisque fortunae*' is likely to have been known to Erasmus, both in Sallust and in its use on the sergeant's ring of Sir John Fineux.[19]

We no longer believe Nolhac's view that Erasmus only became truly aware of the new spirit of humanism on this trip, and that afterwards he had the determination to carry that new spirit north of the Alps.[20] A number of scholars have shown in a substantial body of scholarly work that while still in the Low Countries Erasmus had begun to absorb Italian humanism: from Valla (through Agricola and Hegius, as well as through his own reading), from Neoplatonism (through Colet, and then, thanks to Vitrier, through Origen). But the debt to Italy for a far wider knowledge of Greek is not to be questioned. Renaudet and Cantimori have argued that what he saw in Italy quickened his sense of ecclesiastical abuses,[21] and Tracy has shrewdly observed that 'never does Erasmus seem more a disciple of the northerner, Gerard Groote, than when he recalls the famous Charterhouse (Certosa) of Pavia as a useless pile of marble filled by gawking tourists.'[22] It needs also to be said that Erasmus saw more of the learning and spirituality of Italy than Luther had done, and among this small but significant number of Roman clerics is likely to have been Caraffa (whom he certainly met in London in 1514, *BR*).[23]

He had brought forth his magnificent new *Adagiorum Chiliades*, indeed a vision of the ancient world through a greatly expanded collection of adages and rightly called 'a front-line work of the New Learning': it will merit a chapter for analysis and appreciation (24).

On the road to Italy in 1506 he had meditated on the vanities of scholarship and had written his memorable *Carmen alpestre*. On the road back north after leaving Italy he had his experience in Italy for his meditations: the superstitions of the people and the venalities of the papal court. And so – thinking ahead to staying at the home of a wise man named More – while riding north he began to compose his declamation on folly that he would call the *Moriae Encomium*, or Praise of Folly (chapter 26).

Notes

1) Cf. *Roma Aeterna – Lateinische und Griechische Romdichtung von der Antike bis in die Gegenwart*, ed. Bernard Kytzler (Zürich, 1972); and F. Gregorovius, *Geschichte der Stadt Rom im Mittelalter*, ed. W. Kamp, 3 vols (Basel, 1953–7), and J. Klaczko, *Rome and the Renaissance*, trans. J. Dennie (New York, 1903).

2) *Erasmus*, 60–1, and the praise by Secundus in *Opera* (Leiden, 1631) p. 65; see Reedijk, *Poems*, 281.

3) On Erasmus and humanist medicine, see B. Ebels-Hoving and E. J. Ebels, 'Erasmus and Galen', in *Erasmus of Rotterdam*, ed. J. Sperna Weiland and W. Th. M. Frijhoff (Leiden, 1988) 132–42. Cf. R. J. Durling, 'Linacre

and medical humanism', in *Linacre Studies: Essays on the Life and Work of Thomas Linacre*, ed. F. Maddison, M. Pelling and C. Webster (Oxford, 1977).

4) Huizinga, 60; Tracy, *Erasmus*, 114. Tracy gives Erasmus as 36 by taking a different year as his birth-year: 1467 would give the age of Erasmus as 39, which is a more believable age to think of oneself as *senior*.

5) The problem of interpretation (see ch. 4) is always important in reading the letters and poems of Erasmus. In 'Le Chant Alpestre d'Erasme', *BHR* xxvii (1965), Margolin takes Ep. 189 as more sincere than Huizinga did, and so too do Reedijk (in *Poems*, 122–3) and Tracy (115 & n). In addition to Erasmus' always delicate health (doubtless strained by the exertions of the long ride horseback, the altitude, and rough terrain) there was his frustration at not receiving a benefice in England. This frustration was reinforced by the disruptions because of the papal wars, for the '*papa terribile*', Julius II, was manoeuvering and campaigning against the Venetians. See *NCE* and G. B. Picotti, *La politica italiana sotto il pontificato di Giulio II* (Pisa, 1949).

6) Alluding to the rapidity of the degree-granting (even though it might have had preparatory work by correspondence), Smith recalls an old joke in Germany 'that the train stopped half an hour at Erlangen for the passengers to take degrees, and evidently the standards of Turin were not much more exacting' (103). The diploma (now in the university library in Basel) states that it was the vicar-general of Giovanni Luigi della Rovere, bishop of Turin, who found the candidate sufficient: this ecclesiastic was (as Smith has shrewdly observed, 103 n.) 'doubtless a kinsman of the then reigning Pope Julius II, from whom Erasmus had just procured a dispensation. Perhaps this explains Erasmus' course in stopping at Turin, and his reception there'. Perhaps.

7) See Smith, 104–5 on this point. One wonders whether there is an implied contrast with the humanists' libraries in Paris, England and the Low Countries with which he was familiar.

8) See Smith, 106, and Tracy, 117. The maxim that *cucullus non facit monachum* was everywhere known in the late Middle Ages and Renaissance.

9) See DeMolen 194; and appendix C on Erasmus' Dispensations.

10) *Erasmus and the Northern Renaissance* (1949) 87.

11) It is characterstic of Erasmus that he signs off his letter to Warham with the phrase *meum decus*: this is, as the *CWE* translators note (*CWE* 2:135 n. 31) a quotation, intended to be picked up by Warham, from the dedicatory ode of Horace addressed to Maecenas – a hint for Warham to play the patron.

12) See ch. 40, and Ingram Bywater, *The Erasmian Pronunciation of Greek and Its Precursors* (London, 1908).

13) D. J. Geanakoplos, *Greek Scholars in Venice* (Cambridge, Mass., 1962). On the Ficino indebtedness, see P. O. Kristeller, 'Erasmus from an Italian Perspective', *RenQ* xxiii (1970) 11–12. The passage to which Erasmus was evidently indebted is in Ficino's commentary on Plato's *Symposium*.

14) On the Transylvanian-born Jacobus Piso, see *BR*. After their meeting in Rome in 1509, Piso and Erasmus became friends, and they exchanged many letters, of which only Ep. 216 has survived. Piso 'was one of the main channels through which Erasmian influences entered Hungary' (*BR*).

15) For a description of Rome in 1509, see E. Rodocanachi, *Rome au temps*

de Jules II et de Leon X (1912). I am indebted to Smith, 112, for the population figures.

16) J. K. McConica, 'The Riddle of "Terminus"', *Erasmus in English* 2 (1971) 2.

17) The theory of the climacteric has been advanced by A. C. F. Koch in his discussion of *The Year of Erasmus' Birth* (Utrecht, 1969) esp. 41–2.

18) W. S. Heckscher, 'Reflections on Seeing Holbein's Portrait of Erasmus at Longford Castle', in *Essays in the History of Art Presented to Rudolf Wittkower* (London, 1967) 132 ff.

19) See R. J. Schoeck, 'More, Sallust and Fortune', *Moreana* xvii (June 1980) 107–110. Sallust is not cited in *Adag.* II. iv. 30, *Sui cuique mores fingunt fortunam* ('Every man's character moulds his fortune').

20) Thus Nolhac in *Erasme en Italie*, 94–5, on which see Tracy's summary in *Erasmus*, 115.

21) Renaudet, *Erasme et l'Italie*, 49–53 & passim. For D. Cantimori, see his 'Note su Erasmo e la vita morale e religiosa Italiana nel Secolo XVI', in *Gedenkschrift*, 98–112.

22) Tracy, *Erasmus*, 116, citing 'The Godly Feast' and Groote's *Tractaat Contra Turrim Traiectensem Teruggevonden*, ed. R. R. Post (The Hague, 1966).

The Adages

Well, just as we spend our life seeking to make ourselves better, so we shall not cease to make our writings richer and more accurate until we ourselves cease to live. ... you must decide whether you would rather have it that way, or buy a book from time to time in a revised and expanded form.

Erasmus to John Botzheim, 1523 (Epistle 1 in Allen, I, 37; trans. by M.M. Phillips in *The 'Adages' of Erasmus*, p. xv–xvi)

The Adages was a very large pebble thrown into the European pond, and its ripples are with us still.

Phillips, '*Adages*', 165

I built the house in sections, always following the concrete needs of the moment.

Carl Jung, *Memories*, 225/214

The Adages are many things to many readers. Margaret Mann Phillips launches her introduction with the declaration that the *Adagia* is 'one of the world's biggest bedside books; and a great deal more'. It is an anthology of the ancient world, but an anthology in the unique style of Erasmus. For a generation, indeed for a century and more, it made the whole of the ancient past readable and understandable. It is one of the masterbooks of renaissance humanism, for it both contributed mightily to the revival of ancient learning, provided links between past and present, and established viable parallels between classical learning and christian teaching. For all of these reasons, the *Adagia* is a key work in one's reading and study of Erasmus.[1]

It can be added that the *Adagia* is like the tower of Carl Jung which the modern Swiss built in sections, 'always following the concrete needs of the moment'.[2] So too with the Dutch renaissance humanist, who began with a slender book of adages in 1500 and then added mightily – in individual adages that can be thought of as analogous to Jung's sections – until a larger concept began to emerge. In the process Erasmus was discovering aspects of self; and

in individual adages whose metal, once struck, rang round the European world, he achieved a meaningful form, a symbol of psychic
wholeness.

The *Adagia* is a European book in its genesis and development.
Conceived perhaps even before he left for Paris in 1495, and certainly
worked upon in Paris prior to its publication there in 1500 (for it
was discussed in Oxford in 1499), it was most fully developed in
Venice and continued in Basel (and elsewhere, wherever Erasmus
happened to be, for *'habeo sedem'*, he wrote in Epistle 809, *'ubi
bibliothecam meam habeo'*); and it drew on the collaboration of friends
in several countries as well. Further, it expresses a cosmopolitan view
of the European world of his own time, together with a unique sense
of his excitement in the study of the classical past and in the inte-
grating of that past with christian thought and the urgencies of the
present.[3] Finally, it is also a European book in the wide range of its
readers and its continuing reception: published in many editions in
most European countries and read by students, teachers, and scholars
everywhere, it is a book that helped as much as any other single book
to transform the intellectual landscape of the whole of sixteenth-
century Europe. One must agree with the summary statement of
Sem Dresden: 'It would be difficult to overestimate the significance
of this work within sixteenth-century European culture; for many
writers and scholars these *Adagia* were the chief source for their
knowledge of classical antiquity and they rightly took it for the
reference book it claimed to be.'[4]

For the biography of Erasmus – and are we not all fascinated by
the mysteries of his personality and eager to learn more about the
interplay between his life and career, and above all about his intellectual development? – the *Adagia* has an importance that is surpassed
only by the correspondence for what it tells us about his life and
thought; and at times individual adages will throw light upon key
ideas and lines of development to an even more remarkable degree
than most of the letters. To be sure, a number of the letters that
served as prefaces to individual works are in fact vital guides to the
intentions and methods of Erasmus, and they offer valuable clues to
Erasmus' keen sense of his milieu at that moment.[5] But the individual adages take us more closely to Erasmus' reading, as we shall
see, and the history of successive editions of the *Adagia* provides an
unrivalled view of the writer of the early sixteenth century who
works closely with his printers and learns how to use the printing-
press.[6]

Yet there are problems and dangers in the use of the *Adagia* for
biographical evidence, as well as the possibility of extraordinary

gains.[7] For one thing there is the problem of dating: it is difficult to determine exactly when Erasmus began to conceive his collection of adages (and even to *préciser* his process of defining the sometimes fluid concept of an adage) and then to enlarge and enrich such a collection into the structure of Erasmian *essais* that begin with an adage and proceed to subsume his thinking on related ideas (or relevant recollections), *essais* that sometimes develop over a period of years to the extent that individual adages have their own life-histories (as the textual procedures in the critical edition of the Amsterdam *ASD* make clear).[8] It follows that after 1515 it will be necessary for us (in our archaeological reading of the expanding tower) to discover the context of each newly added adage at the time of its being added – like the sections of Jung's tower that always followed the concrete needs of the moment.

But this chapter cannot be a full study of the whole of the *Adages* (for that enterprise, a separate book will be needed); rather, it is an essay on the bearing of the *Adages* upon our sense of Erasmus' life.

For many readers and scholars the *Adagia* is dated simply by first publication: that is, as from 1500. But there is a very real point in asking how early the *Adagia* was begun. Yes, we can document the beginning at least as early as 1499,[9] but may we not ask whether this project was not one of the several that Erasmus carried with him to Paris in 1495, even though he does not speak of it (in his extant letters) until 1499? For those projects of 1495 often did not see print for years: his work in progress at the end of the Paris period is summarised in chapter 17 (248–9).

We may make a more radical suggestion about their conception. We note that in Erasmus' first recorded letter of about 1484 (Epistle 1), apparently written at the age of seventeen, there are two proverbs which he later listed in his *Collectanea* of 1500. It is very much to the point that it is here Ovid, a school-text author, who supplies the second *paroemia,* and that the allusion quite neatly reinforces the argument of the letter: that things are not being done by the guardian Pieter Winckel to settle the father's estate, and 'time flies by on wingèd feet'. All in all, a remarkable demonstration of rhetorical skill in an adolescent. And let us observe that the pointed employment of the Ovidian allusion established an early attention to adages and that, in fact, it suggests the use of a commonplace book to supply the desired adage for a given context. The first adage in the first letter, 'in case the sky should fall', is also listed in the *Collectanea*, where it is number 558.[10]

The application of this practice, so well known in quattrocento Italy, to Erasmus' reading and writing habits is not new, for many

years ago Preserved Smith remarked that Erasmus 'doubtless followed the practice himself, which he recommended to a friend, of
keeping a commonplace book for the notation of striking sayings
met with in the course of reading'.[11] It is reasonable to suppose that
this practice lay behind the style of the 1500 *Collectanea*, on the draft
for which Gaguin remarked that it was 'too formal and lifeless'.[12]
That remark suggests that the older and more experienced Gaguin
perceived that there was not enough distance between the commonplace book and Erasmus' presentation and striving for a new genre.

The dedicatory letter from Erasmus to Mountjoy[13] which serves as
the preface for the 1500 edition is a very long preface for a slim
volume of only 152 pages, containing the 818 adages of the first
edition; and these adages often carried only a sentence or two of note
or commentary. This edition – with its cumbersome full title of
Veterum maximeque insignium paroemiarum, id est adagiorum collectanea
(Paris: Joan. Philippus Alamannus, xv. June 1500), which is also
notable as one of the first books printed in Paris to use Greek type –
calls attention to Erasmus' working towards a more convenient title
as well as more cohesive concept for his adage-collection. Later, in
the prolegomena to the *Adagiorum Chiliades* of 1508, Erasmus offered
this definition: *'Paroemia est celebre dictum, scita quapiam novitate
insigne'* ('A paroemia is a well-known saying remarkable for a certain
refined novelty of expression').[14] But as Miller observes, 'he is unable
to give any clear and workable distinction between paroemia (or its
synonyms proverbium and adagium) and the closely related
sententia, apophthegma, and scomma'.[15] Yet I suspect that Erasmus
did not want too tight, too restrictive, a definition, in order to allow
his continuing netting of reading to sweep in all kinds of sayings,
though nearly always meeting the criteria of being well-known and
of having a certain refined novelty of expression.

As we mark the quantum leap in Erasmus' intellectual development from 1500 to 1508, there are great changes in thought that are
mirrored in the *Adagiorum Chiliades*, and such changes continue to
the end of his life. Not only are new adages continually added in the
successive editions – especially the monumental editions of 1515 and
1526 – and the subjects or focuses of these additional adages frequently throw a most helpful spotlight on the surfacing of new ideas
or of new perceptions of continuing problems;[16] but there are important revisions of or additions to old essays, and these must be taken
into account in an intellectual biography of Erasmus. One or two
examples are given below.

Thus the *Adagia* is perhaps the best example of the Erasmian
concept of the growing book: for the book of 1500 with its mere 818

adages grows enormously into the *Adagiorum Chiliades* of 1508 with
its 3260 adages – literally, thousands of adages – and on this edition
Erasmus worked with almost ferocious speed and energy during the
winter of 1507–1508, with the help of an international group of
scholars.[17] It is in one of the adages which first appeared in 1526,
Festina lente, that Erasmus relates the kindness of those friends in
lending manuscripts and in assisting him with his Greek; and in this
adage he commends the solicitude of Aldus in helping to make the
edition as perfect as possible. The work continued to grow, as
Margaret Mann Phillips has so lovingly detailed for us,[18] in successive editions down to the 1536 edition in the year of his death, with
the *Opera Omnia* in 1540 offering additional revisions that he had left
in manuscript. In its final form the *Adagia* contains 4151 proverbs, a
number of them short treatises and some in fact printed and sold
separately – the *Dulce bellum inexpertis* (which has its own reception-
history in a century that knew war all too well and yearned for peace
as much as our own century does), the *Scarabeus aquilam quaerit*, and
the *Sileni Alcibiadis* (which offers a daring, and typically Erasmian,
conflation of Socrates and Christ) – and one notes how striking each
of these titles is, in the spirit of that 'refined novelty of expression'
that lies at the heart of the Erasmian adage. In the 1508 edition,
moreover, the Greek was markedly increased and enriched, which
calls attention to Erasmus' mastering, now in his forties, of the
Greek language and literature; but we must note that the first
decade of the sixteenth century was a period that saw the publication
of a significant number of the *editiones principes* of Greek classics, and
Erasmus seems to have kept abreast of that productivity in his
reading and drawing upon an increasingly wider net of authors.[19]
Much of that reading was done in the printing-house of Aldus,
where so many of the Greek authors were receiving their first printed
edition.

   One example may be brought forward to show in yet another way
the workings of Erasmus' mind and his employment of his ever-
growing classical knowledge in the writing of his *Adagia*. In the
1500 *Collectanea Adagiorum* there is the very brief Number 661,
Oleum aure vel ore ferre ('to have oil in the ear or mouth'), which builds
upon a compact distich in Martial. Here Erasmus works almost
exclusively with language; his is an interpretation that very largely
perceives Martial's words as an adage in its own right, and it has been
incorporated into the corpus of Martial textual scholarship. But for
his new explanation in 1508 Erasmus looks outside language to the
physical world: the Dutch Neo-Latin scholar G.C. Kuiper comments
that 'from his immense knowledge of antiquity he produces two

references to make it plausible that Martial's "oil in the ear", taken literally, could evoke the image of a particular position of the head'.[20]

In those crucial years between the appearance of the *Collectanea* in 1500 and the *Adagiorum Chiliades* in 1508, there was the printing of Thucydides, Sophocles and Herodotus in the single year 1502; Euripides was printed in 1503, together with Xenophon's *Hellenica*; and Demosthenes saw print in 1504. The essential biographical point in all this is that Erasmus lived through (and his mastery of Greek grew during) these early years of the century that witnessed a great increase in the number of Greek texts that were being edited and printed; yet, as Phillips has shown in another essay, a close study of the additions to the *Adagia* reveals an increase in quotations from authors long known to Erasmus, from Cicero as well as from Plautus and Sophocles, with less interest in Homer, Lucian, Plutarch, Horace and Terence over the longer span of years. For the intellectual biographer, new editions of the *Adagia* help significantly to establish when a new book has come into his net: 'for instance, all the references to the *Table-Talk* (*Deipnosophistae*) of Athenaeus date from after 1514 when the Aldine edition of the Greek text was printed'. No wonder, Mrs Phillips adds, 'the new editions [of the *Adagia*] were eagerly looked for, and a reader who could not afford the next one went to the labour of copying in the margins of his treasured volume all the latest tit-bits, and on the fly-leaves all the additional proverbs'.[21]

We still lack a definitive edition of the Latin text of the *Adagia* (although the North Holland edition, *ASD*, is moving slowly towards that goal), and that heroic task of editing a work that saw over sixty editions during Erasmus' lifetime alone has been immensely complicated by the appearance of a remarkable copy of the 1523 Basel edition at auction in London.[22] One who has examined the copy recorded that there are so many 'corrections and annotations as well as leaves adding new material in Erasmus' own distinctive hand, that it could almost be considered as an autograph manuscript. Many, but not all, of the 240 or so new passages appear in the subsequent edition of 1526 and a few in the edition of 1528: yet some material present in 1526 has not been added in this copy'.[23] In such a copy one may see Erasmus at work: adding, revising, and adding again.

Erasmus shared in the humanists' hunt for old manuscripts and new texts,[24] and the hunt never lost its excitement for him; and in the *Adagia*, as Phillips has remarked,[25] there is a 'whiff of the intoxication of those days, when he mentions the "poem about spring" which Aldus showed him, freshly unearthed from an old library in

France'. Thus we learn of Erasmus' coming upon that lovely lyric the *Pervigilium Veneris*: how marvellous it was for Erasmus to live in an age when such discoveries were still being made. '*O divitias, si liceat repubescere!*' he cries out ('What riches, if only one could be young again!').[26]

A striking example of Erasmus' intellectual development that is revealed to us in the *Adagia*, as well as an example of how much the work lies at the intersection of interests and influences that were fully European, is provided by one adage which is jurisprudential in its orientation: *Summum ius, summa iniuria* (Loosely: 'the strictest enforcement of the law is the greatest harm'). Erasmus' interest in law was slight enough in earlier years, and the confiscation of precious money at the English border in 1499/1500 (despite expert legal advice from Thomas More and others, see Volume 1, 232–3) did not sweeten his low opinion of lawyers, which even Budé shared, as his prefatory letter to the 1517 Paris edition of More's *Utopia* richly manifests. But that slight interest grew (see Volume 1, 246), and then, in the Basel years after 1521, as Guido Kisch has shown,[27] it matured rapidly; for his friend Cantiuncula was already well established there by the time of Erasmus' arrival in 1521. Cantiuncula's celebrated and much-borrowed doctrine of equity owed much to Erasmus (even to the extent of Cantiuncula's using Erasmus' citations and examples, as Kisch has demonstrated). In the 1500 *Collectanea* Erasmus devoted one adage to equity, and it is only three sentences in length; the title is *summum ius, summa malicia*. In a more extended essay in the 1536 *Adagia* Erasmus has enlarged his treatment to nearly a page, has added detailed references to Cicero's *De Officiis* (which, along with the *De Legibus*, was such a repository on natural-law thinking for the humanists), and also to the *Pandects* (on which Budé and other humanist-jurists had been labouring); the title now becomes *summum ius, summa iniuria*.[28] In this one adage we have an outlining of Erasmus' development in legal thinking from 1500 to 1536. The *Adagia*, in sum, is one of many valuable tools for understanding his intellectual development.

But Erasmus was no legal historian, as some of his younger contemporaries were beginning to become, especially those interested in the *mos gallicus*; nor was he primarily a philosopher any more than he was exclusively a theologian. Rather, as Huizinga so admirable expressed in his justly celebrated biography and as Waszink has more recently reminded us, Erasmus was essentially a philologist, one passionately concerned with language and in love with individual words. His spirit was in the fullest sense of the word philological: *philologia* meaning of course a love of the word and of language; and he loved speech, the right expressions and (as we might now say) *le mot juste.*[29] Erasmus might be intrigued and I hope that he would be pleased to know that a North American professor has found his adage on *summum ius* beautifully heuristic in teaching Shakespeare's *Measure for Measure* (which draws much from, and is indebted to, that humanistic teaching about the nature of justice) to undergraduate students with no awareness of the depth of renaissance thought, and to graduate students in Germany as well as America. Erasmus can serve us well as the forsaken fountain of renaissance wisdom, and in our brave new world that is post-Christian, and long after the fact of the Classical Tradition, we can use the *Adagia* as a resource for the teaching of Shakespeare, Rabelais and Montaigne.

I began by declaring that the *Adagia* was a European work in its genesis and development. It is also a European work in the sweep of application that Erasmus wished to make on vital issues of peace and many others; and it was European also, of course, in its reception. More than sixty editions in Erasmus' own lifetime, and from 1536 through the remainder of the sixteenth century there were nearly four-score.[30] In his longer essays of the later editions, and notably the edition of 1526, Erasmus drew upon the whole wealth of Greek and Roman thought and letters, and he sought to make that wisdom available to his contemporaries in the hope of addressing and helping to solve such urgent contemporary problems as the Turkish question, the endless disputes between the ancients and the moderns, and above all the problems that were rending the seamless coat of Christ.[31]

We need not wonder now that during the sixteenth and seventeenth centuries the book was so widely read, indeed embraced, and that copies of the *Adagia* are to be found everywhere, that so many writers and scholars learned form its superlative style, that so many serious students shared with Erasmus the 'allurements of Antiquity' and the joys of reading. The enthusiasm with which the book was received, especially after 1508, must have given to Erasmus that sense that he was privileged to have a co-creative audience (in the sense of Collingwood's emphasis upon this relationship as a necessary constituent of all great art[32]); and surely that assurance helps to explain the exquisite clarity and authority that characterises Erasmus' mature writing. For us in our own century, the *Adagia* is a work that more than any other, with the possible exception of the *Colloquia*, gives us a sense of the whole intellectual landscape of that most fascinating age in Europe (in which the Christian flowered together with the Classical), and for the biography of Erasmus it is a uniquely valuable index of 'a mind forever voyaging strange seas of thought...'

Keeping in mind not only Rabelais and Montaigne, Shakespeare and Burton, and the legion of renaissance writers who made use of their own well-thumbed copies of the *Adagia*, but also that small army of readers – students and teachers, preachers and prelates – who treasured their own copies as an anthology of classical literature and a guide to the life of the mind, we may well conclude by echoing Dresden's observation that it would be difficult to overestimate the significance of the *Adagia* within sixteenth-century European culture, adding only that the significance carried into the seventeenth century as well, and that the book still holds its renaissance charm to delight and instruct.

Notes

1) I shall use the term *Adagia* for the composite work (and *adages* to call attention to individual pieces); and I shall use *Adagiorum Collectanea* to specify the 1500 edition (and revisions of it) with *Adagiorum Chiliades* to specify the 1508 text and its revisions.

2) Cf. James Olney, *Metaphors of Self* (1972) 140: '*Exegi monumentum* – the self and its creative symbol. The purpose of life is to live it; a life lived, a personality achieved, constitutes its own memorial, a completed process symbolized outwardly in such metaphors as it has struck off spontaneously in the creation of self: in such significant forms as poem and book, square stone and round tower'.

3) *Pace* Lucien Febvre and some others, the *Adagia* is not a pagan, nor even predominantly a secular, work; rather, it is an essential part of the Erasmian programme of christian humanism. See L. Febvre, preface to the French translation of J. Huizinga, *Erasme* (Paris, 1955) and the comment of M.M. Phillips in 'Ways with Adages', in *Essays on the Works of Erasmus*, ed. R.L. DeMolen (New Haven, CT, 1978) 58.

4) Sem Dresden, *Humanism in the Renaissance* (London, 1968) 115.

5) Erasmus' patristic and New Testament prefaces have been usefully collected by Robert Payne, *Desiderius Erasmus, Prefaces* ... (Menston, 1970). There is a comprehensive analysis of the dedicatory preface in Karl Schottenloher, *Die Widmungsrede im Buch des 16. Jahrhunderts. Reformationsgeschichtliche Studien and Texte* 76–77 (Münster, 1953). The classical conventions are presented by Tore Janson, *Latin Prose Prefaces: Studies in Literary Conventions*, Acta Universitatis Stockholmiensis – Studia Latina Stockholmiensia XIII (Stockholm, 1964).

6 Allen's lecture on 'Erasmus' Relations with his Printers' in *Erasmus* (1934) 99–137 is still a necessary starting-point; but now we must consider questions raised by Febvre and Martin, Eisenstein, and others.

7) Cf. the discussion of interpretation of early poems and letters in ch. 4 above.

8) One such example is provided below: the adage *Summum ius, summa iniuria*. The question of consistency must be glanced at, and in the turbulent years of the early sixteenth century all are involved: not only Erasmus but his

contemporaries. In his work on Ulrich von Hutten, Hajo Holborn has quoted from the *Opera* of Hutten (II, 295): 'consistent does not mean that one should always use the same language, but that one should always have the same objective'. Certainly in this light Erasmus was most consistent. Here I use the term *essai* deliberately in order to call attention to the *rapport* between the Erasmian adage in its mature form and the *essai* of Montaigne, which so much derived from the Erasmian concept and form. In the later Erasmian adages there is increasingly a testing of ideas and values against experience.

9) See Eps 113 and 124 of late 1499 and early 1500.

10) See ch. 4 on the early use of Ovid, and the nascent employment of commonplace books. For further discussion of the *1500 Adagiorum Collectanea* see ch. 16 above; the work is now being edited for a facsimile edition by G.C. Kuiper and R.J. Schoeck.

11) Preserved Smith, *Erasmus* (1923) 41; see also C.R. Thompson, Introd. to vol. 23 *CWE*.

12) As Erasmians we would like to know why it is that evidence for such a commonplace book has apparently not survived. But one does not remark in any period on a contemporary's following a common practice – as we do not now ordinarily remark on the use of fiches, or even the adoption of word-processors and all that gear – and Erasmus' commonplace book would thus not have seemed worth noting. If that be true, then we can better understand why his literary executors apparently did not preserve such a notebook (and perhaps it was Erasmus himself who did not): there are few indeed from such an early period, though commonplace books from the later sixteenth century, even those of students, were increasingly preserved and there are valuable collections at the Cambridge University Library and the Folger Shakespeare Library (Washington). On commonplace books: see *Vittorino da Feltre and Other Humanist Educators*, ed. W.H. Woodward (New York, 1963) 173; and Ann Moss, 'Printed Commonplace Books in the Renaissance', in *Acta Neo-Latini Torontoniensis*, ed. A. Dalzell, Charles Fantazzi, and R.J. Schoeck (Binghamton, New York, 1991), with its emphasis on the method of Guarino da Verona. J.B. Trapp has traced the lines of influence in establish-ing a humanist educational programme in early Tudor England through the English pupils of Guarino da Verona: see 'From Guarino of Verona to John Colet', in his *Essays on the Renaissance and the Classical Tradition* (London, 1990).

13) The letter is Ep. 26 (Allen I, 289–97; translated in the first volume of Correspondence, *CWE* 1:255–66). It deals with the value of such 'tiny gems of allegory and allusion', with the many examples the reader would find provided, and with the method he used.

14) Thus *LB* II, 1F–2A (and see further Miller, cited below).

15) Clarence H. Miller, 'The Logic and Rhetoric of Proverbs in Erasmus' Praise of Folly', in *Essays on the Works of Erasmus,* 94–5. Miller's careful study of the *Praise of Folly* underscores the need to read all Erasmus' mature writings with the *Adagia* in view.

16) A notable example is the *Ne bos quidem pereat* of 1526, which contains yet another plea for harmony in Christendom and the universities (see ch. 38 below).

17) See ch. 23. The importance of the colony of Greek scholars in Venice at that time has been studied by Geanakoplos, *Greek Scholars in Venice*; and

the importance of Erasmus' Italian years was narrated by A. Renaudet in *Erasme et l'Italie* (Geneva, 1954). For a fresh picture of Erasmus at work in the household and atelier of Manutius, see Phillips, *The 'Adages'*.

18) Phillips, op. cit. Even before the *Collectanea* appeared in 1500, Erasmus was writing that he planned more than 3,000 (*CWE* 1:255/50–1, Ep. 125, spring 1500). In Ep. 126, the dedicatory epistle, he declared, 'I have published this sample merely in order to see, at comparatively little risk and expense, what this novel work is going to look like' (*CWE* 1:266/297–8; Allen I, 295/254–6). Much later, in 1524, Erasmus wrote to Haio Herman (Allen V, 1479/58–61): 'Last year the Prouerbia came out augmented in not a few places and corrected. And now a new edition is being made ready. I shall do this as long as I live'. He is referring back to the Froben edition of 1523 and looking forward to the next edition, considerably enlarged, of February 1526.

19) Thus Smith, *Erasmus*, 47–8, working from Sandys' now dated *History of Classical Scholarship* (New York, 1958) II, 104 ff., to which one may add the useful appendices in R.R. Bolgar, *The Classical Heritage and Its Beneficiaries* (Cambridge, 1954), though these are neither complete nor completely accurate. It might be added that Plutarch's *Moralia*, a most influential book for renaissance humanists, appeared in 1509; Plato and Pindar in 1513, and so on.

20) G.C. Kuiper, 'Oleum in Auricula ferre (Adagium 463)', *HumLov* XXXIX (1990).

21) 'Erasmus and the Classics', in *Erasmus*, ed. Dorey (1970) 21.

22) This unique copy was auctioned by Sotheby's in a sale of Continental and Russian books and mss on 20 November 1990; I was not able to examine it, and efforts to find out the fate of this copy have not been successful.

23) Thus H.R. Woudhuysen in *TLS* (9–15 November 1990). This copy had been given to Nicolaus Cannius, who preserved it and added notes and annotations of his own; the copy 'does not appear to have been used for the printing of the 1526 edition'. Cannius (Kan), we know, left the service of Erasmus late, by 31 January 1530 (Allen VII, 79n., and VIII, 342/77; and see *BR*). But the central question remains: why did Erasmus not make use of all his corrections and annotations in the 1523 edition for his 1526 edition of the *Adagia*? For he had presumably done this work before Cannius came into his service in 1527: had the volume been mislaid? If so, why did Erasmus not draw upon what he could remember? Answers to these questions would throw further light on Erasmus' late writing habits, for which the Copenhagen codices also tell us a good deal (see ch. 44).

24) A notable example is his discovery of the ms. of Valla's *Adnotationes* at the Abaye du Parc in 1504, which he published at Paris the following year (ch. 21).

25) Phillips, 'Erasmus and the Classics', 19.

26) Allen III, 65 (Ep. 643). I quote from the translation in *CWE* 5:92/29. One is reminded of the perhaps echoing lines in Wordsworth's *Prelude*: 'Bliss was it in that dawn to be alive,/ But to be young was very heaven!' (XI, 107–8).

27) Kisch, *Erasmus und die Jurisprudenz seiner Zeit* (1960). On the critical question of the re-introduction and re-interpretation of Aristotle's

'Epieikeia', see Kisch, 64–5.

28) The citations are to Cicero's 'in actione pro Murena' (25–7), Terence (IV, 5, 47/v.796), and Cicero's *De Officiis* (1.x.33). Next Erasmus adds: *'Citatur et Celsus adolescens libro Pandect. quadragesimo quinto, titulo, De uerborum obligatione, Cap. si seruum Sticum'* (D.45.1.91.3,i.f.; and D.50.17.90). The implications of these citations are discussed by Kisch, *Erasmus*, 59 ff.

29) J. Huizinga, *Erasmus*, German trs. by Werner Kaegi (Basel, 1941) 128, and see Kisch, *Erasmus*, 67–8. Rudolf Pfeiffer has commented on this point in *Humanitas Erasmiana* (Leipzig-Bern, 1931 – Studien der Bibliothek Warburg, XXII). On J.H. Waszink's fine study in 'Erasmus and His Influence on Anglo-Dutch Philology', in *The Anglo-Dutch Contribution to the Civilization of Early Modern Society:* An Anglo-Netherlands Symposium London 1974 (Oxford, 1976) 60–72; see my remarks in *Moreana* XXIII (1986) 91–2.

30) Van derHaeghen, *Bibliotheca Erasmiana*, and the works by S.W. Bijl, *Erasmus in het Nederlands tot 1617* (Nieuwkoop, 1978), and Irmgard Bezzel, *Erasmusdrucke des 16. Jahrhunderts in bayerischen Bibliotheken* (Stuttgart, 1979).

31) There is irony in the fact that those who prepared the *Index Librorum Prohibitorum* years after his death thought the adages were 'a subversive repertory of hidden topical allusions' (Phillips, 'Ways with Adages', 53).

32) See R.G. Collingwood, *Principles of Art* (Oxford, 1938).

England Again, 1509: The 'Period of Silence'

His mind moves upon silence.
W. B. Yeats, 'Long-legged Fly'

We need a reason to speak, but none to keep silent.
Pierre Nicole, *De la paix avec les hommes*

There is no such thing as an empty space or an empty time.
There is always something to see, something to hear. In fact,
try as we may to make a silence, we cannot.
John Cage, 'Experimental Music' in *Silence* (1961)

For it becometh the master to speak and to teach;
but it befits the disciple to be silent and to listen.
Rule of St Benedict, chapter vi

It was probably in mid-July 1509 that Erasmus left Rome, and he travelled north by way of Bologna. From this northern Italian city he crossed the Alps by way of the Splügen Pass, but this time there is no *Carmen alpestre*. Riding across Switzerland to Constance he made use of the Rhine to travel next to Strasbourg. There he is likely to have met the printer Matthias Schürer, who had just opened his own press after his apprenticeship with Prüss and Knoblauch; but it is not clear whether Schürer's 1509 edition of the *Adagia* was totally unauthorised, for it appeared in July, and the edition must have been commenced before Erasmus' arrival in Strasbourg in late July or early August. It has been noted that Erasmus 'gave his work to no other Strasbourg printer during Schürer's lifetime, and the latter had a virtual monopoly on Erasmian publication in the city'.[1] After 1509 Erasmus enjoyed many relations with the humanist circles of Strasbourg and Sélestat (Schlettstadt).

A key figure in the literary circles of the Upper Alsace was Jakob Wimpheling (Wimpfeling), the eldest son of a saddler in Sélestat. In that city that produced so many humanists he attended the well-known Latin school directed by Ludwig Dringenberg, and he had friendly relations with Johann Geiler and Sebastian Brant, men of an older generation who contributed to the humanism of Upper Alsace. By 1509 Wimpheling had retired to a Williamite monastery in Strasbourg, and he is a most likely figure to have greeted Erasmus in 1509. As the focus of the literary society that included the head of the Latin school, Johannes Sapidus, Wimpheling drew together such figures as Paul Volz, Beatus Rhenanus, Martin Bucer, and the printer Lazarus Schürer. Wimpheling did much to continue the early humanist enterprises of the region, although as Otto Herding has noted he remained a stranger to Greek language and thought.[2] One may note, however, his biography of Gerson in 1506: *De vita et miraculis Joannis Gerson*, which gave a fresh spur to the reception of Gerson in the early sixteenth century.

From Strasbourg Erasmus continued down the Rhine by boat to the Low Countries, visiting friends at Antwerp and Louvain before making the Channel crossing he so detested. In Louvain he visited Adolph van Veere, the son of Anna van Borssele whose patronage he had so vainly sought earlier (chapter 18). In a letter of 1512 to Adolph (Epistle 266) Erasmus spoke of that visit: 'How often I have been sorry that I did not eagerly accept the position you offered me at Louvain three years ago [i.e., 1509]! But at that time I had been emboldened by my extravagant hopes and the mountains of English gold I saw in my fancy' (*CWE* 2:237/14–17; Allen I, 519/11–14). Nothing more is known of the position Adolph offered.[3]

It is notable that he did not return to Steyn, as we know from later correspondence with Servatius Rogers. Nor did he inform Servatius that in returning from Italy he had stopped over in Antwerp and Louvain. Perhaps he felt that he would be talking to the seashore, or talking to the wind (*Adagia* I.iv.84, 85) in trying to win the approval of Servatius to remain away from Steyn. Erasmus had his work to do, and he felt, as he had so often told Servatius in his letters (and doubtless in person), that he could do it only away from Steyn.

But now let us press the point that evidence for his biography at this stage of his life is almost non-existent. Some of that lacuna can be explained: we know that some of his letters were lost, and some stolen.[4] It is also clear that Erasmus suppressed some of his letters, particularly those of his youth, as well as that he edited his letters for publication.[5]

Having once again made a miserable crossing – never did he speak with pleasure or admiration either of the Channel or of the white cliffs of Dover – in late July or early August of 1509 Erasmus made the last leg of his thousand-mile journey, travelling from Dover to London. Perhaps he stopped over in Canterbury, as he had done on previous trips. In London he spent some considerable time in More's household, '*apud Morum*'. For some weeks he recuperated from his kidney-stone and rested up from his tiresome and tiring journey. In writing to Martin van Dorp in 1515 (Epistle 337) Erasmus recalled that 'I was staying at the time with More on returning from Italy, and was detained indoors for several days by pain in the kidneys. My books had not yet arrived, and if they had, my illness prevented anything more ambitious in the way of serious study' (*CWE* 3:116/ 134–8; Allen II, 94/126–130). Resting and waiting for his books, he developed the concept of the *Praise of Folly*, delighting in the play of words upon the name of *More* and the word for folly (*Moria*), to which he alludes in the preface to the work.

The last letter from Erasmus before the 'Silence' is the very brief letter to Aldus Manutius (Epistle 213) of December 1508, written from Padua. In the Correspondence there is a long gap; and the next letters are from Warham (Epistle 214, May 1509), Mountjoy (Epistle 215, May 1509), Piso (Epistle 216, June 1509), and the newly discovered letter from Scevola (Epistle 216A, December 1509)[6] – and, what is more, after December 1508 all are letters to Erasmus from his correspondents; nothing from Erasmus. That is all that we know until the letter from Bombasio – and again, like Epistle 213 it is a very brief letter (Epistle 217, March 1511): a period of well over a year (and more than two years of silence on the part of Erasmus himself), during which there are only hints of Erasmus' activities or whereabouts, generally in later writings. Erasmus' first letter after the 'Silence' is Epistle 218 to Ammonio (from Dover in April 1511): this is the first letter from Erasmus since December 1508, a very long hiatus indeed.

To explain the gap in the correspondence J.K. Sowards has written a much-cited essay on 'The Two Lost Years of Erasmus',[7] which does two things. First, it admirably summarises the evidence and reviews the scholarship; and second, it offers some speculation. But the speculative hypothesis rests on two largely unsupported assumptions: that Erasmus was in London and closely in touch with his friends there, and therefore no letters were needed; and that Erasmus' letters during this period were so filled with bitterness towards Julius II, or satirising him, that he thought it prudent to suppress them. But Erasmus often wrote letters to his friends even when he was in the same city with them (as at Paris, Oxford, and elsewhere, as we have already seen), and this alone would not explain why there are no letters extant to Erasmus from places other than London and Oxford. Further, it is difficult to believe that all Erasmus' correspondence during a period of two years was so filled with anti-Julius writing. We do not know the answer, given the evidence that we now possess; and Sowards' hypothesis must remain just that.

May there not in fact be other possibilities? We must keep as a firm bearing first of all what evidence we do possess, and we turn therefore to the issue of Erasmus' health.

Some of the time during this period was spent, as we know chiefly from epistolary evidence, in the houses of Thomas More and then of Ammonio;[8] and it is clear that neither the kidney-stone of which Erasmus now complained,[9] nor the intermittent fever he had suffered from boyhood,[10] was alleviated, much less cured, by the turbulent channel-crossing and that one or the other of these medical problems continued to incapacitate him at various times for the rest of his life.[11] Although he frequently complained of his continuing ill-health, he was not a hypochondriac; it is worth observing that many of his letters that were vividly descriptive of his pain were written to physicians. Besides, he was feeling his age, and in the *Praise of Folly* he ironically pictures the rewards of the scholar, from observation as well as from experience:

> And their futile reward, a word of praise from a handful of people, they win at such a cost – so many late nights, such loss of sleep, sweetest of all things, and so much sweat and anguish. Then their health deteriorates, their looks are destroyed, they suffer partial or total blindness, poverty, ill will, denial of pleasure, premature old age, and early death, and any other such disasters there may be... (CWE 27:124; *LB* IV, 459)

One notes that even here Erasmus works in an Homeric allusion (*sleep*, from *Iliad* 7:289, echoed in Moschus, *Idyll* 2.3). There are echoes of such a lament or *planctus* in many dark corners of renaissance literature, and the whole galaxy of scholarly laments is encyclopaedised by Burton in his *Anatomy of Melancholy* in the next century.

There are further gaps in Erasmus' correspondence, though not so great, in 1512 and in 1513, and Allen has thought that these gaps could again be explained by his illness (I, 524n.).

Yet another plausible hypothesis to explain this period of silence is the thought that he was residing with some patron. Mountjoy has seemed a likely candidate, although there were others whom Erasmus was trying to enlist in his cause: Warham, Fisher, and (with conspicuous lack of success) Richard Foxe, bishop of Winchester. But Mountjoy was gone from England for much of the time under discussion (as Sowards observes, 170–1); he had been appointed commander of the castle at Hammes, and the commission was renewed in 1509. Given Erasmus' erratic correspondence at this time and his frequent moves, it would not be surprising if references to such visiting of patrons, real or potential, had been lost. He does seem to have stayed often with Grocyn (*BR* and Sowards, 172); and this was a period of working closely with Colet on his planning for St Paul's School: we have poems and prayers associated with the school that suggest how much of the time from the summer of 1509 until the spring of 1511 Erasmus spent in London with Colet, perhaps staying with him some of the time.[12]

Still another hypothesis is that Erasmus was in a closed retreat at some religious house for some portion of this period, with an Augustinian house being the more probable.[13] Such an experience is not the sort that would necessarily be recorded, either in letters during the period of retreat or even by recollection later. That Erasmus' first letter after long silence should have been from Dover in April 1511 (Epistle 218) indicates that he was most likely en route to the Continent, for Epistle 219 later in the month is from Paris. Canterbury with its many religious houses is close to Dover, and a stay there is possible.

Finally, it may also be recalled that there was the summoning of French bishops in September 1510, called for Orleans but actually meeting at Tours. In this event and Erasmus' response to it are subsumed concepts of the hierarchical structure of the Church, leading to thinking about the principle of papal primacy and, in time, a General Council of the Church. Erasmus accepted a Church with bishops without question, but he was deeply critical of the abuses of the hierarchy; and while he accepted a certain degree of papal authority it is by no means clear that he believed in a papal primacy *de jure divino* (here I follow Tracy, 188–9): I think that he did not, and it is striking that Erasmus made much of Cyprian's interpretation of Matthew 16:18 – *et ego dico tibi quia tu es Petrus et super hanc petram aedificabo ecclesiam meam* – as referring to Peter himself, not his faith. For Erasmus' thinking on the unity of the Church, hammered out later (as we shall see in chapters 37 ff.) in the many controversial writings of the 1520s and articulated finally in his *De Sarcienda Ecclesiae Concordia* of 1533, his greatest indebtedness was to Cyprian's *De Ecclesiae Unitate*. There Cyprian emphasised the equality of the rest of the apostles with Peter: 'endowed with a like partnership both of honour and of power'.[14] As Quasten soberly concludes, 'it is evident that Cyprian does not recognize a primacy of jurisdiction of the bishop of Rome over his colleagues' (376).

The convocation of 1510 was to consult on the liberties and privileges of the Gallican Church, and obviously canonists and theologians would have been in the forefront at such a meeting.[15] But others are likely to have been called as *periti*, and it is probable that Erasmus had seen Guillaume Briçonnet at Bologna in 1506 (*BR*), who was by then bishop of Rheims and cardinal bishop of Frascati and Palestrina, having just received the French see of Narbonne: clearly in the forefront of French Church leaders. It is further possible that Erasmus met him again in 1509 while in Rome: he was one of the leaders in calling a schismatic council under the sponsorship of Louis XII (*BR*). These were troubled years, and there were other rebel cardinals besides Briçonnet who were joining the schismatic council. We do not know, to be sure, but if Erasmus had consulted with Briçonnet in 1509 or 1510, the pre-empting of the Council of Pisa by Julius II, by his summoning a 'true universal council' to Rome on 9 April 1512,[16] would have put the rebellious French cardinals and all those who were connected with the enterprise in a very poor light, indeed in some danger. In fact, the French cardinals were degraded during the Fifth Lateran Council (Jedin I, 112).[17] There was more than enough reason for Erasmus to suppress references to any activities that included the expression of anti-papal and pro-Gallican sentiment during those years – to that extent I am in agreement with Sowards – but a fortiori, Erasmus would have wanted to suppress references to consultations or similar activities in connection either with the September 1510 meeting of French bishops or the planning for the Council of Pisa.

Having gone to Italy with ambitions and the keen desire for recognition, Erasmus left Italy and arrived back in England in the summer of 1509 having achieved much, including the magnificent Aldine edition of the *Adagiorum Chiliades* that everyone was exclaiming over. He was recognised throughout Europe at last, and he was becoming one of the best known of European, not merely Dutch, humanists. He had immeasurably improved his command of Greek by living amidst the Greek colony in Venice, and through his daily rubbing elbows with emigré Greek scholars and others he vastly widened his reading of Greek literature.

That there is such a zone of silence during this period is frustrating: it reminds us too forcefully of the incompleteness of the biographical evidence, and of the limitations of the evidence we do possess; and it compels us to challenge many of our presuppositions about his thinking during the years of his emerging as the premier humanist of his generation.

Notes

1) *BR*, and see Allen, 'Erasmus' Relations with his Printers', 125; and Miriam U. Chrisman, 'Le métier et la main: Matthias Schürer, humaniste imprimeur', in *Grandes Figures de l'humanisme alsacien* (Strasbourg, 1978) 159–72.

2) Herding, ed. *Adolescentia* (Munich, 1965). See Barbara Könneker in *BR*, and Spitz, *Religious Renaissance of the German Humanists* (1963) 41–60.

3) See Allen I, 62, ll. 216 ff. Thus *CWE* 2:151n & Ep. 266/15.

4) On lost things, including letters, see Ep. 2203 (Allen VIII, 249/23–5), and Allen I, appendix VII, 'The Principal Editions of Erasmus' Epistolae'. On copies of some of his letters that were stolen, see Ep. 3100 (Allen XI, 288/29 ff.). It is to be noted that at least as early as 1505 Erasmus kept letter books (see Ep. 186; Allen I, 415/3 ff.; *CWE* 2:100/4 ff.).

5) The editing of letters for publication was conventional in the Renaissance. Smith, *Erasmus*, 206–7 writes: 'comparison with the manuscripts, where they have survived, shows extensive and important alterations' – but Erasmus usually informed some of his correspondents, esp. More and Mountjoy, that he was altering for publication.

6) In December 1509 Daniel Scevola wrote that he had heard no definite news of Erasmus for about a year (Ep. 216A, *CWE* 2:154/12–13); but he was no great friend and his letter (dated from Ferrara on 22 December 1509, six months after Erasmus' departure from Italy, underscores this observation), and his letter may never have reached Erasmus (see Sowards 162 n. 3). In February of 1512 Ammonio, a much closer friend, complained that 'whereas I myself sent you three letters while you were still in Italy, I have received nothing from you either before or after, save three short words' (Ep. 256, *CWE* 2:217/8–10). Because, as Ammonio observed, 'war interrupts all communications, and also because you never, as I hear, stayed very long in one spot' (*CWE* 2:217/11–13), it is remarkable that as many letters reached Erasmus as did, during his periods of frequent moving.

7) J. K. Sowards, 'The Two Lost Years of Erasmus: Summary, review, and Speculation', *Studies in the Renaissance* 9 (1962) 161–86. See the note in *CWE* 2:156 to the effect that Erasmus seems to have lost touch with his old friends on the Continent (cf. Ep. 256, *CWE* 2:217/3 ff.).

8) Andreas Ammonio like Erasmus was an expatriate, and they shared a passion for Italian humanism; both had been guests in More's household, and they shared lodgings during this period. They had known each other earlier in England (*BR*), and Ammonio proved to be a valuable friend in helping to arrange for Erasmus' dispensation of 1505–6 (see ch. 22 and appendix C) and would be again for the later dispensation of 1516.

9) Erasmus provides some graphic descriptions of kidney-stone attacks that are worthy of Rabelais: in Ep. 1735, ll. 1–18, and 1759. The problems with kidney stone began in Venice, as we learn from Erasmus' brief allusion in the adage '*Festina lente*' (*Adag.* II.i.1), where he writes that 'meanwhile I had had an encounter with a trouble I had not met before, the stone' (Phillips, *Adages*, 186; *LB* II, 405D, and ch. 23). In his 1514 letter to the prior of Steyn Erasmus spoke of this by then long-standing medical problem (for he had had attacks in Cambridge): 'For several years now I have been a prey to the stone, a most troublesome and dangerous ailment ... I can't stand

every kind of food, or even any and every climate. This sickness of mine recurs so readily that I have to be extremely temperate in my habits, and I know the Dutch climate' (Ep. 296 to Servatius, *CWE* 2:296/64–69; Allen I, 567/62–68).

10) The fever that afflicted Erasmus was sometimes called the sweating sickness, sometimes the English sweat (*Sudor anglicus*); sometimes as Pare described the disease, it held for two or three years, and for others all their lives (q. *Cambridge Letters*, ed. Porter and Thomson, 78–9). It could be a killing fever.

11) Erasmus moved among physicians, especially medical humanists, all his mature life; he frequently described his symptoms in professional detail therefore, especially when writing to his doctor friends. The following studies are relevant: of medical studies of Erasmus, E.D. Baumann, *Medischhistorische Studiën over Des. Erasmus* (Arnhem, c. 1953), and Peter Krivatsy, 'Erasmus' Medical Milieu', *Bulletin of the History of Medicine* xlvii (1973) 113–54. On Erasmus' medical friends, see M. Hermanns, *Erasmus von Rotterdam und seine ärtzliche Freunde* (Würzburg, 1937).

12) We have Erasmus' '*Expostulatio Jesu cum Homine*' of 1510 (published in the 1511 volume entitled *Concio de puero Iesu a puero in schola Coletica nuper Londini instituta pronuncianda*) as well as the poem '*Institutum hominis Christiani*', to which Reedijk gives the title 'Precepts for Christians' and suggests that they belong to the 1509–1510 period. With these works should be considered also the epigrams written specifically for Colet's school, the *Carmina scholaria*, which were published on 1 September 1511; see Reedijk 297 & ff., and Tracy 120–1.

13) To be sure, the retreat as a formal devotion of the Roman Catholic Church was introduced only in the Counter-Reformation and was most closely associated with the Jesuits, who were the first order or congregation to include provision for retreats in their rule – in their Spiritual Exercises – see *ODCC* and *NCE*. But provision for spiritual retreat is to be found in chs 49 and 53 of the Rule of St Benedict, and some monasteries served as retreat havens by the end of the Middle Ages. The concept and ideal are consonant with the spirit and goals of the *Devotio Moderna*. The modern Code of Canon Law legislated a closed retreat at least once every three years for most religious (c. 126) and in some cases every year.

14) See J. Quasten, *Patrology*, vol. II (Utrecht, 1953) 349–53, 373–78. See *Opera Cypriani*, 136ᵛ, and *Erasmus' Annotations on the New Testament*, ed. A. Reeve (1986) 70, with Tracy's comment (*Erasmus*, 189). Yet Erasmus 'also praised Cajetan's *De Divina Institutione Pontificatus Romani super totam Ecclesiam*' (Letter 1225, Allen IV, 199–203); see also Ep. 1218, ll. 34–6. But Cajetan's work was published in Rome only in March 1521, by which time the Reformation was heating up. Earlier that same month Erasmus asked Everard, '*Quid Caietano Cardinale superbius aut furiosus?*' (Ep. 1188, Allen IV, 447/23–4). These are complex statements that must be discussed more fully.

15) Gallicanism is but the collective name for the body of doctrine which asserted the more or less complete freedom of the Roman Catholic Church in France from the ecclesiastical authority of the papacy (*ODCC*). The representations of such theologians as Gerson and D'Ailly at the Councils during the Great Schism led to the Pragmatic Sanction of Bourges (issued in 1438 while

the Council of Basel was still in session, but superseded by the Concordat of Bologna in 1516, leaving the French king's right of nomination to bishoprics and other high ecclesiastical offices). Gallicanism was an important issue in the Fifth Lateran Council, owing in part to the French Council of Pisa.

16) The Bull *Sacrosanctae Romanae Ecclesiae* was promulgated 18 July 1511, summoning a General Council of the Church for 19 April 1512 at the Lateran in Rome.

17) The background to the Fifth Lateran Council (1512–1517) is summarised in my essay, 'The Fifth Lateran Council: its partial successes and its larger failures', in *Reform and Authority in the Medieval and Reformation Church*, ed. Guy F. Lytle (Washington, D.C., 1981) 99–104. The modern authority is still H. Jedin, *A History of the Council of Trent,* vol. 1 (Edinburgh, 1957, rptd 1963) ch. v, 'Failure of the Conciliar Attempts of Basel (1482) and Pisa (1511)' 101–16; cf. Hefele-Hergenröther, *Konziliengeschichte,* VIII, 431–97, which is still to be consulted. For the French conciliabulum and the Council of Pisa, see A. Renaudet, *Le Concile gallican de Pise-Milan* (Paris, 1922).

The Praise of Folly

And therefore he imagineth, that Folie shoulde be a Goddesse,
who before all kyndes of men assembled as to a sermon,
shoulde declare how many benefites they receive at hir handes:
and how without hir accesse, nothyng in this life is delectable,
commodious, or tollerable unto us, no not our owne life.

Sir Thomas Chaloner, 'Preface to the Reader' in his first
English translation (1549)

For only when humour illuminated that mind did it become
truly profound. In the *Praise of Folly* Erasmus gave something
that no one else could have given to the world.

Huizinga, *Erasmus*, 78

On returning from Italy in 1509 – as Erasmus wrote, with something of the *sprezzatura* already conventional among Italian humanists, as Castiglione developed that notion in his *Cortegiano*, begun in
the same year:

> as I was returning lately from Italy to England, in order to avoid
> squandering upon vulgar and uneducated talk the whole time I
> had to spend on horseback, I sometimes preferred inwardly to
> savour some memory, either of the studies you [Thomas More]
> and I shared once, or of the learned and congenial friends whom
> I had left behind in this country ... I decided to compose a
> trifling thing, *Moriae encomium*. (Epistle 222, *CWE* 2:161/2 ff.,
> Allen 1, 460/1 ff.)

The conventions can easily be spotlighted: the composition on horseback or after riding, the pretence that the result is a trifling thing,
the recollection of past studies and pleasures, and the closing words
that allude to the country ('*ex rure*').[1]

Erasmus' great classic of irony was played out[2] on the stage of
European thought and letters: 'poised' (as Clarence Miller puts it
quite admirably) 'between the urbanity of the Italian Renaissance
and the earnestness of Northern humanism'.[3] All human life contains
irony, and the complex metaphoric extensions of the *theatrum mundi*
topos has a life in European literature. The ironic double vision is a

perilous equilibrium, because a tipping of the scales too much in the wrong direction leads either to despair and cynicism or, in the other, to preaching and propagandising. The key to the balance, I urge, is rhetoric; but it must be the humanistic rhetoric of renaissance humanism, though even that can be viewed with some irony.[4]

Erasmus' work is about folly, and there is a very large literature on fools and folly. Bakhtin's much-cited book on carnival is stimulating and has some relevance to Erasmus' work, but it makes unsupported assumptions about the nature of late medieval society and its methodology cannot go unchallenged. Yet it usefully reminds the twentieth-century reader of the meaning of carnival.[5] In 1523 Erasmus wrote to Botzheim that he played the fool in the house of Thomas More, but the Latin suggests a greater degree of camaraderie, even co-creativity: *Moriam lusimus apud Thomam Morum* ('we played the fool, or at folly, in the household of Thomas More': Allen 1, 19/6). Earlier, in 1516, in the famous letter to von Hutten, Erasmus spoke directly of his indebtedness to More: 'More was responsible for my writing the *Praise of Folly* – that is, for making the camel dance' (Allen IV, 16/119–20): *'quin et mihi ut Morie Encomium scriberem, hoc est ut camelus saltarem, fuit auctor'.*[6]

Erasmus' modest disclaimer in the prefatory letter to More informs the reader that the *Moria* was composed on the way back to England from Italy; yet even that suggests a reaching for earlier studies, or perhaps conversation, especially between himself and More. Knowing as little as we do about the actual circumstances of composition, we may suppose that some aspects of the work were rooted in Erasmus' Italian experience, and some no doubt in those months about which we know virtually nothing, the period of silence (chapter 25). We may also infer that some of the writing was done in More's house, during a period of illness. To refer to Screech, there is much of More in the work, as indeed Erasmus intimates in his prefatory letter:

> More was not only a close friend; he was a gentleman. Such a man was to be trusted with his friends' most private thoughts and their most private hopes and fears. If ever a man knew what the *Moria* meant, he did. And he championed it throughout his life. But of the circumstances in which it was written he says nothing.[7]

Although sometimes dated to 1509, there is no text of that date. The first printed version is the Paris edition of Gilles de Gourmont of 1511 (of which there are copies in the Dresden and Munich Libraries, as well as the British Library).[8] This text was reprinted in Paris, Strasbourg and Antwerp in 1511, and in 1512 it was reprinted in Antwerp, Strasbourg and Paris. Clearly by 1512 it was already a popular book.[9]

The 1511 version of the *Moria* – even though it does not command our lasting attention by virtue of representing the full development by Erasmus of his concept of a *declamatio*, that is, Dame Folly preaching a mock encomium in praise of herself – nonetheless anticipates his deepest concerns in religious thought and spirituality. It is a work of considerable importance in its own right, and it came into being in the world of 1509–1511, a world dominated in Christendom by Julius II, the warlike pope whom Erasmus so condemned. Further, it is cast in the Lucianesque mode that More and Erasmus together had been generating and engendering in their own writings even more than in their translations: in a real sense *Moria* and *Utopia* are sister works. As we shall see, there are also significant links between the *Enchiridion* of 1503 and the *Moria* of 1509–1511.

But in 1512 the world changed. Having summoned a General Council, Julius II opened the Fifth Lateran Council on 3 May. At the opening session Aegidio da Viterbo preached a powerful sermon on reform, and the pulse of humanists and others who so fervently sought reform was quickened.[10] Although a generous patron of the arts (supporting or commissioning the work of Michelangelo, Bramante and others), and patron and friend to such humanists as Sadoleto and Bembo, Julius was better known as the warlike pope: *Pontifice terribile* he was called in an ultimate oxymoron; for along with his energy and majesty, he was strong-willed and capable of anger.[11] His successor, Leo X, was a son of Lorenzo the Magnificent, and his popular image was that of a peace-loving cardinal. He was a reader and protector of Erasmus, and this was the pope who continued the Fifth Lateran Council and concluded it on 15 March 1517, but failed to implement the reforms that the Council had called for. This pleasure-loving pope was in the Seat of Peter when Luther – disillusioned by the failures of a General Council – nailed his ninety-five theses to the church door at Wittenberg on 31 December 1517, and it was Leo X who excommunicated him in 1521. It was with easy-going Leo as pope that the Reformation arrived in Europe.

By 1514, when an enlarged and revised *Moria* was published, the optimism over the Fifth Lateran Council was cooling off, and there were many other forces threatening the unity of Christendom. It was an age of continuing wars and of many controversies: yet Erasmus still hoped for peace, and he thought his *Moria* would be an instrument for peace and a guiding light to a deeper religion, especially the final pages that convey the thrust of his *philosophia Christi*. But Erasmus failed to realised how many readers could not follow his wit and therefore could not perceive how close in ultimate spirituality the *Enchiridion* and the *Moria* were intended to be. Like so many men and women of wit, Erasmus 'never seems to have realised how wounding his laughter could be to those who lacked his sense of humour'.[12]

But the *Moria* never looked back. Edition after edition and translation after translation rolled of the presses. During the lifetime of Erasmus the work appeared in thirty-six editions from the presses of twenty-one printers in eleven cities, and among these cities were the important printing centres of Europe: Paris, Lyons, Strasbourg, Venice, Florence, Basel, Cologne, Deventer, and Antwerp. Throughout his lifetime Erasmus himself augmented it, and revised it in seven major editions: 1512 (Paris), 1514 (Strasbourg), 1515, 1516, 1521, 1522, and finally in Basel in 1532.[13] The Italian translation by Pellegrini appeared in 1539, and Thomas Chaloner's celebrated English translation in 1549; there have been other translations into German, French, Dutch, Swedish, Danish, Polish, Czech, Greek, and Spanish. It has never been out of print in one or other of the vernaculars or Latin, and as we learn from Margolin's comprehensive bibliography, in the twelve-year period from 1950 to 1962 there were fifty-two reprints or new translations of the *Moria* in sixteen different languages.[14] After 1515 many of the editions included the commentary by Gerardus Listrius (who had attended St Lebuin's School in Deventer while Hegius was still alive, and later became a doctor of medicine; see *BR*), but it is clear that Erasmus wrote much of the commentary himself. There is one copy of Froben's edition of 1515 that has pen-and-ink illustrations in the margins: these were by the young Hans Holbein, and have been reproduced in a handsome facsimile edition (Basel, 1931; the two illustrations in this book are photographed from a copy in the possession of the author). Condemned by Paris theologians in 1527, and put on a list of books condemned by the Sorbonne in 1542 and 1543, *Moria* was condemned in the Tridentine Index of 1564.[15]

Much of the prefatory letter addressed to Thomas More and prefixed to the 1511 edition (Epistle 222) explains the title by establishing that the name of More is close in form to the Greek *moria*, or folly. Much of the remainder of this preface becomes a justification of the mock encomium with an appeal to the authority of Homer, Virgil, Ovid, Synesius, Lucian and Plutarch for the genre of the work – and to what better authorities could one appeal? And, given that everything in the *Moria* is subject to scrutiny, by virtue of the play of genre and the continuing irony, may we not suppose that even the very appeal to authority carries its own ironies? Thus Erasmus feels able to assert further: 'Others will judge me; but unless my vanity altogether deceives me, I have written a Praise of Folly without being altogether foolish' (*CWE* 2:164/59–61). Here, as the Toronto editors note, Erasmus employs for 'vanity' the Greek word for self-love, on which he had already written an adage entitled *Philautoi* or self-lovers (*Adagia*, 1. iii. 92).[16] The adage here, as elsewhere in Erasmus, provides a key to the resonances of his Latin, and it also opens the window to the possibilities of self-directed irony.

One might think that enough rhetorical clues were provided in that letter to More. Yet *Moria* troubled many contemporaries of Erasmus, and it was frequently and bitterly attacked – by Dorp, Edward Lee, Alberto Pio and others – and it led, more than any other of his works, to his image as a jester, one who was not serious and did not deserve to be taken seriously. Erasmus' irony was suspect in the eyes of serious contemporary theologians like Luther, who thought him filled with cunning artifice: '*est vir duplex*', Luther is reported to have said in his *Tischreden* or *Table-talk* (1, no. 131, see *BR*). These contemporaries ignored altogether the genre of the work, despite the preface (and despite their having themselves had some introduction to *declamatio* and mock encomium in their own liberal arts studies), and they missed its irony; for they 'picked various sentences out of their context and labelled them blasphemous or heretical', (thus Miller).[17] But in our own century there are still misunderstandings of Erasmus' writings, and of his purpose in the *Moria*; however, this is not the place to draw up a map of misreadings of Erasmus (see *Erasmus Grandescens*, 129).

The *Moria*, it is agreed, is demanding of its readers, though to be sure it became a celebrated piece which reached a wider audience than one suspects was originally intended – not unlike the widespread popularity of Umberto Eco's *The Name of the Rose* which found its way to the coffee-tables of many who, it would seem self-evident, did not read the Latin quotations or go very far into the historical overtones of the narrative. Erasmus' *Moria* assumes a knowledge of a complex literary tradition, a close familiarity with the Pauline tradition of the paradox of the Christian who is a fool in the eyes of the world but wise in the sight of God (1 Corinthians 3:18, with parallel passages in both the Old and New Testaments, enhanced by numerous commentaries), and, finally, a sophisticated ironic sense that permits the reader to move from one paradox to the next with enjoyment and to arrive at the ultimate ironic double vision, culminating in the comprehension and shared experience of the Pauline ecstasy of which M. A. Screech has written so compellingly in *Ecstasy and the Praise of Folly*.

First of all, then, the *Moria* is a piece of rhetoric, and in fact a masterpiece of rhetoric. It is after all a mock encomium, a *declamatio* of a special kind put into the mouth of Folly herself: it is a praising of folly by the woman (or goddess) Folly. She herself breaks most of the prized rules of conventional rhetoric, and at the end she tells her readers that if they are waiting for an epilogue, 'you are crazy if you think I still have in mind what I have said, after pouring forth such a torrent of jumbled words' (138). If historians have been in error in their interpretations of the *Moria* because of their failure to comprehend sufficiently the irony of the work, literary critics and scholars have in the main failed to understand the importance of rhetoric in the work and – this is the ironic turn, technically speaking – of the manipulations of rhetoric, including but not limited to the medieval school rhetorics that preceded Erasmus' own educational programme that had a new humanistic rhetoric at its centre.

Erasmus would have laughed, one thinks, to read the efforts of moderns to pin down the structure of his *Moria* to a minute following of the structure of a particular classical oration: thus, stressing Quintilian as model, Hoyt H. Hudson in his 1941 translation; or the later efforts of Walter Kaiser, Richard S. Sylvester and Clarence H. Miller to tie the structure into the teachings of Aphthonius and other late rhetoricians.[18] It is not enough, I urge, to call attention to the affinities with structures in classical rhetoric, however close, or to the inconsistencies in Folly's arguments, or to the parodial elements of her own presentation. The *Moria* is also a satirising of the rigidities of much rhetorical teaching in the schools and also a parodying of the pretentious folly and hyper-specialisation of so many professional rhetoricians, who were not so unlike their colleagues, the theologians and lawyers.[19] There is much greater fruitfulness in pursuing the suggestive observations of Sylvester that focus upon the movements from genesis (in detailing, for example, the powers and pleasures of Folly herself) and change, to the catalogue and explosive quality of the ultimate folly of the fool in Christ. This is the main thrust of Screech's splendid reading of the work; and, to quote from the Preface to *Folly and Insanity in Renaissance Literature* by Ernesto Grassi and Maristella Lorch, 'the humanist philosophy of Alberti and Erasmus achieves a kind of meaning that neither poetic nor reflective thinking can achieve. It is a form of reflective thought done through tropes. In this way it is possible to philosophize about the human world without in fact leaving it' (12).

For there is a dynamic in the rhetoric-play and development of the work, and a vital part of that dynamic is the metaphorical stretching that enlarges to include the final metamorphosis possible from an understanding and embracing of the true as opposed to the pretentious or factitious. Folly in herself and by virtue of the concept rooted in her provides the ground for the play and for the final stretching of mind. Rhetoric, I am arguing, becomes a means or path to wisdom; to echo and expand that resonant concept of Professor Grassi, we are here experiencing 'rhetoric as wisdom'.

It is my thesis that not only must we understand such a concept for appreciating the role of rhetoric in the *Moria*, and for the structuring of the work by modes of rhetoric; we must understand the work and its kind of wisdom in order to comprehend the relationship of the *Moria* to the totality of the Erasmian programme.

We have already spoken of the declamation[20] in discussing Erasmus' *Panegyricus* (chapter 19); here it will be useful to speak of the two thrusts of the classical *declamatio* as rhetorical phenomena. The first is the practice of either of the two forms of the *declamatio* originally as part of the rhetorical training of the orator for law courts or senates: these were the *suasoriae*, which were deliberative; and the *controversiae*, which were forensic – these last often subtle and unreal subjects, even (as Baldwin observes)[21] at times indecent and perverted. In the Latin tradition the main sources are to be found in the writings of Seneca the Elder, but there were many practitioners. The other thrust of the *declamatio* is the encomium, intended for such occasions as marriages, birthdays, festivals, and addresses to rulers (as in the *Panegyricus*), funeral orations (as in the oration for Berthe Heyen), and even at athletic games.[22] And mock encomiums were a well-established and well-understood literary sub-genre, as Erasmus takes pains to make clear to his reader.

Thus the rhetorical tradition carried within itself the possibility of playful treatment of serious subjects and of certain aspects of its own tradition: a highly self-conscious rhetoric always contains the seeds of potential parody, satire, or irony.

There is yet another dimension – another rhetorical thrust, if you will – in the *Moria* that has received little attention, and that is the rhetoric of intertextuality, for a general discussion of which I refer to my monograph on *Intertextuality and Renaissance Texts*. The prefatory letter to More – who had not yet won acclaim for his *Utopia* but would have been identified within the republic of letters as the co-translator with Erasmus of Lucian – is notable, and in that letter there are allusions not only to Homer, Suetonius, Catullus, Lucian, Gellius, Seneca, Horace and Aristophanes, but also to Erasmus' own

Adages, which had received a more nearly definitive form in the Aldine edition of 1508 and had won an instant acclaim. If the notables of the classical canon (which was significantly widening in the first decade of the sixteenth century)[23] are also to be found scattered throughout the work proper, allusions to or quotations from the *Adagiorum Chiliades* of 1508 abound on nearly every page. Rhetorically, it seems to me, this underscores the general principles of the Erasmian programme: that classical letters contain much wisdom, and that classical wisdom is not alien to the christian revelation. More subtly, it would seem, the frequent echoing of adages reminds the sophisticated reader of the connections between the *Moria* and another key work in the Erasmian programme: it is another way of stressing the point that the *Moria* at a deeper level shares its purpose with the *Enchiridion* and the rest of Erasmus' writings in the first and second decades of the sixteenth century. To be sure, just as Folly is capable of sleight-of-hand manipulations of the scholastic syllogism,[24] so too she is capable of creative misquotation: for example, she misapplies the proverb about those who display their good character by their deeds to those who boast about their deeds (11); and from time to time she cites ideas or proverbs that are contradictory – the one from the *Adagiorum*, the other, apparently, from the storehouse of proverb wisdom of the Middle Ages:[25]

> But why even bother to give you my name, as if you could not tell at a glance who I am, 'prima facie' as it were, or as if anyone who might claim that I am Minerva or Sophia could not be refuted by one good look at me, even if I did not identify myself in speech, 'that truest mirror of the mind'. (13)

Erasmus came to the conceiving and writing of his *Moria* after years of translating Lucian; irony and satire had become quite natural modes of thought for him. Over the centuries satire has been a mixed bag of literary conventions and devices; one has only to think of the range of satire in English literature, from Chaucer's satire and self-irony in the *Canterbury Tales* (and especially, but not limited to, the General Prologue), or Langland's more biting and angry satire in *Piers Plowman*, to the railing invectives of Skelton, and the wide range of satire in Elizabethan literature, and the elegance of Pope's satirical couplets: examples that are paralleled in Continental literature. If, to attempt a working definition, one conceives of satire as operating across a spectrum of literary modes from direct to indirect, from invective to irony with burlesque and parody somewhere in between, one is equipped to read the range of satire in Erasmus. One must identify his models: in his own preface to the *Moria* Erasmus informs the reader that he will not be like Juvenal, for he will describe the *ridenda* and not the *foeda*, that is the laughable rather than the filthy. Erasmus' later writings from the *Julius Exclusus* to the fully developed colloquies – like, for example, the *Naufragium* ('The Shipwreck') – are charged with irony directed at a range of targets. One brief example must suffice, taken from the adage *A mortuo tributum exigere* (to exact tribute from the dead, *Adag.* I. ix. 12), where the target is the payment to the clergy for religious offices, here burial:

> Among Christians, the dead cannot even be laid in the ground unless you have hired that little scrap of land from a priest, and the size and splendour of the place you are given will be in proportion to the price. A large sum in ready money will buy you the right to lie and rot[26] in church near the high altar; a modest offering, and you will lie out of doors in the rain among ordinary folk. (*CWE* 32:187; *LB* II; 338E)

After relishing the hitting out at grammarians, poets and rhetoricians, at scholars and theologians – all done at length (too much for some modern readers, but apparently never thought long-winded by his contemporaries, who were used to long sermons and found it great fun) – we must turn to reflect that in such satire Erasmus reveals himself to be at the crossroads of the Renaissance with the Reformation. If the literary mode is quintessentially renaissance, the denunciations of abuses by the individuals and the institution of the Church are very much reforming and reformation. Erasmus stood in a well-trod path of late medieval chastising of clerical abuses above all, as much as he drew upon the literary heritage of classical satire. But the *Moria* would not be read today, no more than the now-unread *Letters of Obscure Men*, if there were not a deeper core in the work.

Like the *Enchiridion* written half a dozen years earlier but in a different (and more easily ascertainable) mode, *Moria* is a profoundly christian work. In both the centre of gravity is Christ, and there is a further parallel: the *Enchiridion* directs a layman to the knowing, loving and living of Christ in his daily life, as in its own way does the *Moria*. Erasmus spelled this out in his letter to Dorp of 1515:

> My aim in the *Folly* was exactly the same as in my other works. Only the presentation was different. In the *Enchiridion* I simply outlined the pattern of Christian life. In my little book *The Education of a Christian Prince* I offered plain advice on how to instruct a prince. In my *Panegyric* I did the same under the veil of eulogy as I had done elsewhere explicitly. And in the *Folly*, I expressed the same ideas as those in the *Enchiridion*, but in the

form of a joke [*sub specie lusus*]. I wanted to advise, not to rebuke, to do good, not injury, to work for, not against, the interest of men. (Epistle 337, end of May 1515, *CWE* 3:114–5, but I have here used the translation in *CWE* 27:78. See Allen II, 93/86–94, for the Latin)

What is remarkable in the work is its climactic eloquence after all the satirising of monks, theologians and others, in writing of Christ as the ultimate Fool and of Christianity as the ultimate Folly. For this Erasmus drew upon the New Testament and certain Fathers of the Church, as well as Plato (whom the Greek Fathers knew first-hand). We follow Screech at this point:

> One of the reasons why his contemporaries found his ideas hard to grasp, and so deeply offensive to their traditional piety, is that the theme of the madness of God is more at home in Greek Christianity than in western Catholicism. The *Moria* may well be written in elegant Latin, but its conception of divine folly, in God, in Christ, in his ecstatic followers, is one which emerged more readily from the Greek New Testament than from the Latin Vulgate. It was also given its most authentic slant by Greek Fathers. A favourite among these, for Erasmus, was Origen. From the Latin he preferred those who were open to the influence of these Greeks. His favourites include Ambrose, Jerome and Augustine ... and Bernard of Clairvaux. (xviii) ... For most of the scholastics Plato was a closed book. So too was the Greek New Testament. (*Ecstasy*, xviii–xix)

Despite the fact that Folly herself gives the straight-arm to any conventional peroration, recalling the old saying that 'I hate a drink-ing-companion with a memory' (from Plutarch, Martial and Lucian by way of the *Adages*), I shall try to provide an epilogue. Erasmus never forgot what he tried to instruct Martin Dorp: 'pleasure attracts the reader, and once attracted keeps him reading. For in other re-spects, various men pursue various goals, but all alike are allured by pleasure, except those who are so insensitive that they are completely impervious to the pleasures of literature'.[27] There are the diverse pleasures of folly, then and now. We are amused by the follies of vanity or *philautia* (an Erasmian concept which underlies the *Tiers Livre* of Rabelais, and much of Ascham's *Scholemaster* and many of the writings of later Elizabethans); and we can add our own to the Erasmian *folies de grandeur*, especially in the world of the universities, for we have administrators who are 'educators', those professional non-scholars who have come to dominate the academic world and must take much responsibility for the loss of standards, some of which they do not themselves recognise. It is one thing to be a

Sorbonniste (to juxtapose early sixteenth-century concepts): it is another to be a dean or vice-chancellor of Sorbonnistes.

Just as the *Moria* moves so pleasurably to its surprising conclusion that Christ is the ultimate fool, so too (we may read) Erasmus is dealing with what Screech has called (p. xx) a key moment in his own religious development: his returning from Italy having achieved the major revision of the *Adages* into that monumental and determinative text of 1508, and now looking forward to his intensive and lifelong work on the New Testament (chapter 27). Perhaps too subsumed under a veil there is here an experience of which we cannot speak because of the lid of silence that Erasmus imposed upon the period from 1509 to 1511. Yet having said this, we can observe that the months leading up to the 1511 edition of the *Moria* must have been a remarkable liminal time for Erasmus. In any case, to quote Screech one final time:

> The closing pages are shot through and through with Erasmus' interpretation of the philosophy of Christ, which they expound with a fervour which is enhanced, not hindered, by the subtle humour and Lucianesque laughter. English Christians at least do not need reminding that humour and piety can make very good bed-fellows. Neither did the readers of Brant, Boccaccio and Rabelais. (xx)

Erasmus was a master grammarian and rhetorician. It should not surprise us that this masterwork is so very much a rhetorical *tour de force*. In a world that was so dominated by rhetoric in the schools and universities, in the literary world and in the courts, it is little wonder that the axis about which the structure, the themes and the techniques of the *Moria* turn should be so dominantly and so strikingly rhetorical. Erasmus knew the importance of rhetoric even when he referred to himself with self-irony as *rhetorculus*, 'that little rhetorician'. Recalling that aperçu of C. S. Lewis, that we are separated from the renaissance world by our modern neglect of the classical resources of rhetoric, we might conclude that if Erasmus thought that rhetoric was the *sine qua non* for his perilous equilibrium in an ironic double vision, we ought not to neglect the full pleasures (and demands) of this master-text and to forego the path that leads from rhetoric to wisdom.

Notes

1) On the origins of the *Moriae* see also Ep. 337 to Dorp (Allen II, 94/127 ff.), as well as Allen's introduction to Ep. 222, which is more detailed than the headnote in *CWE* 2:161. For simplicity's sake, in this chapter I shall refer

to the *Praise of Folly* or *Moriae Encomium* as *Moria*. After all, it is the Greek word for folly.

2) Play is a richly complex and richly rewarding dimension of human life, and as Huizinga has shown, it can become a road to knowledge (*Homo Ludens*, 1949). But Folly here too reverses the proper direction or balance, for in her hands, to play is to enjoy, not to learn. See R. S. Sylvester, 'The Problem of Unity in *The Praise of Folly*', *ELR* 6 (1976) 135.

3) *The Praise of Folly*, ed. Clarence H. Miller (New Haven, Conn., 1979) x. Miller's fine translation rests securely upon his critical edition of the Latin text established for *ASD*; one may profitably refer also to the translation by Betty Radice (revised from the Penguin ed. of 1971) in *CWE* 27 (1986).

4) The *theatrum mundi* topos is well outlined by E. R. Curtius in *European Literature and the Latin Middle Ages*, 138–44, and enlarged by Ernesto Grassi in his discourse on Erasmus' idea of life as a spectacle. See *Erasmus Grandescens*, 128.

5) Robert Klein brilliantly analysed the background traditions (esp. in Alberti's *Momus*) in his article, 'Le thème du fou et l'ironie humaniste', *Archivio di filosofia*, No. 3 (Padua, 1963) 11–25; rptd. in *La forme et l'intelligible* (Paris, 1970) 433–50. Comparative studies are given in Walter Kaiser, *Praisers of Folly* (Cambridge, Mass., 1963), and Barbara Könneker, *Wesen und Wandlung der Narrenidee im Zeitalter des Humanismus: Brant–Murner–Erasmus* (Wiesbaden, 1966); and there is a broader study by Joel Febvre, *Les fols et la folie* (Paris, 1968). See also Leonard F. Dean, '*The Praise of Folly* and Its Background', in *Twentieth-Century Interpretations of the Praise of Folly*, ed. Kathleen Williams (Englewood Cliffs, N.J., 1969) 40–60. M. Bakhtin, *L'oeuvre de François Rabelais et la culture populaire* … (Paris, 1970), challenged notably by Richard M. Berrong in *Rabelais and Bakhtin* (1986): see *Erasmus Grandescens*, 129.

6) I am indebted to Sylvester's discussion (1976), 126–7, for an illuminating discussion of the significance of this figure of the dancing camel. As the Adage 'Camelus saltat' (II, vii, 66) points the way, it suggests someone acting indecorously, and Erasmus is apparently suggesting that to dance like a camel is to be out of one's depth; or, to use the terms of Folly herself, to be out of one's mind.

7) See Screech, *Ecstasy*, xix–xx, and Miller, *Praise of Folly*, xxxiii–xxxiv. It is to be observed that the five Italian editions of the *Moria* that were published during Erasmus' lifetime all derived from the Strasbourg edition of October 1512 (Miller, xxxiv); this informs us of the connections of Italian printers with those north of the Alps.

8) Gilles de Gourmont was no Aldus or Froben, to be sure, and his edition is not well printed. But he was a printer of importance, and was himself a humanist who could handle Greek: in 1507 he was the first Paris printer to print Greek, and in 1508 the first to print Hebrew (*BR*). Among his publications was Guillaume du Bellay's *Peregrinatio* (1509), and after the *Moria* he printed the Paris edition of More's *Utopia* (after 1 November 1516). See Screech, *Ecstasy*, 2.

9) Miller, xxxiii–xxxiv.

10) See Schoeck, 'Fifth Lateran Council', cited above.

11) Erasmus frequently compared Julius II to Julius Caesar (*CWE* 2:128/

43n). Most of his contemporaries attributed the dialogue *Julius Exclusus* to Erasmus, and the consensus of modern scholarship is firmly on the side of Erasmus' authorship (see M. J. Heath in *CWE* 27:156–60 for a review of the issues and scholarly interpretations).

12) Screech, *Ecstasy*, xx. The point is an important one; and the majority of Erasmus' opponents were men who never demonstrated a faculty of wit or humour: Béda, Dorp, and others. Luther is more problematic.

13) For a summary of the printing-history of the *Moria* I am indebted to Miller, *Praise of Folly*, xiii, and to Betty Radice, *CWE* 27:78–9.

14) See J.-C. Margolin, *Erasme par lui-même* (Paris, 1965) 5, and *Douze années de bibliographie érasmienne, 1950–1961* (Paris, 1963).

15) See Radice, *CWE* 27:78. She adds (79) that 'only in the Netherlands, England, and Switzerland was it possible to reprint the *Moria* among Erasmus' collected works'. The importance of Listrius' commentary is well argued by J. A. Gavin and T. M. Walsh in *RenQ* (1971) 193 ff.

16) The adage opens with an irony worthy of a Jane Austen first sentence: 'People who are in favour with themselves and who diligently study their own advantage, even to the neglect and detriment of the affairs of others, are gracefully called *philautoi* (self-lovers) in Greek. The vice itself is called self-love or *philautia*'. (*CWE* 31:311/3–5.)

17) Miller, *Praise of Folly* (1979) xii. Quotations are from this text unless otherwise indicated. Hence the importance to some of us of full quotation and, *malgré* the Post-Structuralists and Deconstructionists, of respect for the integrity of the literary work as a whole and of its historical milieu.

18) See especially Miller in *RenQ* 27 (1974) 499–51, and Sylvester in *English Literary Renaissance* 6 (1976), as cited, as well as Chomarat, *Grammaire et rhétorique chez Erasme*.

19) I have sketched this approach to a reading of the *Moria* in *Erasmus Grandescens*, 127 ff.

20) For an excellent brief introduction, see Kennedy, *Classical Rhetoric*, 103; and *OCD* 2d ed., 316–7. S. F. Bonner provides an excellent study of the classical declamation in his *Roman Declamation*; and M. van der Poel has studied the humanist *declamatio* in his *De Declamatio bij de Humanisten*.

21) Charles Sears Baldwin, *Ancient Rhetoric and Poetic* (1924) 93. Both Tacitus and Quintilian protested against the unreal and over-subtle; for, they argued, training of young men to become actual pleaders was 'not to be had from tyrannicide, rape, incest, wizards, pestilence, and stepmothers' (Baldwin, 93).

22) Erasmus had served his apprenticeship in the several kinds of encomium. In addition, in his letters to his students during his Paris teaching years he frequently had recourse to imaginary situations and conversations, the fruit of training in *suasoriae* and *controversiae*.

23) See my 'Intertextuality and the Rhetoric Canon', and '"In loco intertexantur": Erasmus, Master of Intertextualities'.

24) See Miller, xi. To humanist readers who had struggled with the formalities of scholastic logic in their own undergraduate studies, such manipulations would have been yet another source of humour. Like rhetoric, logic is treated with irony.

25) See C. H. Miller, 'The Logic and Rhetoric of Proverbs in Erasmus'

Praise of Folly', in *Essays on the Works of Erasmus*, ed. R. L. DeMolen (New Haven, Conn., 1978) 83–98. May we not see an ironic contrasting of folk and learned?

26) In a fine essay on 'Erasmus as Satirist' in *Erasmus*, ed. Dorey, p. 41, A. E. Douglas has called attention to the verbal ironies of that word *rot* (*putrescere*, which had a wealth of overtones in classical and patristic, as well as medieval, literature); for in small compass it captures that renaissance horror of the death and corruption of the body (with its own echoes of the *de contemptu* theme), as in countless sermons of the age, or in Shakespeare's *Measure for Measure* (III.i.118): 'To lie in cold obstruction and to rot...' Such is the precision and cutting edge of Erasmus' irony in the Latin original.

27) Miller, 148: Allen II, 97/228–31. It is to be noted that the letter to Dorp was often included in early editions of the *Moria*: see Screech, *Ecstasy*, 4 ('a letter which was regularly prefixed to the *Moria* from 1516 onwards'). The significance of this point is that contemporary readers were provided with clear and useful guidelines for reading the *Moria*.

The Cambridge Years, 1511–1514

la liberté que j'ai chez ces étrangers
de dire, d'écrire et de faire ce que je
voudrai; le repos et la tranquillité
de ma conscience.
>> Salmasius (on the reason for his coming to Leiden)[1]

The Bible was the most studied book of the middle ages. Bible
study represented the highest branch of learning.
>> Beryl Smalley, *The Study of the Bible in the Middle Ages*, xi

bright candles over the holy white scriptures.
>> 9th-century Irish hermit poem

The beer in this place doesn't suit me,
and the wines just aren't satisfactory either.
>> Erasmus to Ammonio, 25 August 1511,
>> Epistle 226 (Allen I, 466/5–6)

Et hic, O Academiam!
('And here – what a university!')
>> Erasmus to Ammonio, 27 November 1511,
>> Epistle 246 (*CWE* 2:206/6; Allen I, 493/5)

Erasmus had paid a visit to Cambridge during the academic year
1505–6, as the official records show (Allen I, appendix VI, 590–2);
but little is known of that occasion. It seems that he did contemplate
remaining at Cambridge, as Allen notes, for he applied to the University for admission to the doctorate of theology, with the indication that he was already a bachelor of theology.[2] He doubtless left
because the opportunity arose to visit Italy (chapter 23).

This time, having been in England since 1509, but dependent
upon the hospitality of More, Ammonio, Grocyn, and others, he
readily accepted the invitation to lecture on Greek at Cambridge
when Fisher offered him this appointment in July. To be sure he had
refused offers from other universities in the past – from Oxford in
1499 (chapter 15) and from Louvain in 1502 (chapter 19) – but this
time he felt that the windows of opportunity were closing for him.

He accepted, as he wrote to Roger Wentford from Cambridge in November 1511, because

> Where you are [London] I cannot see how I could live, except with Grocyn; and certainly there is nobody in the world I would sooner live with, but I am ashamed to cause him the expense, particularly when I have no means of returning the favour, and he will not allow me to contribute anything, so kind is he. I was not particularly anxious to leave you, but it was this consideration of price above all that moves me to do it. (Epistle 241, *CWE* 2:195–6/27–33; Allen I, 485/23–6)

Wentford, whom Erasmus had met in 1506 (Epistle 196) or earlier, was headmaster of St Anthony's School.[3] One notes that Erasmus went to Cambridge at about the time of Thomas More's second marriage; he had been living with More in the spring of 1511 before going to Paris for the printing of the *Moria* (Epistle 218). We must look to the second Mrs More, surely, for the reason to explain Erasmus' departure.

Even before his going to Cambridge in 1511 Erasmus had a number of personal contacts there. One of his first Paris pupils was Robert Fisher, and another William Blount, Lord Mountjoy, who had with him Richard Whitford, a fellow of Queens' College. Whitford, who held the offices of dean and bursar of the college before leaving to become chaplain to the bishop of Winchester, Richard Foxe (*BR*), around 1507 entered the widely celebrated Bridgettine monastery at Sion in Middlesex. 'There he achieved note as the author of devotional works and the translator of others (including the *Imitation of Christ*)' (*BR*). To Whitford Erasmus dedicated his declamation against Lucian's *Tyrannicida* (Epistle 191, 1 May 1506). Although Whitford was not at Cambridge at the time of Erasmus' arrival, his combination of piety and humanism commended him to Erasmus, and his career suggests ties between Queens' College and the bishop of Winchester, who founded Corpus Christi College, Oxford. It may have been Foxe who chose Erasmus' translation for certain texts in the windows of King's College, Cambridge (*BR* II, 48, and *CWE* 3:220). But the shaping Cambridge influence was surely John Fisher, who was president of Queens' from 1505 to 1508 and chancellor of the University from 1504 to 1514, at which time he was elected for life. As a token of his affection for the college, in his 1527 will Erasmus stipulated that one of the twenty presentation copies of his projected collected works was to go to Cambridge, for deposit at Queens', and another to Fisher personally.[4]

As part of the Erasmus legend at Cambridge there is the walk named after him, the Erasmus Walk;[5] and Erasmus seems to have had an extensive suite in a tower, described by a seventeenth-century fellow as follows:

> The stairs which rise up to his study at Queens' College in Cambridge do bring first into two of the fairest chambers in the ancient building; in one of them, which looks into the hall and chief court, the Vice President kept in my time; in that adjoining, it was my fortune to be, when Fellow. The chambers over are good lodging rooms; and to one of them is a square turret adjoining, in the upper part of which is the study of Erasmus, and over it, leads. To that belongs the best prospect about the college: viz., upon the river, into the corn fields and the country adjoining. So it might very well consist with the civility of the house to that great man (who was no Fellow and I think stayed not long there) to let him have that study. His sleeping room might be either the Vice President's, or to be near to him, the next. The room for his servitor that above it; and through it he might go to that study, which for the height and neatness and prospect might easily take his fancy.[6]

These three years are a period in which he taught first Greek and then theology, worked on the New Testament, and wrote or revised a number of other works. It is during the latter part of his Cambridge years that he wrote his famous satirical dialogue *Julius Exclusus*. We will take up these activities and accomplishments in turn.

The Scot, John Major, who had been a contemporary of Erasmus at the Collège de Montaigu in Paris during the late 1490s (chapter 11) provided a glimpse of the bells of Cambridge, and of the location on the River Cam:

> When I was a student at Cambridge, I would lie awake most of the night, at the season of the great festivals, that I might hear the melody of the bells. The university is situated on a river, and the sound is the sweeter that it comes to you over the water.[7]

Yet Major thought that Cambridge was 'somewhat inferior to Oxford, both in the number of its students, and in reputation for letters' (23).

To be sure, Cambridge had no printing press until 1520, well after Erasmus had left; and there was, Roberto Weiss has observed, little of 'that taste for Italian learning already present in Oxford by the middle of the [15th] century'.[8] Yet there were both Italians at Cambridge and Cambridge men who had gone to Italy; and Humphrey, duke of Gloucester, who was such a munificent benefactor of Oxford, bequeathed manuscripts to King's College, Cambridge, after his death in 1447.[9]

At the beginning of the Michaelmas term, October 1511, Erasmus began his lectures on the Greek language, which was a large part of the purpose of his being invited to Cambridge. To Ammonio (an important correspondent during these years) Erasmus wrote on 16 October:

> Up to this moment I have been lecturing on Chrysoloras' grammar, but the audience is small; perhaps more people will attend when I start Theodore's grammar. Perhaps also I will undertake lecturing in theology, for that is under discussion at present. The pay is too small to tempt me, but in the meantime I am also doing some service to learning, to the best of my ability...
> (Epistle 233, *CWE* 2:177/10–13; Allen I, 473)

Ammonio had sent Erasmus a cask of wine, and for it Erasmus wrote a longish poem to Ammonio (Reedijk, 301); and much of the exchange of letters in the next three years turns upon Ammonio's gifts of wine. To Ammonio, Erasmus was also indebted for his reporting on the winds of war and events in Italy, especially the schismatic Council of Pisa which began on 4 November after an earlier summons; all of this helped to provide details for the *Julius Exclusus*. Although he voices complaints to his close friend Ammonio, he does write that 'all the same, this place suits me fairly well. Also I see some prospect of earning, if one could act as a man of all work' (Epistle 238, *CWE* 2:187/7–9). Apparently at that time Erasmus was diligently writing to the bishop of Winchester in hope of gaining patronage.[10] In all of this quest for financial aid Ammonio was, as Erasmus put it, 'a most generous friend in everything' (Epistle 240, *CWE* 2:192/50); and Ammonio was at the heart of Erasmus' efforts to secure a stronger dispensation from the pope in 1515–16 that would permit him to accept more than one benefice, and in more than one country.

It appears that Erasmus made his mark upon the University immediately. Fisher wrote on 18 November 1511 (although the dating is not firm): 'I can see how indispensable you are to our university' (Epistle 242, *CWE* 2:197/13–14). Not many modern college presidents would be so quickly aware, or take the time to write so soon after the arrival of a distinguished visiting professor.

But after the first term of 1511 there is little reference in Erasmus' correspondence to his teaching. He was in ill health much of the time, and from Bologna Paolo Bombasio wrote that rumours were circulating about Erasmus' death (Epistle 251, *CWE* 2:212/2; Allen I, 497/1–2). In point of fact, Erasmus had barely recovered from an attack of the sweating sickness in August 1511 when he took up his appointment (see Epistle 225 n. in *CWE* 2:168).[11]

In Epistle 257 from Bombasio, written at Milan in the spring of 1512, there is the news that Aldus has been trying to obtain a lectureship for Erasmus at Padua (*CWE* 2:223; Allen I, 508). These were years of war and upheaval: even Aldus was a fugitive from Venice during 1511–1512. But what is striking is that Erasmus' Italian friends were aware of his critical need for financial support.

Yet Henry Bullock – perhaps the closest of Erasmus' Cambridge friends other than Fisher, who later became a doctor of theology and was instrumental in establishing a printing press at Cambridge, becoming vice-chancellor of the University[12] – wrote to Erasmus in 1516 addressing him as '*preceptor doctissime*', declaring that 'here they are keenly studying Greek' (Epistle 449, *CWE* 4:34/10–11; Allen II, 313–4). Erasmus' Greek class at Cambridge may have been small, but with such students as Bullock he must be counted successful as a teacher.

We shall discuss Erasmus' life-project for the New Testament more fully in chapter 32; what is here important is to make clear that it was never his intention to provide an edition of the Greek New Testament, nor did he translate his own new Latin text of the New Testament directly from the Greek.[13] Mastery of Greek was necessary, he felt, to understand the original text of the Gospels and Epistles.

About 1505 – after his preparation of Valla's *Adnotationes* for publication in Paris that year (chapter 21) – Erasmus set to work to prepare detailed critical notes on the Latin New Testament in the spirit of Valla: that is, philological notes on the language and meaning of the Vulgate. We do not know how much work he did in Italy from 1506 to 1509 (however, it is likely that he consulted some manuscripts); and it seems that much of the work of studying manuscripts, collating, and making his notes was done in England during his 1505–6 visit and still more – far more – during his long stay in London and Cambridge from 1509 to 1514. Not only did he work intensively (although from the viewpoint of modern textual scholarship not always systematically) on New Testament manuscripts both in Latin and, increasingly as he went on in his work, in Greek; but he consulted the Church Fathers and the long line of the Latin exegetical tradition (and again, increasingly studying the Greek exegetes).[14] His work on editions of the Church Fathers went hand in glove with his work on the text of the New Testament.

We may be sure, therefore, that in London and Cambridge, and wherever else he visited during his third and longest English stay from 1509 to 1514, the New Testament was never long out of mind,

and that he would have seized any opportunity to consult manuscripts and scholars whenever possible. Thus in his lengthy letter to
Jacob Wimpheling (Epistle 305) of 21 September 1514, written
from Basel – which is such an interesting catalogue of the Strasbourg
literary circle, and such a telling indication of his regarding himself
as one of the German humanists – he spent a little time on his own
work in progress, speaking of all the works he wanted to get out in
the winter months 'with the same labour and lamp-oil, as the saying
[*Adag.* I. iv. 62] goes' (*CWE* 3:32/225–6; Allen II, 23/220–1). Then
there is this summary passage: 'My *Adagia* [*Adagiorum opus* he calls
it] has now begun to be printed. There remains the New Testament
translated by me, with the Greek facing, and notes on it by me'
(*CWE* 3:32/228–9; Allen II, 23/222–4).

We may pause to note Erasmus' simple declaration for the first
time that the Latin New Testament will be his translation, that there
will be a facing Greek text (a feature that was a late addition), and
that there will be notes by him. Here is his programme for the New
Testament for his age, which would see light in 1516 (chapter 32).

With typical humour Erasmus added – after writing about his
other work in progress, and his hope to visit Italy again – 'I have also
given birth, after most exhausting travail, to a stone ... What, you
say, can you make a jest of anything so painful? Why less so than
Socrates, who jested as he drank the hemlock, and died with a jest on
his lips?' (*CWE* 3:33/251–5; Allen II, 24/243–7).

In the autumn of 1512 Erasmus had written to Pieter Gillis
(Epistle 264) about his scholarly activities, for he liked to keep his
friend informed and at this time Pieter looked after the sums of
money that Erasmus was receiving or investing at Antwerp (Epistle
1654, and *BR*). Enclosing his translation of Lucianic dialogues that
were to be forwarded to Paris and which were published by Bade in
1514 (Epistle 261), Erasmus declared to Gillis:

> I have got ready my work on proverbs [*Proverbiorum opus*, i.e.,
> the *Adagia*], expanding it so much that I have quite changed its
> character – and improved it a great deal, unless I am mistaken,
> though it was not so bad before; so he [Bade] has no need to fear
> editions by others. I intend to finish the revision of the New
> Testament and the letters of St Jerome; if I have time, I will also
> emend the text of Seneca ... I have translated several works by
> Plutarch, which I shall revise and send in addition. (*CWE*
> 2:234–5/7–28; Allen I, 517/6–25)

In a follow-up letter to Gillis (Epistle 265) Erasmus indicates that he
had not heard from him and that he wished to know more about the
conduct of Franz Birckmann, a bookseller of Cologne who was in

London at this time and of whom Erasmus was suspicious. This brief letter speaks of Erasmus' grieving over the war, and especially 'how grieved I am to see our fellow-countrymen gradually slipping into the present conflict'; 'Ah, those tongueless theologians, those mute bishops, who look on at such dire human disasters and say nothing!'[15] This is the period during which Erasmus emerges more and more as an outspoken pacifist.

For years Erasmus had been studying St Jerome (chapter 17), but the bulk of the editorial work for his *Opera Hieronymi* was done during this stay in England,[16] with the edition appearing at Basel in 1516 from the press of Froben (printed and bound sometimes in four and sometimes in five volumes). Having finished the edition, Erasmus dedicated his work to archbishop Warham,[17] together with his celebrated life of Jerome prefixed (*Hieronymi Stridonensis Vita*, which was then separately printed in 1517 and 1519). The significance of Erasmus' life of Jerome must be commented upon. 'When the work first appeared in 1516', one scholar has recently written, 'nothing like the *Vita* had yet been done in England nor would there be anything comparable to it for many years', and it may well be regarded as the starting point for the development of at least one English biography.[18]

It is evident that Erasmus remained close to John Colet and shared in the ambitions for the new school that Colet was founding; certainly Erasmus contributed significantly to the curriculum of St Paul's, which served as a model for English education for generations.[19]

Two important works in Erasmus' educational programme are the fruits of the relationship with Colet: *De Copia* and *De Ratione Studii*. The first official edition of *De Copia* appeared in July 1512, issuing from the press of Josse Bade (who had already published other works by Erasmus). Although the first sketch of his ideas on *copia* – a style of abundance, and the means of attaining it – was in existence at least as early as 1499,[20] Erasmus was pressured by the report that an unauthorised version of his *De Copia*, based upon a manuscript left behind in Italy, might soon appear; thus, being asked by Colet to provide educational material for the new school, Erasmus rather quickly put together this first version of the book, published under the title *De duplici copia rerum ac verborum commentarii duo*.[21] Like other works of Erasmus this one was emended and revised, and it continued to grow through editions of 1514, 1526, and 1534, all published by his authority (from Schürer in Strasbourg and Froben in Basel), and there were a hundred editions of it by the end of the sixteenth century, which gives one a sense of its importance in

renaissance education.[22] For the literature of the sixteenth century
the concept of *copia* is of very great significance, as Cave has demonstrated in his study of *copia* in *The Cornucopian Text*: with its subtitle
pointing to the concern with writing in the Renaissance. For
Erasmus, *copia* was of central importance.

In identifying Schürer as one of Erasmus' printers we pick up yet
another master-printer of significance in his career. Erasmus' relations with Schürer began in 1509 with the printing of a possibly
unauthorised edition of the *Adagia*.[23] Matthias Schürer was born c.
1470 in Sélestat, that home of humanists, and studied at its justly
celebrated Latin school; he became MA at Cracow and returned to
Strasbourg c.1500 to be apprenticed with his cousin Martin Flach.
He next worked with others and finally established his own *atelier* in
1508. From 1509 until his death he had the important monopoly for
publishing Erasmus at Strasbourg: seventy editions of fifteen of his
works.[24] There were others from Sélestat, which Erasmus first visited
in 1514 (Epistle 305) and which thereafter continued to be important in Erasmus' world: Bucer, Gebwiler, Sapidus and Wimpheling
all had Sélestat connections, with Beatus Rhenanus being most
prominent in this respect; and there were close connections with
others in the literary society of Strasbourg, interwoven with the
Sélestat circle. Even before the handsome bequest by Beatus
Rhenanus of his large library to Sélestat (now housed in the municipal library in the heart of the city), the library of the Latin School had
a distinguished collection of humanist texts.

Given the difficulties during the war of getting a manuscript to
Bade in Paris, where the work was published in July of 1512 (and for
forwarding the manuscript Erasmus was indebted to the good offices
of Pieter Gillis), we may be sure that Erasmus began to work on this
edition either in London or very soon after arriving in Cambridge,
with the latter the more likely because of his illness.

De Copia is a very large book: 375 pages in *CWE*. By contrast, *De
Ratione*, the more philosophical work, is far smaller: twenty-five
pages in *CWE*. But it is nonetheless a work of prime importance in
Erasmus' educational programme, and it too had its roots in the
Paris years of tutoring (chapter 14).

De ratione studii ac legendi interpretandique auctores liber (its full title
calling attention to its central importance as a theory of reading and
interpreting authors) was brought out in abridged form in an unauthorised edition by Granjon in Paris, in October 1511, just as
Erasmus was beginning his lectures at Cambridge. Occupied as he
was with other concerns, he nonetheless set to work to provide an
authentic text, which was published July 1512 by Bade in Paris,

with a revised edition appearing in Strasbourg published by Schürer in August 1514. This small work is concerned fundamentally with the relation of christian to classical culture, as was the *Antibarbari* (chapter 8), and as later works would continue to be. For techniques of reading, including analysis and comparison, Erasmus was indebted to Quintilian; but in dealing with the moral dangers for young readers latent in the subject-matter of much pagan literature, Erasmus followed the guidelines of St Basil.[25] Just as *De Copia* was concerned with both words and things (a vital distinction in classical rhetoric), so in *De Ratione* Erasmus begins by declaring that 'in principle, knowledge as a whole seems to be of two kinds, of things and of words' (*CWE* 24:66/4–5). We may echo J.B. Trapp's speaking of *De Ratione* as 'the inheritor of the Italian humanist tradition and the tradition of the schools which were its heirs in an unequivocal insistence that everything worth learning is contained and expressed in Greek and Latin'.[26]

On 21 February 1513 Giuliano della Rovere, pope Julius II, died at Rome. His was the last pontificate before the Reformation, and it was distinguished by most generous patronage of the arts, with Michelangelo, Raphael and Bramante often working under the personal supervision of the pontiff (*CWE* 27:160). But in *Julius Exclusus* Erasmus has little to say of all this patronage: instead, St Peter in this dialogue speaks ironically to the Julius who is trying to enter Heaven (hence the title: *Julius Excluded*): 'You have a band of energetic followers, an enormous fortune, and you yourself are a great architect; build some new paradise for yourself, but fortify it well to prevent the cacodemons capturing it.' To this irony Julius replies: 'Never! I shall be true to myself and wait a few months, increasing my army until I can throw you out by force, if you won't surrender ...' And Peter's last words voice the indignation of the author of the dialogue: 'I'm really not surprised that so few men reach here, when scoundrels like him have seized the helm of the Church' (*CWE* 27:197). But who was the author of the dialogue?

The work did not see print until its appearance at Louvain in September 1518; but its inception was much earlier. There are several undated editions which may date from early 1517, and in December 1516 Thomas More spoke of notebooks of Erasmus, among papers left with Lupset in 1516 when Erasmus left Pace in Italy and returned to England leaving those papers behind: some of that material seems to overlap with the *Julius Exclusus* (*CWE* 27:157). The work does not appear in any of Erasmus' lists and collections of his own writings, and there has been a continuing controversy since 1518 concerning authorship. Some attributed the work to Fausto Andrelini, others to Ulrich von Hutten;[27] and there have been further candidates. Given the existence of a manuscript of the work in Erasmus' own hand, together with other evidence, the probability is strongly in favour of Erasmus' authorship. It is inaccurate to say that he denied authorship at the time (as has been said by more than one Erasmus scholar): what he denied was responsibility for the publication of the work, as Allen and some others have noted.[28]

An admirable summary of the importance of the *Julius* for Erasmus' biography is offered by Heath:

> The journey to Italy [in 1506–09], long anticipated and thus doubly frustrating in its disappointments, was vital to the development of Erasmus' thought. Just as 'it was Julius II who turned Erasmus into a pacifist' and inspired the famous denunciations of war which began with the 1515 *Adagia*, so it was the spectacle of Julius' pontificate which hardened within Erasmus that commitment to the reform of the church which characterizes the works of his maturity. (*CWE* 27:162)

We still do not know all the details of Erasmus' travels in England during this period, but in the colloquy 'A Pilgrimage for Religion's Sake' (first published in 1526) Erasmus describes a pilgrimage to Canterbury that he had made with John Colet. This pilgrimage must have been between the summer of 1512 and the early summer of 1513. Although written some considerable time after the actual visit to the shrine of St Thomas Becket at Canterbury, the main thrust and tone of the dialogue are clear enough (Thompson, *Colloquies*, 286).

It is clear that Servatius Rogers had been pressuring Erasmus to return to Steyn and resume the monastic life and habit of a professed Augustinian canon, and after Servatius had succeeded the kindly and sympathetic prior Nicolas Werner (Claes Warnerszoon) in 1504, Erasmus was careful to keep him informed of his activities (Epistles 185, 189, 200, 203). But from these letters it is also clear that some correspondence on both sides did not reach the person intended, and some doubtless has been lost since. In 1514 Servatius wrote to Erasmus yet again, this time more insistently urging him to return to his monastery. The letter from Erasmus to Servatius on 8 July 1514 deserves attention,[29] for it is a final cutting of ties with his old monastery and has indeed 'something of the air of an apologia written for a wider audience than the comrade of his early days at Steyn who certainly knew the whole story of Erasmus' entry into the monastery' (*CWE* 2:294). But perhaps Erasmus also felt that

Servatius needed to be reminded of the details of that story, and wanted to present them with his own tone and emphasis; and then, with one eye on the canon law and its weighty emphasis on jurisdiction, declared that he would not return (however carefully the thought is expressed in subjunctive and conditional formulations). In a way it adds to the finality of Erasmus' decision that he wrote the letter from Hammes Castle on the edge of the Low Countries, and not from England or Italy. Although copies of the letter were in circulation before his death (according to Allen there were three separate printings of it; I, 564), it is a letter never published by Erasmus himself.

Not only did Erasmus rehearse the story of his entering the monastery, but he included some thoughts about its over-emphasis on place, dress, diet, and a number of petty observances. 'How much more consonant with Christ's teaching it would be to regard the entire Christian world as a single household, a single monastery as it were' (*CWE* 2:297/88–90), anticipating his much-quoted phrase in his 1518 letter to abbot Volz, 'For what is a city but a monastery?' (chapter 34). In this long letter we are given some details of the support Erasmus had been receiving from outside the monastery, then a review of his books. 'These then are the concerns upon which I am bestowing my leisure and my busy hours alike' (*CWE* 2:300/ 169–70). Next Erasmus explains and justifies his dress, retelling the story of his having been nearly mobbed in Bologna during the plague, an experience which compelled him to conceal his scapular; this change of dress, he tells Servatius, was authorised by pope Julius II in the dispensation of January 1506 (chapters 22–23); but in point of fact that dispensation did not mention dress. Erasmus' change of habit seems to have been a very large element in Servatius' unhappiness with his absent canon.

As a final touch Erasmus pleads his age: 'I should become the cynosure of all eyes, returning as a grey-haired old man, and in poor health too, to the place I left as a youth' (*CWE* 2:302/222–4) – indulging in some exaggeration, for he was at least twenty-five when he left the monastery, and at the time of writing he was about forty-seven (middle-age, surely, rather than old age). The letter ends with a final refusal (though it is not so worded) to return to the monastery: 'If I were sure that I could serve him [God] better by a return to your community, I should make ready to depart this very day' (302/251– 4). Erasmus' use of *vestrum contubernium* is notable for the stress on 'your' rather than 'our', but even more in his use of *contubernium* (Allen I, 573/235–6), for he no longer accepts the monastery as 'his' community.[30]

Erasmus was still in Cambridge as late as January 1514, as we know
from the prefatory letter (Epistle 284) to a translation of Plutarch's
De utilitate capienda ex inimicis, a translation made earlier (perhaps in
1512) but still unpublished, so that Erasmus wrote a special copy for
presentation to Wolsey as a New Year's gift in January 1514 (Allen
I, 548).[31] An undated letter to Warham follows in Allen's edition
(Epistle 285), which is doubtless Erasmus' last letter from Cambridge, and in it he speaks of another attack of kidney stone: 'the pest
is still lodged inside my ribs, and when or what the issue will be is
unknown. I suspect that this sickness of mine is due to the beer
which, for the lack of wine, I have been drinking for some time ... I
have merely dictated this letter, and even so with some discomfort;
be sure to look after your own health to the utmost, excellent
Maecenas' (*CWE* 2:276/5–8; Allen I, 549). To this letter Warham
replied with a gift of ten nobles, and concluded: 'Yes indeed, you
still have many important works to publish, and you cannot tackle
them unless you are strong. Look after yourself, and do not by your
sickness deprive us of the splendid promise and sweetest harvest of
your learning' (*CWE* 2:277/16–20; Allen I, 550/13–6).

A fine note on which to end his most productive years in Cambridge. Leaving Cambridge soon afterwards, Erasmus stopped off
briefly in London, visiting the royal palace at Richmond – but
'deterred by the plague from staying long enough to give his present
to Wolsey' (*CWE* 2:277) – and paying his respects to Warham.

From London Erasmus addressed a long letter of protest against
the war, sent to Antoon van Bergen, no doubt because of his influence at the Burgundian court. This letter was soon expanded into the
famous adage '*Dulce bellum inexpertis*' (*Adag.* IV.i.I), which was first
published in the edition of 1515 and then printed separately by
Froben in 1517, with more than a dozen reprintings before 1540.[32]

Erasmus left England with an annuity from Aldington (the rectory in Kent given him by Warham, which he commuted for a
pension in 1512), and a pension from Mountjoy of the same amount:
one hundred ecus d'or, then officially worth £175 tournois (or
£20.16s. 8d. sterling), enough to give Erasmus a foundation of
security (even though his Aldington annuity was paid irregularly), to
which his payments from publishers and other gifts could be added.
To van Bergen Erasmus wrote that 'a considerable amount of further
support is given to me by the generosity of prominent men ... there
could be much more if I were in the slightest degree ready to beg'
(*CWE* 2:279/15–17) – a far cry from the begging letters written
from 1500 to 1504! Erasmus now enjoyed security, not as full as his

growing needs for secretaries and other aids demanded, but a measure of financial independence for the first time since leaving the monastery at Steyn in 1495. It was in anticipation of some of this support that he wrote his refusal to return to Steyn; but it was still an act of courage.

In July 1514 Erasmus left England, his last letter being to Pieter Gillis about his heavy baggage (books and papers) which he had shipped to Antwerp while he himself crossed from Dover to Calais (Epistle 294). Near Calais was located Hammes Castle, of which Mountjoy was the commander, and Erasmus stopped over there for a few days. It was from Hammes that Erasmus wrote the final, and longest, of his letters to Servatius Rogers. Although the letter was written at Hammes, the decision had already been made in Cambridge.

Erasmus' successor as lecturer in Greek was Richard Croke, a student of Eton and King's who continued his study of Greek under Aleandro in Paris. It had been Croke who in the spring of 1511 helped Erasmus with the proofs of *Moria*, and Erasmus did not forget his services. From Paris Croke had gone to Louvain and Cologne, and then in 1515 to Leipzig, where he was that university's first lecturer in Greek. In September 1517 he took his MA in Cambridge, and shortly thereafter was appointed lecturer in Greek, fulfilling Erasmus' prediction to Colet that he had great promise. Croke's *Introductiones in rudimenta Graeca* (one of the first books printed by John Siberch, the new Cambridge printer) was printed in Cambridge in 1520, and it is consequently something of a landmark. Appropriately, the third book printed by Siberch was an edition of Erasmus' *De Conscribendis Epistolis*.[33]

The ripples from pebbles thrown into the quiet waters of Cambridge during Erasmus' years did not altogether disappear. 'Those persons who have never read Augustine or Jerome', Croke declaimed in his second Cambridge oration, printed at Paris in 1520,[34] 'no, nor the Epistles of St Paul! They think they have shown themselves a sufficient preacher if they can fill up their allotted time – or stretch it – so that they themselves grow hoarse with shouting and we exhausted with the listening to folly'. There Croke speaks with the voice of his master.

There were others upon whom Erasmus' teaching had left its mark. In 1530 John Caius, an undergraduate at Gonville Hall, Cambridge, translated some short works of Erasmus into English, including some of the *Ratio Theologiae* of 1519. By the late 1530s, as Ascham wrote later in the 1560s with perhaps an excess of enthusiasm, there was a company of fellows and scholars in St John's

College, 'notable ornaments to this whole realm'. Less well known was John Watson of Peterhouse, who lectured on St Matthew in 1516 using Erasmus' notes as a guide; and the influence of Erasmus upon Robert Barnes, then prior of the Augustinians in Cambridge, and upon William Tyndale, who in the early 1520s translated Erasmus' *Enchiridion* into English, is hardly to be measured.

We shall speak more fully in chapter 45 of the lasting influence of Erasmus in England and elsewhere. Here it suffices to declare that Cambridge was changed by Erasmus' lecturing, and still more we must think by his presence, in Cambridge during those seminal years from 1511 to 1514: Fisher knew whereof he spoke when he wrote that 'I can see how indispensable you are to our university' (Epistle 242, *CWE* 2:197/13–14). *Si monumentum requiris, circumspice* might well be pronounced over the heads, or graves, of all great teachers. Certainly with Erasmus it is not a graven monument; rather one that is to be found in the minds and spirits of those who heard and read him, and in their works and teaching, which carried the spirit of Erasmus to a still younger generation.

Notes

1) A. G. H. Bachrach, 'In Conclusion', in *Sir Thomas Browne M.D. and the Anatomy of Man* (Leiden, 1982) 26, (quoting R.L. Colie, 'Sir Thomas Browne's 'Entertainment' in XVIIth Century Holland', *Neophilologus xxxvi* (1952) 162–71.

2) The bestowing of his baccalaureate in theology is unrecorded, but the presumption is that it took place in Paris.

3) See R. J. Schoeck in *BR* for further details of Wentford's life and career, and of his relations with Erasmus.

4) Although the idea of 20 presentation copies was dropped in Erasmus' final will of 1536 (appendix D), in fact there is a copy of the 1540 *Opera Omnia* in the library of Queens' with a note inside (in a later hand) that it was 'left in his will by Erasmus to Queens' College'; but there is no way to tell how the *Opera* reached Queens'. Porter suggests that it might have been one of the books bequeathed by Thomas Smith, author of *De republica Anglorum* and fellow of the college in the 1530s (*Erasmus and Cambridge*, 34); but the provenance before Smith's ownership remains unknown.

5) There are other traditions: a pine chair known as the Erasmus Chair, Erasmus' corkscrew, etc.; see Porter, 36n. See H.C. Porter, *Reformation and Reaction in Tudor Cambridge* (Cambridge, 1958), for a rich narrative; ch. II is devoted to Erasmus in Cambridge, chapter I presents the Cambridge of Fisher.

6) Q. in Porter, Introd. to *Erasmus and Cambridge*, 37, who observes that 'there is a great deal of 'might' about the description'. Yet J.B. Bullinger wove a fine rhetorical passage about the study in the tower in his history of

the university: *The University of Cambridge from the Earliest Times*, 2 vols (London, 1973–84) I, 506.

7) From Major's *History of Greater Britain* (1521, trans. 1892) 110 (q. by Porter in Introd. to *Erasmus and Cambridge*, 23).

8) R. Weiss, *Humanism in England*, 160. In 1518 Croke claimed 'in all conscience' that at Greek 'Cambridge was better than Oxford' (Porter, *Reformation and Reaction*, 37).

9) See R. J. Schoeck in *NCE* VII, 237.

10) On 8 February 1512 Erasmus even wrote to the bishop of Nantes, Robert Guibé, as yet another potential patron: 'Should there be any matter in which your most reverend Lordship deigns to employ the assistance of the humblest of your servants, pray command and instruct me' (Ep. 253, *CWE* 2:215/21–23).

11) Known as the English sweat (*sudor anglicus*) the disease was described by the French physician Paré: sweating, fever, uneven pulse; 'neither did they leave sweating till the disease left them, which was in one or two days at the most; yet freed of it, they languished long after, they all had a beating or palpitation of the heart, which held some for two or three years, and others all their life after' (q. Porter in Introd. to *Erasmus and Cambridge*, 78–9). It could in fact be a killing fever.

12) See R. J. Schoeck in *BR*, I, 220.

13) See Screech, Introd. to Reeve, *Annotationss* xii–xiii. I am indebted to Dr G.C. Kuiper for clarifying discussion of this complex issue. A full bibliographical note is provided in ch. 32.

14) See Smalley, *Study of the Bible in the Middle Ages*.

15) *CWE* 2:235/8–12 (for the Latin, *'O theologos elinques, o mutos episcopos'*, see Allen I, 518/7–8). Erasmus was well aware of the number of bishops who had been trained as lawyers and so many of whom were involved in the councils of princes and kings. See also Schoeck, 'Canon Law in England on the Eve of the Reformation'.

16) Cambridge, as Porter notes, 'was quite rich in Jerome manuscripts: the University library, for instance, had a volume of the letters, and there were at least seven volumes of Jerome MSS at Peterhouse. Robert Aldrich, then a young scholar of King's, was to remember in 1526 the months he had spent in Queens' reading aloud books of Jerome to Erasmus' (Introd., *Erasmus and Cambridge,* 41).

17) Warham was the last archbishop of Canterbury before the break with Rome, and although he wrote nothing himself he was a patron of scholars; he gave his library to Oxford colleges (*BR*).

18) See John B. Maguire, 'Erasmus' Biographical Masterpiece: *Hieronymi Stridonensis Vita*', *RenQ* xxvii (1973) 265–73. The force of *Saint Jerome in the Renaissance* has been well studied by Eugene F. Rice, Jr. (Baltimore, 1985); and for the depth of Erasmus' devotion to St Jerome we have John C. Olin's Erasmus of Rotterdam Society Lecture (1986) on 'Erasmus and Saint Jerome: The Close Bond and Its Significance', *ERSYB* 7 (1987) 33–53.

19) In September of 1511 Erasmus had written to Colet (Ep. 227) with several enclosures relating to the school, and at the end of it he begged 'a few nobles' for Richard Croke (who doubtless had aided Erasmus in the printing of the *Moria* during the summer of 1511 but is identified by Erasmus as a

former servant-pupil of Grocyn's: *CWE* 2:171/30–34; Allen I, 467–8).This elicited a mixed response from Colet (Ep. 230): he approved of Erasmus' method and longed to have him in his school, but he then somewhat stingily informed Erasmus that he had no loose money to give away (*CWE* 2:174/38 ff.; Allen I, 471/32 ff.).

23) Erasmus himself spoke of this relationship in his letter to Botzheim (Allen I, 17). See the admirable introductory note by Betty I. Knott in *CWE* 24:280–3. The work was dedicated to Colet's new school, in the 1512 edition; the 1514 edition has a prefatory letter to the printer, Schürer, and it ends with a praising of Agricola that is the more touching in its coming at the end of a preface to a key work on education: 'for whenever I read anything he wrote, I feel fresh admiration and affection for that inspired and inspiring mind'. On the force of *De Copia* in 16th-c. education, see Charlton, *Education*, 111.

24) *CWE* 24: 280–3. Strasbourg was an important printing centre.

25) As Brian McGregor recognises in his brief introduction to the *De Ratione* for *CWE* 24:662–4, 'this concern of a Christian for classical tradition is paralleled by T.S. Eliot in his essay on Religion and Literature' in *Selected Essays* (1951) 388.

26) J. B. Trapp, 'From Guarino of Verona to John Colet', in *Essays on the Renaissance and the Classical Tradition* (Aldershot, 1990) XIII, 49.

27) *Julius Exclusus* was roughly contemporary with the hotly controversial *Letters of Obscure Men*, a lampooning of the *Epistolae Clarorum Virorum* that was a collection of letters by prominent humanists in support of his scholarship published by Johannes Reuchlin. Reuchlin, a prominent German lawyer and Hebrew scholar, had been denounced in 1511 by a Jewish convert, Johannes Pfefferkorn in the crudest anti-Semitic terms. The *Epistolae Obscurorum Virorum* attacked the Cologne theologians who persecuted Reuchlin (in editions of 1515, 1516 and 1517); and Ulrich von Hutten along with Crotus Rubeanus was involved in the defence of Reuchlin (and humanism) against the attacks of Pfefferkorn (and the arch-conservatism and malevolence of the scholastic theologians). Thus the mockery of the scholastics came to be fused with a growing cry for a reform in the Church. See H. Holborn, introd. to *On the Eve of the Reformation* (New York, 1964) vii–xiv. Throughout the controversy (on which see also ch. 28) Erasmus defended Reuchlin the man, even though he did not share all his opinions; but he refrained from heaping invective on Reuchlin's enemies.

28) Allen II, 418–9. For a lucid summary of the controversy over the *Julius Exclusus* and of the publication of the work, see M.J. Heath in *CWE* 27:156–7. J.K. McConica has reviewed the problem in 'Erasmus and the *Julius*: a Humanist Reflects on the Church', in *The Pursuit of Holiness in Late Medieval and Renaissance Religion*, ed. C. Trinkaus with H.O. Oberman (Leiden, 1974) 444–71.

29) This letter (Epistle 296, *CWE* 2:302; Allen I, 572) is discussed by DeMolen in *Spirituality of Erasmus*, 194–7.

30) The word *contubernium* is also striking, for in classical Latin very largely it had military overtones; but it was in medieval Latin that it took on ecclesiastical connotations (see Niermeyer). Perhaps by employing this term and not the more conventional *communitas* or *communio* Erasmus wanted to

stress the non-spiritual: for *contubernium* called attention to the fact of living together (or an apartment or tent) shared by a group of soldiers, but it gave no attention to any spiritual bond. And this was the nature of Erasmus' *gravamen* voiced to Servatius: that the monastic institution at Steyn was not sufficiently spiritual, not essentially religious; that it was a living together but not a community in the full sense.

31) It is to be noted that Ep. 297 to Wolsey in the summer of 1514 is a revision and expansion of Ep. 284, for publication in the *Plutarchi opuscula* printed at Basel in that year.

32 For a full and clear analysis of *The Politics of Erasmus* see the book of that title by James D. Tracy (1978), which focuses on Erasmus and Burgundian politics. For a discussion of Erasmus' adage 'Dulce bellum inexpertis' and his role in the pacifism of the age, see R.P. Adams, *The Better Part of Valor* (Seattle, 1962) 82 ff.; but cf. the review by R.J. Schoeck in *ELN* 1 (1963) 133–5.

33) See A. Tilley, 'Greek Studies in England in the early 16th century', *EHR* 53 (1938) 228, and R.J. Schoeck in *BR*.

34) *Orationes Ricardi Croci Duae* (Paris: S. de Colines, 1520) translation by Sir John Sheppard (q. Porter, Introd. *Erasmus and Cambridge* 88). As the *BR* entry makes clear, Croke had an unusual number of contacts with German scholars: with von Hutten and Reuchlin, Camerarius (one of his pupils), and Mutianus.

The Changing World in 1514

It is a kind of exile to live on any island...
Erasmus, Epistle 288 (*CWE* 2:279/22–3;
Allen I, 552/16–18)

Julius was a very great man – the fact that he embroiled almost
the whole world in war shows that...
Erasmus, Epistle 335 (*CWE* 3:103/113–4;
Allen II, 83/109–10)

After many ages persuaded of the headlong decline and impending dissolution of society, and governed by usage and the
will of masters who were in their graves, the sixteenth century
went forth armed for untried experience and ready to watch
with hopefulness a prospect of incalculable change.
Lord Acton, 'A Lecture on the Study of History' (1895)

Having been in England for nearly five years, with only a short
interruption in 1511 to see his *Moria* through the press in Paris,
Erasmus made the Channel crossing that he had always detested
since his first in 1499, and landed at Calais.[1] From there his route lay
through Bruges, Antwerp, Mechlin, probably Cologne, then Mainz,
Speyer and Strasbourg. After his years in Britain – during which he
felt tied down, writing that 'while it is a kind of exile to live on any
island, our confinement is closer still at present by reason of the wars,
so that one cannot even get a letter out' (Epistle 288, 14 March
1514, *CWE* 2:279/22–4; Allen I, 552/17–18) – once back on the
continent he doubtless felt the hunger to travel to old familiar
places. Besides, he had manuscripts to consult and there was still the
need, with his growing requirements for secretaries, for more patronage; so for the next three years, until he settled in Louvain in 1517,
he travelled continually. With the help of his correspondence and
other evidence, we may trace his path.

From Calais, as we have seen, Erasmus went to Hammes on about 7
July, where Mountjoy was commander of the castle as well as bailiff of
Tournai (*CWE* 3:8); and he stopped there for a few days, writing Epistles
295 (to Ammonio), 296 (to Servatius, as discussed in chapter 27), and

297 (to Wolsey). At Hammes he doubtless enjoyed leisure, for he would not catch up with his books until he reached Antwerp.

From Hammes he travelled on horseback to Ghent by way of Rosselare, as we know from Epistle 301 where he describes a painful twisting of his back (*CWE* 3:9/9–15). There he visited the president of the Flemish Council, Jean Le Sauvage, quickly a generous patron of Erasmus (Epistle 436), who dedicated to him a new edition of the *Institutio Principis Christiani* (cf. also Epistle 410). And in Ghent Erasmus also talked with at least two other councillors: one, Anton Clava, alderman of Ghent and a friend during the Louvain years (Epistle 301, cf. *BR*); the other, Robert de Keysere, who had been a schoolmaster at Ghent and then became a printer, in 1511 producing an edition of Erasmus' *Concio de puero Iesu* and probably at the same time an edition of *De Ratione Studii*. Clava was a friend of de Keysere and also of Pieter Gillis; by this time there was a network of friends, and wherever Erasmus went in the Low Countries or along the Rhine he met old friends and made new ones.

From Ghent to Louvain, arriving there probably in mid-July 1514 and staying with Jean de Nève, regent of the Collège du Lys, where Erasmus would later stay during his Louvain residence after September 1517 (*BR*). The following year de Nève became rector of the university, and to him Erasmus dedicated his *Opuscula* (which included *Catonis praecepta* and *Septem sapientium celebris dicta*, two collections of sayings or precepts, as well as the *Institutum christianis hominis carmine pro pueris*); the edition was printed by Martens in September 1514 and was still being printed during Erasmus' lifetime by Froben and Episcopius[2] – indeed there were London printings in the seventeenth century.[3] Addressed appropriately to a rector at Louvain, the book was (in Erasmus' own words in the Preface) 'a scholarly edition of the maxims of some standard authors that might shape the minds of the young for a life of virtue and their lips for correct and fluent speech:' hence the precepts of Cato and Publius and the Seven Sages (*CWE* 3:4/48–52).

Early in August Erasmus was in Liège, from where he addressed a letter to an Andreas van Hoogstraten, who was evidently a younger member of a younger branch of the van Borssele family, someone he had known for a dozen years and with whom he could jest. For in this brief letter (Epistle 299) Erasmus wrote,

> I went somewhat out of my way to see an old friend like you and to enjoy a glimpse of such a famous city, but through some adverse fate I failed of both. You were not at home, and the city made such an impression on me that I never left any place with greater pleasure. (*CWE* 3:5/2–5; Allen II, 3)

He seems to have stopped at Louvain, but there is little record of this visit: it seems likely, however, that his return to Louvain only three years later must have been prepared for by some consultation at this time. By the end of August he was in Basel, as we know from Epistle 300 (to be discussed below). the major part of the journey after Liège must have been on the Rhine, which he described in detail in a number of writings.

Preserved Smith comments that Erasmus, who had been born in the delta of the Rhine, knew the river from its source near Chur (actually at Reichenau, six miles southwest of Chur where two mountain rivers unite to form the principal stream, flowing northward into Lake Constance), and from Basel, where the river turns sharply northward:

> with the great cities strung like beads on its blue filament he was well acquainted, passing through them often in his frequent journeyings. For at that time the Rhine was a principal artery of European commerce and the chief avenue from the northwestern coast to the Alpine lands and to Italy. His ascent of the Rhine in the summer of 1514 was like a triumphal progress. (*Erasmus*, 129)

The river was navigable from its mouth to Basel without interruption, a distance of about 550 miles, and during the late Middle Ages it was one of main arteries of Western Europe. Much of the history of the Renaissance and Reformation is served by the river that connects so much of European culture: Basel, Strasbourg, Baden, Worms, Mainz, Bingen, Koblenz, Cologne, Nijmegen, Rotterdam, Antwerp and Amsterdam – these are the main, but by no means the only, places along the Rhine that helped to shape or nurture the events of the fifteenth and sixteenth centuries. Between Mainz and Bonn the landscape is rich in legendary landmarks like the Lorelei and the Drachenfels. After Cologne the river turns westerly into Dutch regions and divides into two branches, the southern of which is called the Waal. Joined on the left by the Maas (Meuse), it passes Nijmegen and Dordrecht, and one arm of this branch of the river is the IJssel, which moves off to the north, entering the North Sea by way of the Hollandsch Diep. The other branch of the Rhine fans out into several branches: the Oude Rijn (Old Rhine) continues past Utrecht and then enters the North Sea below Leiden. The Rhine was a fortified boundary of the Roman empire and there are abundant ruins and relics of Roman occupation. During the lifetime of Erasmus, boundaries were disputed between France and the Empire, involving especially the claims of Burgundy. Yet throughout history the Rhine has also been a linking of the very different French,

German, and Dutch-Flemish cultures. If Erasmus began as a Dutchman who moved outside his native land and came to think of himself
as a *homo Germanus*, surely the Rhine became for him a symbol of the
possibility of nations living and working peacefully with one another. As he grew older he became more and more of a cosmopolitan,
a citizen of the world, and his travels up and down the Rhine played
their part in this mental and psychological growth.

In England Erasmus had been inconvenienced by the war on the
continent, receiving information regularly from correspondents
about it. But now during the summer of 1514 the actuality of war
was borne in upon him, and his deep feelings of pacifism began to
surface. Completing his epochal and seminal book on *The Prince* in
about 1513, Machiavelli told his prince 'to have no other aim or
thought, nor select anything else for his study, than war and its rules
and discipline.'[4] Machiavelli (1469–1527) was schooled in
Florentine political life; and his commentaries on passages from Livy,
Discorsi sopra le prima deca di Tito Livio, are a distillation of his
political thought and provide yet another example of the conflation
of classical and contemporary thought. Politics were in the air.

At the time of the fall of Constantinople in 1453 the greatest
power in western Europe was the Duchy of Burgundy,[5] consisting of
territories welded together by personal allegiance to the duke; and
this was a political entity of considerable strength that stood between the French monarchy and the Holy Roman Empire; but the
subsuming of the Burgundian territory by the House of Habsburg in
1477 created a new power, with far-reaching consequences for the
Low Countries and Italy (chapter 1)

What followed were years of war, culminating in the League of
Cambrai in 1508 between king Louis XII of France, the emperor
Maximilian, pope Julius II and the king of Spain, for the taking of
territories from Venice. In 1510 peace was made with the Venetian
Republic, and Julius turned to his dream of driving the French from
the Italian peninsula. When he died in 1513 he had succeeded in
establishing a papal monarchy on Italian soil, but his policies had led
to the establishing of the Spanish in the peninsula. Julius' activities
were witnessed by Erasmus during his years in Italy, and they contributed to his bitter reaction to Julius and a secular papacy, a
reaction which produced his *Julius Exclusus* (chapter 27). In simplest
terms, Erasmus was horrified – even more than scandalised – by the
spectacle of a pope who donned armour to lead his soldiers against
christian opponents and cities.

In 1514 Henry VIII of England feared invasion from the French as
a consequence of his unsuccessful campaign against Louis XII; and

he ordered the sheriffs of Dorset and Somerset to issue proclamations that every man between sixteen and sixty should stand ready for armed defence of the realm.[6] Even in the presence of Henry VIII Colet courageously denounced war; and Thomas More, on the eve of his joining the royal Council, wrote in his *Utopia* of 1516 of the folly, futility and beastliness of war and battle (see the chapter 'Of warfare').

In March 1514 Erasmus spoke out in the important letter to Antoon van Bergen already cited (Epistle 288). This protest against war was made to Antoon because of his place in the Habsburg-Burgundian court, which Erasmus thought to have pivotal importance in the strife. The letter is a protest which Erasmus would develop at much greater length in the famous adage *Dulce bellum inexpertis* (of 1515) and his *Querela Pacis* of 1516 (chapter 31). In writing to Antoon, a ducal councillor and later, in 1521, one of the negotiators of the so-called 'Ladies' Peace' at Cambrai (chapter 33), Erasmus declared:

> ... But, you will say, the rights of princes must be upheld. While it is not for me to speak lightly of princes' conduct, I only know that often the greater the right, the greater the wrong, and that there exist princes who first make up their minds what they want and afterwards search for a specious pretext to cover their action. And in the midst of such revolutionary changes in the affairs of men, so many treaties concluded and abrogated, could anyone, I ask, want for a pretext? If the dispute is mainly about the question who exercises sovereignty, what is the need of so much bloodshed? For it is not the people's safety that is at stake, but merely whether they ought to call one person or another their ruler. There are popes and bishops and men of discretion and honour through whom petty issues of this kind can be resolved without conducting incessant wars and throwing Heaven and earth alike into confusion. It is the proper function of the Roman pontiff, of the cardinals, bishops, and abbots, to settle disputes between Christian princes; this is where they should wield their authority and reveal the power they possess by virtue of men's regard for their holy office. Julius, a pope who was by no means universally approved, succeeded in rousing this hurricane of wars. Cannot Leo, who is scholarly, honourable, and devout, succeed in quieting it? Julius' pretext for going to war was a threat to his own safety; but, even though its cause has been removed, the war still goes on ... (*CWE* 2:281/82–282/102; Allen I, 553/68–86)

The notion of the pope as mediator among christian states is a medieval one, as Tracy notes (34); but Erasmus' adducing of the concept of 'the greater the right, the greater the wrong' (on which see his later adage *Summum ius, summa iniuria*) is a new note, and his dismissal of Julius II with the litotes 'by no means universally approved' at the same time that he expresses a pious hope that Leo X will do better is perhaps a *pis aller*:[7] a last resort in a time of crisis, a *faute de mieux*. In writing to Leo on 21 May 1515, in a letter that asked permission to dedicate his edition of Jerome to the pope, Erasmus developed the general thrust of his letter to Antoon van Bergen: 'Julius was a very great man – the fact that he embroiled almost the whole world in war shows that, I grant you; but to have restored peace to the world proves Leo greater still' (Epistle 335, *CWE* 3:103/113–5; Allen II, 83/109–10). This is a remarkable letter to be sent by an Augustinian canon to the Supreme Pontiff of Christendom, and it is a superb example of parrhesia, which might be defined as a dangerous speaking of the truth; but Erasmus had a legitimate excuse for writing (dedicating a book) and he made the most of the opportunity.

The year 1514 was midway of the Fifth Lateran Council, which had begun inauspiciously, summoned by Julius in order to abort the French-inspired Pisan Council.[8] Erasmus heard reports and rumours, and the long-hoped-for reforms with which the Council had begun. He had been invited by Fisher to accompany him to the Council in 1512, but in the end Fisher did not go (*CWE* 2:213n).

Above all else, there was the question of responsibility for reform. To the extent that men took seriously the total structure of *ecclesia* in terms of the metaphor of John of Salisbury (for some the familiar medieval metaphor of the head and its members had become something of a model) they tended to reduce or limit the role and responsibility of the members according to the analogy. Papalists like Durandus saw the pope as a pattern for all; but conciliarists like Heinrich von Langenstein saw reform as one of the tasks of a Council – and so might it have been in the fifteenth century. But by this date there had been a triumph of the papacy in the struggle for power between pope and councils, and at the Lateran the Council was reduced to an instrument of the pope. The price of the concentration of papal energies upon Italian politics was that the unification of the Italian state was set back centuries behind that of the rest of Europe, and that the western Church was still dependent upon an Italian pope and papal court for the initiative to reform.[9]

Jedin has sketched this portrait of Leo X and his court at the time of the Lateran Council, and its colour-tones seem accurate and fair:

Surrounded as he was by the most brilliant court in Europe ...
exalted to the sky by the humanists who enjoyed his favour, Leo
X might well have persuaded himself that schism and Council
were but a bad dream, the anti-Roman opposition of those
beyond the Alps and the cry for a reform of the Curia no more
than a protest of late-comers, malcontents and everlasting fault-
finders. His was a dreadful mistake. The fire of a religious
revolution broke out in the house before its inmates were aware
of it ... For more than a century and a half men had devised
plans for a reform of the Curia and the Church. It had been
discussed and written about, but never had a liberating step
been taken by which the Papacy would have placed itself at the
head of a movement for the Church's renewal. A grand opportunity had been missed.[10]

If the Fifth Lateran Council was an opportunity lost, but one
which was played out on the stage before the whole of Christendom,
the Reuchlin affair was a cause célèbre in Germany and the whole of
the Republic of Letters.

Johann Reuchlin initiated a correspondence with Erasmus in
April 1514, who was at the time of the letter (Epistle 290) still in
England. Reuchlin was about twelve years older than Erasmus, a
doctor of laws at Tübingen who had retired to private life in Stuttgart (although his letter to Erasmus was written from Frankfurt).[11]
By 1514 Reuchlin had become widely known as the leading authority on Jewish literature, having written on the Cabala as early as
1494 and having published the first Latin-Hebrew grammar in
1506. That Reuchlin initiated the correspondence is a sign of
Erasmus' growing reputation.

Epistle 290 provides a synopsis of the controversy over Reuchlin
and the study of Hebrew. A converted Jew named Pfefferkorn had
received a mandate from the emperor Maximilian granting him
power to supervise the destruction of Jewish literature deemed dangerous to Christianity. Reuchlin was called upon as an authority,[12]
and he proposed that while there were a few Jewish books that
condemned Christianity and these might be destroyed, yet there
should be a christian study of both the Talmud and the Cabala and
such understanding would be to the benefit of the christian religion.
Reuchlin's defence of Hebraic studies led to his condemnation by the
conservative theologians of Cologne (and later Mainz), led by the
Dominicans, and even to Reuchlin's trial for heresy. Reuchlin's
original opinion, a 'Ratschlag ob man den Juden alle ihre Bücher ...
verbrenne soll' (6 October 1510) began the controversy, which
erupted into international proportions (although there is no episto-

lary evidence that Erasmus knew of it before 1514 it seems patently unlikely that he would not have heard from one of his German correspondents) and the dramatic event was the burning of Reuchlin's *Ratschlag*. Inquisitorial proceedings on the charge of heresy led to Reuchlin's acquittal by the court of the bishop of Speyer on 29 March 1514; but his accusers took the case to Rome, and these proceedings were halted by pope Leo X in August 1516 (*BR*).

Meanwhile both sides were attacking each other in print, and Reuchlin sought to give evidence of his reputation in the scholarly world by publishing a selection of letters addressed to him: *Clarorum Virorum Epistolae, latinae, graecae et hebraicae* (March 1514). There are no letters from Erasmus in the 1514 edition, but the enlarged edition of May 1519 did contain five letters from Erasmus, who did not appreciate having them included (Epistle 1041 and *BR*). Writing to Wimpheling from Basel on 21 September 1514, Erasmus spoke of Reuchlin in a curious way:

> That really accomplished person, Johann Reuchlin, endowed as he is with such a range of literatures and languages that one might think he has more hearts than Ennius, in my opinion the supreme glory and shining light and ornament of the whole of Germany, is so far from here that it is hardly possible to converse with him in letters; and this I much respect. (Epistle 305, *CWE* 3:33/256–60; Allen II, 24/248–51)

At the time Reuchlin was in Stuttgart and Erasmus in Basel: but perhaps mail was difficult between the two cities, and Reuchlin was under a cloud that made the writing of letters rather dangerous. But there is still another aspect that usefully points up a characteristic of Erasmus himself. Erasmus had no doubts concerning the essential rightness of Reuchlin's case, nor did he doubt that Reuchlin was being treated unfairly; but as Scheible puts it, 'he believed that Reuchlin should have reacted with meekness and patience because the controversy arising from his spirited defence was so damaging to Christianity. He [Erasmus] once said that for the sake of peace he would be prepared to sacrifice the entire Old Testament (Epistle 701; cf. Epistle 703)' (*BR*).[13]

The rising controversy over Reuchlin and the publication of his *Clarorum Virorum Epistolae* coincided with the ever-rising tide of anti-clericalism. The reform movements of the late Middle Ages were frustrated by the failure to call General Councils as enunciated by the decree *Frequens* at the Council of Constance;[14] and the view of Denys Hay that the refusal for so many years before 1512 to hold a General Council – against the will of a majority of Church leaders and at a time when men everywhere cried out for reform – must be judged a reasonable one: it 'resulted in the further development of heresy, near-heresy and indifference'.[15] Thus the most celebrated and most widely read document produced by the Reuchlin affair and its attendant controversy was the famous anti-clerical satire, *Epistolae Obscurorum Virorum*, the principal authors of which were Hutten, Johannes Crotus Rubianus and Philip Melanchthon (*BR*).[16] Other satires and polemics kept coming, but this satirical work did much to discredit rigid conservatism in the Church and university. Around it 'the German humanists formed a single phalanx ready to protect the new learning and education against the ignorance and malevolence of the old-school theologians' (Holborn, xi). As Hajo Holborn has justly observed, 'seldom has human stupidity among scholars been so wittily depicted and a degenerate philosophy so cleverly held up to ridicule' (vii). Despite the fact that many contemporaries looked for Erasmus' hand in the satire, hastily identifying the *Moria* with the *Letters of Obscure Men* by virtue of their sometimes common ends,[17] Erasmus in the main rejected the *Letters* (see Epistles 622, 636, 808), although he was well aware of the biting wit. He felt that Reuchlin had been treated unjustly, but he did not wish to be known as a supporter; yet he did put in good words for Reuchlin with cardinals Riario and Grimani. But, as Tracy observes (165), 'his support for Reuchlin had definite limits. He would not endanger the peace of Christendom for Reuchlin's esoteric Cabala, not even for the whole Old Testament'. In a strikingly suggestive way, Erasmus' stance in the Reuchlin affair anticipated his stance in the controversy between Rome and the Reformers in the 1520s.

As Erasmus was to write in 1518, 'My home, in my opinion, is wherever I keep my library' (*CWE* 5:365/134–5; Allen III, 266/ 117–8). After leaving England, and especially the Cambridge milieu where he had been comfortably settled for several years, he moved continually for the next three years: it took time for his books to catch up with him, and he had to travel to Basel, then back to England, in May 1515, again in the summer of 1516, and a final time in April 1517: all trips necessitated by the need for research on manuscripts, to consult a publisher, or to arrange for and receive the papal dispensation of 1517.

But this liminal period from 1514 to 1517 has its significance in that it marks Erasmus' crossing over into a sense of greater security for his research, wider recognition, and larger and more regular payments. All these elements are reflected in the writings of 1515 and 1516, which manifest a greater assurance in his style. But there was still the necessity to formalise his way of life both because of the pressure from Steyn (chapter 27) and the need to regularise his receipts from livings and pensions.

Erasmus was confronted by the ballooning Reuchlin affair, which can be seen as an extreme and potentially violent example (for force and threats of force were present) of 'a heightened consciousness of the Hebrew tradition. Although outbursts of anti-Semitism had been recurrent throughout the medieval period, Pfefferkorn's particular attempt to destroy Jewish literature was stimulated by the extent to which knowledge of Hebrew sacred books was penetrating Christian thinking'.[18]

The attitude of Erasmus towards the Jews is still a disputed question. Epistle 694 is written against the enemy of Reuchlin, a converted Jew (and now a Dominican), generating such expressions as 'I would not cast the words "half a Jew" in his teeth if he did not behave like a Jew and a half':- full of contempt, to be sure; but they are against one individual for whom Erasmus had no respect, only contempt: they are not necessarily against an entire race. Indeed, rhetorically, Erasmus' charging Pfefferkorn with acting like a Jew and a half was a technique for discharging his attacks against Reuchlin. Quite simply, the final objective study of the question has yet to be made.[19]

Erasmus deplored the tendency towards 'legal Judaism', or 'Judaising', by which he meant an excessive following of the letter, and in this context the term 'Judaism' operates as an historical metaphor that calls attention to centuries of traditional literal interpretation of the Old Testament. As he concludes Epistle 694 to Pirckheimer in 1517: 'Who is there anywhere with any tincture of learning or religion who does not support him [Reuchlin]? Who does not abominate that monster [Pfefferkorn], unless it be someone who does not understand the affair, or who seeks his own advantage at the price of public mischief? ...' (*CWE* 5:171; Allen III, 119/110–12). The number of cross-currents in what I have called the Reuchlin affair defies simple summary or reductive statements of univocal position.

The world was changing, then as always, but the rate of change was now accelerating, as Acton's dictum (one of the epigraphs to this chapter) suggests. Scholars have charged Erasmus with being indifferent to the world around him. To be sure, he does not mention the voyages of Columbus, and while in Italy he said almost nothing at all about the treasures of antiquity or about the monuments to the ambitions of the popes then rising in Rome. But silence in this instance cannot be construed as evidence of ignorance or indifference; for, as we have seen, there are huge gaps in his correspondence, and by the nature of his letters it is likely that Erasmus did not regard his letters of petition, or endorsement, or dedication, to be the proper place for admiration of the world around him. A careful study of his references to places (contemporary, classical and biblical), of which there are many hundreds, reveals Erasmus' keen awareness of place; he often alludes to the place from which his correspondent writes, and he frequently weaves place-references into his letters, the *Colloquies, Adages* and other writings.[20]

In point of fact, Erasmus was keenly interested in Church affairs, in the course of the wars swirling around him, and in general questions of reform. These matters, which do take the scholar out of his study, are frequently discussed in his letters and in those sent to him by correspondents who, in general, shared his interests. In his ascent of the Rhine during the summer of 1514 (the narrative of which will be resumed in chapter 30), Erasmus talked to far more people than are recorded, and even if we cannot identify those with whom he spoke or overhear their conversations through the letters, we must recognise that they took place. Our portrait of Erasmus must allow for shadows in the corners.

Notes

1) After a crossing that he describes as a very good one, but 'distressing all the same, at least for me' (Ep. 295 to Ammonio, *CWE* 2:292/6–7; Allen I, 563/4). The pirates (as he called the sailors) had transferred his 'portmanteau, crammed with my writings' ['*At maritimi praedones illi manticam lucubrationibus meis onustam*'] to another vessel, and he feared the loss of several years' work (*CWE* 2:293/13/–14; Allen I, 563/10–11). Perhaps these lines of Propertius had found their way into his commonplace book: 'so then my tablets, my learnèd tablets are lost, and with them many a gracious writing too is lost' (III. xxiii. 1–2; Loeb ed., 255). The testimony for Erasmus' 1511 trip to Paris is retrospective, coming in a letter of 1526 from Stephen Gardiner to the Dutchman in Basel (Ep. 1669): '*quo tempore primum Moriam edidisti…*'

2) See Devereux, *Renaissance English Translations of Erasmus* (Toronto, 1983) 188–205.

3) The publishing history of these works is complicated, for each of them has its own textual history. Erasmus' account of his editing is to be found in the prefatory letter of 1 August 1514, from Louvain (Ep. 298), where he writes that the proverbs which pass under the name of Cato need not be called Cato's, except that the sentiments are not unworthy of a Cato. For these he compared his text with the version of Planudes, and to these, he goes on, 'I have added the *Mimes* of Publius, wrongly known as the *Proverbs* of Seneca. These too I have corrected, for I found them heavily corrupt, and I have added very brief notes, casting out spurious additions taken from the

books of other men and appending a few from Aulus Gelius and the *Controversiae* of Seneca' (*CWE* 3:3/15–19; Allen II, 2/11–15). Erasmus edited Seneca in 1515 and again in 1529 (passing quickly over the editions of the tragedies in 1513 and 1514). The *Lucubrationes Omnes* of 1515 (published in Basel by Froben) was done in some haste, for Erasmus was working on the last stages of the editions of Jerome and the New Testament. Characteristically, in this edition Erasmus left too much of the copy-editing and proof-reading to others; but for the second edition of 1529 Erasmus demonstrated how much he had gained in knowledge and critical care: 'The second edition, prefaced by an admirably balanced and sensible essay on Seneca, produced two successful emendations for every one in the first edition and provides convincing proof of the judgement and scholarship of its editor', as L.D. Reynolds and N.G. Wilson judge in *Scribes and Scholars*, 2d ed. (Oxford, 1974) 145–6.

4) *Il Principe* (trans. as *The Prince*), ch. xiv.

5) For this summary paragraph I am indebted to M.P. Gilmore, *The World of Humanism*, 78. But the death of Charles the Bold at the Battle of Nancy in 1477 enabled the French king, Louis XI, to seize some of the Burgundian lands, and the Estates General in the Low Countries to strive for greater autonomy. In Holland and the neighbouring provinces there was sporadic but continuing fighting (see ch. 1).

6) Seebohm, *Oxford Reformers*, 163; Hughes, *Tudor Proclamations*.

7) Tracy writes (*Politics*, 150) that 'the bitterness with which Erasmus later speaks of Leo X ... may well be the counterpart of his idealised view of the pope's role in 1514'. But the idealisation may have been of the pope's character as well as of his role.

8) All the bishops of France had been summoned to meet in Orleans in September 1510 (see Schoeck, 'The Fifth Lateran Council', 100–1), and in May 1511 delegates of Maximilian and Louis XII were notified of a Council to open in Pisa on 1 September 1511, in compliance with the decree *Frequens*. In July 1511 Julius II summoned a 'true universal council' to meet at the Lateran in Rome on 19 April 1512, thereby smothering the abortive revolt, or even potential schism, of the dissident bishops and cardinals (101–2).

9) For fuller discussion and documentation, see Schoeck, 113–4.

10) Jedin, *A History of the Council of Trent*, I, 137–8. For the preceding paragraph I have drawn upon my account in 'The Fifth Lateran Council' (1981) 99–126.

11) Reuchlin (1454/5–1522) had studied widely, even in an age of wandering scholars: Freiburg, Basel, Paris (where he studied Greek under Erasmus' Paris teacher, Georgius Hieronymus), Orleans, Poitier, and again Tübingen. On a trip to Italy in 1482 he visited Florence and Rome with the count of Würtemberg and studied with Pico. After a diplomatic career, and legal practice, he held an appointment as professor of Greek and Hebrew in Ingolstadt, and the next year in Tübingen (*BR*).

12) He was one of several whose advice was sought by Maximilian, but Reuchlin was the only one to oppose Pfefferkorn in his assessment (*BR*). The comparative nature of the study of grammar is revealed by Louis Kukenheim, *Contributions à l'histoire de la grammaire grecque, latine et hébraïque à l'époque de la renaissance* (Leiden, 1951).

13) Johannes Caesarius (c. 1468–1550) to whom Ep. 701 is addressed, was a very successful teacher of Greek in Cologne and other places, among whose students were Glareanus and Mosellanus (see *BR*). In this letter Erasmus has been carried away by his rhetoric (ll. 15 ff.), and his argument is that he would be prepared to sacrifice *even* the Old Testament for the sake of preserving the peace of Christendom; but the opponents of Reuchlin were seeking to protect Christianity (*tutiorism*, the safer way, again) by destroying all of Hebrew Literature. See *CWE* 5:181 n. 40 to the effect that 'there is no evidence that Erasmus ever wished to endorse the tenets of the Marcionite heresy which included a rejection of the Old Testament; cf. Ep. 798:26–30'. The complexity of the milieu at Cologne is set forth by James V. Mehl in 'Humanism in the Home Town of the "Obscure Men"', in *Humanism in Cologne*, ed. J.V. Mehl (Cologne, 1991) 1–38.

14) In the Bull *Frequens* (COD 414). Conciliarism continued to draw theological as well as canonist supporters: see H.O. Oberman, *Forerunners of the Reformation* (Philadelphia, 1981) 214–5.

15) Denys Hay in *New Camb. Mod. Hist.*, 1, 11.

16) See F. G. Stokes, ed., *Epistolae obscurorum virorum* (New York, 1909), and the introduction by Hajo Holborn to a new edition of this translation (New York, 1964). For a more recent discussion see Peter Schäffer, 'Letters of Obscure Men', in *The Renaissance and Reformation in Germany*, ed. Gerhart Hoffmeister (New York, 1977) 129–40 and n. 13.

17) Reuchlin's role in the edition of Jerome needs to be recognised during the years from 1510–1516 (see *BR*), and Reuchlin did send Erasmus a New Testament ms. that Erasmus needed (Ep. 384); and besides, much of the period of the controversy found Erasmus still a member of the theological faculty of Louvain, which had taken an official stand against Reuchlin (Ep. 713). There seems to be a silence in their correspondence between November 1517 and November 1520: perhaps, in fact, Erasmus was reviewing relationships in the light of the advent of Lutheranism, and, further, Reuchlin's case was under review at Rome. Reuchlin died in ill-health in 1522. See Heinz Scheible's excellent bibliography of Reuchlin in *BR*.

18) Thus Gilmore, *World of Humanism*, 198. Gilmore continues: 'Like the revival of Greek, Hebrew scholarship introduced changes of decisive importance in the evolution of the Christian tradition... The assimilation of Greek and Hebrew learning could then in the long run only redound to the purification of Christianity. Scholarship has thus its practical uses in the service of the church. It was this conviction that underlay the hopes of the early sixteenth-century reformers and it was these ideals which inspired the Christian humanists' (198–9). See now the survey-article by David B. Ruderman, 'The Italian Renaissance and Jewish Thought', in *Renaissance Humanism*, ed. A. Rabil, Jr. (1988) I, 382–433 with its rich documentation.

19) On Erasmus' attitude towards Jews in general, see Guido Kisch, *Erasmus' Stellung zu Juden und Judentum* (Tübingen, 1969). More recently Heiko Oberman charged Erasmus with anti-Semitism: *The Roots of Anti-Semitism in the Age of Renaissance and Reformation*, trans. by J.I. Porter (Philadelphia, 1984) 38–40 and 58–9; to which should be added Shimon Markish, *Erasmus and the Jews*, translated by A. Olcott with afterword by Arthur A. Cohen (Chicago, 1986). There has been more heat than light in the charges

by Oberman and the rejoinders in the Dutch periodicals. Erasmus often spoke against 'Hebraizing': an excessive devotion to the letter of Scripture; and he was bitter towards Pfefferkorn as a renegade Jew. But he warmly supported Hebrew studies, and I do not think a case can be proved against him on the charge of anti-Semitism.

20) Such a study – provisionally entitled *The Geography of Erasmus* – is now in progress, and I plan to send the manuscript to the printer in late 1992.

Vocation and Life-style

Faber est suae quisque fortunae.

Sallust

Therefore, when we have read and studied all things, let this be
our final resolve: 'that through much tribulation we must enter
the Kingdom of God'.

Thomas à Kempis, *The Imitation of Christ*, chapter 12

How much more consonant with Christ's teaching it would be
to regard the entire Christian world as a single household, a
single monastery as it were, and to think of all men as one's
fellow-canons and brethren, to regard the sacrament of baptism
as the supreme religious obligation, and to consider not where
one lives, but how one lives.

Erasmus to Servatius Rogers, Epistle 296
(*CWE* 2:297/88–93; Allen I, 568/84–8)

Although the terms 'canon' and 'monk' were frequently confused,
even in medieval times, it is well to reserve the term monk for those
who live in a monastery and have taken vows of obedience, as well as
of poverty and chastity. With the wide adoption of the Rule of St
Benedict in the western Church, the term *monachus* was for some
time reserved for individuals living under that rule; but it had a
broader and less precise signification. Until the Reformation
monachus was understood to apply to Benedictines, Cistercians, and
Carthusians, but not to other orders and communities.[1] 'Friar' is the
term applied to a member of a mendicant order, especially after the
thirteenth century; the larger number were members of the Dominican, Franciscan, Carmelite and Augustinian orders.[2]

Canons were clerics attached to cathedrals (where they were generally priests), or, as in the case of the Canons Regular of St Augustine, they served parishes, taught in schools and colleges, and also
served at times as chaplains. At the same time, as DeMolen stresses,
they 'enjoyed a community life based on the rule of St Augustine.
Neither wholly active nor fully contemplative, they were in Erasmus'
view,"amphibians"'.[3]

Erasmus' unique sense of vocation put forward earlier must be understood in terms of his lifelong commitment to the Canons Regular of St Augustine. For, having made his decision not to return to the monastery at Steyn, as we have seen in Epistle 296 (discussed in chapter 27), Erasmus still had to work out the economy of his modified life-style and to decide where he should live in order to work best. But, to repeat, he remained a priest and a canon all his life; and thus in 1524 he referred to himself *'ut demus canonicos regulariter viventes esse monachos'*.[4]

In one of the colloquies there is a striking exchange on monks and canons. First published in the 1526 edition of the *Colloquies* was one of the most famous of them all: 'A Pilgrimage for Religion's Sake', which describes a pilgrimage to the shrine of Our Lady of Walsingham in northern Norfolk, about sixty miles north-east of Cambridge (not on the north-west coast of England as Erasmus wrote in error).[5] It is known that Erasmus had visited the shrine in the summer of 1512 and possibly again in 1514 (Reedijk, 302) before leaving England. Rather than reading the colloquy only as an attack upon relics and superstitions (as it has been much cited), one should – without discounting the attack on relics – perceive that it has an appreciation of the proper place of respect for the Virgin Mary and saints, and for holy places. It is notable that he may have visited the shrine twice, as is also the fact that he composed a Greek poem in honour of the Blessed Virgin (Reedijk, 303, with the note that the poem was first printed in the Strasbourg edition of the *Lucubrationes*, September 1515). He was not iconclastic or anti-religious, it is manifest, during these years.

Let us turn to the colloquy itself:

> By the northwest coast of England, only about three miles from the sea ... The village has scarcely any means of support apart from the tourist trade. There's a college of canons, to whom, however, the Latins add the title of Regulars: an order midway between monks and the canons called Seculars ... You tell me of amphibians, such as the beaver ... Yes, and the crocodile. But details aside, I'll try to satisfy you in a few words. In unfavourable matters, they're canons; in favourable ones, monks. (Thompson, 292)

Further on in the colloquy the principal speaker declares that canons have no provost [*praepositum*]: 'And that's why colleges of canons reject the name of "abbot". That of ["prior"] they accept willingly' (300). Erasmus is able to make sport out of the ambiguities of the term 'canon', and to include himself in that light. Yet until 1506 he continued to maintain ties with his monastery. As late as 1501 Erasmus could write to Hendrik van Bergen that after visiting his brethren at Steyn for more than a month, 'They have decided that I ought to spend a year longer on my studies; they think it will be discreditable to themselves as well as to me if I return after all those years without acquiring any qualification at all' (*CWE* 2:35/49–51; Allen I, 360/45–7). Within the limits of this letter, Erasmus indicates his acceptance of the authority of his brethren and superior, and his place in that disciplinary structure. That will change, of course; but for the time being, Erasmus does not challenge his status.

Let us review his status according to canon law. In 1492 or 1493 Erasmus had accepted an appointment as Latin secretary to Hendrik van Bergen, bishop of Cambrai (chapter 7): this had been done with the approval of the prior of Steyn and of the bishop of Utrecht, who had ordained him in 1492. Although details are lacking we may be sure that canonical permission was granted for Erasmus to enrol at the Collège de Montaigu in Paris for an advanced degree in theology (chapter 13); others of the Augustinian Canons Regular did so, and there was nothing extraordinary about that. The 1501 letter just cited apparently manifests Erasmus' sense of having to 'report' to Hendrik van Bergen: his canonical seconding was still in effect. But when Erasmus interrupted his formal studies at Paris, and especially when he went to England in 1499 (chapter 15) and to Italy in 1506 (chapter 23), Erasmus was going beyond the norm, and his new prior in 1504 obviously thought so. It is for this reason that Erasmus continued to keep Servatius Rogers informed of his movements (in Epistles 185, 189, 200 and 203). We have no evidence that formal permission was ever granted for this enlarged and extended stay away from his monastery, but it would appear that Erasmus was making a case by keeping his prior informed.

In 1506 Erasmus received a dispensation from pope Julius II (Epistle 187A). This brief is a dispensation freeing Erasmus from any canonical impediment to his accepting ecclesiastical benefices on account of his illegitimate birth (see appendix C). Henry VII apparently had promised a benefice, and Julius' brief sanctioned his accepting any benefice 'even if it be a parish church or the perpetual vicarage thereof or a chantry, free chapel, hospital or annual duty normally assigned to the same clerks by way of perpetual ecclesiastical benefice and by right of lay patrons ... '[6] Although the dispensation was never used to sanction receiving a benefice, Erasmus appears to have regarded it as authorising him to live outside the monastery at Steyn and warranting a change in dress (see Epistle 296/196–9). But after 1504 the new prior of Steyn, Servatius Rogers, appears to have insisted with increasing urgency that Erasmus return to Steyn.

When one knows that Erasmus was the son of a cleric (chapter 2), it is self-evident that the validity of the 1506 dispensation could be questioned, for in his application Erasmus had referred to his parents as 'a single man and a widow'; on the basis of this wording Julius had referred in his brief to Erasmus' affirmation that he suffered 'from a defect of birth being the offspring of an unmarried father and a widow' (*CWE* 2:105/9–10; Allen III, xxix–xxx, line 5). It would seem self-evident as well that the knowledge of his illegitimacy had been general in Holland: it must have been taken into consideration in his acceptance into the monastery and in his ordination. But if the prior and others at the monastery had reason to believe that Erasmus was the son of a cleric, if not a priest, the validity of the dispensation could be challenged.[7] Servatius' letters to Erasmus, which are lacking, doubtless pressed this point, and according to the letter of canon law Erasmus was obliged to obey his superior and to return to Steyn. But Erasmus refused, as we have seen, and even when he returned to the continent after several years in England he stayed at a distance from Steyn.

In the two years after 1514 Erasmus laid the groundwork for a second petition to the pope for a stronger dispensation, one that would clearly dispense him from the obligation to reside in the monastery at Steyn. The dedication of his New Testament translation to Leo was a strong oar for moving in this direction, and it would appear that he had worked out a campaign strategy with Ammonio while still in London in 1513 or 1514; and it was Silvestro Gigli, the Italian bishop of Worcester, 'who was to put Erasmus' case to the pope by word of mouth' (see Epistle 446, lines 41–2; *CWE* 4:7). The fictitious letter to Grunnius of August 1516 was a final piece in the campaign, providing Gigli with a detailed and somewhat witty narrative of Erasmus' history.[8]

The resulting dispensation of 1517 implies approval of Erasmus' change of habit as well as his living away from Steyn, and indeed (as McConica puts it in the commentary on Epistle 446), 'it does indicate approval of the shift implied in Erasmus' abandonment of his Augustinian habit: a move away from the dependency on his religious order and in the direction of self-support in the manner customary to secular priests' (*CWE* 4:3 n). Erasmus, it is clear, took the dispensation to the limits of interpretation: to mean not only freedom to wear a modified form of dress (but one appropriate to priests), and to accept benefices anywhere; but also freedom to live where he chose and to obtain independent sources of income. But all said and done, he continued to be a member of the Augustinians and subject to their rules, and under a certain obedience.[9]

However, Erasmus could not live in a monastic community because of his sleep habits, his finicky diet, and, as he put it to Servatius Rogers, a reluctance to 'exchange my studies for drinking parties' (Epistle 296/255–6). What is not fully clear is whether he had hoped his application to Leo X would produce a dispensation altogether from his vows as an Austin Canon, as McConica declares in his commentary on the letter to Grunnius (Epistle 447, *CWE* 4:7). If that had been his intention or wish, surely he would have made his request more explicit. Further, there is Erasmus' own conviction about having a true vocation, which DeMolen doubts in his chapter on Erasmus' commitment to the Canons Regular (197): but that dubiety is expressed in the much discussed letter to Servatius of July 1514 (chapter 28), which is something of an apologia and clearly strongly rhetorical, for it is pleading Erasmus' case for not returning to the monastery. In letters to others, among them Colet, he wrote of the slowly developing sense of vocation that he did have.

The story of Erasmus' life of prayer has not yet been written fully, and the concept of his spirituality has scarcely been studied;[10] yet he wrote many prayers and religious poems, and even a manual of prayer.

In his sense of the interior life Erasmus was very close to the spirit of the *Devotio Moderna*. Doubtless glancing at his own profession at Steyn, he wrote in an autobiographical aside in the *Moria* that 'Long ago, not speaking obliquely in parables but quite openly, I promised my Father's inheritance not to hood, or trifling prayers, or fast, but rather deeds of faith and charity' (Miller's translation, 100). This echoes the words of Thomas à Kempis in the *Imitation of Christ* that the monk's habit and tonsure are by themselves of little significance, for 'it is the transformation of one's way of life and the complete mortification of the passions that make a true Religious' (chapter 17, Sherley-Price's translation, 45). In a letter to Martin Lipsius, Epistle 2045 of September 1528, Erasmus recalled a passage in his own *Enchiridion*: there 'I had stated that it was no great thing to be buried in the cowl of St Francis and that the habit would have no value unless one had imitated Francis' life'. Simple but courageous words.[11]

It has already been noted that there are very few references to the celebration of the Mass by Erasmus. The lack of such references may or may not be an accurate indication of attendance at or celebration of the Mass; I think it rather weak testimony one way or the other. But even if it were an indication of non-celebration of the Mass, or celebration only infrequently, this was not uncommon before Trent.

What mattered to Erasmus beyond measure was a daily life of prayer. It is out of such a prayer-life based upon the reading of Scripture that such works as his *Method of Praying to God* (*Modus Orandi Deum*, first published 1523) directly proceeds. In a letter to Jacopo Sadoleto, by 1536 a cardinal, Erasmus expresses his sense of a life of prayer most strikingly:

> [speaking of the reading of a Psalm and the turning to many interpretations] The results are much more felicitous if, after studying the general theme, one surrenders his whole being secretly to the Spirit and at the same time turns his mind not only from moral faults but from all external and less important concerns and retires into a lofty seclusion that is peaceful and quiet and removed from all the roar of worldly passions. It is of no little importance to utter a prayer at frequent intervals, for that in a marvellous way gives fresh vigour and enthusiasm to the spirit. God immortal! How happy would we be if we could banish all disagreement of thought and feeling! Being one at heart we might seek refuge in the fertile fields of Scripture and play in its lovely meadows – if that word should be used in a matter that is not at all playful ... (Epistle 2443, Haworth translation 246–7; Allen IX, 166/362 ff.)

There can be no questioning his own piety or his own life of prayer.

In his final effort at winning peace for Christendom, the treatise *On Mending the Peace of the Church* of 1533, Erasmus stressed piety (which he understood and taught in the spirit of the *Imitation*), and he emphasised that piety must be acquired in stages. For this there are external steps, but these are useless unless they are disposed in the heart.

Especially after his Cambridge years Erasmus was again and again offered various ecclesiastical posts, not only in teaching but also as a bishop. There was in place a papal civil service during the Renaissance, and Erasmus would have come into contact with it during his service with the bishop of Cambrai, during his negotiations with the papal curia leading to his 1517 dispensation, and at various other occasions in his public career.

In Italy particularly, humanists sought employment as secretaries in the service of popes and cardinals. Erasmus knew many of these over the years, and after his service with an important bishop he would have learned about the ways (and costs) of entering papal service. For all too many the prime motivation for getting into the civil service of the Church was personal aggrandisement or (and sometimes both that and) cupidity. The influence of these officials in supporting scholarship, building libraries and helping to provide access to manuscripts, and other activities was enormous. A study of Erasmus' carefully framed letters to cardinals, curial secretaries, and bishops and abbots reveals how clearly he understood the rules of the game.

Perhaps a case of familiarity breeding contempt, Erasmus' experience with the civil service of popes and cardinals – like his experience with princes – led him to see how much freedom the humanist would have to surrender in entering such service. For many, as Peter Partner has written in his recent study of the papal civil service, 'saw it all as a choice between the active and the contemplative life [and it is striking how much of the writing by secretaries during the fifteenth century is concerned with this dichotomy], rather than a choice between God and mammon'.[13]

We do not have to depend upon the arguments of Raphael Hythlodaeus in More's *Utopia* for an expounding of humanistic arguments against entering the service of a prince or prelate. Erasmus knew all this at first hand, and we can well believe that his declining of all invitations to ecclesiastical service was founded upon his own experience.

This was not the direction in which he would turn, any more than the monastery. Erasmus chose to shape his own way of life as a scholar.

Remain true to his profession as a Canon Regular of St Augustine he would, and he kept his vows of chastity and, with qualifications, of obedience. Poverty is a grey area: after Paris he struggled, but certainly after Cambridge he lived well above the poverty line – but then, so do most religious (although not parish vicars and priests who live in poor communities). Erasmus owned property of several kinds: books, furniture, later even a house, and he purchased annuities: he was anything but poor after 1514. But he never strove simply to accumulate wealth; he felt that to achieve his goals in editing and writing he needed more than one secretary, and that required a house and housekeeper. Whatever he accumulated by the time of his death, he distributed to friends and to the poor.

It is therefore misleading to say that Erasmus was a failed monk or that he had defected from a monastery (*CWE* 66:xix); and perhaps, in a different way, it is also misleading to say that 'throughout his own religious life, Erasmus sincerely doubted that he had a true vocation' (DeMolen, 197). Rather, may we not say that Erasmus shaped his own vocation: in the spirit of Sallust's well known *Faber est suae quisque fortunae*, but made religious, even spiritual. That wise churchman Warham early recognised the potential of Erasmus, and the essential rightness of his way of life: 'You still have many important works to publish', he wrote to Erasmus in 1514, 'and you cannot tackle them unless you are strong. Look after yourself, and do not by your sickness deprive us of the splendid promise and sweetest harvest of your learning' (Epistle 286, *CWE* 2:277/17–20; Allen I, 550/13–16).

From what we know about Erasmus, the following line of interpretation concerning his vocation seems eminently reasonable. Having taken the bold step of not returning to his monastery in 1499, Erasmus had to prove to his superior that his decision was the right one. But perhaps even more he had to justify to himself his act of conscience in making his own independent judgment: not openly defying canon law, but circumventing it; not openly defying his prior, but not agreeing with him; and, although remaining an Augustinian Canon, not living with other canons. He was moving towards becoming an independent cleric living in but not of the world, not only supporting himself from his books (and the patronage they brought him) but holding up the scholarly vocation as a *bona fide* vocation for himself, recognising as well that he was serving as a model for others.[13] Is that not the view we are given by Metsys, Holbein and Dürer in those masterly portraits that show the humanist at his desk? – not at prayer (though of course he did pray), not teaching (though he had done that), not caring for the sick or aged (which are also acts of mercy) – but studying and writing. Above all writing: the focus in those portraits (and on this see appendix F further) is iconographic, and it is an image of the humanist-scholar in the act of writing.[14] That is the reality of Erasmus the humanist, now in the period immediately following 1514 and for the rest of his life.

We may then take it as most meaningful that Erasmus did not return to Steyn after his return from England, and that instead his route took him up the Rhine to Basel, where he would set in motion major publication plans.

Notes

1) See J. Olphe-Galliard in *Dict. Spir. Ascet. Myst.* 2:404–16, and, more popularly but knowledgeably, Peter Levi, *the Frontiers of Paradise – A Study of Monks and Monasteries* (London, 1988).

2) See W. B. Ryan in *NCE*.

3) R. L. DeMolen, 'Erasmus' Commitment to the Canons Regular of St Augustine', in *The Spirituality of Erasmus*, 191–7. To be sure, the term 'amphibian' occurs in a dialogic work (specifically, 'A Pilgrimage for Religion's Sake' in the *Colloquies,* ed. C. R. Thompson, 292).

4) Erasmus, Ep. 1436 to Geldenhouwer (Allen V, 427/19–21), cited by DeMolen, *Spirituality*, 196 (but without noting that the phrase he quoted was a part of an *ut* clause and that the sentence ends with '*in me certe non quadrat, qui nunquam fuerim monachus*' , 20–1).

5) See the bibliographical note in Thompson, *Colloquies* (1965) 287.

6) *CWE* 2:106/20–23. I have supplied some punctuation lacking in the translation.

7) It is doubtful that Erasmus knew before 1505 that he was the son of a cleric – which is to say that he was sincere in his petition for the first dispensation of 1506 – and I have earlier suggested that he may well have learned this fact during his sojourn in Italy.

8) It is not merely conceivable but even probable that Erasmus' letter to Grunnius – which may be fictitious only in the name of the addressee (but with exaggerations on a number of key points) – 'was in intent a memorandum for the instruction and amusement of Silvestro Gigli' (*CWE* 4:7); but in Ep. 453/16 Ammonio calls a letter of Erasmus to the pope (perhaps this letter to Grunnius; Allen II, 318/13) 'a fiction' (*commentum*: for which an English rendering simply as 'fiction' may be misleading: it could mean something devised by careful thought). In September 1516 Ammonio sent Ep. 447 to Rome along with Erasmus' Ep. 446 for the pope, and with it his own covering letter. Gigli wrote to Ammonio that the matter had been well received (Eps 498/11 and 505–6) and Erasmus made suggestions on the draft that was enclosed. After it was returned to Rome, the final documents were prepared at the end of January 1517 and they reached Erasmus in mid-March (Ep. 552), with the indication that he had to go to London to receive the official act of dispensation from Ammonio. And so Erasmus yet again made the dreaded Channel crossing in April, evidently his last trip to England.

9) See DeMolen, *Spirituality*, 196, and Allen V, 427/19.

10) See DeMolen, *Spirituality*.

11) *Erasmus and His Age*, trans. M. A. Haworth, 218; Allen VII, 480/220–2.

12) See Peter Partner, *The Pope's Men: The Papal Service in the Renaissance* (Oxford, 1991), ably reviewed by D. S. Chambers in *TLS* (12 April 1991).

13) In March of 1529 Erasmus wrote to Ludwig Baer (Ep. 2136) that he never gave his approval to monks who left their order without serious reason and without papal authorisation. In fact, he wrote, 'I have consoled or encouraged many who were wavering in their vocation' (Haworth trans., 224).

14) As I have written in ERSYB X (1990) 166, there is the fascinating matter of the three Copenhagen codices: whether these codices represent, as the most recent interpretation by a Danish scholar argues, an attempt to memorialise the most celebrated renaissance humanist by making permanent the state of his papers at the time of his death (a remarkable kind of textual icon comparable to the iconic features of the great portraits by Metsys, Dürer and Holbein, which dramatise the scholar writing, *humanista scribendus*, analogous to the portraits of St Jerome in his cell), the hand of Beatus is surely to be seen. I have commented on the codices more fully in an essay forthcoming in the proceedings of the 1991 Congress of the International Association for Neo-Latin Studies.

To Basel, Summer 1514

His ascent of the Rhine in the summer of 1514 was like a
triumphal progress.

> Preserved Smith, *Erasmus*, 129

Once a general Council was held in Basel, which continued for
nearly eighteen years. There is also in the city an extremely fine
printing house owned by the famous Johannes Frobenius. Indeed, if one considers the beautiful square in front of St Peter's
Church, the magnificent trees, the bridge which unites the two
towns and the healthy air, one can understand that Basel can
bear comparison with many other towns, but perhaps it deserves the first place because of the pure air.

> from the late 16th-century *Civitates Orbis Terrarum* of
> Georg Braun and Franz Hogenberg

After his visits to friends in the Low Countries (chapter 28) Erasmus
proceeded to the Rhine, and the first place to visit was Mainz, at that
time the seat of a prince-archbishop and the home of one of the leading
universities and centres of learning in Germany. The recently elected
(1514) archbishop – and also holder of the titles and powers of Elector of
the Holy Roman Empire, Imperial Arch-Marshal, and Primate of Germany – was the ambitious Albert of Brandenburg, with whom Erasmus
later corresponded (*BR*). But while it is not known whether Erasmus
met him on this first visit to Mainz, Albert's support of humanism,
derived from his early contacts with Ulrich von Hutten, Wolfgang
Capito and others, led him to a warm sympathy for Erasmus' *philosophia
Christi* (chapters 3 and 20). Elevated to the college of cardinals in 1518
during a diet at Augsburg, Albert was the prelate who condoned the
indulgence-selling of Tetzel in the diocese of Magdeburg, and it was he
who forwarded a copy of Luther's Ninety-Five Theses to Rome; his
relations with Erasmus will be discussed in subsequent chapters, and
especially in chapters 34 and 37. Albert, it must be added, had a strong
commitment to humanist education, and he supported Grünewald,
Simon of Aschaffenburg, Dürer, Cranach, and a number of other humanists and artists sympathetic to humanism (*BR*).

The university at Mainz was one of the new universities, having been founded in 1477. But Mainz is most famous as the place where Johann Gutenberg developed the art of printing in the 1450s. Erasmus' prefatory letter of February 1519 (Epistle 919) is the preface to a new edition of Livy, printed by J. Schöffer at Mainz in 1518, although not published until after the death of the emperor Maximilian; the edition was based on a newly discovered manuscript in the library of the Mainz cathedral chapter. In this preface Erasmus praised Johann Fust (or Faust) and his partner Peter Schöffer (who was succeeded by his son Johann) as inventors of this 'almost super-human art: So that this honour in one way descends tó Johann Schöffer as it were by right of inheritance, and in another is part of the glory of the city of Mainz, which has so many titles to distinction'.[1]

It was at this time that Erasmus first met that romantic courtier of the ecclesiastical court, the talented but violent-minded Ulrich von Hutten (chapter 28), and other German humanists. Word of the visit to Mainz reached London; on 20 October 1514 Colet wrote Erasmus (Epistle 314), 'That in Mainz they thought as highly of you as you say, I can well believe'.[2]

In the spring of 1515 Erasmus would visit Mainz again, this time stopping to attend the famous book fair held in March or April of each year.

From Mainz Erasmus ascended the Rhine to Strasbourg, which was an important Free Town of the Empire: 'one city watered by three rivers, nobly fortified, flourishing, rich and populous; above all, distinguished by such admirable institutions and governed by such admirable leaders', as Erasmus courteously wrote to Jakob Wimpheling (Epistle 305) on 21 September from Basel, following his visit there.[3] The glory of Strasbourg was its cathedral with a spire 465 feet high, already venerated in the early sixteenth-century, with its remarkable clock that was spared by the iconoclasts a decade after Erasmus' visit. Chief among the circle of humanists were Wimpheling, a theologian interested in reform; Sebastian Brant, whose *Ship of Fools (Narrenschiff)* was everywhere read; and the humanist-educator-statesman, Johann Sturm. Strasbourg was a notable centre for the printing trade, and at the end of the century the schoolmaster Frischlin entertained the town with an academic play in which Cicero was laughed at because he did not understand the printing press.[4]

In the same letter to Wimpheling, Erasmus wrote:

Again, I am well aware that I owe it to you, if the two distinguished magistrates at the head of the city of Strasbourg, who

gave me such a warm welcome when I was with you and treated
me with no common respect, honour me with their good wishes
now that I am absent and indeed far away [writing from Basel].
Here was the image of one of those cities we read of in the ancient
philosophers, Erasmus went on to say: 'with its noble citizens displaying at first glance (as they say) and in their whole deportment
exceptional wisdom, complete integrity, and almost a kind of majesty, tempered however with admirable discretion' (*CWE* 3:25/62 –
26/76; Allen II, 18/45 ff.). To say that Erasmus was well pleased is
an obvious understatement, and he went on in his letter to
Wimpheling to recall the importance of advisers like Nestor, Scipio
and Cato, and the ancient senators of the Areopagus: such a wonderful balance (he felt) between Roman severity and Greek refinement –
altogether an example of civic virtues. He was especially struck by
the harmony of different classes and ages: 'a great throng of men but
no crowd'; and 'O divine Plato, how I wish that you had had the
good fortune to light upon a city-state like this!' (lines 92 ff.).

So impressed indeed was Erasmus that he composed poems in
commemoration of the occasion, (*Poems*, 95–7), and these must have
been written either in preparation for the visit or during it (see
Reedijk, 313), and the three were printed by Matthias Schürer in his
edition of *De Copia* published at Strasbourg in December 1514.

In Strasbourg there was business to be done with Schürer, who
had been reprinting Erasmus' *Adagiorum Collectanea* (the 1500 version) almost every year since 1509.[5] Schürer was a faithful admirer of
Erasmus and they soon became staunch friends; he had just printed a
book in which 'the printer lauded him as "Germanorum omnium
eloquentissimus Latinissimusque", with a fine publisher's flourish.'[6]
Schürer apparently obtained permission from Erasmus to add a note
on the title-page of a new edition of the *De Ratione Studii*: '*ex
recognitione autoris, dum mense Augusto degeret, MDXIII*' (Epistle 66).
To this admiring printer Erasmus entrusted a new work, the
Parabolae (Epistle 312), as well as a revised edition of the *De Copia*
(Epistle 311).

Beatus Rhenanus, the German humanist, was one of the finest and
most attractive scholars of his generation, whom Erasmus was later
to call his *alter ego*.[7] In his literary sketch of Beatus, in writing to
Konrad Heresbach in Epistle 1316, Erasmus described him as witty,
good-humoured, and the most endearing of friends (*BR*).

Born in Sélestat in the Upper Alsace in 1485, Beatus was well-
schooled at the justly celebrated Latin school of his native city (where
he is commemorated in the municipal Bibliothèque humaniste), and

where foundations for his later achievements in scholarship and for his commitment to a scholarly life outside the university[8] were solidly laid by Crato Krafft Hoffmann and Hieronymus Gebwiler. Of the first of these teachers Beatus wrote, *literas cum sanctis moribus docebat* (*Briefwechsel*, 163). With Beatus as with Erasmus, the study of classical and humanistic texts also served moral development. At Paris Beatus studied with Jacques Lefèvre d'Etaple and received the MA in 1505 (*BR*).

The story of the relationship between the two scholars who collaborated over so many years, and the younger of whom indeed served as Erasmus' *alter ego*, has yet to be studied in all its fullness.[9] However, Erasmus and Beatus Rhenanus seem not to have met in Paris during Beatus' student years of 1503–6. To answer that anomaly we must turn to and concur with the argument of Robert Walter: Beatus was still a student and very much a disciple of Lefèvre, with whom Erasmus had remarkably little direct contact before 1511 despite their sharing many common aims and friends (not least Bade), and despite their having been in the same city over a period of some years. But even if they did not meet, Beatus would have heard about the Dutch scholar, not only from Lefèvre but from common friends; and Beatus soon began to add the books of Erasmus to his impressive humanistic library.

When did they meet? Probably in Strasbourg, where Beatus had been working with Schürer, who had been an active publisher of Erasmus well before Froben. Notably Beatus collaborated with Schürer, who was also from Sélestat, in an edition of Andrelini. The printer, as one dedicated to the printing of the classics (producing 101 editions of Latin and Greek authors in the twelve-year period before his death in 1520), was praised by Erasmus for being willing to print books for the use of the scholarly community without thought of profit (Epistle 311, Reedijk 98, and *BR*).

Beatus travelled back and forth from Sélestat to Strasbourg and Basel, moving to the latter city in 1511, partly to work with the press of Johann Froben, partly to be closer to the distinguished Greek scholar Johannes Cono. In 1513 Beatus saw his first edition through the press of Froben: the *Sententiarum* of Paolo Cortesi (a commentary on the *Sentences* of Peter Lombard), which contained a dedicatory letter from Konrad Peutinger to Beatus and a preface by Beatus (BR). The next year he began his own major scholarly work in editing Pliny's letters (which he published with Schürer, having doubtless begun the work while still in Strasbourg); in 1515 he published his commentary on Seneca's *Ludus* with Froben.[10] When Erasmus left Basel to return to the Low Countries in 1517 he empowered Beatus to act for him in editorial as well as personal matters.

From Strasbourg Erasmus continued his progress up the Rhine toward Basel stopping off in Sélestat (Schlettstadt).[11] It was then a small town of only four or five thousand inhabitants, but it possessed a splendid Latin school and could point with pride to a number of humanists of note. The greatest of these was Beatus Rhenanus, just mentioned, and others were Matthias Schürer and Johannes Sapidus, in 1512 appointed rector of the Sélestat grammar-school. Johannes Sturm, to be encountered later, was the son-in-law of Sapidus. The warm friendship between Sapidus and Erasmus began on this 1514 visit and was deepened by Sapidus' escorting Erasmus to his destination in Basel; it was Sapidus (and Johann Witz) who introduced Oecolampadius to Erasmus, which led to Oecolampadius' staying on in Basel to help Erasmus with the editing of the New Testament (Epistle 354).

A fourth poem written by Erasmus on this journey was his *Encomium Selestadii carmine elegiaco* (*Poems*, 98). It seems to have been finished after Erasmus wrote to Wimpheling on 21 September (Epistle 305), and it is a eulogising of the humanistic circle, with these mentioned by name in the poem: Wimpheling, Johann Kierher (*BR*), Seidensticker, Beat Arnold (who studied at Paris with Beatus), Johann Storck – a remarkable group to come from so small a town. The poem concludes with this graceful couplet that plays on Erasmus' slowness in writing the poem:

> *Haec memor hospitii tibi carmini panxit Erasmus*
> *Haud lepida, at grata qualiacunque cheli*. (Reedijk, 318)

From mid-August 1514 until the middle of 1516 (with a trip away in 1515), again from 1521 to 1529, and then for the final year before his death in 1536, Erasmus spent many years of his life in Basel.[12] It was the closest that he came to having a permanent home.

Basel was, and is, both a city and a canton in northern Switzerland, but it was not always Swiss, though it has been overwhelmingly German-speaking since the Middle Ages. After many years of war and negotiations it pulled out of the Habsburg alliance and was admitted into the Swiss Confederation in 1501, having long wavered between the pull to the Rhine cities and the political-economic ties with the Confederation. The death of Zwingli in 1531 at the head of his troops fighting the Catholic cantons demonstrates the hard fact that the traditional stability of the Swiss Confederation was not easily achieved.

Originally a Roman *oppidum*, the city's name is thought to derive from the *castellum* or *Basilia* (city by the water) built by the emperor

Valentinian in the fourth century AD. Not a native of the city, Beatus
Rhenanus described it as 'a royal residence, the queen of cities', for it
had, even then, pleasant and handsome houses, clean streets, gardens,
splendid views over the Rhine, and a relatively mild climate. The
cathedral (later münster) sits on a terrace high above the Rhine, and
public meetings of the fifteenth-century Council of Basel were held
in the choir whilst committees worked in the chapter-house; and it is
in the cathedral that Erasmus is buried (chapter 44).

An Ecumenical or General Council of the Roman Catholic
Church met in Basel from 1431 to 1439, and Smith speaks of its
memories animating the place 'with a sense of freedom and reform'
(138). Certainly there was an impact on the city in learning and
education as well, for secretaries came with the prelates, and with
them they brought the new Italic script and a keen hunger for
humanistic texts.

At the end of the fifteenth century Basel was a centre for many
guilds, leading to its pre-eminence in modern times for its chemical
works. Above all, Basel was famous for its printers.[13] Johann
Amerbach – an MA at Paris by 1464, with a 'vigorous Latinity' and
some knowledge of Greek – had begun his press about 1475 after
studying in Rome and apprenticeship in Venice. In his trade, in
which he rapidly prospered, 'he collaborated with other printers,
editors, and booksellers, corresponding with business friends and
agents as far away as Paris, Nürnberg, and London' (*BR*). Amerbach
was supportive of humanism and corresponded or collaborated with a
number of contemporary scholars: Trithemius of Sponheim,
Wimpheling, Sebastian Brant, and Reuchlin (*BR*). Amerbach was
also closely connected with the nearby Carthusian monastery and its
rich collection of manuscripts (many of which derived from the years
of the Council), and these served the printing-press for many editorial enterprises. Still dreaming of his great aim of publishing the
Fathers of the Church, Amerbach was working on editions of
Ambrose, Jerome, Gregory and Augustine when he died in 1513.
Among the several sons of Johann Amerbach the youngest is the
most notable for connections with Erasmus: Bonifacius was born in
1495, attended the school at Sélestat, and received his BA and MA
from the University of Basel. He met Erasmus soon after the latter's
arrival in Basel, and their correspondence was steady and important
(*BR*). In his final will of 1536 (appendix D) Erasmus named
Amerbach his legal heir and one of the executors.[14]

Johann Froben filled the vacuum left by the death of Amerbach,
and in fact Froben and his partner Petri had often collaborated with
Amerbach in joint ventures; as Guggisberg has observed, Froben

took over Amerbach's shop and his uncompleted projects.[15] In 1510 Froben married the daughter of his partner Wolfgang Lachner, forging an additional link binding the commercially minded Lachner with the more idealistic Froben. Then in 1511 Petri died, and in 1513 Amerbach: it seems probable that by 1514, the date of Erasmus' arrival, Froben was able to turn to other publishing ventures outside their usual line of Bibles, theological *summae*, and like works appealing to the clerical market (*BR*).[16] The timing of Erasmus' arrival in Basel could not have been more opportune.

We know from several epistles (219, 163 and 283) that Erasmus had been planning a reprinting of his *Adages* in 1511 (to be done by Bade in Paris); but Birckmann (to whom Erasmus had entrusted a copy of the revised edition) had taken it to Froben instead of giving it to Bade (Epistles 258 and 283, see chapter 27). In Epistle 283, writing to his trusted friend Ammonio on 2 December 1513, Erasmus recounted the events:

> A certain person printed them [the *Adages*] at Basel, but so much in imitation of the Aldine edition that to a careless eye it might seem identical. I had entrusted an emended and enlarged text to Franz, who is accustomed to import almost every book into this country [England], intending him to hand it over to Bade or, if he advised it, to another publisher. That worthy immediately carried it off to Basel and put it in the care of the man who had already printed it [Froben], so that he will publish this edition only when he has sold all the copies of his own, that is, ten years from now. (*CWE* 2:273/182–189; Allen I, 547/152–9)

But Erasmus' fears were unfounded: Froben published the new edition in 1515 (see Epistle 269, introduction). This new edition of 1515, in which a goodly number of essays are enlarged and several long essays included, tended (as Phillips had observed, 96 ff.) to introduce a new note of criticism of contemporary society and culture.

On the face of it, then, Erasmus does not seem to have planned the action he did in putting the revised copy of the *Adagia* into the hands of Froben and Lachner. This raises the question of Erasmus' travelling to Basel in the summer of 1514: how much had been negotiated beforehand, how much of the cooperation between Froben and Erasmus prepared for in advance?

At least a partial answer is provided by a passage in Epistle 305 to Wimpheling where Erasmus tells of arriving in Basel and at first seeing those he wanted to see: Beatus Rhenanus, Gerard Lyster, and Bruno Amerbach. He continues by inventing a *persona*:

I gave Johann Froben a letter from Erasmus, adding that I was very closely acquainted with him, that he had entrusted to me the whole business of publishing his work, and that whatever steps I took would have the same authority as if they had been taken by Erasmus himself; in fact, I said, Erasmus and I are so alike that if you have seen one, you have seen the other. He [Froben] was delighted later on when he saw through the trick.[17]

It is evident that Erasmus had admired Froben's printing, and I follow Bietenholz in concluding that 'it is not likely that he came to Basel in the fall of 1514 (Ep. 305) without an invitation of some kind since the Froben firm was then anxious to secure a new academic director for the great edition of Jerome (Epp 326, 396; Allen I, 63–4)' (*BR*).

The university of Basel was founded by Pius II in 1460 and is the oldest in Switzerland.[18] In the university library are the archives of the fifteenth-century Council of Basel. After the Council strong ties with Italy continued, especially in law; but there were also links to Paris and Orleans, and to the German universities to the north.

Soon after his arrival in Basel, as Erasmus wrote to Wimpheling (Epistle 305),

> the doctors of this university, through the dean of the faculty of theology and another man, invited me to supper next day. All the doctors of all the faculties, as they call them, were there. Ludwig Baer (Ursus, if you prefer it in Latin) was there too; he is rector of this university, a distinguished graduate in theology from Paris , a man still in the prime of life ... [19] [it also gains] lustre from the character and learning of Guillaume Cop, the new Hippocrates of our age ... [20] There has also come here on purpose to see me one Johannes Gallinarius, a man of wide learning with a character to match.[21] And a poet laureate is here, Henricus Glareanus, who has an admirably frank and gay disposition and is a young man of high promise.[22] I have had two or three letters from Udalricus Zasius, the well-known professor of civil law at Freiburg.[23] (*CWE* 3:31/200 ff.; Allen II, 22/195 ff.)

With such a warm reception Erasmus was much taken by Basel, and this introduction, he wrote in the same letter to Wimpheling, 'makes me more and more charmed and attracted by my Germany'.[24] And so he wrote,

> I can easily be induced to stay here for the winter until the middle of March; and then, when I have finished the business I want to do in Italy, I will return to you about the middle of

May. And this I would do the more readily, if it should prove possible to get all my works out in these winter months with the same labour and lamp-oil, as the saying goes.[25]

What were the works he wanted to get out?

Even as early as 21 September (the date of the letter to Wimpheling) Erasmus could write that 'My *Adagia* has now begun to be printed' (*CWE* 3:32/228). Clearly arrangements must have been made in advance for this to proceed so quickly; and this edition appeared early in 1515 from the presses of Froben. At about the same time Schürer produced a reprint during the month of April, but this was not the revised edition that found its way to Froben and Lachner; it is likely that Beatus Rhenanus helped to see Froben's edition through the press.

The *Parabolae* or *Parallels (Parabolae sive similia)* too is a work that had roots in the Paris years, but its immediate genesis lay in the collection of proverbs for the 1515 revision of the *Adagia* and in working on the collected works of Seneca, also published in 1515. It was all, as the learned and wise R. A. B. Mynors writes in his introductory note to the Toronto edition (*CWE* 23:124), 'potentially material for the man who wished to learn from the ancients to live wisely, but also to think clearly and to write compellingly, the destined beneficiary of the *De copia* and *De conscribendis episolis*'. The emphasis consequently in the *Parabolae* is all on content, not on form.

Erasmus was reading widely – for the revision of the *Adages*, for his work on Seneca, and for various other projects in progress – and the aphorisms in the *Parabolae* are apparently set down in the order in which he collected them from Aristotle, Pliny, Plutarch, and others. By April 1514 he had gone as far as he meant to, at least for the time being, and he either left it with Schürer as he passed through Strasbourg or he sent it on.[26] In December 1514 a small quarto volume appeared that contained the *Parabolae* and also *De Copia*, plus letters and verses about the author's visit to the literary circles of Strasbourg and Sélestat during the preceding August. The volume in its special way is a tribute to the *sodalitas literaria* of the city and to Schürer's active role in it (Mynors, 125); and it is also a mark of the quickness with which Erasmus could respond to a situation or occasion for putting together a number of his works. Schürer sold out his edition in less than a year, and it was reprinted in February and November of 1516, and again in 1518. But Erasmus had been revising the work and turned over his revised edition this time to Thierry Martens, who published a *Parabolae* in June 1515 .[27] Over fifty later editions are known, with the last in Erasmus' lifetime being the Basel edition of 1534 by Froben.

Erasmus also brought with him to Basel his work on the letters of St Jerome, and this found its way into the edition of the works of St Jerome that Froben had been planning. The edition would appear in nine volumes during the summer of 1516 (chapter 31). Here it rests only to say that the work of Erasmus was joined to that of Reuchlin, Pellican, Reisch, and Kuno, who had been at work for several years (see the introductory note to Epistle 396, the dedicatory letter to Erasmus' part of the Froben edition of 1516: *CWE* 3:252–4). His work on Jerome went hand in hand with that on the New Testament, and had done so since 1498 (see Epistles 67, 141, and 373).[28] His responsibility was the letters and other treatises of Jerome, filling up the first four volumes of the edition; but he served, more or less, as general editor of the project throughout (Olin, 41). The editorial work was finished in the summer of 1516, and with amazing speed the edition was on the market by late September. Erasmus' editing of the letters and his Life of Jerome will be taken up in chapter 31.

Besides his notes on the New Testament, the remaining work on which he had brought material was on the *Lucubrationes* of Seneca.[29] Published in August 1515 by Froben, this edition was dedicated to Thomas Ruthall, a prelate with great influence who had been bishop of Durham since 1509 (and often figures in Erasmus' English letters) and secretary to the king from 1500 to 1516. In this letter of 7 March 1515 (Epistle 325) Erasmus surveys his editorial work on the *Lucubrationes* on which he had worked while in England, having now published the Tragedies in 1512 and revised that faulty edition in 1514. Erasmus here describes his editorial method for the *Lucubrationes* in fascinating detail:

> One thing however helped me: they [manuscripts of Seneca provided by Warham and King's College, Cambridge] did not agree in error, as is bound to happen in printed texts set up from the same printer's copy;[30] and thus, just as it sometimes happens that an experienced and attentive judge pieces together what really took place from the statements of many witnesses, none of whom is telling the truth, so I conjectured the true reading on the basis of their differing mistakes ... (*CWE* 3:64/ 45–50; Allen II, 52/38–43)

Erasmus tells us nothing of his method of collation – of reading one manuscript or printed text against another – but he has clearly done just that. Collation he might have learned from Valla, who consulted manuscripts and compared their readings. His work, technical analysis, however, 'pointed the way to a complete textual critical method rather than demonstrated how to devise such a system'.[31] Only with

Poliziano was there the foundation of a scholarly method of textual criticism: he even conceived of arriving at the archetype of manuscript families after careful investigation of individual manuscripts (D'Amico, 25).

Erasmus was absent from Basel during the greater part of the time that Seneca was actually being printed, as Allen has noted: 'the proofs were corrected by Beatus Rhenanus and a young man named Nesen'.[32] Although freed from the burden of correcting proofs, Erasmus still 'boils over with annoyance against the correctors for the blunders they let pass'.

This autumn of 1514 saw Erasmus living at the 'Haus zum Sessel', where Froben had both his press and living quarters for his family and – much like his earlier experience of living in the Academy of Aldus in Venice (chapter 23) – Erasmus became part of a community of scholars, all devoted to the cause of good letters. In Epistle 391A to Witz in the latter part of 1516, Erasmus described the spirit of this community:

> You say how fortunate so many scholarly and warm-hearted friends are in my society, but you do not say how happy I am in my turn in seeing so much of them, as though the good fortune in this were less mine than theirs. I seem to myself to be living in some delightful precinct of the Muses, to say nothing of so many good scholars, and scholars of no ordinary kind. They all know Latin, they all know Greek, most of them know Hebrew too; one is an expert historian, another an experienced theologian; one is skilled in the mathematics, one a keen antiquary, another a jurist. How rare this is, you know well. I certainly have before never had the luck to live in such a gifted company. And to say nothing of that, how open-hearted they are, how gay, how well they get on together! You would say they had only one soul.[33]

Coming on the heels of Erasmus' decision not to return to Steyn, his discovery of such a fine community must have been not only pleasant and stimulating but a great source of strength for him. This community was very different from Steyn: there were no vows, obviously, and not even the formality of membership. In his fine book on Basel Hans Guggisberg has written that 'a lot of scholarly work was done, but there was also a great deal of conversation, conviviality, merriment and gossip'.

Work proceeded with intensity, at times at fever-pitch. Allen has detailed Erasmus' rapid pace that made possible his extraordinary productivity:

His work was always done in heat, under the passion of his
demand for knowledge. He read, he wrote, *tumultuarie,
praecipitanter.* When he had formed a design, he liked to carry it
out *uno impetu* [in one attack]. To those around him he was the
leader, whose will was their driving force, sweeping them on to
keep pace with him. His sense of what was business-like led
them to the newest methods of sparing labour, his view that
economy may be of time rather than money prompted them to
avoid petty savings.[34]

At times Erasmus complained of working hard, and in the prefatory
letter to an edition of the *Institutio Principis Christiani* he wrote of
'always sweating for the public good', and he and some of his friends
referred to the 'treadmill'[35] – not unlike the private names at Yale for
the scholarly projects in the old Sterling Library: the Franklin Factory, the More Factory. Thus in one letter of 1516 to Bruno
Amerbach we read: 'How goes our treadmill? what news of the cave
of Trophonius? ...' (*CWE* 3:335/1; Allen II, 279/1).

Erasmus had had the experience of living in the house of Aldus
during his Venetian period, working on the revision of the
Adagiorum Collectanea into the *Adagiorum Chiliades,* and in many
ways it had been important and valuable. Yet his experience in the
Froben press was even more communal, and apparently much more
fun. Further trips were necessary back to the Low Countries and to
England for various reasons, and Erasmus remained in Louvain for
several years (chapter 33). But for the rest of his life Basel was a more
permanent home than he had known. He had to leave it in the spring
of 1515, but he was soon back in the summer of that year and
remained until May of 1516; there was another quick visit in the
summer of 1518 from Louvain. Then he was back again in Basel
from late 1521 until early 1529, and again during his last months
from late spring 1535 until his death in mid-1536. Whenever he
was in Basel, however, the activity of the Froben press revolved
around Erasmus and his projects. Through correspondence he remained in close communication with Froben and Bonifacius
Amerbach, as well as the editors and scholars: he was never unconnected, never left out of the major planning of editions.

It would be a mistake therefore to think of Erasmus' activity *chez
Froben* merely in quantitative terms: the quality of his editorial work
continued to improve, and one result of his close association with the
company of scholars was a widening of his intellectual horizons.
Most of all he matured as a textual scholar. In all his editorial activity
Erasmus made mistakes, partly from working too rapidly, partly
because of his imperfect understanding of principles for judging one

manuscript superior to another, and partly because there was not yet an articulated theory of textual emendation and editing. But Erasmus learned from his mistakes: the revised edition of any one of his major editions is always an improvement over the earlier one.

For all of this, the unique association with Froben is at the heart of the matter, and Erasmus' tributes to Froben upon his death in 1527 express the closeness of their relationship and the depth of his respect, even love, for the great master-printer who had helped Erasmus to become a master-editor. Within a short span of two years after his arrival in Basel a number of Erasmus' long-term ambitions would be brought to fruition: the editing of Jerome's letters and the writing of a life of Jerome, and the editing of the New Testament, and several other projects.

Notes

1) *CWE* 6:255/15–18l; Allen III, 494/14–17. The names of Faust, Scheffer [sic], along with those of Albert, Frederick, and Tzobel (Zobel) are in large caps that stand out on the printed page: see the illustration facing p. 255 in *CWE* 6.

2) *CWE* 3:48/5–6; Allen II, 36/4 – 37/5. Allen notes that Ep. 314 is 'the answer to a letter written from Basle on the same date as Ep. 301 and narrating the events of the journey', but that is a letter not preserved.

3) See *BR* and Miriam U. Chrisman, *Strasbourg and the Reform* (1967) and *Lay Culture, Learned Culture* (1982), both discussed in Dickens and Tonkin, *The Reformation in Historical Thought* (1985) 302–3.

4) See Nicodemus Frischlin, *Julius Redivivus* (1585). Erasmus is mentioned in III.1.

5) Given that Schürer and Erasmus probably met in July or August 1509, when Erasmus was on his way from Italy to England, post-1509 printings were therefore doubtless done with Erasmus' permission.

6) See Allen, 'Erasmus' Relations with his Printers', 125.

7) *CWE* 8:219/76; Allen IV, 500/69–70. This letter was public, for it was the preface to the 1521 edition of Erasmus' letters. Erasmus wrote (to quote more fully): 'And so in this business [of preparing the correspondence for publication] I implore you in the name of our friendship, dear Beatus, the most learned of my friends, to be in truth my second self and to do for me what I should have done myself had it been possible'.

8) Is it not most likely that Erasmus was Beatus' model in this sense of vocation? Beatus' master at Paris, Lefèvre d'Etaples, in later life lived in a monastery *(BR)*.

9) The account in John F. D'Amico, *Theory and Practice in Renaissance Textual Criticism* (1988) needs to be supplemented by the valuable article by Robert Walter (whose dissertation on Beatus seems to be unknown in the UK and North America): 'Une amitié humaniste: Érasme et Beatus Rhenanus', *Annuaire de la Société des Amis de la Bibliothèque Humaniste de*

Sélestat, 36 (1986) 13–23. See my review of D'Amico's book on Rhenanus in *ERSYB* 10 (1990) 163–8.

10) Until 1519, it is noted in *BR*, Beatus appears to have lived in Froben's house. For much of the detail in the preceding account of Beatus I am indebted first to the compact essay by Beat von Scarpatetti in *BR*, and secondly, in far greater detail, to the work of Dr Robert Walter, who has kindly provided me with his publications.

11) The vernacular name for the city during Erasmus' time was Schlettstadt, but today (Alsace being part of France) it is Sélestat. For convenience and simplicity, we shall use only the modern Sélestat.

12) Note the French spelling *Bâle*, and the English Basle.

13) See Peter G. Bietenholz, *Der italienische Humanismus und die Blütezeit des Buchdrucks in Basel* (Basel, 1959) and his *Basle and France in the Sixteenth Century* (Geneva-Toronto, 1971). Shipping of books down the Rhine and over long-established trade routes to France, Italy and beyond made printing the more profitable.

14) Owing to the complete preservation of the Amerbach family papers in Basel, Welti has observed, 'the extant letters in the correspondence between Bonifacius and Erasmus are more numerous than those of any other epistolary exchange the latter had' (*BR*). To Welti's excellent bibliography should be added Guido Kisch, *Bonifacious Amerbach* (Basel, 1962).

15) See Hans R. Guggisberg, *Basel in the Sixteenth Century* (St Louis, 1982).

16) As Beatus wrote to Erasmus on 24 April 1517 (Ep. 575), 'It is impossible to say what a passion they have for really huge tomes' (*CWE* 4:341/29; Allen II, 550/26).

17) Erasmus adds that Lachner paid all that was owing in the inn and took Erasmus, complete with horse and baggage, to stay in his house (*CWE* 3:39/192 ff).

18) There were many connections between Froben and the University: see Earle Hilgart, 'Johann Froben and the Basle University Scholars, 1513–1523', *Library Q* 41 (1971) 141–69. Walter Rüegg has written eloquently on the spirit of humanism in Basel in the early years of the 16th c.: see his *Die Beiden Blütezeiten des Basler Humanismus*, (Basle, 1960).

19) Baer (1497–1554) studied theology at Paris at the same time as Erasmus, though it is not known whether they met at that time; he received his MA in 1499, and his doctorate in 1512. He returned to Basel to join the theology faculty, where he does not appear to have published, beyond a treatise *De praeparatione ad mortem* (Basel, 1551). It must be noted that he left Basel after the triumph of the reformers and withdrew to Freiburg in January 1529, where he spent the rest of his life and where Erasmus soon joined him (Allen II, 381 n).

20) Cop (c. 1466–1532) was a physician Erasmus respected and liked, and to him was dedicated his poem on growing old, *Carmen ad Gulielmum Copum* … (Reedijk, 122, and poems 83 & 131). It is doubtless, as Reedijk comments, written from his own painful experience under Cop's care.

21) Gallinarius was a kinsman of Wimpheling, who received his MA from Heidelberg.

22) Glareanus (1488–1563) studied at Cologne, receiving his MA in

1510, and in 1512 was laureated by the emperor Maximilian. Because of his support of Reuchlin he felt it desirable, or necessary, to leave Cologne, and he made his new home in Basel in 1514. See Ep. 440 and note in *CWE* 3:336–7.

23) Udalricus (Ulrich) Zasius (1461–1535) was born in Constance and studied arts and theology at Tübingen, after which he moved about as notary and town clerk in many towns in Germany and Switzerland. In 1501 he was made doctor of laws at Freiburg after an unusually brief period of formal study. Erasmus and Zasius each respected the work of the other, and Erasmus appears to have encouraged him to publish. The publication in 1526 of his *Intellectus singulares* established him as one of the leading legal scholars of Europe. (See *BR* and Kisch, *Erasmus und die Jurisprudenz*): also several articles by Steven Rowan cited in *BR*.

24) *CWE* renders the line in Erasmus' letter 'attracted by my native Germany' (4:32/220–2), but the Latin has simply *mea Germania* (Allen II, 23/216). The point is perhaps a small one, but it is nonetheless important: Erasmus came increasingly to think of himself as German (in the terms of the early 16th c. and especially of the Holy Roman Empire), but he would not have called himself a native of Germany. Cf. James D. Tracy, 'Erasmus Becomes a German', *Ren Q* 21 (1968) 281–8.

25) *CWE* 3: 32/222–227; Allen II, 23/217–221. The last phrase is an allusion to *Adagia* I. iv.62; *oleum et operam perdidi*. There is no explanation for 'the business I want to do in Italy': it is not impossible that Erasmus is now casting about for a stronger dispensation in order not to have to return to Steyn (see app. C), and that his thinking was to begin the process at Rome. However, he also had manuscripts to consult.

26) The classic essay on Erasmus and his printers is still by P. S. Allen: 'Erasmus' Relations with his Printers', *Transactions of the Bibliographical Society* 13 (1913–15) 297–321, rptd in *Erasmus* (1934) 109–37. See also Eileen Bloch, 'Erasmus and the Froben Press: The Making of an Editor', *Library Quarterly* 35 (1965) 109–20; and S. Diane Shaw, 'A Study of the Collaboration between Erasmus of Rotterdam and His Printer Johann Froben at Basel during the Years 1514 to 1527', *ERSYB* 6 (1986) 31–124.

27) See Allen, 'Erasmus and his Printers', 125; and Mynors, Introd. to *CWE* 23:125. Mynors provides a detailed analysis of the early editions.

28) On St Jerome during the Renaissance period, see Eugene F. Rice, Jr., *Saint Jerome in the Renaissance* (Baltimore, 1985; rptd 1988); for Erasmus and Jerome, John C. Olin, 'Erasmus and Saint Jerome: The Close Bond and Its Significance', *ERSYB* 7 (1987) 33–53.

29) See W. Trillitzsch, 'Erasmus und Seneca', *Philologus* 109 (1965) 270–92, and L. D. Reynolds, *The Medieval Tradition of Seneca's Letters* (Oxford, 1965) introduction.

30) Erasmus must have been a part of stop-press corrections in the printing-house, but he does not seem here or elsewhere to be cognisant of or sufficiently appreciative of consequent differences in printed texts.

31) D'Amico, *Theory and Practice in Renaissance Textual Criticism*, 16.

32) Allen, 'Erasmus' Life-Work' in *The Age of Erasmus*, 159. Rummel generalises: 'Erasmus very rarely acknowledged his mistakes and regularly offered lame excuses or half-hearted retractions' (*Erasmus and His Catholic Critics II*, 53); but this is too sweeping, at least for the full range of his writings.

33) *CWE* 3:243–4 /7–18). This is a letter redated by *CWE* to the second half of February 1516; Allen had dated in October 1515.

34) Allen, 'Erasmus' Services to Learning' in *Erasmus*, 56.

35) See the prefatory letter for the edition of *Institutio Principis Christiani*. *Pistrinum* in Erasmus' Latin is translated by *CWE* as 'treadmill'; but in medieval Latin *pistrinum* also meant *bakery* or *bakehouse*, and there were doubtless extensions of the metaphor that were current enough.

1516, the Annus Mirabilis

The next year, 1516, was the year of triumph of the Erasmian reformers.

> R.W. Chambers, *Thomas More*, 121

... yet I have had far more from you – besides an infinity of other things, one above all, that you taught me to seek the philosophy of Christ, and not to seek that only but to imitate Him, to worship Him, to love Him...

> Glareanus to Erasmus, 5 September 1516,
> Epistle 463 (*CWE* 4:69/10–12; Allen II, 341/8–11)

Greetings, my dear Erasmus, most learned of men, shall I say, or most eloquent? You have achieved such a partnership with both Venus and Minerva, such an alliance between the graces of style and universal knowledge, that all men rightly yield the palm of eloquence to you ...

> Reyner Snoy to Erasmus, 1 September 1516,
> Epistle 458 (*CWE* 4:57/2–5; Allen II, 332/1–4)

1516 was a year of many fulfilled ambitions for scholarly projects: the New Testament, the *Education of a Christian Prince*, the work on Jerome, and a couple of other lesser projects – on each of which the average scholar would have spent years. It was also a year of honours and invitations. Early in 1516 Erasmus received a call (German universities still speak of a *Ruf* or *Berufung* for the offer of a chair or a professorship) to the University of Leipzig, and in the spring the University of Ingolstadt made efforts to lure him there. Correspondents had voiced expectations of preferment in France, which included the possibility of a canonry at Tournai (and that involved a dispute between the French and English governments); and – not least – came his appointment as a member of the privy council of prince Charles, soon to become king of Spain and then Holy Roman Emperor.[1] Regarded by some historians as a sinecure,[2] this was an appointment that Erasmus took seriously enough to complete his *Institutio Principis Christiani* and dedicate it to Charles; and there are references to his seriousness of purpose. It was also the year at the end of which More's *Utopia*, on which Erasmus had expended much labour and time, was finally published. Leaving the New Testament for chapter 32, let us take up the other works in turn.

The *Institutio* or *Education* is concerned with the education of princes, but with a particular one in mind, the person to whom the work was dedicated: the young prince Charles, future Charles V, to whom Erasmus had been appointed a councillor just months earlier. While the work may be compared with profit to other treatises on statecraft of the Renaissance – obviously Machiavelli's *Prince* (written about 1513, but not published until 1532), Thomas More's *Utopia* (also published in 1516), and Claude de Seyssel's *Grant Monarchie de France* (1519) – Erasmus' *Institutio*, dedicated as it was to a sixteen-year old prince, is above all devoted to keeping clearly in view an ethical ideal for him.[3] One copy bears the date 1515 (van der Haeghen, 111), but this is a printing error (*CWE* 27/8:508/1). Erasmus asserts quite clearly twice that he did not write the work until after he had been appointed (ibid., n. 2).

Erasmus was forty-nine when he wrote the *Institutio*: at the peak of his powers, and in the process of being recognised as the intellectual leader of Europe. Not surprisingly then the work represents his mature thinking on topics of war and peace, the education of princes, and those elements which constitute the hopes of Christianity in the political world: peace, harmony, ethical values, education, and true prosperity. As always with Erasmus, we find the roots earlier: in those years leading up to 1500–1501 when he was forging his tools and clarifying his humanistic ideas. In 1498 he had addressed a long letter to Adolph, prince of Veere, a young boy of about ten. Erasmus thought the letter important enough to reprint in the *Lucubratiunculae* of 1503 (chapter 21), seeing that edition reprinted seven times in eleven years under the title, usually, of *Exhortatio ad virtutem*, or *Oratio de virtute amplectenda*. In the *Adagiorum Collectanea* of 1500 are several adages on ethics, war, peace and related subjects. In the *Panegyricus* of 1503 Erasmus addressed Philip of Burgundy directly, and the work is fulsome in its praise of the prince; but under the flattery (Erasmus himself argued more than once) was much correcting of a prince. This work too was frequently reprinted. Along with the printing of the *Institutio* in 1516 Erasmus was writing several new adages parallel in thought: the well-known *Dulce bellum inexpertis* (expanding a letter to Antoon van Bergen, Epistle 288), the *Scarabaeus quaerit aquilam*, and the *Sileni Alcibiades* – all published in 1515, and all concerned with peace and offering the possibility of arbitration as a substitute for war.

The *Institutio* thus provides a summing up of Erasmus' thoughts on the role of the prince at the end of many years of war, and at the heart of that thinking is his experience and sense of identity as a Hollander and Burgundian. In Tracy's words:

> Despite his claim to be a citizen of the world, despite sentimental ties to England, home of his dearest friends, his political views and his closest contacts with statesmen were often those of a Netherlander, or, as one might say in the sixteenth century, a 'Burgundian' from the 'landen van herwarts over' [i.e., roughly equivalent to the twentieth-century Benelux concept, Tracy notes]. When he speaks of abuses of royal power, his most biting comments are reserved for the Emperor Maximilian's rule in the Netherlands. His frequent contention that princes will sometimes 'collude' with each other to oppress their peoples by war could perhaps be ignored, were it not for the fact that he resolutely applies this conception of princely perfidy to the interpretation of a local conflict in Holland in 1517. (Tracy, *Politics of Erasmus*, 6–7)

It cannot be forgotten then that Erasmus was writing as a Netherlander, recently appointed to the Council of a young prince who had succeeded to the Netherlands possessions and the duchy of Burgundy upon the death of his father Philip in 1506, and although he lived under the 'strenuous guardianship' of Margaret as vice-regent until he was declared of age in 1515, he continued to live in the Netherlands. Nor, *pace* the many critics of Erasmus who misleadingly charge him with ignoring the world around him, may the modern reader forget that the *Institutio*

> has many references to contemporary matters in its discussions of the corruption of the laws and the law courts, the malfunctioning of the customs service, the monetary system, the difficulties of safe and convenient travel, the organization of the armies, the recommended program of road making, and sanitary engineering. (Born, *The Education*, 43)

The roots for the published work on Jerome run deeply into the past. The Brethren of the Common Life were called *Hieronymiani* because of their devotion to Jerome, and Erasmus' life interest doubtless is to be traced to this association.[4] At Steyn he read and copied all the letters of Jerome, and to Berta de Heyen (Epistle 22) he declared that Jerome was his model. At Paris, it is clear from the brief letter to Gaguin (Epistle 67), he had begun to work on Jerome, and by 1500 he was hard at work correcting the text and preparing a commentary (Epistle 138, *CWE* 1:138/45; Allen I, 321/39–40). In a number of

letters in 1500 he declared and explained his intention to restore and
edit the letters of Jerome and to write a commentary on them. To a
Lübeck merchant (identified in *BR*), Greveradus, to whom he writes
from Paris on 18 December 1500, Erasmus explained his ambition
and his scholarly effort (perhaps in the greater detail because he does
not seem to be writing to a humanist-scholar):

> Yet of course I am quite well aware what a rash enterprise I have
> taken upon myself. First of all, how difficult it will be to wipe
> away the errors which in the course of long ages have so pro-
> foundly penetrated the text. Secondly, look at the classical
> learning, the Greek scholarship, the histories to be found in
> him, and all those stylistic and rhetorical accomplishments in
> which he not only far outstrips all Christian writers, but even
> seems to rival Cicero himself. For my part at any rate, unless my
> affection for that saintly man is leading me astray, when I
> compare Jerome's prose with Cicero's I seem to find something
> lacking in even the prince of prose writers. There is in our
> author such variety, such solidity of content, such fluency of
> argument, and while it is very difficult to demonstrate this kind
> of artistry in the works of good stylists, it is nevertheless ex-
> tremely helpful. This is what I trust I may be able to do,
> provided the saint himself comes to my aid; and I hope that, as a
> result, those who have hitherto admired Jerome for his reputa-
> tion as a stylist may now admit that they never before under-
> stood the nature of his stylistic power. (*CWE* 1:309/40–55;
> Allen I, 332/35–49)

It is not so remarkable to find Erasmus extolling Jerome as a stylist
(though the comparison with Cicero, to the Roman's disadvantage, is
striking); but what is remarkable indeed is the emphasis on Jerome's
stylistic power without mentioning his other qualities.[5]

At Cambridge Erasmus taught Greek and lectured on theology,
doubtless emphasising Jerome. During the years from 1511 to 1514,
as we saw in chapter 27, he returned with renewed energy to the
edition of Jerome's letters; for the work of collating, emending,
annotating, he wrote, 'I seem to myself inspired by some god'. At
Basel Erasmus learned of the ambition of Amerbach, taken over by
Froben, to publish an edition of Jerome (begun as early as 1507) to
go along with the firm's editions of Ambrose (1492) and Augustine
(1506). Towards this end Amerbach had gathered manuscripts of
Jerome and had employed several scholars: Johann Reuchlin, Conrad
Pellican, Gregor Reisch, and Johann Kuno. At this time Erasmus
appeared on the scene in Basel, and he became more than an adviser
to the project and in fact seems to have been the general editor of it.

His own special responsibility was for the letters and other treatises by Jerome in the first four volumes of the edition. Writing to Raffaele Riario, Cardinal of San Giorgio (in Epistle 333 dated 31 May 1515 from London, and first published in the *Damiani Elegeia* of August 1515), Erasmus declared 'At least I have thrown myself into this task so zealously that one might almost say that I have worked myself to death that Jerome might live again' (*CWE* 3:90/86–8; Allen II, 71/79–81). The edition, finished in the summer of 1516, appeared on the market in late September. To echo Olin, 'one of the great ambitions of Erasmus had been realised, one of his most significant enterprises had been accomplished'.[6]

One would think that the New Testament project, the writing of the *Institutio*, the editing of Seneca and Jerome – not to mention the several hundred letters he had written by this date – would be enough for a mortal scholar to hold together and work on simultaneously during one year; but, Erasmus being Erasmus, there was more.

During 1516 he was pressing his petition for an enlarged dispensation from the pope. This necessitated not only the letter to Leo X (Epistle 446) but also, whatever its exact purpose, the letter to Grunnius (Epistle 447); and conferring with Ammonio about the tactics for obtaining the dispensation occupied a fair amount of time,[7] along with an ever-increasing volume of correspondence. In the summer of 1516, for example, a letter came from Melanchthon in the form of a Greek poem (Epistle 454); these new correspondents, like Reuchlin as well (Epistle 457), had to be answered, and Erasmus spent an ever-increasing part of each day keeping up the flow of letters to old friends.

The editing of More's *Utopia* occupied Erasmus throughout much of 1516, although it is still difficult to be precise about Erasmus' involvement in the final casting and printing of *Utopia*. But let us try.

The Louvain edition of 1516 by Dirk Martens was only the first of four early editions of *Utopia* in which Erasmus had some involvement[8] – the others being the Paris edition of 1517, and the Basel editions of March and November 1518 – but it is our immediate concern.

The genesis of the work is to be traced with certainty to 1515, to talks with humanists like Pieter Gillis while More was on a trade mission representing England in negotiations in the Low Countries, but the roots run deeper: surely back to his lectures on the *City of God* a decade earlier. Elsewhere I have tried to suggest the immediate historical and intellectual milieu in which More wrote his seminal work; surely one must also consider the currents in the universities, and the reactions to the Fifth Lateran Council, as well as works being published in the first and second decades of the new century.[9] These were years in which intellectuals everywhere felt the urgency of the times, and humanists would most likely have tried to persuade civilians and canonists of the reasonableness of their approaches to current problems. We do not stray far from the evidence within the text of *Utopia* and in the introductory letters to the successive editions of the work if we see *Utopia* at least in part as a product of months of discussion by More and the humanists he met in the Low Countries during the long months of trade negotiations. The work is a contribution to that ongoing dialogue, together with the letters from Geldenhouwer, Budé and others.

Erasmus in fact had been involved in the preparation of *Utopia* for publication from the beginning; and on 17 October 1516 he wrote to Gillis, 'I am preparing the *Utopia*' (*CWE* 4:98/7–8: 'I am getting the Nowhere ready'; Allen II, 359/5–6: 'Nusquamam adorno'). This general statement, Surtz glosses, 'could include some possible polishing of the style, the addition of some marginal notes (see the title page of the Paris edition of 1517 but see also note to 22/21 below), and, above all, the provision for commendatory letters and poems by Giles, Busleyden, etc.' (Yale edition, 267–8). All of these efforts were crucial to the success of the book.

We cannot claim co-authorship for Erasmus: *Utopia* is too much a part of More for that. But for that essential completion of moving a work from concept to text, and for the necessary business of readying a manuscript for the printer and seeing it through the press, Erasmus must be given a lion's share of the credit. Further, he was an author experienced in dealing with a printer, as More was not; and he would have known the truth of the German saying that *Ein Buch ist erst ein Buch wenn es ein Buch geworden ist* (a book is first a book when it has become a book).

Little wonder that there are so many correspondences and analogues between the *Moria* and the *Utopia*: the role of irony, the playing with the genre of the dialogue and *declamatio*, the richly allusive Latin style, and the dealing with complex ideas of power, the city, and humanism itself. The spirit of Lucian hovered over both Erasmus and More during these years as well.

Lucian, we can say, was the godfather of *Utopia*. Erasmus continued to work on the translations of Lucian that he and Thomas More had begun in 1506. Then, besides those translations which were printed in the volume of 1506, he made Latin translations of seven other Lucianic pieces, and these appeared in the edition published by

Bade in mid-1514.[10] In 1516 Aldus printed an edition of Erasmus' *Opuscula*, which is a reprint with minor changes of the 1506 text. It is not known whether 'Erasmus had been aware of Aldus' plans or was consulted about them, but a member of the firm reports that Erasmus was pleased with the book' (Thompson, lviii–lix).

During some of 1516 and continuing into 1517, Erasmus was engaged in correcting the 1514 edition. In fact, there is a copy of the 1514 edition now in the Universitätsbibliothek, Basel, which contains the familiar inscription of one of Erasmus' own books: 'Sum Erasmi', on the last leaf. Further, there are marginal corrections and additions to the text scattered throughout the volume: twenty bear on More's text, and all were adopted; about a hundred marginal annotations are in the Erasmus part of the book. Thompson concludes that the marginalia in this volume are in Erasmus' hand (lx). The result was the edition by Froben in December 1517.

In May 1516 Erasmus was on his way to the Low Countries to take up in an active way his appointment as councillor to prince Charles, and as Tracy has made clear in his perceptive book on *The Politics of Erasmus* the political events of the Netherlands form a background to his life. The business that took him briefly to London in August 1516 (Epistle 446) was the need for a new dispensation that would enable him to hold more than one benefice, since as an Augustinian canon he was still technically bound to the obligations of a canon under vows (*CWE* 4:Preface, xi). By mid-August he was in Rochester, staying with the bishop for other reasons besides Fisher's having asked for help in the study of Greek. Leaving Rochester about 24 August, Erasmus wrote to Reuchlin from Calais on the 27th (Epistle 457), having yet again crossed the Channel. To Reuchlin he wrote about the reception of the New Testament in England: 'The New Testament has made me friends everywhere, although some people protested forcibly, especially at first; but they protested only in my absence, and most of them were the sort who did not read my work, and would not understand it if they did' (*CWE* 4:57/53–7; Allen II, 331/48–51).

From Antwerp on 5 September Erasmus wrote to the Froben corrector, Wilhelm Nesen (Epistle 462, a letter accompanying the new Froben edition of *De Copia*, published in 1517) that he was revising proofs while on shipboard – that is, either on the Channel crossing or perhaps by barge from Calais to Antwerp, for Erasmus was still in Antwerp at the end of September (Epistle 470). He wrote to Busleyden that the chancellor, Le Sauvage, had summoned him again to Brussels, where he arrived not later than 6 October.

Erasmus now decided to remain in Brussels for the winter, as he announced to Ammonio (Epistle 475) and in a letter of the same date to Pieter Gillis he told of being almost made a bishop by Charles. 'All the same', he wrote, 'I thanked them for their kind feelings, warning them however not to waste vain efforts in future on any business of this sort, for I was unwilling, I said, to exchange my liberty for any bishopric however distinguished. There's a daydream for you to laugh at!' (CWE 4:96/27–30; Allen II, 357/23–4).

Despite the annuity from his appointment as councillor to Charles, Erasmus' financial security was not much better for payments of the annuity were slow in coming; and thus far there was little to show from other promises and assurances. Thus, in a long letter to Guillaume Budé (Epistle 480 from Brussels on 28 October) Erasmus complained about being able to afford only one servant for copying his letters and manuscripts:

> ... is it not somewhat inhuman, when a man is busily occupied in the copying out of great volumes and on top of that sometimes has twenty letters to write in a single day, to demand that he should take great pains over the penmanship of his letters as though he had nothing else to do? If I undertook the labour of copying out my things a second time, the burden would be much more than I could carry; if I delegated the duty to others, five servants would hardly be enough. Yet that wife of mine [poverty, as he sustains the figure through the rest of the letter], at whose expense you wax so merry, barely allows me to keep a single one; such is the hen-pecked life I lead from an imperious mistress rather than a wife. (*CWE* 4:103/28–36; Allen II, 263/25–32)

It must have been frustrating to receive a letter from Alaard of Amsterdam offering to obtain any book Erasmus might want from the library of Agricola (now in the hands of a merchant named Pompeius Otto) at a time when Erasmus could not afford to buy any books (see Epistle 485).

Finally, from Westminster Andreas Ammonio wrote to Erasmus on 4 December that the business of the dispensation had progressed to the point of having a copy of it, and a draft for the approval of Erasmus and Ammonio was to be returned to Silvestro Gigli in Rome. Letters from More gladdened the spirit of Erasmus as well.

Erasmus was busy at the 'treadmill' of Froben's factory, working with the energy of several men, and keeping a whole team busy. Yet he continued to be a moral teacher, and the letter from Glareanus written from Basel on 5 September 1516 (Epistle 463) contains these illuminating words:

A great thing indeed it was to have learnt morals from Socrates and set one's life in order under his instructions; yet I have had far more from you – besides an infinity of other things, one above all, that you taught me to seek the philosophy of Christ [*quod me Christum sapere docuisti*], and not to seek that only but to imitate Him, to worship Him, to love Him. (*CWE* 4:69/8–12; Allen II, 341/7–10)

And further on in the letter Glareanus stresses that it was not merely good letters that he learned from Erasmus, but *caritas:*

It was not eloquence or learning on which you taught me to rely, it was on truly Christian love; and accordingly I owe you a debt of gratitude the most abundant, undying, superlative and all the other long words our common throng of stylists are so fond of, and which (more to the point) I pray Christ may repay to you in view of all that you have done for me. (lines 33–37)[11]

Here is a flowering of christian humanism. In all these months of being bone-weary in work on the editions, Erasmus evidently had not lost sight of the larger goals: all his labours were towards the end of knowing and loving God, and of leading others to that philosophy of Christ as well. Erasmus had been a teacher of grammar and rhetoric in Paris (chapter 14) and of Greek and theology at Cambridge (chapter 27), and through his books he continued to be such a teacher – even, a teacher of teachers. But he was also a moral teacher, as Glareanus so vividly testifies.

Notes

1) According to Ep. 370 from van Borssele the appointment had been proposed in November 1515 (*CWE* 3:191/18: this is the first mention of Erasmus as a councillor; Allen II, 161/18); and by February 1516 he regarded himself as having actually entered upon his office (Ep. 392/15–16). It is likely, as Allen suggests (II, 161/18n) that his actual appointment is to be dated from January 1516.

2) See, e.g., Tracy, *Erasmus*, 129, citing Ep. 370. Allen dates the first proposal to Erasmus as May 1515, and late January or early February 1516 as the date by which Erasmus had entered upon his office (II, 161 n. 18). It is worth noting that the salary of 300 florins had not been paid by 1517 and Le Sauvage advanced 200 florins from his own pocket (Ep. 597/26). See *CWE* 5:9 and 63, for discussion of the transaction, which left most of the annuity unpaid.

3) One begins with the long-standard edition of Lester K. Born, *The Education of a Christian Prince* (New York, 1936), with its careful tracing of the sources for Erasmus: Isocrates, Xenophon, Plato, Aristotle, Cicero, Seneca, Suetonius, Plutarch, Dio Chrysostom, Pseudo-Sallust, Marcus Aurelius, Dio Cassius, the *Panegyrici Latini*, Julian, Synesius, Augustine, to

which must be added the patristic and medieval Isidore of Seville, John of Salisbury, Thomas Aquinas, Aegidius Romanus and others, although Cheshire and Heath question whether Erasmus made any use of medieval writings on the subject (*CWE* 27:508/6). The Latin text has been well edited with full noting of sources by Otto Herding in *ASD* IV–1 (1974); and there is now an English translation, with introductory note by Neil M. Cheshire and Michael J. Heath (in *CWE* 27).

4) Allen II, 210. Part of the devotion of the Brethren was in their study of Jerome (see ch. 5 above).

5) Indicating that nothing is known of the name *Greveradus*, Allen suggests that it is perhaps a local name derived from *Greverath*, a small town about 25 m. NE of Trier, and that the person seems to have resided near Paris and to be something of a scholar; but it seems equally valid to perceive the recipient as not a scholar (although there were many religious institutions in and around Trier). However, the letter concludes with an invitation to join 'this splendid enterprise' (ll. 65–6), but what kind of collaboration or aid is not specified: it may be an early letter to a potential patron: see *BR*.

6) John C. Olin, 'Erasmus and Saint Jerome: The Close Bond and Its Significance', *ERSYB* 7 (1987) 41.

7) There is a cluster of letters to and from Ammonio in 1516, and in Ep. 453 from Ammonio to Erasmus (c. 19 August 1516) Erasmus is reassured: 'on that business of yours, nothing has occurred to me beyond what we agreed on. That fiction of yours [the letter to Grunnius?] I approve without reserve; and about who is to take charge of it, I urge you as they say, not to lose a wink of sleep ...' (*CWE* 4:40/15–18). 'A wink of sleep': cf. *Adag.* I. viii. 19.

8) Edward Surtz has given an account of each of the first four editions in the edition of *Utopia* by himself and J.H. Hexter: vol. 4 in the *Collected Works of St Thomas More* (New Haven, Conn., 1965) clxxxiii–cxc). To the Basel edition of March 1518 Erasmus added his own preface dated 25 August: Epistle 635, CWE 5:82–83; Allen III, 56–7.

9) See 'The Intellectual Milieu of More's *Utopia*', *Moreana* 1 (1963) 40–6; and the article on *Utopia* as a humanistic masterpiece (48–55).

10) See Craig R. Thompson, *Translations of Lucian*, vol. III.1 in *Complete Works of St Thomas More* (1974) lv–lviii.

11) Erasmus' Latin original for 'truly Christian love' is *'amori vere Christiano'* (Allen II, 341/30) – a more active expression.

1. Portrait of Sir Thomas More in 1527 by Hans Holbein the Younger.
(Reproduced with permission of The Frick Collection, New York.)

2. Portrait of Pieter Gillis in 1517 by Quentin Metsys. This portrait is part
of the diptych which Erasmus sent to Sir Thomas More in September 1517
(see chapter 33). The companion piece, of Erasmus himself, is to be found in
Volume 1. (Private collection: Courtauld Institute of Art.)

    Gillis was a friend of both More and Erasmus. Here he is seen holding a
letter from More, and with his forefinger resting on Erasmus' *Antibarbari*, a
work evidently known in 1517 but not published until 1520.

3. Portrait of Martin Luther in 1525 by Lucas Cranach. (Reproduced with permission of the Öffentliche Kunstsammlung of the Kunstmuseum, Basel.)

Gramaticis qnq genera, qnq casus, et qnq deuotiones.

uotionibus. Allusit autem ad Graecu Epigrama, quod iocatur Gramaticis esse, τῶϊ τ ϱυκ πεντε πωσας καὶ πεντε καταρας.i. quinꝗ genera, qnꝗ casus, & qnꝗ deuotiones, ob quinꝗ primos uersus Homericos, quorum primus incipit a μῆνιν, quod iram significat. Secundus, ουλομενlυ, qd ꝑ nicie significat, habet & μυρια αλγεα.i. innuceros dolores. Tertius, anias mittit ad inferos. Quartus, canu laniatione, Quintus, auium, & iram Iouis. Atꝗ his auspicijs ingrediuntur suum munus. Epigra-

Tyrānis ludi magistro rum.

q tantum diris obnoxij sutt isti, queadmodum indicat epigrama graecum, uerum sexcentis, ut qui semper famelici, sordidiꝗ in ludis illis suis, in ludis dixi, imo in φροντιςκριοιε, uel pistrinis potius, ac carnificinis, inter puerorꝛ greges, cosenescant laboribus, obsurdescat clamorib9, fetore paedoreꝗ cotabescant, tame meo beneficio fit, ut sibi primi mortaliu esse uideant, Adeo sibi placet, dum pauida turba, minaci uultu uoceꝗ, territant, du ferulis, uirgis, lorisꝗ coscindut miseros, dumꝗ modis omibus suo arbitratu, saeuiut, asinum illum Cumanu imitantes, interim sordes illae, merae munditiae uidetur, paedor amaricinu olet, miserrima
illa seruit9

ma autem est libro primo Palladae titulo huiusmodi, Αρχη γραμματικης πεντασιχος οσι καθαρα πρωτ, μῆνιν εχ{ε} δευτερ, ουλομενlιυ και μετ τα δ ουλομενlιυ, δαναῶν παλιν αλγεα πολλα. ο ξιτατ, ψυχας εις αδι δκρ καθαγ τω δ{ε} πταρταις τα ελωρια, ε κανες αργοι πεμπτ, οιωνοι, κη χολ οσι διος πως ουν γραμματικος δυναη μετα πεντε καθαρας κη πεϊ τ πωσης, μη μεγα πενθ εχειη.i.Principium grammatices, quinꝗ uersi-
bus contenta, est deuotio. Primus iram habet, secundus pniciosam. Et post perniciosam, Graecorum rursum dolores multos. Tertius animas in infer-
nu deducit. Quarti aut, tractus, & canes ueloces. Quinti, aues, & ira est Io-
uis. Quomo igit Gramaticus pot post qnꝗ execratioes, et qnꝗ casus, no magnu luctu habere? In φροντιςκριοιε, Aristophanes, ϊν νεφελαις, Socratis schola uocat φροντιςκριου, qsi dicas solicitudinis locu, qd illic tristes ac cogi-
tabundi sederent. Et Socrates dicere cosueuit, φροντισου, hoc est cogita, hoc dicto adhortans, ad diligete rei cosyderatione. Asinu illu Cumanu) Is re-
pertu leonis exuuiu, adaptarat corpori suo, atꝗ ita leo creditus, timebatur.
Donec quida ex auriu, pminentiu inditio, sensit asinu esse, deinde fuste cotu-
sus, ad stabulum reductus est. Amaricinu olet.) De compositione ungenti Amaricini, quod & sansucinu uocant, uide Diascoridem in primo. Hoc Pli-
nius in de

Phrontisterium.

Asinus Cumanus.

Amaricinu suauissimi odoris unguenti e. Un proueri:: Nihil nisi amaricino sui.

4. *The tyranny of a schoolmaster*. This and the following illustration are from the earliest known drawings by Hans Holbein the Younger, in the margin of a copy of the 1515 edition of *In Praise of Folly*, printed in Basel by Froben. The volume belonged to the humanist Myconius.

ac uelut umbra quædã, fit ut præmij quoq; illi⁹ aliqñ guſtũ,
aut odoré aliqué ſentiãt. Id tãetſi minutiſſima quædã ſtillu
la eſt ad fonté illũ æternæ felicitatis, tñ longe ſupat uniuer⸗
ſas corpis uoluptates, etiã ſi oés omniũ mortaliũ delitiæ in
unũ cõferant. Vſq; adeo præſtãt ſpiritalia corpalib⁹, inuiſi⸗
bilia uiſibilib⁹. Hoc nimirũ eſt, qd pollicet̃ ꝓpheta, oculus
nõ uidit, nec auris audiuit, nec in cor hois aſcédit, quæ præ⸗
parauit deus diligétibus ſe. Atq; hæc eſt Moriæ pars, quæ
nõ aufert̃ cõmutatióe uitæ, ſed pficit̃. Hoc igit̃ qbus ſentire
licuit (cõtingit aũt ꝓpaucis) ij patiunt̃ qddã demétiæ ſimilli
mũ, loquũtur quædã nõ ſatis cohærétia, nec humano mo⸗
re, ſed dant ſinc méte ſonũ, deinde ſubinde totã oris ſpecié
uertũt, Nũc alacres, nũc deiecti, nũc lachrymãt, nũc rident,
nũc ſuſpirãt, in ſũma uere toti extra ſe ſunt. Mox ubi ad ſe
ſe redierint, negãt ſe ſcire, ubi fuerint, utrũ in corpe, an extra
corp⁹, uigilãtes, an dormiétes, qd audierint, qd uiderint, qd
dixerint, qd fecerint, nõ meminerũt, niſi tãq̃ p nebulam, ac
ſomniũ, tantũ hoc ſciunt, ſe feliciſſimos fuiſſe, dũ ita deſipe
rét. Itaq; plorãt ſeſe reſipuiſſe, nihilq; omniũ malint q̃ hoc
inſaniæ genus ꝓpetuo inſanire. Atq; hæc eſt futuræ felicita
tis tenuis quædã deguſtatiuncula. Verũ ego iãdudũ oblita
mei ὑπὲρ τὰ ἐσϰαμμένα πηδῶ. Quãtq̃; ſiq d petulãtius aut loqua
cius a me dictũ uidebit̃, cogitate & ſtulticiã, & mulierem di
xiſſe. Sed interim tñ memineritis illius Græcanici puerbij,
πολλάϰιοι ϰαὶ μωρὸς ἀνὴρ ϰαʈαϰαίριον ἔιπεμ. Niſi forte putatis hoc
ad mulieres nihil attinere. Video uos epilogũ expectare,
ſed nimiũ deſipitis, ſi qdé arbitramini me qd dixerim etiã
dũ meminiſſe. Cũ tantã uerborũ farraginé effuderim. Ve⸗
tus illud, μισῶ μνάμονα συμπόταμ. Nouũ hoc, μισῶ μνάμονα ἀϰρο⸗
ατὼ, Quare ualete, plaudite, uiuite, bibite, Moriæ celeberri⸗
mi Myſtæ.   MΩPIAΣ EΓϰΩMIΩN Feliciter abſolutum.

5. *Folly leaving the pulpit*. Pen-and-ink drawing by Hans Holbein the
Younger (see Figure 4).

6. Autograph letter from Erasmus to the reformer Ulrich Zwingli, May 1516. The original is in the Staatsarchiv, Zürich (Ms. E. II. 360), with whose permission it is here reproduced.

7. Erasmus' living-room at Basel. (Reproduced with permission of the Historischesmuseum, Basel.)

8. An early Dutch printing-press (engraving by J. Luiken, 1705, in possession of the author).

The New Testament: a Life Work

Holy Scripture is above all other books, not only by its authority because it is divine, or by its utility because it leads to
eternal life, but also by its antiquity and by its literary form.
Bede, *De Schematibus et Tropis*
(*Rhetores Latini Minores*, ed. C. Halm, 1863, 607)

The Bible was the most studied book of the Middle Ages.
Beryl Smalley, *The Study of the Bible in the Middle Ages*
(1978) xi

Textual criticism and Christian doctrine stand in a complex
and reciprocal relation, as a striking epitome of the delicate
balance between scholarship and theology.
Jarislav Pelikan, *The Melody of Theology* (1988) 248

Erasmus devoted half his life, and more, to the study of the New
Testament; and many moderns would ask why? To the believing
Christian, textual criticism of the New Testament – which may be
said to have been founded by Origen in the third century AD, and
greatly advanced first by Valla in the fifteenth century and then by
Erasmus in the early sixteenth century – is necessary because of the
thousands of variants to be found in existing manuscripts and versions of differing age and authenticity. Textual criticism is important for christian theology first in contributing to the determination
of the canon of the Bible: what belongs in the Bible and what does
not (although the authority for that determination is not exclusively
a matter of textual scholarship). Textual criticism also helps the
believing Christian to know what the New Testament says, and it
thus guides him to understand what it means. And from this massive
scholarly effort, Erasmus felt, there would be a reforming of the
individual and of Christendom.[1] But an account of Erasmus' life-
work must begin with the patristic and medieval traditions of the
Bible.

The importance of the Bible in the Middle Ages cannot be over-
stated, though the manner of its filtering into the life of the
lay-person can be misconstrued and questions of interpretation not

perceived clearly enough.[2] From the time of the early Church until that of Erasmus, the Gospels and Epistles entered into the liturgical life of the clergy and indeed the whole of the people, and parts of the Old Testament were regularly read in the Mass and other services; the Psalms especially were an integral part of the medieval fabric, and there were some besides the religious who knew them by heart. One sees the imbedding of the Bible in sermons and homilies, and especially in the Latin hymns and sequences; and after the early thirteenth century (in part because of the Fourth Lateran Council, and in part because of the rise of the friars), in an increasing number of translations and adaptations in verse, prose and drama. There was as well the visual presentation in the frescoes and stained-glass windows of the churches, in the carved altars, pews, and other parts of the church buildings; and of course there were the magnificent carvings in stone over the doors of the larger churches and cathedrals. One could not escape the Bible and its teachings.

Yet the Bible was not a simple text. There were books of different composition and genre, and there was the complex relationship of the New Testament to the Old. Interpretation of the Vulgate Bible, therefore, occupied a central place in the intellectual life of the whole of the Middle Ages, everywhere in Christendom.[3] Failure to understand all that a writer like Erasmus could take for granted often creates an even greater distancing between the modern reader and the correspondent or reader of Erasmus' age. An adage like the '*Ne Bos Quidem Pereat*', for illustration,[4] depends for the fullness of its meaning upon the reader's recognition of the scriptural source and context (as well as the traditional interpretation) of the figure of the maidservant that so powerfully concludes the adage:

> Let them warn, and help, and correct, as a conscientious maidservant warns, and helps, and corrects her mistress. Theology is by rights the queen of all the sciences, but she will have more honour and more learning if she receives such useful waiting-women with proper kindliness into her household. (trans. by Phillips, *The 'Adages'*, 380)

In the Breviary and elsewhere in the liturgy, Psalm 122 (123) is recited or chanted (antiphonally, in some orders, when it is part of the Office); and the prayer that begins with an act of humble submission and rises to a prayer for help, is widened by the figure of the conscientious maidservant who offers a warning, a kind of parrhesia: correction for the theologians of the times. The adage was added to the *Adagiorum Chiliades* of 1526, perhaps the high-water mark in the flood of controversies in which Erasmus was involved for a decade of attack and criticism.

Inside the churches – in the liturgical life of the Church, in the visual renderings of the Bible and its stories in windows and statues and other carvings, as well as in sermons and prayers – and outside the churches, in pageants, mystery-plays and moralities, and in the private or family prayers within the home: the teaching of the Bible was never far away from the pious. Many laymen and laywomen knew large portions of it by heart. The Bible was not the exclusive province of the clergy.[5]

'The Bible was the most studied book of the Middle Ages', so Beryl Smalley begins her magisterial book, *The Study of the Bible in the Middle Ages*; and, she continues, 'bible study represented the highest branch of learning.' So Bede, and Boniface, as captured in a ninth-century hermit poem: they must have seen

   ... bright candles
  over the holy white scriptures.

We must add, Smalley concludes her first paragraph, 'the host of obscurer persons, the monks, canons, friars, and secular masters who expounded Scripture in the cloister or the school. Their biblical commentaries and aids to study account for a good proportion of the monastic or cathedral library'.[6]

For convenience one may separate two overlapping and inter-twined, yet distinguishable, traditions in the later Middle Ages: that of the universities, and that of the monasteries and other religious institutions. Within the medieval schools the Bible was the pre-scribed 'set book' for theologians, and a student wishing to become a master of theology (after the universal arts course) had to attend lectures on the *sacra pagina* (sacred page) as well as fulfil statutory obligations for those academic functions which supplemented the lecture, that is, the university sermon and disputation (chapter 11). In all of this the Bible played its part: in furnishing texts and quotations, if nothing more. But even before his theological studies the student, so often a member of a religious community, would have been prepared for further Bible studies by much Bible reading, both communally and in private. (See chapters 5, 11 and 13.)

Within the institutions of the professed religious there were dif-ferences. Among those orders 'friendly to learning' – the Benedic-tines (especially earlier), the Victorines, the Dominicans and the Franciscans (the two major orders of friars) – there was a scholarly or 'scientific' (in the European sense) study of the Bible, at least (now speaking of the late fifteenth and early sixteenth centuries) in theory; and (as Smalley observes, xv), such orders produced biblical scholars. But when a religious community distrusted learning (as was the case with the Brethren of the Common Life, as we have seen in chapter 5

and appendix B), the reading of the Bible was of a very different
kind: 'its reading was 'holy' without being 'serious' in a scientific
sense' (Smalley, xv). This kind of Bible reading, as distinguished
from a scholarly study of the Bible, has been described at Steyn in the
1490s (chapter 5). Unless new manuscripts are discovered to dis-
prove present conclusions,[7] one may rather sharply divide Erasmus'
study of the Bible into two quite distinct periods. Up to and including his years at the monastery at Steyn, he lived, worked, prayed and
studied with men whose calling it was to read the Bible and to
meditate upon it – no one can question the dedication of a Thomas à
Kempis to such a life of study. But it was never their intention to
question the text, and indeed that was hardly to be permitted, for the
manuscript-oriented Windesheim congregation felt that it already
had a 'perfect' copy of the Vulgate. Only rarely, it seems, was there
serious study of the Bible, for there are no major traditions of biblical
commentary among the Brethren of the Common Life or the Augustinian Canons of the Windesheim congregation. Erasmus' second
period of Bible study began at Paris in 1495; but I have already
suggested limitations in the study of the Bible at that time in the
universities (chapters 11 and 13). Much of the energy for such study
was given to lectures and commentaries on Lombard's *Sentences*,
rarely to whole books of the Bible or to textual problems, and there is
little indication of critical commentary or textual interest before
about 1500. Jacques Lefèvre d'Etaples, whose road of scriptural studies so interestingly parallels yet differs from that of Erasmus, was
still at the end of his life learning from the rich resources of the
Abbey of St Victor in Paris (on which, as a major centre for scriptural
studies, see Smalley, xvii and her chapters III and IV). Erasmus' Paris
years were scarcely more than a bridge from Brethren of the Common Life and Windesheim traditions to his mature biblical scholarship; the real crossing-over, in terms of scholarship and critical
attitude towards the biblical text, must be marked by his discovery
of Valla's *Adnotationes* in 1504 (chapter 21). After his reading of
Valla for method as much as for inspiration, his future work on the
New Testament soon became clearly charted.

   Until the end of the fifteenth century, then, there was a con-
tinuum of patristic and medieval biblical scholarship,[8] but one faith-
fully reflecting (as Bentley has written) 'medieval assumptions, values, and doctrines'.[9] The effort of humanist scholars during the
Renaissance was a double one: to understand the Greek of the Gospels and Epistles, and to 'recover or reconstruct the assumptions,
values, and doctrines not of the Middle Ages but of the earliest
Christians' (Bentley, 31). It was an historical as well as philological

effort, but the best philology has always been historical.

Perhaps the most widely and most popularly known scriptural exegete at the end of the Middle Ages was Nicholas of Lyra (1270–1340), criticised yet used by Erasmus. Nicholas of Lyra was a French Franciscan who taught at the Sorbonne, and he was remarkable for his knowledge of Hebrew and the rabbinical tradition, particularly the eleventh-century scholar Rashi. 'It is plain', Smalley observes, 'that Lyra represents the culmination of a movement for the study of Hebrew and rabbinics. He owed much to the past' (355). His highly esteemed *Postillae* was the first biblical commentary to be printed (Rome, 1471–2, a folio of five volumes), thereby making his distillation of older commentators and his emphasis on the literal-historical meaning more widely available to Erasmus, Luther, and others. There is a well-known medieval distich which has little historical validity (it has in fact been called a *dicton absurde*), but it points to Lyra's historical importance and calls attention to his implications for the Reformation, as his much-reprinted and often-cited work merited:

> *Si Lyra non lyrasset,*
> *Lutherus non saltasset.* (Smalley, xvi)[10]

Nicholas had as his prime concern an exact understanding of the literal sense of Scripture, 'and at the beginning of his *Postillae*, which were a recognised supplement to the *Glossa Ordinaria* and printed along with it in a number of early editions, he declares:

> The beginning of Genesis is involved in many extremely difficult matters, and their obscurity is proved by the variety and the number of interpretations offered by Jewish and Christian scholars. And, since confusion of this sort is harmful to understanding and memory alike, I propose to avoid this multitude of interpretations and in particular those which seem remote from the literal sense, since it is this sense which I propose to stress in accordance with the grace which the Lord has bestowed upon me.[11]

It is striking that the main thrust of medieval Biblical commentators was on the Old, and not the New, Testament.

Unquestionably the pioneer in the new humanistic study of the New Testament was Lorenzo Valla (see chapters 9 and 21), whose study of the Bible paralleled his original studies in other areas: the relation between dialectic and rhetoric (arguing in his *Dialectical Disputations* that dialectic, so supreme in medieval scholasticism, ought to be subordinated to rhetoric); traditional moral teaching (in his *De Vera Bono* arguing that traditional ascetic moral teaching could benefit

from Epicurean teaching, however ironical he meant to be, or however christian Valla's interpretation of Epicurus was understood to
be); conventional scholarship and teaching in Roman law; monastic
vows, where he argued (on philological as well as theological
grounds) that laymen might be at least as pious as monks. Valla's
notes on his study of the New Testament manifest the same independence of thought, not least because he was not a doctor of theology and yet he was writing on the problem of understanding and
interpreting the New Testament.[12] He was of course primarily a
philologist, but one who felt that a mastery of philology qualified
him to read, annotate and interpret all kinds of texts.

Erasmus' discovery of the *Adnotationes* of Valla in 1504 (chapter
21) crystallised his thinking about the questions of biblical interpretation which had been discussed with Colet in 1499 and with Vitrier
two years later (chapters 15 and 19), and his perhaps still vaguely
formulated ambitions took more concrete shape. Put quite simply,
'Erasmus was so deeply influenced by the *Adnotationes* that he devoted much of his career to the task of developing, refining, and
extending Valla's methods' (Bentley, 69).

Erasmus had of course known Valla's *Elegantiae Linguae Latinae* –
that erudite essay on Latin words and the proper use of them, working
with meanings and nuances and forms of individual words, and facing
up to problems in philology at least as early as his monastery years
(chapter 5) before going to Paris; at which time he announced himself
rather fiercely as a defender of Valla. But it is with the *Adnotationes* that
we are here concerned, and in recalling his edition of it in 1505 we
must give credit to Erasmus for his courage in publishing such a work:
the preface to that edition is something of an apologia, but it significantly recognises that there will be instant opposition to Valla's
method. That preface, Epistle 182 to Christopher Fisher, is vital to our
understanding the link between Erasmus and Valla:

> But, it will be said, it is sinful to change anything in the Holy
> Scriptures; for no jot and tittle therein is without some special
> import. On the contrary: ‚the sin of corruption is greater, and
> the need for careful revision by scholars greater also, where the
> source of corruption was ignorance: but it must be done with
> the caution and restraint with which all books, and particularly
> the Holy Scriptures, deserve to be treated. (*CWE* 2:95/179–
> 184; Allen I, 411/158–162)

Until 1505 Erasmus had been prepared for the study of the Bible by
the medieval traditions of Steyn and Paris; after 1505 his master was
Valla, strengthened by years of study and editing of Jerome and
other Church Fathers.[13]

Everything, as McConica puts it, 'points to the fact that it was this received Latin text – the Vulgate – which was the final object of Erasmus' concern. The road to it led, therefore, through Jerome' (*Erasmus*, 35). His work of so many years on the letters of Jerome was, as we shall see further, thus no detour or evasion of a long-standing commitment to devote the rest of his life to the study of the Bible: it was a necessary propaedeutic for a humanist who wanted to edit the text of the Vulgate.

When Erasmus arrived in Basel in mid-August of 1514 he carried with him precious cargo. He was weighed down with his books and manuscripts that included his revision of Jerome's letters, his commentary on Seneca, revisions of and additions to the *Adagia*, some translations which included Plutarch, the book called *Parabolae*, and extensive notes on the New Testament text. He could not have known in advance the fullness of Froben's response to his proposal for work on the New Testament, though doubtless there was some correspondence (either direct or through an intermediary) which led Erasmus to make the journey to Basel. That there had been negotiations is indicated by the statement of Beatus Rhenanus, on whatever grounds, made on 2 September, so soon after Erasmus' arrival in Basel, that there was an agreement between them: '*Novum Testamentum Graece hic imprimet Frobenius cum annotationibus illius*'.[14] But the idea of the Greek New Testament seems likely to have been added after his arrival in Basel.

In May of 1515 Erasmus described a less ambitious work to cardinal Grimani (Epistle 334):

> Next summer I intend to issue various not unprofitable annotations of mine (or so I think them) on the New Testament, together with my version of the apostolic Epistles, designed to make them intelligible; a task which I have performed in such a way that, even after Lorenzo Valla and that learned and industrious man Jacques Lefevre, I hope I may be thought to have had good reason to undertake it ... (*CWE* 3:98/172–8; Allen II, 78/164–170)[15]

But this passage clearly describes the pre-Basel stage of the planned work, that is, without a Greek text; for in his letter to Wimpheling on 21 September 1514 Erasmus described a work that combined his Latin version with a Greek text and annotations (Epistle 305/228–9). Clearly the work had grown (as Erasmus' works so characteristically did), doubtless because of the suggestion, possibly even the insistence, of Froben that a Greek text be incorporated in the edition. Another element in this complicated picture is the death of Aldus on 6 February 1515, which doubtless strengthened Erasmus' resolve to proceed with Froben as the printer of his New Testament. Further, while Erasmus was in England in April 1515 Froben apparently obtained a copy of Erasmus' complete Latin translation of the New Testament; thus, by the time Erasmus returned again to Basel decisions about publisher and composition of the volume were made firm.[16]

For our present discussion what is important is Erasmus' notes on the New Testament, which were on the Vulgate but were consistently, and increasingly, keyed to Greek texts.[17] In this work Erasmus was manifestly following in the footsteps of Valla, but his effort was more extensive, more constant, and far more painstaking. Rummel has conjectured that when Froben saw Erasmus' notes on the New Testament he moved at once to a further and grander plan: to include the Greek text of the New Testament along with Erasmus' annotations. Aldus had projected a New Testament in Greek and Latin, but without completing the project;[18] and both Erasmus and Froben knew of that projected edition. Froben doubtless saw the possibility of demonstrating his capacity to set up in type an important Greek text – for a Christian the most important of all – and saw this as a way to bring special fame to his press.[19] For Erasmus it was a challenge to bring to fruition both his annotating of the Vulgate and his Greek studies and years of consulting Greek manuscripts.

Froben's enthusiastic response led consequently to modifications in Erasmus' planned New Testament work. When he arrived in Basel, Erasmus intended to publish the Vulgate text of the New Testament together with his annotations on that text. Erasmus' annotations were neither translations nor paraphrases,[20] nor were they the early commentaries that he envisaged; these 'seem not to have survived, except insofar as Erasmus might have included them in his later works' (Bentley, 115). Erasmus' annotations depended upon a thorough knowledge of Greek, and they could have been begun only after he achieved that level of competence in Greek, that is, not earlier than 1506 (chapter 22). But from about 1507, while in Italy, Erasmus began to study and collate a number of Greek manuscripts. In early 1506, however, he appears to have made his own fresh translation of the Greek New Testament – he had always advocated translation as a teaching aid – and this translation was copied by the scribe Pieter Meghen in 1506 and apparently again in 1509, according to the colophons; but Erasmus did not publish this translation until 1519, in the second edition of the New Testament, replacing the Vulgate.[21]

We recall that in July 1514 Erasmus had written to Servatius

Rogers: 'I have also revised the whole of the New Testament from a collation of Greek manuscripts and ancient manuscripts and have annotated over a thousand places, [adding with dry but barbed irony] with some benefit to theologians' (*CWE* 2:300/164–6; Allen I, 570/155–7).[22]

For his work of collation in England Erasmus had available to him four Greek manuscripts, one of which was the Leicester Codex (Codex 69) of the entire New Testament (see Epistles 264/16, 270/67, and *LB* IX 986E-F: '*in codice, unde contuli in Anglia*'.)[23] In Basel Erasmus had additional manuscripts. The five he primarily used are listed below; all are now in the Öffentliche Bibliothek der Universität Basel (*CWE* 3:219):

AN III 11 Omont Nr 11 (Pauli Epistolae) 7p
AN IV 1 Omont Nr 7 (Evangelia IV) 2e
AN IV 2 Omont Nr 8 (Nov. Test. praeter Apoc.) 1eap
AN IV 4 Omont Nr 9 (Acta et Epist. Apost.) 2ap
AN IV 5 Omont Nr 10 (Acta et Epist. Apost.) 4ap

In addition, Erasmus borrowed another manuscript from Reuchlin for the text of Revelations: the 'Codex Capnionis' (1. r; in Schloss Harburg, Donauwörth, Üttingen-Wallersteinsche Bibliothek 1.1.40.1). But this last manuscript lacked the final leaf, which contained the final six verses (22: 16–21) of the text of Revelations; to complete the text he translated the missing verses from the Vulgate into Greek.[24] Curiously, most of Erasmus' own notes for the printer in his first edition of the Greek New Testament did not find their way into the edition: 'some of them the printers either ignored or modified, possibly on later instructions of Erasmus or his collaborators, Gerbel and Oecolampadius' (Bentley, 131). Printers and editors alike were working under great pressure.

Mistakes there were in the first edition of 1516, but Erasmus did not rest his editorial oars; for the rest of his life he continued to consult new manuscripts and to collate their variant readings. Some of this was done in the Low Countries while preparing the text for the second edition;[25] he noted thousands of variants, in both the Latin and Greek texts, and for his third edition of 1522 he consulted the Aldine 1518 edition of the Greek and occasionally cited it. From this edition onwards, Erasmus increasingly applied variant readings from his study of Patristic texts. Although he never saw the very important Codex Vaticanus, he made use of collations by Bombasio and Sepulveda (Epistles 1213, 2873). He knew the truth of the old dictum that the manuscript librarian at the Bibliotheca Nazionale in Florence told an initiate in manuscript studies in 1968: 'One is never finished'.

Returning to the work for the first edition, we may note Epistle 322 of January 1515 to Willibald Pirckheimer, which tersely summarises Erasmus' work in progress; and of the New Testament he writes, 'I have corrected the whole New Testament and added notes' (*CWE* 3:60/25–6; Allen II, 47/25–6). For the Basel manuscripts with which he worked we can begin with the important Greek text of the New Testament he had asked Reuchlin for (Epistle 300, August 1514, which also asked that Reuchlin allow Froben to have access to it). This letter is also important evidence that very soon after his arrival in Basel Erasmus had added the idea of printing the Greek New Testament text: 'I have written annotations on the entire New Testament, and so have now in mind to print the New Testament in Greek with my comments added' (*CWE* 3:7/33–4; Allen II, 4/31–5/33). To emphasise the central point: very soon after arriving in Basel Erasmus modified his project, for until then he had not planned an edition of the Greek text.

On 30 August 1515 Erasmus felt able to report to Wolsey (Epistle 348) that the New Testament was in the press: 'In the press also is the New Testament in Greek, as it was written by the apostles, and in Latin, as translated by me, together with my notes' (*CWE* 3:168/13–4; Allen II, 137/10–2). But this was optimism on Erasmus' part, for on 11 September Gerbel wrote from Strasbourg (Epistle 352) that the business of the production was just then being worked out: 'the arrangement of the page, the type faces, and the order in which you have thought best to print it, with columns corresponding to one another, so that everything is mingled together, Greek-Latin and Latin-Greek' (*CWE* 3:172/8–11; Allen II, 140/5–141/9). Erasmus had wanted the texts in parallel columns, and he won out. But, as he told Pieter Gillis at the end of September, printing had to be interrupted in September because of a lack of proof-readers (Epistle 356). On 2 October (Epistle 360) Erasmus wrote to Ammonio that work had been resumed: 'They have started on the New Testament at last. I can neither stay here to face the intolerable reek of their hothouses [*ob intolerabilem nidorem aestuariorum*], nor go away with so much work on hand which cannot possibly be finished without me' (*CWE* 3:181/3–6; Allen II, 149/2–5).

Subsequent letters complain of the work. To Zasius in October (Epistle 366) he wrote, 'I am almost overwhelmed with work and so badly caught in the double pressure of Jerome and the New Testament that I think Hercules had less trouble with his hydra and his crab' (*CWE* 3:187/3–6; Allen II, 157/2–5). In a long letter to Budé the following summer (Epistle 421, mid-June 1516), Erasmus wrote an explanation that confirms our present interpretation, declaring that he had been encouraged by certain people 'to change the Vulgate text by either correcting or explaining it' (*CWE* 3:305/51–2; Allen II, 253/ 46–48); and Allen's explanation holds firmly the interpretation that originally he had not thought to publish his Latin version with a Greek text and that this change had required much additional work. For this decision he put the blame on members of Froben's team, namely Gerbel, Oecolampadius and Beatus Rhenanus. Besides, he takes pains to explain to Budé, he had to take upon himself the final checking of forms (the type secured in the chase and ready for printing): 'I was already weary and well-nigh exhausted when I came to the annotations' (*CWE* 3:306/72–3; Allen II, 254/67).

Erasmus' revisions and his expanded annotations moved through the clattering presses of Froben, and on 3 February he wrote to Wimpheling (Epistle 385) that 'the New Testament is hastening to its finish' (*CWE* 3:225/4; Allen II, 187/2–3). At long last he wrote in Epistle 394 on 7 March 1516 to Urbanus Regius, 'The New Testament is published' (*CWE* 3:252/38; Allen II, 209/36): a folio volume of approximately a thousand pages had been revised extensively and seen through the two presses of Foben in six months. The Toronto editors note in *CWE* (3:216n) that a copy reached Budé in Paris on 26 April (Epistle 403), and a week later the work was for sale in the Paris market (Epistle 403) and Reuchlin found the book at the Frankfurt spring fair (Epistle 418).

Despite the herculean efforts in producing and helping to print the first edition, almost at once Erasmus set to work making corrections for a new edition of the New Testament (Epistles 417, 421). The second edition appeared in 1519 with some 400 changes, and for this Erasmus revised the Greek text, and revised it again for the third edition of 1522, again published by Froben. The fourth edition by Froben in 1527 is regarded by many as the definitive text; but there was a fifth edition in the year 1535, which seems to some scholars to contain only minor alterations to the fourth, but some of those alterations are interesting.[26]

Erasmus lamented that this first edition had been rushed into print rather than edited with care ('*Novum Testamentum praecipitatum est verius quam aeditum*': Epistle 402 to Ellenborg, from Basel, April 1516), Allen adding that nonetheless in this kind of work he was superior to all his predecessors (II, 226/1–2). A year later, in Epistle 694 to Pirckheimer (from Louvain, 2 November 1517) he repeated his words about the haste with which it had been printed: '*Novum Testamentum quod pridem Basilae praecipitatum fuit verius quam editum*' (Allen III, 117/17–8).

Let us sum up Erasmus' New Testament work by looking very briefly at his title, the role of the Greek, the nature of the annotations and their quality, and the Latin version by Erasmus. (The *Paraphrases* came later and are to be considered separately.)

When it first appeared, Erasmus' work was called *Novum Instrumentum,*[27] a bold title which contributed no doubt to the challenging by unfriendly critics of some of Erasmus' textual readings, as well as the notes and the Latin translation. For the second edition of 1519 Erasmus gave up the much-criticised title. Changes in the 1522 and 1527 editions, the third and the fourth, were in part in response to the barbs of his critics (and these will be discussed in the context of those controversies, in chapters 34 and 39); but the changes were in large part also owing to Erasmus' continuing work with Greek manuscripts.

For all its faults, and despite the hostility of some modern classical scholars, Erasmus' Greek text remained the established text: it was the *textus receptus* for the great edition of the French scholar-printer Robert Estienne in 1550,[28] and it was not challenged or 'castigated' until the late-nineteenth-century labours of Tischendorf, Westcott and Hort to restore the original Greek text on principles of sound textual scholarship. The consensus of current scholarship on the role of the Greek in the 1516 edition is summed up by M.A. Screech's penetrating observation that 'inside the volume the Greek original plays much the same role as the *Annotations* alone were originally intended to do: to justify the improvements and emendations to the Latin Vulgate' (*Annotations*, xix).

What are properly speaking the *Annotations* of Erasmus are very full notes: extremely varied, and often quite copious – amounting, in effect, to a modern commentary (although Erasmus himself maintained that they should not be considered such; *CWE* 3:198/14). Justifying his attention to minutiae (might he not today repeat the Warburg dictum that God is in detail?), he wrote in his Preface to the Reader:

> If Christ's sayings survived in Hebrew or Syriac, handed down, that is, in the same words in which he first uttered them, who would not love to think them out for himself and to weigh up the full force and proper sense of every word and even every letter? At least we possess the next best thing to this – and we neglect it. If anyone shows us Christ's robe or his footprint, we fall down and worship it and kiss it. But even could you produce his every garment and all the furniture of his mother's home, there is nothing that can so exactly represent, so vividly express, so completely show forth Christ as the writings of the

evangelists and apostles. (*CWE* 3:203/187–204/196; Allen II, 170, 170–80)

And Erasmus added more and more detail as he worked on successive editions. Thus Screech summarises, 'The *Annotations* are the work of a man both *passionné* and *engagé*. This sense of engagement increases from edition to edition, as new texts are studied, new enemies arise, new defences are erected, old defences strengthened'.[29]

The Latin of Erasmus' 1516 *Novum Instrumentum* is not a new translation: it is a revision of the Vulgate based in large part on the evidence of the Greek text; and the annotations are on the Vulgate.

It would take a large monograph to enter into Erasmus' Latin version and to show where and how it differed from the Vulgate, and to explain why it was so harshly attacked by a few critics. But two examples must serve to illustrate and represent a host of others. In John 1:1, Erasmus substituted '*sermo*' for the traditional Vulgate '*verbum*', – a substitution which stirred the ire of many critics perhaps more than any other single change that he made, for he felt that on philological grounds the word '*sermo*' had the connotation of rational discourse which is in the original λογος; and he argued that *sermo* was rhetorically and theologically a better rendering of the Greek than *verbum*.[30] This Erasmian touch was much attacked (by Edward Lee in particular, but also by Henry Standish and others);[31] but in his *Apologia de 'In principio erat sermo'* (1520, with at least five reprintings in the same year) Erasmus stood fast and marshalled strong witness to his use of *sermo* from scriptural and patristic authorities.

Another, less well-known, translation occurs in Matthew 3:2 (and elsewhere), with the Greek μετανοειτε translated in the Vulgate as '*penitentiam agite*', lending an ambiguity to the original thought; for Latin had but one word for 'repentance', and 'penance' did not carry over the force of the Greek. The traditional catholic interpretation took the line 'do penance': which supported the Sacrament of Penance, and in effect the whole sacramental system. Erasmus did not accept the Vulgate translation and instead offered either '*resipiscite*' or '*ad mentem redite*': that is, 'be mindful' or 'come to yourselves'. The leaven of this new rendering, Smith comments, 'worked so powerfully in Luther's mind that it became the starting point of the Reformation and thus leavened the whole loaf of Christendom'.[32]

There are many other instances of Erasmus' meticulous translation, to be sure; for, as he wrote in the introductory epistle (373), theologians could err in the smallest points, and thus it was necessary to examine each word individually with the utmost care.

Erasmus' great enterprise of 1516 consisted of both the Jerome and the *Novum Instrumentum*, for both were worked on for a number of years together, beginning no later than the course on Jerome that he gave at Cambridge in 1511 (chapter 27, but the roots of course were earlier). While Erasmus was far more aware of medieval traditions of scriptural scholarship than was previously thought,[33] he manifests his medieval kinship 'particularly in the psychological and moral bent of his interpretation of Scripture, reacting against a theology in which speculation had gone over into pure abstraction. In this he was faithful to the *Devotio Moderna*; and indeed he even intensified its main lines'.[34] Jane E. Phillips has shown in her recent translation of and introduction to Erasmus' *Paraphrase on John*, how indebted Erasmus was to the *Glossa ordinaria*, St Thomas Aquinas' *Catena aurea*, the commentary of Hugh of St Cher, and the *Postilla* of Nicholas of Lyra. Despite his objections to them and their mistakes, 'Erasmus was taught by them before he outgrew them, and their influence stayed with him' (*CWE* 46:xiv). Each of these medieval sources merits intensive study.

But, that having been said (for it needs to be said), Erasmus was far closer to the ancient patristic writers, as Bouyer has argued, 'and to the Greek Fathers especially, than to the medieval writers, in the living sense which he recovered of the Church's tradition, and of Scripture seen, as it were, inside that tradition' (505). In sum, Erasmus manifests and managed excitingly to communicate the humanist ideal of the 'revival of traditional patristic culture, made new again, so that Scripture too should be rediscovered, and be at the heart of a reform of the Church entirely from within' (504–5). First Jerome – to be joined later by Cyprian, Hilary, Chrysostom, Irenaeus, Origen (first his fragments on Matthew), Ambrose, Augustine, Basil, and then at the very end, a complete Origen – contributed to understanding Christ and his teaching. From the method of Valla Erasmus moved to an even fuller concept of historical context: employing the fullest and most accurate philological examination possible at that time to arrive at a truly historical understanding of all ancient texts, biblical and other. It is worth observing that while he maintained his youthful love for Valla, he was able to look critically at Valla's work on the New Testament, often differing sharply from it;[36] in fact it has been argued that Erasmus was the first scholar to develop the principle of the harder reading – *difficilior lectio potior*, 'the more difficult the reading the better', because a scribe was more likely to substitute an easier reading for a difficult one – and he employed this principle in his own textual criticism of the Greek New Testament.[37]

So we may agree, in the words of Bouyer one final time, that

'Erasmus offers one of the finest examples of a "return to the sources" without taint of archaism: where what is newest ministers to a fresh and better understanding of what is oldest' (505).

The implications for his age of Erasmus' *Novum Instrumentum* – in the several senses of the word *instrumentum* – will be given attention in subsequent chapters.

Notes

1) There is an admirable (and brief) essay for the general reader on the text of the New Testament in Jaroslav Pelikan's *The Melody of Theology*, 245–8.

2) For a general survey of the Biblical tradition, see *The Cambridge History of the Bible: the West from the Fathers to the Reformation*, ed. G.W.H. Lampe (Cambridge, 1969), and its valuable bibliography (509–35).

3) For many years I have been greatly in debt to Beryl Smalley, *The Study of the Bible in the Middle Ages* (1941; 2d ed., 1952, rptd 1964), and, rather less so, to C. Spicq, *Esquisse d'une histoire de l'exégèse Latine au Moyen Âge* (Paris, 1944). A full study is given by Henri de Lubac, *Exégèse Médiévale: Les quatre sens de l'écriture*, 3 vols (Paris, 1959); for a Catholic theological analysis, see Louis Bouyer, *The Meaning of Sacred Scripture* (Notre Dame, Ind., 1958).

4) 'Not even an ox might perish' (*Adag.*, IV. v. i, *LB* II, 1049A; see the trans. by Phillips in *The 'Adages'*, 368–80).

5) There is an admirable, well-documented survey by Jean Danielou, *The Bible and the Liturgy* (Notre Dame, Ind., 1956). For the late Middle Ages and Renaissance the standard work was the *Rationale Divinorum Officiorum* of Gulielmus Durandus (printed in Paris 1475, and much reprinted), the first book of which is translated into English as *The Symbolism of Churches and Church Ornaments*, by J.M. Neale and B. Webb (London, 1906). See also M.D. Anderson, *Drama and Imagery in British Churches* (Cambridge, 1963), and G.R. Owst, *Literature and Pulpit in Medieval England*, 2nd ed. (Oxford, 1961).

6) Smalley, *Study of the Bible*, xi.

7) One must always bear in mind Smalley's caveat that 'the bulk of medieval commentaries remains in manuscript' (xii), and necessarily this includes commentaries from the Low Countries. A watershed is marked by Bainton's observation that in the age of the Renaissance and Reformation 'commentaries on the Sentences gave way to commentaries on the Bible' – a partial truth: see 'Biblical Scholarship in the Renaissance and Reformation' rptd from *Church History* x (1941) in Bainton, *Collected Papers in Church History*, Ser. 1 (Boston, 1962) 210–216.

8) One must stress that the standard Gloss (*Glossa ordinaria*) of the high Middle Ages was a standard reference for both Roman Catholic and Anglican divines as late as the early 17th c.: 'the medieval Bible survived intact into the Counter-Reformation period' (Smalley, 367).

9) Jerry H. Bentley, *Humanists and Holy Writ – New Testament Scholarship in the Renaissance* (Princeton, 1983) 31.

10) Writing his letter 'To a Monk' (c. 1519) Thomas More played with this proverbial saying: '*sicubi quis vel Carrensem* [Hugo of St Cher] *conuincat*

errasse, vel delirasse Lyranum (*Correspondence of Sir Thomas More*, ed. E.F. Rogers [Princeton, 1947] 172). Thomas More at ordinary mealtimes had scripture read by one of the family, together with the commentaries of Nicholas de Lyra (Chambers, *Thomas More*, 179), which was perhaps a habit established in his Carthusian years.

11) Translation by R.L.P. Milburn in *The Cambridge History of the Bible*, ed. Lampe (1969) 305.

12) One striking point is that the main thrust of medieval Bible study was on the Old, not the New, Testament. In his monograph on *Humanists and Holy Writ*, Bentley has devoted a chapter to Valla as Biblical philologist. Also important are S. Camporeale, *Lorenzo Valla – Umanesimo e teologia* (Florence, 1972) which views Valla as a proponent of Pauline theology; and C. Trinkaus, *'In Our Image and Likeness'* (Chicago, 1970) which stresses the potentially undermining aspect of Valla's philological approach.

13) On the genesis of Erasmus' NT studies and publication, see the following: C.A.L. Jarrott, 'Erasmus' Biblical Humanism', *Stud. in Ren.* 17 (1970) 119–52; and, building on Jarrott but to be used with reservations, Marjorie O'R. Boyle, *Erasmus on Language and Method in Theology* (Toronto, 1977). Essential are Erika Rummel, *Erasmus' Annotations on the New Testament* (Toronto, 1986) and Albert Rabil, Jr., *Erasmus and the New Testament* (San Antonio, 1972); and the chapter on Erasmus in Bentley's *Humanists and Holy Writ*, 112 ff., is intelligent and lucid. In 1986 a facsimile edition of Erasmus' annotations on the Gospels (the first of several volumes) by Anne Reeve with introduction by M.A. Screech, was published (London, 1986), and the problem of the dating of Erasmus' Latin translations has been studied by Andrew Brown in 'The date of Erasmus' Latin translations of the New Testament' in *Transactions of the Cambridge Bibliographical Society*, 8.4 (1984–5) and by H.J. de Jonge in two important studies, 'Novum testamentum a nobis versum. De essentie van Erasmus' uitgave van het Nieuwe Testament', *Lampas* 15 (1982) 231–48, and 'Wann ist Erasmus' Übersetzung des Neuen Testament Entstanden?', in *Erasmus of Rotterdam,* ed. Sperna Weiland and Frijhoff (1988), 151–7. In approaching this key chapter in the biography of Erasmus – 'key' because of the centrality of New Testament scholarship in all the mature work of Erasmus – we have already noted the frequent statements of his intentions or ambitions, together with references to manuscripts, or discussions of problems of interpretation: these are all listed in the index to this volume.

14) *Briefwechsel des Beatus Rhenanus*, ed. A. Horawitz and K. Hartfelder (Leipzig, 1886, rptd 1966) 40; q. *CWE* 3:217n. It would appear from Eps 328 and 330 that he wrote on behalf of Froben (*CWE* 3:80/36–81/37, and 3:82/2; Allen II, 63/36–7, and 65/1; *'Frobennius Novum Testamentum a te cupit habere'*. But these letters do not necessarily mean that Erasmus was still dickering: only that he had not yet given Froben the ms. and that Froben was afraid Erasmus might take it to Italy or elsewhere for printing.

15) This letter to Domenico Grimani is addressed to one of Erasmus' most influential patrons in Rome (*BR*). Allen has commented on the possibility that the sentence on Valla was added at the time of publication, possibly to answer Dorp's charge that the work of Valla and Lefèvre on the New Testament was sufficient; but at the beginning of Ep. 337 Erasmus

asserts that he did not see the letter from Dorp until after his arrival in Antwerp the following May (cf. *CWE* 3:98/176n, and 3:111n).

16) Ep. 328 from Beatus in Basel to Erasmus (17 April 1515) is key evidence in this matter, for there Beatus reports that Froben is asking for Erasmus' New Testament; and this information is repeated in Ep. 330. See further Rummel, *Erasmus' Annotations on the New Testament*, 24–25. Allen suggests (II,183) that one of the objects of Erasmus' journey to England in March 1515 may have been to 'fetch a copy of his translation': quite possibly the Dutch humanist did not have the complete translation with him in Basel.

17) To speak of 'the' Greek NT is to represent as monolithic what is in fact a many-layered but long-lasting plastering-over of a complex textual problem. The editorial work of Lucian of Antioch (d. 312) harmonised conflicting Greek texts of the New Testament and became the standard edition of the Byzantine Empire. For a convenient summary, see Bentley, *Humanists and Holy Writ*, 15–18; and B. Metzger, *The Text of the New Testament*.

18) In one of his letters to Aldus (Ep. 207, 28 Oct. 1507), Erasmus wrote, 'I very much wonder what has prevented the publication, long before now, of your New Testament, a work which, unless my guess is mistaken, will please even the general public and especially those of my own sort, that is, the theologians' (*CWE* 2:131/17–21; Allen I, 437/16–438/19). Allen notes (I,438n) that Aldus had projected an edition of the NT as early as 1499, but one did not appear from his press until February 1518.

19) Rummel, *Erasmus' Annotations*, 23.

20) His *Paraphrases* came later: the first of them, on the Epistles of St Paul, came in 1517; the first on the Gospels, that on John, came in 1523, with all the Gospels published together in 1524. The *Paraphrases*, it is self-evident, were written on the foundation of his editorial work.

21) Pieter Meghen (1466–1540), who had been a student at Louvain, was a one-eyed scribe (thus variously called 'Unoculus', 'Monoculus', 'Cyclops', etc.) who also served at times as a courier for Erasmus. We know from one letter that he was not only robbed but beaten (*CWE* 4:131/4–5; Allen II, 385/4). At the end of his life he was Writer of the King's Books, and so remained until his death in 1540. It was to Meghen that the Metsys diptych was entrusted (ch. 33), and very likely it was Meghen who carried Erasmus' *Novum Instrumentum* to Leo in Rome (Ep. 701). The NT manuscripts copied by Meghen are Cambridge Dd. vii. 3 (Erasmus' version of the New Testament comprising Matthew and Mark); British Library 1 Reg. E.v.1 (Luke and John, dated 7 September 1509); Corpus Christi College, Oxford, E.4.9, 10 (another copy of Erasmus' version, but without colophons); Hatfield House, Cecil Papers, MS 324 (Acts and Apocalypse, undated). J.B. Trapp suggests that the Corpus Christi manuscript was prepared between 1514 and 1520 (*BR*). See J.B. Trapp in *BR*, and his 'Notes on Manuscripts written by Pieter Mieghen', *The Book Collector* 24 (1975) 80–96; and 'A Postscript to Matsys', *Burlington Magazine* 121 (1979) 435–7. To Pieter Meghen's copying Simon Bening of Bruges provided illuminations: Screech, Introd. to *Annotations*, xiv; and on the workshop of Bening, see Vol. I, 22 n. 39.

22) At this point Erasmus added: 'I have begun a series of commentaries [*commentarios*] on Paul's epistles, which I will finish when I have published

this other work'. To Colet he had written in July 1513 that he had finished his collation of the NT (Ep. 270, *CWE* 2:249/66; Allen I, 527–58).

23) This passage in Erasmus' *Responsio ad Collationes Cujusdam juvenis gerontodidascali*, carrying over to 987B, speaks in detail of his editorial work with the annotations. Its significance is stressed by de Jonge in his 1988 paper.

24) This act, which violates the letter, spirit and law of textual scholarship, Erasmus admitted in the *Annotations*: see Bentley, 128n.

25) He spoke of mss examined in Brabant (*LB* 9: 277A, & 986 F). See also Ep. 597.

26) On the mss used by Erasmus for these different editions, see Allen II, 164–6; see the underscoring of the significance, by Screech (q. in n. 29 below).

27) In classical Latin *instrumentum* meant tool or instrument, but also furniture, supply or store; tropologically, a writing as an instrument, a document. But in medieval Latin it also meant a lesson or teaching: thus, *instrumenta virtutum* in the *Regula Benedicti*, c. 73. Yet it was still a bold thing to call a new edition of the New Testament a *novum instrumentum*.

28) See Metzger, *Text of the New Testament*, 2d ed. (1968) 95–106.

29) Screech, Introduction to *Erasmus' Annotations on the New Testament* (1986) xxii–xxiii. Screech rightly stresses the importance of the edition of 1535, the last of a series and completed only months before Erasmus' death: 'Each of these five editions represents his very last word on particular questions at the date of writing. In all of them he was adding, correcting, re-thinking, re-casting up to the moment of printing the final proofs' (xxiii).

30) Reeve, ed. *Annotations*, 218; Bentley, 170.

31) In Gemany the attack was led by Johann Eck, later Luther's famous antagonist; in Spain, by Zuñiga (Stunica). See Rummel, *Erasmus and His Catholic Critics I* on Dorp, Lee, the friars, and Stunica; *Catholic Critics II* on critics in Brabant and Germany, Béda and the Paris faculty, the Spanish religious orders, and the Italians. Some of Erasmus' arguments in defence are presented in the *Apologia de 'In principio erat sermo'*: first published by Froben in 1520 and reprinted at least five times that same year, again in *Opera Omnia* (1540) and *LB* IX, cols. 111–22.

32) Smith, *Erasmus*, 168, citing Luther's *Resolutiones* of 1518 (*WA*, I, 530). For further discussioln, see Bentley, 161 ff.

33) To suppose him ignorant of medieval tradition is to ignore his years of study with the Brethren of the Common Life and at Steyn and Paris. This principle bears on the trivium and theology as well as on the study of Scripture.

34) Fr. Louis Bouyer, 'Erasmus in relation to Medieval Biblical Tradition', *Cambridge Hist. of the Bible*, 2 (1969) 505. Phillips quite rightly stresses the importance of Erasmus' patristic editing for his annotation of the Bible: 'The great names of the patristic era were not the only ones to write running commentaries on Scripture. Indeed, Erasmus' first introduction to the Fathers of the Church is likely to have been through the excerpts, compilations, and epitomes of their work in the form of the biblical commentaries that were the school texts of the medieval Church: the compilation known as the *Glossa Ordinaria* or *Gloss* (twelfth century), the collection of excerpts made by

Thomas Aquinas (d. 1274), and entitled *Catena aurea*, the commentary, heavily dependent for the Fourth Gospel on Chrysostom, by Hugh of St Cher (d. 1263), and the *Postilla* of Nicholas of Lyra (d. 1340). Though he objected to most of these works for many reasons – their fondness for allegory, their pettiness, their out-and-out mistakes, the naivete of their interpretive principles – Erasmus was taught by them before he outgrew them, and their influence stayed with him' (*CWE* 46:xiv).

35) A model for such research is the excellent analysis of H.J. de Jonge, 'Erasmus und die Glossa ordinaria zum Neuen Testament', *Nederlands archief voor Kerkgeschiedenis*, n.s. 56 (1975) 51–77.

36) See Chomarat, *Grammaire et Rhétorique*, I, 252 ff.

37) See Jerry H. Bentley, 'Erasmus, Jean LeClerc, and the Principle of the Harder Reading', *RenQ* 31 (1978) 309–21.

Years of Travel: from Basel to Brabant, 1516–1521

> My home is wherever I have my library.
>
> Erasmus to Mark Lauwerijns, 1518, Epistle 809
> (Allen III, 266/117–8)

> In 1517 Erasmus' fame was at its zenith; and in consequence
> visitors came to him from every side, some to seek counsel,
> others to adore.
>
> P. S. Allen, *The Age of Erasmus*, 277–8

> Yet I shall feel that I have made good use of the life I live, the
> air I breathe, for I have seen Erasmus my great patron deity;
> and since the days of Cicero and Quintilian no age has known a
> greater scholar or one who could surpass you in divine and
> human learning and great gifts of style.
>
> Zasius to Erasmus, 1518, Epistle 857
> (*CWE* 6:71/28–31; Allen III, 361/23–7)

Erasmus lived in Brabant[1] from 1517 to 1521, making frequent trips
to Basel, varying his residence from Louvain to Anderlecht, and
visiting Bruges and Antwerp often. Perhaps more than any other
period, these might be called his nomadic years. But there is a ready
explanation. Erasmus wrote to one of his correspondents that the
emperor's chancellor wanted him close to the court: certainly he did
not want to lose the chance of securing a final appointment to a
prebend that would at last give him financial security; after all, his
appointment as imperial councillor was not permanent and there
were continuing problems about payment of the promised stipend.
Despite assurances from England, promises from the court at Brussels, and attractive invitations from many other quarters, Erasmus
was still not financially secure.

There was another compelling reason. The dream of a Collegium
Trilingue in which the great classical languages (Greek, Latin and
Hebrew) would be taught, was one in the planning of which
Erasmus was long involved, and in the last months of the life of
Jerome de Busleyden, who shared that dream, the two were close
friends. With the death of Busleyden in August of 1517, the College

came into being, and Erasmus not only continued to take an interest in it, but he actively campaigned for it and had a hand in the search for its first professors of Greek, Latin and Hebrew. It appears that for Erasmus the existence of such a College under the umbrella of a major university like Louvain offered the possibility of a real community that he had been seeking, and the lack of which at Steyn he lamented to Servatius Rogers. The experience a few months later of having the Louvain theologians turn against the idea of the Collegium and seek to block its development was a bitter one for Erasmus.

Meanwhile it was a period of much travelling: there were half a dozen trips to Basel (in August 1514, March, August and September 1516, May and December 1518). Twice his horse carried him safely from the Low Countries to Basel and back again, a horse now at least as wise as Ulysses, he wrote in 1516.[2]

That Erasmus was by choice a nomad has often been alleged, but – despite the fact that the period from his departure from Basel in May 1516 to his arrival in Louvain in July of 1517 is marked by much travel – a considerable amount of that apparent restlessness is attributable to his feeling, even sense of duty, that his appointment as councillor to Charles required him to be close to the court in Brussels. Some of that movement can be linked to visiting friends in Antwerp and elsewhere (often in connection with his research), and some to other reasons or motives. Some of the travelling had to do with the publication of his work, and his quick trips to England in the summer of 1516 and again in April of 1517 were for laying the foundations for and then receiving his papal dispensation (appendix C). As we shall see, he continued to work while travelling, and he frequently consulted manuscripts even on trips for other purposes.

In the winter of 1516–17 humanism was at its zenith in western Europe, for the challenges of the Reformation and the stiffening of conservatism in the pre-Tridentine Church had not reached their flood. There was, to be sure, some continuing of reform and of the humanist spirit among those loyal to the Holy See; but the main force in Rome and among those still staunch to Rome was a growing conservatism. Erasmus was recognised everywhere as the prince of humanists and the leader of reform within the Church. The Dutch humanist might have remained in Basel, where he had found one of the two or three finest presses in Europe, and, more important, one with which he could work with great productivity by virtue of the team of scholars that Froben had gathered around him. Had he returned to Rome or Venice, he would have found things much changed in a dozen years. He had many invitations: why did he choose to leave Basel and return to the Low Countries?

He had not gone to Basel in 1514 with the intention of making it his permanent home. Indeed, when pope Leo X – that 'amiable hedonist'[3] – wrote to him, the letter was addressed to the Low Countries.[4] But there were still promises made that were not being kept: the payment of this living, and that pension; and Erasmus was still pressed for money. He was living beyond his means, no doubt, but his need for additional secretaries kept increasing (see chapter 38 below on his *famuli*, the secretaries who lived with him in Basel). Not least, as we have seen, he seems to have taken seriously the responsibilities that went along with his appointment as councillor to Charles. Doubtless largely owing to the request of Jean Le Sauvage, Charles' chancellor, Erasmus wrote his *Institutio Principis* in late 1515 (chapter 31), and that was before the death of Ferdinand in early 1516 made Charles presumptive king of Castile and Aragon.[5] Charles did not forget.

Let us first trace his movements in broad outline from the time he left Basel until his arrival in Louvain. Then, against this background, we shall examine his accomplishments and look at the happy months at Anderlecht.

Erasmus left Basel in May 1516: turning aside for Kaisersberg (Epistle 412/3), a town just northwest of Colmar, he reached the Rhine again at Strasbourg and passed through Speyer (Epistle 563/21), Mainz (Epistle 412/16) and Cologne (Epistle 412/7), arriving at Antwerp on 30 May. In all, as Allen observes (II, 240n), the journey took no more than seventeen days, and much of it was by boat. From Antwerp, where as before he stayed with Pieter Gillis, he went on to Brussels, paying his respects to Jean Le Sauvage, president of the privy council and since January 1515 chancellor of Burgundy. Erasmus was careful to keep his fences mended in Brussels, but here there were other places to bear in mind, for the two most important prelates in the Low Countries were among his friends: Philip of Burgundy in Utrecht, and Erard de la Marck in Liège.[6] In Brussels there were other old friends to visit: Anton Clava, a member of the council of Flanders, and Nicholas Everardi, president of the council of Holland and Zeeland, and of Friesland.[7]

From Brussels he went on to Saint-Omer and returned to Antwerp in mid-June (Epistle 421), not only visiting friends but working: the Preface to *Primus liber grammaticae institutionis Theodori Gazae ... translatus per Erasmus – Gaza's Grammar*, published by Martens in Louvain in July 1516 – is a product of this brief visit: but the actual translation had probably been made at Basel (Allen II, 264n), and earlier Erasmus had used Gaza's grammar in teaching Greek at Cambridge (chapter 27, and see *BR*, s.v. 'Gaza'). About 10 July Erasmus went to Brussels in response to an invitation from Jean Le Sauvage (Epistle 436), which was more than an invitation, it was a promise or assurance:

> If you can come here at the first available opportunity, it will be to your advantage, because, if you have determined to remain in these parts and to live a peaceful and pleasant life in honourable leisure, as you could not hope to elsewhere without great effort, I will cause to be conferred on you forthwith a prebend or canonry of Courtrai. Nor will that be the only thing you can expect with sure and certain hope from the generosity of his catholic majesty, my master.[8]

But by mid-July Erasmus was back in Antwerp, preparing to travel to England, for he wanted to confer with Ammonio and to visit Fisher and others; he seems to have then remained in England only five or six weeks, ten days of which were spent visiting Fisher in Rochester (Epistle 456). However, the major purpose in his making the trip to England was undoubtedly the final composition of his appeal to Rome for a fuller dispensation (Epistles 446 & 447, appendix C). These papers he gave to Ammonio, and from Rochester he set out for Dover and reached the French coast about 27 August (Epistle 457). Upon landing at Calais he hastened to Brussels (Epistle 463) to visit the chancellor, Le Sauvage, and to try to make more secure his promised Courtrai prebend. He then went to Antwerp, where he spent a month with Gillis, who had a lingering illness.

Apparently upon his departure from England Erasmus had made known his intention to settle in Louvain. In mid-September 1516 Warham wrote to Thomas More (Epistle 465) that he, the archbishop, proposed to send money to Erasmus in Louvain (*CWE* 4:75/3–77/5); and More expected (Epistle 468) that Erasmus would by then be in Louvain, writing that Colet was very busy with his Greek, with help from Clement, and 'I think he will make progress and achieve his aim by hard work, especially if you encourage him steadily from Louvain' (*CWE* 4:80/17–8; Allen II, 347/13–14). In this letter More also writes about a horse that Christopher Urswick, a leading churchman and patron of humanism (*BR*) had promised Erasmus and about which Erasmus had written to both Ammonio and More earlier; and so the horse wanders across the pages of the correspondence of the travelling Dutch humanist, with More writing in another letter (Epistle 467) that he had spoken with Urswick about 'your horse, He says he will see to it that you get one soon, but that he has not yet found one of the sort he would wish to send you'

(*CWE* 4:79/13–15; Allen II, 346/12–13). In the shadow of war and
rumours of war, three men of prominence were occupied with finding the right horse for the frail but demanding Dutchman.[10]

But Erasmus did not yet turn to Louvain; for some reason he felt,
in Allen's words, that the 'auspices were not favourable, and he
preferred to spend the winter between Brussels and Antwerp' (Allen
II, 281n). Again, Erasmus may have been drawn to the court either
in hopes of preferment or out of a feeling that he owed attendance
because of his council appointment. Thus, on 6 October he wrote to
Ammonio from Brussels (Epistle 475), affecting to laugh at the
possibility of a bishopric in Sicily; but Le Sauvage had told the
councillors present at a gathering that the prince was trying to secure
this bishopric for Erasmus. Perhaps Erasmus made it clear to Le
Sauvage that he would not turn away from his scholarship;[11] the
matter of this episcopal preferment was not raised again. In the letter
to Ammonio, ever his confidant, Erasmus also wrote that he now
meant to spend the winter in Brussels, having 'turned somewhat
against Louvain', one of the reasons being the bothersome and
drearisome presence of Martin van Dorp; another, the call on his
time to correct verses and vet letters. From other letters we know
that Erasmus remained in Brussels into the New Year (Epistles 483
and 491, and intermittently through 528).

In January 1517 Erasmus was invited, so it appears, to Louvain,
and he paid a short visit and had some kind of interview with the
theologians who had been criticising him harshly. Allen suggests
that the intermediary was doubtless Dorp, as Epistle 509 suggests.[12]
The visit cleared the air, at least for the time, although Erasmus still
expressed some apprehension to Gillis, writing on 20 January that
Louvain,

> although I have made my peace with the theologians, more or
> less, would give me a grim reception in Lent. To sit here
> [Brussels] any longer I simply have no spirits. If without incon-
> venience to yourself you could let me have one room which has a
> privy, maybe I will move over and join you, in order to get
> ready what I can send to Basel. Anything you may find you have
> spent beyond your usual level I wish to be charged to me; thus I
> shall not be too much of a burden on you, nor you on me. (*CWE*
> 4: 187/7–13; Allen II, 433/6–12)

In mid-February of 1517 Erasmus was in Antwerp, writing to
Etienne Poncher, bishop of Paris, from there (Epistle 529), and
ending the letter with an inimitable Erasmian touch of familiarity:
'You see how frankly I write to you, as though I had forgotten your
high position. So spoilt have I been by your kindness, which has

taught me this lack of shame; you must either forgive it entirely, or take a great part of the blame at least upon yourself (*CWE* 4:221/ 132–5; Allen II, 458/121–4).

At a time when official correspondence was so highly formal, and the ability to write in such a style was for many a grace beyond the reach of their art, the letters of Erasmus were a despair to those who sought to imitate him slavishly, but an inspiration to those who responded more creatively. Collections of his letters began to appear in 1516 (an edition by Martens at Louvain), and individual letters – such as that to Dorp of 1514, or the letter to Wimpheling in praise of the literary society of Strasbourg – were reprinted many times; and many others circulated privately in manuscript.[13] Even while moving about, Erasmus managed to sustain his large and demanding correspondence; as he wrote just a few years later in his *Catalogus lucubrationum*, published by Froben in 1522: 'I have written, and today am still writing, such a mass of letters that two wagons would hardly be equal to carrying the load. Having come into possession of many of them by chance, I myself burned them, for I realised that very many people were preserving them.'

His letters were indeed prized. In October 1514, writing from Freiburg-im-Breisgau, Zasius wrote to Erasmus about his letters being passed from hand to hand all round his university:

the faculty are clamouring for it, full of admiration for such a great fountain of the purest style, for genius of the divine Rotterdam, and for the fire of inspiration that comes down from heaven. Even a Zasius is highly esteemed: people point me out: 'This is the man', they say, who has had a letter, a kindly and friendly letter, from Rotterdam, the Cicero of our modern Germany' [*Cicero Germaniae nunc aetatis nostrae*] ... (*CWE* 3:41/13– 18; Allen II, 31/8–15)

Even then he was not yet ready to make the move to Louvain. To Ammonio (with whom he was always quite free in expressing himself) at the end of February he wrote a frank and intimate letter (Epistle 539):

In Louvain they were creeping up on me with their knives drawn,[14] in a conspiracy (what is more) led by Athensis [Jan Briaert of Ath], who was all the more dangerous because he was an enemy disguised as a friend ... But in the end I went to Louvain myself and blew all the clouds away, ending up on most friendly terms with the theologians, both great and small. (*CWE* 4:256/3–257/9; Allen II, 484/2–7)

Little wonder that Erasmus should write to his old friend Anton Clava from Antwerp in mid-February (Epistle 530): 'As for me, I have been so much distracted on all sides by illness, by the efforts of research on more fronts than one, and by frequent changes of abode, that I have been almost beside myself' (*CWE* 4:222/6–9; Allen II, 458/3–5). A rare *cri de coeur* from Erasmus: to complain not only of his illness (which was frequent enough), but also of his changes of residence, and of keeping going several lines of research at the same time (*'hinc studiorum non unus labor'*). Behind his optimism and the ironies that he presented to the world, he was human and could suffer.

In the midst of his hesitation about going to Louvain Erasmus wrote to Ammonio on 15 March (Epistle 552) that he had received letters from the pope and the bishop of Worcester,[15] indicating that he should see Ammonio:

> If this is necessary, let me know as soon as you can, though I really hate that Channel crossing. Never mind, I will face it, I will be a second Theseus who, according to Virgil 'so oft by that sad road goes and returns', and do what I have to do in person. (*CWE* 4:284/7–10; Allen II, 504/5–8)

As he feared, it was mandatory that he receive the dispensation in person from the hands of Ammonio, the apostolic delegate;[16] and so he left Antwerp on about 1 April, and the brief legal ceremony conferring the dispensation took place on 9 April at Westminster in the house of Ammonio. At most Erasmus remained in England four weeks. Epistle 577 to Thomas Wolsey was written from London just 'when the wind was blowing fair for him to cross the Channel' (Allen II, 553n, who dates the letter c. 28 April). Of this letter to the now powerful Wolsey, cardinal of York (and since 1515 lord chancellor of England, succeeding Warham), McConica writes in his note: 'Erasmus' confident tone in dealing with the powerful Wolsey (over some proposal to provide for him in England, cf. 574/64–5) shows his new confidence after the favours shown him in the Netherlands and the successful outcome of his request for a dispensation from Rome' (*CWE* 4: 344n).

The year 1517 also marks a turning-point in Erasmus' expectations from Henry VIII and Wolsey, and Cecil H. Clough has noted that Erasmus in his programme for the reform of western Christendom, founded on lay piety, was swimming against the current of vested interests of influential clerics, who were opposed to that Erasmian reform, including Wolsey himself. Although Erasmus received a gift of £20 for the presentation of the *Institutio Principis Christiani*, no other patronage was forthcoming, despite blandishments made to the Dutch humanist in April 1517. Quite simply, then, 'Erasmus turned his back on the possibility of a position not only at the English court but in England in any capacity'.[17]

Erasmus was still in Antwerp in early June (Epistle 586), as he signed the preface to an edition of Suetonius that was included with the *Historiae Augustae Scriptores* printed the following year by Froben. In this preface he returned to his familiar themes in advising princes: 'For a man who limits a great emperor's part to the exaction of revenue is anything rather than a true emperor' (*CWE* 4:382/252–3). Erasmus followed the court to Ghent (Epistle 584) to Louvain (597) and to Bruges (608 and 651), where it was suggested – very likely by Le Sauvage – that he follow prince Charles to Spain, but this he refused to do, Spain being at worst a cemetery for many humanists at this time, and at very least a major distraction from his scholarship. Later Erasmus maintained that his residence at Louvain complied with the wishes of Charles (see Epistle 1225: 'As you know I have moved to Louvain,' he writes to Barbier, 'for such was at that time the emperor's wish', *CWE* 8:272/30).[18] Thus, as he wrote to his old friend Thomas More on about 10 July 1517,

> I have moved bodily to Louvain, intending to spend several months among the theology faculty, who have given me quite a kind welcome. The chancellor [Le Sauvage] has paid me part of my retainer out of his own pocket – two hundred florins, that is – with the intention of securing a refund by some means or other. I am still hoping for another hundred; but who will produce the cash now they have all departed? The chancellor's parting advice to me was to be optimistic. He intends, I gather, to confer a bishopric on me. So much easier is it for these people [*istis*] to make one a bishop than to pay one the money they have promised to pay. (*CWE* 5:28–36; Allen III, 5/25–31)

Thus after visits to London and several towns in the Low Countries, attendance at court, following it to two or three other places, Erasmus had settled down to a more regular way of life, planning to stay for several months. In fact he remained for several years: with the exception of some months at Anderlecht, and allowing for trips to Flanders in April 1518 and again in May 1519, as well as visits to Basel in May and December 1518, Louvain was his home until 1521, at which time he would move to Basel for the most extended residence of his life. The university had already invited him to come in the spring, for – unlike the theology faculty at Cologne which was dominated by Dominicans – it was composed largely of secular priests, for whom Erasmus always had more respect.[19] Perhaps at Louvain even more than at Basel Erasmus hoped to erect a kind of school of letters – in the twentieth century it would be called an institute – to provide 'within the very university system that was the mainstay of scholasticism – a solid institutional basis for the study of good letters' (Tracy, 171). In a very real way Erasmus was anticipating the profound conclusion of Beryl Smalley at the end of her study of the Bible in the Middle Ages: 'biblical scholarship in the strict sense has depended on institutions which imply a certain level of material prosperity and security'.[20]

Here attention must be given to the *Method of Theology* (*Ratio seu compendium verae theologiae*, published by Froben in January 1519), which was an expansion of his Preface to the New Testament. This seminal work, reprinted about eighteen times before the *Opera Omnia* of 1540, presents the core of the Erasmian programme for the study of theology. One should begin with a good life and reverence, and there must be a firm foundation provided by the knowledge of the original languages of scripture built firmly upon rhetoric, dialectic, arithmetic, music, physics, cosmography and history (following the medieval tradition of the trivium and quadrivium). Erasmus emphasises the importance of exegesis, and for this the ancient fathers were to be preferred to modern authorities; then church history, dogmatics, civil and ecclesiastical law were to follow.[21]

At very much the same time Erasmus was writing the letter to abbot Paul Volz, which is a preface to the revised edition of the *Enchiridion* published in 1518; and here we have the image of the christian community in three concentric circles, all focusing on the person of Christ at the centre like the rings of a target: in the innermost, the priests, bishops, cardinals, and popes; these are to experience the intense purity of the centre and to pass it on. In the second circle there are the secular princes, who contribute to the restoration of the true ends of a christian society. In the third circle are the laity, the 'most earthy portion of this world, but not so earthy that they are not members of Christ's body just the same' (*CWE* 66:15).

As McConica comments on this striking metaphor in the *Enchiridion*, all is centred on Christ, and the christian commonwealth is a polity of the baptised, without elaborate institutional structure (*Erasmus*, 62).[22]

From July to September of 1517 Erasmus stayed with Jean Desmarez (also known as Paludanus), who was president of the college of St Donation, a fine Latin scholar and an old friend whom he trusted, as well as one who also enjoyed the patronage of Le Sauvage.[23]

Let us now see what Erasmus managed to accomplish during the period between his leaving Basel in May 1516 and his arrival in

Louvain in July 1517. A considerable amount of energy went into correcting and enlarging the uncompleted works of past years. Erasmus was a master of the growing book, and during 1516–17 he never ceased to work at more annotations for the New Testament, and on revisions of older books; but these were never old in the sense of having ceased to grow.

First on the list were his annotations for the New Testament. On 6 March 1518 Erasmus wrote to Le Sauvage that 'My New Testament has been made new a second time; the toil of revision is now finished, and it remains to take equal care in the printing' (Epistle 793, *CWE* 5:337/34–5; Allen III, 246/33–34).[24] In the preceding chapter the manuscripts in the Low Countries consulted by Erasmus were noted.

A new edition of *De Copia* was published by Froben in April 1517, and in Epistle 462 of 5 September 1516, which had been written to accompany the text, Erasmus writes of the proof for it: 'I have therefore revised them as you wished, while on shipboard [*inter navigandum*: perhaps on the Rhine in May, though by barge from Calais to Antwerp is possible], so that even that space of time might not be wholly lost to my programme of work'.[25]

A new edition of the *Moriae Encomium* had been in progress, and it came forth from Froben's presses in 1516. It is worth pausing to note how much revised the new *Moria* was, for after the unauthorised Paris edition of 1511 Erasmus revised and added to the *Moria* seven times (1512, 1514, 1515, 1516, 1521, 1522, and 1532), and there were other reprintings during his lifetime.[26] Froben's 1515 edition was undated, but it was on sale early in 1515; and this is the edition, as we saw in chapter 27, in which Holbein drew his famous illustrations (see illustrations 4 and 5; the copy is now in the Kupferstich-kabinett, Basel, and a facsimile edition of it was edited by H.A. Schmid and published by Henning Oppermann of Basel in 1931).[27] The third of the 1515–1516 Froben editions is described by Screech:

> The text of this edition has been carefully expurgated, as far as the closing pages devoted to ecstasy are concerned. It is presented as being *pro castigatissimo castigatius* – the more absolutely correct text, better even than previous editions. In significant ways it differs from all others; as far as ecstasy is concerned, these differences are very important. In addition, the text is accompanied by even more marginal notes attributed to Listrius. They are the most interesting ones. This must be the edition that Froben refers to in his letter to Erasmus, which P.S. Allen dates as 17 June [1516]. He stresses what personal attention he gave to its printing. (Allen II, 251/15–16)[28]

Throughout this period from 1517 to 1521 there were criticisms of
the *Moria*, the most notable of which was made by Martin van Dorp,
and Dorp was answered in a long letter which was afterwards prefixed to the *Moria* (that is, from 1516 onward) – see Epistle 337,
May 1515 (*CWE* 3: 111 ff; Allen II, 90 ff.).[29]

After a number of years of slack, *Enchiridion* sales were picking up
rapidly. There had been three editions in 1515, and now two in
1516. Nesen reported to Erasmus from Basel (in Epistle 473, late
September 1516), 'Schürer has reprinted your *Enchiridion*' (*CWE*
4:90/22).[30] This increase in sales can be attributed in large part to
Erasmus' rising reputation; readers now wanted anything by
Erasmus of Rotterdam. But times were changing as well, and there
was more interest in reform, of the individual as well as of the
Church; above all the *Enchiridion* addresses the spiritual needs of the
laity.

Jerome was nearing completion, and on 17 October 1516 Erasmus
wrote to Pieter Gillis (Epistle 477), 'Pray hasten to see that Jerome is
sent here properly bound for the addition of notes' (*CWE* 4:98/2–3;
Allen II, 358/1–2). It was sold out by November 1516 (Epistle 483,
CWE 4:120/31; Allen II, 375/27–8).

Under so much pressure the handwriting of Erasmus was deterio-
rating steadily, and in late October he wrote to Budé (Epistle 480)
with some irony that 'it is by writing so much that I have learnt to
write badly.' He continued: 'is it not somewhat inhuman, when a
man is busily occupied in the copying out of great volumes and on
top of that sometimes has twenty letters to write in a single day, to
demand that he should take great pains over the penmanship of his
letters [*literas accurate scriptas*] as though he had nothing else to
do?...' (*CWE* 4:103/23 ff.; Allen II, 363/22 ff.) Yet upon occasion he
not only could but did turn out a professionally written document,
as with his letter to Cop on 24 February 1517 (Epistle 537).[31]

For some time Erasmus had been working on Suetonius, and his
edition of the *Historiae Augustae Scriptores* was printed by Froben in
June 1518 (Epistle 648). This edition included an index (a new
thing in the early sixteenth century) and included a number of
emendations; various editions with his annotations, and later those of
others, were reprinted steadily throughout the sixteenth century.

Along with editions of the *Institutio Principis Christiani* (twice in
1515, four times in 1516, twice in 1517), his *Querela Pacis* was
printed in Basel in 1516.[32] Written by order of Le Sauvage (as
Erasmus tells us in a later letter), the *Querela Pacis* cuts to the heart of
the disputes among Maximilian, Francis I and Henry VIII, with Leo
X standing on the sidelines in the role of a peacemaker, praised for

that role by Erasmus after the pope was instrumental in arranging a peace between England and France in 1514. Despite the *Institutio*, written for the young Charles, and despite Erasmus' presence on the council, Charles had an upbringing typical of a French or Burgundian prince during the long waning of the Middle Ages – indeed, a Burgundian like Maximilian would doubtless have thought of his lifetime as the harvest of the Middle Ages[33] – Charles did not have a humanistic education under his tutor, Adrian of Utrecht (the future Adrian VI) who was a professor of theology and a scholastic. Tracy has called attention to the fact that 'the real influence in Charles's life after 1509 had been Guillaume de Croy, Lord of Chièvres, scion of a family long prominent in the chivalric culture of the Burgundian court. One contemporary reports that Chièvres actively discouraged Charles from studying Greek or Latin.'[34] Instead, he was taken on hunts at the age of ten and read chivalric romances, like other nobles.

Quentin Metsys' name is variously spelled (Quinten; Matsys, Massys or Metsijs). He was born in Louvain a year or so earlier than Erasmus. The son of a blacksmith, he is said to have started in that trade then changed to painting and metal engraving in Antwerp, becoming a master in the painters' guild of St Luke in 1491. Some of his mature work is still to be seen in Brussels and Antwerp, among them two multiple altarpieces, the former signed and dated 1509, the latter 1509–1511. A friend of Pieter Gillis, Metsys is thought of as 'probably the most talented painter of his generation in Flanders'.[35]

When the idea occurred of sending their mutual friend Thomas More a double portrait (as Erasmus informed More in Epistle 584, dated Antwerp 30 May 1517) – 'Pieter Gillis and I are being painted on the same panel' (*CWE* 4:368/8; Allen II, 576/6), describing the problems of working during the sitting – very likely the choice of painter was due to his being the friend of Gillis. But owing to Gillis' illness the finishing of the painting dragged on: 'Tell Quentin he really must finish', Erasmus wrote to Pieter from Louvain on about 1 August (Epistle 616); 'and when it is done, I will hasten over to consult with you how it can be most easily and safely dispatched to England, and also to square up with Quentin' (*CWE* 5:50/10–12; Allen III, 33/9–11). In response to Erasmus' letter of May, Thomas More wrote that he awaited the panel 'with indescribable impatience and curse the ill-health that so long keeps my hopes unfulfilled' (Epistle 601, *CWE* 5:18/56–8; Allen III, 11/50–12/52). The portrait was finally sent off to More from Antwerp on 8 September (Epistle 654, *CWE* 5:106), doubtless to Calais where More still languished, as a present from both Erasmus and Pieter. More's enthusiasm (expressed in Epistle 683 to Erasmus, and 684 to Pieter) reflects the accuracy of detail in the two portraits (see illustration 2, and Volume 1 frontispiece);[36] and More added verses on the diptych (for which see *CWE* 5:149–50).

The double portrait of Erasmus and Gillis has several points of importance. It marks the strong bonds of friendship between Erasmus, Gillis and More. It confirms for us the accuracy of the portrait as seen by Thomas More. And it is the first important stage in creating an image of Erasmus as the scholar at work: the iconography of Erasmus in the act of writing (on which see further appendix E).

Erasmus lived in Anderlecht for five months, from mid-May to mid-October 1521. He had planned to stay only a few months, perhaps as long as three (Epistle 1208/9–10), but he had brought his whole library with him, indicating that he might not return to Louvain, at least not directly. As he had previously written, 'Wherever I keep my library, there is my home'.[37]

Despite the description in Baedeker of Anderlecht as a suburb lying to the south-west of Brussels, it has been swallowed up by the twentieth-century growth of the city. What Erasmus found in 1521 was a rather splendid country house next to a parish church, in a village outside the limits of the sixteenth-century city of Brussels, close enough for access to the court, yet far enough from the growing hostility of the theology faculty at Louvain with its noisy chorus of critics.[38] At Anderlecht his health improved dramatically, and he sang the praises of the purer air.[39] His host was Pieter Wichmans (Wychman), canon of St Pierre, who had studied at Orleans and Louvain, and in 1515 had built himself a fine house in Anderlecht (*BR*). This mansion, 'De Zwane', was purchased in 1931 by the municipality of Anderlecht and now houses the Erasmushuis Museum, which memorialises the Dutch humanist who lived there in 1521; it is furnished in period style with many mementos and some significant bibliographical items. The house is on the east side of the square where the parish church of St Pierre (late 15th- early 16th-century) still stands. It is appropriate that this, the most perfectly preserved of Erasmus' dwelling places, should be in the last of his Brabant locales.

Were it not for the rising clamour of the increasingly hostile Louvain theologians (see chapter 34), Erasmus would doubtless have thought this one of the most pleasant periods of his life. Again and again he closed a letter with the phrase 'from my country retreat in Anderlecht' (e.g., Epistles 1211, 1212). Perhaps he enjoyed the resonance that suggested a Roman writer at his country villa; perhaps Erasmus, who had always lived in a town or city after his monastery years (except for brief visits to the bishop of Cambrai's country house, and one or two others), was finding the experience of living outside a city very interesting and relaxing. Certainly his health improved.[40] Thus in Epistle 1216 he wrote of the experience 'which has turned me from a townsman into a countryman [*nunc ex urbano factus rusticus sat suaviter ago*], and this I find quite agreeable' (*CWE* 8:252/86–7; Allen IV 536/81–2). And as he wrote in August 1521 (Epistle 1223), as he was beginning to prepare for his move to Basel, and reflecting on this new experience for him at fifty-three:

> I used to think in the old days that it was merely for the pleasure of it that the Ancients spoke so highly of life in the country. Experience has now taught me that it is not so much enjoyable as healthy… Scarcely had I spent two days here and my fever had departed to the devil, and my digestion was sound again. I really seemed in this country to grow young again… My dear Goclenius, I never did anything in my whole life of which I had less reason to repent. (*CWE* 8:269/2–4, 12–6; Allen IV, 552/1–3, 9–12)

In October, writing to Nicolaas Everaerts, he looked back upon his time in Anderlecht: 'This whole summer I have spent in the country, and never was anything a greater success'.[41]

Yet soon after arrival in Anderlecht, having given up his lodgings in the College of the Lily in Louvain, Erasmus had written to Goclenius not to forget about renting a house for him there – provided it has a garden (Epistle 1209). *In totum*, Erasmus anticipated being away from Louvain for an extended period, perhaps a year, and wanted a place to return to; and even after his arrival in Basel he kept open the possibility of returning to Louvain (see Allen V, 12/10). And as he wrote to Bombasio as late as September 1521 (in Epistle 1236):

> I am still in two minds whether to go to Basel. For whole years now I have been going there, but something always crops up to keep me here [in Anderlecht]. Just now, I had quite made up my mind to take to the road, with the idea of finishing what I wished to do in Basel, and then migrating entirely to Rome, there to devote what time is left me to the society of great scholars and the resources of great libraries.[42]

Like every true scholar he knew the vital necessity of access to great research libraries and the need for serious conversation with fellow scholars.[43]

However pleasant the summer in Anderlecht and the lure of remaining there, Erasmus felt obliged, or driven, to move to Basel.

The period from May 1516, the time of his leaving Basel, to July 1517, the date of his arrival in Louvain, was a period of much movement; we observe the nomadic Erasmus and have almost the sense that his books and papers never catch up to him for very long. Yet he continued to work even on the move, and we have already caught a fascinating glimpse of him reading proofs on shipboard. This period of movement is followed by his settling down in Louvain, but with the atmosphere of criticism and growing conspiracy worsening; and the 1517–21 years conclude with an almost pastoral idyll in Anderlecht.

It is a period in which one must be struck by the amount of revising, annotating and translating that Erasmus managed to keep going, and at the same time to turn out new work: three new Adages, for example. This is the time when he laboured over the final touches to ensure the best possible reception for More's *Utopia*, and much of its initial success must be attributed to his editorial expertise and attention. There is another work of about these years (although the date of composition is even more uncertain than the authorship): the *Julius Exclusus* that surfaces in the correspondence in a letter from Thomas More (Epistle 502 of 15 December 1516), which expresses no opinion at that time about the dialogue, only that it was included among notebooks of Erasmus given to More by Lupset. Erasmus did not deny authorship, but only denied that he had authorised publication of it; but he did not include it in any of the official lists or collections of his writings (*CWE* 4:169n).

Following upon the tremendous acclaim given in most quarters to the *Novum Instrumentum*, Erasmus enjoyed a great surge of fame. In January of 1517, for example, duke George of Saxony wrote to Erasmus (Epistle 514):

> Since the report reached me of your eminence over the whole of Germany and every other nation, and how you are such a brilliant example of learning and scholarship that you more than any other man might well be called a light of the world, the desire has grown in me day by day to set eyes on the great man of whom such things are told. (*CWE* 4:183/1–5; Allen II, 431/1–4)

In March 1517 Giustiniani, the resident Venetian ambassador to England from 1515 to 1519, wrote: 'It is indeed surprising, the quality and quantity of what is wrought in your workshop' (Epistle 559, *CWE* 4:296/37; Allen II, 515/34). And Germain de Brie exclaimed from Paris in April 1517, 'Never did the world on our side of the Alps produce anything more richly gifted with every literary endowment than Erasmus' (Epistle 569, *CWE* 4:317/62–3; Allen II, 532/61–2). The great scholar Budé declared to Tunstall in May (Epistle 583), 'Erasmus has now for many years gathered a rich harvest of that solid and well-defined reputation which will endure down the centuries' (*CWE* 4:360/320–2; Allen II, 568/296–7). Others from every country joined the chorus of praise.

Invitations poured in from every country of Europe. To Pierre Barbier he wrote from Louvain in March 1518, in a summing up that is worth quoting in full:

> I am overwhelmed here with loving proposals from all quarters. I have had a letter from the archbishop of Mainz, one or two from the bishop of Utrecht, others from the bishops of Liège and Bayeux. They invite me to share bed and board. Invitations come from the king of England and his *fidus Achates* the cardinal of York, and from the king of France. I have so many suitors that it is difficult even to answer all their letters. (Epistle 704, *CWE* 5:342/74–343/80; Allen III, 249/68–73)

It was indeed the zenith of his fame, and there had been nothing before quite like it.

Yet there were dark clouds on the horizon with the imminent failure of the Fifth Lateran Council, which led Erasmus to think less and less of the efficacy of General Councils for achieving reform.[44] He had lost none of his zeal for reform, and one of his immediate targets was war and its frightful cost; he was becoming a more and more confirmed pacifist.[45]

The saddest news for him personally was always the death of a close friend, and especially one whom he entrusted with those thoughts and expressions of emotion that he could share with few others. Such a friend was Andreas Ammonio, whom he trusted enough to manage all the details of his petition for dispensation. He died on 17 August 1517, and the news was communicated by Thomas More on 19 August (Epistle 623). In an epidemic of 'sweating sickness' many died, More wrote, 'among them (which I am sorry to think will bring you sorrow too) our dear Andrea Ammonio, who is a very great loss to learning and to all right-thinking men...' (*CWE* 5:68/12–14; Allen III, 47/10–12).[46]

A second loss that moved him deeply was the death of Colet on 16 September 1519. Erasmus wrote immediately of his grief to Budé in Epistle 1023, and to friends in England in Epistles 1025–30. To Budé he was utterly simple in his direct statement: 'John Colet, best of men and most reliable of my friends, has died in London of the dropsy' (*CWE* 7:96/7–8; Allen IV, 87/6–7). To his English friends he was more free in revealing the depth of his emotions: to Pace he

wrote, 'I feel only half a man, with myself alive and Colet dead!'
(*CWE* 7:97/3); and to Thomas Lupset, who was a protégé of Colet, he
wrote, 'It must be thirty years since I feel any man's death as I feel
Colet's' (*CWE* 7:98/2). Erasmus's memorial of Colet in his letter to
Justus Jonas of 13 June 1521 (Epistle 1211) is a moving tribute and
a beautiful portrait.

This was the period during which Erasmus can well be said to
have been recognised universally as the prince of humanists, but he
had worked mightily for this accolade, and he was beginning to feel
keenly the passage of years. There was also the darkening cloud of
criticism, which by 1521 had become a constant concern.

Notes

1) The term 'Brabant' is used here by design, in place of the broader term
'Low Countries', which would include Holland. But Erasmus did not return
to Holland after 1501 (the reason, for a number of years, largely to stay away
from Steyn). He would not have thought of himself as Brabantine by birth, of
course: north Brabant reached only as far as 's-Hertogenbosch and a little
north, and his home was in south Holland (see ch. 1 on the names for
Erasmus' homeland). Brabant was a duchy until 1430, when it was united
with the duchy of Burgundy, and the chief city of Brabant, Brussels, became
the residence of the court under Maximilian and the capital of the Netherlands. For these years, from 1517 until late 1521, Erasmus was highly
conscious of his status as a member of the council of Charles, and he wished
to (perhaps he was in effect directed to) live within a relatively short radius of
Brussels, except for his required trips to Basel. Louvain was very much
Brabantine, and the University of Louvain came into being under several
auspices, for its foundation was authorised by the pope on 9 December 1425
at the request of duke John IV of Brabant, and also the chapter of St Peter's
and the city council of Louvain (*CWE* 8:374 n. 41).

2) In a fine intertextual allusion (weaving Horace's line that copied
Odyssey 1.3): 'he is now at least as wise as Ulysses in Homer, who knew the
"cities and the minds of many men", so many are the universities he has been
to' (*CWE* 3:298/4–6, Ep. 416).

3) The admirable phrase is owing to J.H. Parry, from his *Establishment of
European Hegemony*, 50.

4) It is remarkable that so many letters to Erasmus were safely forwarded.
He was better served, because of his international reputation, than many of us
are today.

5) See Pierre Mesnard, *L'Essor de la Philosophie politique au XVIᵉ Siècle*
(Paris, 1936; 2nd. ed., 1952) 86–140. The most satisfactory analysis of
Erasmus' politics, focusing upon the Low Countries, is by James D. Tracy,
The Politics of Erasmus (Toronto, 1978).

6) See note by Tracy, *Erasmus*, 171. Although according to Halkin (*BR*)
Erasmus had not visited Liège before 1519, in fact he was there in Aug. 1514
(cf. ch. 28).

7) Clava was one of Erasmus' frequent correspondents during this period (*BR*). Everardi (Tracy notes, 171n) had been chancellor to Hendrik van Bergen; Erasmus met him again during his stay in Louvain from 1502 to 1504 (ch. 19), noting that he had been named rector of Louvain in 1504. Everardi was supportive of humanism and contributed to making Mechlin a humanistic centre with his five sons, Cranevelt, Scheppter, Dantiscus (*BR*) and, one must add, Busleyden.

8) This letter dated Brussels 8 July 1516 (Allen II, 2/6) speaks of a prebend, which Erasmus planned to have converted into an annuity: see *CWE* 3:333/6n for explanation of the monetary value of this prebend. It is apparent that Le Sauvage hoped that the living would encourage Erasmus to take up permanent residence in the region.

9) While in Rochester he wrote a very long letter to Henry Bullock (Ep. 456) in defence of the *Novum Instrumentum;* for criticisms – the first serious criticism in a long history of criticism – were reaching his ear. In this letter there is the anecdote of the English priest who, in the prayer after communion during Mass, is supposed to pronounce the words '*Quod ore sumpsimus Domine',* but for twenty years he has been saying *mumpsimus.* When told that *sumpsimus* was what he ought to say, he refused to change a habit of twenty years (*CWE* 4:46/81 ff.; Allen II, 323/72 ff.). Erasmus uses the story to illustrate the difficulty of persuading people to change old habits, even when shown to be wrong.

10) For the later fortunes of this horse, see below.

11) To Gillis he wrote (Ep. 476, 6 October, from Brussels): 'I was unwilling, I said, to exchange my liberty for any bishopric however distinguished' (*CWE* 4:96/29–30; Allen II, 357/23–4). Much of the letter to Gillis was concerned with his health, and there is some irony in the long-ailing Erasmus writing to his friend, 'Good health, believe me, is mainly in your hands' (*CWE* 4:96/44; Allen II, 357/37) – or as we would now say, mainly in the mind.

12) Allen II, 426n. In Ep. 474 to Thomas More, Erasmus had spoken of 'that stupid fool': this and other passages critical of Dorp were removed from the *Epistolae ad diversos* (printed by Froben in August 1521), doubtless (as Allen remarks) in 'an endeavour to preserve the better understanding arrived at in 1517'. Dorp is worth at least the attention of a footnote, for in 1514 and 1515 there had been a lengthy controversy between him and Erasmus, with Thomas More taking up the matter in one of his most important humanistic letters (cf. More's letter to Dorp, written from Bruges 21 October 1515, in *St Thomas More, Selected Letters*, ed. E.F. Roberts [New Haven, Conn., 1967, 2d ed.] 8ff.). More's letter is a point-by-point reply to Dorp on the importance of Greek, the place of grammar and its relation to theology, the meaning of the *Moria,* and the reading and value of classical literature: it is a defence of humanism and of Erasmus. On Dorp and the involved story of his relationship with Erasmus, which developed ultimately from reconciliation into friendship, see the valuable essay by J. IJsewijn in *BR.*

13) In Van der Haeghen it is noted that the letter to Dorp was reprinted at least four times in 1515, again in 1516, 1519, 1520, and 1521 (and included in the 1540 *Opera omnia*); the letter to Wimpheling was reprinted twice in 1514, twice in 1516, once in 1517, twice in 1519, twice in 1521, three times in 1522, and so on.

14) Literally (as Mynors notes in *CWE*), 'in the spirit of gladiators', thus invoking the metaphor of *Adag.* I. iii. 76, recurring in later adages as well. Echoes of his adages are rarely absent from his letters, but there are times, doubtless when he has been working at revision or composition of his adages, when the atmosphere of a letter is especially full of these echoes.

15) Erasmus wrote them individually in Eps 566 and 567, in appropriate language, from Brussels in early April, where he arrived after leaving Antwerp on about 1 April (Ep. 572/16–7 & n).

16) Ammonio was a man of many offices: in 1509 he became secretary to Lord Mountjoy, and by 1511 Latin secretary to Henry VIII. In 1515 he was appointed by Leo X as subcollector of papal taxes in England; and his connections with Gigli, bishop of Worcester and English ambassador to Rome (and later papal collector for England) were close. See *BR*.

17) See Cecil H. Clough, 'Erasmus and the Pursuit of English Royal Patronage in 1517 and 1518', *ERSYB* 1 (1981) 126–40.

18) Barbier was an old friend (*BR*), who by 1521 was in the service of cardinal Adrian of Utrecht; Erasmus seems to have kept in view the cardinal as also reading the letter.

19) Tracy, *Erasmus*, 172, who notes that 'since their reconciliation in January his contacts with Dorp and Briard had been friendly'. The friars are not kindly treated in the *Colloquies*.

20) *The Study of the Bible in the Middle Ages*, 356, and she continues with the words of Andrew of St Victor, speaking (as he says) for scholars of all periods: '*Ab otiosis et in tempore otii et non a discurrentibus et perturbationis tempore sapientia discitur*': wisdom indeed is learnt from the leisured, in time of leisure, not from the hurried in time of disturbance. William Latimer, writing to Erasmus in January 1517 (Epistle 520) exclaimed in much the same vein: 'And besides this interruption in my studies, which I believe to be the greatest of all enemies to scholarship...' (*CWE* 4:199/44–5). William Latimer (d. before 17 Oct. 1543), was a friend of More, Grocyn and Linacre, as well as Erasmus (McConica in *BR*). Interestingly, only his letters to Erasmus survive of his writings. These reflections have a direct bearing on our thinking about the structures for research and teaching of the humanities in our own age when the isolated scholar may well find a 'a mere dead-end' (Smalley, 356).

21) In the 1523 edition there is an interpolation on marriage, which is to be related to his *Encomium Matrimonii* of 1526 and other writings on marriage.

22) Here too Erasmus could be perceived as threatening the traditional teaching of many theologians: by denying the essentiality of scholastic theology, by reducing the emphasis on the sacramental system, and by conceiving of Christendom as existing without an elaborate structure: there is a place for the hierarchy, in the innermost part of the structure, but it is they whose 'duty is to follow the Lamb wherever he shall go'. There is more commentary on this theme in the letter to Volz prefixed to the 1518 rev. ed. of the *Enchiridion*. Volz was a Benedictine abbot whose monastery had undergone reform. Kent Emery discusses the metaphor of a *scopus* and fixed sighting taken from the sailor's navigational art (via Boyle?) in the *Ratio*: see his *Renaissance Dialectic and Renaissance Piety* (1987) 46.

23) For Erasmus' earlier friendship with Desmarez, see ch. 19 and *BR*. Desmarez had urged Erasmus to publish his *Panegyricus* (if Erasmus ever needed encouragement to publish anything); this Erasmus dedicated to him as well as his subsequent translation of Lucian's *De mercede conductis* in 1506. Listris' very important commentary on the *Moria* (published in the Froben edition of 1515) was dedicated to Desmarez; and Geldenhouwer, associated with Desmarez in the *parerga* of the 1516 edition of More's *Utopia*, dedicated a work to Desmarez in 1517 (*BR*). Erasmus grieved over the death of his old friend in 1526 (see Ep. 1694).

24) That the work of revision spread out over many months is witnessed by Erasmus' letter (Ep. 649) to Gigli (7 Sept. 1517) in which he speaks of having the New Testament in hand once more (*CWE* 5:100/10; Allen III, 72/8–9).

25) *CWE* 4:68/8–9; Allen II, 340/5–6. Nesen's reply (Ep. 473) at the end of the month was reassuring: 'I will do my very best to see that the *Copia* appears in Froben's type as quickly and as neatly as can be' (*CWE* 4:89/18–9; Allen II, 352/17–8). In his April 1517 letter (Ep. 575) Beatus Rhenanus wrote: 'Your books on *Copia* have been printed quite neatly' (*CWE* 4:342/47; Allen II, 551/44).

26) See C.H. Miller, trans. with introd. of *The Praise of Folly* (New Haven, Conn., 1979) xxxiv.

27) Illustrations taken from this edition were photographed from a copy in the possession of the author.

28) M.A. Screech, *Ecstasy and the Praise of Folly*, 4.

29) Dorp's criticism and Erasmus' reply occasioned More's letter to Dorp, discussed above (n.12).

30) This was a reprint of the second ed. of the *Lucubratiunculae* (Strasbourg, 1515), supervised by Gerbel.

31) On the handwriting of Erasmus, see H. Callewaert, *Physiologie de l'écriture cursive* (Bruges, 1937), and van Damme, *Erasmus*, 162. The portraits by Metsys, Dürer and Holbein all exhibit Erasmus as a writer (see appendix E).

32) It is a kind of *declamatio*, relatively short (cols. 625–42 in *LB* IV), and much reprinted in the 16th c. See the definitive edition by Otto Herding in *ASD* 4:1 (1974), of both the *Institutio* and the *Panegyricus*, together with his valuable introduction.

33) Here it is appropriate to note that Huizinga's celebrated book on *The Waning of the Middle Ages* (first published in Dutch 1919 and translated into English 1924) had as its original title *Herfsttij der Middeleuwen*, which means more nearly *harvest-time* than *waning* (though the French translation is like the English in being entitled *déclin*); it is a book, as the subtitle clearly indicates, about 'forms of life, thought and art'. The final paragraph of Huizinga's great book makes clear this intellectual thrust and confirms the relevance for understanding the Burgundian court and the upbringing of Charles: 'the fifteenth century in France and the Netherlands is still medieval at heart. The diapason of life had not yet changed. Scholastic thought, with symbolism and strong formalism, the thoroughly dualistic conception of life and the world still dominated. The two poles of the mind continued to be chivalry and hierarchy. Profound pessimism spread a general gloom over life.

The gothic principle prevailed in art. But all these forms and modes were on the wane. A high and strong culture is declining, but at the same time and in the same sphere new things are being born. The tide is turning, the note of life is about to change.' (p. 308). These are themes discussed in Vol. 1, and to which we shall return in our final chapter. Huizinga's work has had a powerful effect upon 20th-c. views of the renaissance period, especially in the Low Countries; attention should be called to the essay by F.W.N. Hugenholtz, 'The fame of a Masterwork', in *Johan Huizinga 1872–1972*, ed. W.R.H. Koops, E.H. Kossmann, and Gees van der Plaat (The Hague, 1973) 91–103.

34) Thus Tracy in *The Politics of Erasmus*, 59. Many fathers among the aristocracy were reluctant to have their sons study the humanities, and we recall that More's father pulled him away from Oxford after two years so that he could get to the serious business of studying the common law.

35) I am indebted to the entry on Metsys in *BR* by Marcel A. Nauwelaerts and P.G. Bietenholz. See further the bibliography cited in appendix E.

36) See further J.B. Trapp, et al., 'Quentin Matsys, Erasmus, Pieter Gillis, and Thomas More', *Burlington Magazine* 120 (1978) 716–25; and J.B. Trapp, 'A Postscript to Matsys', ibid., 121 (1979) 437–7; and Larry Silver, *The Paintings of Quinten Massys* (Montclair, N.J., 1984).

37) *'Habeo sedem, ubi bibliothecam meam habeo'* (Ep. 809, April 1518, Allen III, 266/117–8). Still, Erasmus had vacated his lodgings in the college at Louvain, and very likely he did not wish to leave his papers and books there for too long, whatever his plans.

38) Cf. Halkin, *Erasme, Sa Pensée*, I, 85: 'Dans la dernière de ces localités brabançonnes, il trouve une maison de campagne ou il vit heureux, à deux pas de Bruselles, la cour s'interposant entre lui et Louvain'.

39) As he wrote more than once, *'hoc coelo puriore'*: cf. Allen IV, 591/11 (letter of late summer 1521), and V, 95/15–8 (from Basel in July 1522).

40) This note is repeated throughout the Anderlecht letters (Eps 1208–1240), though not in every letter.

41) Ep. 1238 October 1521 (*CWE* 8: 311/12–4). In this letter Erasmus observed that 'never before was it so clear to me that climate and not food dictates our life' (ll. 11–12). One wonders whether some of Erasmus' illnesses and malaise may not have been due to polluted water in the cities.

42) *CWE* 8:308/197–202; Allen IV, 587/177–82. As Bietenholz notes (at 446/39): 'the war in Italy ruled out even a visit to Rome'. Erasmus had particularly wanted to visit Pyrrhus d'Angleberme, a pupil during his 1500 visit to Orleans (*BR*), but he died in 1521: 'for his sake I particularly longed to visit Milan, if that blockhead the god of war did not reduce everything to chaos with his furious uproar' (333/10–11).

43) For Erasmus with his many works in progress, including revisions of editions that demanded more and more Greek type, the need to work closely with a printer and his staff was an urgent consideration.

44) Erasmus commented on its conducting of business in Ep. 456 and elsewhere. The council's final session was on 16 March 1517: see R.J. Schoeck, 'The Fifth Lateran Council', 116.

45) On the pacifism of Erasmus, see Leon-E. Halkin, 'Erasme, la guerre et la paix', rptd. in *Érasme. Sa pensée et son comportement* (London, 1988) xvi; Pierre

Brachin, '"Vox clamantis in deserto" – reflexions sur le pacifisme d'Erasme', in *Colloquia Erasmiana Turonensia,* ed. J.-C. Margolin (Toronto, 1972); and Robert Adams, *The Better Part of Valor: More, Erasmus, Colet and Vives on Humanism, War and Peace* (Seattle, Wash., 1962).

46) Johannes Sixtinus (who had witnessed the dispensation ceremony) reported the news in a separate letter (Ep. 624). A graduate of Siena (*CWE* 5: 69n), he had close ties with Ammonio and was as well an old friend of Erasmus (*BR*). Erasmus was saddened by the news of Ammonio's death, and he asked Sixtinus and another friend, Vannes (a cousin of Andreas Ammonio), 'to collect his correspondence with Ammonio lest it should fall into the wrong hands' (Eps 655 & 656) having in mind particularly papers relating to the papal dispensation, which contained privileged information.

The Rising Storm of Controversy: Erasmus and his Catholic Critics, 1517–1522

for here a great revolution seems to be in prospect ...
Erasmus to Thomas More, March 1517,
Epistle 545 (*CWE* 4:274/11; Allen II, 496/10)

We often see how from such a small spark is kindled a mighty conflagration.
Erasmus to Pirckheimer, 2 November 1517,
Epistle 694 (Allen III, 118/82–3)

One thing ought to be a great consolation to you, that, as you well know, none of the ancient Fathers, even the most saintly of them, found his efforts so successful that he had no experience of these quarrelsome gentry; and your situation is in a way better than that in which the ancients found themselves, because in those days there were so many more men of great learning that they could not achieve such an outstanding reputation, and so were an easier target for their enemies and those who lay in wait for them. But you, as the leading light of our generation, stand above all the hazards of ill will, so that, let them bark as loud as they please, they cannot weaken your authority, for such accusations find credence nowhere. Go valiantly on your way then, and continue to support the republic of letters as you always have.
Alciati to Erasmus, c. 29 May 1522,
Epistle 1288 (*CWE* 9: 103/37–47; Allen V, 72/34–44)

Not but what I have maintained my record of not writing to hurt to the extent of never drawing sword against anyone except under insufferable provocation; nor have I ever answered anyone without overcoming by forbearance an adversary who had the advantage of me in scurrility. ...
Erasmus to Botzheim, January 1523,
Epistle 1341A (*CWE* 9: 325/790–7; Allen I, 21, 27–32)

Every schoolboy knows, or should know, that Martin Luther tacked his Ninety-Five Theses to the church door in Wittenberg on the Eve of All Saints, October 1517, since known to Lutherans and others as

Reformation Day. He was a professor at the University of Wittenberg, and he chose the customary way of publicising theses he wished to defend in disputation, and the door of the castle church (Schlosskirche) was the most public place imaginable.[1] The immediate cause for Luther's posting of the theses was the preaching by the Dominican Johann Tetzel on papal indulgences. In writing to Thomas More in March 1518 (Epistle 785) Erasmus first alluded to Luther's Ninety-Five Theses (calling them 'the Conclusions on Papal pardons': *Conclusiones de veniis Pontificum* – *CWE*: 5:327/39; Allen III, 239/37). But in the same letter to More Erasmus declared that the 'German presses have gone mad' and the impact of Luther shows more and more in his writings.

Reform was not new in 1517, nor was it born only in Germany. Well before the end of the fifteenth century there had been strong expressions of the need for reform in the Netherlands, and in a number of these protests or criticisms the influence of the Brethren of the Common Life can be seen. One of the leaders of the pre-reform movement – to give it a limping title that comes from an excess of historical hindsight – was Wessel Gansfort (1419–1489), who had been schooled under the Brethren at Zwolle, where he grew up under the influence of Thomas à Kempis and later went on to study theology at Cologne, Heidelberg and Louvain (*BR*). But there were others, of course: Jan Hus, Nicolas of Cusa, and Jean Gerson among them.[2]

The *de rigeur* journey to Italy for early humanists was followed for Gansfort by a lengthy sojourn in Paris, after which he lived in Basel and Heidelberg, where he was a professor. He was disputatious (but modest) and was known as the *Magister Contradictionis* (master of contradictions), and in fact he took a number of strong positions on theological matters or disputed questions. In 1479 Gansfort was forced to leave Heidelberg 'on account of the persecutions of his opponents among the Dominicans',[3] who were nearly always on the side of tradition and conservatism (hence disliked or distrusted by Erasmus), and he returned to his native town of Zwolle, where he was under the protection of bishop David of Utrecht, who took his part against the Dominicans of Groningen.

Gansfort opposed the use of excommunication, and questioned the strict doctrines of transubstantiation, absolution, veneration of saints, and the use of the rosary (Blok, I, 301f). He had many followers among Dutch priests and schoolteachers, among whom was Rudolph Agricola (an associate in the Aduard Academy), who also questioned transubstantiation and certain other doctrines promulgated by the fifteenth-century Church. Gansfort exemplifies the thrust of much of the early reform thought, and the questioning of the teaching authority of the Church cannot be minimised.

There is a line, then, from Gansfort through Agricola to Erasmus – even directly so, for Erasmus owned some of Gansfort's work and mentions him (*BR*) – on the need for reformation within the Church and on the desirability of simplifying the doctrines which it preached and proclaimed. From Groningen south, even to Louvain in Brabant, there were many who were sympathetic to the idea of reform, lay as well as religious, rich as well as poor.

Erasmus contributed vitally to the quickening of this spirit by his *Moria* and *Colloquies*, which criticised abuses and excesses, and his challenging of the authoritative Vulgate shook the confidence of many in an absolute authority of the Church. Further, his letters constituted a unique clearing-house of ideas and news of individuals and events.

Erasmus was steeped in the values of the *Devotio Moderna*, not only through the teachings and writings of the Brethren of the Common Life (see appendix B), but also directly through his own reading of the *Devotio* masters. Perhaps it is when he seems furthest from the *Devotio*, as when he so obviously is not quoting them, that Erasmus is closest in the spirit.[4]

What was new in 1517 was Martin Luther, who burst upon the European scene with the boldness and clarity of his Ninety-Five Theses, and the acceleration provided by the printing-press. If as late as 1519 Erasmus could claim to Campeggio that he knew little about Luther as author and had not yet read the book through (Epistle 961; *CWE* 6:351/36 ff.; Allen III, 574/30–333) and in the same year he could write to John Fisher that he reserved judgment (Epistle 937/107–8: 'On Luther I will write at more length another day'); the pressure of events would not permit him to maintain his detachment or objectivity for long. There was already a swarm of pamphlets, and the Reformation was well under way.

It is against this background that Erasmus now became embroiled in controversy. Controversy is both the act and the form of disputing, conducted in public between sides that hold opposing views. Controversy was built into medieval scholasticism and the medieval *disputatio* was one of the three characteristic modes of argument and writing (chapter 11); but scholastic debate and dialectic had its rules, as reformation controversy did not. Shakespeare's lines in *Julius Caesar*, I.ii.109, might have been written of the early sixteenth century, which introduced an age of passionate, sometimes violent, nearly always longwinded, controversy: 'The Torrent roar'd, and we did buffet it … stemming it with hearts of Controversie'.

Erasmus disliked the scholastic disputation which he was obliged to participate in during his student years in Paris, and in its place he wrote declamations and dialogues. Besides, he turned increasingly to irony, and there is no room for irony in scholastic dialectic. Had Erasmus had his way, he would not have given so much of his time and energy to controversy. But the catholic critics of Louvain and England – so called to distinguish their criticism from that of the Reformers of the 1520s – thrust controversy upon him. He did not respond to every criticism, but he felt obliged to answer those that he felt challenged *bonae litterae* or imputed false motives to his way of life or scholarship.[5] Out of controversy there may perhaps come a greater precision of language, or a clarifying of one's premises: not always, for there are too many ways to respond to argument, and the sixteenth century quickly adapted scholastic logic as well as classical rhetoric to serve in the battles that were joined.

With some of his critics Erasmus chose to respond in letters, and with others there is the group rebuttal in the *Colloquies* (as, for example, with the Carmelites and Dominicans). There are, however, several with whom the controversy has a greater lasting-power and a greater importance. Among them are Standish, Latomus, Lee, the friars – and always the theologians of Louvain. These we shall take up *seriatim*.[6]

One of the earliest of Erasmus' opponents in controversy was the Franciscan Henry Standish (born not later than 1468, and died 1535). He received his doctorate in theology at Oxford before January 1502, and from 1505 until 1518 he was provincial of his order in England; he was no straw man. He was a popular preacher, often delivering sermons before the court; and in 1515 he became embroiled in the notorious Hunne affair,[7] into which he entered on the side of royal and parliamentary authority. He was charged with heresy by a convocation at Canterbury, but charges were dropped. The affair became a burning issue in the polemics of Thomas More, William Tyndale, and Christopher Saint-German from 1529 to 1534.

Erasmus probably met Standish on his trip to England in 1515, and it is apparent that he disliked the Franciscan from the first, both for the rigidity of his views and for his unscrupulousness in debate. He let pass few opportunities to ridicule him, beginning perhaps as early as his letter of May 1515, where he speaks of drinking wine with a certain Franciscan, 'a Scotist of the first rank', who criticised Erasmus' plans for the edition of St Jerome despite his own obvious ignorance of the works of the saint (Epistle 337). More too joined in the ridiculing of Standish (Epistle 481), and in letters to Henry Bullock (Epistle 777), Maarten Lips (Epistle 843), and Philip Melanchthon (Epistle 1113), Erasmus further referred to Standish as a 'beast' who spoke against his editions of Jerome and the New Testament, and supported his arch-enemy Edward Lee. In 1517 he made Standish the butt of the adage *'Esernius cum Pacidiano'* (*Adag.* II.v.98).[8] By July 1520 Erasmus heard that Standish had attacked his rendition of John 1:1 as *'in principio erat sermo'* in a sermon at St Paul's (that most public of pulpits), and More took Standish to task at court. That Standish was made a bishop in 1518 and remained a favourite of the king (perhaps because of his siding with royal authority and taking arms against ecclesiastical interference) was doubtless a source of irritation to Erasmus (Epistle 2205).[9]

Jacobus Latomus (Jacques Masson, c. 1475–1544) studied in Paris under Standonck, an ancient enemy of Erasmus (chapter 12), and he was one of the Louvain theologians who welcomed Erasmus, as we have seen. After the first edition of his New Testament and while preparing the second, Erasmus asked Latomus and others for their comments (Epistles 1225, 1571, 1581), but none of them gave him any serious criticism. Their previously amicable relations apparently broke down over the question of the teaching of Greek and Hebrew, which became an issue in 1517 with the founding of the Collegium Trilingue. Latomus thought the teaching of Greek and Hebrew dangerous rather than useful (*BR*).[10]

The primary disagreement between the two men began with the Erasmian emphasis on the teaching of the three languages, which Latomus strongly disputed, despite the bull *'De Magistris'* of Clement V enjoining universities to teach all three. In fact, Latomus balked at the Erasmian emphasis on language studies,[11] for this disturbed the all too traditional concept of theology as not only above but distinct from the liberal arts. There was also the matter of the ranking of patristic authors, with Latomus preferring Augustine and suspicious of Erasmus' high regard for Origen, who was suspect in orthodox quarters. Finally, Latomus thought that Erasmus' emphasis on the textual study of Scripture, with its concentration on source readings, was 'dangerous because of the underlying idea that doctrine need not be accepted unless it was clearly founded on Scripture' (Rummel, 17): this was close to the later Lutheran *sola Scriptura*.

The spark that flashed the fire would seem to have been an anonymous satire, in which Erasmus may not have had an active hand, but some of whose ideas are certainly Erasmian: *Dialogus bilinguium ac trilinguium*.[12] It was in circulation not later than July

1519 (*CWE* 9:330 ff.), and there were three early editions. It seems evident that Erasmus was not aware of the publication of the dialogue, but he did not specifically either admit to or disavow its authorship (332).[13] Given that there is no evidence to suggest that Latomus had even a modicum of a sense of humour, we may take it that he was not pleased by the dialogue.

But clearly Latomus reacted strenuously to Erasmus' *Ratio Verae Theologiae* in November 1518 (published by the Louvain printer Dirk Martens), and he responded with his own dialogue *De trium linguarum et studii theologici* (Antwerp, Hillen, 1519), on which in March 1519 Erasmus wrote: 'I send a pamphlet by Jacobus Latomus, a scholarly and elegant performance which many people suspect to be not his own unaided work but put together by the theologians in conclave, and aimed at me.'[14] Erasmus replied to Latomus with the rather temperate *Apologia contra Latomi dialogum* (Louvain, 1519).

Friction between Erasmus and Latomus, and the Louvain theologians *en bloc*, worsened, leading to the official condemnation of Luther in November 1519 and the beginning of an investigation of Erasmus' writings. Vives confirmed Erasmus' view that Latomus was leading the attack and was continuing to rant and rave against Erasmus (Epistle 1256). Over the next several years there are many references to Latomus and the Louvain attacks against him in Erasmus' correspondence.

Latomus continued a campaign against what he thought was heresy with 'unrelenting vehemence' (*BR*); and it hurt Erasmus' reputation to be included among the targets. One view of Latomus is that of a bitter and unrelenting opponent (Tournoy in *BR*), and it is a persuasive one. It is to be noted, as G. J. Donnelly has done, that Latomus was a dedicated defender of orthodoxy as well as a gifted Latin scholar, and that he wrote tracts not simply against Erasmus but against a range of individuals: Johannes Oecolampadius, Beatus Rhenanus, Jean Gerson, Bartholomew Batnus, and William Tyndale.[15]

The controversy between Erasmus and Edward Lee was one which added nothing to the reputation of either, although it did catapult Lee to the front of the scholarly stage in 1518 and 1519, and it cost Erasmus a great effort. His letters for the next several years are filled with direct and veiled allusions to Lee, and Erasmus felt it necessary to justify his action to Henry VIII, Thomas More, and others.

Although of good family and with an MA from Cambridge in 1504, Lee had no professional degree or office, not receiving the doctorate in divinity until 1531; and yet he set about reviewing the New Testament of Erasmus at a time when Erasmus was preparing the second edition. Before Erasmus left for Basel in the spring of 1518, Lee had worked up some 150 notes, copies of which he carefully kept, but waited for a response from Erasmus before sending him more. By the time Erasmus returned in September 1518, Lee had increased his notes to between 200 and 300. Erasmus offered to incorporate Lee's corrections in the revision, for which he was about to send Froben revised notes and final corrections (Rummel, 97). There was a standoff: Lee did not show Erasmus his additional notes and was indignant over Erasmus' behaviour towards him (as Lee told the story later), and Erasmus, while willing to incorporate Lee's corrections with proper acknowledgments, was not prepared to treat him as a collaborator.[16] Letters passed back and forth with advice from Fisher, Colet and More (Rummel, 98). The *Apologia contra Latomi dialogum*,[17] published in 1519, angered Lee, and the satirical *Dialogus bilinguium ac trilinguium* annoyed him further, for he saw himself ridiculed there. The upshot was that Lee sent off to Paris a manuscript incorporating his notes, and it was published by Gilles Gourmont in February 1520.

A narrative of the events is provided by Lee in Epistle 1061, which is a point-by-point rebuttal of points raised in Erasmus' Epistle 998. Bietenholz writes that 'Lee's recollection of facts and dates appears to be accurate, while in the analysis of these events bias stands against bias' (*CWE* 7:171, introductory note).

What can be learned from Lee's writings against Erasmus? It is clear that he felt from the beginning that Erasmus had acted patronisingly: doubtless he had, for Lee had little Greek and no real credentials in theology.[18] Lee seems also to have felt that Erasmus did not take his criticisms seriously enough, while those with merit were in danger of being taken over by the older scholar. On the side of Erasmus, it must be noted that again and again Lee charged him with going counter to church dogma and acting in defiance of the Church: on this score Erasmus was already sensitive and would grow ever more so as the Reformation developed. The exchanges and developing controversy call attention to Erasmus' characteristic response to criticism: it was difficult enough for him to accept criticism from anyone, but impossible for him to take it from one whom he regarded as brash, unqualified and ambitious. Yet Erasmus admitted to his friends that his New Testament needed revision, and he continued to revise it, as already seen in chapter 32.

Soon after the publication of the New Testament Erasmus felt that there was a conspiracy of friars against him.[19] To More he wrote in the summer of 1517: 'the Dominicans and some of the Carmelites are beginning actually to call on the mob to start throwing stones, and nowhere do those pestilent folk flourish more than in my native land ... ' (Epistle 597, *CWE* 5:12–13/63–6; Allen III, 6/56–58). Once in Louvain he wrote further: 'Men of motley garments, especially some of the Preacher, and Carmelite gang, are putting their heads together and baying in the distance; to my face, not a word from anybody.'[20]

The friars were of course international, and among those whom Erasmus had in mind we must count the English Henry Standish, the Franciscan whom we have just encountered; the Carmelite Nicolaus Baechem, a fellow Dutchman; and a number of Louvain Dominicans, among them the Spanish Jorge Ateca (confessor of queen Catherine) and Johann Löblein from Leipzig. But one must be singled out from this crowd: Nicolaus Baechem Egmondanus, a Carmelite who studied at Louvain and from 1510 onwards was prior of the Carmelites there. His opposition began with the appearance of the New Testament in 1516; as Erasmus wrote in a letter to More that is remarkably vivid in its account of the confrontation with Baechem before the rector (Epistle 1162/98), he 'tore into me even before I moved to Louvain'. According to Erasmus in another letter, 'when the New Testament had appeared, he cried out that I was the Antichrist' (Epistle 1581, Allen VI, 93/241–2). The violence and rancour of such reactions to the New Testament can only be interpreted as stemming from resentment and fear. Such a world of new readings derived from intimate knowledge of the Greek was, for professional theologians who knew little or no Greek, beyond their philological reach: it was a threat. Erasmus continues that when urged to point out the offensive passages, Baechem remained silent until pressed, and then 'this reverend father said that he had never read my annotations'.[21] But Baechem could not be dismissed, for he was a person of power, and in 1520 he was appointed assistant inquisitor of the Netherlands by Charles (*BR*); thereafter he began as a matter of habit to link Erasmus' name with that of Luther. When the 1522 edition of the *Colloquia* appeared, Baechem inveighed against such 'Lutheran heresies' as the writing against indulgences, fasting and auricular confession. With Baechem Erasmus had just cause in complaining about his defamatory preaching to Rosemondt and others.

One must note Erasmus' getting back at the Carmelites in a number of colloquies. In 'The Godly Feast' (1522), for one, there are amusing world-plays on camel/Carmelitic.[22]

Another Carmelite and apparently a co-conspirator with Baechem was the suffragan bishop of Cambrai, Jean Briselot, who in 1517 became confessor to the future Charles V and thus had a power base for his hostility.[23] In fact, as Farge notes in *BR*, 'from the time he left the Burgundian court and settled down in Louvain (the summer of 1517) Erasmus considered Briselot as one of his prominent enemies, doubly dangerous because of his influence with Charles (Epistles 608, 628, 641, 1040) and especially critical of the *Moria* (Epistles 597, 7 39); in consequence he spoke of him with frank animosity and also irony (Epistles 695, 794).' The death of Briselot in 1520, only five months after receiving the archbishopric of Oristano in Sardinia, removed a powerful enemy; and of his passing Erasmus wrote with dripping irony in Epistle 794: 'I have heard a most damnable rumour, at which I almost fainted away, about Briselot, that he had departed for the Elysian Fields, and I was preparing a suitable lament to commemorate the loss of such a leading light.' (*CWE* 5:339/227–30; Allen III, 247/25–98). Erasmus' *Apologia de 'In principio erat sermo'* is a part of this affair. It saw the light of day in Froben's edition of 1520 and was then reprinted more than six times in the next year and a half, indicating the widespread interest not only in scriptural matters but the controversy that was growing in intensity.[24]

An anonymous pamphlet entitled *Consilium cuiusdam ex animo cupientis esse consultum et Romani pontificis dignitati et christianae tranquillitati* appeared in Cologne and was printed at least five times in 1521 and 1522, and soon translated four times into German. Erasmus was thought to be the author, and Luther credited the pamphlet to him without hesitation. It is apparent that Erasmus endorsed its views, summarised the ideas extensively in Epistle 1156, and echoed some of the statements verbatim in his letters (*CWE* 8: introduction to Epistle 1149). We can safely take Erasmus to be the co-author, along with Johannes Faber of Augsburg, prior of the Dominican house there.[25] The essence of the views of Faber and Erasmus that is embraced in the *Consilium* is the belief that Luther had not had a fair hearing from the ecclesiastical authorities, and that a peaceful solution could come only through an independent commission that would enquire into the Lutheran matter and arbitrate between Luther and the authorities.

Even if Erasmus was probably not the author of the entire document, the *Consilium* is significant in manifesting Erasmus' irenicism in an early form. The full title is a clear signal of the thrust of the argument: 'Counsel of a Certain Man Sincerely Concerned for both the Dignity of the Roman Pontiff and Christian Peace'.[26]

Following on the heels of the *Consilium* was another anonymous writing, *Acta Academiae Lovaniensis contra Lutherum* (also Cologne, November 1520), which is an insider's account of the Louvain controversies (Tracy, 185 n). It contains the threatening statement – granted it is assigned to Hoogstraat (318) – *qui illam bestiam {the papacy} non adorarint*', which Tracy takes as 'implying Luther's belief that the papacy is Antichrist, [which] is utterly out of character for Erasmus ... ' (185 n). But as Tournoy notes in *BR*, Hoogstraat was indicted by Erasmus together with Baechem 'as a principal enemy of the *bonae literae*' whose unthinking zeal against Luther he deplored. The statement quoted from the *Acta Academiae* is not far from what Erasmus thought Hoogstraat capable of.[27]

While neither the *Consilium*, almost certainly co-authored by Erasmus, nor the *Acta*, less certainly from Erasmus' hand (though the publication was not at his instance) is a work of prime importance in charting the development of Erasmus' thought, both are of great interest in displaying the cross-currents of these months: the manoeuvrings and the accelerating pace of events. Faber's entrance upon the stage is symptomatic: Erasmus wrote letters of introduction for him, and he showed the *Consilium* to Albert of Mainz, Erard de la Marck, and Mercurio Gattinara, who had succeeded Jean Le Sauvage as the chancellor of young king Charles in 1518 (Epistle 1150, in which Erasmus introduces both Faber and himself). In Cologne there were important meetings (Tracy, 186; Smith, 234–6), and on 5 November 1520 Erasmus was summoned to an interview with the elector of Saxony, Frederick the Wise, with Spalatin present as interpreter.[28] Erasmus spoke in Latin, which Frederick understood but preferred to put his questions in German through Spalatin.[29] The first question was whether Luther had erred, to which Erasmus replied, 'Luther has erred in two points – in attacking the crown of the pope and the bellies of the monks'.[30] When the papal envoys, Aleander and Eck, called on 6 November, Frederick gave them a complete refusal of their demands (Smith, 237).

At Frederick's request Erasmus drew up a series of short propositions that might serve as the basis for settling the whole affair; these he called '22 Axioms on behalf of Luther'. Erasmus' essential sympathy with Luther – at that time – is shown in this document, which declares:

> That the origin of the persecution [of Luther] was hatred of learning and love of tyranny; that the method of procedure corresponded with the origin, consisting, namely, of clamour, conspiracy, bitter hatred, and virulent writing; that the agents put in charge of the prosecution were suspect; that all good men and lovers of the Gospel were very little offended with Luther; that certain men had abused the easy-going kindness of the pope.

Thus the summary by Smith (236), who adds:

> The author advised that precipitate counsels be avoided, as the fierceness of the Bull had scandalised all and was unworthy of the gentleness of Christ's vicar, and that the cause be examined by impartial and experienced persons ... Erasmus added orally that Luther had been too violent; and Spalatin promised to remonstrate with him.[31]

Aleander tried to win Erasmus over to the direct and outspoken support of the pope, but Erasmus refused, and he also declined all his invitations to dinner – fearing, as he later declared, that he would be poisoned.[32]

Erasmus still tried to remain neutral, writing to Reuchlin on 8 November (Epistle 1155) from Cologne:

> You can see what a desperate tragedy is now being enacted, and what will happen in the last act is uncertain. Whatever the outcome, I pray it may tend to the glory of Christ and profit the truth of the Gospel. I would rather be a spectator of this play than one of the actors; not that I refuse to undergo some risks for Christ's sake, but because I see clearly enough that the business is too big for a small man like me ... The truth must win. And the unspoken judgments of men of good will acquire an authority which will retain their force even among posterity. (*CWE* 8:78/7–12; Allen IV, 371/5–10)

After the three strenuous and anxious weeks at Cologne, Erasmus returned to Louvain in a journey made treacherous by floods, the horses being 'almost shipwrecked' as the humanist wittily put it (Epistle 1169).

All this business, and his failure in Cologne to win an arbitration, marks indeed a turning point for Erasmus. He had not joined the Roman strategy of attacking and destroying Luther. For the sake of peace he wrote five personal letters to Luther enjoining mildness, but saving one (Epistle 1041) they have perished. The event that produced his total turning away from the Lutheran cause was the double shock of Luther's burning of canon-law books at Wittenberg on 10 December 1520, and his *On the Babylonian Captivity of the Church*. Erasmus' letters to Everaerts of 25 February 1521 (Epistle 1186) and March 1521 (Epistle 1188) sum up his feelings: 'What a load of unpopularity Luther is piling both on liberal studies and on true Christianity!' (*CWE* 8: 155/1/–2; Allen IV, 444/1–2: '*rem Christianam*').

One last act remained to be played out before Erasmus would leave Louvain for a more tranquil place: the Diet at Worms in January 1521. This was the first Diet opened by Charles, and it was here that Luther came on 17 April and again on the 18th and refused to retract one whit of his doctrine. Erasmus had been invited to be present but declined, as he explained, partly because of the plague in that crowded town but more because of not wanting to meddle with the religious question (Smith, 245). While the Diet was in session, Erasmus was a spectator at Louvain and Antwerp. After the Diet Luther was returning home when he was seized by retainers of the elector Frederick and taken to the Wartburg, a castle near Eisenach, for his safety. In Epistle 1218 Erasmus wrote to Pace that the Germans wanted to drag him into the affair. On 6 May Aleander published the Bull *Decet Pontificem Romanum* that placed Luther under the ban of the Church, and on 26 May the emperor signed the Edict of Worms that placed Luther under the ban of the Empire and commanded his books to be burned and him to be given over to the authorities. Charles returned to the Netherlands with Aleander, where a programme of stamping out heresy was at once begun (Smith, 248). There was a real fear of the inquisitor in Antwerp, which doubtless precipitated Erasmus' removal to Anderlecht.

Erasmus' letter to the theologians of Louvain (Epistle 1301) written from Basel in July 1522, well after his departure from Louvain, is so remarkable that it deserves more attention than it has received in Erasmus studies. There are two versions of it: the shorter was first published in the *Vita Erasmi* by Merula in 1607; and this is the version that was most probably sent. There is also a longer version, which was printed in April 1523 with the first edition of the *Catalogus lucubrationum* (Epistle 1341A).[33] Although the longer version may not ever have been sent to Louvain, Erasmus added further information that arrived after the composition of the short version, and Erasmus appears to have been 'content to publish it as his considered defence of the points attacked' (*CWE* 9:129 introduction). We turn to it here because a life like Erasmus' is not lived in a straight line, and his biography cannot be unilinear or even unilateral.

The gist of the matter is that Baechem had attacked Erasmus for passages in the *Colloquies* that he judges even worse than heretical, and Erasmus' first argument is that he is not to be identified with the characters in his colloquies: 'I suppose he would also ascribe it to me if, in the dialogue, I had put into the mouth of Arius some words which conflicted with the teachings of the church' (*CWE* 9:131).

Then Erasmus explains his views on three central matters: first authority, stressing that there are certain practices on which the chain of authority is not clear: 'I myself am not entirely clear that the church laid it down that the present practice of confession is of

Christ's instituting. For there are very many arguments suggesting the opposite which I at least cannot resolve' (*CWE* 9:132/78–81). And the question of authority for the practice and teaching of the Church enters into baptism and the episcopacy, where the apostles instituted the practices, 'doubtless in accordance with Christ's teaching' (132/89–90). And yet, Erasmus notes, 'it cannot be denied that much in the practice of confession depends on the legislation of the bishops, namely, that we make our confession once a year' (132/91–3).

Erasmus' own practice in fasting, and his teaching concerning it, is clearly under fire. One of the characters in his colloquy 'The Profane Feast' raised the question 'whether it was the bishop's intention to lay all men equally under an obligation to abstain from meat' (*CWE* 9:133/110–12). There are those who cannot eat fish, just as there are those who react to wine: 'If someone who is affected by fish in this way is prevented from having meat or dairy foods, will this [hell-fire] not be harsh treatment? Will anyone want to make such a person liable to the punishment of hell if he eats meat in response to the needs of his body?' (133/117–120).[34]

Erasmus insists that neither in the *Colloquies* nor elsewhere had he simply condemned episcopal indulgences: 'I believe nothing could serve religion better than to tell the public not to put their trust in papal bulls, unless they take serious steps to change their way of life and amend their corrupt affections' (134/146–8).

What was the reason for his writing the letter? Early in the letter Erasmus spoke of a story reaching him not only by hearsay 'but in letters from friends of standing, who tell me precisely the language, the place, and the audience for a slanderous attack on me' (*CWE* 9:129/3 ff.). Part of those reports included news of impending action against him, and the Epistle makes a strong defence out of attacking Baechem and Latomus. Erasmus' quickness in writing provides evidence for his concern, for even in Basel such action by the theologians of Louvain could be harmful to his cause. What is striking is the obvious point that he is writing not just to an individual – not even the dean of the faculty – but the body of Louvain theologians and assuming that his letter would be read aloud to the entire faculty.

It is clear that in the years from 1517 to 1522 Erasmus expended a great deal of energy in his controversies with these and other catholic critics. His own account in the letter to Botzheim quoted at the head of this chapter is not the complete story: to be sure, he was provoked by Baechem and other friars, and Edward Lee clearly aroused his resentment and ire. With these men, he could justly claim not to have drawn his sword without provocation. But the same cannot be said of Standish, in relations with whom Erasmus seems clearly to have taken the initiative in expressing his dislike and in ridiculing him.

The heaping up of pages in these endless controversies calls attention to a flaw in Erasmus' personality. He did not take kindly to criticism, and he resented it strongly from certain quarters. Thin-skinned he has been called, and thin-skinned he often was. For some of the criticism he was responsible. His rapidity of work led him to make mistakes, yet one must quickly add that in subsequent editions of all his works he endeavoured to correct his mistake, something which neither his contemporary nor his modern critics have been always willing to recognise.

One must also add that Erasmus paid the price for his biting wit. Opponent after opponent had been angered by the *Moria*, and some by the *Julius Exclusus*: satire and irony do not generally make friends. Further, Erasmus was far more open and uninhibited in his letters than a prudent man should have been, and these letters circulated widely. The publication of many of these indiscreet letters in the collections of 1517, 1519 and 1520 made even more public his witty opinions and cutting remarks.[35]

Further, at Louvain there was opposition to the Collegium Trilingue; many of the Louvanistes condemned the concept out of hand and for some it served as a ready target for their attacks on the basic trilingualism of late renaissance humanism. It is clear, also, that the appearance of the New Testament was a challenge to many conservative theologians, whose career had been built upon a study of the Vulgate text only: if Erasmus is right, some doubtless felt (if they did not so word it), my career as a theologian, or scripture scholar, is threatened.[36]

There is another aspect to the involved experience that Erasmus had with his catholic critics. For several years before the Lutheran crisis erupted, he had already been under fierce criticism then attack: he had justification for feeling that there was a conspiracy against him. Then, in 1518, when Luther burst upon the consciousness of Europe and he was gradually but inevitably drawn into the complexities of that controversy, he had to respond even while his business with the catholic critics was continuing; and some at Louvain compounded the matter by careless linking of Erasmus with Luther.[37] Erasmus was not paranoid, but one can understand the pounding that his ego or psyche took over several years of criticism, vilification, and entreaty from both sides to speak out, while all his instincts were for finding a peaceful solution, for remaining quiet, for seeking the peace and gentleness of Christ. Erasmus never claimed to be a martyr, but his fortitude was prodigious, especially for one who suffered continuing ill-health. He was a man of faith who lived the life of scholarship heroically in those times.

As the controversies with the catholic critics began to heat up, it was at best unfortunate that the merry *Dialogue of the Two-Tongued (Dialogus bilinguium ac trilinguium)* appeared in public when it did: 'the dialogue was the kind of lively and learned lampoon that could not fail to be noted in humanist circles as soon as it became available' (*CWE* 7:330). Erasmus was embarrassed in the debate with Lee, and it did not help his cause with others at Louvain. Yet there is a positive side to the controversies. As More across the Channel was later to find in his polemics with Tyndale and Saint-German, Erasmus learned in these early controversies that anything theological which could be misunderstood, would be misinterpreted. Let us bear in mind that not only Erasmus' opponents but the humanists as well, including Erasmus himself, had all been schooled in the rigorous scholastic disciplines of disputation and dialectic. Erasmus had not enjoyed these scholastic rigours at Paris, and in these early controversies we find that he had no real heart for drawing swords against scholastics.

1520–1521 was a time of crisis: a crisis in Christendom, and for Erasmus a crisis in the life of the mind as well as the life of faith. Nothing could be more intolerable than the atmosphere of vindictiveness that he now breathed in Louvain, as we have seen in Epistle 1164 . He had tried to answer his Louvain critics and would make one final effort from Basel in writing to the theological faculty as a *collegium*, appealing to them to oust Baechem. He had tried to mediate the growing Lutheran crisis with the *Consilium* of 1521 and the many letters and conversations between the parties. There was little more that he could do (*Opuscula*, 341).

Before the year 1520 was out, Erasmus was ready to admit defeat (Tracy, 186). More than one biographer has read Epistle 1218 of July 1521 as a confession of weakness, in that Erasmus evidently drew back from martyrdom. But, quite simply, he did not want to be a martyr for Luther who, he thought, acted as if he did not wish to be saved.

The months in Anderlecht were doubly welcome for their peace and quiet, but he could not stay there forever: it was too close to Louvain, and there was imminent danger. Now it was too close to the court, and there was the likelihood that he would be asked by chancellor or emperor to write against Luther. By 1521 he was sure that he could not write for Luther, but he was not yet ready then to write against him. The actions and intentions of Erasmus, even his wanting to take a middle path, are crucial for our understanding of his temperament and character. Thus in writing to Richard Pace on 5 July 1521 he seems to have felt that he had to answer charges that he was supporting Luther, and he did not lose the opportunity to speak out strongly against Aleandro that he had fathered some of the pamphlets now appearing, 'What a ready pen I must have, to be able to run off all these tracts! – though all the time I am burdened with the great difficulty of revising my New Testament and correcting the works of Augustine, as well as other sections of my research' (*CWE* 8:258/19–21). While admitting that much of Luther's teaching and even many of his denunciations are admirable, he admitted to his friend Pace, at a distance from events in England (where perhaps Erasmus still had some hope of going, if Wolsey's promised support materialised, though by this time he was hoping against the grain of what we now know Wolsey's real interests were):

> Even had all he wrote been religious, mine was never the spirit to risk my life for the truth. Not everyone has the strength needed for martyrdom. I fear that, if strife were to break out, I shall behave like Peter. When popes and emperors make the right decisions I follow, which is godly; if they decide wrongly I tolerate them, which is safe. I believe that even for men of good will this is legitimate, if there is no hope of better things. (*CWE* 8:259/35–40; Allen IV, 541/30–37)

'Never the spirit to risk my life for the truth': Bietenholz comments (in *CWE* 8:431) that 'the significance of this statement, and a similar one in Epistle 1167/488–9 should perhaps not be overrated; both were made in an effort to contrast Erasmus' caution with Luther's rashness. Erasmus said at the same time that he would gladly give his life for the faith and the "gospel truth", see Epistles 1225:272–4, 1236 : 133–4'. Prudence on the part of Erasmus? Yes. But moral weakness, no.

He completed his rural retreat in Anderlecht, and in the autumn he was ready to go to Basel.

Notes

1) So much controversy has swirled around the figure of Luther for four and a half centuries that it is not surprising to find that even the matter of the theses is hotly disputed: whether they were in fact nailed to the door – a bibliography is provided by Kurt Aland in his *Die 95 Thesen Martin Luthers und die Anfänge der Reformation* (Gütersloh, 1983).

2) An introduction to the question of reform is provided by G. B. Ladner, *The Idea of Reform* (Cambridge, Mass., 1959; rev. ed. 1967), supplemented by the essays in *Reform and Authority in the Medieval and Reformation Church*, ed. Guy F. Lytle (Washington, D.C., 1981); and one may recommend the lucid treatment of complex issues in Alister E. McGrath's introductory *Reformation Thought* (Oxford, 1988). For the documents of a number of the figures involved, see H. Oberman, *Forerunners of the Reformation* (Philadelphia, 1966; rptd. 1981). Various theories and histories of the Reformation are ably discussed by A. G. Dickens and J. M. Tonkin in *The Reformation in Historical Thought* (Cambridge, Mass., 1985).

3) The Dominicans were widely perceived to be enemies of reform by virtue of their rigid insistence on scholasticism and authority; and one finds few reformers among them. In the spring of 1517 it was the Dominican Johann Tetzel who moved about Germany preaching the famous papal indulgence that triggered Luther's response with his *95 Theses*.

4) See F. Pijper, *Erasmus en de Nederlandsche Reformatie* (Leiden, 1907), and G. J. Hoenendaal, 'Erasmus en de Nederlandse Reformatie', *Vox Theologiae* 30 (1969) 126–44. The dissertation of C. Augustijn, *Erasmus en de Reformatie* (Vrij Universiteit, Amsterdam, 1962) has not been available to me; and his *Erasmus* (Ambo, 1986) reached me too late to be of use in the writing of this chapter.

5) The outline sketch by Erika Rummel, 'A Reader's Guide to Erasmus' Controversies', in *Erasmus in English* 12 (1983) 16–19, has proved to be a useful tool; and it has been followed by her monographs on *Erasmus and His Catholic Critics I, 1515–1522* (Nieuwkoop, 1989), and *II, 1523–1536* (Nieuwkoop, 1989), to which I am greatly indebted, even beyond the frequent citation of this work in my notes.

6) Context is always important in reading Erasmus, as he himself implied in Ep. 1206 to Beatus Rhenanus (see esp. ll. 150–1), and a colloquy like 'A Godly Feast' is illuminated by an awareness of the controversies with friars.

7) Richard Hunne, a prosperous merchant tailor suspected of Lollard sympathies, was found strangled in the Lollards' Tower while in the custody of the bishop of London late in 1514. The bishop declared Hunne a suicide, exhumed the body and burned it as that of a heretic; but a London coroner's jury returned a verdict of murder against the bishop's chancellor. See R. J. Schoeck, 'The Affair of Richard Hunne', in *Proceedings of the Third International Congress of Medieval Canon Law, Strasbourg 1968*, ed. S. Kuttner (Rome, 1971) 237–54, with full documentation.

8) This adage was written while Erasmus was in London during 1517 and added to the edition of the *Adagiorum* published by Froben in Nov. 1517. Standish is mentioned by name a dozen times, and Phillips writes that 'this story stands alone in the *Adages* as a satirical attack on a person mentioned by name' (*Adages*, 361).

9) For this account of Standish I have drawn upon my own account in *BR*.

10) Studies which set forth the background for the quarrel between Latomus and Erasmus, and hence between the Louvain theologians and Erasmus, are the following: H. de Jongh, *L'Ancienne Faculté de théologie de Louvain* (Louvain, 1911); J. Etienne, *Spiritualisme érasmien et théologiens*

louvanistes: Un changement de problématique au début du xvi e siècle (Louvain-Gembloux, 1956) esp. 91–102.

11) Thus E. Rummel, 'Erasmus' Conflict with Latomus: Round Two', *ARG* 80 (1989) 17. Cf. ch. 4 in her *Erasmus and His Catholic Critics I*.

12) The first English translation is to be found in *CWE 7:* appendix. A critical edition of the three early editions is in W. K. Ferguson, *Opuscula*, 205–224.

13) Authorship is a disputed question, but the consensus appears to be that Erasmus was responsible for at least a share of the dialogue, but was not the single and perhaps not even the main author. Still the best discussion of the question is by Ferguson in the Introduction to his edition, in *Opuscula*, 191–203.

14) Ep. 934 to Maarten Lips, who noted 'ironically' in the margin alongside 'scholarly': *CWE* 6:285/3–6 & n. 4.

15) *NCE*, noting that his works were edited by his nephew, J. Latomus, and published at Louvain in 1550. He was significant as a forerunner of the Counter-Reformation in the Netherlands: see P. Kalkoff, *Die Anfänge der Gegenreformation in den Niederlanden*, 2 vols. (Halle, 1903).

16) Erasmus declared that the notes he saw before his own second edition was published were worthless (Ep.886/65 ff.; cf. also 765/1–2).

17) Reprinted three times in 1519 and included in the *Erasmi apologiae omnes* published by Froben in 1521–22.

18) In Erasmus' view, 'He is young, so far distinguished by no remarkable literary service; as for theological affairs he neither has, I think, a doctorate nor has be achieved for himself a single degree beyond mediocrity; he discharges no public office' (*Opuscula,* 299; q. in *BR*).

19) See Ch. 6 in Rummel, *Erasmus and His Catholic Critics I*.

20) Ep. 826/5–7, *CWE* 5:398/4–7; Allen III, 293/3–5. The metaphor of garments patched together with lies is used in *Adag.* II. iv. 58, as *CWE* notes (5:398/4). Attacks by and on Dominicans and Carmelites figure in a number of Erasmus' writings, not least the *Colloquies* (see, e.g., 'The Godly Feast').

21) Ep. 1581/242–4. Rummel notes (235) that in Ep. 948/141–9 the same episode is related.

22) In *BR* it is suggested that the play on *camel* may 'perhaps also [be] alluding to the camel's nasty habit of spitting in one's eye'; but the punning goes deeper, as shown in the dialogue on 'the Godly Feast' by Schoeck and Meagher, already cited. In the 'Apotheosis Capnionis' ('Apotheosis of Reuchlin') we read 'at Louvain I heard a certain camel preaching that anything new was to be shunned. A saying fit for a camel!' (Thompson, 81). The stupidity of camels is taken up in *Adag.* II. vii. lxvi (*'Camelus saltat'*).

23) See Rummel, *Erasmus and His Catholic Critics I*, 143, and *BR*.

24) It was included in the collection of *apologiae*: *Erasmi apologiae omnes* (Basil, Froben, 1521–2), a folio collection which had a second edition later that year.

25) In *BR* the view is presented that when Faber and Erasmus met in Cologne, later October 1520, they discussed the ideas that Faber had put into writing concerning a possible trilingual college in Augsburg, as well as the Luther question, and that this writing was revised and published as the *Consilium*: cf. Ferguson, *Opuscula*, 338–61.

26) The term *tranquillitas* (here translated as 'peace') is one of the key

concepts in Erasmian thought: see Tracy, *Erasmus*, 35–6 (viewing *tranquillitas* as the dominant motif of the *De Contemptu Mundi*), 43 (calling attention to the closeness of *tranquillitas* and *humanitas*), and 99 (on 'the happy tranquillity of an innocent soul' in the *Enchiridion*). Thus *tranquillitas* has a multi-layered signification, for it operates within the human being, it conditions his relating of self to the *studia humanitas*, and it is vital for the individual's existence in a society. Like other key concepts in Erasmus it also has active intertextualities, evoking expressions of the concept in classical and patristic thought.

27) A reasonable balancing of the contradictions in the question of authorship of the *Acta* is by Tracy (186 n): 'Perhaps *Acta* was published without Erasmus' knowledge by another person who added some opinions of his own'. Writings like the *Acta* were passed from hand to hand, and it would be easy to make such conjectured additions in copying a manuscript. Jacob of Hoogstraaten, to give his full name, was another Dominican who taught for some time in Cologne (that hotbed of conservative theology), where as inquisitor of the archdioceses of Cologne, Mainz and Trier he supported Pfefferkorn in his campaign against Reuchlin and even pleaded their cause at Rome. Soon after his arrival in Louvain he was instrumental both in the condemnation of Luther by the theological faculty and in their breaking the peace temporarily made with Erasmus (*BR*).

28) The seriousness of the interview cannot be minimised, for the papal nuncios had visited Frederick at his lodgings and demanded that the heretic's books be burned and he himself be either punished by the elector or be delivered to them.

29) Georgius Spalatinus (1484–1545) was a member of the humanist circle of Mutianus Rufus. In September 1516 he became private secretary to the elector Frederick the Wise of Saxony. It is to be noted that in 1520 Spalatin had translated several of Erasmus' shorter works into German: the *Querela pacis*, the *Institutio Principis Christiani,* and the adage 'Sileni Alcibiadis' (III.iii.1) – prime examples of Erasmus the pacifist – so that he was already familiar not only with Erasmus' ideas but also with his language.

30) Spalatin's account is our source, and I am dependent here upon Smith's rendering of it (Erasmus, 235 & n).

31) Erasmus was sent a chamois gown by the Elector, who 'was both surprised and pleased by the boldness of the *Axioms*' (Smith, 236). Aleander, who had known Erasmus in Venice (ch. 23), had become librarian of the Vatican on 27 July 1519, and in the summer had been dispatched to Germany to implement the papal bull, *Exsurge Domine*. His was an uncompromising attitude (*BR*).

32) Smith 237, citing Ep. 1188. This letter (from Mechlin, March 1521) is 'unusually unguarded': it was written in a hurry, and it was transmitted by a man Erasmus felt he could trust; moreover, it was first published only in the collection of 1697 (*CWE* 8:159 introd.; Allen IV, 446 n).

33) Allen prints the shorter version (V, 90–4, with his reasons); *CWE* prints the longer version (*CWE* 9:129–36), as 'the more interesting historically'.

34) It is to be noted that Erasmus received papal permission to eat meat during Lent.

35) There was the collection of 1516, published by Martens in Louvain, but Erasmus could plead that he had not authorised it.

36) Academics often respond to something different out of fear for their own prestige, position, or years of training and specialisation. Questioned a few years ago about a new approach to medieval literature, a prominent Chaucerian declared that if it were right, 'My thirty years as a Chaucerian go down the drain'.

37) It has been said that during the 1520–1521 period 'the obsession with Luther predominates' in his correspondence. But it would be more accurate to say that Luther imploded into his world: at first Erasmus paid as little attention as possible, next he pleaded insufficient acquaintance with Luther's writings – 'I had scarcely leisure enough to read what I write myself, and if there were any time left over, I would rather devote it (to speak frankly) to the reading of the Ancients', he wrote to Campeggio (Ep. 1167 in December 1520, *CWE* 8:115/244–46; Allen IV, 405/219–221). As early (or as late) as July 1520 he wrote that 'Luther has rendered a great service by pointing out so many abuses, but I wish he had done so in more civil language'; and he gently remonstrated to Justus Jonas in May 1521 that Luther's violence was far from the 'courtesy and meekness of the spirit of Christ in the Gospels' – in the context, what understatement, what irony!

The Colloquies

A small book appeared in November 1518 from the presses of Froben in Basel: *Familiarium Colloquiorum Formulae*, with a preface by Beatus Rhenanus. This *libellus* had turned up in the hands of Lambert Hollonius of Liège, who may have purchased the manuscript or even (it has been suggested) 'simply have taken the manuscript from Erasmus' rooms, where he lived in Louvain' (*BR*).[1] Beatus Rhenanus wrote the preface to the unauthorised edition, which displeased Erasmus, but that action led to the first authorised and expanded edition of the work published at Louvain by Martens on 1 March 1519.[2] Such are the bare facts of first publication. From such a modest beginning came one of the great books of the Renaissance, and one of Erasmus' most popular and enduring works.

The genesis of the book lay in Erasmus' tutoring in Paris in the last years of the 1490s (chapter 14). Part of his teaching method was the use of simple exercises to learn correct conversational and written Latin, and some of this effort is to be found also in his letters of the same years. Thus we find such short exchanges as the following:[3]

Peter Thanks. I commend you. Therefore I invite you to dinner tomorrow. Therefore I ask you to dine with me tomorrow. Therefore I beg you to have lunch with me tomorrow. Therefore I want you for my guest tomorrow.

Christian But I fear it won't be possible. I'm afraid I can't. I'll
come if I can. But I'm afraid I can't.
Peter Why can't you? Why so? Why thus? For what reason?
What's to prevent you? (Thompson, *Colloquies*, 583–4, under
'Have Lunch With Me Tomorrow')

From this example it is evident that the essence of the early *Formulae*
was simply to provide formulas for conversation, like a Berlitz lesson,
and not a developed dialogue: not yet. Also evident is the emphasis
on directness and casualness. But two extended treatments in the
November 1518 edition indicate how much the generic concept of a
colloquy was already in being by that date.

The first is 'The Profane Feast', first printed in 1518 and revised
with additions in March 1522. Thompson observes,

> In its observations on hospitality and banter about culinary topics
> this supper party resembles others described in the *Colloquies*, and
> like them often recalls Athenaeus and Aulus Gellius. Its discuss-
> ions of fasting and allusions to ecclesiastical authority anticipate
> more elaborate treatments in *The Godly Feast* and *A Fish Diet*.
> These passages have an underlying seriousness... (592)

When the Sorbonne included these passages on fish-eating in listing
objectionable parts of the *Colloquies* (1526), Thompson continues,

> Erasmus pointed out that Augustine's light talk is answered by
> Christian, and he accused his critics of ignoring the dramatic
> character of the passage: they should not assume he shares all
> the opinions of his speakers. Even so, however, Augustine says
> nothing very improper.[4]

It must be stressed that Erasmus himself felt that the Church was too
stringent in its views about dieting, and that what mattered was the
spirit of the Law, not its letter.

Another more fully developed section of the early *Formulae* was
the 'Short Rule for Copiousness' (615–20 in Thompson), a first
version of what Erasmus expanded into *De duplici copia verborum ac
rerum*, developed after the Paris years and published in 1512, before
the publication of the *Formulae*. But even in a somewhat routine
section, 'Forms of Wishing Well', in which there is a grouping of
good wishes to a pregnant woman, we find the following witty, if
earthy, expression:

> God grant you luck in your bearing. God grant you make your
> husband the parent of a lovely child. May the Virgin Mother
> grant you good fortune in becoming a mother. I pray that this
> swelling may subside luckily. Heaven grant that whatever this
> burden you carry, it may slip out with no more trouble than it
> slipped in. God give you a good delivery. (Thompson, 549–60)

At some stage before the edition of March 1522 Erasmus began to see the potentialities of the colloquy that may be perceived in 'The Profane Feast', and soon he began to write dialogues, some of them long and fully developed. In fact, after the March 1522 edition, no more formulae were added (Thompson, xxv), whereas eleven colloquies were written for inclusion in the 1522 edition. Attention will be given in later chapters to key ideas which are rendered in the colloquies, for these need to be considered in the changing contexts of controversy, humanistic developments and the shifting political scene of the 1520s and 1530s. At this point, it seems appropriate to consider the genre of the Erasmian colloquy and to look to conditions between 1517 and 1522, as well as emerging aspects of Erasmus' own mind and personality, that will help to explain the flowering of the genre, most remarkably for a man in his mid-fifties.

The appearance of the *Colloquies* in 1522 at Basel obviously calls attention to the milieu of that Swiss city which provided both stimulus and relief for the beleaguered humanist who came there from Louvain. In the immediate atmosphere of Froben's printing establishment and its community of scholars Erasmus, we may safely assume, enjoyed to the fullest conversation that could be unguarded and uninhibited, yet learned.

A part of Erasmus' personality leaned towards the dramatic: to see himself in terms of a relationship with a listener, to cast even letters in a dramatic mode, and to make use of the dramatic to present more than one angle of thought on a given idea, situation or belief. The earliest colloquies, and certainly the mature ones even more, confirm other testimony concerning Erasmus' love of conversation; and we perceive Erasmus leading his students into an enjoyment of learning Latin. There is always in Erasmus an appreciation of conversation as the appropriate expression of friendship (as we saw earlier in his recasting of the *Antibarbari* into this mode, chapter 8), and a growing appreciation of the dialogue as a genre.

The psychological roots for Erasmus' attraction to the dialogic lie deeper in his personality. His work on the colloquies emphasised the conversational – and, increasingly, the dramatic – thus moving him more and more to directness and simplicity, at the same time that he was enabled to pursue his bent for the familiar. It is after about 1518 that his prose style becomes simpler and less ornate: much of that change in his Latin style can be attributed to his growing interest in the dramatic, and to his experience in working with the dramatic.[5] Perhaps we should look to his profound study of the New Testament and to his experience in writing the Paraphrases for a general audience as well.

An increasingly sure sense of audience is also a part of Erasmus'
development that we mark in the radical shift from the *Formulae* to
the *Colloquia*, or from his earlier to his later letters: a growing
awareness of the presence of an audience, marked by the obvious
addresses to the 'Dear Reader' but more deeply by the subtle rhetorical involvements of the reader. Yet I do not know of any passages
(with the exception of the *Moria*) that would indicate a sense of his
works being read aloud to groups, in the way that More gives us
indications in the *Debellation* and *Confutation* that his own works
were read aloud; and that sense or awareness in More helps to explain
the embedding of anecdotes and quasi-dramatic elements in the long
exposition of those works. Certainly Erasmus would have understood
Virginia Woolf's words in her diary at the start of World War II:
'No audience. No echo. That's part of one's death'.[6]

The history of the renaissance fondness for dialogue is a manifold
story. The word itself is Greek: *dialogos* defines a discussion among a
number of speakers, typically investigating a philosophical problem
or a complex idea. Despite the medieval belief that the form was
limited to two persons, the Greek practice had more, often a goodly
number, as in Plato. Among the writings of Xenophon, Plato and
Aristotle there are many dialogues; characteristically, 'at this first
stage of the genre's development, a topic is discussed in a historical
setting, usually the Athens of Socrates' day, and a single speaker of
superior logical and rhetorical talents, often Socrates, dominates the
discussion'.[7] Erasmus was of course familiar with the full range of
classical dialogue, Roman as well as Greek, and especially with the
dialogues of Cicero that were constructed on the model of the Aristo-
telian dialogue that explored established doctrines. He was deeply
familiar with Augustine's four Cassiciacum dialogues, Boethius'
Consolation of Philosophy, and Petrarch's return to the Augustinian
dialogue in his *Secretum.* It seems likely that he would also have been
familiar with such medieval dialogues as those of Alcuin that were
for teaching purposes, and doubtless with some of the late medieval
exemplars. Despite Erasmus' attack upon the Barbarians (chapter 8),
scholasticism continued to dominate the universities, and bad poets
of the twelfth century were still being read: of these a number were
quasi-dialogue.[8]

But in the dozen years just preceding his development of the
genre of the colloquy Erasmus was much taken by the ironic dialogues of
Lucian, that Greek of the second century AD who so brilliantly
attacked the superstition and philosophical error of his age with a
rich sense of the irony of life, slashing wit, and boldness of irreverence. We also know that Erasmus was familiar with the dialogues of

Valla and other Italian humanists of the fifteenth century.[9]

The colloquy as Erasmus developed it had its life on three different, but interrelated, planes: literary, with its manifold functioning
as a new literary genre; religious, with its cries for reform and
criticism of abuses, endeavouring to present a guide to the christian
life; and educational, providing a teaching method for learning to
speak, then write, proper and idiomatic Latin. That threefold division can serve for further discussion.

As literature, and I bring to bear Eliot's dictum that the greatness
of literature cannot be determined solely by literary standards,[10] the
Erasmian colloquy came into being during a literary period of immense flexibility in terms of genre.[11] Rosalie Colie sees the adage as
'a sub-literary small form intended to transfer culture and to communicate important values, more a literary "device" than a genre,
and workable into any kind of literature an author might choose
…'(33). Then, following Colie (despite reservations about the re-
strictiveness of her view of the adage as 'a sub-literary small form',
which is adequate for the earlier, brief adages, but not for the later
and more developed ones), the movement is from the level of pedagogical exercise in *De Copia* and *Formulae* to the mature colloquies,
where 'Erasmus taught European schoolboys how to make use of his
adages to best rhetorical advantage. The adages, then, become *orna-
ment, copia*, figures for alluding to a large meaning from an important
context. They are keys to culture, or convenient agents of cultural
transfer'(33).

For the genre of the colloquy Erasmus drew from two millenia of
literary tradition, with a wide range of exemplars. He declined the
gambit of only one or two precedent forms. For example, he does not
choose to make use of Petrarch's genre-experimenting, and there is
nothing in the colloquies like the *Secretum* (c. 1350) with its 'solilo-
quy-like interchange' between the literary *persona* of the author and
his inner conscience, that is so very Augustinian.[12]

The *Colloquies* were a great spur to the writing of dialogues during
the later Renaissance, and manifestly in Elizabethan and Jacobean
drama (for so many of the writers, and of the audiences, had been to
school with Erasmus' *Colloquies*);

> Writers have found in it a fertile source of scenes, plots, or
> dialogue. Rabelais borrowed freely from it. Lyly, Webster,
> Nashe, and Jonson knew it, as did other Elizabethans. Sterne,
> Scott, and Reade used whole colloquies for scenes in novels.
> That Shakespeare missed such a book is most improbable, even
> though his familiarity with it cannot be proved beyond ques-
> tion. In short, it was one of the books most educated men were

expected to know, whether they had read it in or out of school.
(Thompson, *Colloquies*, xxxi)

A most useful focus is that of Franz Bierlaire, whose study of the
Colloquies of Erasmus carries its thesis in the sub-title: *réforme des
études, réforme des moeurs et réforme de l'Église au XVIe siècle.*[13]

Thus the *Colloquies* have a thrust in the religious thought and life
of the sixteenth century, as well as in its literature, and this is a
major issue to be taken up as the ideas in individual colloquies
surface in subsequent chapters. To call attention to continuing
themes or principles in Erasmus' writings after 1517 can be of
service at this point, however. He encouraged the new when it was
sound and maintained continuity with tradition; but he attacked
fossilised concepts of tradition that refused to see the need to relate
tradition to the living moment. It follows then that he attacked
scholasticism for its rigidities and abstractions, and he opposed
strenuously its hold on the academic system; for only very slowly
were humanists able to win positions within the universities.
Erasmus carried with him the emphases of the Brethren of the
Common Life, despite his bitterness against certain Brethren whom
he had encountered as teachers at 's-Hertogenbosch and elsewhere,
valuing the spirit rather than the letter of the law, as taught by
Thomas à Kempis in the *Imitation of Christ*. This love of simplicity
and valuing of the essentials rather than the trappings carried over
into his views on the teachings of the Church: emphasise the essentials, not the superficial things. He attacked the monastic and religious orders not because he disbelieved in the ideal of monasticism,
but because he condemned the abuses and shortcoming of the monastic orders, and still more of the friars. All of this we find in the
Colloquies, summed up in the principle of *philosophia Christi* (discussed in Volume I, pp. 50–1, 111–12, and 268–70). Erasmus
emphasised christian living, not (echoing Thomas à Kempis) speculation about theology and piety and ethics; and above all, living in
accordance with the teachings of Christ in the Gospels. And in such
individual colloquies as 'The Epicurean' Erasmus brought to bear
those resources learned from Valla: 'haven't I convinced you yet that
none live more enjoyably than those who live righteously?'
(Thompson, *Colloquies*, 549).[14] We do not do wrong if we think of
the *Colloquies* as a guide to the christian life, as Erasmus understood
it to be.

From 1522 onwards Erasmus explored (and perhaps at times
exploited) the genre of the colloquy for the presentation of ideas on a
very wide range of contemporary issues and questions (as we shall see
in chapters 38 and following). To say that he expressed his own ideas

is to simplify the very nature of the form in which he exercised the potentialities for playing ideas against one another, and for dramatising both the very difference in points of view and often the open-ended quality that left a difference as a disputed question, but now in an atmosphere of civility, play, and tolerance.[15] From 1522 onwards, then, the colloquies added plot and structure, and the characterisation becomes more impressive. Even the quite brief 'Rash Vows', first published in 1522,[16] sketches a character named Cornelius who confesses to the 'vast pleasure of impressing both myself and others at meetings or drinking parties by telling lies about my travels', who has conversation with Arnold, back from visiting Rome and Compostella after a rash vow made after drinking. This is as sharply etched as a piece in *The New Yorker*. With some talk about indulgences and bulls – Arnold speaks of his fellow-drinker who 'pinned his whole hope of salvation, so to speak, on a piece of parchment instead of a moral life' – the colloquy ends with Cornelius planning to arrange 'a little drinking party, invite the men of our order, compete in lying, and have a good time by taking turns telling whoppers'.[17] Other concerns that emerge in the 1522 *Colloquies* are benefices, military affairs, servants, manners, sport, schooling, hunting, with religion always an element. 'The Godly Feast' is perhaps the most developed and polished of the early colloquies; and it is here that we find the celebrated 'Saint Socrates, pray for us' speech.[18]

There is, finally, the enormous importance of the *Colloquies* for education. It had its beginning as simple formulas for the teaching of good Latin through conversation, and it never lost that central function. While it became many things to many readers – 'a book for all seasons' Thompson called it (xxvii) – it never forfeited its central and controlling purpose. There were competitors,[19] and it was not the only popular collection of Latin dialogues in sixteenth-century schools, but no other collection rivalled Erasmus' in popularity: there were approximately a hundred editions or reprints by the year of his death in 1536 (see Thompson, xxiv–xxv).

In the earliest library of Yale College, Bainton has noted, Erasmus was better represented than either Luther or Calvin.[20] However, as the tide turned against Erasmus at Louvain and Paris, the *Colloquies* was often singled out for attack, and in 1528 the University of Paris forbade its use in teaching (Thompson, xxx). As early as 1538 it was a prohibited book, and in the first Roman *Index librorum prohibitorum* the *Colloquies* was included; the Council of Trent followed suit, as did the *Index* of Paul IV in 1559, which condemned not only the *Colloquies* but all of Erasmus' commentaries, annotations and translations.[21]

In sum, the *Colloquies* represent Erasmus most completely, for we find Erasmus the conversationalist, always free to bring into the conversation a remembrance from his schooling or childhood; Erasmus the master-rhetorician, inexhaustibly energetic, fecund, inventive, and always exhibiting a marvellously supple Latin style; and Erasmus the reformer. Here the reader – contemporary as well as modern – is entertained by Erasmus' often slashing wit and earthy humour; but always the wit and humour are for the sake of provoking thought, for the sake of exploring a question. Here too is Erasmus the apostle of conscience and the enemy of false piety; seeking to restore theology to its earlier simplicity and vigour, combating those who would undermine liberty and peace. Here, finally, is Erasmus the humanist: always defending good letters, the *studia humanitatis*, which was such a dependable road to sound ethics and christian living, and ever demonstrating to his readers the vitality and beauty of the classical tradition. 'Saint Socrates, pray for us' captures the spirit of not only 'The Godly Feast' but the main part of the *Colloquies* as well.

In an age torn apart by strife – warfare among christian nations, bitter animosities within the universities and religious orders, and the growing split between the Reformers and Rome – Erasmus chose the dialogue and brought it to its perfection in the colloquy: a testimony to civility and humour, and always to a conviction in the rightness and viability of tolerance. If he spoke vividly to his own times, he speaks no less clearly to ours.[22]

Notes

1) See F. Bierlaire in *BR*, where Hollonius' act is called unscrupulous. In his 1519 preface Erasmus wrote, 'As for Hollonius, if he scraped together a little coin out of this, I do not grudge it him. But I do not propose to thank the man, unless he does something else to earn my gratitude; and if he continues, I shall reckon him not so much Hollonius as wholly felonious' (*CWE* 6:219/60–64; Allen III, 466/54–57: ' ... ex Holonio faciemus holopolam aut, si malit, holopolium' is elaborate word-play).

2) The *Formulae* was reprinted within a few months in Paris and Antwerp, then by Froben in 1519. Other reprints (either of the 1518 or the 1519 edition, which has a few pages of new material) appeared during 1519 in Antwerp, Leipzig, Vienna, and Cracow; it clearly caught the interest of the times, and there were more than forty editions during Erasmus' lifetime, well after the appearance of the *Colloquia* (or *Familiarium colloquiorum opus*) in 1522.

3) In these earliest formulae the speakers are Christian, Augustine and Erasmus. Christian and Heinrich Northoff of Lübeck were students of

Erasmus at Paris. Augustus Vincent Caminadus was more than an acquaintance but less than a friend, slightly older but still receiving tutoring from
Erasmus; it would seem that he saved copies of exercises that Erasmus had
never intended for publication. Craig R. Thompson, *The Colloquies of Erasmus*
(Chicago, 1965) xxii–xxiii. All my work on the colloquies stems from this
splendid edition, soon to be complemented by that in *CWE*.

4) Ibid., citing *Declarationes ad censuras*, *LB* IX, 933B–934B.

5) I would agree therefore with the conclusion of O. Kluge in his 'Die
Neulateinische Kunstprosa', *Glotta* xiii (1964) 67–8, that the prose style of
Erasmus after 1519 becomes simpler and less ornate; but obviously it is not
possible to pinpoint too precisely the year of that change, not only because
such changes cannot be described in a smooth line of development but also
because Erasmus was forever revising older scripts.

6) See Herbert Blau, *The Audience* (Baltimore, Md., 1990) 1, quoting
from *A Writer's Diary* (New York, 1954) 323. Blau goes on to declare that
'the advent of an audience is, on the visible surface of the normal course of
things, a ratification of the social' (9). This question needs further discussion,
obviously: even in the highly professional forms of the medieval commentary
(perhaps the most characteristic form of the Middle Ages) there is an implied
audience of fellow-scholars; with necessary qualifications, this is also true of
such related forms as the disputation, and even in the *declamatio* there must
be (rhetorically speaking) a sense of audience, though Erasmus' *Panegyricus* is
not strongly developed in this respect. But one thing we never get with
Erasmus is a sense of a mass-audience; nearly always it is the individual
reader whose presence and participation is felt.

7) I am indebted to the lucid discussion by David Marsh in *The
Quattrocento Dialogue* (Cambridge, Mass., 1980) 2. The history of the form is
studied by Rudolf Hirzel, *Der Dialog* (2 vols, 1895; rptd. Hildesheim, 1963).

8) As late as 1551, Curtius writes, 'an Italian Humanist feels himself
obliged to be on guard against the "bad poets" of the twelfth century. So they
were still being read!' Curtius, *European Literature and the Latin Middle Ages*,
27. In late medieval thinking about the liberal arts there are strong elements
from the quasi-dialogic *De Nuptiis Philologiae et Mercurii* of Martianus
Capella, which after a thousand years was still enjoying something of a vogue
(with eight editions between 1499 and 1599, Curtius notes, 38n), as well as
mss and early printed editions of the once popular *Psychomachia* of
Prudentius, and Alan de Lille (Alanus de Insulis), *Anticlaudianus* (c. 1183).
There were printed editions of the *Psychomachia* in c. 1475 (Strasbourg), 1500
(Paris), c. 1500 (Zwolle), and of the *Opera* in 1497 (Deventer). The interest in
the Low Countries is apparent. On the *Anticlaudianus* see the critical edition
of R. Bossuat (Paris, 1955) and the reflections of Gilson in *La Philosophie au
moyen âge* (1930) 77. How very different Erasmian dialogue is from the
relatively static medieval *débat*, the contention of two or more parties on a
moot point; for the debate is with few exceptions static and frigid. Despite
their conventionality of thought and sentiment, the dialogues of Christine de
Pisan achieve a freshness and simplicity: perhaps, as Huizinga suggests
(*Waning*, 274 ff) it is by virtue of their closeness to the popular song.

9) On Quattrocento Dialogue, see Marsh (n. 7 above).

10) 'The "greatness" of literature cannot be determined solely by literary

standards; though we must remember that whether it is literature or not can be determined only by literary standards' – 'Religion and Literature', in *Essays Ancient and Modern* (1936), where it is the opening paragraph.

11) I am indebted to Rosalie Colie's posthumously-published lectures entitled *The Resources of Kind: Genre-Theory in the Renaissance* (Berkeley, Cal., 1973), especially in teaching renaissance literature over the course of many years. One clue is in the heavily rhetoric-oriented educational and literary theory of renaissance humanists: 'Rhetorical education, always a model-imitating enterprise, increasingly stressed *structures* as well as styles to be imitated in the humane letters – epistles, orations, discourses, dialogues, histories, poems – always discoverable to the enthusiastic new man of letters by kind' (4).

12) Skipping a few centuries, there are 20th-c. counterparts to the *Secretum*: one thinks of Paul Valéry's 'Colloquy Within a Being' (*Dialogues*), or his 'drama of consciousness' in narrative form, his *Monsieur Teste*. More recently there is the example of William Plomer's use of the dialogue form in *Electric Delights* (1977), with a young self engaged in dialogue with the older self. If it is true that 'nothing is clear-cut in South Africa except diamonds' (as one of the interlocutors remarks in a Plomer dialogue), perhaps we can make use of that aperçu and, by adaptation, remark that for Erasmus in his *Colloquies* the process of cutting the diamond is never completed: all colloquies are more or less open-ended. The colloquy of Erasmus is quintessentially many-faceted, and there is more than one way to look for its brilliance and fire (L. von Berquen of Bruges, we may observe, was in 1476 the first to introduce the use of powdered bort and the lapidary's wheel for faceting diamonds, *EB*).

13) *Les Colloques d'Erasme* (Paris, 1978).

14) Thompson, *Colloquies*, 535–6, where it is noted that this was the concluding colloquy in 1533 (the final edition in Erasmus' lifetime), and that it opens with a classical text: appropriately Cicero's *De Finibus* (On the Ends of Goods), for Erasmus' first edition of a classical text was Cicero's *De Officiis*.

15) Cf. Erasmus' insistence in *Declarationes ad censuras* (cited earlier) that critics 'should not assume he shares all the opinions of his speakers'. L.V. Ryan has noted Erasmus' point-by-point defence of the colloquy 'Convivium Profanum' in *RenQ* xxxi (1978) 1–16.

16) In 1522 it was published without a title (as Thompson notes, 4), but in later editions it was called *De visendo loca sacra* and *De votis temere susceptis*.

17) The translation is that of Thompson, 4–7. Thompson suggests that the names may be those of two friends of Erasmus: Arnoldus Bostius, a Carmelite, and Cornelius Gerardus, a native of Gouda and an Augustinian canon (but the conjecture has not been accepted by Tournoy and some others: see *BR*). Erasmus' ideas on pilgrimage are fully developed in the 1526 colloquy 'A Pilgrimage for Religion's Sake'.

18) The play of meanings in this colloquy has been explored in a modern dialogue: see R.J. Schoeck and John C. Meagher, 'On Erasmus' "The Godly Feast"', in *Erasmus in English* 3 (1971) 10–12. We learn from the Copenhagen Codices that 'Saint Socrates, pray for us' is a second-thought, for it is an idea that is added vertically in the margin after the main text had been written (see my article in the forthcoming ACTA of the 1990 Congress of IANLS).

19) Vives wrote one in 1538, and later Cordier (Corderius): see Thompson, xxviii. Both are of course in the main line of educational tradition in the sixteenth century.

20) R.H. Bainton, *Yale and the Ministry* (New York, 1957) 43. But Erasmus continued to be used in colonial America: see W.H. Woodward, *Desiderius Erasmus Concerning the Aim and Method of Education* (Cambridge, 1904) and Thompson, xxviii.

21) See further chapter 44 below, on Erasmus in history.

22) I am indebted to the monograph of Prof. Bierlaire on the colloquies of Erasmus, and in my conclusion to this chapter I have drawn from this (pp. 306–7).

36

Erasmus and his Friends: his Audience and his Geography

Wishing to be friends is quick work, but friendship is a slow-ripening fruit.

Aristotle, *Nicomachean Ethics*, 8.1

Friendship cannot exist except among good men.

Cicero, *De Amicitia*, v. 18

... yet in friendship there is nothing false, nothing pretended; whatever there is, is genuine and comes of its own accord.

Cicero, *De Amicitia*, viii. 26

History will mean more to you if you have a taste of geography first.

Erasmus, January 1518, Epistle 760
(*CWE* 5: 275/14–15; Allen III, 197/13)

'As the living man is known by the company he keeps, so the mind of the great dead can be surely placed by observing the character of those among posterity who praise and follow and of those who depreciate and detest him': so Smith writes in approaching the question of the genius of Erasmus and his place in history (421).We are not yet ready to examine the place of Erasmus in history, for that will be the concern of chapter 44. But it is appropriate to pause in the narrative of Erasmus' life and to consider the company he kept; and this topic will lead to consideration of his audience and his sense of geography.

Erasmus commented on the ideal of friendship in the *Adages*, where the theme occurs frequently (as it does in the *Familiar Letters* of Petrarch in an earlier century, and in the writings of Cicero and Seneca in a still earlier age); and themes of friendship are to be found in his letters from the very earliest.[1] In one of the letters to a friend while still in the monastery, written at the age of twenty or twenty-one, Erasmus wrote that 'there is nothing on earth more pleasant or sweeter than loving and being loved'; and on the theme of friends separated by great distances he wrote a year or two later to another friend, 'it was by such means [the exchange of letters] that the two famous Fathers of the Church, Jerome and Augustine, prevented as they were by enormous temporal and spatial distances from being together and enjoying each other's embrace as they would have wished, still managed never to lack each other's presence; and each was ever aware of the other's feelings of good will'.[2]

Even through many revisions the pride of place in the *Adages* was kept by the adage 'Between friends all is common' ('*Amicorum communia omnia*', I. i. 1), which leads into notions of equality and community of possessions. Indeed, quoting Cicero in the first book of the *De Legibus*, 'friendship is equality', he points to the Latin word *coenobium* which expresses the ideal of a community of life and fortunes. The second adage is 'Friendship is equality. A friend is another self' (I. i. 2), which becomes an *omnium gatherum* essay.

Among Erasmus' many friendships several stand out. Certainly the long relationship with Thomas More, which was a friendship for all seasons; but there were others, perhaps most notably with Beatus Rhenanus.

In chapter 15 we witnessed the first meeting of Erasmus and More and the beginning of their friendship. We know too of their collaborative work in translating Lucian, which continued for several years (chapter 22).[3] The first achievement in their collaboration is the 1506 volume published at Paris by Bade, containing eighteen brief dialogues and ten longer ones translated by Erasmus, with four translated by More; and, in addition, an original *declamatio* by each.[4] The role of More in Erasmus' *Moria* has been pointed to in chapter 26, and the role of Erasmus in More's *Utopia* briefly commented on in chapter 33. The reciprocal giving and sharing is itself a remarkable thing in the history of thought and letters.

After Erasmus' return from England in 1517 there were few meetings, and much of their correspondence has been lost.[5] A key letter is that from Erasmus to Ammonio of March 1517, in which he lamented the pressures of business that had torn both Ammonio and More away from the Muses that might have possessed all their genius: this is the lament of a friend of both, who cares about the loss of potential contributions to literature. Then there is the prefatory letter from Erasmus in the Froben March 1518 edition of *Utopia*: 'What could this wonderful, rich nature not have accomplished if his talent had been trained in Italy, if it were now totally devoted to the service of the muses, if it ripened to its proper harvest and, as it were, its own autumnal plenty?'[6]

The year 1520 seems to mark a shift or turning in their relationship, so far as present fragmentary evidence suggests. In More's rather foolish quarrel with Brixius, Erasmus may well have annoyed

More by not taking his side; but the August 1521 letter from Erasmus to Budé did praise More while it admonished Brixius, and he did publish the letter in his *Epistolae ad diversos*, printed by Froben in late 1521. 1520 is also the year of the Field of the Cloth of Gold that found the two friends in opposite camps: More with the entourage of king Henry VIII, and Erasmus in that of Charles V.[7]

But in fact More was increasingly caught up in his duties to the king; he had been snatched away from friends and good letters, as Erasmus had prophesied in 1517.[8] For his part, in 1521 Erasmus moved to Basel, where he found not only the new challenges and new pressures of working directly with Froben (see chapter 38), but also experienced a widening of intellectual horizons by his entry into the Basel circles of the Frobens, Cantiuncula, Zasius and others.

Besides, after 1520 the world changed. Luther had come upon the scene, and one has only to examine the titles of books published in the year 1520 to see that books by and about, or against, Luther now dominated the world of thought and letters.[9] Still, when More and Erasmus met for the last time in the summer of 1521 during More's mission to the continent and Erasmus' visit to Bruges in the court of Charles V, there was still much of good spirits and friendship: that had not changed, it had only ripened, and the two friends had grown older.[10]

But Luther drove a wedge between them. On 19 October 1519 Erasmus wrote a long letter to Albrecht, archbishop of Mainz, in which he said that Luther in fact had much right on his side – in condemning the sale of indulgences, on the pronouncements and use of Aquinas, on the contemporary practice of the sacrament of confession – although it is simplistic to say that Erasmus never changed 'the fundamental convictions expressed in his letter to Albrecht of Mainz' (Marius, 271). The expression of those convictions was necessarily modified by changing events, and Erasmus became less optimistic in the 1520s and 1530s. In 1523 More wrote his *Responsio ad Lutherum* which is suffused with a tone of 'almost unbearable hatred of Martin Luther and of anything else that might threaten the authority of the Catholic Church' (Marius, 281; Schoeck, 'Telling More', 14). Erasmus insisted upon far fewer points of dogma, a result in part of his training with the Brethren of the Common Life, but also in part from his own disposition. On the eve of Erasmus' opening the debate with Luther on the freedom of the will (scarcely an attack though that came later, see chapter 39) he wrote to Tunstall, who as bishop of London had asked More to join the battle against Luther, and one feels that Erasmus was aware of More reading the letter over Tunstall's shoulder: 'In Luther's writings are some things I hear reproved which, in sober debate among the learned and the honest, might strengthen the spiritual and evangelical life from which the world has surely fallen as much as it can' (Epistle 169, Allen V, 295/15–18; Marius, 287).

Here is the voice of moderation in a storm of controversy, division and hatred: probably intended to be a mild reproof of More's unsober attack, but certainly an expression of willingness to listen to the validity of Luther's writings. There are clear differences between them, but the falling off of their correspondence cannot logically be laid at that door (though it may well have been an element); for More was far too engaged in public and private matters to resume the full freedom of the earlier correspondence with Erasmus. Nonetheless, Erasmus wrote with deep sadness over the deaths of Fisher and More in 1535 (chapter 43).

It must be added that a number of the writings of Erasmus during this period after 1520 are testimonies to friendship. Most notable is the memorial letter on Colet, so full that it is a miniature biography, and so personal in tone that it is a eulogy by a friend, in Epistle 1211 of 13 June 1521, written to Justus Jonas in response to a request for an account of Colet's life. Jonas, a professor of law at Erfurt who moved in the intellectual circles of Mutianus and Eobanus, tried to preserve ties with Erasmus despite his joining the Lutheran cause; and as late as 1527 Luther himself reported that Jonas had said to him, 'Doctor, sir, you have no idea what a noble and reverend old man he is' (*BR*). But even Jonas changed under the pressure of events and controversies.

As for More, Erasmus gave several pen-portraits of More and his household in Epistles 118, 999, 1233 and 2750 (*BR*). Significantly, the two friends had played parallel roles earlier when the other was involved in controversy: More tried to defuse Erasmus' quarrel with Edward Lee, and Erasmus reciprocated in More's quarrel with Germain de Brie. (The long letter from More to Dorp, discussed above, is a defence not only of humanism but of Erasmus.) In his last extant letter to Erasmus (Epistle 2659), More informed him of his resignation from the chancellorship, although he concealed the true reasons which, because of Erasmus' wanting to believe in the good will of Henry VIII as well as continuing friendly relations with some of Henry's chief advisers, Erasmus could not, or simply did not choose to know. While More was jailed in the Tower, discretion dictated a refraining from correspondence. Together with Philippus Montanus and Gilbert Cousin, Erasmus seems to have been involved in the publication and circulation of the *Expositio fidelis de morte D. Thomae Mori et quorundam aliorum insignium virorum in Anglia* (*BR*) – the so-called Paris Newsletter.

It may seem difficult for the modern person to comprehend that two humanists could have lived in the same city, and so largely contemporaries, for a dozen years without having met, especially since they had a number of common interests and friends. But Jacques Lefèvre d'Etaples (Jacobus Faber Stapulensis) was at least half a dozen years older than Erasmus, and he taught at a Paris college other than Montaigu, the Collège du Cardinal Lemoine; and Lefèvre, we recall, was away in Italy in 1500, and again in 1507. Yet there was the common ground of friendship and dealings with the Parisian printer Josse Bade, in whose atelier many humanists came to meet and talk.[11]

However, following Lefèvre's return from Italy in 1507 he was invited by Guillaume Briçonnet, now his patron, to reside in the Abbey of Saint-Germain-des-Près, of which Briçonnet was abbot; and Lefèvre was able to devote himself to scholarship without the burden of daily teaching (*BR*). Although Erasmus visited Paris a number of times after he had lived there as a student from 1495 to 1499, his visits were sometimes hurried or filled with printing business and he could easily have missed meeting Lefèvre. The abbey was no great distance from the university, but it was enclosed behind its walls.

It is therefore only on Erasmus' seventh and final visit to Paris in 1511 that we have evidence of his meeting Lefèvre. Both by that time were famous. In the years between 1503 and 1511 there were several shared contexts in which the work of the two men must be related:[12] their shared notion of a purified Christianity, their working towards textual theory, and their textual criticism of Scripture. But Lefèvre had tendencies towards mysticism which Erasmus did not share, and Lefèvre's work on Aristotle would have struck little enthusiasm in Erasmus, nor would his dedicated editing of many medieval texts. One point of contact does need to be identified, however, and that is their common relationship with Beatus Rhenanus. Beatus had been a student and follower of Lefèvre, especially in the years from 1503 to 1507 when Beatus studied under Lefèvre, Fausto Andrelini and Clichtove.[13] He was a fellow student of the scholarly but retiring Michael Hummelberg of Ravensburg, who learned Greek and worked with Josse Bade on several editions (Epistle 263).[14] To cite but one instance, Beatus is mentioned in 1515 as one of the correctors for a volume of works by Ramón Lull that was edited by Lefèvre. About the year 1512 Beatus seems to have transferred some of his admiration to Erasmus, and apparently in 1514 Beatus and Erasmus finally met.

Other members of the Lefèvre circle were Robert Fortune, Guillaume Castel, Johannes de Molendino and Gerard Roussel – minor figures, perhaps, on the stage of the history of the age – but Charles de Bovelles (Bovellus) was a stronger figure, especially in the history of philosophy, and his is the key work in the rediscovery of Nicolas of Cusa (Cusanus) and the building of fresh philosophical work upon it.[15]

The publication of Erasmus' *Novum Instrumentum* in 1516 precipitated a quarrel between them, possibly (as Henry Heller has conjectured in *BR*) because 'Lefèvre felt intimidated by the evident superiority of Erasmus' scholarship'. Erasmus criticised Lefèvre for reading Hebrews 2:7 as 'Thou madest him a little lower than God' instead of 'a little lower than the angels': a seemingly minor point which illustrates how far-reaching textual detail could be. Lefèvre based his view on an awareness of the dignity of Christ, generating a sense of the deep gap between God and man; Erasmus stressed the historical and theological implications of Christ's suffering on the Cross. Many letters passed between them, and Erasmus' *Apologia ad Iac. Fabrum Stapulensem* (Martens in Louvain, 1517) issued from their differences. Yet Erasmus felt that *parrhesia*, the necessity of speaking frankly, compelled him to answer Lefèvre in his *Apologia*; and as he wrote to Barbier in Epistle 652 (c. 7 September 1517 from Louvain), 'I cannot say how much it grieves me, how I regret this necessity which compels me to answer him. I would rather write a large book in praise of my old friend Lefèvre than this short *apologia* in support of my own position' (*CWE* 5:104/8–11; Allen III, 74/7–10).

Lefèvre had a large following, especially in France, and his public disagreement (and for Erasmus disagreeableness) could not be allowed to pass in silence. Even private letters were often handed around, and many of the letters of humanists like Erasmus and Lefèvre were public, intended to be read by others. It would be a mistake to think that only with the *Apologia* did Erasmus 'go public'.[16]

Lefèvre 'believed that Erasmus had sacrificed piety to scholarship' (*BR*), and this is the core of their differences after 1516. But it is ironic that Lefèvre should think this, for the Brethren of the Common Life would never have sacrificed piety to scholarship and Erasmus would not have thought that the two were self-excluding.

Lefèvre too came under fire from the Paris theologians, especially from Béda, and at the beginning of 1521 he withdrew from Paris and moved to the diocese of Meaux, where his patron Briçonnet had become bishop in 1516 and wanted his assistance in reforming the diocese. In Meaux he headed the leproserie (1521) and the next year became vicar-general *in spiritualibus* (*BR*). He too turned to commentaries on the New Testament: in 1522 publishing *Commentarii initiatorii* on the Four Gospels, and in 1525 *Commentarii in Epistolas catholicas* (published by Cratander in Basel). By this time he was questioning the spiritual authority of the priesthood, the efficacy of the sacraments apart from faith, the sacrificial character of the Eucharist, and the doctrine of the real presence, rejecting the invocation of the saints and the veneration of images (*BR*), so far had he moved away from the position of, let us say, Thomas More, and towards that of Luther. Reactions forced Lefèvre to flee Meaux for Strasbourg later in 1525, and Erasmus intervened on his behalf at Rome in Epistle 1650A. 'It is not impossible that this act prepared the way for a meeting of the two at Basel prior to Lefèvre's return to France in the spring of 1526' (thus Heller in *BR*, citing Epistle 1713). Recalled by Francis I, who appointed him head of the royal library at Blois, Lefèvre finished translating the Bible into French, and it was printed at Antwerp in 1530. During his final years Erasmus referred to him as '*bonus vir*' (Epistle 1821) and made a number of efforts to preserve a relationship; but if there were replies from Lefèvre they are not extant.[17] He died in retirement at the court of Margaret of Navarre in 1536.

The story of Erasmus and Jacques Lefèvre remains the story of a friendship largely failed: there was obviously much in common, but there were too many distances between them – not only spatial, but intellectual and spiritual – and friendship, that slow-growing fruit, never fully ripened. We would probably put it in our modern way that there was a clash of personalities.

Beatus Rhenanus was a major northern humanist and nearly a generation younger than Erasmus. They became close friends, and Beatus performed many services that were at the expense of his own scholarly work, although he emerged as a classical scholar and historian in his own right.

Born in Sélestat in Upper Alsace in 1485, Beatus was well-schooled at the celebrated Latin school of his native city.[18] From there he went on to study in Paris, where he became a disciple of Lefèvre. Curiously, Erasmus and Beatus Rhenanus seem not to have met in Paris during Beatus' student years from 1503 to 1506; but, as Walter has argued, he was still a student and very much a disciple of Lefèvre, with whom Erasmus remarkably had little or no contact before 1511, despite their having lived in the same city over a period of many years.[19] Beatus worked with Schürer in Strasbourg after leaving Paris, and there he prepared his own edition of Pliny's letters (published 1514), and a commentary to Seneca's *Ludus* for Froben (Basel, 1515).

The role of Beatus in the preparation of Erasmus' correspondence for publication has no parallels in renaissance letters up till then. To glance at the high points: in August 1518 Froben printed the *Auctarium selectorum aliquot epistolarum* with a preface by Beatus, and that edition was followed the next year by *Farrago nova epistolarum Erasmi*. The first contained sixty-three new letters not in the smaller collections printed by Martens at Louvain, and the second a total of 333 letters. The third Froben edition of 1521, *Epistolae … ad diversos*, contained 617 letters of which 171 were new. This is striking testimony to the hunger of readers for letters by Erasmus (and perhaps contributed to the sending of letters to Erasmus by strangers who had hopes of being included in this quasi-Who's Who of humanism). As Erasmus revealed in the preface to the third Froben edition, which was addressed to Beatus (Epistle 1206, from Louvain 27 May 1521), this is an edition which includes some revising of his own letters (*CWE* 8:218/42): 'I have revised the *Farrago...*' From Erasmus' letter it is clear that Beatus was a trusted friend by this time – 'entrusting the choice to you and even giving you the right to alter anything … that you might think would damage my reputation or rouse passionate resentment in anyone' (*CWE* 8:217/12–14). Erasmus was most relieved at being able to leave the 'drudgery' of reworking old letters for publication (a not unusual renaissance practice) to a person like Beatus who was both loyal and scholarly. One must further note (as Walter does, 18–19) that the zeal of Beatus led to the printing by Froben of the *Familiarium colloquiorum formulae* in November 1518, and the *Verae theologiae compendium* in April 1519.

Then there is the idea of an edition of Erasmus' collected works, to which he had given much thought in his later years and for which he made a provision in his second will of 1527 (see appendix D); with modifications, Beatus supervised this enterprise and brought forth the *Opera Omnia* in 1540.[21]

Finally there is the fascinating matter of the three Copenhagen codices, which are discussed further in chapter 44. If these represent, as recently argued, an attempt to memorialise the most celebrated and beloved renaissance humanist by making permanent the state of his papers at the time of his death – a remarkable kind of icon, a fixing of a scholar's work in progress, comparable to the iconic featuring of Erasmus *Scribendus* in the great portraits by Metsys, Dürer and Holbein, which dramatise the scholar writing by establishing analogies with the traditional portraits of St Jerome in his cell – the hand of Beatus is surely to be seen.

The deep and complex relationship of Beatus Rhenanus to Erasmus was central to the full development of Beatus as a humanistic scholar in his own right, and his self-sacrificing work as a friend facilitated much of Erasmus' publication of his letters and other writings at a time when he was greatly busy and under pressure. Erasmus' gratitude and tribute are contained in Epistle 1206, where he writes,

> And so in this business [of preparing the correspondence] I implore you in the name of our friendship, dear Beatus, the most learned of my friends, to be in truth my second self and do for me what I should have done myself had it been possible... (*CWE* 8:219/75–77; Allen IV, 500/68–70)

Erasmus gave much to individual friends, and he gained much from them. One dimension of this enriching experience is to be found in the strong sense of audience that his writing manifests. Erasmus wrote so many letters which are informal, direct and often frank to the point of indiscretion, always easy and familiar in their style, that this habit affected his writing in other forms. His growing correspondence provides valuable testimony that he was made aware of his work being read by students and non-professionals, and that awareness contributed to his striving for clarity and simplicity.

A parallel can be drawn with Petrarch, ever so acutely aware of audience. 'A writer, sitting alone, facing a blank sheet of paper, puts on that paper words that are the words of speech but not spoken'.[22] But there is nearly always with Erasmus the sense of 'absent presences' (to borrow a lovely oxymoron from Kerrigan and Braden). At about this time Erasmus began his practice of often dictating to a secretary, as well as dashing off letters in his rapid (and increasingly illegible) hand. But we don't know whether he habitually read aloud, or whether he would have spoken aloud, as he wrote: given the reading habits of the day, reinforced by Erasmus' fondness for the figures that depend upon sound, it seems likely. What does matter is that like Petrarch Erasmus translated into the silent medium of words upon a page the sense of actuality in speaking to someone – even at times implying, or incorporating the gestures of speaking – so that the writer endeavours to imagine the presence of the reader, as the reader in turn vividly participates in the reciprocal act by imaging Erasmus speaking.[23]

One can scarcely picture Erasmus except speaking and writing, yet there is one conspicuous difference between him and Petrarch in the well-nigh compulsive flow of words upon the page, in the letters to correspondents widely scattered, and in the case of Erasmus (thanks in part to the printing press) endless flow of books: he did not write, as Petrarch did, to imagined recipients.[24] The iconography of Erasmus' portraits is striking, in each individual portrait and in the shared view of Erasmus by all three portraitists (discussed in appendix E). The hypothesis that the purpose of assembling manuscripts into three codices at the time of Erasmus' death was to provide three separate – each unique, but each manifesting the same reality – representations or icons of the humanist in the act of writing, of making his books, seems to be unique for Erasmus.[25]

It is worth returning to Huizinga's aperçu that 'Erasmus' public was numerous and of high culture.'

> He was the only one of the Humanists who really wrote for all the world, that is to say, for all educated people. He accustomed a whole world to another and more fluent mode of expression: he shifted the interest, he influenced by his perfect clarity of exposition, even through the medium of Latin, the style of the vernacular languages, apart from the numberless translations of his works. (191)

From this fluency of expression with its perfect clarity there emanated a special kind of authority, and for readers of Erasmus this subsumed those values which he proclaimed and provided so many examples of: the excitement of the antique world and the immense storehouse of wisdom contained in the classical writers, the concept of education and faith in human nature, of civility and tolerance, and above all of Christ: 'Christ dwells everywhere', Erasmus wrote in his own echoing of the *Devotio Moderna*.

The authority of an author resides ultimately in his text, not in his personality, which evaporates next year, or (in the twentieth century) sooner. The Erasmian text, to borrow from Steiner, flourishes in a context of authority.[26] This is not the place to discuss the textual theory of Erasmus, although that is a significant part of his achievement (for that, see chapter 44 on textual scholarship as part of his achievement). What matters here is his unique 'productivity', not so much the quantitative aspect (though that must have had its impact upon his contemporaries, and continues to daunt us today), but the qualitative. Everywhere in the final text, from the prefatory letter to the final words, there is the Erasmian voice: immensely learned and impressively buttressed by his scholarship, and almost seductively expressed in that flawless Latin style that was the envy of all (see chapter 40).

He has spoken of his own awareness of his audience:

> From all parts of the world I am daily thanked by many, because they have been kindled by my works, whatever may be

their merit, into zeal for a good disposition and sacred literature; and they who have never seen Erasmus, yet know and love
him from his books.[27]

Each of Erasmus' correspondents deserves at least an essay, some a
book. *Contemporaries of Erasmus* (cited throughout as *BR*) serves to
identify and to provide biographical information about each of the
more than 1,900 people mentioned in his correspondence and works.
There is a wealth of evidence about his remarkable relationships with
so many of his contemporaries, and vital clues for establishing a
multiplicity of networks.[28] Perhaps one metaphor that can serve is
that of interlocking circles; as for example Beatus Rhenanus was a
member of the Erasmian circle in Basel and provided links to other
circles in Sélesat and Strasbourg and to individuals in the Lefèvre
circle earlier in Paris; or Thomas More, also a lifelong member of
Erasmus' 'inner circle', who had his own circles of friendship and
influence in England.[29]

There were always and everywhere networks of Erasmus' friends,
in the sense of a chain or linking of individuals inter-connected by
virtue of their shared friendship with him. We have spoken of the
network in England: Colet, More, Grocyn, Fisher, Urswick,
Mountjoy, Warham, Ammonio while he was alive and in London,
and others. In France there had been in earlier years the circle of
Robert Gaguin that included Fausto Andrelini, and later there was
the circle of Josse Bade (by virtue of their common background as
well as their shared interest in publishing humanist books); and we
have spoken of Guillaume Budé and Jacques Lefèvre. There were
others. In Italy Erasmus had made a number of friends, with some of
whom he kept up a correspondence: Aldo in Venice, Celio
Calcagnini (whom Erasmus met in the house of Richard Pace during
his Ferrara visit in 1508), and Calcagnini provided links with Hun-
garian humanists. We have spoken in earlier chapters of Erasmus'
friends in the Low Countries, who were legion. There were already
many friends in Strasbourg, Nürnberg, Augsburg and Cologne, and
after 1517 there would be many Swiss.[30] We must not neglect the
Spanish, Polish, and Luxembourg links of friendship forged by
Erasmus. His correspondence after 1517 becomes very full and rich,
and intricately inter-connected.

The most effective and famous news agency of the period was that
of the Fuggers of Augsbug, whose branches were spread into such
areas of economic importance as the Tirol, Hungary, Italy, England,
the Netherlands, and Spain (and included American ventures); and
to inform all their branches of news of all kinds they circulated the
Fugger-Zeitungen, the forerunner of the modern business news like the

Economist or the *Wall Street Journal*. Anton Fugger (1493–1560) tried for several years to move Erasmus to Augsburg, but Erasmus declined; to Anton's gift of a gold cup he responded by dedicating his Latin rendering of Xenophon's *Hieron* (Epistle 2273), and some of Erasmus' far-flung correspondence was forwarded by the Fugger network (*BR*).[31]

Following an indication of the copious networking of Erasmus' friends it is appropriate to speak of his full and rich sense of place: an awareness of cities and countries, both past and contemporary, and the extent to which he often identifies places in his correspondence and other writings. A consideration of Erasmus' place-references *tout ensemble* will give the twentieth-century reader an appreciation of how extensive and how detailed his geographical knowledge was: how informed a sense of his physical world he possessed.[32] He was fond of maps.

Erasmus was familiar with the ancient geographers, and Epistle 2760 to Theobald Fettich, a doctor of medicine from Worms, forming the preface to Ptolemy's *Geographia* (Basel, 1533), as well as Epistle 2938 from Sepulveda, which explains several place-names, chiefly Biblical, are but two of the letters in which his interest and expertise in geography is manifested. The texture of the *Adages* and *Colloquia* are often dense with place-references, and that awareness together with his interest in the cosmographers is revealed by this passage in the colloquy 'A Problem':

> If some god bored straight through the middle of the earth – through the centre to the Antipodes, as cosmographers are wont to do when representing the position of the whole earth on globes with lines – then, if you threw a stone into the hole, how far would it be carried?[33] (first printed in the 1533 edition, Thompson, *Colloquies*, 530)

Cosmography leads on to thoughts of the infinite, and *Adag*. I. viii. 59, 'You join thread with thread', is just such a reaching from the known world of sun and stars to the infinite:

> ... Aristotle in the third book of the *Physics*, in a discussion of the infinite, where he prefers Parmenides' opinion to that of Melissus (for Melissus had held that the universe as a whole was infinite, while Parmenides said it was finite, equidistant from the centre), says 'For it is impossible that the infinite should be connected with the universe as a whole, just as thread is with thread'. (*CWE* 32:158)

How simply and how lucidly Erasmus writes even of the complexities of physics!

Erasmus' life was one of ideas and ideals; and, to use a nineteenth-century term, we would now want to call him an intellectual. But he would have insisted rather that he was a humanist, in the sense defined in chapter 12 and used consistently in this biography.

Yet his life was filled with movement from place to place, and it was enriched by friends: he was always trying to cultivate the old ones and always eager to make new ones. A deep and fervent belief in friendship as one of the supreme virtues of the human condition was one of his most consistent characteristics.

The flow of letters to Erasmus wherever he was, and the prodigious number that he sent out – more and more of them transcribed by his secretaries either from dictation or from his rapidly scribbled first drafts – were vital to individual friendships and to the maintaining of the networks everywhere of friends. No wonder that he spoke of spending half his days in the writing of letters. Those letters, I have suggested, were instrumental in the development of his unique familiar style and to the heightening of his sense of readers, of having an audience of friends with shared interests and convictions, and vitalised too by his rich sense of geography. Some friendships, one reflects years later, are limited to the place shared – as with Aldus, which lasted, really, only so long as he was in Venice (many of us would add some Army friendships) – but others are not so limited. In the years immediately following 1517 when Erasmus was at the pinnacle of fame, universally recognised as the prince of humanists in Europe, he had an abundance of friends everywhere; and that abundance mattered greatly to him.

Notes

1) It is striking that among Erasmus' contemporaries there were others who were acutely conscious of friendship and reflected upon it. In Ep. 744 from Budé there is a memorable metaphor for friendship: 'I preferred to deal with you by the strict letter of the law under the provisions of the Statute of Friendship' (*CWE* 5:248/97–8), alluding to the requirement of giving true advice with frankness (*parrhesia*): cf. Cicero, *De Amicitia*, 13. 44–5. A fine metaphor for a lawyer.

2) The first quotation is in *CWE* 1:17/3–4 (Ep. 13, Allen I, 86/1–2); the second, *CWE* 1:36/15–20 (Ep. 23, Allen I, 104/13–18). But monastic discipline (as I have observed in ch. 5) 'cautioned against too much human friendship that might impede the love of Christ, as in *The Imitation of Christ*, I. vi, on inordinate affections (*Opera* II, 13–4)' (104).

3) Which of the two friends knew Lucian first and which first proposed translating his writings into Latin, as Craig R. Thompson has observed, we simply do not know: *Translations of Lucian*, vol. 3/1 in *Complete Works of St*

Thomas More (New Haven, Conn., 1974), xxviii.

4) Described by Thompson, xxviii ff.

5) For their meetings, see index. On their lost correspondence, see Hubertus Schulte-Herbrüggen in *Erasmus und Europa* (Wiesbaden, 1988) 110.

6) Letter of Erasmus dated Louvain 25 August 1517, to John Froben: *Utopia*, ed. E. Surtz and J.H. Hexter, vol. 4 in *Complete Works of St Thomas More* (New Haven, Conn., 1965), 3. The bitter-sweet letter of Erasmus is quite short, and yet it serves as both a tribute to More's great talent and a lament for the lost 'autumnal plenty' ('*si ad iustam frugem ac uelut autumnum suum maturuisset?*').

7) See Richard Marius, *Thomas More* (New York, 1984) 201, and J.J. Scarisbrick, *Henry VIII* (Berkeley, 1968) 74f, 76–80, 94, 106, 119f, 135, 306.

8) Ep. 829, c. 23 April 1518 (*CWE* 5:401/8; Allen III, 295–6).

9) As can be done by consulting the invaluable chronological short-title catalogue in the Herzog August Bibliothek (Wolfenbüttel). Very roughly, in 1520 a majority of the titles are by, against or about Luther.

10) Both had read Petrarch and might have recalled the many passages in his *Familiar Letters* on friendship. One is resonant, 'Friendship ever was and ever will be strong in might, nothing is difficult, nothing impossible to it' (Bk XIII, letter 10).

11) See R. Wiriath, O.P., 'Les rapports de Josse Bade Ascensius avec Erasme et Lefèbvre d'Etaples', *BHR* XI (1949) 66–71.

12) I write in agreement with Tracy's analysis, *Erasmus*, 173.

13) Fausto Andrelini is discussed in ch. 12. Clichtove, a disciple of Lefèvre (see *BR*), emerges later as one of the critics of Erasmus: see chapters 38 & 39.

14) After Hummelberg's return to Germany, Botzheim enabled Erasmus to keep in touch with him, for he had impressed Erasmus (Eps 1316 & 1342 where he is called a 'Second Rhenanus', *CWE* 9:381/463). On Hummelberg's career in Paris, see Renaudet, *Préréforme, passim*.

15) See Renaudet, esp. 410 ff., and *Cambridge Hist. Ren. Philosophy*.

16) See Ep. 814, which is an appeal in the spring of 1518 begging Lefèvre not to allow a difference of opinion to make them enemies. Erasmus tried to have mutual friends mediate, and there are letters to and from Glareanus (Ep. 766) and Budé (Eps 778 & ff.), which touch on the dispute with Lefèvre. Even Luther commented on it, observing that in this instance the Dutch humanist had the better of it (18 Jan. 1518, q. Smith, *Erasmus*, 179).

17) Heller, for whose essay on Lefèvre in *BR* I am much indebted, notes that in a sculpture in the Belle-Chapelle in the Abbey of Solesmes, Lefèvre is represented as St Jerome attired in a cardinal's dress. See further the following by Eugene F. Rice, Jr.: *Prefatory Epistles*, and 'The humanist idea of Christian antiquity, Lefèvre d'Etaples and his circle', *Stud. in Ren.* 9 (1962) 126–60; as well as M.M. Phillips in *Érasme et les débuts de la réforme française* (Paris, 1934) 23–46.

18) I draw from my discussion of Beatus Rhenanus in *ERSYB* X (1990) 163–6, in reviewing J.F. D'Amico's study of *Theory and Practice in Renaissance Textual Criticism: Beatus Rhenanus Between Conjecture and History* (Berkeley, Calif., 1988). See also *BR*.

19) See Robert Walter, 'Une amitié humaniste: Érasme et Beatus Rhenanus', *Annuaire de la Société des Amis de la Bibliothèque Humaniste de Sélestat* 36 (1986) 13–23.

20) See the introd. to Ep. 1206 in *CWE* 8:215–6, for a succinct account of the publishing history of the *Farrago,* as well as Bietenholz's preface to *CWE* 8:xiv–xv.

21) The history of the *Opera Omnia* has been discussed by C. Reedijk, in his unpublished Oxford lectures of 1968.

22) William Kerrigan & Gordon Braden, *The Idea of the Renaissance* (Baltimore, 1989; rptd. 1991) 163.

23) One of the striking features of the diptych painted by Metsys in 1517 is the composition: Erasmus facing Pieter Gillis, and each seeming to be in a suspended state that is the act of writing, yet each on the brink of speech (see illustration 2 and Vol. 1 frontispiece).

24) One possible exception that might be advanced is the Letter to Grunnius, but there was an actual situation for which this fictive letter was written. We still cannot say whether there was a real person for whom the name Grunnius is surrogate, nor can we be sure of the exact purpose for that letter.

25) That hypothesis was discussed at the congress for Neo-Latin Studies (IANLS) in Copenhagen (August 1991) and will be presented in the *Acta* of that Congress.

26) Cf. George Steiner, *On Difficulty & Other Essays* (New York, 1978).

27) This quotation is from a letter presumably written towards the close of his life, and I have made use of the translation in Huizinga (191), but I have been unable as yet to locate the original in the text of his writings.

28) I use networking in the current sense of the interrelationship of members of a community or profession who not only communicate with one another but also actively support each other.

29) My review of *BR* in *Moreana* xxv 97 (1987) pays tribute to the great usefulness of these volumes for further study; for me in the writing of this biography they have been indispensable. As one example, in an appendix to the review in *Moreana* I extracted the names of British humanists and their patrons, and certain others: some ten dozen names, a list which strikingly demonstrates the interconnected friends and others with whom Erasmus had some degree of association. What is shown as the 'British network' can be repeated, *mutatis mutandis*, for other countries.

30) One notes Erasmus' friendly connections with Ludwig Baer, Cantiuncula, Zasius, Glareanus, Wilhelm Nasen, and Nikolaus Briefer; but, again, there were many others. See Bietenholz, *Das italienische Humanismus und die Blütezeit des Buchdrucks in Basel* (Basel, 1959), and *History and Biography in the Work of Erasmus of Rotterdam* (Geneva, 1966); and Guido Kisch, *Erasmus und Jurisprudenz.*

31) For a general study of renaissance banking one may begin with R. Ehrenberg, *Das Zeitalter der Fugger, Geldkapital und Creditverkehr im 16. Jahrhundert* (Jena, 1896), although it needs to be supplemented by a number of more recent specialised monographs. On the achievement of Jakob the Rich (d. 1525), uncle of Anton Fugger, see J. Strieder, *Jacob Fugger der Reiche* (Leipzig, 1926). Like Erasmus' earlier and long-lasting connections with the

Burgundian court and the various strata of society in the Low Countries, the Rhineland and England, his connections with the Fuggers (and others like them) must be kept in view to counter the bald and erroneous assertion that Erasmus was a recluse in an ivy tower who had little knowledge of the so-called 'Real World'.

32) The author plans to complete a monograph on Erasmus' geography in 1993.

33) First printed in the 1533 ed.; see Thompson, *Colloquies,* 530.

Reform and Reformation: Ecclesia semper reformanda

Luther at Worms is the most pregnant and momentous fact in
our history.

> Lord Acton, *Lectures on Modern History* (1906) 101

Would to heaven that the Church of Christ today had no false
apostles! Would to heaven that all men who assumed the duty
of preaching the gospel followed the example of Paul in
preaching Jesus Christ, not for personal gain, not out of self-
seeking, not to win the favour of men of influence, not out of ill
will or to gain the approval of men, but with single-minded
sincerity. ... If the shepherds turn into wolves, what hope is
there for the herd?

> Erasmus to Erard de la Marck, 5 February 1519, Epistle 916
> (Allen III, 488/306 ff)

[in the Augustinian idea of reform] The monk-priests and
conversi were the *sancti* of the *Civitas Dei* on its earthly pilgrimage, whose teaching and example should bring about a *mutatio
vitae*. The end of this 'change of life' may be safely identified
with the key idea of patristic reform ideology: *reformatio ad
imaginem Dei*. The Augustinian road then leads from *doctrina
christiana*, the receiving of 'Christian instruction', to pre-bap-
tismal conversion, to baptismal regeneration, to reformation
and postbaptismal conversion, to a monastic or at least ascetic
way of life in the City of God on earth, and through it all back
to *doctrina christiana*, the giving of 'Christian instruction'
within the *Civitas Dei*.

> G.B. Ladner, *The Idea of Reform,* 377

It is historical hindsight to say today simply that the Reformation
happened. For Erasmus and his contemporaries it would be more
accurate to say that 'the Reformation was happening'. Reformation
and Counter-Reformation, as Patrick Collinson has wisely expressed
it, 'are not terms which we can easily dispense with and yet they are
deceptive, especially when preceded by the particularising definite
article'.[1]

Reform, by contrast, was a familiar and accepted term long before

1500. Its roots are embedded in the rich earth of patristic tradition, and much of the discussion concerning reform during the sixteenth and seventeenth centuries was enriched by a deepening study of patristic literature. In this, as in everything connected with reform, and much connected with the historical Reformation and Counter-Reformation,[2] Erasmus was a potent force.

In an impressive book that bears indeed the marks of greatness, Gerhart B. Ladner has given a magisterial analysis of the basic christian idea of reform and its impact upon the thought and action of the age of the Church Fathers.[3] Drawing in many instances upon older notions of cosmological renewal, and occasionally upon concepts of millenarian renewal, the fundamental christian idea of reform stressed the process of conversion and the potency of baptismal regeneration, followed in christian living by penance. Further enlargements or extension of the fundamental idea of reform were made by St Augustine and then by the various formulations of monasticism that began with the Augustinian Rule, a monastic regime that profoundly influenced the spiritual development of Erasmus (see chapter 5).

There were conspicuous movements that strove for reform in the fifteenth century, and these can readily be identified.

The reform of the individual, so stressed in early sixteenth-century literature, had been almost a constant in the patristic and medieval periods. Its core was the Pauline teaching of the replacement of the sinful Old Man with the converted New Man, leading to a restoration of the original image of God in the tarnished soul of sinful man and emphasising a conforming to the model of Christ. There were numerous movements that shared these goals, but one that has direct relevance to Erasmus was the *Devotio Moderna* that came out of the Low Countries and Rhineland in the fourteenth century and flowered in such compositions as *The Imitation of Christ* (see appendix B). Erasmus never lost his concern for the reform of the individual nor his zealous teaching of Christ as the perfect model for sinful man, as in the *Enchiridion.*

Monastic reform was closely linked to this. The initial ideal of monasticism was not so much a withdrawing from society as striving to lead a life of perfect devotion to God. The history of monasticism after the time of Augustine in the fifth century is marked by pronounced shifts of emphasis, and there were several reforms from within. The foundation of the monastery at Cluny in about the year 910 was inspired by a strict interpretation of the by then venerable Rule of St Benedict. In the eleventh century there was a powerful reform movement, known as the Hildebrandine, which aimed at nothing less than a universal reform of the Church; one aspect of its strategy was the making of reform a Rome-centred programme. This movement was followed by the Cistercian reform of the twelfth century, a return to literal observance of the Benedictine Rule and a greater strictness. The remainder of the High Middle Ages is marked by a series of constantly renewed reforms: the Franciscan and Dominican of the thirteenth century, and a widening and deepening analysis of the need for reform, as in William Durand, who coined the phrase *reformatio in capite et in membris* (reform in head and members), a by-word for the Conciliarists who, like Marsiglio of Padua in his *Defensor Pacis* in 1324, proposed changes that would diminish the monarchic authority of the episcopate and papacy and introduce representative principles. John Hus in the fifteenth century can be seen as a part of this reforming tradition.[4]

Although there had been earlier reforming councils (such as that held at Vienne, 1311–12) the fifteenth century was pre-eminently the period of Conciliarism: the long series of more or less representative gatherings concerned both with reform and with the schism which racked the Western Church.[5] In 1409 a council was convoked at Pisa to deal with the scandal of two rival popes, and in fact it produced a third, Alexander V, who at least promised to work for the reform of the Church. The Council of Constance (1414–18) proclaimed the superiority of a General Council over the pope and called for councils to be held at fixed intervals (the decree *Frequens* specified ten years); and with the election of Martin V in 1417 the schism was for the moment healed. However, it was this council which condemned as heretical the reforming doctrines of John Wyclif, and had that other pioneer of reform, John Hus, burned at the stake.

The Council of Basel was summoned by Martin V in response to the decree *Frequens* and convened in 1431, and was later transferred to Ferrara and Florence before being dissolved in 1449.[6] Although some progress was made in regulating the higher echelons of the Church, the papacy and the curia, and the principle of conciliar superiority to the pope was once again affirmed, the council spent much of its long career at loggerheads with Eugenius IV. Little was done to address the problems which affected the lives of the faithful: frequency of receiving the sacraments, the teaching of the faith to local congregations, the education of parochial clergy, the duty of bishops to reside in their dioceses and visit parishes and religious houses in their jurisdiction regularly; and above all the state of theological teaching in the universities.[7] Three successive General Councils spanning half a century had failed to provide effectively for the reform of the Church.

The Fifth Lateran Council convened in 1512 and sat for five years, its closing session coming only seven months before Luther's Ninety-Five Theses against indulgences and other abuses.[8] Although the theme of the council was reform, and it was launched by a stirring oration by Giles of Viterbo on the reform of the individual and Church, reform cannot be said to have been achieved, although the council concluded its final session by congratulating itself on having done so. 'Nowhere', it has been said (Hughes, 279), 'is it a more tragic disappointment than in the reform decrees of its ninth and tenth sessions [1514/15]'. The Fifth Lateran Council must be judged a failure, and yet ironically (as has been said elsewhere)[9] in a real sense it cleared the air for reformers of both the protestant Reformation and the Counter-Reformation. After 1517 what answer could be given to the just charge that a General Council of the Church had so recently failed? The road to reform, one could reasonably conclude, lay elsewhere than through a council.

As we have already seen (chapter 34) the Reformation may be said to have begun with that dramatic event, the posting of the Ninety-Five Theses on the door of the Castle church in Wittenberg on 31 October 1517. Even as they were being nailed to the door they were being printed, and they circulated like wildfire. Only four months later Erasmus sent copies to his friends More and Colet. Two books that had appeared before that help us even today to chart the already turbulent climate of ideas. In 1516 Martin Luther discovered and published a selection of the German mystics – Ruysbroeck, Suso, Tauler, and especially Meister Eckhart – and in a completed edition of 1518 he gave it the name *German Theology* (*Eyn deutsch Theologia*, Wittenberg, 1518).[10] In the preface he declared that he had not learned more about God, Christ, and man except from the Bible and St Augustine.[11]

A second influential work widely read in 1517 was the posthumous printing of Lorenzo Valla's treatise on the so-called 'Donation of Constantine', which demonstrated, largely on philological grounds, that the donation had been a forgery (chapter 9). For this edition Ulrich von Hutten wrote an insolent preface addressed to Leo X: it constituted nothing less than an attack upon the papacy by a liberty-loving German patriot. Von Hutten's gravamen was far more political than doctrinal: in diatribes against the papal legates at the Diet of Worms, Caracciollo and Aleander, von Hutten thundered: 'all you Roman legates are robbers of our people, betrayers of Germany, destroyers of law and justice!'[12] The list of complaints drawn up by the Diet of Worms in 1521, the so-called *Centum gravamina*, was in a very real sense independent of Luther's Theses and was the summing-up of complaints accumulating over the preceding century.[13] But they corresponded almost point by point with Luther's incisive pamphlet *To the Christian Nobility of the German Nation* that had appeared six months earlier.

Earlier, in 1517, the Dominican Johann Tetzel preached on the Indulgences[14] granted by Leo X for contributions to the re-building of St Peter's in Rome, and for the repayment of a loan from the Fugger banking house for the installation fee of Albert of Brandenburg to the archbishopric of Mainz in 1514. Tetzel had a rough and ready eloquence, but he preached with a commercialism and extravagance that supported the widely held opinion that a mere money payment could be applied with unfailing efficacy to deliver a soul from purgatory. Although he did not preach in Wittenberg (for the indulgence had been forbidden in electoral Saxony), he preached nearby at the town of Jüterbog, where Luther heard him and was scandalised.[15]

The years before 1517 had been crowded ones for Martin Luther, who was educated at Erfurt University from 1501 to 1505, in which year he entered the monastery of the Augustinian Hermits at Erfurt.[16] Ordained priest in 1507, he was sent as lecturer in 1508 to the very newly founded University of Wittenberg, where he continued his studies and lectured on moral philosophy.[17] In 1510 he went to Rome on business of his order, and soon after his return in 1511 he became a doctor of Scripture (*Doctor in Biblia*) and was made professor of Scripture, a post that he held until his death. In 1515 he became vicar of his order, which entailed responsibility for eleven Augustinian houses. Of being busy he wrote in October 1516:

> I could use two secretaries. I do almost nothing during the day but write letters. I am a conventual preacher, reader at meals, parochial preacher, director of studies, overseer of eleven monasteries, superintendent of the fish pond at Litzkau, referee of the squabble at Torgau, lecturer on Paul, collector of material for a commentary on the Psalms, and then, as I said, I am overwhelmed with letters. I rarely have full time for the canonical hours and for saying mass, not to mention my own temptations with the world, the flesh, and the Devil.[18]

Out of such labours, and out of such a coming together of pastoral, scholarly and administrative activities, was born the arch-reformer of the Reformation. He had criticised indulgences in his sermons three times during the year 1516, but his anger reached a high pitch during the summer and early autumn of 1517.

In accord with contemporary practice in university towns, Luther posted a printed placard in Latin listing ninety-five theses for debate, mostly on indulgences. The posting of theses merely invited scholars to dispute them in scholastic fashion and presumably in Latin, but their translation into German was altogether another matter. Later he asserted that he had meant them only for those concerned. Albert of Mainz forwarded the theses to Rome, where pope Leo X is supposed to have said that Luther was a drunken German who would feel different when sober.

Far less well-known than the Ninety-Five Theses are the Twenty-Eight Theses for the Heidelberg Disputation. Having been asked by Johann Staupitz,[19] the German vicar of the Augustinian order, to join in a discussion of the new evangelical ideas at a meeting of the general chapter of the Augustinians of Germany at Heidelberg in April 1518, Luther drew up these theses.[20] He was apprehensive about the meeting, where he was received as guest of honour; and about the trip he observed, 'I went on foot. I came back in a wagon'.[21] Although triumphant at Heidelberg, Luther was tried in Rome for spreading heretical doctrine in the same year and summoned to appear before cardinal Cajetan at Augsburg; but he fled to Saxony, under the protection of the elector, Frederick III. At a disputation with Eck in 1519, held at Leipzig, he denied the primacy of the pope and, less surprisingly, the infallibility of a General Council.

1520 marks Luther's complete break with Rome. He himself published three foundational reforming tracts during the year. The first was *An Appeal to the Nobility of the German Nation*, a pamphlet of tremendous popularity[22] that called upon the German princes to take the reform of the Church into their own hands, and to abolish the tradition of paying tribute to Rome, the celibacy of the clergy and Masses for the dead. He also condemned pilgrimages and other catholic practices and institutions. That first pamphlet was followed by *On the Babylonian Captivity of the Church,* the 'Babylonian Captivity' being a metaphor for the captivity imposed upon the laity by denying them Communion under both species, and by the doctrine of Transubstantiation in the sacrifice of the Mass. The third of the year's pamphlets was *The Liberty of a Christian Man*, in which Luther enunciated his teaching of the liberation of the Christian by faith, and the priesthood of the laity; at the core was the concept of justification by faith alone. In emphasising liberty in this third pamphlet Luther was careful to stress that he meant the liberty given to live in obedience to God and by service to one's neighbour. One may read the first of the pamphlets as a logical progression from the failed conciliar movement of the fifteenth century: if popes and councils had failed to achieve reform, it was now up to the princes.

To this point there was not a great difference between Luther's views and those of Erasmus; but in the second pamphlet Luther directly challenged the sacramental system of the Church, and his concept of the Mass was in direct opposition to the main lines of catholic teaching; here his radicalism showed forth, and Erasmus now declared that there was no possibility of peace between Luther and the papacy. In his letter to Nicolaas Everaerts, Epistle 1186 of February 1521, Erasmus wrote: 'His *De captivitate Babylonica* alienates many people, and he is proposing something more frightful every day. I do not see what he is hopeful for in setting this on foot, unless perhaps he is relying on the Bohemians [Hussites]' (*CWE* 8:157/8–11; Allen IV, 444/7–9).

Subsequent letters develop his alienation from Luther after this point, and his fear that something worse might happen.[23] Not yet wishing to take sides, however, Erasmus tried to keep open lines of communication with Lutheran supporters, and to clarify his stand to Rome.

Although Leo X procrastinated and mishandled the crisis, a bull of condemnation – *Exsurge Domine*, with its metaphor of a wild boar raging in the vineyard – was issued in Rome by Leo X on 15 June 1520, and Johann Eck, who had been Luther's opponent in a disputation at Leipzig in 1519, was commissioned to promulgate it throughout the Empire. Instead of submitting, Luther again appealed to a general council. But in a final bull of excommunication, *Decet Romanum Pontificem*, sentence was pronounced on Luther on 3 January 1521. The bull *Exsurge* was one of the documents burned by Luther at Wittenberg on 10 December 1520, along with books of canon law. The bull of excommunication was not put into effect in the Empire, where he was not officially prosecuted, nor was the condemnation of the diet at Worms (April 1521). From late 1520 until 1525, the reform movement flourished. Events of 1524, such as the peasant revolts in the Black Forest, will be discussed in a later chapter.

With the issuing of *Exsurge Domine* and Luther's defiance of papal authority by the burning of the bull and books of canon law in December 1520, the Reformation can be said to have begun. While Luther was at the Wartburg near Eisenach for ten months (from 4 May 1521 until March 1522, when he returned to Wittenberg), he was attacked by Latomus, the University of Paris (its condemnation came 15 April 1524), Emser, and Albert of Mainz.[24] Spalatin was the go-between, and all communications to and from Luther at the Wartburg went through him, as secretary to the elector Frederick of Saxony (*BR*); and it was while at the Wartburg that Luther trans-

lated the New Testament into German (published 1522), working
from Erasmus' second edition of the Greek New Testament of 1519.

Luther's earlier influences, spiritual and intellectual, were scholas-
tic (especially Gabriel Biel), Augustinian (and as noted above the
German mystics of the Rhineland), and Pauline.[25] From about 1511
until 1521, Erasmus was the chief guide of the Wittenberg reformer.
'After 1521, the humanist was indeed read carefully, but generally
with dissent and reprobation' (Smith, 212). Among the works of
Erasmus read with care by Luther were the *Enchiridion*, the *Praise of
Folly*, the *Julius Exclusus,* and the letters in edition after edition.

> The *Adagia* was one of the first works of its author to be
> thoroughly read by the Wittenberger, and was one which he
> took care always to have in the latest and best edition. There
> may be a quotation from it in Luther's works as early as 1510–
> 11; quotations from it become very numerous after May, 1518.
> (Smith, 213)

But it was the Greek New Testament which from the moment he
put his hands on a copy in April 1516 became Luther's 'chief guide
and authority in exegesis for some years…' (and for his German
translation he used the 1519 edition). Yet Luther read the edition
critically, and he was not happy with the treatment of the Epistle to
the Romans, for his own doctrine of justification of faith rested on
Romans 1: 17. Where Jerome read 'the just shall live by my faith',
Erasmus read the passage as 'by his faith' (Smith, 214–5).

Luther's enthusiasm for Erasmus had begun to cool in 1517, as we
mark in a letter of 1 March of that year:

> I read our Erasmus and my respect for him daily decreases. He
> pleased me because, constantly and learnedly, he convicts and
> condemns monks and priests in inveterate sloth and ignorance;
> yet I fear he does not sufficiently reveal Christ and the grace of
> God, in which he is much more ignorant than Lefèvre d'Etaples,
> for human considerations prevail with him much more than
> divine. (Smith, 215)

Erasmus' attitude to 'this business of Martin' remained enigmatic.[26]

Much attention has been given in the twentieth century to Martin
Luther's Lectures on Romans (given 1515–1516), but these have
been published only in the twentieth century and therefore cannot be
considered in an evaluation of his impact upon his own age, although
it must be recognised that they are central to his theological development. In 1517, at about the time of the Theses, Luther lectured on
the Epistle to the Hebrews, and in 1519 he wrote a Commentary on
Galatians which provides his analysis of the question of the law and
the gospel; this commentary was reworked in 1523, and again in

1535. But, to repeat, these are dimensions of Luther's work that Erasmus did not know.[27] Here we must concentrate on the theses and the three seminal tracts of 1520 to establish the image of Luther that Erasmus and others would have formed. In chapter 39 we shall come to grips with the famous controversy between the two men on the freedom of the will, which provides such a decisive and clear-cut line between the theology of Luther and that of Erasmus; and for that we shall draw upon subsequent writings of Luther. By that time, the year 1524, patterns and issues will have emerged far more clearly.

The first of six surviving letters that passed between the German reformer and the Dutch humanist is Epistle 933 from Luther to Erasmus. Written at Wittenberg in March 1519, Luther's letter acknowledges Erasmus' 'wonderful spirit' that 'has so much enriched me and all of us' (*CWE* 6:282/26–7); and he asks Erasmus to write to Melanchthon, who prospers but burns too much with the ardour of youth 'both to be and to do all things for all men' (48–9). Then, strikingly, he closes:

> 'But you must bear in mind that it is not always the scholarly letters [*eruditas ... epistolas*] that deserve to be read; sometimes you must be weak with those that are weak [*cum infirmis infirmandum*]' (*CWE* 6:283/55–7; Allen III, 509/46–7)

Erasmus replied in Epistle 980 from Louvain at the end of May 1519:[28] a somewhat guarded letter written in more cautious terms than Epistle 939[29] where in his April letter to the elector Frederick of Saxony he had explained (in 69 ff.) that he knew little of Luther and had read his writings only 'in snatches' (*nisi carptim*: Allen III, 530/ 69, which is more ambiguous). To Luther he writes bluntly, 'No words of mine could describe the storm raised here [in Louvain] by your books' (line 4); and he added the caution or admonition,

> Everywhere we must take pains to do and say nothing out of arrogance or faction; for I think the spirit of Christ would have it so. Meanwhile we must keep our minds above the corruption of anger or hatred, or of ambition; for it is this that lies in wait for us when our religious zeal is in full course. (*CWE* 6:393/54– 58; Allen III, 606/47–51)

Incomplete though this segment of Erasmus' correspondence with Luther obviously is, Epistles 933 and 980 are crucial in demonstrating Luther's belief even this early that there was a gulf between Erasmus' humanism and his own christian love: he apparently had not perceived how necessary classical studies were for Erasmus' editing and annotating of the New Testament, and he remained disturbed by his *Moria*. For his part, Erasmus – not familiar with Luther's lectures on Romans or his commentary on Galatians[30] – may not have realised the power of Luther's study of Scripture; but he was still prepared to defend Luther's right to criticise the Church.[31]

The Reformation is usually seen as a number of distinct but inter-connected and often antagonistic movements, ranging from Luther's activities on the one hand, to the emergence of the reformed tradition (principally in Switzerland to begin with), the radical reform of the Anabaptists and kindred sects, and the catholic Counter-Reformation on the other. It was only after Luther's return from the Wartburg to Wittenberg in 1522 that a thoroughgoing and institutionalised 'Lutheranism' began to take hold in various parts of Germany and elsewhere. In the case of the reformed churches there was a progressive shift of focus from Zürich to Berne, and from Berne to Geneva, stretching over a generation from about 1520 to 1560, leaving John Calvin for a time as the pre-eminent figure. Erasmus' life touched the men, movements and cities involved in the complicated cross-currents of the Reformation at many points. Here a handful only can be indicated, reserving a discussion of Basel for chapter 38.[32]

On 11 December 1518 Zwingli was elected minister at Zürich, and he remained there until his death in 1531. The influence of Erasmus has been judged decisive for Zwingli (see *BR*), and the two met in Basel during the spring of 1516 (Epistles 401, 404), and their correspondence continued until 1523; Zwingli repeatedly stressed that his work as a reformer had begun before his first acquaintance with Luther's writings late in 1518. There was enthusiasm between Zwingli and Erasmus in the years from 1514 to 1520, a growing alienation from 1520 to 1522, and then open hostility (*BR*).

Another key figure was Johannes Oecolampadius (1482–1531), who had studied Greek and Hebrew at Tübingen and further with Reuchlin at Stuttgart. During this formative period he met Melanchthon and made friends with Wolfgang Capito. Moving to Basel in 1515, Oecolampadius worked as a corrector for Froben and assisted Erasmus on the New Testament. In 1518 he received a doctorate in theology at Basel (Epistle 904) and took up an appoint-ment as cathedral preacher in Augsburg. For some time he became a supporter of Luther and wrote two tracts on the Mass and Confession and in 1522 returned to Basel, where he became a leader of the reform movement. Very much a supporter of Zwingli at Baden (1526) and Berne (1528), he also helped to bring about reformation at Ulm, Memmingen, and Biberach. Erasmus criticised Oeco-lampadius in several writings (*BR*), but Epistle 2147 was a friendly letter. They met in Froben's garden before Erasmus left for Freiburg in 1529, and the two parted in peace (Epistles 2158, 2196).

Willibald Pirckheimer (1470–1530) was born in Eichstätt and studied Greek and law in Italy. In 1497 he became a town councillor at Nürnberg,[33] and one of the leading German humanists of his age, translating from Greek into Latin and from both classical languages into German. Apparently Erasmus never visited Nürnberg, but a friendship developed through their correspondence, beginning with Epistle 322 from Erasmus and 318 (to Beatus Rhenanus) from Pirckheimer (see *BR* on continuing letters). Pirckheimer initially approved of Luther and continued to complain about repressive measures taken by Rome against reformers; consequently he was viewed with suspicion by the nuncio, Chierigati. In about 1524 he changed from a Lutheran supporter to an opponent of the Reformation, and this 'realignment' strengthened his friendship with Erasmus. Epistle 2493 is in effect Erasmus' obituary for his friend Pirckheimer. The significance of Nürnberg as an imperial free city is well developed by Gerald Strauss.[34]

Born in a small village on the Mosel between Koblenz and Trier, Petrus Mosellanus (Schade) was a student of the University of Cologne; learning Greek by private study, in 1514 he moved to Freiburg in Saxony as a teacher of Greek. He then studied under Richard Croke to perfect his Greek, and in 1517 succeeded Croke as a lecturer in Greek at Leipzig, although he then still lacked his MA, which was awarded in 1520. In 1520 and 1523 he was rector of the University of Leipzig. Erasmus respected Mosellanus' qualifications in Greek learning, and his letters (Epistles 911, 948, 1123, 1305) dealt with the advancement of Greek studies and the opposition to them at Leipzig and Louvain. Mosellanus, who died in 1524, was pulled into Erasmus' controversy with Luther (*BR*).

Justus Jonas (1493–1555) was a native of Nordhausen, north of Erfurt, and studied at Erfurt, obtaining an MA in 1510 at the age of sixteen, and went on to study law at Wittenberg, where he received a baccalaureate in law in 1514–15, returning to Erfurt for further studies. In the spring of 1519 he visited Erasmus at Louvain, carrying with him Martin Luther's first letter (Epistle 933). In his absence on a long trip Jonas was elected rector of the University of Erfurt (such elections *in absentia*, or appointments to committees, happened in the sixteenth as in the twentieth centuries). Jonas was involved in much of the early reform movement: the Leipzig disputation between Luther and Eck took place while he was rector at Erfurt. In March 1521 he was appointed provost of the chapter and professor of law in Wittenberg, and he was then involved in many of the debates and concerns of the university in reformation matters. It was Jonas who gave the oration at Luther's funeral in Eisleben in 1546. Not until 1527 did he remove himself from the influence of Erasmus, on which occasion Luther wrote, 'I congratulate you on your recantation … I am glad that you have gained so much insight reading his *Hyperaspistes*, and that you have changed your opinion of him' (*BR*). Erasmus had a special regard for Jonas, and in Epistle 1211 to him he gave his account of the lives of Vitrier and Colet.

In 1520, as Smith has observed, Erfurt was still thoroughly Erasmian:[35] besides Jonas there was a circle of humanists which included Eobanus Hessus, Mutianus Rufus, and Johann Lang (some of whom later became Lutherans). Eobanus lectured on the *Enchiridion*, and another professor on the *Moriae*. Erasmus was asked by the university, one of the newest of German universities with a young faculty, to advise on the reform of the curriculum.

Philip Melanchthon (1497–1560) had his second name given him by Reuchlin, his great-uncle, in place of the family name Schwarzerd (Schwartzerdt). He studied at Heidelberg, then Tübingen, where he received his MA. In 1518 he was appointed to the new chair of Greek at Wittenberg and was from the outset a leader in curriculum reform. In the *Annotations* of 1516 Erasmus gave extravagant praise to the young scholar of nineteen (but, Scheible notes in *BR*, that praise was later removed). Several letters testify to their mutual high opinion (Epistles 454, 556, 563, 605). Although they apparently did not correspond for four years, there was mutual respect, even consideration, and Erasmus was kept informed of Melanchthon's affairs and publications (Epistles 1128, 1168, 1198). When his *De Libero Arbitrio* was published in September 1524, Erasmus sent it to Melanchthon rather than to Luther (Epistle 1496). There was again a period of no correspondence for more than three years; and although Melanchthon disapproved of Erasmus' theology, there was a warm exchange in 1528. In his last years Melanchthon honoured Erasmus, and on his deathbed repeated Erasmus' last prayer (*BR*). If Melanchthon can be rightly called the *Praeceptor Germaniae*, Erasmus can be called the teacher of Melanchthon.[36]

Few Erasmian scholars, it has been remarked, know how many ties attached the master humanist of Rotterdam to the countries of eastern Europe.[37] Even the dispersion of Erasmus' library in Poland is still an incomplete story, for of several hundred volumes in the Erasmus-Laski library, only about fifteen have been located today. In Epistle 1039 (of November 1519) to Jan Šlechta, Erasmus dealt with the troubles in Bohemia, and in October 1520 he received a letter (1154) from Arkleb of Boskovice, a nobleman of Moravia, soliciting his opinion concerning the Czech Brethren. These two letters illustrate the desire of humanists in eastern Europe to win Erasmus' support, and of his effort to maintain ties with that part of Christendom.

Adrian of Utrecht (1459–1523) has already been introduced (chapter 19). Like Erasmus a Dutchman, Adrian Dedel was a native of Utrecht and like Erasmus he was schooled by the Brethren of the Common Life at either Deventer or Zwolle. At Louvain he became a doctor of theology in 1492, and later *rector magnificus*. Margaret of Burgundy appointed him a member of her household in 1515, and he was named tutor to the future Charles V. While in Spain on a diplomatic mission – where he became a friend of Ximénez, bishop of Tortosa, viceroy of Spain and cardinal – he was unanimously elected pope in 1522 on the death of Leo X. Worn out by the frustrations and burdens of the papacy at a time of great crisis, and a stranger to Italy as well as to the papal court, he died twenty months after ascending the papal throne.

Erasmus knew Adrian during his first sojourn in Louvain, 1502 to 1504,[38] but during much of the time that Erasmus was in the Low Countries from 1517 to 1521 Adrian was in Spain. While Adrian valued Juan Luis Vives as well as Erasmus, and tried to enlist the support of Erasmus (in several letters strongly urging him to come to Rome) there were pronounced differences between them. Adrian was a conservative theologian, and his two publications were the *Commentarii in IV libros Sententiarum* (1516) and the *Quaestiones quodlibeticae* (1515).[39] He appreciated Erasmus' scholarship in the *Novum Instrumentum*, but there is little evidence that he felt warmly about the *Adagia* or the *Colloquies*. We turn to the exchange of letters between them in 1522 and early 1523 for the light they throw on a number of significant points.

In Epistle 1324 of 1 December 1522,[40] which was sent to Brabant and may not have reached Erasmus in Basel until the end of January, Adrian first reassured Erasmus on his not lending 'a ready ear to information reaching us to the discredit of learned men who are noted for their holiness of life' (*CWE* 9:205/20–1; Allen V, 145/17–19); and praising his 'great intellectual powers, extensive learning, and a readiness in writing' (29–30). He then urged Erasmus to write to confute Luther: 'you must confound them [his heresies], abolish them, explode them by all the powers of reason and all the authoritative texts of Holy Scripture' (53–5). In closing (lines 120 ff.) Adrian repeated the invitation: once winter is past, 'do come to us as soon as you can, but come in good health and spirits'.

Erasmus' letter, Epistle 1329 of 22 December 1522 (which is not a reply to Adrian's letter), strikes a note of obedience: 'If your

Holiness will deign to test my loyalty, give me what task you will, and unless my obedience is prompt and cheerful, do not count the name of Erasmus among your servants' (*CWE* 9:220/41–3; Allen V, 220/41–3). In Epistle 1337A of perhaps mid-January 1523, Erasmus wrote to Prierias, the pope's theologian, that he should like to be in Rome and would come if his health could stand it (*CWE* 9:283/55–8). Adrian's reply came in Epistle 1338 of 23 January 1523, urging speed and urgency upon Erasmus in expounding his position, and then, again, urging him to come quickly (285/61).

To Adrian's last letter Erasmus replied with some deliberateness (Epistle 1352 of 22 March 1523), asking what weight could be attached to a mere individual like himself: 'Will the authority of Erasmus have any effect on people who give no weight to the authority of so many universities, so many princes, and the supreme pontiff himself?' (CWE 9:435/35–7; Allen V, 258/30–32). His next statement has a double interest, not only for its weight as a reply to the pope, but also for the light it throws on his own awareness of his rapidly changing image:

> Time was when hundreds of letters described me as greatest of the great, prince of the world of literature, bright star of Germany, luminary of learning, champion of humane studies, bulwark of a more genuine theology. Now I am never mentioned, or am painted in far different colours. (*CWE* 9:435–6/ 39–43; Allen V, 258/34–7)[41]

'What good should I do in Rome?' Erasmus asked the pope. If a rumour were started and circulated that Erasmus had gone to Rome, 'what a hubbub instantly ... everyone saying that I was skipping off to your part of the world for my share of the spoils!' (439/151, 158–9). Instead Erasmus offered positive advice:

> The first thing will be to investigate the sources from which this evil so often springs up afresh; for they must be set right before all else. And then it will not be found ineffective if once again a pardon is offered to those who have gone astray through the persuasion or influence of others; better still, an amnesty of all wrongs previously committed, which seem to have come about by some sort of destiny ... (193/198). At the sweet name of liberty all men will breathe afresh. (*CWE* 9:440/206; Allen V, 261/170–182)

Apparently Adrian never replied to Epistle 1352 – at least none is extant – and Erasmus, with reason, feared that his advice had offended Adrian; certainly the notion of an amnesty was not in curial thinking. No further communication between the two is known in 1523, and Adrian died in September of that year.

The letter indicates Erasmus' capacity of *parrhesia*, and it witnesses to his constant irenicism and emphasis on liberty.[42]

As Luther's theological thought matured and as he himself began to present his differences with traditional catholic doctrine and his objections to Erasmus, their lines of development diverged (for Erasmus too had to clarify many points of his thought and belief after 1520). But for several years Luther had drawn extensively from the writings of Erasmus and was dependent upon Erasmus' editorial work on the Greek New Testament; and even after 1517 he continued to be interested in editions of the *Adages* and collections of Erasmus' letters.

At first Erasmus was sympathetic to Luther; but 1520 was a landmark year, and Erasmus' objections became more outspoken in those semi-public letters that were read by more than the named recipient and often passed from hand to hand (as the writer knew that they would be), and then, especially after 1518, circulated widely in the printed collections of his letters that people everywhere in Europe were avid to read. Until his final years Erasmus felt keenly the need for reform, provided the institution of the Church itself were not threatened.

After 1518 there were followers of Luther everywhere in Germany and neighbouring countries. After his excommunication in 1521, and with knowledge of the fact that he was not only still unpunished but actually remained alive, the numbers of Lutheran supporters multiplied. Some like Pirckheimer, who were at first greatly attracted to Luther, later returned to Rome. But for the first half-dozen years after 1517 the undisputed leader of the reform movement was Martin Luther.

Under Leo X the Roman reaction was hesitant, uninformed, and procrastinating. Only Luther's condemnation by the bull *Exsurge Domine* on 15 June 1520 was clear-cut and decisive; but the promulgation of it in Germany was assigned to Eck, whose abrasive methods stirred up fierce opposition at Leipzig (29 September) and Wittenberg (3 October), exacerbating the friction between Germany and Rome, and accelerating the pace of events. By the time of the death of Leo and the election of Adrian VI in 1522 the Lutheran movement was in full stride, and Adrian was the first pope, consequently, to feel the full impact of the reformation movement; but his pontificate was only twenty months in duration. He did begin the reform of the papal curia, but achieved little else.

Erasmus played a unique role at the eye of the hurricane. No one else remained in such continuing and vital communication with very nearly the full spectrum of reformers, and yet all the while remaining in touch with Rome and church leaders throughout Christendom, as well as princes, everywhere else. One needs a detailed chronology as well as a sense of geography to read the crowded correspondence of Erasmus after 1518 with anything like fullness of understanding.[43]

To borrow a metaphor from a later century: events were in the saddle, and they moved with bewildering speed. The tide was clearly running in favour of the reformers; Erasmus feared that the humanists were losing out rather badly and that the cause of true learning was becoming desperate.

Notes

1) See his illuminating essay on 'The Late Medieval Church and its Reformation (1400–1600)', in *The Oxford Illustrated History of Christianity*, ed. John McManners (Oxford, 1990) 235. He adds: 'Yet Martin Luther was not aware that he had inaugurated something called "the Reformation" and no one spoke in that way of the Reformation before the seventeenth century': of reformation, yes; but of The Reformation, no.

2) Yet another variable in this complex of problems is that of the conceptualising of the Reformation as a movement in modern Western history: so complex that there is even questioning of whether there was but one Reformation, or many. See the survey of this immense scholarly area by A.G. Dickens and John M. Tonkin, *The Reformation in Historical Thought* (Cambridge, Mass., 1985).

3) Gerhart B. Ladner, *The Idea of Reform* (Cambridge, Mass., 1959; rev. ed., New York, 1967).

4) The literature on the reform movements before Luther is itself vast. For a useful introduction with selected key documents and a useful bibliography of primary and secondary sources, see Heiko Oberman, *Forerunners of the Reformation* (1966; rptd. Philadelphia, 1981).

5) Convenient bibliographies are given in *ODCC, NCE* and *LThK*. The authoritative works in the field are E.F. Jacob, *Studies in the Conciliar Epoch* (Oxford, 1943), and Brian Tierney, *Foundations of Conciliar Theory* (Cambridge, 1955). There are more specialised studies by Joseph Gill, Margaret Harvey, Edith C. Tatnall, A.N.E.D. Schofield, and A.J. Black in *Councils and Assemblies*, ed. G.J. Cuming and Derek Baker (Cambridge, 1971). The documents of the conciliar decrees are given in *COD*, with English translations of a large number of the decrees in H.J. Schroeder, O.P., *Disciplinary Decrees of the General Councils, Text, Translation, and Commentary* (St. Louis, 1937). The first 165 pages of volume I of H. Jedin, *History of the Council of Trent* (London, 1957) offer a marvellously compressed history of the conciliar movement and of concepts of *Reformatio capitis*. Among recent studies that of A.E McGrath, *The Intellectual Origins of the European Reformation* (Oxford, 1987) is noteworthy. Erasmus has a large role in the study of Jean-Pierre Massaut, *Critique et Tradition à la Veille de la Réforme en France* (Paris, 1974). The volume *Latran V et Trente* by O. Brosse, J. Lecler, H. Hostein and Ch. Lefebvre (tome 10 of

L'Histoire des Conciles Oecuméniques, sous la direction de G. Dumeige, Paris, 1975) offers a wide perspective on the history and historiography of the councils.

6) Hughes, *The Church in Crisis,* 273. The impact upon Basel itself is discussed in ch.30.

7) I am indebted to Hughes, 272–3, for this summary.

8) To say that Martin Luther was disappointed by the Fifth Lateran Council is an obvious understatement. His posting of the theses can be seen as an act by an individual after the grievous failure of the highest level of the Church, and the council of the Church having failed to achieve reform or even viable reform measures to confront the larger problems was a catalyst for him and many others.

9) See 'The Fifth Lateran Council' (1981).

10) *Eyn deutsch Theologia*, ed. M. Luther (Wittenberg, 1518) was reprinted more than nine times before 1538 in Augsburg, Strasbourg, Wittenberg, Frankfurt and Rostock.

11) See Rufus M. Jones, *Spiritual Reformers in the 16th and 17th Centuries* (Boston, 1914; rptd. 1959) 6: 'He had already in his convent days come under the spell of St. Augustine, St. Bernard, Gerson, and many another guide into the deep regions of inward personal religion, and his intimate friend, the vicar-general Staupitz, had been to him in some sense a personal embodiment of this type of religion. But the German mystics of the fourteenth century, with their mighty experience and their extraordinary depth, carried him still farther in this direction'. Cf. L.W. Spitz, *Religious Renaissance of the German Humanists,* (Cambridge, Mass., 1963) 238.

12) In *Opera Hutteni*, ed. E. Böcking (Leipzig, 1859–70) 11, 12–21. He had hoped to win over archduke Ferdinand to the cause of the Reformation; failing, he was dismissed by the archbishop of Mainz, Albert of Brandenburg. Under an order of arrest from Rome, he fled to Franz von Sickingen, who offered his castles as places of refuge to the reformers (thus, even the medieval church-sanctuary had become laicised). He sought the protection of Erasmus in 1522 and was refused; in the end he went to Zwingli, who gave him a refuge on the island of Ufenau in the Lake of Zürich (*ODCC, BR,* and *LThK*). In addition to the edition of Hutten's work by Böcking, the standard scholarly biography is that of Hajo Holborn, *Ulrich von Hutten and the German Reformation* (New Haven, 1937; German ed., 1929); and there is a lucid examination of Hutten's religious ideas in Spitz, *Religious Renaissance.* The relationship between Hutten and Erasmus is succinctly given by Barbara Könneker in *BR.* The two key works in the confrontation of Hutten and Erasmus – the *Expostulatio* of the former, and the *Spongia* of the latter – are translated and annotated by R.J. Klawitter in *The Polemics of Erasmus of Rotterdam and Ulrich von Hutten* (Notre Dame, Ind., 1977).

13) See B. Gebhardt, *Die gravamina der deutschen Nation gegen den römischen Hof* (Breslau, 1895), esp. 103 ff.

14) Theologically, an indulgence is the remission by the Church of the temporal punishment due to sins that have been forgiven by virtue of the merits of Christ. Much false doctrine was peddled along with the virtually unrestricted sale of indulgences, especially in connection with the raising of funds for the rebuilding of St Peter's. This practice was finally prohibited by pope Pius V in 1567 (*ODCC*).

15) Tetzel (c. 1465–1519) was a German Dominican at Leipzig, who had been appointed subcommissary for the regions of Magdeburg and Halberstadt in 1516. After Luther's posting of the 95 Theses, Tetzel took up the challenge in two sets of counter-theses, which merely flamed the controversy. The attempt by Carl von Miltitz, a Papal nuncio, to restrain him in 1519, in an effort towards conciliation, was a failure (*ODCC*). Interestingly , Tetzel does not figure in Erasmus' correspondence.

16) The Augustinian Hermits or Friars were formed in the Middle Ages from several Italian congregations of hermits who were banded together by pope Alexander IV in 1256 under the Rule of St Augustine, their constitution being modelled on that of the Dominicans. Thus, although Luther and Erasmus could both loosely be called Augustinians, there were profound differences between their orders; the chief common bond was the Rule of St Augustine, although even with that there were differences: i.e. different versions of the Rule (see ch. 5), and it was variously interpreted.

17) The newness of the University of Wittenberg needs comment: a new university favours innovation (see, e.g., the role of the new universities in logic and rhetoric, as examined by Terrence Heath in *Stud. in Ren.* 18 [1971] 9–64), and Luther would not have found support as he did at Wittenberg, had he been at Paris, Cologne or Louvain. See n. 19 and Spitz, 249.

18) Q. by Bainton, *Here I Stand*, 52–3.

19) Staupitz (see n. 11 above), whose dates are c. 1468–1524, played a leading role in the founding of the University of Wittenberg, where he was from the outset professor of theology and dean of the faculty. After some years as Luther's spiritual director, Staupitz gradually withdrew from support of Luther and resigned as vicar-general of the German Augustinians in 1520, moving to Salzburg, where he entered the Benedictine Order. See A. Jeremias, ed., *Johann von Staupitz, Luthers Vater and Schüler* (Berlin, 1926), and *LThK*.

20) These 28 Theses, which avoided some of the more controversial issues of the 95 Theses, are available in English translation in John Dillenberger, ed., *Martin Luther, Selections* ... (New York, 1961). See further Walter Koehler, ed., *Dokumente zum Ablass Streit von 1517,* 2d ed. (Tübingen, 1924).

21) Bainton, *Here I stand*, 65–6.

22) The first edition of some 4,000 copies (phenomenal itself) sold out between 18 and 23 August (*NCE*).

23) See Eps 1203, 1217 & 1244.

24) See Martin Brecht, *Martin Luther – Shaping and Defining the Reformation, 1521–1532* (Minneapolis, 1990) 6 ff.

25) Luther's heritage from Gabriel Biel and the nominalism of the late Middle Ages has been thoroughly studied by Heiko A. Oberman in *The Harvest of Medieval Theology* (Cambridge, Mass., 1963). See further Leif Grane, *Contra Gabrielem – Luthers Auseinandersetzung mit Gabriel Biel in der Disputation Contra Scholasticam Theologiam 1517* (Gylendal, 1962).

26) 'Do not, I beg you, exaggerate this business of Martin into a public issue', Wolfgang Faber Capito wrote to Erasmus on 8 April 1519 from Basel, Epistle 938 (*CWE* 6:294/1) – 'this business of Martin' (*Martini negotium*: Allen III, 527/1) – on which Bietenholz comments, 'It [the letter] also forecasts the future disagreement between Capito and Erasmus, since they evidently differed sharply in their advice to Froben as to whether or not he should continue to publish Luther's writings' (Introd. to Ep. 938).

27) Our 20th-c. view of Luther is the result of much change. For a straightforward introduction to 20th-c. perspectives on Luther, see, briefly, J. Pelikan, *The Melody of Theology,* 154–7; and, more historically, *Wandlungen des Lutherbildes,* by Erwin Iserloh et al. (Würzburg, 1966).

28) This letter was promptly published in Germany without Erasmus' knowledge. Such unauthorised publication, along with the underground circulation of manuscripts of letters and other writings, makes it difficult to chart the movement of ideas with precision. See the n. following.

29) A copy of Ep. 939 was made by Spalatinus and sent to Wittenberg, where Melanchthon acknowledged it with much satisfaction. On 30 July Martin Bucer saw a copy of it at Heidelberg (*CWE* 6: introd. to Ep. 939).

30) But he was soon to be conversant with Luther's lectures on the Psalms: see Allen III, 606/53n. The public lectures, *Operationes in Psalmos* (1519) carried a prefatory letter from Melanchthon which testified to the debt owed to Erasmus for his Latin and Greek scholarship.

31) However, here one must take note of his threat made later (in 1520) to end his cooperation with the Froben press if it continued to publish Luther's writings: cf. Allen IV, 345/20.

32) The purpose here is to call attention to the rapid diffusion of reform ideas and activities throughout Germany and Switzerland. There is no attempt at completeness, only at an overview through selected examples.

33) Barbara Könneker records in *BR* that Pirckheimer did not complete his studies in Italy, 'because his father was planning that he should have a civic career at Nürnberg, where men with doctorates were ineligible to sit on the city council'.

34) See Gerald Strauss, *Nuremberg in the Sixteenth Century* (New York, 1966). See further, Spitz, *Religious Renaissance.* 155–96, & passim.

35) Smith, 157. In May 1520 friends of Erasmus published a volume of epigrams in which Lee was called a son of Cerberus and of Fury: *In Edwardum Leeum Quorundam e sodalitate Erphurdiense Erasmici nominis studiosorum Epigrammata* (Moguntae, J. Schoeffer, 1520); from *BM Cat.*

36) See Leo Stern, et al., *Philipp Melanchthon, Humanist, Reformator, Praeceptor Germaniae* (Berlin, 1960); C.L. Manschreck, *Melanchthon the Quiet Reformer* (New York-Nashville, 1958); Wilhelm Maurer, 'Melanchthons Anteil am Streit zwischen Luther und Erasmus', *ARG* 49 (1959) 89–114, rptd. in Maurer, *Melanchthon-Studien* (Gütersloh, 1964), 137–62. The analysis of Wilhelm Schenk, 'Erasmus and Melanchthon', *The Heythrop Journal* VIII (1967) 249–59, stresses the point that 'the Erasmian trinity of concepts became firmly established in Melanchthon's thought: tradition, nature, and reason – the voice of enlightened mankind throughout the ages' (257–8). But Schenk also identifies their differences.

37) See Istvan Vida, 'Erasmus in eastern Europe today', in *Erasmus in English* 2 (1971) 14, and, in the same number, Maria Cytowska, 'Erasmian Studies in Poland 1969–70: the Erasmus Quincentenary', 13–4.

38) We recall that it was Adrian who had persuaded the magistracy of the city of Louvain to offer Erasmus a lectureship in rhetoric (ch. 19).

39) On the significance of the traditional genre of these published writings see ch. 11.

40) This was a letter of great importance to Erasmus and he frequently cited it (*CWE* 9:203 introd.). Allen has commented at further length: nearly

a year had elapsed since Adrian's election and Erasmus was apprehensive about Adrian's feelings towards him. Ep. 1324 was a *Breve Aureum* indeed, and it marks the importance of the letter to Erasmus to observe that he had it printed in the *Exomologesis* and thereafter in the collected volumes of letters (Allen V, 143–4).

41) Allen's notes to these lines give references to letters in which these epithets had been used.

42) Would Erasmus at this point have been thinking of the Augustinian formulation: 'In necessary things, unity; in doubtful things, liberty: in all things, charity'? (the motto, by the way, of Richard Baxter in the 17th c.).

43) The complexities of geography and chronology are admirably demonstrated by the analysis of Henri Gibaud, 'Les tribulations d'Erasme de Bâle à Louvain: 4–21 septembre 1518', in *La Correspondence d'Erasme et L'Epistographie Humaniste* (Brussels, 1990), 25–36.

The Basel Years, 1521–1529:
The Reformation Storm Rising

This sorry business of Luther ... *[Lutherana tragoedia]*
Erasmus, 27 May 1521, Epistle 1206
(*CWE* 8:218/50; Allen IV, 499/46)

New factions constantly arise, not to say persecutions. The laity are hostile to the clergy, and the clergy regard the laity almost with abomination.
Caesarius to Erasmus, 14 July 1522, Epistle 1291
(*CWE* 9:107/14–6; Allen V, 75/14–6)

'I laid the egg; Luther hatched it.' Indeed a surprising statement, made by those Minorites – but it does suit their fat bellies. What I laid was a hen's egg; the bird Luther hatched was altogether different.
Erasmus to Caesarius, 6 December 1524, Epistle 1528
(trans. M. A. Haworth in Hillerbrand, 183;
Allen V, 609/11–14)

Long before Erasmus arrived in Basel on 15 November 1521 he had talked of returning there. In Epistle 1236, writing from Anderlecht in October 1521, he spoke lightly of the decision facing him in the early part of the year:
> Just now, I had quite made up my mind to take to the road, with the idea of finishing what I wished to do in Basel, and then migrating entirely to Rome, there to devote what time is left me to the society of great scholars and the resources of great libraries. (*CWE* 8:308/198–202; Allen IV , 587/178-182)
But, he added in this letter to Paolo Bombasio, the 'cruel war' was a deterrent. In Basel Froben had expected his arrival before Easter (Introduction to Epistle 1242, *CWE*); in Rome and Wittenberg it had for some time been assumed that Erasmus was already in Basel.

Epistle 1239 of 14 October 1521 is the last dated letter by Erasmus from Anderlecht. About a week was given to financial and other matters in Louvain and Antwerp, and he set out from Louvain for Basel on the 28th of October (Epistle 1241A). His route was much the same as on previous trips; from Tienen (about 15 km. south of Louvain) to Speyer he travelled with a troop of disbanded soldiers (Epistle 1248), which reminds us in the twentieth century of the turbulent times that existed then in much of Europe. From Speyer he could travel safely up the Rhine by boat, arriving in Basel on 15 November.[1] It was a trip now quite familiar to him, and there were old friends who had been impatiently awaiting his arrival for months.

For the first ten months he lived with Froben, but he was meticulous in paying 150 gulden for his room and board (something like a thousand dollars today),[2] being sensitive to rumours that he was living off the kindness of Froben. Froben's property was the 'Zum Sessel' that consisted of several houses and a yard reaching from the Nadelberg to the Totengässlein; in October 1522 the house 'zur alten Treu' was purchased for Erasmus' use (Epistles 1316 and 1371), and for that Erasmus paid 400 gold florins. As Epistle 1422 indicates, it was doubtless in 'Zum Sessel' that Froben had built an open fireplace in one of the rooms in place of a stove (Epistle 1422/28–9) to please the demanding Dutchman with his outspoken dislike of German stoves.[3] Erasmus detested the stoves that he found in Germany and Switzerland, and wherever possible he preferred an open fireplace – largely for reasons of health, but possibly also for aesthetic reasons.[4] 'On 12 June 1526 Froben purchased a garden against the city wall only a short walk away from his house. This was greatly appreciated by Erasmus (Epistle 1756, 2147)' (*BR*). Allen adds that 'as the Nadelberg is close to St Peter's Church, it may be inferred that Erasmus was still there when his first will was attested' (V, 133/38 n).

In the final analysis, Erasmus came to Basel to complete his projects by being closer to Froben and his scholarly team. But he was also fleeing Louvain, which had become increasingly hostile to him and his ideals, and where because of its proximity to the court and the arch-conservatism of Louvain's school of theology he was being pressured to write a book against Luther.[5] At first he did not plan to remain in Basel beyond the winter.[6] In September 1522 he moved to a separate house, close enough to Froben, but apart. Here he had space enough to establish his own household: a housekeeper, his secretaries, and room for visitors. The inventory attached to his will, dated 10 April 1534 (see appendix D) is later, but it will serve to indicate his rising prosperity. In the will are indicated a considerable collection of gold and silver vessels and ornaments given him over the years, as well as ample clothing, and a goodly supply of furniture and household utensils. By this time his library was well stocked. He lived comfortably indeed.

We speak of the 'family' of Erasmus in the sense conveyed by the Latin *familia*, which in medieval Latin had taken on further meanings beyond those of classical Latin where the main thrust of signification was to cover the servants and domestics, not the family in a modern sense. In medieval times the word meant 'the aggregate dependents of different kinds subservient to a lord' or 'the whole of the residents of a monastery, including the monks' (Niermeyer). Allen made use of the term *servant-pupil* for *famulus* to describe the relationship of a number of young men who lived with Erasmus, learned from him, and served him in different capacities.[7] Some in fact paid a pension for the privilege of living with him and learning. Before 1511 he often had no *famulus* (although there had been two in Paris), but from 1516 to 1518 he had as many as three or four at a time, and in Basel he often had four or five. Customarily they read to him during dinner; in Epistle 1756 of 1526 he wrote that 'after dinner I try not to work too intensively – perhaps I converse without wearying myself, or walk, listening to a *famulus* reading' (Epistle 1759, Allen VI, 423/55–7).[8] It is in this letter that he speaks of his twenty-year habit of writing standing, despite the fact that his portraits may show him standing or seated (appendix D).

A number of Erasmus' servant-pupils went on to further education and distinction. One such was Robert Aldridge, who worked with Erasmus at Cambridge and afterwards became bishop of Carlisle; another was Thomas Lupset, whom we have already encountered; and still another, the nobleman Jan Laski. To one, his service with Erasmus mattered so much that the fact is engraved on his tomb.[9]

But the *famulus* to whom he was most closely attached was Gilbert Cognatus (Cousin) of Nozeroy in the Franche-Comté, who was with Erasmus during the Freiburg years and left him in 1535 to take on the duties of a canonry to which he had been appointed (*BR*). A later woodcut shows him taking dictation from Erasmus, and between them there is a vase of flowers, which Erasmus loved to have before him while writing. Cognatus wrote a small treatise on a servant's life and duties, *Οἰκέτης*, published by Oporinus at Basel in 1535; and in that he speaks of being trusty in everything as the prime virtue of a servant.[10]

And there was Margarete – Margarete Büsslein – who looked after the household of Erasmus from about 1521 until 1535. She was difficult to live with (as Erasmus etches her in Epistle 2735: '*Margarete furax, rapax, bibax, mendax, loquax*') yet energetic and indispensable enough that Erasmus moved her with him to Freiburg in 1529. But when he left Freiburg to return to Basel, he did not take her back with him: she was elderly by then, and a grumbling settlement was made with her (*BR*). She figures in the colloquy *Convivium poeticum* of 1523, which also features Hilarius Bertholf (Bertulf), Erasmus' secretary at that time, and she is present also in the colloquies *Diversoria* and *Synodus grammaticorum*. Erasmus felt warmly about Bertholf, and in Epistle 2735 played affectionately on his name: '*ubicunque erit, Hilarius erit*'. Thompson sees Margarete as 'a woman worth notice by those interested in the ancestry of comic characters in Elizabethan dramatic literature' (159), presenting her as a forerunner of such characters as the Nurse in *Romeo and Juliet*.

Erasmus made Basel his home for nearly eight years, but until the sack of Rome in 1527 he had in mind the possibility of one more trip to Italy, even of settling there (as he had written in Epistle 1236), devoting his remaining days 'to the society of great scholars and the resources of great libraries'. In September 1522 Erasmus visited his friend Botzheim in Constance, and he quite fell in love with his house and the setting of the town. About the house he wrote: 'The house he lives in you would take to be a real home of the Muses; no part of it but displays something in the way of polish and elegance, no part without a voice – all speaks in paintings that attract and retain the attention' (Epistle 1342 to Marcus Laurinus, 1 February 1523, *CWE* 9:378/375–78; Allen V, 212/339–42).[11]
    Moreover:

> the situation of the place itself was full of charm too. Constance is dominated by a wonderful great lake, which stretches both far and wide for many miles and at the same time loses none of its beauty. Its attractions are increased by the forest-clad hills prominent in all directions, some distant and some near at hand. For at that point, as though wearied by its rocky headlong passage through the Alps, the Rhine seems to have found an agreeable resting-place to recuperate in, through the middle of which it makes its gentle progress; at Constance it gathers again into its proper channel and therewith resumes its own name – though the lake as a whole has always preferred to take its name from the city, being the Lake of Constance now but in the old days the Lake of Bregenz, as long as Bregenz was the name of the city which is now called Constance.[12]

So much for Erasmus' alleged lack of interest in scenery![13] He obviously could respond to natural beauty; but doubtless he rarely had the time, or occasion, or audience, to write about it.
    He seems to have had it in mind to go on to Rome, but at Constance he had a bad attack of kidney stone, and so he abandoned

thoughts of travelling across the mountains, especially after the first snows. He stayed in Constance about three weeks,[14] and then returned to Basel.

Only a few months later Erasmus set off again, this time to visit Besançon, at that time an Imperial Free City and only about 150 kilometres from Basel. The city lies east of Dijon on the river Doubs, with a university founded in 1287, and the seat of an archbishopric. He had been invited by Ferry de Carondelet (c. 1473–1528), the youngest brother of Erasmus' patron Jean de Carondelet, archbishop of Palermo, who had been born in Mechlin and raised in the Netherlands, where his father was chancellor of Burgundy.[15] Erasmus had met Ferry in Rome (Epistle 1359) and probably visited him in Flanders. He greeted Erasmus with great warmth (Epistle 1610) and later was asked for any scriptural materials that might help in revising the New Testament for the 1527 edition (Epistle 1749). Ferry was a friend and correspondent, and the two men were closely linked (*BR*).

At much the same time Erasmus travelled to Freiburg at the invitation of his friend Ulrich Zasius, professor of law in the university and one of the most famous jurisconsults of the time. Zasius had initiated their acquaintance, which ripened into friendship, with a letter in 1514 (Epistle 303) addressed to the 'great Rotterdamer', for Erasmus' friend Bonifacius Amerbach was the favourite student of the civilian (*BR*).

In the colloquy 'A Fish Diet' there is a description of a visit to Freiburg (under the name of Eleuthereopolis) during Lent; the speaker in the dialogue (a butcher) tells of an old man in his sixties who was so averse to eating fish and so impatient about fasting that he possessed a papal brief permitting him to eat whatever he liked. Making ready to leave (for he felt his sickness coming upon him) he accepted an invitation to the house of a man of vast learning and of high authority in the community – on condition that nothing be provided except a couple of eggs, planning to mount his horse and depart as soon as he had eaten them. Upon arrival he was annoyed to find a chicken had been prepared, but he ate only the eggs. Somehow the rumour of the chicken spread, and his host had to satisfy a magistrate with the explanation (Thompson, 349–50).

Not a favourable introduction to a city; but Erasmus enjoyed its peaceful setting and its charms. Only three years after the publication of the colloquy in the edition of February 1526 Erasmus left Basel and moved to Freiburg (see chapter 42).

Pope Adrian VI, who was a known quantity, died unexpectedly in

1523 and was succeeded by Clement VII, the illegitimate son of Giuliano de'Medici who had been raised by his grandfather, Lorenzo the Magnificent. The best that can be said for his pontificate is that patronage continued for such artists as Raphael, Michelangelo, Bandinelli, and Sebastiano del Piombo; the worst, that he told less than the truth in important matters (like sending Campeggio to London on the affair of the annulment of Henry VIII's marriage to Catherine of Aragon, with instructions to keep the proceedings from reaching a final solution); a balanced historical judgment would be that he was weak and indecisive. It was during his pontificate (1523–1534) that the Church suffered the humiliation of the sack of Rome by mutinous imperial mercenary forces in 1527 (*NCE*).

Erasmus himself summed up the world picture in his colloquy 'The New Mother' (*Puerpera*, first published in 1526):

> If he weren't God I don't think he could get through so much business. King Christian of Denmark, a devout partisan of the gospel, is in exile. Francis, King of France, is a 'guest' of the Spaniards. What *he* thinks of this I don't know, but surely he's a man worthy of a better fate. Charles is preparing to extend the boundaries of his realm. Ferdinand has his hands full in Germany. Bankruptcy threatens every court. The peasants raise dangerous riots and are not swayed from their purpose, despite so many massacres. The commons are bent on anarchy; the church is shaken to its very foundations by menacing factions; on every side the seamless coat of Jesus is torn to shreds. The vineyard of the Lord is now laid waste not by a single boar [an allusion to Luther, from *Exsurge Domine*] but at one and the same time the authority of priests (together with their tithes), the dignity of theologians, the splendour of monks is imperilled; confession totters; vows reel; pontifical ordinances crumble away; the Eucharist is called in question; Antichrist is awaited; the whole earth is pregnant with I know not what calamity. The Turks conquer and threaten all the while; there's nothing they won't ravage if their undertaking succeeds ...
> (Thompson, *Colloquies*, 269–70)

Most of these crises are taken up elsewhere by Erasmus, in tracts, adages, and other colloquies, as well, of course, as in his letters; here in the unlikely place of a colloquy dealing with the care and feeding of babies[16] he has given a concise picture of a world everywhere in shreds.[17] In Erasmus' view, there was little to support optimism.

The year 1525 was perhaps the worst in Erasmus' life,[18] for the terrible events of the Peasants' Revolt moved with frightening speed across Southern Germany.[19] Commencing in the autumn of 1524 in the high country between the Rhine and the sources of the Danube, the revolt swept in all directions, and eventually nearly the whole of the Empire was affected by it. On 4 April 1525 it was first checked, and after that there was fearsome slaughter. To Lupset he wrote in Epistle 790 that the revolt was like a hydra, with nine heads springing up to take the place of the one cut off. In late October 1525 he put the number slaughtered at 100,000 and declared that some of the shooting was within earshot of Basel.[20] Earlier, in August, writing to Pirckheimer in Epistle 1603, Erasmus had commented on uprisings in Holland, Zeeland and Flanders, and he thought that the princes would use the suppression of the rebels to curtail still further the liberties of their subjects.[21] Epistles 1483 and 1630 are later comments. Erasmus did not blame the Reformers directly for the revolt, but he felt that too much blood had been spilled and that 'never have I seen a more pestilent or intractable kind of men' (Epistle 1483/8–10; Allen VI, 199).

In the peasants war are caught up a number of historical problems, for it involved the crisis of the old agricultural order and hostility towards the new early modern state, a crisis of feudalism over its treatment of serfs and tenants, conflicts of civil with other laws, and the consciousness of the common man that was stimulated by Luther. The War has now its own historiography and bibliography.[22] Although we cannot take up the issue in a biography of Erasmus, it is relevant to identify core aspects of the movement, for some derive from his own roots. Blickle deliberately employed the term 'revolution' in his title, for the concept expresses 'the conviction that the movement of 1525 was not just a series of inexplicable, individual actions on a level of no more than regional significance. Rather, what happened in 1525 was a deliberate movement, proceeding on a rational course, and with challenging ethical claims, for human self-realization' (193). Erasmus deplored the bloodshed, but he was in sympathy with any striving for 'human self-realization', provided that it was Christ-oriented.

The *Colloquies* are the great achievement of the Basel years. Having argued in chapter 35 that the form of the mature *Colloquies* rose out of the rhetorical formulas of the 1518 and 1519 editions, it is to be noted further that because the edition of March 1522 must have gone to the printer quite soon after his arrival in Basel, we must assume that Erasmus' work had been largely done (if not prepared for the printer) earlier. Once the 1522 edition appeared it was apparent to all that Erasmus had created a new genre, and he continued to work on the *Colloquies* until his final years. Ten colloquies were added in 1524, five in 1526, and two more in 1527. The 1529 edition incorporates a dozen new colloquies, and the 1531 edition five. Two more colloquies were added in the final edition before Erasmus' death, the 1533 edition.[23] Some of the additions made in the Basel editions – or changes in the texts of colloquies already published – reflect attacks and censure by different critics, and especially by the theology faculty at Paris which formally censured the *Colloquies*: '(along with passages from other writings by Erasmus), denouncing sixty-nine passages as "erroneous, scandalous, or impious" and describing their author as a pagan who mocks at the Christian religion and its sacred rites and customs' (Thompson, xxx). Although the censure by the Sorbonne was not printed until 1531, hints of its deliberations reached Erasmus – the world of learning buzzed with rumours as never before, and rarely since, and the networking of which we have spoken was important for such communications – and so to the June 1526 edition he added a letter to the reader in defence of his book.[24]

Beginning with the Basel edition of March 1522 then, there are now dialogues rather than sets of formulae: a giant step in exploring the potentialities of the genre. Some of these dialogues, Thompson comments (xxv) – 'The Whole Duty of Youth' (*Confabulatio pia*), for example – 'are rather long and are fully developed compositions'. One of the best of all the dialogues, the most sharply delineating in its characters and the fullest in the exploration of intellectual positions, 'The Godly Feast' (*Convivium religiosum*) first appeared in complete form in the August 1522 edition. After publication of the March 1522 edition, in fact, no more formulae were added. It had become a book that would appeal to men and women as well as to schoolboys: 'it became a book of colloquies instead of exercises' (xxv).

The genius of the mature *Colloquies* is in part their richness of texture, giving such a superbly rendered sense of everyday life in the 1520s and 1530s (with occasional flashbacks to Erasmus' childhood and schooldays). There is genius in the characterisation, no less brilliant in its way than that of Brueghel or Holbein, and the range of characters provides a brilliant picture of the men and women of the period from every part of the spectrum of renaissance life. Many of these colloquies are still capable of giving intense pleasure to the twentieth-century reader:

> The pages of Erasmus permit us to know that epoch as well as we can now hope to know it from a single witness. They take us through words into that milieu made familiar to us by Brueghel, Holbein, Dürer, Cranach, and Metsys, whose pictures are the ideal companions to the *Colloquies*. (xxvi)

Much further study lies ahead in understanding the genius of Erasmus, and his letters and adages offer clues of one kind to the highly developed familiar style that he mastered and that was the despair of his contemporaries, whose imitations rarely achieve the same level of gracefulness beyond the reach of art. One area for comparative studies is the analysis of scenes by the artists named by Thompson with like scenes in the *Colloquies*; and much work remains to be done in perceiving the intertextualities of Erasmus, the linkages between the *Colloquies* and the letters, adages, and other writings.[25]

It remains to be said that the language of these colloquies is wonderfully informal and full of life, flexible to accommodate a very wide range of thought, and a supple instrument that moves effortlessly from wit and irony to simple statement, often to eloquence, even more often to bantering. When T. S. Eliot wrote that the poet's duty 'is only indirectly to his people: his direct duty is to his *language*, first to preserve, and second to extend and improve',[26] he might well have had Erasmus in mind. In the *Colloquies* even more than elsewhere in his writings Erasmus has rendered in full his duty to his language, preserving all the wonders of the classical literatures but also extending it by his use of allusions and puns and by involving the language and thought of patristic and medieval writers, and by his mastery of every kind of rhetorical device: thus improving the Latin of his generation. Later Neo-Latin writers manifest their debt to Erasmus' Latin, and so do the vernacular writers who had been schooled in Latin and inspired by Erasmus. The pity, in effect, is that it is no longer a language that is much mastered in our own age; but the wonder is that through such translators as Thompson, Mynors, and a few others, we are able not merely to understand but to share the experience of that humanistic language.

Let us turn to the two artists with whom Erasmus was closely associated, especially during his long Basel period.

Erasmus' relations with Hans Holbein the Younger of Augsburg (1497/8–1543) most probably began in the autumn of 1515, when the artist arrived as a young journeyman in Basel. Holbein's earliest surviving work is probably the drawings he made in the margins of a second edition of Erasmus' *Moria*, printed by Froben in the spring of 1515. (See illustrations 4 and 5.) Myconius noted that when Erasmus saw the drawing of himself at work he exclaimed, 'If Erasmus now looked like that he would immediately take a wife'. In 1523 Holbein painted two portraits of the humanist that were sent to England (see Epistle 1452, frontispiece, and appendix E), one of them intended for Archbishop Warham (Epistle 1488).

When Holbein left Basel for England in 1526, during the rising tide of the reform movement there, Erasmus gave him a letter to Pieter Gillis (Epistle 1740), asking that Holbein be introduced to Quentin Metsys. By December 1526 More is writing the praises of Holbein (Epistle 1770), who by this time has done his sketch of the More family group and was engaged in painting the famous portrait of More that now hangs in the Frick Collection in New York. More wrote to Erasmus: 'Your painter, dearest Erasmus, is a remarkable artist; but I am afraid he will not find England as fertile and fruitful as he expected. Still, I shall do my best to see that he does not find it altogether barren.'[27] Upon Holbein's return to Basel in 1528 Erasmus commissioned the Augsburg artist to execute various versions of his device Terminus. This had been done first in a glass painting (1525) and then in Holbein's woodcut portrait, perhaps in 1532.[28]

Son of a goldsmith to whom he was at first apprenticed, Albrecht Dürer (1471–1528) was in 1486 apprenticed to the leading painter of Nürnberg, Michael Wolgemut, and in 1490 he began to travel about Germany and Switzerland, until 1494, when he visited Italy. By February 1507 he was back in Nürnberg, where he resided except for a visit to the Netherlands in 1520–21 (apparently to see to the renewal of his imperial salary). In Antwerp the artist and the humanist met, and they exchanged presents (with Dürer's being perhaps a portrait drawing, *BR*). There were several drawings of Erasmus, of which one is extant in the Louvre (Allen IV, 330). In 1526 Dürer, having been much pressed by Erasmus, made an engraved portrait, curiously reversing the pose of Erasmus in the Metsys painting of 1517; but Dürer could not have seen the original, which had gone to England in 1517 (*BR*).

Although the idea of a Christian as a knight was a traditional one, it seems likely that Dürer was inspired by Erasmus' *Enchiridion* for his famous woodcut. There are, as Rowlands notes in *BR*, several references to Dürer's published treatises in Erasmus' writings, and the praise of Dürer in *De Pronuntiatione* of 1528 (*ASD* 1–4, 40) became a eulogy for his dead friend, for the artist died soon after publication.[29]

The Terminus emblem just mentioned, reminds us of his ambivalent reputation, as McConica has written.[30] It is also a splendid clue to Erasmus' personality and self-image.

As we saw in chapter 23, while staying with Aldus in Venice in 1508, Erasmus was given a gold ring by Alexander Stewart, illegitimate son of James IV of Scotland. The ring contained an antique gem depicting a young man's head on a block of stone.[31] Erasmus at once adopted the Terminus emblem as his personal seal, adding the motto *Concedo nulli* ('I yield to no one') in 1519. Metsys placed the figure of Terminus on the reverse of a medal-portrait of Erasmus, which delighted the humanist, who used the ring and seal to authenticate his most important documents.[32]

Even the literal meaning of the Terminus emblem is far from certain, and the resonances of it as an emblem – especially at different periods of Erasmus' life – have been much debated. Harking back to a riddle in Aulus Gellius' *Attic Nights* (XIII, 6:2) the Terminus emblem establishes its primary meaning as the ancient god of boundaries, who had refused to yield his place for the construction of a new temple of Jupiter: perhaps, as Wind has suggested, it was at least in part 'an emblem of defiance', and it was so taken by Erasmus' enemies.[33] But it is evident that the theme of Death became attached to the emblem, appearing in the 1519 medallion by Metsys, which adds the Greek motto 'Keep in view the end of a long life' and the Latin 'Death is the boundary of things'.[34] In the later Holbein portrait of 1525 Erasmus' hands rest on a book labelled in Greek 'The labours of Hercules' (McConica, 5). The iconography of this portrait has been studied by W. S. Heckscher, who sees the theme of Stoic *tranquillitas*, of being in harmony with self and the world.[35] According to Heckscher the portrait speaks 'of the humanist's self-denying suffering ... reveals his constancy and tranquillity amidst tribulations, and ... proclaims the ultimate triumph of man's dignity in spite of all the vagaries of Fortune'.[36] This biography sees Erasmus in that light, and it is urged that this is indeed Erasmus' concept of himself; the Terminus emblem thus provides a direct mirroring of his personality.

One final employment of the Terminus emblem needs to be brought into view, and that is the moving woodcut executed by Holbein in 1535, not long before Erasmus' death.[37] By that time Erasmus was bedridden for the most part, praying for release from 'the raving world' (Huizinga, 184). Holbein displays Erasmus standing in an archway of renaissance style, dressed in the scholar's gown lined with fur, held together by a narrow sash, and his customary headpiece. His right hand rests on the stone figure of Terminus that is the focal point of the composition, but the left hand is poised in mid-air and Erasmus appears to be leaning away from the column: perhaps ready to depart.[38]

Although he continued to complain about the smallness of his income, Erasmus lived comfortably in Basel: he had horses and servants, good wine, and of course his own excellent library. In 1525 he resorted to selling his books in order to raise money, and perhaps anticipating his death, but reserving the right to use them during his lifetime. The fact of the sale of the library to Jan Laski was duly noted in Erasmus' will of 1527 (appendix D).[39]

In earlier years his agent for financial matters had been Pieter Gillis, who handled the transfer of his English annuities (Epistles 1583, 2159); but long before Gillis' death in 1533 Erasmus asked Erasmus Schets, a merchant and banker in Antwerp, to take over his finances (*BR*). A relationship of mutual trust and affection developed; in 1527 Erasmus observed that Schets' Latin might sometimes be at fault, but never his trustworthiness (Epistle 1862).

The world was troubled in the 1520s, but at Basel Erasmus was away from Louvain and his catholic critics, and at a remove from Wittenberg; but the post kept events clearly in view. Erasmus lived comfortably, and he kept up his remarkable productivity. We recognise the prodigious effort of his revisions, and the creativity of the mature *Colloquies*. Although the zenith of his fame had passed by 1521, he did not cease to work as hard as ever.

His *De Libero Arbitrio* was published at the mid-point in his Basel years. Nearly everything appears to lead up to that work, and after it there is a sea-change, a crystallising of his stance and of attitudes towards him in both camps; and at times we perceive in his writings, apart from the *Colloquies*, a loss of intellectual play or suppleness. The work on freedom of the will has great biographical significance for understanding Erasmus, and it of course launched one of the great theological debates in the history of Christianity. It deserves a separate chapter.

Notes

1) I follow the account in the introd. to Ep. 1242 (*CWE* 8:321); the reconstruction was first attempted by Allen on the strength of Erasmus' own information in Eps 1302 & 1342.

2) See John Munro's valuable appendix on 'The Purchasing Power of Coins and Wages in England and the Low Countries from 1500 to 1514', in *CWE* 2.

3) Here I have conflated Allen's account in V, 133/38n with that of Bietenholz in *BR*. It would seem that there was an open fireplace in 'zu alten Treu' as well.

4) One thinks of Santayana's lovely note on fireplaces: 'in northern climates [an obligatory fire] made the poetry of indoor life. Round it you sat, into it you looked, by it you read, in it you made a holocaust of impertinent

letters and rejected poems' – George Santayana, *Persons and Places* (New York, 1944) 193.

5) What are we to make of his statement to archbishop Warham in August 1521 (Ep. 1228) that he intended to read all the works of Luther, doubtless with a view to writing something against him? Erasmus was always careful to touch base with his influential patrons, and perhaps here he wanted to reassure Warham of his not having joined the Lutheran faction. Perhaps expressing feelings at the English Court, Mountjoy had asked him to act decisively by writing a book against Luther; in Ep. 1219 of mid-summer 1521, Erasmus wrote that he would keep this request in mind when he went to Basel: 'when I have finished what I have in hand [the New Testament and St Augustine] I may attempt something that may help to heal this discord' (*CWE* 8:263/135–7). But Erasmus does not promise something against Luther; rather, something to help heal.

6) Here again one must read the letters of Erasmus in terms, at least in part, of Erasmus' relationship with the addressee: all too often he wrote – on matters like this – what he thought his correspondent wanted to hear. See introd. to Ep. 1242, which was written to Stanislaus Thurzo, bishop of Olomouc in Moravia, an ecclesiastic whom Erasmus praises; he also belonged to a family of some wealth, owing in part to its connections with the Fuggers of Augsburg. Thurzo was a strong supporter of the house of Habsburg and a patron of learning (*BR*).

7) 'Tous font partie de la *familia* de l'humaniste et sont à la fois ses disciples, ses collaborateurs et ses factotums': Franz Bierlaire, *La Familia d'Érasme* (Paris, 1968) 7. For a tabulation of Erasmus' servant-pupils over the years, see Bierlaire, 'Tableau Recapitulatif' (between pp. 39 and 40), and the individual discussions following. Some of these are dealt with individually and more fully by Bierlaire in *BR*.

8) See Allen, 'Erasmus' Servant-Pupils', in *Erasmus – Lectures and Wayfaring Sketches* (Oxford, 1934) 99–108.

9) Andreas Zebridovius, who served Erasmus in Basel, returned to Poland to become a canon of Cracow and later a bishop until his death in 1560. He also served as chancellor of the University of Cracow. On his tomb in the cathedral are the words: *magni illius Erasmi Roterodo: discipulus et auditor* (Allen VII, 73, introd. to Ep. 1826; cf. Bierlaire, *La Familia*, 85).

10) Allen, 'Erasmus' Servant-Pupils', 105, with the supplementing data of Bierlaire already cited.

11) But Allen's introd. to Ep. 1342, conjecturing that Erasmus may have conflated two letters in preparing Ep. 1342 for publication in the *Catalogus Lucubrationum* (1523): the full passages from which the two quotations above have been excerpted have the literary air of a *locus amoenus* and invocation of nature (on which see Curtius, *European Literature*, 92–8, 192 ff., 195 ff., 201).

12) Ep. 1342/419–30; Allen V, 213/381–91; *CWE* editors note that 'Bregenz is, of course, a city at the other end of the lake': this may have been a slip of the pen on Erasmus' part, or he may have misunderstood his guides (doubtless not having sailed the full length of the lake from Constance to Bregenz).

13) Allen comments (213/381) that 'this expatiation is a measure of Erasmus' enjoyment of his visit. He hardly ever halts to descant on natural

scenery'. Quite simply, because of his illnes he had the leisure to do so.

14) See introd. to Ep. 1316 (*CWE* 9:187–8).

15) In addition to *BR* and the references there given, see Richard Walsh, 'The Coming of Humanism to the Low Countries', 187, and J. -M. Suchet, 'Jean Carondelet, grand chancelier de Flandres et de Borgogne, 1428–1501 [sic]', *Mémoires de l'Academie des sciences, belles-lettres et arts de Besançon* (1898) 280–99.

16) Perhaps Erasmus deliberately set his treatise on the question of why babies should be suckled by their own mothers against war and social upheaval in order to argue the universal need of the human race to reproduce and care for its young, especially in such times. Erasmus was then dealing with courtship and marriage in his *Colloquies*; the three colloquies together 'constitute a brilliant and entertaining addition to the vast literature of Renaissance feminism' (Thompson, 267).

17) Cf. among others the '*Scarabeus aquilam quaerit*' (the beatle searches for the eagle, *Adag.* III. vii.1) of 1515, often printed separately, which is a biting satire of war and makers of war.

18) I echo Tracy, *Erasmus*, 199.

19) In England, as Marius observes (*Thomas More*, 307), 'More and others learned of the Peasant's Revolt with shuddering horror. They saw it as a direct consequence of Luther's doctrines and a confirmation of their conviction that the advent of Lutheranism in England would bring violence and revolution. In a royal proclamation, Henry VIII declared that Martin Luther was the cause of all the slaughter'.

20) Cf. Ep. 1633/17–8 ('*locatur ille in crisim sanguinis; verum ea crisis Orco dedit agricolarum plus minus centum millia*': Allen VI, 199/17–18).

21) Allen VI, 155, Ep. 1603/10 ff. '*Incipiunt nunc ferocire*', he added: now they are raging, or becoming ungovernable.

22) For an admirable interpretation of this phenomenon, see *The Revolution of 1525* by Peter Blickle, trans. T. A. Brady, Jr., and H. C. Erik Midelfort (Baltimore, Md., 1981; rptd. 1985).

23) C. R. Thompson, whose *Colloquies of Erasmus* (Chicago, 1965) is the indispensable introduction and guide to serious reading of the colloquies, summarises that at least sixteen editions of the early colloquies had appeared by March 1533 (xxiv–xxv).

24) After the censure was printed, Erasmus then replied to it in his *Declarationes ad censuras ... facultatis theologiae Parisiensis* (Antwerp, 1532). See Thompson, xxx. This work is also given the title *Declarationes ad censuras Lutetiae vulgatas*, and it was twice reprinted before its appearance in the *Opera* of 1540.

25) See my essay on intertextuality in Erasmus: '"In loco intertexantur": Erasmus as Master of Intertextuality', in *Intertextuality,* ed. Heinrich F. Plett (Berlin, 1991) 181–91.

26) From 'The Social Function of Poetry', in *On Poetry and Poets* (1967) 20. One may begin a study of the language of Erasmus with the pioneering essay by D. F. S., Thomson, 'The Latinity of Erasmus', in *Erasmus*, ed. T. A. Dorey (London, 1970) 115–37.

27) Trans. by M. A. Haworth in *Selected Letters of St Thomas More*, ed. E. F. Rogers (New Haven, Conn., 1967) 164.

28) See A. Gerlo, *Erasme et ses Portraitistes*, 2d ed. (1969) 29–44.

29) See further appendix D, Gerlo (1969) 29–44, and E. Panofsky, 'Erasmus and the visual arts', *JWCI* 32 (1969) 200–27.

30) J. K. McConica, 'The Riddle of "Terminus"', in *Erasmus in English* 2/ 1971, 2–7.

31) For the historical context see A. Renaudet, *Érasme et l'Italie*, 86 ff., and Ep. 2018 to Valdes on 1 Aug. 1528, although the 1528 explanation is disputed.

32) Thus McConica (1971) 2, pointing to his first and last wills, as well as a February 1535 letter which he signed with the seal alone because of gout in his right hand.

33) Edgar Wind, 'Aenigma Termini: The Emblem of Erasmus', *JWCI* 1 (1937–8) 66–9, reviewed and enlarged by N. van der Blom, 'Erasmus en Terminus', *Hermeneus* 28 (1957) 153–8.

34) See McConica 7, n. 9. In *The Imitation of Christ* there is often a flowing together of classical (esp. Stoic) and Christian thought. Erasmus may well have kept in mind the injunctive and admonitory words of Thomas à Kempis: 'The end of all is death, and man's life passeth away suddenly as a shadow' (1.23).

35) *Tranquillitas* (meaning quietness or stillness, but also serenity and tranquillity of mind, as in Cicero and Seneca) is seen by Tracy as one of the 'thought-terms' of Erasmus: see *Erasmus*, 35–6, 43, 99, 224.

36) Heckscher, 'Reflections on Seeing Holbein's Portrait of Erasmus at Longford Castle', in *Essays in the History of Art Presented to Rudolf Wittkower* (London, 1967) 132, 144–5. Cf. McConica's note (7 n.30) on the question of whether Erasmus is standing behind a table or a parapet.

37) McConica notes (7 n.10) that in 1525 Holbein made a large design for a stained-glass window in Basel making use of the Terminus and showing an armless torso of a youth with flowing hair; see Allen VII, 430, and *Catalogus, Erasmus en zijn tijd* (Museum Boymans-van Beuningen, Rotterdam) I no.350 & plate I.

38) I am grateful to McConica's comprehensive essay on Terminus.

39) The sales contract is dated 20 June 1526 (according to *BR*, 1525 according to Smith, 260). Smith translates the contract of sale: 'I, Erasmus of Rotterdam, have sold my library to the illustrious Polish Baron, John Laski, for three hundred crowns ... on condition that as long as I shall live the use of the books may amicably be allowed to me as well as to him, but that they shall permanently belong to him and to his heirs. As a pledge he has an inventory of the books. All additions to the library shall belong to him, except future purchases of high-priced manuscripts, for which a special agreement must be made. In witness whereof, I, Erasmus, have written this with my own hand and affixed the seal of my ring representing Terminus.' Laski paid half the purchase price immediately, the other half was to be paid after Erasmus' death. Smith adds that after the second half of the agreed-upon money had been paid on 12 Nov. 1536 to Boniface Amerbach, the books were sent in three boxes early in 1538. In 1573 they passed to the University of Ingolstadt, and a few are now in the University of Munich Library.

Erasmus and Luther: On the Freedom Of the Will

Nos distractos sub peccatis:
Liberet lex charitatis.
Ex perfectae libertatis
Dignos reddat munere.

Adam of St Victor, De sancto spiritu [attributed]

And this same noble faculty it is
Beatrice calls Free Will.

Dante, Purgatorio, xviii. 73–4

La grâce sera toujours dans le monde (et aussi la nature), de
sorte qu'elle est en quelque sorte naturelle. Et ainsi toujours il
y aura des pélagiens, et toujours des catholiques, et toujours
combat; parce que la première naissance fait les uns, et la grâce
de la seconde naissance fait les autres.

Pascal, Pensées, 521 [423]

Luther had a teleological view of the historical role of humanism in relation to the Reformation. He believed that the culture of classical antiquity bloomed under benign Providence in
order to prepare the way for the New Testament Revelation
and the success of the Christian mission.

Lewis W. Spitz, The Religious Renaissance of the
German Humanists (1963) 245

After Luther's initial admiration of Erasmus, and despite his continuing use of the Greek New Testament, *Adages* and letters, the
widening split between them first became alienation and then developed into hostility on Luther's part. From the beginning there was a
pronounced difference of personality and style, strongly projected in
the different rhetoric of their writings, with Luther always suspicious
of Erasmian wit and irony and distrustful of the author of the *Moria*.
Increasingly their stormy relationship involved fundamental issues
of theology and churchmanship: that is, the role of the priest as a
member of the Church, the question of hierarchy, and proceeding
from those issues the larger question of the role of priest and laity
together in the Church.[1] It might be thought that Augustine would

be a bond between them, for he was greatly favoured by both theologians. Erasmus never flagged in his enthusiasm for Augustine, which began in his monastery years and continued through the completion of his edition of the bishop of Hippo in 1528–29; but Augustine permits of differing interpretations. Luther too shared an admiration bordering on veneration for Augustine, but his reading was filtered through different lenses, especially the late medieval nominalism of Gabriel Biel's *via moderna*.[2]

There were for Erasmus external reasons to write against Luther: pressures from England and the Low Countries, and exhortations by a number of his correspondents. Concerned less with the rhetoric of Luther (which, however, he deplored) and more with the thrust of Luther's teaching and the effects of it upon his followers, Erasmus went public. Perhaps, in the final analysis, he now felt that after so long he had to do so, but more likely he was being his most parrhesiastic self: warning Luther in what he doubtless thought was a moderate and avuncular mode concerning the disturbingly fatalistic determinism entering into his writings.

In Augustine, it can be put somewhat summarily (and without having space to prepare the background and context in detail), grace as a healing gift is central. Grace was at all times necessary, since (Augustine taught in *De spiritu et littera*)[3] by himself man could only sin, as a consequence of the Fall. But Augustinian theology is coloured by the fact that much of his theological thought is to be found in his theological writings against the Manicheans and Donatists.[4] In reacting against Manichaean dualism, Augustine stressed the reality of free will in spite of human sin, and in opposing the Donatists, who had charged that the catholic episcopate had betrayed the faith and thus invalidated the concept of a ministry, Augustine insisted that the holiness of the Church depended not upon the clergy but upon the objective gift of grace conferred through the sacraments: that is, grace as healing – which is fundamental both in the Greek *sōtēria* and in the Latin *salus* – which was seen as meaning that grace was a gift freely given.[5]

Augustine continued to be read continuously throughout the Middle Ages and into the reformation period (not least by members of the Augustinian orders), as the huge number of manuscripts and early printed editions attests. One has only to call attention to Anselm in order to underscore continuing discussion of and theological debate over grace and free will.[6] Augustine's thought percolated through the distillation of Peter Lombard's *Sentences*, which contained a wealth of quotations from Augustine, and it became the standard textbook of christian theology in the medieval universities – and still for Erasmus and Luther (see chapter 11), with commentaries on the *Sentences* being produced by reformers in the sixteenth century and as late as 1635. Augustine was also excerpted and read in the *Breviary* of the religious, and even more powerfully than in Lombard, Aquinas accommodated the theological doctrine of Augustine to the metaphysical writings of Aristotle and his commentators.

With William of Ockham (c. 1300–c.1349) scholasticism experienced a sea-change: his nominalism denied reality to universals and granted it only to individual things. He taught an extreme form of the Augustinian doctrine of grace and free will, holding that the Divine will was the cause of all things. God, according to Ockhamism, did not will things because they were good, but they were good because He willed them. His separation of faith from reason helped to prepare the way for a number of the intellectual and theological positions in the Reformation.

Via moderna is the name given to the movement that in philosophy was known as nominalism as taught by William of Ockham, and in theology as taught by Pierre d'Ailly (1350–1420) and Jean Gerson (1363–1429). Nicholas of Cusa (c. 1400–1464) added a distinctive voice to the cross-currents of fifteenth-century thought. A native of Cues on the Moselle, Nicholas was schooled with the Brethren of the Common Life and then studied at Heidelberg and Padua before moving to Cologne in 1425, where he became a doctor of canon law. He was active in the proceedings of the Council of Basel in 1433, and in the same year wrote his *De concordantia catholica*, which outlines a full programme for reform of Church and empire. Influential in achieving the Concordat of Vienna in 1448, which won a reconciliation between pope and emperor, he was made a cardinal by Nicholas V. Among his many writings, *De Docta Ignorantia* (completed 1440) is an important philosophical probing of the nature of the truth accessible to the human intellect, which is (Nicholas argues) but a knowledge that is relative, multiple, complex, whereas the Truth is absolute and unknowable to man. God is where all contradictions meet, the *'coincidentia oppositorum'*: the centre and the circumference of the world, everywhere and nowhere, neither One nor Three but Triune. A pivotal distinction between Luther and Cusanus can be drawn in the concept of *'Deus absconditus'*: hidden and revealed in history.[7]

Yet Luther was not simply following Augustine: he was extending the Augustinian doctrine of grace by his intensive reading and interpretation of the New Testament (a reading that owed much to Erasmus' *Novum Testamentum*), and he did so to the point where from Erasmus' perspective it began to enter the realm of determinism –

for if all was the act of God, then mankind could do nothing by his own free will.[8]

Perhaps rather prematurely Luther wrote to Oecolampadius[9] (who was in Basel where word of Luther's letter spread quickly to Erasmus),

> He [Erasmus] has accomplished what he was called to do: he has introduced sacred letters among us and called us from sacrilegious studies. Perhaps he will die with Moses in the plains of Moab, for he does not go on to better studies (which have to do with piety).[10]

Erasmus now let it be known that he would respond to the pressure of patrons and the urging of friends, and would write against Luther's teachings. Word of this decision soon reached Luther, and in Epistle 1443 from Wittenberg in April 1524 he sent Erasmus a letter that is mixed warning and challenge. Erasmus replied to Luther in a rather cool fashion (Epistle 1445, 8 May 1524), and concluded it with the wish that Jesus Christ direct Luther's mind in understandings which may be worthy of the Gospel (Allen V, 453/61–2).

An advance copy of the text was sent to Henry VIII in March 1524, at about the time that it went to the printer.[11] The text was completed on 13 May 1524, and its author thought of keeping it in manuscript – perhaps in the spirit if not the strict letter of Horace's advice to put the parchment back in the closet and hold it back until the ninth year.[12] As he wrote to Willibald Pirckheimer in Epistle 1466 (21 July 1524), he had now decided to publish it.[13]

Erasmus was aiming at moderation, which was surely the reason for his title; and as he wrote in the *Catalogus Lucubrationum* (Allen I, 17), 'I have never renounced the friendship of anyone either because he was inclined to Luther or because he was against him' (Smith, 346).

In September 1524 Erasmus' *'De Libero Arbitrio'* was published in Basel, and there were half a dozen reprintings of it in the same year and one more in 1525. In the full title it is called a diatribe: in classical Latin *diatriba* meant a learned discussion (or a school for rhetoric or philosophy).[14] A year later he stressed that he had taken great precautions not to denounce anyone by name, and that he had given the book a most modest title by calling it a discussion or conference.[15]

The work divides into four parts of unequal importance.[16] In the introduction the problem is put, with an indication of two theses that are in opposition to each other, with Erasmus aiming at a middle solution, a *via media*. The discussion of the freedom of the

will (*liber arbitrio*) has always been an open question with philosophers and theologians; and Erasmus recalls the general nature of the
catholic tradition on this point of moral theology. Erasmus takes the
opportunity of reminding his readers that he has never been a Lutheran. What follows is a model of brevity (thirty-three columns in
LB) in an age of excessively long controversial treatises, and throughout there is genuine moderation and real wit. In the introduction, to
illustrate, Erasmus admits that the Bible must be the authoritative
text, but he shows that many things in the Bible are difficult to
understand. His attempted strategy of defence is one utterly consistent with the spirit of the *Devotio Moderna*: it would be better to leave
the whole disputed question of grace and free will at the level of
simple piety ('*satis erat ad Christianam pietatem*', *LB* IX, 1216E), for
when two sides of a controversial argument appeal to Scripture, who
can tell with certitude what Scripture means? And when appeal to
Scripture will not referee disputed questions, neither will the appeal
to the guidance of the Holy Spirit – for can there be proof that the
people making the appeal are truly and infallibly inspired? – nor will
the example of a good life, for the reformers now claim justification
by faith, not good works.

The main problem, then, is the liberty of choice and its relation to the
grace of God. Free will is defined as the power to act in those matters
that look to salvation. Its importance lies in its being the basis for
believing in man as a person and as unique among creatures. On the
operation of free will is founded much in the Judaeo-Christian tradition
of law and ethics. For determining his position on this problem Erasmus
had undertaken a course of reading: Augustine, Aristotle, Aquinas,
Wyclif and Biel;[17] but he heaps up his authorities among the Greek
Fathers also: 'Origines, Basilius, Crysostomus, Cyrillus, Joannes
Damascenus, Theophylactus; apud Latinos, Tertullianus, Cyprianus,
Arnobius, Hilarius, Ambrosius, Hieronymus, Augustinus, ne recenseam
interim Thomas, Scotus, Durandos, Capreolos, Gabrieles, Aegidios,
Gregorios, Alexandros' (*LB* IX, 1218E). To these names are added those
of Wyclif and Lorenzo Valla. It is hard, Erasmus concludes this section,
to say that the will has power only to sin; but it is much harder to deny
altogether – as Wyclif and a few Manichaeans and Luther have done –
the existence of free will. This is either a misunderstanding on the part of
Erasmus or an exaggeration for purposes of debate; for Luther had
granted freedom to natural man in all of the ordinary affairs of life.[18]
Whether Luther or Erasmus had the more authentically Augustinian
sense of sin has been much debated; against Melanchthon's argument
that 'flesh' as employed by Paul signified the whole of man in all his
faculties, Erasmus followed Origen in the interpretation that 'flesh' in

the physical sense was indeed corrupted by sin, but man is also possessed of *spiritus* 'by virtue of which we strive for noble things (*honesta*)'.[19]

McSorley has observed that Erasmus does not follow Augustine's account of Pelagianism any more than he did Jerome's account of Arianism.[20] This questioning of secondary sources reflects the desire of Erasmus to get to the heart of the matter in a scholarly issue. But what is here involved is even deeper: a view of man that stresses the spirit as much as the flesh, and yet allows for the efficacy of grace. Erasmus freely acknowledged that this had been an open question (in effect a *quaestio disputata*) when he took it up, and he confessed to difficulties in his own position. Writing to Thomas More in 1527, Erasmus spoke of trying to arrive at an equilibrium between free will and grace: 'But if I follow Paul and Augustine, what is left to free will is very little' (Epistle 1804, Allen VII, 8/81–2).

Therefore, in speaking of a good defence of the freedom of the will, Erasmus moves in that direction but without arriving at resolution: 'The opinion which thinks that we can initiate grace [*gratia posse de congruo*] of our own powers without special grace, would not displease me – except that Paul opposes' (8/91–94). Tracy's view is that 'in other words his own inclination was to the "more-than-Pelagian" view ascribed in *De libero arbitrio* to the "Scotists"; and his final impression is most apt, "that Erasmus has reluctantly and without too much success attempted to superimpose a Pauline theology on a moral optimism derived from the classics and the Greek Fathers' (231).[21] Erasmus had arrived at a point where ambivalence was no longer tenable, and he found the ultimate necessity for resolution of classical teaching in the *studia humanitatis* and the different rigours of Pauline theology: the *philosophia Christi* necessitated this kind of resolution, and it offered a path of wisdom in following the model of Christ.

One summary of Erasmus' effort is that he 'defended an attractive position with his familiar grace, courtesy, and clarity' (McConica, 74), which is true enough, but it is not the whole story. Erasmus had carefully chosen a form that he thought would keep discussion on an even keel of moderation, and his own tone is, while graceful, almost deliberately non-rhetorical; it deliberately refrains from the colours and devices of rhetoric, and it makes a reasonable appeal through reason.[22]

In a cluster of letters written from 4 to 6 September Erasmus sent copies of his book to his more important patrons on the Continent and in England. On 6 September (Epistle 1495) he sent a copy to duke George of Saxony with the comment that up till then he had not written against Luther because he had thought of him as a

necessary evil, a scourge for the manifest corruptions of the age
(Allen V, 543/7 ff.). Vives wrote to Erasmus almost immediately and
informed him that he had observed Henry VIII reading it with
delight (Epistle 1513, Allen V, 576/4–6).

From Freiburg Zasius reported that opinion of *De Libero Arbitrio* was
favourable (on 19 September), and he delivered an oration against Luther
at the university that was doubtless influenced by Erasmus' diatribe; and
then the university condemned Luther on 12 October.[23] From Ferrara,
Calcagnini wrote to praise Erasmus' work and to blame the author for
the long delay in the writing of it (Smith, 350).

Among the reformers, however, Melanchthon was the only one to
praise Erasmus (see Erasmus' reply to Melanchthon in December,
Epistle 1523), after which there was apparently a silence of three
years between the two humanist-reformers. The Erasmus-Luther debate compelled Melanchthon to re-examine man's will in terms of
conversion and predestination, however.[24] Luther, as he wrote on 1
November 1524, was resolved to answer what he thought so un-
learned a book by so learned a man; but he was preoccupied with the
Peasants' Revolt, with a controversy with Carlstadt over the sacrament, and with other concerns, until late in 1525. Luther's reply, *De
Servo Arbitrio* (On the enslaved will), was printed in December 1525 and
went through about nine editions in Latin and German within a year.

Luther could not accept the notion that different texts in the
Bible are often contradictory; to him all of Scripture was one gar-
ment, a single unit, all inspired, and all to be taken literally.

In the main section of his polemical treatise, he expounded a view
of the human will that took one step further the Augustinian teaching that God inclines men's hearts either to good or evil according to
their foreseen merits,[25] and from this he went on to develop a concept
of the total impotence of the natural man:

> The human will is like a beast of burden.[26] If God mounts it, it
> wishes and goes as God wills; if Satan mounts it, it wishes and
> goes as Satan wills. Nor can it choose its rider, nor betake itself
> to him it would prefer, but it is the riders who contend for its
> possession. (Smith, 352)

In an outburst of rhetoric Luther sums up:

> God foreknows nothing subject to contingencies, but he fore-
> sees, foreordains, and accomplishes all things by an unchang-
> ing, eternal and efficacious will. By this thunderbolt free will
> sinks shattered in the dust. (Smith, 353)

It is immediately apparent that a biography of Erasmus is not the
place to attempt to do full justice to the power of Luther's argument,
nor to its theological structure.[27]

There were other answers to Erasmus, but Luther's polemical treatise was the spearhead of the reformers' attacks on Erasmus' *De Libero Arbitrio*; though in fact a now well-nigh forgotten French reformer François Lambert had already written on *The Captive Will* against Erasmus (Smith, 353). Others like Bugenhagen and Capito had planned to write answers to Erasmus, but with Luther's *De Servo Arbitrio* published they withdraw their plans.

Stung by Luther's strong reply[28] (sent to him with a letter expressing what seemed to be arrogant assurance in the rightness of his own opinion), Erasmus replied in Epistle 1688 of 11 April 1526 that Luther was now employing the same ferocity against his book that he had used against Cochlaeus and Fisher. The main charge of this letter was that Luther had put the entire world in conflict by his arrogant, insolent and rebellious nature (Allen VI, 307/26–29). This, in point of fact, is the main thrust of the *Hyperaspistes*, which appeared in March 1526, and is about three times as large as the *Diatribe* that it defends, as the full title indicates: *Hyperaspistes Diatribae adversus Servum Arbitrium Martini Lutheri*. Luther is now named in the title of the anti-Lutheran work. The work contains 312 pages, 156 leaves, and at the rate of printing indicated it was produced in a week and finished early in March, ready for the Frankfurt fair.[29] Working in such haste, Erasmus regarded the *Hyperaspistes* as only a first reply to Luther, and a second part was promised to follow. The first part was reprinted at least four times in 1526, and translated into German by a protégé and secretary of duke George, Hieronymus Emser (who had been a member of the Wimpheling circle in Strasbourg, *BR*). The second part of the *Hyperaspistes* is six times as long as the *Diatribe*, appearing in September 1527. This was never answered by Luther.[30]

The full aftermath of the debate between Luther and Erasmus is to be seen in the proceedings of the Diet of Augsburg, which will be discussed in chapter 42.

It is true enough to declare, as McConica does (74), that Erasmus 'was the more skillful debater, Luther, the more practised theologian'. But that is not exactly what happened. Erasmus did not begin as a debater, whereas Luther did. What has to be charted is the change of tone and direction from Erasmus' initial moderation to the final anger and invective of the *De Servo Arbitrio* and *Hyperaspistes*, for this marks a new phase of the Reformation. There were attempts at conciliation at Augsburg, and as late as May 1531 Julius Pflug wrote from Leipzig that if Erasmus would intercede with Melanchthon some concessions might be made on the catholic side. For that effort

Erasmus dedicated his *De Sarcienda* – on the 'Mending of the Peace of the Church and Quieting Dissent', 1533 – to Pflug.[31] But after 1526 Erasmus lost much heart in attempting conciliation or mediation, although in writings like the *De Sarcienda* he would continue to plead for concord. On 20 August 1531 Erasmus replied to Pflug that never had there been so wild an age: one would think six hundred Furies had torn loose from hell; clergy and laity are mad together (Allen IX, 318/20 ff.). For this worse than tumult, Erasmus blamed Luther – blamed him as the cause of the Peasants' Revolt and as the cause of the lack of unity even among the leaders of reform and still more for the dissension and lack of concord in Christendom. Concord mattered increasingly to Erasmus.[32]

Would Erasmus not smile at the wry reply of Isaac Bashevis Singer to questions about theology and philosophy: 'We must believe in free will. We have no choice'?[33] Erasmus would smile and doubtless agree, but Luther would not.

Notes

1) See Pelikan, *Melody of Theology*, 73. The early attitude of Luther towards Erasmus has been indicated in the preceding chapter.

2) On Biel and his impact upon young Luther, see the argument of Oberman in *The Harvest of Medieval Theology*. There were strong currents of nominalism in Paris during Erasmus' student years, but he was many years older than Luther was at Erfurt and less likely to accept a rigid curriculum (chapter 11). Besides, it has been argued in Volume 1 that Thomas à Kempis played a significant role in shaping the spirituality of young Erasmus (see esp. ch. 5), and in the writings of Thomas and especially in the *Imitatio Christi* there is a pronounced vein of anti-intellectualism. Luther's progress towards advanced studies in theology and philosophy had not been interrupted, as had those of Erasmus, and nominalism clearly influenced him strongly. On the *via moderna* (largely made up of nominalists and followers of Ockham), see *Antiqui und Moderni: Traditionsbewusstsein und Fortschrittsbewusstsein im späten Mittelalter* (Berlin, 1974).

3) *PL* xliv, 201–46, *De spiritu et littera ad Marcellinum*. A brief exposition is given in *ODCC*, with bibliography. For a lucid discussion of the development of this notion in Augustine, see Peter Brown, *Augustine of Hippo* (1969), ch. 15. A fuller analysis is provided in *DTC* vi (1920) cols. 1554–1687. So central is the doctrine of grace in Augustine's teaching that in the Middle Ages he was known as *Doctor gratiae*.

4) For a firm sense of that background and conflict, see Brown's magisterial biography.

5) See *DTC* and *DSAM*.

6) Anselm's arguments for the existence of God are contained primarily in his *Proslogion* and *Monologium* (see *PL* 158–9, and *Sancti Anselmi Opera Omnia*, Edinburgh 1938–1949). Anselm of Canterbury (1033–1109) was

challenged by a monk named Gaunilon, in his *Liber pro insipiente*, to which Anselm replied. Known as the father of scholasticism, Anselm argued, finally, that liberty is given back to free choice through grace: E. Gilson, *Christian Philosophy in the Middle Ages*, 138–9 (with rich bibliography). In addition to the Anselmian tradition (linked to his ontological argument), one would have to consider the Boethian tradition, which had considerable currency at the end of the Middle Ages (see, e.g., Chaucer's examination of free will in *Troilus and Criseyde*).

7) But (as Spitz notes, 259) 'The *Deus absconditus* of Luther's *theologia crucis* is not the subject of a speculative *theologia negativa* as in the case of Dionysius or of Cusanus. Rather, the God of history is *abscondite* because he works behind many masks (*larvae*) and he works deviously and by contradictions or antitheses (*a contrario*), not in a straight line and in a detectable manner'. Erasmus mentions Cusa in his *Apologia ad Fabrum* (Louvain, 1517), where he indicates that Lefèvre followed Cusanus' interpretation of a passage from Psalm 30 (*LB* IX, 6D); *BR*.

8) Down the centuries so much theological writing has been done in terms of opposing a previously-stated position or view, however old: Luther can be seen as reopening the old Pelagian controversy that so concerned Augustine and other early fathers of the church. Pelagianism may be understood as holding that a human being by his or her own effort takes the initial and essential step towards salvation, apart from the assistance of divine grace. Pelagius, a British lay monk of the late 4th– early 5th c., wrote a *De libero arbitrio* that was condemned by African councils in 416 and then by the Council at Carthage in 418. The main writing by Augustine against Pelagian teaching on grace and free will is his *De natura et gratia* (see further Brown, *Augustine of Hippo*). The roots of Pelagianism have been alleged to be at least as old as Theodore of Mopsuestia (c. 350–428); the story is a complicated one, and the scholarly literature very large. For Pelagius and Pelagianism one may start with the *ODCC* and the works cited there; see further O. Bardenhewer, *Patrology* (Freiburg, 1908), and Johannes Quasten, *Patrology III* (Utrecht, 1960) 419, 438, 442.

9) Oecolampadius had left Basel for Augsburg in 1518, but in 1522 had become chaplain to Franz von Sickingen. In November of that year he returned to Basel, worked for the printer Cratander, and began his double career as teacher at the university (lecturing partly in German) and preacher (*BR*). He was soon the leader of the reform movement in Basel. Cf. Luther's allusion in Ep. 1443/43.

10) E. Gordon Rupp in *BR*, citing *Briefwechsel* III, Ep. 626, Weimar ed.

11) McConica (74), with the implication that a lost letter from Thomas More had impelled his decision to write on the freedom of the will, a subject 'suggested by Henry VIII, and it had the merit of addressing an issue of deep importance for Erasmus' personal approach to reform'.

12) *Ars poetica*, 388–9. Besides, he was completing his revised edition of Jerome (published by Froben 1524–6): see his prefatory letter to Warham, Ep. 1465 (Allen V, 492–3), for the suggestion that he was hurrying to complete the printing in time for the September book fair at Frankfurt.

13) As the rumour of his having written it was out and people might think it worse than it was, Smith comments (346).

14) The modern English sense of a bitter or violent criticism seems to have arisen only in the early 19th c. (see *OED* sb.2). But is it not likely that Luther's quick temper bridled at having a *diatriba* written for him (even if he is not specifically named in the title)? Erasmus' intention seems clear: to keep his work a learned discussion, a conversation even.

15) *Titulum indidi libro modestissimum, disputationem siue collationem appelans* (Allen VI, 268/10–11). Allen notes (267) that the original letter to the duke of Saxony dated 2 March 1526 is followed by a contemporary German translation signed by Erasmus, and that the original Latin did not appear in print until 1883.

16) I have found Pierre Mesnard's 'Introduction au libre arbitre' in *Érasme: La philosophie chrétienne* (Paris, 1070) 175 ff., most helpful. I have also consulted the following: Alister E. McGrath, *Reformation Thought* (Oxford, 1988); Bainton, *Here I Stand*; Smith, *Erasmus*; McConica, *Erasmus*; Tracy, *Erasmus*; John B. Payne, *Erasmus: His Theology of the Sacraments* (1970); and T. M. McDonough, *The Law and the Gospel in Luther* (Oxford, 1963). I have not consulted Jean Boisset, *Érasme et Luther: Libre ou Serf Arbitre* (Paris, 1962).

17) See E. W. Kohls, 'La Position theologique d'Erasme et la tradition dans le *De Libero Arbitrio*', in *Colloquium Erasmianum*, 82–5. The list of authorities writing on this question is far fuller, however, than Erasmus indicates.

18) *LB* IX, 1248C indicates Erasmus' willingness to accept Luther's teaching that man places all his hope and trust in God's will and immense mercy. Cf. also 1241EF.

19) Translation by Tracy, *Erasmus*, 231, whose exposition on this point I follow.

20) Harry McSorley, *Luther, Right or Wrong*, 289; Tracy, 231.

21) Payne argues that Erasmus finally expressed his preference on this point in the second part of the *Hyperaspistes*: *Erasmus, Theology of Sacraments*, 198, citing *LB* X, 1500E, 1524E–1525A, 1525CE, 1531C, 1534AB; cf. Tracy, 231.

22) A modification of Erasmus' concept of the proper role of rhetoric is indeed involved: after 1519, Otto Kluge declares, his prose style does become simpler – 'Die Neulateinische Kunstprosa', *Glotta*, xxiii (1934) 67. One would want to except his controversies as a whole.

23) Although, as Smith notes, 349–50, the theological matter in the condemnation was largely taken from the earlier papal bull *Exsurge Domine*, and the University of Paris *Censura*.

24) *Melanchthon on Christian Doctrine – Loci communes 1555*, trans. & ed. by Clyde L. Manschreck (1965; rptd. Grand Rapids, Mich., 1982), introd. by Hans Engelland, xii.

25) Augustine, *De gratia et libera arbitrio*, ch. 20. Even, Augustine elsewhere writes, God may will men to sin in order to punish them: *Contra Julianum* V. iii. § 10–13.

26) The figure of the donkey and of God as the rider of the will is an ancient one, and Eck and others attributed it to Augustine, see Smith 352n.

27) On Luther's argument, see the second volume of Brecht's biography in which he examines the context and structure of Luther's *De Servo Arbitrio*: Martin Brecht, *Martin Luther: Shaping and Defining the Reformation, 1521–*

1532 (Minneapolis, 1990) 213–238.

28) And irritated by its coming so late in the year that he thought the author had held it up so that Erasmus could not answer it before the spring Frankfurt book fair. But with tremendous energy, Erasmus completed his answer within two weeks and set the six Froben presses to work turning out 24 pages a day, finishing it in a week's time.

29) Allen VI, 262 introd. to Ep. 1667, the pref. to the reader.

30) See now C. Augustijn, 'Le dialogue Erasme-Luther dans l'*Hyperaspistes* II', in *Actes du Colloque International Érasme* (Tours, 1986) ed. J. Chomarat et al. (Geneva, 1990) 171–83.

31) *Liber de Sarcienda Ecclesiae Concordia* (Antwerp, 1533). At least 8 editions were printed in 1533 and 3 more before Erasmus' death.

32) See McConica 75–6: 'in the *Paraclesis* he even suggested that the health of the whole social body depends on it'.

33) Q. in *Time* (5 August 1991), 61, on the death of Singer.

Language and Style

We may say that the duty of the poet, as poet, is only indirectly
to his people: his direct duty is to his *language*, first to preserve,
and second to extend and improve ...

　　　　　　　T.S. Eliot, *On Poetry and Poets* (1967) 20

Style is ... the ultimate morality of mind.

　　　　　　　A.N. Whitehead, *The Aims of Education* (1949) 24

Things fall apart; the centre cannot hold;
Mere anarchy is loosed upon the world ...

　　　　　　　W.B. Yeats, 'The Second Coming'

In this early letters we have witnessed the enormous concern of
Erasmus with style (chapter 4). All young writers have such a concern; but in the twentieth century it is usually conceived in terms of
finding one's own voice. For the Renaissance the guiding light came
in studying Latin authors and learning the art of *imitatio*.[1] That is a
very large question, and to be discussed elsewhere.[2]

For Erasmus, in the final analysis, language expresses the essence
of human reality, and in this he may be compared with the twentieth-century poet Seamus Heaney, throughout whose work *lingua* is
perhaps the central reality of man *qua* man: the physical tongue and
its marvellous workings producing sibilants, gutturals, plosives, and
all the wonders of man-produced sound.[3] And also the power of
speech: the language enjoyed and enriched as though following the
guidelines of T.S. Eliot's sentence quoted as epigraph to this chapter.
Language for Erasmus is the source of good order, civility, the path
to concord, and the means for understanding in human culture and
society; through the Word – *logos* in Greek, *sermo* in Latin[4] – truth
and salvation, he believed, came into the world, through the incarna-
tion and the divine Word.

But through misuse of language and all that this implies – and
the fuller implications and growing consequences impinged upon
Erasmus' thought in the years following 1517 – have come lying,
disorder and dissension, violence, and the corruption of civil order.

To repeat an old proverb attributed to Augustine (but to be found in Gregory the Great's *Moralia*), *corruptio optimi pessima*: in corruption the best becomes the worst. Thus language becomes an essential part of the teleology of Erasmian thought; it not only expresses order but it actually becomes, in its proper functioning, a means to retrieve a sense of order and to strive for still higher goals. In the two works taken up here for discussion we shall pursue the use and misuse of language.

De linguae usu ac abusu (concerning the use and abuse of language)[5] was first published in August 1525 and, at the urging of Jan Łaski, dedicated to Krzsztof Szydłowiecki, an adviser to king Sigismund of Poland.[6] Szydłowiecki was a diplomat, then chancellor, who accumulated great wealth and was a fine patron of art and literature (*BR*). Following the dedication, Erasmus and the Polish patron of the arts became good friends and Erasmus was sent a number of expensive gifts. The letters from Erasmus are extant (Epistles 1593, 1622, 1660, 1752, 1820, 1918, 2032, 2177, 2376), but none from Szydłowiecki to Erasmus. As Epistle 1810 demonstrates, Erasmus also admired him as a statesman devoted to maintaining peace.

The years leading up to August 1525 were filled with attacks on Erasmus: from the so-called catholic theologians (such as Béda at Paris and Latomus at Louvain) and with increasing rancour from the reformers, with the bitterest coming from Luther himself, although the *De Servo Arbitrio* did not appear until late November or early December of 1525, three months after the first publication of *Lingua*. There were even minor disputes with fellow humanists: with Lefèvre and Budé, with whom there was substantial agreement on the main points of the basic humanistic programme, but much disagreement on details of interpretation or expression. Erasmus was compelled to enter into long-drawn out and exhausting controversial writings at the very time that much of his own work was moving to fruition.

Much of the criticism, Erasmus felt (perhaps especially that closest to home at Louvain and Paris), was not a responsible – certainly not a scholarly – examination of the evidence; and all too often his words were taken out of context. Still more, Erasmus thought that he was the victim of slander and defamation, and there was increasingly the threat of violence. The experience of the nasty quarrel with the stormy Ulrich von Hutten, leading to Erasmus' *Spongia* in 1523, the year of Hutten's death, disturbed Erasmus greatly. Margaret Mann Phillips viewed *Lingua* as Erasmus' omnium-gatherum defence against all these adversaries, under the aegis of viewing the damaging effect of language that was uninformed and intemperate, and in some instances malicious (114).

By *lingua* Erasmus means both the organ of speech and the language that it brings to life, as it did in classical Latin.[7] The second half of the title, *usu ac abusu*, pointed to the proper use but also the abuse:

> When it is used properly, the tongue can build communities, cement friendships, soothe hurts, educate, admonish, and represent God's will as it preaches the Word. When abused, it destroys communities, ruins relationships, inflicts mortal wounds, spreads pestilential lies and false flattery, and finally, becomes the agent of Satan himself by creating the opposite of Christ's kingdom on earth. (Carrington, 108)

In the dedicatory epistle that precedes the work proper, Erasmus drew the bold analogy with syphilis (*ASD* IV. 1, 235/76–88); and this serves to call attention to the spiritual diseases caused by the misuse of the tongue: 'the sickness of an unbridled tongue is widespread, deeply embedded in its sufferer, highly contagious, frequently uncontrollable, and incurable' (Carrington, 109–110).

In describing the physiology of the tongue in the main part of his little treatise, Erasmus marvels at its versatility; at the number of voices it can assume and the different languages it can speak, at the different emotions it can project, and at the amusing fact that any other animal can be imitated by the human voice. But that very versatility is cause for restraint, and he takes up an idea to which he returns again later: nature intended the tongue to be the moderator of human life (*ASD* 244/216–8). Various abuses of the tongue violate this intended purpose: garrulity (a kind of overuse) and mendacity (a misuse), moving as he tells his reader from misuse that is the result of *stultitia* to misuse that results from *malicia*. This tactic permits Erasmus to attack theologians who accuse other people of heresy, and monks who spend their precious time in gossip instead of uttering the Word. Coming to the peak of his analysis of the tongue's potential for good and evil, Erasmus declares that no kind of lie is more destructive than those inspired by Holy Scripture, which is the *fons et regula* of eternal truth (*ASD* IV. 1, 300/236–8). There is a cure for the diseased tongue in the right kind of study of the Gospels. Yet, perhaps pessimistically as Carrington judges (116) but perhaps realistically, Erasmus declares that the tongue being itself flesh can never entirely transcend the flesh.

To view the work as a whole and in the whole of Erasmus' work, Phillips concludes, 'We might look at *Lingua* as a complete example of the Erasmian approach. All his work can be seen reflected in it'

(225). What is at stake is not only the right kind of reading of the Bible but also the programme of christian education that builds upon language; and both can be threatened by ignorance and malice. (Writing in 1525 Erasmus has had rich experience with malice directed at himself and his work.) Again, *lingua* as speech can build, but it can also destroy.

Perhaps the ultimate irony is that Erasmus depended upon his own tongue to cry out against the abuse of the tongue by others, and to keep open the doors for dialogue with all men of good will. *Lingua* is not totally a pessimistic work.

The dialogue or colloquy *Ciceronianus* looks back to Erasmus' own years in Italy and to Italian Ciceronianism that by the mid-1520s had come so much to be the vogue. Although it was essentially an Italian phenomenon at that time, young Ciceronians were appearing in other countries as young men influenced during their time of study in Rome, Padua or Bologna returned home, converted by their Italian tutors who proclaimed that they alone could possess the true quality of writing a Latin worthy of being called Ciceronian. In the sphere of *lingua* Ciceronianism provides the ultimate example of the proverb that became commonplace by the time of Roger Ascham's *Scholemaster* in 1570: '*Inglese Italianato e un diabolo incarnato*' (Schoeck ed. 1966, 65).

For Erasmus there was one young man in particular who was spoiled by an excessive adherence to Ciceronianism; this was Christophe de Longueil (1488–1522), a gifted native of Brabant who had studied law in Poitier and received a doctorate in 1514 at Valence (*BR*). Moving to Paris about 1514–15, he was taken into the humanist circles of Nicolas Bérault and Louis Ruzé. Then he left Paris for Rome to study Greek under Musurus and Lascaris, and after about a year (c. 1518) he met Pietro Bembo and Jacopo Sadoleto, the two most distinguished Ciceronians in Italy, who introduced him to the Ciceronian circles of the Roman Academy (*BR*). Having stirred up a hornets' nest Longueil fled Rome for Venice, and from there went to Louvain in October 1519 to make the acquaintance of Erasmus, armed with a letter of introduction from Budé. But Erasmus was not impressed by a young man who on the question of style had compared him with Budé, to Erasmus' disadvantage. Returning to Italy, Longueil settled with Bembo in Padua. In 1522 he died at the age of thirty-three. Richard Pole, in whose house he died, saw to the publication of his collected writings in 1524;[8] and Erasmus was sent a copy in 1525, as a letter from Thomas Lupset (Epistle 1595 of 23 August) explains. In that letter Lupset spoke of the imitation of Cicero (lines 129–30) and of Longueil's devotion to Ciceronianism (lines 130–2). To add to the unfortunate example of a dedicated Ciceronian who died young,[9] in 1527 Erasmus 'was receiving reports of Italians who were criticising his style as un-ciceronian, labelling him *barbarus* and *Batavus*, and holding the most eloquent of northerners to be not Erasmus but the deceased Longueil'.[10] Enough to have led Erasmus to his resolve against the Ciceronians. The dialogue was published by Froben in 1528, following *De recta latini graecique sermonis pronuntiatione dialogus*. The volume included an edition of *De recta* together with minor pieces in Greek and Latin by various hands (Erasmus composed three of them: epitaphs on or tributes to Bruno Amerbach, who died in 1519, and Dorp, who died in 1525, and *Epistola consolatoria in adversis*): a miscellaneous volume but one with a strong focus on 'true classical scholarship'. The work was dedicated to Johann van Vlatten, who had been provost of St Mary's, Aachen: a humanist who worked to promote Erasmian ideals in education and religion (*BR*).[11]

The basic plot of the dialogue is simple. The target-figure is named Nosoponus (translated by Knott as Mr Workmad, by Smith as Morbid Toiler); the other two speakers are Bulephorus (the Counsellor), and Hypologus (the Arbiter, or perhaps Back-up). Nosoponus is dedicated to the task of learning to imitate Cicero – at whatever cost, and with unremitting determination – to the end that he will be hailed even by Italians as a true Ciceronian. By adopting the Socratic method Bulephorus leads Nosoponus to admit that there are other writers who in particular points are superior to Cicero; and in terms of vocabulary there is a great deal in the world of which Cicero knew nothing – why should we be bound by Cicero's vocabulary?

The humour of the satire is enjoyable today. Nosoponus describes his devotion:

> I have a picture of him, nicely painted, not only in my private chapel and in my study, but on all the doors too; and I carry his portrait about with me, carved on gems, so that all the time he's present to my thoughts. I never see anything in my dreams but Cicero. (*CWE* 28:346)

There is a great deal of satirising of the study of Cicero's vocabulary, presented with many examples and commented upon with dry irony by both Bulephorus and Hypologus. To Nosoponus' declaration that he plans to remain a bachelor because he could not stand the intrusion of love into his sacred vocation, Bulephorus retorts:

> That was wise of you, Nosoponus. If I were to start giving that amount of attention at night to Cicero, my wife would break

down the door, tear up my indexes, and burn all my papers with my Cicero exercises on them. Worse than that, while I was giving attention to Cicero, she would invite in a substitute husband to give her a little attention in place of me. And so, while I was aiming to make myself the image of Cicero, she would produce a child who was anything but the image of Bulephorus. (*CWE* 28:252)

To a catalogue of names of those who had written in Latin, Nosoponus replies with scorn, displaying his lack of realistic stand-ards. At the end of this review, there is an assessment of Italian classicisers – writers in neo-Latin who practise *imitatio* – and Erasmus praises especially Bembo and Sadoleto, whom he respected. But it is Longueil who is now criticised as a thorough-going Ciceronian in all his foolishness. Erasmus brings to bear the anti-Ciceronian views of Poliziano, perhaps the greatest of fifteenth-century philologians, who had characterised those who merely copy Cicero slavishly as the 'apes of Cicero'; and the metaphoric 'Ciceronian apes' is repeated nearly a dozen times in the dialogue, for not only is the intelligent study of Cicero not well served by Ciceronianism of the Longueil sort, the true nature of renaissance *imitatio* is violated as well. Margolin wisely observes that 'Le principe de l'imitation n'est pas seulement d'ordre psychologique ou littéraire (cf. le *Ciceronianus* et sa querelle): il a une valeur universelle, il est d'essence métaphysique'.[12]

In France there were angry responses to the linking of Budé and Bade (with Bade found superior in terms of the Ciceronian style); and many came to feel increasingly that Erasmus deliberately deni-grated French scholarship in the person of Budé. Erasmus' letter to de Berquin, with a copy sent to de Brie, leaked out and worsened the situation by widening the talk.[13] A storm arose: there were defama-tory epigrams attacking Erasmus, and Erasmus made some changes in the second edition of March 1529 (*CWE* 28:331). Other people complained at being omitted, and some names were added in the second edition; and in the third the names of Cantiuncula, Cornelis de Schepper, and Zasius were added too (*CWE* 28: 332).

But the real fury came later. In 1531 the Italian-born J.C. Scaliger published his *Oratio pro Marco Tullio Cicerone contra Desiderium Erasmus Roterodamum*, a vitrioloic attack indeed, and so much *ad hominem* (taking up the matter of illegitimacy discussed in chapter 2, for example, but in a particularly nasty way) that Erasmus thought his old friend turned adversary, Aleandro, had written it. In 1535 Etienne Dolet continued the controversy, writing a *Dialogus de imitatione ciceroniana*, which was both a loyal defence of Longueil and a vigorous, sometimes bitter, attack upon Erasmus.[14] There were others as well, and the full history of the *Ciceronianus* and its reception, including commentaries upon it, is an important chapter in sixteenth-century scholarship and letters.

Once again Erasmus' wit had won enemies. Years earlier his *Moria* had antagonised many who remained enemies all his life, and the *Colloquies* added to the growing company of anti-Erasmians; and now humanists in Italy and France were alienated by Erasmus' witty writing too. It did little good to explain that he was criticising only the rigid and doctrinaire extremists, and that his lists of names appeared within a dramatic dialogue and – in naming men of literary eminence – there was no effort at completeness: as Knott comments, 'most of the contemporary persons mentioned appear simply because they were friends or acquaintances of Erasmus whose names sprang to mind whether or not their literary eminence warranted their inclusion'. But there are enough names that omission was the more noticeable: 'to have been mentioned in the *Ciceronianus* became an accolade'. But after all the criticism and controversy Erasmus 'soon felt that it had been mistaken generosity to include more than one or two representative names, or indeed to mention the living at all' (*CWE* 28: 333). As he tried to make clear in his prefatory letter to the revised edition of 24 January 1529, 'I am taking issue only with those who are so committed to this irrational creed that they reject with incredible disgust anything that does not conform'.[15]

To *Lingua* and *Ciceronianus* we might add certain other writings by Erasmus on rhetoric which call attention to the qualities of good writing: *De Copia* (1512), *De Constructione octo partium orationis* (1514), *Antibarbari* (1518), *De Conscribendis Epistolis* (1521), *Paraphrasis in elegantias Laur. Vallae* (1529; see chapter 9), the *Ecclesiastes* (1535), and the *Compendium Rhetorices* published posthumously. All of these contributed to the laying out of a programme for *bonae literae*: not a 'system', for that would be too un-Erasmian, but a programme making clear the place of rhetoric in education and providing guidelines for good writing and good speaking. Classical rhetoric was heavily tilted towards speaking; with Erasmus the tilt was towards writing. And the importance of rhetoric carries over into preaching and prayer as well as letter-writing and the other forms of expression.

At the core of rhetoric and the educational programme is the concept of language, which as Erasmus viewed it (and in the spirit of T.S. Eliot) was first to preserve, and then to extend and improve the language. For the abuse of language is detrimental to the social order and destructive of civility and concord. The right use of language is the source of good order and civility, and it is the path to concord, and to wisdom.[16]

The *Ciceronianus* and its consequent quarrels highlight an important aspect of Erasmus' thought and personality. Both temperamentally and philosophically he was against extremes. In the religious differences leading up to the final splitting away by the reform groups from Rome, he strove to mediate, to keep a middle position between the extremes. Within devotional practice he complained of excessive devotion to Mary – in one of his characteristic rhetorical questions he asks, who canonised the Virgin Mother? (Thompson, 85) – though he himself had a devotion to her and composed prayers and poems in her honour.[17]

But with the hardening of differences between the reformers and Rome it was ever more difficult to find and keep a *via media*, and more dangerous. In matters of literature – if one can ever completely separate literary concerns from those of society, politics and religion – it was increasingly difficult as well. One of the sad consequences of the misreadings of the *Ciceronianus* is that concord and consensus were disappearing among the humanists, as well as among the religious reformers. When the centre gives way, as Yeats intoned,

Things fall apart; the centre cannot hold;
Mere anarchy is loosed upon the world ...[18]

Notes

1) See R. J. Schoeck, '"Lighting a Candle to the Place": On the Dimensions and Implications of *Imitatio* in the Renaissance', in *Italian Culture* 4 (1983) 123–42.

2) One of the recurrent themes in my *Erasmus Grandescens* (1988) is the process of Eramus' learning through *imitatio*; see also Vol. 1 of this biography, 63–7 and 121 ff.

3) Cf. Seamus Heaney, 'My tongue moved, a swung relaxing hinge', in 'Sibyl', *Field Work,* and many other instances of a rich awareness of *lingua*. See Johanna Tetzlaff, *The Poetic consciousness: A Reading of Seamus Heaney's Poetry and Prose* (MA thesis, Trier 1991).

4) The close relation of these two words is discussed in ch. 32. See the discussion of language in terms of the early letters and poems in ch. 4.

5) See M. M. Phillips, 'Erasmus on the tongue', *ERSYB* 1 (1981) 113–25; Jacques Chomarat, *Grammaire et Rhetorique* (1981) II, 'La verité et la violence', 1118–55; and Laurel Carrington, 'Erasmus' Lingua: The Double-Edged tongue', *ERSYB* 9 (1989) 106–18. The text has been edited in *ASD* IV. 1 (1974) by F. Schalk.

6) The work was immediately popular, especially in Poland (thanks to Szydłowiecki) and in Spain: there were four editions in 1525 (two in Paris),

and six in 1526; a total of fourteen editions by Erasmus' death. There were numerous translations into Flemish and Dutch as late as 1633.

7) *Lingua:* 1) the tongue; 2) the tongue as the organ of speech; 3) the use of the tongue – speech; also, an utterance. (*Oxford Latin Dictionary*).

8) Christophorus Longolius, *Orationes...* (Florence, 1524).

9) 'Erasmus might even have felt a mixture of admiration and genuine pity', *BR*.

10) Betty I. Knott, Introd. note in *CWE* 28:327, a commendable essay on the gestation of the dialogue as well as its literary achievement, and an introduction to which I am indebted in a general way. In *BR* M.-M. de la Garanderie notes his irregular birth and his absolution from its consequences by a brief from Leo X.

11) For the second authorised edition of March 1529, Erasmus wrote a second letter of dedication to van Vlatten, defending his motives in certain passages which had offended and provoked some individuals (Knott, 335). He did modify some of the offending passages and made minor improvements in the Latinity. In this edition the *Ciceronianus* was combined with an edition of the *Colloquia*, indicating a wish to identify it as a dialogue or colloquy. The third edition was published in Basel in October 1529, with a number of changes; the fourth, March 1530, was in effect a reissue of the third. In addition at least four editions appeared elsewhere (twice at Lyon) before the *Opera* of 1540; and there were several further editions in the 16th & 17th c. In *ASD* 1.2 there is a critical edition of the first edition (1528) with *apparatus criticus* showing changes in subsequent editions. Knott's translation in *CWE* 28 is based upon a collation of *ASD* with *LB* (tom. I). In his essay on van Vlatten for *BR*, Anton J. Gail conjectures that it may have been his encouragement that led to the composition of such works as the *Explanatio symboli* of 1533 and, at least in part, of the *Ecclesiastes* of 1535.

12) J. -C. Margolin, in *Recherches Erasmiennes* (Geneva, 1969) 16 n.34.

13) Eps 2046 and 2048. See the long Ep. 2046 to Brixius (September 1528, Allen VII, 483–93) and a shorter letter to de Berquin at about the same time (Allen VII, 494–6). Erasmus tried to placate Budé in Epistle 2047 at the same time (Allen VII, 493/ 1–5), but Allen observes that 'Erasmus' soft words did not soothe Budaeus' feelings'.

14) Etienne Dolet of Orléans (1508–1546) was educated at Paris for several years, then became a disciple of Villanovanus at Padua (1527–30), where he became a dedicated, even passionate, Ciceronian. The attack upon Erasmus in Dolet's *Dialogus de imitatione Ciceroniana* (Lyon, 1535) came too late for Erasmus to spend much time in responding, and he blamed Dolet's and Scaliger's attack of 1531 upon Aleandro. Dolet was abusive, accusing Erasmus of garrulity and Lutheranism and calling him a 'toothless old food-for-worms'. See J.R.Henderson in *BR*.

15) *CWE* 28:41. Erasmus adds a final note about the troublemakers and detractors: 'Some persons are born for nothing except to cause trouble to people trying to do something decent, while they have nothing to fill their own time except gambling, whoring, guzzling, and boasting' (ibid.). This is obviously a final fillip that could easily be misunderstood and would have added to the wave of resentment against the treatise.

16) Luther too had a high regard for languages, as Spitz notes (*Religious*

Renaissance, 253), but 'for Luther the utility of languages was functional and not substantive'. However, for Luther language played a role analogous to that of speech, and its highest function 'was its service as a vehicle for the Word of God' (253–4): this is not different from, but it is less than, Erasmus' even loftier concept of *lingua*.

17) Early, Erasmus' devotion to Mary was manifested in prayers and poems (see ch. 4), and it continues even in his *Annotations on the New Testament*. See Halkin, *Érasme*, 330–40. One of the Colloquies is an attack upon the false application of religion, not upon religion itself: see 'An Examination Concerning Faith' (*Inquisitio de fide*, 1524), with Erasmian explanation of why it was fitting for God to be born of Mary (Thompson, 182). Critics at the Sorbonne and in Spain accused him of irreverence in dealing with the invocation of saints and the Virgin Mary; his defence that he was attacking silly superstitions failed to appease his enemies: Thompson, 139, citing *LB* IX 942C–943E, and 1086C–F.

18) Yeats, 'The Second Coming'.

The Basel Years: Humanism and Religion

I see a new kind of men appearing that my spirit vigorously
abhors. I do not see anyone getting better, instead everybody is
getting worse – at least those I know.

> Erasmus to a monk, October 1527, Epistle 1887
> (Allen VII, 199/9–11)

The most prominent of the accomplishments of Erasmus lie in
the area of 'sacred philology'. Many of the Church Fathers,
Greek as well as Latin, owe the first printed editions of their
writings to his tireless activity as scholar and publisher.

> J. Pelikan, *The Melody of Theology*, 71

That the Lutherans destroyed by their violence the culture of
humanism, the refinement of letters, was the constant com-
plaint of Erasmus.

> Edgar Wind, in *JWCI* (1938)

As late as 1527 Erasmus still toyed with the idea of going to France
or England where there were excellent prospects, even assurances
from the French and English kings and their spokesmen. The sale of
his library in 1525 doubtless had several motivations: he could use
the money,[1] and very likely he was clearing his house and ordering
his affairs as he became older and approached the ever-nearer inevita-
bility of death. In 1534 his *De praeparatione ad mortem* was published
in Basel,[2] and it marks his thinking about old age (about which he
increasingly complained) and death (see chapter 43).

More positively, the English annuity was paid regularly, although
on the death of Warham on 22 August 1532 Erasmus was to fear
that the annuity might cease.[3] Yet he was able to live in comfort; and
he carefully continued to preserve close relations with both England
and France, needing the protection of the French king especially
because of the unrelenting hostility of the Sorbonnists. He played
with the idea of going to France as late as 30 March 1527 (Smith,
275); but after the censures of the Sorbonnists in 1529, and their
forbidding the sale of his editions of Ambrose and Augustine in
1530, followed in April 1532 by yet another censure, he relin-

quished his desire to go there even with the king's protection: the situation was too dangerous. In April 1529 a moderate writer with sympathies for reform ideas was burned at the stake. The story of de Berquin is a long one, well summarised by Gordon Griffiths in *BR*. A follower of Erasmus, Berquin was doubtless targeted because it was seemingly he who had extracted from Béda's writings against Erasmus twelve propositions that were allegedly heretical (*BR*): this proved to be a bold attack on a dangerous opponent. In Epistle 2188 Erasmus gives an account of Berquin's execution and of his relations with him (writing from Freiburg on 1 July 1529 to Charles Utenhove, Allen VIII, 210/11 ff).

As for England, that scene was complicated by the question of Henry VIII's divorce. In either 1524 or 1525 Mountjoy, ever Erasmus' faithful patron and now chamberlain to the queen (*BR*), asked Erasmus to write a book on marriage for her (Epistle 1624, the important letter to Lupset which is so informative on a number of issues); Erasmus responded with his *Christiani Matrimonis Institutio* of 1526, the prefatory letter to which is addressed to Catherine of Aragon (Epistle 1727). Not surprisingly, given the delicate politics involved,[4] Erasmus wrote carefully about marriage and divorce.[5] In the prefatory letter Catherine was extolled as the most perfect wife of that generation, and he went on to define marriage as the perpetual and legitimate union of man and woman, calling attention to how binding it was both in law and religion. There are impediments to marriage, he recognised, and some of them can break a marriage contract (but not consummated wedlock). The thrust of the work tilts slightly, but definitely, in favour of the queen. By 1528, when Mountjoy wrote to convey the queen's thanks (for which she had had to be reminded), he expressed his hope that Erasmus would come to England and alluded to an invitation from the king. But on 1 June 1528 Erasmus wrote to Henry (Epistle 1998) declining the invitation with several excuses. To both Henry and More he wrote that he was feeling old, too old to take up a new place to live.

Erasmus remained in Basel, and it is well to survey its attractions for him.

Greek had come as early to Basel as it did anywhere else north of the Alps, and one should look to the lasting influence of the secretaries and scribes who had been in Basel during the Council (chapter 38). Between 1470 and 1480 Greek was taught at the university by the Greek Andronikos Kontoblakas. Towards the end of the century one may identify such names as Johann Ulrich Surgant, a philosopher and jurist from Altkirch, Johannes Geiler from Kayserberg, and Sebastian Brant from Strasbourg. (It was because Brant did not approve of Basel's accession to the Swiss Confederacy in 1499 that he returned to Strasbourg, where he began a new career the following year, *BR*.) There was, demonstrably, a *Blütezeit*, a blossoming of Basel humanism even before the arrival of Erasmus.[6] There were other scholars: Matthaeus Adrianus, a baptised Jew of Spanish origin who published a Hebrew grammar in Venice in 1501 and claimed both Reuchlin and Pellicanus as students. He gave lessons to the Amerbach sons as well as to Wolfgang Faber Capito, and later in Heidelberg to Oecolampadius and Johann Brenz. Having delivered an oration in defence of the three languages at Louvain, where he was the first professor of Hebrew in the Collegium Trilingue, he left suddenly in July 1519 and appears to have gone to Wittenberg (*BR*). With such teachers from Kontoblakas to Adrianus, the three languages were well served in Basel.

A few key individuals must serve to establish the vigour of humanistic studies in Basel during the 1520s: Ludwig Baer, Cantiuncula, Glareanus, Pellikan, and Beatus Rhenanus. Additional names will serve to complete the picture of the scholarly milieu during Erasmus' Basel years.

Christoph von Utenheim (d. 1527) was a native of Alsace, who obtained his MA from Erfurt in 1466 and a doctorate of canon law in 1474. In 1502 he was elected bishop of Basel. A close friend of Johann Geiller and Jakob Wimpheling, he was also a patron of Sebastian Brant. He was known for a commitment to ecclesiastical reform (but in this he was only moderately successful) and to humanistic learning, bringing to Basel exponents of reform and humanism such as Limperger in 1498, Johannes Fabri in 1513, Capito in 1515, and Oecolampadius in 1518. Thus Utenheim had established a firm base for Erasmus' decision to move to Basel, and he was instrumental in establishing links between the Basel circle and those elsewhere, especially in Switzerland (see *BR*).

Ludwig Baer (1479–1554) came from a family of wealth and high office and was sent off to Paris with a view to a career in the church. At Paris he graduated BA in 1497–8 and MA in 1499, teaching arts courses for seven years while earning his degrees. In 1511 he ranked first among those obtaining the doctorate in theology, and he returned to Basel at the beginning of 1513, beginning lectures as *professor ordinarius* of theology. By 1514–15 he was rector of the university, and in the following year dean of divinity. Baer had his own network of friends, as well as being a friend of some of Erasmus': Guillaume Cop and Aleandro from Paris, and from Germany Cochlaeus, Eck and Pelargus. Glareanus was a life-long friend. Baer supported the invitation for Erasmus to settle in Basel, and he adopted the Erasmian *philosophia Christi* to the full. In a noble tribute Erasmus declared that 'Baer managed to exercise his academic duties as a theologian without the slightest hostility towards classical and biblical scholarship'.[7]

Conrad Pellicanus (1478–1556) was an Alsatian who first studied at Heidelberg then entered the Franciscan house at his home town of Rouffach and in 1495 was sent to Tübingen for further studies. He was soon interested in philology by Paulus Scriptoris and in 1499 began to study Hebrew, establishing personal contacts with Reuchlin. In 1501 he took holy orders and finished his Hebrew grammar, printed in 1504 by Schott in Strasbourg: *Do modo legendi et intelligendi Hebraeum*. He became a lecturer in theology in the Franciscan friary at Basel in 1502, and was soon a collaborator at Froben's press. Elected warden of the Franciscans in 1519, he made his house a centre of reformation ideas in Basel. In 1523 he and Oecolampadius were appointed to professorships in theology at the University; three years later he moved to Zürich (where the Reformation had already been established) and taught Greek and Hebrew until his death. He had known Erasmus from 1515, and after 1521 was a member of the close circle of friends surrounding him. But in 1525 there was a falling out over views on the Eucharist; the break was not repaired, and the former friends did not communicate for ten years, becoming reconciled shortly before Erasmus' death, on the initiative of Pellicanus (*BR*). The figure of Pellicanus calls attention to the changing dynamics of the reform movement and the ease with which even friends could misunderstand each other and become hostile.[8]

Born near Glarus in Switzerland, Heinrich Loriti (1488–1563) is better known under the Latin name Glareanus, which he adopted after 1511 and used universally thereafter. After earlier schooling Glareanus was instructed in Latin and music at Rottweil in Würtemberg, where he was a student with Myconius. In 1507 he matriculated at Cologne, obtaining his BA in 1508 and his MA in 1510. In 1512 the emperor Maximilian I crowned him poet laureate, an honour he always cherished. When Glareanus moved to Basel in 1514 Erasmus 'welcomed him at once as the foremost of the Swiss humanists' (BR), and except for five years in Paris (1517–1522) he remained in Basel until 1529, and then moved with Erasmus to Freiburg, where he remained until his death. Glareanus was an important connection with Zwingli, who was active in Glarus from 1506 to 1516. In all his work,[9] Fritz Büsser writes in *BR*, he 'considered himself Erasmus' friend and comrade in arms but also his admirer'. When the time came for a break with Rome, or a decision to remain, he followed Erasmus' lead in remaining with the catholic Church; 'he severed his relations with Zwingli and later Oecolampadius but remained on friendly terms with Beatus Rhenanus, Pirckheimer, and Zasius' (*BR*).

Cantiuncula – Claude Chansonnette – was born around 1490 in Metz and studied law at Louvain, being elected dean in 1516; and in Martin van Dorp he had a common friend with Erasmus. Arriving at Basel in 1517 he established contact with Erasmus; at the university he rose rapidly and became professor of civil law in 1518 even though he did not win a doctorate until the following spring. In October 1519 he was elected rector and entered upon a busy career at the university and in the town council. In his writings Cantiuncula is notable for stressing the relationship between canon and secular law, and as an exponent of humanistic jurisprudence, the *mos gallicus*.[10] For his career after leaving Basel in 1524 (a decision he later regretted), which took him to Metz, Speyer, Vienna and elsewhere – see Thieme and Rowan in *BR*. Two points of scholarship especially link Cantiuncula with Erasmus. He translated Erasmus' *Exomologesis* into French (*Manière de se confesser*, Basel, 1524), and More's *Utopia* into German (Basel in the same year). Cantiuncula's influential teaching on equity, as Kisch has shown,[11] owed much to Erasmus', even to the point of his using the same citations and examples. Erasmus had deep respect for Cantiuncula, and theirs was a warm intellectual relationship.

Beatus Rhenanus of Sélestat we have already met several times; here it is only necessary to stress his Basel connections. Throughout his years in Basel (from 1511 to 1527) Beatus visited Sélestat frequently, and he maintained links with the Strasbourg circle. When Erasmus moved to Basel in 1521, he called upon Beatus in Sélestat and they travelled together to Basel. The visit to Botzheim in Constance was a joint visit by Erasmus and Beatus. Both Beatus and Erasmus remained on close terms with Sturm more than the rest of the Strasbourg community; and Beatus maintained a frequent correspondence with Bonifacius Amerbach. In 1530 he visited Augsburg in the year of the Diet, and on this visit he examined 'Peutinger's famous road atlas of the Roman Empire and also the art collection of the Fugger family' (*BR*).

Joachim Vadianus (1484–1551) studied at Vienna, graduating BA in 1504 and MA in 1508, and he belonged to the humanist circle of Conrad Celtis. At Vienna he was vice-chancellor of the university in 1514, and in 1516–17 he was appointed rector and professor of rhetoric. A native of St Gall, he was inspired by Zwingli and led the establishment of the reformed church there, where he was elected mayor in 1525. In an edition of Pomponius Mela, Vadianus placed a complimentary mention of Erasmus (Epistle 1314) and Erasmus returned the compliment in the 1526 edition of the *Adagia (BR)*.[12] Erasmus was always most conscious of the ties between Basel and other Swiss centres of learning and religion; and Vadianus, who had met Erasmus in 1522 and contributed to a new edition of Glareanus' *Helvetiae descriptio*, maintained and preserved a voluminous correspondence also reaching to Poland and Italy.

Wolfgang Faber Capito (d. 1541) was taught first at the Latin school at Pforzheim, then in the universities of Ingolstadt (MA by 1505) and Freiburg (MA in 1506), taking a licentiate in theology at Freiburg in 1512. Between the MA and the licentiate he took minor orders as a Benedictine. While on leave from Freiburg (1506–9) he became associated with the humanist group of Wimpheling and Brant and served as a proof-reader for the press of Heinrich Gran in Hagenau. Upon his return to Freiburg he became part of the circle of Zasius; at Bruchsal he was started in the study of Hebrew by Pellicanus. In mid-1515 he was called to Basel as cathedral preacher by bishop Christoph von Utenheim, and simultaneously was appointed professor of theology at the university. For the next five years he moved in the company of Oecolampadius, Pellicanus, and the Amerbachs. He and Erasmus had a mutual admiration for each other (Epistles 459, 541), but in October 1518 it was he who persuaded Froben to publish a Latin edition of Luther's early works (Epistle 904), and he then in 1520 moved to Mainz as preacher, confessor and adviser to Albert of Brandenburg. His conversion to Luther's evangelicalism broke his earlier warm relationship with Erasmus, yet it matters that Capito was one avenue for Erasmus' continuing influence on the mainstream of the Reformation *(BR)*.[13]

Although neither of the great master-printers, Johann Amerbach (c. 1443–1513) and Johann Froben (c. 1460–1527) was a scholar,[14] each developed a circle of scholar-editors that bears comparison with the famed academy of Aldus in Venice (chapter 23). In Epistle 2215 written to Mountjoy in his first year at Freiburg, which expresses gratitude to Mountjoy and Mary of Hungary, Erasmus looked back upon the advantages he had enjoyed at Basel in working with the press of Froben and the team of scholars (Allen VIII, 278/32–4).

It is apparent that there were several humanist circles in Basel, and Erasmus played a key role in each of them and in binding them together. Clearly they also mattered to him, in obviously differing ways. Baer was an important adviser in theological and ecclesiastical affairs, and he tried to mediate some of Erasmus' conflicts. Several broke away and joined the reform movement: Pellicanus and Capito, for example, yet an Erasmian influence continued through them. Several were deeply loyal to Erasmus – Glareanus, Beatus Rhenanus, Cantiuncula, among others – and their closeness continued even after geographical separation. Vadianus followed Zwingli yet remained respectful of Erasmus, and Erasmus of him. Finally, through Froben, Erasmus (who served as a kind of literary director for the publisher) had even more contacts than we yet know, and his influence upon what was printed (or, as with Luther, not printed) was very great. In Basel the bulk of Erasmus' correspondence began to increase almost geometrically, and he observed from time to time that he spent half his days in writing letters; this was scarcely an exaggeration. The wonder is that without our modern tools he was able to keep his correspondents and all of their details of publishing and living reasonably straight: only occasionally does he forget the name of a brother or a wife, or confuse two individuals or two places.

Bucer and the reform of Strasbourg during Erasmus' lifetime were indissolubly bound together. Martin Bucer (1491–1551) was born in Sélestat and attended the Latin school,[15] after which he joined the Dominican order and was trained in the rigorous scholastic methodology of disputations and *lectura*, and the disciplines of Albertus and Aquinas. Sent to the Dominican centre in Heidelberg, he studied Greek with Johann Brenz and read the works of Erasmus. In 1518 he was present at Luther's defence of his Theses before the Augustinians at Heidelberg, and Luther became a major influence upon him. Released from monastic vows he became a member of the secular clergy, and he next joined Heinrich Motherer in establishing the Reformation in Lorraine. In 1523 he moved to Strasbourg and was chosen pastor of the parish of Ste Aurelie, having married; from that time onwards he played a major role in the reform movement in Strasbourg (*BR*), and although influenced by Luther in achieving reform in the Church, he remained close to Erasmian teachings on baptism (*BR*).[16] As late as 1527 he was still attempting to win over Erasmus to the side of reform; Erasmus' Epistle 1901 carefully and courteously gives three reasons for not joining him. The first was his conscience, the second the fact that many in Bucer's company were too far removed from evangelical sincerity, and the third, the terrible dissension among reform leaders. Erasmus spoke of all this, he wrote from Basel on 11 November 1527, in deep sorrow.

The arrival of Geldenhouwer in the city caused a serious rift between Bucer and Erasmus. For Geldenhouwer published an Erasmian tract (*Apologia adversus ... monachos*) without asking Erasmus' permission, and added to it his own plea for toleration

towards the evangelicals (*BR*). Miriam U. Chrisman writes in *BR*
that 'Erasmus was deeply angered and responded with his *Epistola
contra pseudevangelicos* (Freiburg, 1529), which attacked not only
Geldenhouwer but also the Strasbourg and other south German and
Swiss reformers. He condemned them for having destroyed the cause
of the Gospel among the princes and those in authority'. Letters from
Erasmus followed, reflecting his hatred of Geldenhouwer and his
scorn for the Strasbourg reformers. Early in 1536 Bucer and Capito
paid a courtesy visit to Erasmus, that is described as 'jovial and
intent on avoiding serious topics' (*BR*). Strasbourg went its own way
in matters of doctrine, and after 1548 Bucer was forced to leave,
going to England where he assisted in the revision of the Book of
Common Prayer. The expense of friendship in a waste of religious
conflict is a bitterness that does not heal. Erasmus could not but
lament the direction taken by a graduate of the Sélestat Latin school,
with its humanistic stress that had also produced such men as Beatus
Rhenanus.

At least a glance at the Reformation in Switzerland is needed to
complete the picture, for events there affected Erasmus greatly during his 1521–1529 years in Basel.

Oecolampadius (1482–1531) is the key figure as the reformer of
Basel, as we have already seen. There was never an open break
between the reformer and Erasmus, although the earlier close friendship cooled. A new element was added to the rising tide of reform in
Basel by the arrival in 1524 of Guillaume Farel (1489–1565), described by Smith as 'a man on fire with zeal from the crown of his red
head to the sole of his gospeller's feet upon the mountains' (376–77).
Having just called Erasmus 'a chameleon and a pernicious enemy of
the gospel', Farel called upon him to argue hotly over the invocation
of the Holy Spirit. Erasmus avenged himself by giving him the name
Phallicus, and by seeing to it that in July he was asked to leave, if not
actually expelled from, the city.[17] Not surprisingly, Erasmus was
turned away from the reform movement by such reformers. Meanwhile the influence of Zwingli from Zürich continued strong. In
1525 Erasmus was requested by the Town Council for an opinion
concerning certain reforms, and the result was his *Erasmi Rot.
Consilium Senatui Basiliensi in negotio Lutherano* (see Smith, 387) – the
consilium being a widely practised form by means of which
jurisconsults and others rendered their opinions on issues of the
day.[18] But moderation did not prevail, and in 1527 Oecolampadius
published a pamphlet branding the Mass as worse than theft,
harlotry, adultery, etc. The so-called breaking of the idols in 1529
was the last act in a long series of violent and disruptive actions.

Ironically, perhaps, Erasmus had left Basel long before the death of Zwingli on the field of Cappel on 11 October 1531, to be followed only a few weeks later by the death of Oecolampadius from a fever. Erasmus saw these twin events as tolling the death of the Swiss Protestant cause:

> Here [he wrote to Olaus in Hungary on 11 December 1531] we are freed from great fear by the death of the two preachers Zwingli and Oecolampadius, whose fate has wrought an incredible change in the mind of many. This is the wonderful hand of God on high: may he complete what he has begun to the glory of his holy name! (Epistle 2582, Allen IX, 399–400/38–42, trans. by Smith, 395)

In the eight-year period at Basel Erasmus was prodigiously productive. Many of his old projects came to life (often without authorisation) and were revised by him for publication. A number of editions of long standing were at last coming forth from the presses. There were new challenges, and fresh ideas. There were also great distractions. His health continued fragile, and in 1526 he consulted with Paracelsus, the famous and controversial physician who had come to Basel as a consultant to Johann Froben.[19]

As he was entering his sixtieth year Erasmus drew up his first will on 22 January 1527. The details are examined in appendix D; here what is to be noted is the provision for a complete edition of his works along the guidelines of the *Catalogus Lucubrationum*, and copies were to be distributed to named individuals and libraries. What is striking too is the centering of the executors in Basel: Bonifacius Amerbach was to be his trustee, and the executors were to be Basil Amerbach, Beatus Rhenanus, and Hieronymus Froben. In 1527 Erasmus clearly felt that Basel was his final home.[20] After his unanticipated move to Freiburg in 1529 he perceived the necessity for a new will, and his second was made and on 26 November 1533 signed in his Freiburg home; this will has not survived. Upon returning to Basel he made a third will on 12 February 1536, which is that executed after his death (see appendix D).

There were new editions of the *Adagiorum Chiliades* in 1523, 1526, 1528. In 1526 the most notable addition is the long adage 'Ne bos quidem pereat', but there were fifty others added in this edition. In the adage 'Ne bos...' Erasmus widens the concept of a neighbour and inveighs against the current craze for what is new; and he concludes with a plea for peace within the universities:

> that the study of languages and of good letters, coming back to take their place amongst us and spring up again from the roots,

as it were, should courteously and peaceably work their way into the company of those disciplines which have held sway for so many centuries in the universities, and without disparaging anyone's particular study, should be of use to the studies of all. (Phillips, *'Adages'*, 379–80)

Erasmus surely had in view the hostility towards the Collegium Trilingue at Louvain, and the animosity of the Sorbonists towards humanism at Paris and elsewhere; and, published by Froben in their own city, the adage can be taken as an admonition to the university in Basel. The marvel is that Erasmus' tone here is so relatively calm and cool, despite the rancorous attacks against him in Louvain and Paris. Elsewhere in his writings he often enough gave way to cutting irony or biting scorn.

There were editions of classical authors: second editions of Cicero (1520) and Seneca (1529), embodying much work over a number of years. There was a translation from Galen's Greek into Latin (1526). Some of Erasmus' most notable educational work appeared during these years: the much-reprinted *De Conscribendis Epistolis* in 1522, and the *De Pueris Instituendis* in 1529. A work of remarkable influence was the treatise entitled *Dialogus de recta Latini Graecique sermonis pronuntiatione* (1528), for it has been called 'one of the foundation charters of the classical education that reigned supreme in European schools from the sixteenth to the twentieth century'.[21] It bears repeating that while all too often the first printing of an Erasmian edition of a classical author will bear marks of haste, or inattentiveness in seeing a book through the press, the second edition bears witness to a returning to the manuscript, a making of corrections, and an effort towards improvement.[22]

Adjectives like 'cavalier' and 'spasmodic' have been applied to his critical use of manuscripts that came his way, and it must be noted as well that much of the drudgery of collation, and other aspects of preparing and correcting the editions to which he put his name, were turned over to assistants inevitably less qualified than he. Yet one would not do justice as an editor without recognising, as Thomson has done, 'an exquisitely sensitive linguistic attunement both to the *nuances* of the Latin written (and spoken) at various periods, and to the personal style of the author against the background of contemporary usage'; a second critical tool was 'Erasmus' wide *historical* grasp'.[23]

The edition of Jerome, first published in 1516, was revised in 1524 and would see yet another edition (1533) before Erasmus' death. There were also editions of Arnobius (1522), Hilary (1523), Ambrose (1528–9), and Lactanius (1529). Augustine appeared in ten stout folio volumes during 1528–9, straining even the presses of

Froben. Still other Church Fathers received editorial attention from Erasmus while he was in Freiburg after 1529, among them Chrysostom, Basil, and the thirteenth-century Franciscan, Haymo of Faversham.

In 1527 Erasmus published an edition of the *Chrysostomi Lucubrationes*, dedicated to king John III of Portugal.[24] In the dedicatory epistle Erasmus wrote of Chrysostom that there is nothing in Sacred Scripture so deeply buried that Chrysostom cannot make it dramatic: 'He digs out hidden aspects, displays them and presents them to the eye, and does so as one might hold the attention of the viewer with an exceptionally well-executed painting' (Epistle 1800, 24 March 1527, translated M.A. Haworth in Hillerbrand, 195).

These patristic editings alone would win honours for an average scholar, then or now; but of course they were only part of Erasmus' steady flow of scholarly output. Rudolf Pfeiffer has justly commented that 'If we brought together all these editions of Erasmus, it would be a mountain of volumes. We can hardly imagine how difficult it was to explore the world of manuscripts at that time and to make careful collations. Later editors usually complain that Erasmus did not make sufficient use of manuscript readings, but relied too much on conjectures'.[25] One may accept the evaluation of J. de Ghellinck on Erasmus' edition of Augustine and other Church Fathers: that Erasmus did not aim at an absolute precision of text, as a modern textual scholar would do, nor did he aim at making his annotations a work of pure learning, as later scholars like J.J. Scaliger would do.[26] A more gracious evaluation is that of Pelikan: 'the most prominent of the accomplishments of Erasmus lie in the area of "sacred philology". Many of the Church Fathers, Greek as well as Latin, owe the first printed editions of their writings to his tireless activity as scholar and publisher'.[27] Pfeiffer rightly stresses the effort of his editions to provide instructions to the reader for the understanding of both the language and the subject-matter (78).

By 1529 Erasmus' educational programme was firmly in place. He himself drew up lists of his writings, in the letter to Botzheim of 1523–4 (Allen I, 38 ff.), and in the proposed edition of his works after his death (*CWE* 24: 693–702). In the first volume of his collected works were to be those *'quae spectant ad institutionem literarum'*: 'that concern literature and education'. *De Copia* and *De Ratione Studii, Parabolae* and *Antibarbari* had all already appeared before 1521; these works are all in volume 23 of *CWE*. To them must be added *De Conscribendis Epistolis* of 1522 (in *CWE* 25) and the dialogue *De recta Latini Graecique sermonis pronuntiatione* of 1528 (in *CWE* 26). The first is the better known work in the twentieth century, and it can be taken up summarily.

De Conscribendis was immediately popular, and there were more than twenty-eight editions in Erasmus' lifetime, and at least another sixty in the rest of the century (*CWE* 25:1ii). It was used in both Lutheran and Jesuit schools and adopted in dozens of English grammar schools for boys in the upper forms. It has sensible categories of letters, and for each Erasmus commented on such concerns as style, arrangement and tone, using examples taken from his own letters or of his own devising. Throughout there are vivid passages and many anecdotes that give us glimpses of the life and people of his age. Near the end of the prefatory essay of the manual – for such it is – Erasmus declares, 'my remarks have been intended more for the teachers than for the pupils' (38). The epistle was one of the most popular literary forms of the age, and Erasmus was a vital force for many student-generations, providing examples and instructing them on the art of the letter.[28]

De recta Latini Graecique sermonis pronuntiatione is a lively dialogue in which an emended pronunciation is argued for. The so called Erasmian pronunciation (for which he was not the first)[29] means that 'modern Greeks to a man – except for the few trained philologists among them – curse him loud and long. Having learnt the language from books, rather than from the lips of Greeks, he very naturally insisted on the pronunciation that had been current at the time when the script was formed'.[30] The foundation for all that follows the first introduction to classical languages is the ability to read and write, and – an innovative stress with Erasmus – to speak those languages.[31] The second part of the dialogue is a spirited and clear presentation of the principles of classicism. There are anecdotes from the ancients as well as from contemporary life. The dialogue was immediately popular, and it has remained a major text in the twin worlds of education and scholarship. After the first edition of 1528 it was reprinted in 1529, 1530, 1531; and in France, Italy, and Germany as well as Switzerland (*CWE* 26). The *Ciceronianus* was also published in 1528, and it was discussed in the previous chapter, in a context of concerns of style.

What Thompson has called a bold claim for the achievement of Erasmus has been made by R.R. Bolgar: that Erasmus is 'the greatest man we come across in the history of education'.[32] It is bold, Thompson comments (*CWE* 23:1xviii), 'because education is an activity as old as civilization; and Erasmus himself knew the mettle of Greeks before Plato (whom he probably would have named for the highest honour as an educator), and there have been great names in education since Erasmus'. When John Colet wrote to thank Erasmus for his *De ratione studii* in 1511, he expressed the hope that Erasmus might be one of his teachers; failing that, he would be grateful for 'some assistance, if only in training teachers' (Epistle 230, *CWE* 2:174/15–16; Allen I, 470/13): 'O Erasmus, how I have longed to have you as a teacher in our school!' He was a teacher (thus chapter 14 argues), but in the programme that was being unfolded at Basel he comes forward as a teacher of teachers.

The reformers were gaining power everywhere, it seemed: in Basel as also in Bern and Zürich, in Strasbourg and in so many places in Germany. But the exodus from Basel would not happen until 1529 (chapter 42).

Yet there had been other changes painful to Erasmus. One such was the death of Froben in October 1527, and earlier in 1527 the death of his bishop, the loyal friend and man of integrity, Utenheim, had been another blow. On Froben, Erasmus wrote a formal letter that is eulogistic: to Jan van Hemstede, a member of the Carthusians in Louvain.[33] Froben is praised for his love of learning; he seemed born to honour and illuminate learning (lines 68 ff.). His death is described in the loving detail of a saint's life (92–120): thus was our Froben released from mortal affairs, and thus has he passed to a happier life. We should pray for the deceased, celebrate his memory, and support the publishing house of Froben ('*officinae Frobenianae*') – may that which he instituted move forward to something even better. The death of Froben moved Erasmus greatly, and that year his mood oscillated from optimism to pessimism, sometimes even in the same letter. Thus in writing to the Spanish humanist Maldonatus in Epistle 1805 (30 March 1527) he spoke of the world awakening from lethargy and exclaimed that all the young were turning to languages and *bonae literae* (lines 209–211). Yet towards the end of the letter Erasmus laments that no one is reforming his life, and everyone is out for his own advantage (lines 244–45).

Despite distractions and the pitch of strife and disorder that led him to say in Epistle 1805 that 'we priests scarcely dared set foot outside our doors' (lines 241–2), and despite almost constant pain – a steady note in the story of his life – Erasmus had been prodigiously productive during his Basel years. Not only was there a great number of writings during these years, but some of his most original and most characteristic works came into being or flowered.

Notes

1) The annuity granted by the emperor continued, though Erasmus did not regularly receive the moneys, partly because of the disorder of imperial finances, partly because the agent Pierre Barbier was untrustworthy. In letters of July 1529 (Ep. 2192 to Fugger, Allen VIII, 225/96) and August 1534 (Ep. 2961 to Justus Decius, Allen XI, 30 ff.) Erasmus complained that his pension had been seven years unpaid, and that Barbier had once robbed him of one hundred florins: '*Adhuc verbis amicus est, sed in pecuniaria re perfidissimus*' (Allen XI, 32/55–6).

2) There were half a dozen editions of this late work during Erasmus' final months, and there have been many more, with translations into French, Spanish, Czech, Dutch, German and English.

3) See Smith 259 & nn. 2 & 3 on funds from England.

4) Preserved Smith has written on Erasmus' role in the divorce business: 'German Opinion of the Divorce of Henry VIII', *EHR* (1912) 671 ff. It is interesting to note that Catherine was impressed by Erasmus' *De Libero Arbitrio* (Ep. 1513) and read his *De praeparatione ad mortem* only a few months before her own death (Ep. 3090); *BR*.

5) The problem of Henry's divorce did not go away, and Thomas More was ineluctably caught in its meshes; but Erasmus' silence apparently was construed by some to mean he approved of it. In 1533, writing to Damian a Goes from Freiburg (Ep. 2846), he mentioned a visit two years earlier by two members of the emperor's court who had asked for his views on the case; and there is reason to believe that he had been approached by an envoy interested from the point of view of Henry (Allen X, 271). To the emperor's courtiers Erasmus answered that he had not given his attention to this question – an equivocation – and he went on to say that it would be very easy to pronounce what she would like, but to declaim on what the divine or human law might permit would require not only a lengthy study but also a knowledge of the circumstances of the case (Allen X, 273/73–6).

6) See August Rüegg, *Die beiden Blütezeiten des Basler Humanismus* (Basel, 1960), esp. I. Teil, 'Der Humanismus im Renaissancezeitalter und die Gründung der Basler Universität'. Among the several studies of Guido Kisch that bear on Basel and its university, one should cite *Erasmus und die Jurisprudenz seiner Zeit* (Basel, 1960).

7) Thus Bietenholz in *BR*, who adds valuable information on Erasmus' seeking theological advice of Baer, and Baer's careful examinations of Erasmus' positions on key questions. Baer, Bietenholz further notes, 'attempted to mediate in Erasmus' conflicts with Hutten, Eppendorf, and Pelargus'.

8) See H. Meylan, 'Erasme et Pellican', in *Colloquium Erasmianum* (Mons, 1968) 244–54.

9) Two areas of his scholarship merit special attention, geography and music. Glareanus published a map of the world in 1510, which presents the eastern coastline of America with considerable accuracy, and in 1527 he published his *De geographica*, a scientific description of Asia, Africa, and Europe; see my monograph on *The Geography of Erasmus* (forthcoming). It is in the field of music that he won a permanent reputation, and his *Dodecachordon* (1547, but written between 1519 and 1533) offers a harmonis-

ing of christian religion and classical education (cf. the work of Meier and Lichtenhahn cited in *BR*).

10) See my essay on 'Humanism and Jurisprudence' in *Renaissance Humanism*, ed A. Rabil (1988).

11) See Guido Kisch, *Claudius Cantiuncula: Ein Basler Jurist und Humanist des 16. Jahrhunderts* (Basel, 1970). He points out that the Erasmian *philosophia Christi* was vital for Cantiuncula's concept of equity (which was greatly influential), and that Cantiuncula was also indebted to the *Ratio verae theologiae* (90). See also *Erasmus und die Jurisprudenz seiner Zeit* (1960), esp. 1 ff. on '*Summum ius, summa iniuria*'.

12) See Ernst Gerhard Rüsch, 'Erasmus in St. Gallen', in his *Vom Heiligen in der Welt* (Biel, 1959) 57; and G. Kisch, 'Vadians Valla-Ausgaben' in *Aus Vadians Freundes- und Schülerkreis in Wien* by Conradin Bonorand (St. Gallen, 1965).

13) J. M. Kittelson, *Wolfgang Capito: From Humanist to Reformer* (Leiden, 1975).

14) One must distinguish, however, between the two in terms of learning. Amerbach received an MA from Paris and had what Allen calls a 'vigorous Latinity' with some knowledge of Greek, whereas Froben had little Latin and doubtless little formal education, and Erasmus scorned his Latin and may have written publisher's prefaces for him. Yet each in his way was supportive of humanistic scholarship: Amerbach with his dream of editing the Fathers of the Church (completed by Froben), and Froben with his support of Erasmian and other humanistic scholarship. Each secured the support of the best possible scholars and made his press into a publishing-scholarly team: with Amerbach, Trithemius, Wimpheling, Brant and Reuchlin; with Froben, Reuchlin, Erasmus and other scholars, and there was a '*sodalitas*' that included the talented Amerbach sons, Beatus Rhenanus, Glareanus, Pellicanus, Nesen, Listrius and others.

15) What a heritage there was from that one small school in a modest Alsatian city!

16) E. -W. Kohls, 'Martin Bucer: Erasmien et Martinien', in *Strasbourg au coeur religieux du XVIᵉ siècle* (Strasbourg, 1977) 167–83.

17) See Smith 377, with citations from a number of sources.

18) See G. Kisch, *Consilia*: and Schoeck, 'Humanism and Jurisprudence', in *Renaissance Humanism*, ed. A. Rabil (1988) III, 310 ff. Smith notes that Erasmus' *consilium* is not published in his works but is preserved in the Basel archives (387 n. 1); it is not in Ferguson's *Erasmi Opuscula*, however.

19) Froben died in October 1527, and Paracelsus lost a valuable supporter in Basel; the following year he was dismissed from his post as town physician and lecturer in medicine at the university. Paracelsus was an innovator: he lectured in Swiss German rather than Latin, rejected much of Galen, and publicly burned Avicenna (*BR*).

20) Smith 261, and appendix 25 in Allen XI.

21) Thus Maurice Pope in *CWE* 26:348.

22 P.S. Allen has remarked on the techniques employed by Aldus in his printing of Erasmus: 'In the translation he invited Aldus to correct evident mistakes, and even to make more disputable changes if he had a clear view: but typographical accuracy the author felt to be no part of his own responsi-

bility. "You will probably find a number of printer's errors: please have a sharp lookout kept for these".' ('Erasmus' Relations with his printers', in *Erasmus* [1934] 120.) I am not so confident as Allen that the text of Erasmus indicates that he felt no responsibility for typographical accuracy: rather that the major responsibility was Aldus'. In later letters we read of Erasmus reading proof himself. Kenney observes that the tendency to rely on printer and printing-house staff 'to see to the correctness of details persisted long after Erasmus' day' – E.J. Kenney, *The Classical Text* (1974) 51, citing Percy Simpson, *Proof-reading in the sixteenth, seventeenth and eighteenth centuries* (1935, rptd. 1970) ch. III, 'Correctors of the press', 110–68.

23) D.F.S. Thomson, 'Erasmus and Textual Scholarship in the Light of Sixteenth-Century Practice', in *Erasmus of Rotterdam: the Man and the Scholar,* ed. J. Sperna Weiland and W. Th. M. Frijhoff (Leiden, 1988) 158–71.

24) 'Since there was no acknowledgment of the dedication, Erasmus withdrew it when he published the works of Chrysostom in 1530' (Hillerbrand, 195n); but Allen notes (VI, 483n) that the central portion was incorporated in Erasmus' fuller edition of Chrysostom (Basel, 1530).

25) R. Pfeiffer, *History of Classical Scholarship, 1300–1850* (1976) 78. But textual criticism was in its infancy and in fact Erasmus was instrumental in bringing it to its maturity. See Reynolds & Wilson, *Scribes and Scholars*, 146, where we find the judgment that 'he made judicious use of such manuscripts as he could muster, but they seem to have been an indifferent lot...'

26) Beatus Rhenanus stands between Erasmus and the late-16th.c. scholars like Scaliger: see D'Amico, *Theory and Practice in Renaissance Textual Scholarship* (1988); and A. Grafton, *Joseph Scaliger: A Study in the History of Classical Scholarship*, I (Oxford, 1983). See J. de Ghellink in *Miscellanea J. Gessler* (1948) I, 530 ff.

27) Thus J. Pelikan: 'The most prominent of the accomplishments of Erasmus lie in the area of "sacred philology". Many of the Church Fathers, Greek as well as Latin, owe the first printed editions of their writings to his tireless activity as scholar and publisher': *The Melody of Theology*, 71.

28) See the concise introduction in *CWE* 25. For a general view, see Cecil H. Clough, 'The Cult of Antiquity: Letters and Letter Collections', in *Cultural Aspects of the Italian Renaissance: Essays in Honour of Paul Oskar Kristeller,* ed. C.H. Clough (Manchester, 1976). In this essay Clough remarks that 'by the turn of the fifteenth century the letter was replacing the oration as the prime means by which scholars, and particularly those devoted to the cult of Antiquity, disseminated their ideas and made their case in scholarly controversy' (33). Judith Rice Henderson, 'Erasmus and the Art of Letter-Writing', in *Renaissance Eloquence*, ed. J.J. Murphy (Berkeley/Los Angeles, 1983) 331–55, is an admirable bibliographical survey of scholarship on the renaissance epistle and introduction to Erasmian theory.

29) That was the Spanish humanist Antonius Nebrissensis (or Nebrija): see Ingram Bywater, 'The Erasmian pronunciation of Greek and its precursors' (London, 1908). On Nebrissensis (1444–1522) see *BR*, which notes Erasmus' praise of Nebrija in Ep. 1111 to Vives.

30) Pfeiffer, *History of Classical Scholarship*, 42.

31) The emphasis is on Latin and Greek – 'the only languages where the standard of excellence is permanent and which are immune from change or

decay' (*CWE* 26:349) – but vernacular languages received attention as well, for they have their usefulness for everyday needs. The greatest number of vernacular words in *De Pronuntiatione* come not surprisingly from Dutch, but there are examples drawn from English, French, Frisian, German, and even Swabian, the dialect of the region around Freiburg (*CWE* 26:640–1); and there are discussions of pronunciation in these languages and also Italian, Polish, Scots, Spanish, and even the Westphalian dialect (see Index, 642–4).

32) Bolgar, *The Classical Heritage and Its Beneficiaries* (Cambridge, 1954) 336.

33) Jan Symons was a native of a village named Heemstede near Haarlem, who studied at Cologne and received an MA from Louvain. He had some reputation as a painter, but (having entered the Charterhouse in 1521) he also became a member of a circle of humanists. Jan wrote to Erasmus after the death of Dorp (Ep. 1646 of November 1527), and there are traces of other letters sent to Heemstede (*BR*). This letter of 1527 was followed by two epitaphs by Erasmus (Reedijk, *Poems*, 116–7; Allen VII, 119). Erasmus dedicated to him an edition of the commentaries on the Psalms attributed to Haimo of Halberstadt (1533), Ep. 2771. Still, Erasmus' writing the eulogy of Froben in a letter to Jan is rather puzzling: why him, who does not appear to have known Froben? Perhaps Froben had shared Erasmus' respect for the Carthusian order and there is a Carthusian connection.

The Freiburg Years, 1529–1535

God is like the brilliant chorus-leader of a play who introduces
various characters on to the stage of life and has a reward ready
for all who properly play the role He has assigned.

> Erasmus to Jacopo Sadoleto, 7 March 1531, Epistle 2443

The greatest good fortune, even greater than health, for the old
person is to have his world still inhabited by projects; then,
busy and useful, he escapes both from boredom and from
decay.

> Simone de Beauvoir, *Old Age*, 548

To give me a position of rank would be like piling up treasures
on the back of an old worn-out nag, now that the course of my
life is almost run.

> Erasmus to Bernard of Cles, May 1532, Epistle 2651
> (trans. M. A. Haworth in Hillerbrand 261)

Basel had become a city of factions. The leader of the conservatives
was Ludwig Baer, still rector of the university but 'a living corpse'
who had just married a widow of twenty.[1] Against the pressuring of
Oecolampadius, who had become the minister of St Martin's church
and leader of the reform movement in Basel, Baer strove for moderation. The position of the town council of Basel was that no one
should be compelled to go either to Mass or to the reformed services,
and everyone should be free to follow his own conscience. As
Wackernagel notes, this meant – or would have meant – pluralism
within a single city.[2] But such a compromise was unacceptable to
extremists like Oecolampadius. A violent turn came on 9 February
1529.

Several hundred men gathered in the Barfüsserkirche and demanded the abolition of the Mass; the council began its deliberations
but reached no decision by nightfall. Next day while the council
again sat, the mob moved angrily from the Marktplatz to the cathedral square and began smashing the images of the Münster and other
churches. The scene has been described by Bainton:

> In the morning Basel looked upon the broken idols, torsos,

heads, arms and legs in wood and stone, shreds of painted
canvas, fragments of stained glass and glittering decorations, all
in heaps of rubble. The wood was offered to the poor and when
they quarrelled over the pieces, the council ordered all to be
burned. For two days and two nights fire consumed the residue
of generations of piety. The images were gone. The Mass was
gone.[3]

Erasmus was happy that no blood had been shed in the iconoclasm;
writing to Cricius from Freiburg in July of that year (Epistle 2201)
he looked back at the memory of the violence and then exclaimed
that when he thought of what had happened to those who mocked
the wounds of St Francis he could only wonder at the patience of
Christ and the Virgin (Allen VIII, 245/44, 246/49). Out of a characteristic regard for civility and consensus he refused to join the radi-
cals, and quietly but firmly began to think in terms of moving to
Freiburg: not too distant from Basel, and under the jurisdiction of
the archduke Ferdinand, who had been inviting him to come to
Vienna. Others felt much the same; almost immediately after the
riotous smashing of statues in the Münster and other churches, there
was something of an exodus by the university faculty, who were
largely catholic.[4] He set about shipping his books down the Rhine.[5]

On the 13 April a quiet crowd gathered at the Rhine bridge to
watch their Erasmus, the famous scholar known to all Europe, as he
said goodbye to friends, and embarked.[6] Even Oecolampadius, 'that
most implacable reformer',[7] begged him to stay.

Situated above sixty kilometres north of Basel by road – but it was
possible to travel most of the distance by boat[8] – Freiburg-im-
Breisgau is located at the foot of the Schlossberg in the Schwarzwald;
it is an archiepiscopal see with one of the finest Gothic minsters in
Germany; and its university was founded by archduke Albert VI of
Austria, in 1457.

There were other possibilities. England, as always (though there
would have had to be the dreaded channel crossing, now too threatening to his health); but no longer France. The Low Countries, but
Louvain was a nettle. Italy, but it was now too far, and still dangerous. Freiburg was close, and there were several warm friends, among
them Ulrich Zasius, professor of jurisprudence, who in 1518 had
addressed Erasmus as 'my great patron deity' (Epistle 857, *CWE*
6:71/29; Allen III, 361/24–5).

A house awaited him through the good offices of Johannes Fabri, a
native of the Allgaü in Upper Bavaria,[9] whom Erasmus had known
since about 1513. Fabri, adviser to archduke Ferdinand since 1523,
arranged for him to have what was reputedly the finest house in

Freiburg, having been built by the Imperial Treasurer in 1516, and known then as the 'White Lily'. But there were two drawbacks: he had to pay a substantial rent, and he had to share the place with Othmar Nachtgall (Luscinius).[10] Nachtgall had already been assigned the ground-floor apartment, and Erasmus was then given the floor above. But personalities flared: Erasmus felt that he should have the whole house, and there was trouble between him and Nachtgall.[11] An uneasy peace was restored, at least on the surface (Epistles 2676, 2818); and Nachtgall withdrew to the Carthusian monastery near Freiburg, to which he left all his property (*BR*).

Erasmus moved out of the 'White Lily' into a house on Schiffstrasse (now number 7, and occupied by a brewery but with an inscription to mark the residence of Erasmus). He rented it at first, then bought it for a thousand gulden, and he sold it when he returned to Basel in 1535.[12] A chapter of canons came with him from the Basel cathedral, and some of them were given teaching positions. Erasmus was enrolled on 5 August 1533 as 'Desiderius Erasmus Roterodamus theologiae professor',[13] thus enabling him to secure the (then) professional privilege of freedom from taxes (Smith, 405). He had a few students with him as *famuli*, as was his habit.[14] The most important of these, and closest to Erasmus, was Gilbert Cousin, or Cognatus, whom we have already met.

Despite his failing health, Erasmus made one more trip away from home, this time it was another visit to Besançon in the autumn of 1531, perhaps to 'quench his thirst with good Burgundian wine'. But the invitation had come from the secretary to the town council of Besançon, Jean Lambelin,[15] and the venerable humanist was well received; even, apparently, receiving an invitation from the magistrates to settle there (Smith, 405). Erasmus had thoughts of going on to Lyon, which he had visited a quarter-century earlier; but the war between Savoy and Bern, and a letter from Charles V, prevented him (Smith, 405). Partly through Desprez, a relative, Erasmus kept in touch with Lambelin (*BR*).

The happy product of this or an earlier Besançon visit was his meeting Cognatus, who became more than a *famulus* and something like a companion and associate in scholarly study.[16]

During his stay in Freiburg Erasmus suffered the death of many friends: not only in Rome but also in England, France, Germany and Poland (Epistle 2867/12–3). This inevitable consequence of growing old was part of his general sense (as he told Tunstall) that there is little time left to live.[17] Events in England were especially disturbing, and at the end of 1532 he wrote to Johannes Fabri, bishop of Vienna, about the rumour (spread all the way to Vienna) that Sir

Thomas More had been removed from office; and in this letter he gave a conspectus of More as an officer of state.[18] Erasmus was aware that he was in prison for many months, thus explaining one of the periods of silence between the two friends, for he would not have risked writing to him there. In August of 1535 Erasmus wrote to Bartholomaeus Latomus, commenting on his own old age and the death of More:

> If I should number my years, I have lived long ... whereas the King gave Fisher his red hat by beheading him ... it is all too true that Thomas More has been in prison for a long time, and that his properties have been forfeited to the royal treasury. It is also rumoured that he has suffered the ultimate penalty, but I do not know that for certain. *Would that he had never mixed with this perilous business, and had left a theological matter to the theologians.*[19]

The letter ends with a return to the question of Erasmus' own health:

> ... I am living only from day to day, expecting death and even sometimes desiring it, so severe are my sufferings. It is scarcely safe for me to put a foot outside my bedroom, and I am upset by the most foolish little things. This thin and fragile little body cannot bear a breeze unless it is balmy. (Allen XI, 217/94–8)

When the definite word of the death of Fisher and More did reach Erasmus only a short time later,[20] he spoke out unequivocally: 'In England, what happened to the Bishop of Rochester and to Thomas More, the holiest and sweetest pair of men that England ever had ...' (Allen XI, 221/160–2). With utmost simplicity and directness of feeling he added: 'In More I feel as if I myself had died, for there was but one soul between the two of us, as Pythagoras says' (lines 163–4). But such are the tides of human affairs (164).

Together with Philippus Montanus and Cognatus, Erasmus was involved in the publication and circulation of the so-called Paris Newsletter: *Expositio fidelis de morte D. Thomae Mori et quorundam aliorum insignium virorum in Anglia* (BR, with references given there).

When his friends suffered family losses, Erasmus was quick to write a letter of consolation. To Botzheim he wrote in August 1529 an epistle (2205) filled with consolation from Scripture, and the message is to accept what the Lord has sent, and to find solace in the thought that He knows what is best for us. Even in the political troubles we should cry out to the Lord and not to this or that ruler, and certainly not to armies. Erasmus rose to the occasion by turning to the music now heard in churches – a subject on which he had pronounced views (Epistle 1756/83–112) – and on illiterate priests who say Mass like a cobbler making shoes. Perhaps such thoughts would take Botzheim away from his grieving. To an even closer friend, Bonifacius Amerbach, Erasmus wrote in July 1532 (Epistle 2684) on the death of his dear daughter, and after other consolatory thoughts he gave the example of the mother of John Colet, a woman of rare piety, who had borne eleven sons by the same husband, only one of whom, John Colet, survived to adulthood; yet in her ninetieth year she was full of gaiety, eventually outliving even her son John. It was piety, her devotion to God, that sustained her. I know you will say (he goes on), 'that I am late to console, and even offering scolding instead of consolation' (lines 89–90). God sometimes takes away what we have loved excessively: in human affairs, and in this occurrence, there is a certain Nemesis (118–23).

Again and again, as we have seen, Erasmus spoke of his own frailty, and he was at times quite detailed in describing his illnesses (and not only in writing to friends who were physicians). Perhaps the most moving is the self-portrait or sketch that he sent in 1533 to Eustace Chapuys, the imperial ambassador to England from 1529 to 1544: 'I do not know what picture you have seen in my writings that led you to form such a strong affection, for I know that everything about me is less than mediocre', he wrote in this first extant letter between them.

> You would not see a human being, but a mass of wrinkled skin, and one who is utterly wretched, unless we could convince ourselves that once this hide is sloughed off there will emerge a fresh creature with the gleam of youth. Evidently you also realize the waves that toss me about and the winds that buffet me. But a harbour is coming into sight, not far away, which with Christ's blessing will put an end to all my woes ... [21]

Not long after moving to Freiburg he had fallen seriously ill, and to Melanchthon in July 1530 he described his symptoms graphically:

> This is now the fourth month of my illness. First I suffered from colic, then from vomiting, and the vomiting ruined my whole stomach. This poor little body of mine does not get along very well with doctors. All the medicines they gave me did me harm. The colic was followed by an ulcer, or more accurately, by a hard swelling which first extended all along the lower right groin. Then it centered on the pit of my stomach, almost like a dragon with its teeth biting my navel while the rest of its body was writhing and its tail stretching towards my loins; when its head was fastened tight it coiled around to the left side of my navel, with its tail almost encircling it. It caused constant, sometimes unbearable pain. I could not eat or sleep or write or read or dictate or listen to anyone reading: I could not even

converse with friends. A surgeon was called and almost murdered me with his powerful plasters. Finally I underwent surgery. After that I was reconciled with sleep as the pain was relieved. I am still crawling around feebly, and the surgeon has not as yet released me. (Epistle 2343, Allen VIII, 474/5–19; translated by M. A. Haworth in Hillerbrand, 239–40)

Erasmus continued to work, although not surprisingly (given his long bouts of severe illness) there are strong indications that he did not keep up with the flood of publications just after 1530. Vives provides one example, which can be illustrative. Bietenholz has observed that his *De disciplinis*, published in 1531, with a Cologne printing of 1532 (BM Catalogue) – an encyclopedic survey of the world of learning –

> contains an original inquiry into the working of history, based upon texts which Erasmus never bothered to analyze more fully, in particular Cicero's *De oratore* but probably also Politian's preface to Suetonius mentioned above. Nor did Erasmus ever discuss the views of Vives and he may not have realized that Vives' grasp of the subject of history, in keeping with the whole book, was outstanding.[22]

The bulk of the *Ecclesiastes* was written in Freiburg, but it was finally printed at Antwerp in late August 1535. This was the manual on preaching that for many years he had been exhorted to write,[23] and not only was it Eramus' last major work (other than editions that saw light in Basel the next year), it was his longest work. Through the years preceding 1535 Erasmus worked on *Ecclesiastes* off and on, and although the writing was not completely congenial he considered it an important work. It had a very wide circulation: within the year there were three additional printings in Antwerp and Basel, and three more before the *Opera* of 1540. After an initial printing of 2,600 copies, which was quite unusual for the time, 'it ran through nine other editions – some authorized, some pirated. It was, without doubt, one of the best sellers of the decade' (O'Malley, 2). O'Malley concludes his careful study by declaring it 'a major monument in the long history and continuing influence of the classical tradition in western culture. Above all, it is a major monument – perhaps *the* major monument – in the history of sacred rhetoric. Its only rival is the *De doctrina christiana* of Augustine' (29).

A new edition of the New Testament appeared in 1535, and there were several editions of classical authors during his Freiburg period: Suetonius (1533), Aristotle (1531), and Ptolemy (1530). Several editions by him of the Church Fathers came to fruition during these years: Chrysostom (1530, 1536), Algerus (1530), Basil (1532), Haymo (1533). Remarkably, and well-nigh heroically, for an old man in poor health, he continued to work at almost his old pace.

Works of a moral or religious nature can also be cited. In 1533 his *Explanatio symboli apostolorum sive catechismus* was published, dedicated to Thomas Boleyn, father of Anne, who also requested the *Praeparatio ad mortem*, which reached him in time to be of practical use for his own execution.[24] The first work, a catechism, is a brief exposition of what Erasmus saw as the essential articles of faith, and predictably it was hotly denounced by Luther, who remained bitter towards Erasmus even at his death. The essential articles are contained in the Apostles' Creed, on which he stresses two main points. Although it is not the work of the apostles, the creed is to be received because it carries the consensus of the Church, and Erasmus was almost always deferential to the principle of consensus. The second point is the stress on the inwardness of religion: Faith (as Bainton glosses it, 267), is not mere belief, but rather total commitment; and the inner reality of belief is the overwhelming reality.

The *Praeparatio ad mortem* takes us back to the spirit of the *Enchiridion*, for 'meditation on death is meditation on true life'.

There is almost a fascination in Erasmus' descriptions of his own illness: the relish of the novelist who describes his own feeling and symptoms. It may be that at a time when Melanchthon was writing to Erasmus from the Diet of Augsburg, opened by the emperor Charles V on 25 June 1530, he took advantage of his legitimate excuse. But in the same month he was writing to Johannes Rinck, a staunch Roman Catholic from Cologne, in much the same vein.[25] Erasmus did not attend the Diet, but he was plied with letters from both sides; fourteen are extant from Erasmus to members of the Diet, and there are eight replies. As Bainton remarks, 'Erasmus had sharp comments for them all. He cannot be accused of trimming in this instance'(26). He did indicate that he approved of certain reforms, including having the Eucharist administered in both kinds, allowing the marriage of priests, and regulating or abolishing private masses.

As a final effort towards mediation the Diet must be judged a failure. The Protestants read their Confession (so much the effort of Melanchthon) on 25 June, but the Catholic majority voted that they were to recant before the following April or be treated as schismatics.[26]

Gattinara, grand chancellor of Charles V since 1518 and elevated to the cardinalate on 13 August 1529, died at Innsbruck en route to the Diet; sympathetic to the moderate views of Erasmus[27], he would have been a peacemaker there. The absence of Erasmus was also felt, and even after the close of the Diet appeals were made to him to act as arbitrator.[28]

Erasmus' *Liber de sarcienda ecclesiae concordia* ('book on mending the peace of the Church') appeared in 1533, but it had been in progress for some time. Perhaps the most attractive of the appeals made to Erasmus after the Diet of Augsburg was that of Julius Pflug, who on 12 May 1531 wrote from Leipzig that if he would intercede with Melanchthon (or some other good man), concessions might still be made on the catholic side. Erasmus replied, with characteristic wit, that he was tired of trying to mediate and felt like the man who in trying to separate two gladiators is himself killed by their swords (Epistle 2522, Allen IX, 322/173).

But his book on mending the peace was nonetheless one final effort. The prefatory letter to Pflug is dated 31 July 1533 (Epistle 2852). In this little book he begins by discoursing on the words of Psalm 84 (85), v.11: 'See, where mercy and faithfulness meet in one; how justice and peace are united in one embrace!' He recommended above all tolerance in trifles, and also the prohibiting of books likely to disturb public order; and he harkened back to a constant theme of his, that the best way to end schism and to restore order was for everyone to lead a good life.

A harmless essay Smith has termed it (364), but it produced a storm of anger from the reformers, and a condemnation years later by the Roman Catholics (364). It was reprinted at Antwerp, after its first edition in Basel, then Leipzig and Paris; within months it had two German translations, one Flemish, and one Danish.[29] It is interesting, if puzzling, Himelick writes (2), that 'such editions and translations as there were remain limited to areas most closely identified with evangelical reform' – except for Antwerp and Paris. More accurately described by Allen than by Smith, the *Concordia* is 'as torrential as the most fluent orator's tongue, whirling along in eddies and backrushes which sometimes return almost to their starting-point';[30] in sixteenth-century terms, it is a model of *copia* and good construction.[31]

A *famulus* of Erasmus named Hilarius Bertholf (Bertulf), who had been with Erasmus from 1521 until about 1527, moved to Lyon and apparently worked with Rabelais as well as for the printer Gryphius; he, his wife and their three children died of the plague in the summer of 1533 (*BR*).

It was apparently Bertholf who provided the connection between Rabelais and Erasmus that engendered the remarkable letter from Rabelais dated 30 November 1532 from Lyon:

George d'Armagnac, the famous Bishop of Rodez, recently sent me Flavius Josephus's *Jewish History of the Sack* [i.e., of Jerusalem] and asked me, for the sake of our old friendship, that, when I found a reliable man setting out I would send it to you at the first opportunity. I gladly seized that handle and occasion, kind father, of showing by a pleasing service with what devotion and piety I love you. I call you father; for, as we daily see that pregnant women nourish offspring which they have never seen and protect them from the harsh outer air, *the same has happened to you* who have educated me who am unknown to you and of simple estate. Thus have you hitherto nourished me with the most chaste breasts of your divine learning, so that, did I not ascribe to you alone my whole worth and being, I should be the most ungrateful of all men who are now alive or ever will be. Hail again and again, most beloved father, father and glory of your country, champion and *defender* of letters and unconquered fighter for the truth.[32]

If Erasmus did reply to Rabelais, the letter is not extant; if not, it may be that the letter arrived during one of his serious bouts of illness. Nonetheless, the indebtedness of Rabelais to the works of Erasmus is well known, and a modern editor of Rabelais' *Le tiers livre*[33] (to point to a single example) has demonstrated the quarrying of the *Adages* and other writings of Erasmus on every page. Erasmus wrote to Jean de Pins, an ecclesiastic who was a humanist himself and patron of a humanist circle at Toulouse, to thank him for the Josephus, having written to him in 1532 (Epistle 2628) to request the manuscript for Hieronymus Froben (*BR*).[35]

To be sure there was important work yet to be done at the Froben press in Basel, but that might have happened even with Erasmus in Freiburg. However, a vital edition and one more treatise would see the light of day in Basel, and Erasmus felt that he must be on hand.

The decision to return to Basel was thus less for reasons of religion than had been the case with the decision to leave the city in 1529. Every place, it seemed, was becoming more intolerant, and he had even advised a catholic at Augsburg to leave the city if it became Protestant.[36]

Even more likely is the interpretation that it was a call for help from Bonifacius Amerbach, who was made rector of the university on 1 May 1535, that pulled Erasmus back to Basel. The university (as Bainton notes, 264) was nearly extinct: 'the enrolment in the university of Basel in 1521 was sixty, in 1528 only one, and in 1529 none at all'.[37] Two weeks after being made rector Amerbach went to Freiburg in order to bring back Erasmus to Basel, and as Reedijk has plausibly suggested, the help of the aged scholar – whose reputation was still high away from Wittenberg, and whose learning was still impressive – was sought for the sake of the university.[38]

And so back to Basel he went in the summer of 1535, probably between mid-June and early August (see Epistles 3028 and 3032).[39]

Notes

1) So described by Bonifacius Amerbach (q. by Bainton, *Erasmus*, 218–9).

2) See R. Wackernagel, *Geschichte der Stadt Basel*, III (Basel, 1924) 490, 496.

3) Wackernagel, 494, 501, 507, 509–11; Bainton, 220. See now C.M.N.Eire, *Against the Idols: The Reformation of Worship From Erasmus to Calvin* (Cambridge, 1986) especially ch.4.

4) See Tracy, *Erasmus*, 211 and the authorities there cited.

5) Afterwards in Freiburg he lamented (Ep. 2203, the prefatory letter 'To the Reader' for his *Opus Epistolarum* of 1529), 'Because of moving (*migratio*) I have lost many things that I would now like to have; everything has really been confused' (Allen VIII, 250/24–6). We who have moved much in the 20th c. can sympathise.

6) See 'A Fish Diet' (*Ichthyophagia*, first published in 1526) for its expression of christian liberty (Thompson, *Colloquies*, 349–50) and with its sharply etched anecdote concerning hypocritical piety over fasting.

7) Bainton, 223. Guggisberg in *BR* calls attention to 'a last meeting [that] took place in Froben's garden shortly before Erasmus' departure for Freiburg. The two men parted in peace (Eps. 2158, 2196)'.

8) This was of importance, for Erasmus had been unable to ride horseback for two years and on the move from Basel to Freiburg he had to be carried in a litter (Ep. 2192 to Fugger, 7 July 1529; Allen VIII, 224/64 ff.).

9) Not to be confused with the Dominican Johannes Faber, our Fabri (1478–1541) was schooled at Constance and then Ulm, where he received the BA and possibly MA; at Tübingen, where he enrolled in theology and law, he came under the influence of a professor who directed him towards the *via antiqua* (the revised Thomist, Albertist, and Scotist schools [see *CHLMP*, 269] so that he was known to friends as a Scotist) and where he was ordained. In 1509 he matriculated at Freiburg and studied theology and law under Gregor Reisch, the author of the long-lived *Margarita philosophica* (1496), and Erasmus' predecessor as adviser to Froben on the great edition of Jerome, as well as Ulrich Zasius; he was awarded the doctorate of both laws (civil and canon) in 1510–11. In 1521 he was appointed suffragan bishop of Constance, in time for Erasmus' visit there. An adviser to archduke Ferdinand from 1523, Fabri had a wide range of duties and in 1530 he was to become bishop of Vienna, where he estabalished the Collegium Trilingue of St Nicholas (*BR*).

10) Nachtgall/Nachtigall (1487–1537) was a humanist, but a sometimes

testy one, who remained a Catholic but was bitter at the Church's failure to encourage and support humanists like Wimpheling and Erasmus – and himself. Born in Strasbourg he received his early education from Jakob Wimpheling and Johann Geiler; in 1508 he went to Paris to study philosophy and literature, becoming interested in classical literature; and he went on to study theology and canon law at Louvain and Padua. At Vienna he studied musical compositon under Wolfgang Grefinger. After a trip to Hungary and Greece he returned to Augsburg in 1511, and in 1514 to Strasbourg. He was a friend of Sturm, Gerbel, Brant, Wimpheling and Vogler, and himself a member of the Strasbourg humanist circle. Erasmus respected him for his knowledge of Greek and he prepared his own Greek grammar; he also worked on an edition of Aulus Gellius. Alienated from the Strasbourg literary circles for religious reasons, he left there in 1523 for Augsburg, and through the patronage of the Fuggers was named preacher and canon of St Maurice's, where he became a spokesman for the catholic cause; in September 1528 he denounced Luther and the Anabaptists from the pulpit, and for this he was forbidden to preach and retired to Freiburg (Ep. 2264, *BR*).

11) See Erasmus' letter to More (Ep. 2211) of 5 Sept. 1529 (Allen VIII, 273/72 ff.).

12) Smith, 404–5, with the documentation there cited.

13) H. Mayer, *Die Matrikeln der Universität Freiburg-im-Breisgau, 1460–1656* (1907); Smith, 405 n.

14) See F. Bierlaire, *La Familia d'Érasme*, 'Tableau Recapitulatif' between 39 & 40. During the Basel and Freiburg years he had the largest numbers of *famuli*; when he returned to Basel in 1535 he had only three.

15) Jean Lambelin (d. 1538) was sent to the Diet of Worms in the course of his duties as secretary to the town council, and he returned sympathetic to Lutheranism, stirring antagonism between the town on the one side and the archbishop and chapter on the other. After he signed a council edict against the Lutheran sect on 3 February 1537, he himself was 'charged with heresy, embezzlement, and abuse of his political powers. He was tortured with a new instrument of his own invention and beheaded on the market square, giving witness to his Protestant faith' (*BR*).

16) It is possible that Erasmus had actually met Cousin (1506–1572) in Freiburg where he may have been studying. In any case, he was badly needed in the summer of 1530 (Eps. 2348, 2349, 2381), and he became a valuable member of Eramus' household. Between Oct. and Nov. 1533 he visited Burgundy to accept a benefice, and brought back wine; in Dec. he went home again with letters pleading the case that he be allowed to hold the benefice while remaining in Erasmus' household (who would be a guarantor for his orthodoxy). There was a third trip to Burgundy around December 1534 to secure a canonry in Nazeroy; again he returned to serve Erasmus, with whom he moved from Freiburg to Basel in the summer of 1535. In Sept. he returned to Freiburg on business pertaining to the dissolution of Erasmus' household (Eps. 3052, 3055, 3059), planning a visit for Easter 1536, then autumn (Eps. 3104, 3122, 3118), but Eramus' death intervened. See the excellent essay on Cousin in *BR*, and Bierlaire, *La Familia* for his duties in the household. Cousin's own treatise on the office of *famulus*, Οἰκέτης (1535), is printed in Bierlaire.

17) Ep. 2263, 31 Jan. 1530: 'I have little time to live, for I am old and nursing a stone in the bladder, which is certain death'.

18) Ep. 2750 Allen X, 135–9, a summary which leads into a brief discussion of true nobility, a popular theme of the day.

19) Ep. 3048, Allen XI, 215/38–216/59–60. I have italicised the sentence dealing with More because it has been much quoted: taken out of context it has been much misunderstood. First, at this point Erasmus is not certain that More had been executed. Here, to a fellow Latinist, Erasmus is expressing a private opinion that in the Reformation too much has been taken out of the hands of trained theologians; see his letter of July 1533 to Damian a Goes (Ep. 2846 quoted above) to the point that the divorce question was a subject of debate among learned men for years. There is also implied the old wish that More had not been the King's Councillor so that he might have safely kept his own counsel. All of Europe was horrified when the news of More's execution reached them. Erasmus and Latomus (Bartholomaeus is not to be confused with Jacobus, who was an early 'Catholic critic' and remained opposed to Erasmus' scholarship and teaching) had been out of touch with each other for some years when Erasmus wrote an encouraging letter on the publication of Latomus' *Oratio de studiis humanitatis* (1534), the inaugural lecture upon Latomus' appointment to a professorship in Latin at Paris (see Ep. 3029 from Latomus on 29 June 1535). Erasmus' letter of August of the same year (Ep. 3048) is his reply (*BR*).

20) News from England was usually slow: Allen XI, 194 n. Correspondence between More and Erasmus had been interrupted, and Erasmus was careful not to put his friend in further jeopardy by writing to him in prison. It is the more striking therefore to note that More made a significant borrowing from Erasmus in his last Tower work, *De Tristia*, and one may well think of the whole of the *De Tristia* as a farewell message (although it is virtually certain that Erasmus never read his friend's final work). See Louis L. Martz, *Thomas More* (New Haven, Conn., 1990) 86–7, and the ed. by Clarence H. Miller (New Haven, Conn., 1976) on parallel passages between More's *De Tristia* and Erasmus' *Disputatiuncula de tedio, pavore, tristicia Jesu* ... (notes to 41/5–43/4, etc.).

21) Ep. 2798, Allen X, 206/26–35; trans. M. A. Haworth in Hillerbrand, 273–4. On Chapuys see *BR*. In this letter Erasmus is combining aspects of the humility *topos* with familiar classical *topoi* of sailing in high seas and looking forward to coming into safe harbour. Aspects of the description also suggest Job, but Erasmus does not presume to compare himself with Job, and when he does on his death-bed it is in jest.

22) P. G. Bietenholz, *History and Biography in the Work of Erasmus of Rotterdam* (Geneva, 1966) 16.

23) Fisher was among the friends making the request. J. W. O'Malley writes that Erasmus would have dedicated the work to Fisher had he not been executed shortly before it was published: 'Erasmus and the History of Sacred Rhetoric: The *Ecclesiastes* of 1535', ERSYB 5 (1985) 1–29.

24) See Smith, 285, citing several letters.

25) It was at the request of Rinck (whose father was a patron of Brant and Wimpheling, and who was himself a friend of Cochlaeus) for Erasmus to state his views on the Turkish question that Erasmus most promptly wrote

his *De bello turcico*, which is dedicated to Rinck (Ep. 3004, and *BR*).

26) Erasmus discussed these issues in a letter to an abbot at Lyon, Antoni (Ep. 2410, on 27 Nov. 1530). Antoni, or Antoine d'Albon/Dalbanus (1507–1574) had since 1525 been abbot of the ancient abbey of St Martin-de-l'Ile-Barbe (*BR*).

27) See J. M .Headley, 'Gattinara, Erasmus, and the imperial configuration of humanism', *ARG* 71 (1980) 64–98. On Gattinara, see *BR*.

28) See Smith, 363, and the citations there given.

29) Himelick, introd. to *Erasmus and the seamless coat of Jesus* (Lafayette, 1971) 2.

30) P. S. Allen, *Erasmus* (1934) 82.

31) Himelick, 2. As Himelick remarks, some of the passages can be seen as examples of *copia*; but the work has not received a full rhetorical analysis.

32) The original is printed by Allen (X, 130 with facsimile of the manuscript); translation is in Smith, 414 (the words in italics are in Greek in the original).

33) See further M. A. Screech, 'Rabelais, Erasmus, Gilbertus Cognatus and Boniface Amerbach ...' in *Études Rabelaisiennes* 14 (1977) 43–6.

34) M. A. Screech, ed. *Le tiers livre* (Geneva, 1964).

35) See Eps. 2628 & 2665, as well as 2757 and subsequent letters, for the continuation of the friendship of de Pins and Erasmus (*BR*).

36) Writing to Choler on 19 Feb. 1544 (Ep. 2906). That it was 'written throughout and even signed by a secretary, probably Cognatus' (Allen X, 356 n) must be taken as a sign of Erasmus' failing energies; but that it was written is a token of his affection for Choler (Koler), with whom he maintained a 'lively and frequent correspondence' and who served Erasmus in a number of ways: see *BR*.

37) Other Swiss and German universities suffered because of the disturbances and growing schism: Erfurt declined, as did Vienna and Wittenberg. 'There were sometimes more professors than students', Bainton observes, 264. Before too long there was indeed a resurgence, but in 1530–35 there was a crisis at Basel.

38) See C. Reedijk, 'Das Lebensende des Erasmus', *Basler Zeitschrift* VII (1958) 23–66.

The Final Act at Basel: Summer 1535 to July 1536

> Behold, death is at your doorstep, ready to dash you to the
> ground from the height of your glory; swooping up all your
> possessions and yourself like a swift-flowing whirlpool. Thus
> our dear Rudolph Agricola wrote elegantly no less than truth-
> fully: Death scatters all, what is born must die again. Only
> virtue knows no death, and good deeds abide.
>
> *De Contemptu Mundi*, 6. Of the inevitability of death
> (*CWE* 66: 149)

> If I should count the number of years, I have lived a long time.
> If I should calculate how much of that time I have spent
> wrestling with fevers, the stone, and gout, then I have not lived
> very long.
>
> Erasmus to Latomus, 24 August 1535, Epistle 3048
> (Allen XI, 215/38–42; translated by
> M. A. Haworth in Hillerbrand 285–6)

Once again Erasmus came to Basel with no intention of making a
long stay, only long enough to take care of the business of seeing to
his publications. There were still impossible thoughts of one more
visit to Italy, of visiting Besançon (that home of good wine), and
possibly a return to the Low Countries. But his health dictated
otherwise.

In the summer of 1535 he was greeted by the university upon his
return to Basel,[1] and there were gifts of spiced wines and salutations
by a delegation of professors. Oporinus, in fact, shook his hand so
heartily that it made him cry out with pain (Smith, 419).

He lived in the house 'Zum Luft' that was the home of Hieronymus
Froben, son of his close friend Johann. After the death of Johann in
1527 Erasmus had worked even more closely with Hieronymus; and
Bietenholz comments that 'it seems that it was chiefly Hieronymus
who on his frequent trips to Freiburg persuaded Erasmus that he
should return to Basel ... and it was in his house "Zum Luft" that
Erasmus spent the last thirteen months of his life'.[2]

His letter to Latomus on 24 August 1535, Epistle 3048, gives us a reading of Erasmus' state of mind and health soon after his return to Basel. To Latomus, a Greek and Latin scholar recently made a royal professor of Latin at Paris,[3] he wrote,

> If I should count the number of years, I have lived a long time. If I should calculate how much of that time I have spent wrestling with fevers, the stone, and gout, then I have not lived very long. But it is right for us to bear patiently whatever the Lord sends us; for no one can oppose His will and He alone knows what is best for us. (Epistle 3048, Allen XI, 215/38–42; translated by M. A. Haworth in Hillerbrand, 285–6)

In the same letter Erasmus went on to say that he was living from day to day, expecting death at any moment; and that, so painful his suffering, he at times even desired to die. Also, it is in this letter that Erasmus commented on the rumour that his life-long friend Thomas More had been put to death, and as we saw in the previous chapter in this context of weariness with the world, distance from his old and dear friend, and his own resignation to death he wrote the often quoted (and often misconstrued) wish that More 'had never become involved in this perilous business and had left a theological matter to theologians' – and that much in a time of fear ('my other friends ... are now too fearful to write or to send anything as if under every stone lay a sleeping scorpion' (Haworth translation, 286); that much, but not more than that. In another letter (Epistle 2867 of late 1533) he lamented the death of many friends in England, France, Germany and Poland.

In Basel Erasmus stayed mostly indoors, rarely leaving 'Zum Luft', and during the winter he was always close to the fireplace in the large upper room where he received his small circle of friends: Bonifacius Amerbach, Hieronymus Froben, and Nicolaus Episcopius, who in 1529 had married Justina, the daughter of Johann Froben, and worked with Hieronymus in the publishing of books (*BR*).

But some visitors could not be kept away, and some could not be kept off much-debated topics of theology. One, in fact (as Erasmus complained in a letter to his *famulus* Gilbert Cousin in Epistle 3095 of 12 February 1536), dropped in for a visit after lunch, and he (unnamed)

> kept me three hours sitting by the fire discussing doctrines of faith. The combination of paying attention to him and sitting close to the fire brought on a relapse, for both were harmful to my health. He was not going to quit before nightfall; I interrupted his discourse [*sermonem*] and sent him away. But soon I had an ache in both ears, and upset stomach ... (Allen, XI, 282/26–32)

He found the winter hard, and in the late spring suffered from a bout of dysentery from which he did not recover.

On that same day, 12 February, he made final preparations for his death. The second will of 1527 had given detailed instructions for the printing of his complete works by Froben (see appendix D), and in 1534 he made a careful inventory of all his belongings. But now to die in Basel required a different will because of the change of jurisdiction from an imperial city to one in the Swiss Confederation.[4]

The 1536 will marks two things which played important roles in his life, as Huizinga observes (186): his relations with the printing-house of Froben, and his appreciation of friendship. Bonifacius Amerbach is his principal heir, and the executors are to be Hieronymus Froben and Nicolaus Episcopius, the managers of the press. *Pro amicitia*, to each of his surviving good friends he bequeathed a trinket recalling his fame with the great of the world, especially to Louis Baer and Beatus Rhenanus. He remembered the poor, the sick, and the young – especially young girls about to marry, and young students of promise – this charity was left to Amerbach to work out, with his connections at the university.

Yet another aspect of his will remains for comment (although strictly speaking it was not enjoined by the legal document). After his death the work in progress on his desk was assembled and then bound into three codices, and it has been thought that the purpose was a final and unique remembrance of Erasmus the writer: an icon of Erasmus at work, *humanista scribens*.[5]

There are several key questions to ask about Erasmus' state of mind in his last months. Had the Erasmian optimism of the years from 1508 to 1517 in fact surrendered, 'did it fall victim to events?' as Tracy asks (232). Earlier, in such works as the rather youthful *Antibarbari* (chapter 8), Erasmus had expressed an unbounded optimism in the power of humanistic education to open the mind and to uplift the quality of living for each individual. Together the classical *studia humanitatis* and the pure message of the Gospel would nourish man's natural instincts for piety; with the reforming of the individual, piety and good fellowship would flourish, and from that would come good order in society and government. But the events after 1517, the failure of the Fifth Lateran Council, the posting of the Ninety-Five Theses on a church door in Germany (and the storm that arose from that act), the attacks upon Erasmus himself, and the outbreaks of violence by Catholics and Evangelicals alike in the 1520s – all these events in christian countries that tore the unity of the Church and challenged the foundations of authority, all shook Erasmus' optimism. If man cannot control events, will he not turn to a stronger, even evangelical, trust in God?[6] Tracy argued (and I share that view) that Erasmus' faith in the 'gentle qualities of human nature' and their ultimate triumph, 'owed less to Cicero than to the Gospel teaching, so imbedded in Netherlandish piety, that the meek shall inherit the earth' (233).

One can examine the change, or development, or tempering, of Erasmus' thought in several ways. One is to study closely the works completed after 1530, especially *De sarcienda concordia* (1533), *Enarratio in Psalmum 38* (1532), and the *Ecclesiastes* (1535). His *De puritate tabernaculi sive ecclesiae christianae* was first published in 1536, and in this very late work he indicates that he is no longer sure that men can be educated or led to the good:

> The prohibition of evil suits hard and rebellious men; the teaching of good suits those who are obedient and spontaneously roused to piety ... Great is the rudeness and sluggishness of the human mind: so much so that the Decalogue, which was given to a coarse and rebellious people, has but three precepts commanding what is virtuous, while the others prohibit manifest crimes. (*LB* V, 297D; translation by Tracy 232)

These are strong words from a humanist who years earlier had thought men could be persuaded to the good, that education could reach all, and that the *studia humanitatis* had a nobility of purpose and substance. The very foundations of belief in *humanitas* have been shaken by 1536. Erasmus continues in the same work to discuss those who abuse *libertas*: they must be constrained.[7] There are some men who are suited for autonomy: they are 'born to better things' than monastic discipline – a theme not unfamiliar to readers of the *De Contemptu Mundi* (especially its final chapter) and of his later writings on monasticism (see Tracy, 232). Erasmus concludes with his consistent word on monasticism: 'But there are others born of such a nature that they should be coerced with ten cowls rather than left to their own choice' (Epistle 1459, Allen V, 482/86–110; Tracy 232).

In the *Ecclesiastes*, which expresses thoughts about preaching and the priestly office held for many years, Erasmus comes back to the classical slogan that 'the people is a great beast'.[8] If the concept is an old one, the words doubtless echo his nightmarish images of the mobs in Basel in 1529.

Involved as well is a modification in the Erasmian concept of the nature of man. Thus the point in *De sarcienda concordia* that 'the whole man (for Paul includes all faculties in one) is incapable of celestial gifts':[9] does this not sound as though he has learned something from the Lutheran emphasis? It is not simply the flesh (in the

Pauline sense of body distinguished from spirit) that is corrupted by
sin:

> Whatever in man seems of more solid nature is nothing in the
> sight of God. The soul is the more solid part of man, and in the
> soul reason. Yet this faculty also counts for nothing before God,
> without Whom human powers can do nothing. It too is cor-
> rupted by sin; despoiled of the grace of God, by which it was
> made something, it has become nothing, needing a Redeemer
> as it needed a Creator before coming into existence. (*LB* V,
> 481AD; Tracy 233)

Some of this language and thinking is the result of a closer study of
Paul made for the revisions in the 1532 *Paraphrase of Romans*.

We might put it that the question is not so much whether
Erasmus learned from his exchanges with Luther, Melanchthon and
others in the 1520s (as doubtless he did), but rather that he has
returned to the deeply imbedded teachings of the *Devotio Moderna* to
which Luther was also indebted. Much of the *De sarcienda* rings with
the resonances of Thomas à Kempis and his masters.

Changes and revisions will also provide clues to shifts in Erasmus'
theological thinking. In 1517 Erasmus wrote in his *Paraphrase of
Romans:* ' ... some part of it depends on our own will and effort,
although this part is so minor that it seems like nothing at all in
comparison with the free kindness of God' (CWE 42:153, with the
1532 text at 55/15n). In 1523 Luther accused Erasmus of
Pelagianism on the strength of this passage; in 1532, Tracy notes
(234) it was deleted. Erasmus continued to work with his *Annotations*, and revisions in the *Paraphrases*, and those changes that he
made in 1532 and as late as 1535 merit continuing study.[10]

To respond to Tracy's question put earlier in this chapter: the
earlier optimism was not surrendered to events, but it clearly had
been modified.

In his later years Erasmus brought together prayers composed
over a long period of time, many associated with particular occasions,
some with the liturgical calendar and seasons. His prayers were long
used in devotional manuals in Germany, perhaps elsewhere as well,
often without attribution of Erasmus' authorship.[11] His prayer for
winter seems especially appropriate for evoking his spirits during the
last winter of his life:

> O God most wise, founder and governor of the world, at whose
> command the seasons revolve in stated changes, like unto sere
> death is winter, whose desolateness and hardship are the better
> endured because they are soon to be succeeded by the amenity of
> spring. Like the year our outward man is in childhood vernal, in

youth torrid, in maturity ripe, and in age declining. But the horror of death is softened by the hope of renewal of which we are most certainly assured by the promise of Thy Son, who is eternal truth, who can no more deceive or be deceived that he can not be Thy Son, through whom our inward man knows not age and through his constant aid is vernal in innocence, fervent in the zeal of piety, bears fruit, and passes on to others that which it has received. The more the vigour of the body declines, by so much more the spirit flourishes. We beseech Thee that what Thou has conferred upon us through Thy Son, Thou wilt deign to guard and increase through the same one who reigns with Thee, world without end. Amen. (*LB* V, 1201F–1202A)

If it be true that the letters of Erasmus – full as they are of his immediate day-to-day concerns of publishing, finances, sickness, controversies, and news of all kinds – yet do not give us the whole of his experience (as Bainton notes, 244), and that they do not record his having said Mass, they do nonetheless tell us that he carried his prayer book with him, and from that knowledge and from our reading of the prayers and religious poems he composed, together with such last works as the *Ecclesiastes*, we must rightly build a picture of a man who was deeply religious. It is inconceivable that one who wrote the prayer '*Pro Gaudio Spirituali*' – with its memorable chiming of the words *gaudio, laetitia, delectatio* (familiar though they are in themselves) – did not himself experience and nurture spiritual joy, and the exhilaration of a rich inner life: '*ut unctio tui Spiritus mihi frequenter excutat malorum taedium, ac mentem meam salutari gaudio exhilaret ...*'

There is a numerical pattern in the life of Erasmus which is followed in this biography that ends Volume 1 after thirty-three years, and Volume 2 after thirty-six. In his *Historia Ecclesiastica* the Venerable Bede

begins the story of Abbess Hild by calling attention to the numerical patterns in her life. Hild died at the age of sixty-six. This span was divided into two equal parts of thirty-three years each, the first devoted to a secular life, the second to her monastic vocation (iv.21 [23]). That thirty-three is the sacred number that corresponds to the number of years Christ lived on earth is taken for granted. Furthermore, Hild suffered from a prolonged illness of seven years before she died. The illness sent by the Lord 'so that like the apostle, her strength might be made perfect in weakness' [*ut iuxta exemplum apostoli virtus eius in infirmitate perficeretur*][12]

To some modern minds such attention to numerical patterns may seem quaint, even superstitious; but Erasmus was one who accepted much of Bede's number symbolism in Biblical interpretation, and who besides is likely to have applied such numerical notions as that of the climacteric to his own life.[13] And such a line of thought may well have contributed to his deep sense of being ready for death when he reached sixty-six, and of awaiting death patiently thereafter.

Erasmus kept on working until the very end. It is too easy to play the cynic with Dr Johnson and say that no one ever wrote except for money. Erasmus no longer needed to write for money, as he had to do earlier; and he was beyond the seeking of a fame whose rewards he would not accept. But he had projects to complete, and he doubtless believed in the Benedictine *laborare est orare*. And therefore he continued to work on his unfinished projects, and to continue revising his several continuing works and editions.

Of all his attributes, none is more impressive than his extraordinary capacity for work. Froben, who had worked closely with him at the press in Basel, wrote

> Gracious Heavens! Have we not seen Erasmus, when he was with us a year and a half ago, partly employed in turning Greek into Latin, partly in correcting the Epistles and Gospels; now compiling his notes to the *Novum Instrumentum*, anon penning scholia upon St Jerome? What laborious, what incessant study! What fatigues were his daily portion![14]

There are many tokens of his all but unbroken work. In a letter to Amerbach of 11 April 1534 (Epistle 2920) we see him apparently writing while at dinner (*'mox a prandio'*). He seems to have been able to write, dictate, and talk all at the same time, such were his powers of concentration. To have produced as much as he did in the course of his lifetime was prodigious; to have achieved that record of work in spite of poor health, physical pain, and much criticism and even hatred, was heroic. May we not (thinking of the 'Saint Socrates' of the Colloquies) murmur our 'Saint Erasmus'?

The huge *Ecclesiastes* (his longest work) was seen through the final stages at the press after Erasmus' arrival in Basel; and he was also working on his *De puritate tabernaculi*, which came from Froben's press in 1536.[15] The writing and dedication of this last work provide eloquent testimony to Erasmus' regard for friendship; for *De puritate* is not dedicated to 'prelate or prince, no great wit or admired divine' (as Huizinga observes, 186), but to Christoph Eschenfelder, a customs officer at Boppard, who in 1518 had cleared a boat descending the Rhine and entering the ecclesiastical jurisdiction of the bishop of Trier. Erasmus was a passenger on that boat, and he was delighted to meet an avid reader of his writings, as he narrated in Epistle 867, and he followed up with a letter to Eschenfelder (Epistle 879). Over the years more letters passed between the great humanist and the simple customs officer on the Rhine (later *Brückenmeister* of the bridge across the Rhine at Koblenz, *BR*). Towards the end of 1535 Erasmus remembered the request of Eschenfelder to dedicate to him his interpretation of some psalm. Choosing, he says, at random, Erasmus wrote his commentary on Psalm 14(15) and called his little work 'On the purity of the Tabernacle or Christian Church': it proved to be the last of his writings. The psalm begins, 'Who is it, Lord, that will make his home in thy tabernacle, rest on the mountain where thy sanctuary is?' The work is an illustration of true piety, that of the interior life. With this composition Erasmus returns yet again to the spirit of the *Devotio Moderna*.[16]

There was one final edition of the New Testament, incorporating even at the end revisions and additions; the 1535 edition in fact is the most complete. One must realise the vocation of Erasmus' work of more than a quarter-century: 'he was convinced that scholarship, aided by the secret workings of the Spirit, would enable him to open up a text which was the jewel in the treasure-house of the Church ... A Renaissance scholar working on the New Testament who saw Christ as his *adjutor* (his 'helper' in the task of spreading the Gospel) was probably thinking of himself as in some way a successor to the *Adjutores Dei* who were the Apostles' (Screech, xxiii).[17]

Finally, there was the edition of Origen that appeared in two volumes from the Froben presses in September 1536 after Erasmus' death. To be sure, in 1527 he had published an edition of Origen's fragmentary commentary on Matthew, but he had been working on his edition of Origen's *Opera* for many years,[18] and the use of Origen as a resource is manifest in Erasmus' ideas concerning allegory, the nature of man, Christology, and the freedom of the will. If Valla was his master for philological method, Origen can be thought of as his master for the interpretation of the Bible.[19] He continued to work on the edition until a month before his death, and it was published in two stout folio volumes about two months after his death.

Dying in Protestant Basel Erasmus did not have, and there is no evidence that he desired to have, a priest at his bedside at the hour of death. To say, however, that he did not die a Catholic in the formal sense is to go beyond what the evidence at hand means in itself.[20] His dying was consistent with his beliefs concerning the sacraments of the Church, which he thought were limited to Baptism, the Eucharist, Marriage, and Holy Orders; for he did not place much importance in the last rites, the final Roman Catholic sacrament for the dying. In his *De praeparatione ad mortem* two years earlier, he differed from conventional manuals on dying by implying that the acts of the final hour are not the determinant: it is the nature of one's whole life that will count for more than his feverish thoughts *in articulo mortis*.[21]

Years earlier, in Epistle 1211 to Justus Jonas, written from Anderlecht in June 1521 when feeling his age, he wrote full of praise for Jean Vitrier (see chapter 19), a learned and devout Franciscan who was totally absorbed 'by a kind of incredible passion for bringing men to the true philosophy of Christ' (*CWE* 8:228/77–8); and those that he had won for Christ 'differed from the common run of Christians' on their deathbeds. 'There you might have seen his disciples meeting death in the most cheerful spirit and, like swans that sing before they die, uttering words that proved how the divine spirit had touched their hearts ... ' (229/126–9). Such was Erasmus' concept of Christian dying.

He suffered the final indignity of an attack of dysentery. In a letter of 6 June 1536 he showed that he knew himself to be dying, after years of ill health. Writing to Tiedemann Giese on that date (Epistle 3126), he wrote '*saltem veniam dabis morienti*' (Allen XI, 332/6–7).[22] Giese had sent a manuscript of his three-volume but unfinished work *De regno Christi*, hoping for a favourable opinion from Erasmus on it; but as Epistle 3126 makes clear Erasmus was now too ill to give attention to scholarly matters (Allen XI, 332/2–5).

A few days before the final end three of his closest friends – Amerbach, Froben and Episcopius – came to his sick-bed, and he jested with them about being Job's comforters: why were they not tearing their garments and sprinkling ashes on their heads?

The end came on the night of 11–12 July. The account of Johann Herwagen a Basel printer,[23] to Erasmus' very close friend Beatus Rhenanus tells us much of what we would want to know:

> The day after I reached Basel – I had arrived in the evening – Erasmus of Rotterdam exchanged life for death. It was July 11, close to twelve o'clock midnight. His death was due to various causes, of which you know; the immediate cause was dysentery. The funeral was attended by every scholar, by one of the two mayors, and by a large number of members of the town council. The place selected for his burial in the cathedral had previously been consecrated to the Blessed Virgin. There a short eulogy was delivered by Myconius,[24] which reviewed briefly a large number of Erasmus' laudable achievements. Next Tuesday (the day chosen by the city government) according to our custom his funeral celebration will be held. On August 23, with God's blessing we shall sing the nuptial song in honour of our beloved

Erasmus. You will, I hope, join us in honouring him. (Epistle 3135, Allen XI, 344/11–21, translation by M. A. Haworth in Hillerbrand 290).

On his deathbed in the large room with the open fireplace that he took pleasure in, Erasmus repeated over and over the prayers 'O Mother of God remember me!' and 'Jesus Christ, Son of God, have mercy upon me! I will sing the mercy and judgment of the Lord'. Then with his expiring breath he said in the language of his childhood, 'Lieve God!' ('Dear God'), and so he died.[25]

It is fitting to end with the words of P. S. Allen in the chapel of Corpus Christi College, Oxford, speaking of Chrysostom (thus combining the voice of his great editor to whom Volume 1 was dedicated, and the figure of Erasmus' beloved Greek Father):

He turned – as others have turned before him – to man's imperishable part, his only property and all his treasure: the soul which this life ended he must render up to God – not merely unspotted from the world, but worn and weary after a life of service, yet looking forward to new service beyond the gate of death. (*Letters of P. S. Allen* [Oxford, 1939] 298)

Notes

1) He had arrived in Basel no later than 28 June (the date of Ep. 3028), and in his letter to Erasmus Schets he speaks of the discomfort of the trip (Allen XI, 144/17 ff.). See Smith, 419 and the sources there cited.

2) In *BR*, citing Eps. 2755 & 2756, which are however not conclusive. The role of Bonifacius Amerbach in persuading Erasmus to return to Basel must also be recognised (see chp. 42).

3) After Erasmus' death Latomus entered the service of the archbishop of Trier, now Johann Ludwig von Hagen, a former student of his (*BR*). There had a been a conflict between Erasmus and Latomus, but after 1527 it died down and it seems to have been Erasmus who re-opened their friendship after Latomus' tribute in *Oratio de studiis humanitatis* (his inaugural lecture at Paris on 1 November 1534). Both Ep. 3029 and Erasmus' response in Ep. 3048 were included in the last selection of Erasmus' correspondence published Feb. 1536. See E. Rummel, 'Erasmus' Conflict with Latomus: Round Two', *ARG* 80 (1989) 5–23.

4) To sum up the complications: Erasmus was born in Holland, lived in the Holy Roman Empire (where there were some funds and one bequest), and died in the free imperial city of Basel. See P. P. J. L. van Peteghem, 'Erasmus' Last Will', in *Erasmus of Rotterdam*, ed. Weiland and Frijhoff (1988) 88–97, and appendix D.

5) I have briefly discussed this phenomenon in a paper on the Copenhagen

codices given at the 1991 Copenhagen Congress of IANLS, and to be published in the ACTA of the Congress.

6) Tracy has suggested (234) the parallel in the reasoning of Venetian patricians studied by Bouwsma from a sense of man's helplessness to control events to an 'evangelical' doctrine of trust in God. Much of this is figured in the debate between Erasmus and Luther on the freedom of the will (ch. 39).

7) I am indebted to Tracy for his emphasis on the 'thought-terms' of Erasmus, among which *humanitas, libertas, simplicitas,* and *spiritus* are paramount.

8) *LB* V, 776E, 805EF; cf. 855B, 812B, 779A, 781F; Tracy, 232.

9) In Tracy's interpretation, Erasmus in the 1530s 'abandoned the effort to restrict Paul's term "Flesh" to the body, thus leaving the higher faculties untouched by sin. *De sarcienda concordia* (1533) avers that "the whole man" (for Paul includes all faculties in one) is incapable of celestial gifts'. At the very last, *Ecclesiastes* 'declares that those who think "Flesh" in St Paul refers to concupiscence are mistaken: it means not merely coarse emotions, such as lust or drunkenness, but man's very reason, indeed all his faculties, as long as the spirit of Christ be absent' (Tracy, 233).

10) Vols 43, 46 & 49 in *CWE* now provide splendid translations, introductions and commentaries for the *Paraphrases on Romans and Galatians, Paraphrase on John,* and the *Paraphrase on Mark. CWE* 42:32n. 117, 153 for several further examples.

11) See Helen C. White, *Tudor Books of Private Devotion* (1951), and Paul Althaus, *Forschungen zur Evangelischen Gebetsliteratur* (1972; rptd. Hildesheim, 1966).

12) Colgrave and Mynors ed. (1969) 410–11; cf. Calvin B. Kendall, 'Bede's Historia Ecclesiastica', in *Medieval Eloquence,* ed. J. J. Murphy (Berkeley/Los Angeles, 1978) 169.

13) On Erasmus and the theory of the climacteric, see ch. 2 and app. A.

14) Bruce, *Erasmus*, 35. See further Allen, 'Erasmus' Relations with his printers' in *Erasmus* (1934) 109 ff.

15) An edition at Antwerp that same year may have been earlier; the two editions at Leipzig and Paris were doubtless later. The work was translated into Dutch and German in 1537. Charles Béné has recently interpreted this composition as a double testament: a spiritual testament on the Church, through a meditation; and a personal testament to defend himself against calumnies and to affirm his fidelity to the Church, but ultimately to reassert his personal concept of the writer and the Christian. See Béné, 'Le *De Puritate Tabernaculi,* Testament spirituel d'Érasme', in *Actes du Colloque International Érasme* (Tours, 1986) ed. J. Chomarat, A. Godin and J. -C. Margolin (Geneva, 1990) 199–212.

16) See app. B . It is to be noted that a folio *Opera* of Thomas à Kempis was printed in Paris by Bade (1523); general interest in his writings continued.

17) Screech, Introduction to Erasmus' *Annotations on the New Testament*, xxiii.

18) Origen (c.185–c.254) – the Alexandrian Biblical scholar and theologian, perhaps 'the outstanding teacher and scholar of the early Church' (Quasten, 11, 37) – was certainly a thinker of originality, to the edge of

boldness in philosophical speculation. His work has often been misunderstood and at times condemned, hence the loss of many of his writings.

19) See Halkin, 402. Erasmus had read Origen's homilies and his commentary on Romans before writing the *Enchiridion*, which contains many quotations from Origen (ch.20).

20) Cf. Reedijk in 'Das Lebensende des Erasmus', 33: that there is no proof that he died a Catholic in the 'formal sense'.

21) Thus Tracy, 227, following Thomas Tentler, 'Forgiveness and Consolation in the Religious Thought of Erasmus', *Stud. in the Ren.*, 12 (1965) 22.

22) The story of Giese and Copernicus has considerable bearing on the question of Erasmus' interest in science. Tiedemann Giese of Gdansk (1480–1550) wrote an unpublished and now lost *Hyperaspisticon*, in which he defended the heliocentric theory of his friend and fellow canon in Frombork, Nicolaus Copernicus, and apparently pointed out that Erasmus had spoken highly favourably of Copernicus, perhaps through the thought and writings of his Ferrarese friend Celio Calcagnini, see *BR*; and on Calcagnini's *Quod caelum stet, terra moveatur*, which philosophically defended the notion of the rotation of the earth upon its axis, see F. Hiper, 'Die Vorläufer des N. Copernicus, inbesondere C. Calcagnini', *Mitteilungen des Copernicus-Vereins zu Thurn* 4 (1882) 51–80. In turn Copernicus mentioned Giese's support in the dedicatory preface to *De revolutionibus orbium coelestium* (Nürnberg, 1543), *BR*.

23) Johann Herwagen (1497– c.1557) was a printer who had married Gertrud Lachner, the recent widow of Johann Froben (*BR*), and that marriage and his enhanced role in the business explain his being one of the small number of close friends gathered at the death of Erasmus. The date of death is here given as 11 July; the monument on his tomb gives it as 12 July. There was a discrepancy of one hour between the city and its suburbs, as Bainton straightforwardly explains (272) in those days before Greenwich Mean Time and precisely fixed zones.

24) Myconius – Oswald Geisshüssler (1488–1552) – was a native of Basel and successor to Oecolampadius in 1532 as professor of divinity (*BR*). It is worth underscoring the remarkable fact that the funeral services for Erasmus included a Roman Catholic Mass in the now reformed Münster. A remarkable tribute to him.

25) There is dispute over his last ejaculations. According to another report they were '*O Jesu, misericordia! Domine, libera me; Domine, miserere me!*' (See the literature cited by Smith, 420.) It is the report of his Belgian *famulus* Lambert Coomans that his last prayers were as given above. It is of course possible that two different witnesses were at the bedside at different moments and heard different prayers. As to his final words, there is scholarly dispute as to whether 'Lieve God' would have been a customary expression in the Dutch prayers of his day; it seems probable that it was. Dr J. Trapman declares that 'the combination "lieve God" does occur in Dutch medieval prayers, for example in prayers where Jesus' suffering and wounds are meditated upon' ('Erasmus' Precationes', in *Acta Conventus Neo-Latini Torontonensis* [Binghamton, 1991]) 778.

44

The Achievement of Erasmus and his Place in History

> He is the greatest man we come across in the history of education.
>
> R.R. Bolgar, *The Classical Heritage* (1954) 336

> It is in the biographies of Erasmus and Lorenzo Valla that we must find consolation. They were willing to work at foundations. They did not give the crowd what it wanted.
>
> Ezra Pound, *The Renaissance* (1915)

> The name of Erasmus will never perish.
>
> John Colet (1516)

The achievement of Erasmus was manifold and prodigious, and we shall have to consider his work as a teacher and rhetorician, as a renaissance humanist and classical scholar, as biblical scholar and theologian, as literary artist, and as player on the European stage of world-shaking and world-shaping events during the early reformation period. His place in history is also complex, and we shall summarise and evaluate the main bibliographical evidence, his impact upon his own contemporaries, and his direct and indirect influence upon the thought and letters of the sixteenth and seventeenth (and subsequent) centuries. To complicate matters, the image of Erasmus in different periods has changed radically.[1]

Fundamentally, as Thompson has rightly suggested (xxv), Erasmus was a teacher of teachers, which Colet recognised in expressing his longing to have Erasmus as a teacher in his new school but – even more than that – 'I am hopeful that you may lend me some assistance, if only in training my teachers' (Epistle 230, *CWE* 2:174/14–16; Allen I, 470/12–14). One must recognise that he had spent several years teaching and tutoring in Paris, and then several more years as a 'visiting professor' of Greek and theology at Cambridge: he knew teaching first hand, and his success with a substantial number of individual students was remarkable. But the greater thrust of his work in education is to be found in many writings, which had phenomenal success for reasons that Colet saw clearly: 'I am full of admiration for your gifts, as well as your masterly technique, erudition, fluency, and power of expression' (*CWE* 2:173/5–174/7; Allen I, 470/4–5). For a quarter of a century, in that new era of the printing press, Erasmus was able to reach his wider audience of teachers and scholars without delay by virtue of the new technology of printing; thus, his books always had a strong sense of immediacy that went hand in hand with his directness of style. His books were quickly printed, for Erasmus at times was able to hand his manuscript directly to the printer who had his press at the ready, and to keep up to the daily demand of the voracious presses. His books of increasing popularity were thereby put into the hands of hundreds of teachers and students everywhere, and in the next generation his texts for teachers served as models for fresh texts, and the circles of his pedagogical influence continued to widen.

In the *Adages* – even in the compressed version of 1500 (which itself went on being printed for several decades), but far more in the 1508 and subsequent editions of the *Adagiorum Chiliades* that greatly increased the number of adages (*Chiliades:* literally, thousands) and expanded many of them into book-length essays, often separately published – Erasmus provided a unique introduction to and survey of the moral teachings of antiquity, presented in a form that was at once readable and instructive. Implicit in the *Adages* was the belief that the best of the ancients taught an ethic compatible with and even supportive of christian teaching. In the *Colloquies* Erasmus developed the dialogue form into something marvellously entertaining and endlessly instructive: schoolboys who read or sometimes acted out the dialogues learned more than they realised about moral situations in sixteenth-century living, and as with the *Adages* the capability of the Latin to respond to the demands of the contemporary was demonstrated at every step. It was not only schoolboys who read the *Adages* and *Colloquies*, of course, but read them they did and doubtless they were inspired in many ways by them. Writers and scholars also used them as handbooks and quarries for ideas, reference, and guides.

In a series of treatises which nearly all had roots in his Paris teaching experience, Erasmus laid out his educational programme: *De Ratione Studii* (1511), *De Pueris Instituendis* (1529), *De Civilitate morum puerilium* (1530) and other works, all of which have their grounding in a theory of language (*Lingua,* 1525) and a rhetorical theory embodied in a rhetorical curriculum and programme beginning with *De duplici Copia verborum ac rerum* (1512).[2] Each of these works has an impressive publishing history, for the copies circulated everywhere in Europe. At the core of his educational programme was rhetoric, rhetoric conceived as a pathway to wisdom.[3]

When we speak of Erasmus and education, or of Erasmus and the humanistic curriculum, we are speaking of an educational concept and of cultural values which are now under close examination on both sides of the Atlantic, and sometimes even under violent attack. Some may wish to question the appropriateness of a liberal-arts curriculum for twentieth-century British or North American society – although to attack it (for whatever reasons) and advocate discarding it (with alternatives poorly conceived) before fully understanding it is foolish and unscholarly – but its central role in shaping modern culture down to the twentieth century cannot be questioned. Matthew Arnold, A.N. Whitehead, Paul Valéry, Aby Warburg, Ernst Robert Curtius, and T.S. Eliot (to name only a few, but those are among the shapers of the modern mind) are all products of the liberal-arts curriculum, as were Marx, Freud, and a host of others; and the indebtedness of their thought to, and indeed the shaping of their imagination by, the resources and forms of the liberal arts – and, ultimately, therefore, Erasmus – is very great.

As Craig R. Thompson writes in his wise introduction to the literary and educational volumes in *CWE*,

> If by education is meant liberal-arts education as known in the West during the past five centuries, a training whose basis was grammatical, rhetorical, and literary, the primacy of Erasmus can be accepted without demur... Everything he wrote on education and much that he wrote on religion and ethics must be taken into account if we want to understand his conception of education and estimate his contribution to it... All the pieces are needed before we can pronounce judgment. Meanwhile what should be kept in mind, in reading these and other volumes in the [*CWE*] series, is the controlling idea set forth in the *Antibarbari*, that the best pagan wisdom and culture were not only good in themselves but good for the Christian society that inherited the wealth of antiquity. If we can see what Erasmus meant by the relationship between learning, Good Letters [i.e., the *studia humanitatis*], education and religion we are on the road to understanding him and his purpose. (*CWE* 23:lxviii)

'All the pieces are needed': this is true in a double sense, both to understand Erasmus, and to perceive that for the renaissance humanists learning was not purely utilitarian, and there was a whole greater than the sum of its parts.

It is too easy and simplistic to assert that the Erasmian programme of humanistic education was a failure because it is no longer much alive today. But look at what that programme produced in the schools of England (from St Paul's School to its many offshoots and beneficiaries, and the reforms of Dr Thomas Arnold in the nineteenth century), Germany (where the educational philosophy of Sturm and Melanchthon drew deeply from Erasmian teachings), and elsewhere (not least in the schools of the Jesuits around the world, whose *Ratio Studiorum* names many masters, but not the key name of Erasmus to whom their philosophy is most deeply indebted). Consider the central role of Erasmus himself and of the humanism to which his name is attached in the writings of Rabelais, Montaigne, Lipsius, Shakespeare, Grotius, and countless other writers of the Renaissance. The argument that his programme was a failure because it does not exist today is shallow on the face of it, and it comes ironically from many whose first line of attack upon it – were it still to exist *in toto* – would be that it has existed too long. One line of response to that criticism is the massive evidence of several kinds of influence upon master-theologians and thinkers of the renaissance period. Luther studied and digested much of the works of Erasmus, especially the earlier ones, but he kept buying and reading later ones as well, as did Zwingli, Melanchthon and Oecolampadius. Although he does not praise him, Calvin took some of his ideas from Erasmus and cited him heavily on matters of exegetical authority; and he leaned on Erasmus for his notion of the contempt of the world, for his humanistic Platonism, and for his concept of faith.[4] In England William Tyndale took much from Erasmus, especially in translating the New Testament into English,[5] which contributed so mightily to the language of the King James version of the Bible. Castellio offered Erasmus as a major support for his plea for tolerance (as he was also the support for Postel's imaginative concepts of tolerance), and Semler, the eighteenth-century father of German rationalism, declared that 'everything which the newer theology had painfully won for itself was already to be founded in the great and admirable Erasmus'.[6] In the nineteenth century the historian J.S. Brewer even claimed that in one respect (that of applying to the editing and translating of Scripture the same rules that scholars were applying to the texts of Cicero and Virgil), 'his influence on the Reformation was greater than Luther's; as the application of the principle of criticism introduced by Erasmus must, under favourable circumstances and in more vigorous hands, lead to consequences more important'.[7] Many have seen Erasmus as an early champion of the independent scholar, a judgment voiced early by George Burton Adams, the American historian:

> By no means the least of the great services of Erasmus to civilization had been to hold up before all the world so conspicuous an example of the scholar following, as his inalienable

right, the truth as he found it, wherever it appeared to lead him, and honest in his public utterances to the result of his studies.[8]

To these somewhat random indications can be added more systematic studies. Much can be made of the massive, and accelerating, record of Erasmian scholarship provided by the three volumes of Margolin's invaluable bibliography, and by the testimony of the Erasmus collection of more than 5,000 volumes in the Gemeentebibliotheek of Rotterdam. The remarkable number of biographies of Erasmus is an eloquent testimony to his enduring appeal and significance, and in these biographies that have appeared every two or three years since the mid-sixteenth century can be studied the changing tides of interpretation and also the conviction that Erasmus has an enduring significance. Bruce Mansfield has given his survey of interpretations of Erasmus to the year 1750 in volume one of his study, *Phoenix of His Age* (1979), a second volume will carry the narrative into the early twentieth century. The evidence is indeed massive.

The printing record of his books is impressive to a staggering degree. Central works like the *Adagia, Colloquia, Moriae Encomium,* and *Novum Testamentum* were printed in his own lifetime in a very large number of editions, and that publishing history continues in reprints, abridgments, selections, translations, critical editions, and the like, to our own day. Some individual works have numbered hundreds of editions. To consider the meaning of this kind of influence we may again turn with profit to the penetrating comment of Thompson:

> A book may be a best-seller, a popular success, and forgotten in a few years. It may be a standard work for a long time, as *De copia* was, and then either superseded by other manuals or abandoned because the subject itself goes out of fashion or is approached in new ways. Influence is harder to judge than popularity.[9] When influence is discussed, the word may prove to mean simply being the source of passages or scenes or plots... Or influence may refer to a memory of, respect for, affinity with, one writer by a later writer... Influence has many nuances, such as half-conscious recollections, indirect or mingled borrowings, or adopted techniques which a well-read writer may use for his own purposes without knowing or caring whence he derived them. Influence of ideas is easy to suspect, notoriously difficult to prove. We can scarcely avoid talking about influence but, bearing in mind that its importance is more qualitative than quantitative, we must not expect the term to be more than suggestive unless accompanied by the sort

of detailed analysis of text which belongs to specialized studies... (*CWE* 23:liv–lv)

The concept of the influence of Erasmus covers all the above categories, and evidence is mounting through bibliographies and bibliographical studies to support the conclusion that Erasmus' influence
in the sixteenth century alone was well-nigh incalculable. In the
field of education only, an exhibition like that mounted in Liège in
1969, *Exposition Le Livre scolaire aut temps d'Erasme et des Humanistes*
(with catalogue by René Hoven and Jean Hoyoux, and introduction
by L.-E. Halkin) demonstrated most vividly the impact of Erasmus:
through his own books first, and then through the books inspired by
him and his work. *Si monumentum requiris, circumspice*. All of this
having been said then, we can accept with the kind of understanding
here indicated Bolgar's otherwise bold-seeming declaration that
Erasmus 'is the greatest man we come across in the history of education'.[10]

Education is but one area of influence: we must look also to
further studies in scriptural scholarship and interpretation, the development of irony and satire, theology, classical scholarship and
interpretation, humanistic resources in expanding studies of jurisprudence and medicine, and more. Influence, in fact, is an inadequate concept to describe the stature of Erasmus; his presence was
everywhere felt during his lifetime, and his ideas, writings and
personality have cast a long shadow upon subsequent thought and
letters.

So how do we explain the ups and downs of fortune, and the
neglect of Erasmus in the schools and universities of today, given his
manifest greatness? Since his death his place in history has never
been absolutely secure, and there are historical explanations for this.
Twentieth-century secular humanism has only a developmental connection – in the biological sense of a later stage that can be traced
back to a previous stage in a long line of development – with the
christian humanism of the Renaissance that Erasmus espoused; and
to use the single term 'humanism' for both phenomena confuses
many important issues and values. It blurs necessary distinctions and
it makes the mistake of taking one stage of a development as representative of the whole.[11] It must be accepted that with the exception
of a very small number of pockets of authentic christian and jewish
studies that combine religious belief with learning, the late twentieth-century in Western Europe and the United States and Canada is
an almost completely secularised culture. It is not surprising that
twentieth-century secular humanism is not the christian humanism
of Erasmus.

Erasmus' religious beliefs can be summed up in the celebrated phrase, almost a slogan, *philosophia Christi*. At its simplest and most direct it can be seen in his very basic, lay-oriented work of pastoral theology, the *Enchiridion,* written at the age of about thirty-five or thirty-six (see chapter 20). The *philosophia Christi* carried the simplicity of the message of Christ, but that too has often been misunderstood. *Philosophia Christi* was strongly moral, drawing strength from stoic teachings as well as christian, but it was not puritanical. Above all it valued the role of classical learning and wisdom, and fundamentally there was a lasting commitment to the study of the christian scriptures and a deep, abiding love of Christ: a complete acceptance of the actuality of Christ and of the presence of Christianity in the world in which he lived. Christ was always the centre of that world. The end of christian life for Erasmus was human will made free by Grace, and its purpose was to develop an interior devotion towards the following of Christ.

Simplicity meant the fundamental teachings of Christianity, without unnecessary trappings of dogma or ceremony; and a style that grew more simple, less adorned with the 'colours' of rhetoric, more direct. Erasmus was consistent in this category, as in nearly all aspects of his thought and living.

He thought of himself as a theologian (as well as a poet and a rhetorician), in part because one had to be a professional theologian (that is possessing a doctorate) in order to be privileged to speak and write about sacred matters; but he was not a school theologian, not a follower of the scholastics. He was not interested in speculative theology; what he was fervently concerned to do was to teach the story of Christ in the New Testament; and his life-work of more than three decades was the editing, translating and interpreting of the New Testament for all readers of his own age.

The scope and continuity of Erasmus' writings on religious matters is impressive, and it cannot be ignored in studying or judging him. Those highly original genres developed by Erasmus – the *Adagia* (chapter 24), the *Moriae Encomium* (26), and the *Colloquia* (35) – are remarkable writings designed to teach christian values to different audiences in very different modes; but the central teaching, as Erasmus himself insisted, was the same as in the straightforward *Enchiridion*. The *Ratio Verae Theologiae* began as a preface to the New Testament edition and was expanded into its present form and published separately in 1519; only the Gospels and Epistles of the New Testament, it instructs its readers, truly and efficaciously bring back the whole Christ to us. Of this work Zwingli wrote (in words that may serve to indicate the reaction of a whole generation): 'I do not remember having found elsewhere so much fruit in such small space'. Erasmus was also a writer of prayers and liturgy, and no one can read his prayers without the strongest conviction of his intense spirituality. Finally, his longest work came at the very end of his life: *Ecclesiastes*, and it is not simply a magnificent treatise on christian preaching, it embodies much of the experience and spirit of Erasmus himself.

But Erasmus' vocation as a humanist-scholar, his way of life, and his writings went against the grain of an academic world still committed to rigorous scholasticism and of an ecclesiastical order that recognised no place for an independent scholar who was a cleric. His evolved vocation as a christian humanist, still faithful to his vows as an Augustinian canon, required him to say 'no' to his prior and to achieve his own space in which to work. His, again, was a lifetime of dedication to the study, editing and teaching of the Church Fathers and the New Testament.

Erasmus without his religion would be inconceivable, and Erasmus without his humanism would not be possible. His complete mastering of the humanism of his age made it possible for him to recover – or at very least, to strive to recover – the original teaching of Jesus in the New Testament by applying the ever more rigorous methods and standards of humanistic scholarship forged in the editing of classical texts (in which he played no small part) to the Greek as well as Latin texts of Scripture. The *sola scriptura* of Martin Luther was inconceivable without Erasmus' *Novum Instrumentum* of 1516 and subsequent editions in which he continued to make corrections, even as our modern biblical scholarship that is incomparably more accurate and scholarly owes much to the scholarship of Erasmus.

Finally, there was (as we are slowly beginning to appreciate) a rich spirituality in Erasmus, the roots of which lay partly in his schooling by the Brethren of the Common Life – and in his readings in that great master of Augustinian spirituality, Thomas à Kempis, although he never cities the *Imitation* directly – and by such humanist-masters as Agricola who were themselves deeply imbued with the humanism and spirituality of the *Devotio Moderna*

Understanding Erasmus' christocentric thought, and keeping clearly in view the concept of the *studia humanitatis* with which we have been concerned throughout this biography, we can better understand misreadings of Erasmian humanism that have tried to create a false antithesis and to stress either the humanism or the religion at the expense of the other. Here we must call attention to the central role of Latin and Greek in that humanism, for true humanism has always been at least bilingual. Much is due to Erasmus for the continuing of Latin as the living language – or at least the literary language – of educated Europeans in the sixteenth century (with the emphasis on Latin in schools and universities continuing through the seventeenth and eighteenth centuries, and even into the twentieth in some quarters). The impact of Latin upon intellectual habits, patterns of thought and imagination, and standards of culture is still incalculable[12] for it remains the main road (even if in disrepair and little used) to the vast wealth of classical learning. A large part, but not all, of the glorious story of European literature as an entity has been charted by E.R. Curtius in his magisterial study of *European Literature and the Latin Middle Ages*. 'The bases of Western thought are classical antiquity and Christianity', Curtius has written; and he adds that 'the function of the Middle Ages was to receive that deposit, to transmit it, and to adapt it' (596). The humanism of Erasmus took as its charge the reception and refinement of that deposit in a greater measure and more directly than had been undertaken for hundreds of years; it removed impurities, and it directly experienced for the first time in a millennium the whole of classical antiquity; then, with a sense of great excitement, it presented that refined deposit to his own age. That too is the role of Erasmus, and it justifies his high place in the long chain of tradition.

To transmit tradition, the received wisdom of the past (I return one final time to Curtius) 'is not to solidify it into an immovable body of doctrine or into a fixed choice of canonical books' (597); for tradition, as I have written elsewhere (in 1970), is a continuing process, and a living one, of change, adaptation, reception, and transmission. But, as Erasmus stressed, there is necessarily continuity as well as innovation.

Latin was the medium in the West – for Erasmus, the quintessential medium – for the whole of that process of making tradition live. The language, which includes respect for language itself, the poetic sense of form and the rhetorical stress on audience, together with the spirit of play in the educational enterprise are all vital parts of the Erasmian legacy. All of this was achieved through an incomparable style, one of directness and simplicity: style as the enabling stance and voice, the ultimate morality of mind. Erasmus was the recognised master of Latin language and style (the true disciple of Valla), and the familiar ease and clarity of that style were at once the model and the despair of his contemporaries. Without Erasmus, one reflects, the Latin of scholarship and the international *respublica litterarum* might well have continued its downward slide of the fifteenth-century's exaggerated prose in both Latin and the vernacular; the *florida venustas*, the exaggerated Ciceronianism that is familiar to us in the pedantry and posturing of Johnsonian sesquipedalian words, phrases and sentences. Later centuries have witnessed the virtual disappearance of Latin as the *lingua franca* of the learned world, which is to be lamented; but one cannot understand Erasmus fully without a careful reading of his living Latin and its superlative style, and without a reasonable comprehension of the classical, patristic, medieval and Neo-Latin resources of his Latinity.

Another reason for the neglect of Erasmus today is to be found in the structures of the institutions of learning that have changed so remarkably since the sixteenth century, although too many faculties and *a fortiori* the administrators of the late twentieth-century university are unaware of how the process of change has carried the university away from its earlier ideals of dedication to learning and structures for learning and teaching. Much falls through the nets when university, departmental and other structures are changed: new disciplines come into being, and older ones are pushed aside. Relationships which a renaissance humanist took for granted are forgotten, and Salutati's charge – *Connexa sunt studia humanitatis* – takes on a further meaning. To read the writings of Erasmus with these changes in mind will inevitably bring fresh perspectives.

Renaissance humanists would have been the first to emphasise that knowledge (the expressed goal of the typical twentieth-century university although it tends to conceive of knowledge only in quantitative terms) is not wisdom (which was the ideal of the renaissance university), and that the well-educated human being requires a command of the disciplines and resources of the liberal arts, from grammar and rhetoric to logic and dialectic, and from arithmetic to music and astronomy. Computer literacy must follow verbal literacy, and the use of the computer is only one more superior tool for learning and communication. As Alan Bullock wrote in his wise book on *The Humanist Tradition:*

> It is the study of history and the humanities that keeps alive our sense of a future which is still open. This was what happened when, quite unpredictably, in fourteenth-century Italy, a handful of men felt the impulse to recover the world of antiquity and from that derived the confidence to create a new world of their own.
>
> This is what, throughout these 600 years, the humanist tradition has represented, a refusal to accept a determinist or reductionist view of man, an insistence that in some measure men and women, if they do not enjoy complete freedom, none the less have it in their hands to make choices. (197)

Given the explosion of specialised knowledge, and the restrictive force of departments of specialisation, it is not surprising that many of Erasmus' works do not fit into modern academic structures (as I have commented more fully in 'The Place of Erasmus Today'). There are gains from specialisation, to be sure, but we must realise how high a price is paid by the individual for those gains. Erasmus stands above, or outside of, the departmentalisation of our present-day structures, yet in the modern university we further contribute to our misunderstandings by setting up disciplinary requirements and walls to discourage the reading in Latin of Erasmus' writings as a whole, or of those of his masters and contemporaries. There is, indeed, a growing body of translations of Erasmus into English and French, but departmental reading-lists and like requirements militate against all but the gifted students 'doing' Erasmus on their own. A reading of our Dutch renaissance humanist can give broader perspectives to all specialists and generate fresh insights. For the ideas that Erasmus and the main stream of renaissance humanism expressed are powerful both in the historical view and for our own situation: the insistence on the unique value and centrality of individual human experience, so superbly rendered by Montaigne in his *Essais* and so unforgettably captured by the wealth of Dutch Old Masters from Brueghel to Rembrandt; the dignity of man, quarried from the classical discussions of the *studia humanitatis*, but carried to fresh expression in the enthusiasms, even at times the glories, of literature from Pico della Mirandola to Shakespeare. These are powerful ideas, and they still have importance for us today; and it is in the humanities and arts that we will find the human condition addressed directly and uniquely. Therefore I echo and applaud the words of Alan Bullock: 'I believe they [the humanities and the arts] ought to remain an essential part of our education and lives' (188).

How do we evaluate Erasmus and his many controversies, and what importance can they have for us today, those hundreds upon hundreds of pages of controversy on what are all too often obscure topics for us in the twentieth century? For a person who professed the goal of peace, it must be said that Erasmus was engaged in a great deal of controversial writing, some of it petty and personal. For the last two decades of his life he spent an inordinate amount of time and energy in addressing enemies of humanism – but had not his very early work *Antibarbari* been directed against just such enemies, the barbarians? – and in responding to direct attacks upon himself and his work. He knew all too well from experience what Edward Gibbon called 'the exquisite rancour of theological hatred'. But then, we can now look at the cumulative impact of Luther and his followers upon the life of the period: it became a world of peasants' rebellions, iconoclasms, civil disorder and upheaval. If our contemporary Ursula LeGuin can write in all sincerity 'my goal has always been to subvert as much as possible without hurting anybody's feelings', we must respond that no one who subverts can think that she or he will not hurt someone's feelings; and after 1520, if not earlier, Luther no longer cared about hurting the feelings of those who opposed or differed from him. Although Erasmus was neither perfect nor totally blameless – one can only guess at the host of enmities generated by the *Moriae Encomium*, as well as the many other barbs of his often biting wit (written paradoxically by one who had a thin skin himself), with the witticisms of his letters often reaching a wide audience – Erasmus in his controversies tried, in general, to keep to the higher levels of discourse.

Again and again Erasmus did try to be a peacemaker, and his irenic spirit shines through many of his writings; and much of his energy in his last years was given to work specifically aimed at mending the torn coat of Christendom, and to countless letters which tried to mediate. Thus a passage like the following strikes a note that is fairly consistent in his later years, and it can be found echoed in works of the mid-1520s, such as the adage *'Ne Bos Quidem Pereat'* discussed earlier. In his Paraphrase on the *Epistle to the Romans*, where he is addressing Jews by name but others by implication, and expanding the Pauline injunction 'welcome him, but not for disputes over opinions', Erasmus says,

> Nevertheless, if there is someone among you, perhaps a Jew by race, who, because he has grown accustomed for so long to his former practice and life, is still rather superstitious, and whose faith has not grown in him enough to enable him to exclude all observance of the former law, he must not be immediately excluded with contempt, but instead he must be attracted and encouraged by gentleness and courtesy until he too begins to advance and receive the strength of faith. This will come about more readily through good-will than through contentious arguing... In order that peace and concord exist everywhere among you some things must be ignored, some endured, some interpreted with more kindness. This forbearance and sincerity has great force to produce a mutual fellowship of life. Peace will never remain firm among many unless in some things one gives way in turn to another, inasmuch as there are various opinions among people. (*CWE* 42:77)

If this passage might seem to fall short of our high standards of ecumenism and tolerance (on which see Pelikan, *The Melody of Theology*), it must be affirmed that Erasmus was a monument and a beacon for his own age.

All Erasmus' controversial writings, it must be emphasised, were in Latin (like all of his other writings): in his controversies he was exchanging opinions among professional colleagues and not trying to sway a popular audience. But his paraphrases of the New Testament, together with his irenic writings, can be read as parables for our times that have deep-seated hatreds bred in the bone in so many parts of the globe. A text for discussion of long-standing political strife such as we find in the Near East, in the Indian sub-continent, in Northern Ireland, and elsewhere, might well be Erasmus' final words on Romans 14: 'But whenever error arises out of weakness, he who is held in the grip of error deserves to be taught and admonished; he does not deserve to be despised or ridiculed' (*CWE* 42: 82).

For one caught in the maelstrom of the Reformation to write of the mutual fellowship of life was neither weak nor foolishly optimistic: it was at its heart's core Christian, and it was strengthened by the traditions of civility that run through Cicero into the main stream of the western traditions of politics and into the thought that produced the casting of the American Declaration of Independence and Constitution (as Ernest Barker has so eloquently shown in *Traditions of Civility*). That ideal of mutual fellowship was still possible in 1519, the date of the Froben revision of the New Testament paraphrases, and in 1521 in the collected edition of the Pauline letters; and we find it in 1532 and 1534 in the collected editions of all of the paraphrases. For Erasmus it was still possible, though increasingly difficult, even in the year of his death.

Some today might wish that the author of the *Moriae Encomium* had allowed freer rein for his imagination in his later years and had spent less time on the controversies; or that the author of the *Adagia* and *Colloquia* had given us still more of that bounty. But he would not have been Erasmus if he had not tried with all his rhetorical skills to make clear his own position and to attempt to correct the views of others: 'I cannot be other than what I am', he said.

The notion that Erasmus was an 'intellectual' has already been put forward, but it is a view that needs further exploration and greater qualification.

In one of the more interesting recent books on the intellectual in the modern European world, Paul Johnson has written as follows:

> Over the past two hundred years the influence of intellectuals has grown steadily. Indeed, the rise of the secular intellectual

has been a key factor in shaping the modern world. Seen against the very long perspective of history it is in many ways a new phenomenon. It is true that in their earlier incarnations as priests, scribes and soothsayers, intellectuals have laid claim to guide society from the very beginning. But as guardians of hieratic cultures, whether primitive or sophisticated, their moral and ideological innovations were limited by the canons of external authority and by the inheritance of tradition. They were not, and could not be free spirits, adventurers of the mind.[13]

If one defines an intellectual as a person guided by ideas and by the use of the intellect rather than by emotion or experience, then neither Erasmus nor Rabelais nor Montaigne was an intellectual in the pure sense of a *doctrinaire*: one who subordinates individual experience to the formulation of a doctrine. (Besides, in the narrower sense, who would be more of an intellectual than a medieval schoolman, ringed as he was by authority?) There are disadvantages in applying such modern terms to a man or woman of the Renaissance; yet there may be gains at the same time, provided that our use of the term intellectual is clearly defined and understood. With Erasmus as later with Montaigne, ideas are tested by experience (where more dramatically than in the *Adages?*), and experience through memory is brought to bear, to be probed and tested in the act and art of the *essai*: which is a trying-out, a probe, something tentative or at least provisional ('*La maladresse est la loi de toute essai, dans n'importe quel genre*', Alain). And of the three sixteenth-century figures it seems patent that it is with Erasmus far more true that the person mattered very nearly as much as the idea; and at times, more so.

Perhaps the ultimate gain in looking at Erasmus in the light of the modern concept of the intellectual is, paradoxically, to understand the extent to which he fought off intellectual formulations. There is more than a hint of the anti-intellectualism which is so characteristic of Thomas à Kempis and so much of the *Devotio Moderna*: 'I would prefer to love the Trinity than to be able to define it'.

Partial and partisan judgments of Erasmus have been made with great facility and great regularity over the generations.[14] Slowly these inadequate judgments are being pushed aside by the scholarship of P.S. Allen and the other Erasmians who have devoted years, lifetimes even, to the study and interpretation of Erasmus' writings. If it be in part reasonable (though less than fully fair) that Erasmus can be seen as a Hamlet figure who found it difficult at times to arrive at a decision for action, a more valid answer lies in the fact that in some situations no action can be taken that is in accord with one's values. There are some situations that are morally indifferent. Thus, like Plato, Erasmus can be taken to be 'the tragic symbol of the wise man who cannot support either of two opposing issues, not because he lacks strength and courage, but because his mind is too unimpeachable to conceal to itself the defects on either side'.[15] Rather than a cowardly figure, then – in Pastor's influential view, 'a great scholar but a weak character'[16] – let us recognise the integrity of the man. And to that recognition let us add understanding in the light of Lord Acton's judgment of Erasmus as the greatest figure of the Renaissance, not only eminently international but also of all men the most capable of living by historical imagination in other times.[17]

Yet in stressing his imagination and his quality of mind, and in perceiving the indomitable courage that lay in that frail body, let us not neglect that aspect which was for Erasmus of supreme importance: the reality of Christ, and the centrality of Christ in his vision of Christianity. We have not yet reached a consensus on the spirituality of Erasmus, or on his unique sense of vocation,[18] but in this biography it has been argued that he in fact had a rich spiritual life and that his vocation was that of a religious, an Augustinian canon, living outside his monastery and devoted to a life of scholarship. The end of that scholarship was simple and constant: to live a life infused with a love of Christ and to teach others how that love might be reached and supported through a lifelong study of the Bible and the classical heritage of wisdom.

The magnificent portraits of Erasmus by Metsys, Dürer and Holbein project the living presence of a scholar at work, *scribendus*, and in some of the paintings we can even read the titles of the work at hand: *New Testament, Paraphrases, Adagia, Antibarbari*. To speak of the 'presence' of Erasmus immediately connotes the quality of self-assurance and confidence, which are there in the portraits, to be sure; but the word also denotes the area immediately surrounding a great personage, which for Erasmus was everywhere that his books and letters reached, that is, all of Christendom from Spain to Poland, and from Italy to the regions north of the Alps, including Scandinavia. Just as Erasmus never lost his sense of the presence of God in his world and everyday life, so humanists around the map of Europe were also aware of Erasmus – whether he was at the moment in Paris, England, the Low Countries, Basel or Freiburg – continuously at work, always producing something new and exciting, yet always growing out of a rich sense of tradition.

Thus the younger scholars of Europe never lost sight of the courage of this humanist, and of his willingness to engage hostile critics and enemies of himself and of the humanism he espoused and they shared, in order to make clear what it was that he espoused. Of the fifteen hundred known letters written to Erasmus by a cross-section of educated European society of the period, one remarkable letter stands out and can serve as an example for the host of others. At the end of 1532 a young French friar and scholar, then a proofreader for the printer Gryphius in Lyon, wrote to Erasmus, whom he had never met, and that autograph letter is extant in Leipzig. That young humanist on the threshold of his own greatness was François Rabelais, who addressed the great Dutch humanist whose writings (especially the *Adagia*) he had been studying:

> I gladly seized that occasion, kind father, of showing by a pleasing service [forwarding a manuscript] with what devotion and piety I love you. I call you father; for, as we daily see that pregnant women nourish offspring which they have never seen and protect them from the harsh outer air, *the same has happened to you* who have educated me who am unknown to you and of simple estate. Thus have you hitherto nourished me with the most chaste breasts of your divine learning, so that, did I not ascribe to you alone my whole worth and being, I should be the most ungrateful of all men who are now alive or ever shall be. Hail again and again, most beloved father, father and glory of your country, champion and *defende*r of letters and unconquered fighter for the truth.[19]

Colet's prediction that the name of Erasmus would never perish was fulfilled by such a reader then and in such a remarkable way (for the pages of Rabelais' own masterpiece are filled with marks of his indebtedness to the *Adagia*), and the prediction continues to be fulfilled by countless readers around the world today.

Nomen Erasmi ...

Notes

1) For the earlier period see A. Flitner, *Erasmus im Urteil seiner Nachwelt: Das literarische Erasmus-bild von Beatus Rhenanus bis zu Jean Le Clerc* (Tübingen, 1952). Bruce Mansfield's survey covers from about 1550 to 1750: *Phoenix of His Age* (Toronto, 1979). See also 'The Genius of Erasmus and His Place in History' in Preserved Smith, *Erasmus,* 421–41. In addition to the bibliographical coverage in Van der Haeghen, *Bibliotheca Erasmiana*, there is a complete bibliography of Erasmian scholarship in the three volumes edited by J.-C. Margolin: *Douze années de bibliographie érasmienne, 1950–1961* (Paris, 1963); *Quatorze années de bibliographie érasmienne, 1936–1949* (Paris, 1969); and *Neuf années de bibliographie érasmienne, 1962–1970* (Paris-Toronto, 1977).

Of the several tools for Erasmus research one must be mentioned at this point: the *Catalogue of the Erasmus Collection in the City Library of Rotterdam* (Gemeentebibliotheek Rotterdam), published by Greenwood Press, New York, 1990, on the significance of which I have written in *Libraries and Culture* (1992). Appropriately located in a city that honours Erasmus in a number of ways – a fine statue in the heart of the city, a university that bears his name, an old gymnasium with a fine classical tradition – the Erasmus Collection holds the world's largest collection of works by and about Erasmus, including rich holdings in early 16th-c. printings.

2) On Erasmus as rhetorician, see R.J. Schoeck, '"Going for the Throat": Erasmus the master-rhetorician', [in press].

3) Ernesto Grassi has written persuasively on this concept in *Rhetoric as Philosophy: The Humanist Tradition* (University Park, Pennsylvania, 1980).

4) Cf. M. Schulze, *Calvins Jenseits-Christentum im Verhältnis zu den religiösen Schriften des Erasmus* (1902). Smith, *Erasmus* 425, cites the index to *Calvini Opera*, vol. lix, p. 76, for citations of Erasmus by Calvin.

5) Tyndale spoke nastily of Erasmus as one 'whose tongue maketh of little gnats great elephants and lifteth up above the stars whosoever giveth him a little exhibition' – A.W. Pollard, *Records of the English Bible* (1911) 96; but as Smith notes, 425 n.5, Tyndale borrowed from Erasmus himself (*ex musca plusquam elephantem: Adag.* I. ix. 69) in the very act of slighting him (cf. Ep. 1148).

6) E. Troeltsch, *Protestantism and Progress* (1912) 201.

7) J.S. Brewer, 'Passages from the Life of Erasmus' (1881) 346.

8) *Civilization during the Middle Ages*, 423 ff. That opinion is echoed by Mark Pattison in the article on Erasmus in the *Encyclopedia Britannica*, 9th ed. (rev. by P.S. Allen for the 11th ed.).

9) The debate between J. van Dorsten and R.J. Schoeck can be seen as turning about a difference between popularity and influence.

10) 'Erasmus dominated his age. He is the greatest man we come across in the history of education. Those particular qualities of sympathy, mental grasp and imagination which an educator requires if he is to be completely successful, are in practice rarely found together. He possessed them all in a perfect combination and on a gigantic scale' – R.R. Bolgar, *The Classical Heritage*, 336.

11) Bullock has commented judiciously on the careless, ignorant or imprecise linkage (to the point with some of claiming an identity) between the humanism of the 16th c. and that of the 20th (160): 'None the less, while accepting that the humanist tradition inherits from the eighteenth and nineteenth centuries a current of anti-Christian feeling as one of its historical characteristics, the claim sometimes made by both secularists and fundamentalists that secularism *represents* humanism is a travesty – as much a travesty as to take fundamentalism to represent religion. Humanist attitudes towards religion in fact cover a much wider spectrum than rationalist hostility to anything which smacks of the supernatural or the mystical' (160).

12) Much of the effort of recent Neo-Latin Congresses (IANLS) has been given to exploring that impact, and the recent work of J.W. Binns is significant: see *Intellectual Culture in Elizabethan and Jacobean England* (Leeds, 1991).

13) To other discussion of the problem of influence one should add the perceptive comments of Peter Burke on terms like 'spread', 'diffusion', 'impact' or indeed 'reception': 'like much of the historian's vocabulary, they are of course metaphors, dead or at any rate sleeping and sometimes inappropriate for the tasks they are required to perform' ('The Spread of Italian Humanism', in *The Impact of Humanism on Western Europe,* ed. A. Goodman & Angus Mackay (London, 1990) 2. I have commented on the question of metaphors in 'Metaphors, Models and Mobiles for Interdisciplinary Study' (16th-c. Studies Conference, October 1991).

14) Paul Johnson, *Intellectuals* (London, 1988) 1. Johnson goes on to speak of 'the decline of clerical power in the eighteenth century': but that power was in intellectual matters already being eroded in the early sixteenth century, and Erasmus had played a significant role in the recognition of the capabilities and rights of the laity. One could write pages of commentary on the last two sentences of the quotation: intellectuals like Erasmus extended, if in fact they were not already breaking through the canons of external authority; and he for one would not have felt limited by the 'inheritance of tradition', though he did not spurn the concept of a dynamic tradition. If Erasmus in works like *Moriae Encomium*, the Colloquies and the major Adages was not an adventurer of the mind, I do not know what he was – nor can I think of one more entitled to be called one.

15) Thus Robert Ulich, *Educational Wisdom,* 250. Cf. T.S. Eliot on Henry James: 'He had a mind so fine that no idea could violate it' (from 'Henry James', in *Selected Prose*, ed. Kermode, 151).

16) Ludwig von Pastor, *History of the Popes*, Engl. trans. by Kerr, VIII, 315; see Smith, *Erasmus,* 423.

17) Lord Acton, *Lectures on Modern History* (Cambridge, 1906) 86 ff.

18) See R. DeMolen, *The Spirituality of Erasmus;* R.J. Schoeck, *Erasmus Grandescens*, and Vol. 1 of this biography on his unique sense of vocation.

19) Ep. 2743, 30 Nov. 1532; Allen X, 130/5 ff. I follow Smith in italicising the words originally in Greek, for Rabelais was doubtless intending them to establish his humanistic credentials. Cf. Halkin's aperçu (367) that the enthusiasm of Rabelais's eulogy of Erasmus was justified by the service of Erasmus in establishing the 'voice' for the early Gargantua. The study of the letter by L. Thuasne in *Revue des bibliothèques* 15 (Paris, 1905) 203–25 is still relevant; and the relationship of Rabelais to Erasmus has been further explored by M.A. Screech in 'Folie érasmienne et folie rabelaisienne – Comment Rabelais a exploité les travaux d'Érasme', *Colloquia Erasmiana Turonensia* (Paris, 1972) I, 44–61.

APPENDIX C

Erasmus' Dispensations

A dispensation in Roman Catholic canon law is a relaxation of a law in a particular case. Such a relaxation can be made only by the competent authority, and it involves an act of jurisdiction (*CIC* c. 80). Erasmus must have received four dispensations: the first for his ordination; the second in 1506; the third in 1517; and a fourth much later. These will be discussed individually.[1]

1. Dispensation for Ordination

Erasmus was ordained on 25 April 1492 (ch. 5), despite his illegitimacy. Normally illegitimacy is a hindrance or impediment for ordination, and Erasmus' illegitimacy (discussed in ch. 2) was such an impediment, or, more technically, an irregularity by defect. Such an irregularity is regarded as perpetual, but it may be dispensed by competent authority. This dispensation presumably was given by the ordaining bishop, David of Utrecht (ch. 5).

This dispensation is glanced at in the letter from Leo X to Ammonius (Ep. 517): Erasmus 'advanced in holy orders even so far as the priesthood under license from his superior' (*CWE* 4: 190/10–11; Allen II, 434/8–9: '*et presbyteratus ordines promotus de licentia sui superioris*').

2. The Dispensation of 1506

Having struggled against the insistence of his prior that he return to the monastery, Erasmus applied to the pope for a dispensation that would permit him to live outside the cloister and to hold ecclesiastical offices outside the monastery. That dispensation was granted in a bull from Julius II to Erasmus, dated 4 January 1506 (*CWE* 2:105–6; Allen III, xxix).[2]

This dispensation is primarily a freeing of Erasmus from any canonical impediment to his accepting ecclesiastical benefices on account of his illegitimate birth, and at this time the essential concern of Erasmus was for freedom to accept a benefice in England (*CWE* 2:103–4; Allen III, xxix); but he did not in fact use the dispensation for this purpose until he was given the rectory of Aldington in 1512 (Ep. 255).

The papal dispensation is for 'a defect of birth being the offspring of an unmarried father and a widow': it is not only possible, it is very likely that in 1505 at the time of applying for the dispensation Erasmus had not been aware of the full circumstances of his birth, although that he knew of his own illegitimacy is of course clear (ch.2 and app. A).

3. The Dispensation of 1517

Not only did circumstances change after 1506, as we note, but it seems probable that in Italy Erasmus gained knowledge about his father that made clear to him the true nature of his birth.[3] First, owing to his long residence in England Erasmus improved his chances for clerical patronage. Especially after the Cambridge period (1511–1514) he now had increased hopes of one or more benefices in England; he was promised a canonry at Courtrai; and he writes of talk about his being given a bishopric. The 1506 dispensation did not cover these possibilities. Accordingly Erasmus sought a dispensation from Leo X that would be fuller in its scope, and also more specific in addressing the worrying issues of having to return to his monastery and wear the monastic garb. Secondly, it seems most likely that while in Italy from 1506 to 1509 he learned more about his father's clerical status (and perhaps the family relationships of his mother); for in applying for the 1506 dispensation he had spoken of his father only as a bachelor (*solitus*) and of his mother as a widow (*CWE* 2: 105/9–10; Allen III, xxix/5: '*de soluto genitus et vidua*').[4] In the *Compendium Vitae* Erasmus acknowledge that his father eventually became a priest, and this is congruent with the statement of Leo X about Erasmus' illegitimacy: 'And being thereafter, although he suffers from a disability of birth being the offspring of an unlawful and (as he fears) incestuous and condemned union ...' (*CWE* 4:190/8–10; Allen II, 434/ 6–8).

The Toronto editors have rightly pointed out that 'even if the phrase [*'de illicito et ... coitu'*] did imply 'spiritual incest', such a relationship could be incurred in a number of ways, including the obligations of godparent to godchild...' (*CWE* 4:note to Ep.517). But the possibility of his father's having been a priest at the time of his conception and birth is not ruled out by the letter from Leo X, nor are other possible affinities (on which see appendix A). The phrase *as he fears* is a conventional one.

Clearly the main motive for the 1517 dispensation was the need for a new, and stronger, dispensation to enable him to hold more than one benefice anywhere. It did not free Erasmus from his monastic vows, except for permitting him to live away from the monastery and to wear a modified dress; and it did not in any way alter his status as a priest.[5] See illustration in *CWE* 4:192/3.

4. A Dispensation for the Making of a Will

Ex professo, Erasmus had taken vows of poverty, chastity and obedience in becoming an Augustinian Canon – the vow of absolute poverty originally agreed upon in the Rule of St Augustine was mitigated by the pope in 1257 to permit property to be held in the name of the community when deemed necessary (*NCE* I, 1072). But the dispensations of 1506 and 1517 authorised Erasmus to hold benefices and to receive 'of whatsoever valuation or annual value the fruits, revenues and proceeds thereof' (*CWE* 2:106/23–4).

For the making of a will that involved his property, however, Erasmus required and evidently obtained a licence from the pope, in order for him as a cleric to dispose of that property without violating any of the many provisions of canon law that touched upon this question.[6] Erasmus' donation of monies to Goclenius was contested by his Westphalian family and the university of Louvain, owing to Goclenius' having been intestate. Erasmus took great pains to insure his testamentary provision for the disposal of his estate (see appendix D and the discussion of his 1536 will).

Notes

1) See J. Lederer, *Der Dispensbegriff des kanon. Rechtes* (Mainz, 1957); E. Reilly, *The General Norms of Dispensation* (Washington, D.C., 1939); and *NCE*. Stupperich's strongly argued article on canonical aspects of Erasmus' entry into the monastery and priesthood (*ARG* 65 [1974], 18–36) has already been discussed in Vol. 1 (32, 39, 261).

2) In his letter to Servatius Rogers of 1514 (never published by Erasmus, which contains his apologia for not having returned to his home monastery) Erasmus invoked the dispensation of Julius II in order to justify his change of habit (Ep. 296, *CWE* 2:301/197 ff.); but in point of fact this dispensation did not warrant his change of dress (*CWE* 4:2 headnote). This was not a major problem, however; and Erasmus received permission from the bishop of Utrecht to do so (*CWE* 2:300/182–5), probably from the successor to David of Burgundy, who had died in 1496.

3) But this probability still lacks documentary evidence, and it must be acknowledged that information might have reached Erasmus at any time after 1506, especially in the Low Countries.

4) Even the term *vidua* is ambiguous (see ch. 2).

5) On these last points see DeMolen, 'Erasmus' Commitment to the Canons Regular of St. Augustine', ch. 8 in *The Spirituality of Erasmus of Rotterdam* (Nieuwkoop, 1987) 191–7: 'It is important to recall that Erasmus remained a member of the Austin Canons throughout his adult life. His life-style harmonized with the spirit of the Austin Canons even though he lived outside of their monastic walls' (191). Yet it cannot be declared, except with careful qualification, that Erasmus remained 'subject to its rules and under obedience to its religious superiors' (196); but certainly in 1524 he declared himself a living member of the Austin Canons, in his letter to Geldenouwer (Ep. 1436, c. 2 April 1524, Allen V, 427/19).

6) Our lack of clear understanding on this matter is reflected in the remark of van Peteghem that 'ambiguous laws, conflicting customs and special privileges and institutions helped to fashion a legal order which was for *a layman and immigrant* like Erasmus rather confusing' (91, italics mine): but whatever else his status, Erasmus was not a layman, and canon law had its jurisdiction by virtue of his being a cleric (see ch. 1).

APPENDIX D

Erasmus' Wills

One's first will may be a *rite de passage*, something required in difficult times (as with the military in time of war) or expected in normal times (for reasons of family or business). Given Erasmus' change of home and fortune, it is not surprising that he made more than one will. It is surprising, in fact, that there were not more than three and that he had not made out a will during his earlier periods of severe illness, when he thought of the imminence of death.[1]

1. The Will of 1527

On 22 January 1527 Erasmus drew up his will, naming Bonifacius Amerbach as his trustee,[2] with three executors Basil Amerbach, Beatus Rhenanus, and Hieronymus Froben. His rings were to go to Boniface, together with a spoon of pure gold and a golden double cup given him by duke George. Other friends were remembered with token bequests: Glareanus, Baer, Basil Amerbach, Hieronymus and Johannes Froben, Sigismund Galen (a proofreader at the Froben press), Botzheim and Goclenius – all friends of some years' duration. His servant Quirinus was remembered with a legacy of two hundred pounds, and there were directions for a funeral 'neither pretentious nor sordid' ('*sumptu nec sordido nec ambitioso*'). Erasmus also speaks of the sale and shipment of his library to Johannes a Lasko (See Epistle 1593/133).

For this will Erasmus had taken pains to have legal sanction to make such a will: in 1525 from pope Clement (permission to leave his property as he wished), and from the tribunals of Basel in 1527.[3]

In this will Erasmus made provision for Froben to print a collected edition of his works, following the plan laid down in the *Catalogus Lucubrationum*. The editors were to be Glareanus, Goclenius, Rhenanus, the two Amerbachs, and Sigismund Galen. Then, interestingly, provision was made for copies of the work to be sent as follows: six to England (Warham, Tunstall, More, Longland, bishop of Lincoln, Fisher, and to Queens' College, Cambridge); five variously in Europe (the Royal Library in Spain, to Croy, bishop of Toledo, to Ferdinand, Bernard von Cles, bishop of Trent and to Baptista Ignatius); and eight to recipients in the Low Countries (the Collegium Trilingue and the College of the Lily at Louvain, to the college to be founded at Tournay, to Francis Craneveld in Mechlin, to the abbot of St Bavon at Ghent, to Laurinus for the library of the College of St Donation at Bruges, to Everard the President of the Estates of Holland, and to the monastery at Egmond).[4] All in all, a total of twenty copies of what would be an expensive *Opera Omnia*: a fine remembrance of old friends, or (in the case of libraries) old debts.

2. The Will of 1533

In moving from Basel to Freiburg – although the distance was only a hundred kilometers – Erasmus changed not only political jurisdiction, from a city in the Swiss Confederation whose *Reformationsordnung* was creating fresh problems to an imperial city functioning in the light of the Roman legacy of law and still professing obedience to the emperor and pope. There were other changes as well, involving intricacies of legalities and jurisdiction.[5]

At Freiburg on 26 November 1533 Erasmus revoked his earlier will and made a new one. Unfortunately that will has not survived, although the attestation by a Freiburg notary has been preserved (Allen XI, 362, Appendix XXV).

3. The Will of 1536

Back in Basel and in failing health, Erasmus needed a new will, and this was drawn up on 12 February 1536 (Allen XI, 362–5).[6] This legal act was done only several months after his return to Basel in the summer of 1535, doubtless because of ill health. What cannot be discussed here is the extent of consultation (notably with doctors of law in Louvain, and doubtless in Basel as well), and the donation to Goclenius, a Louvain professor and intimate friend who lived in the Low Countries.[7]

The main differences between this 1536 will and that of 1527 have been noted by Allen (XI, 362). The provision for the publication of the *Opera Omnia* has been dropped. The naming of executors calls for comment: Basil Amerbach (one of the three named in 1527) died in 1535, and only one of the remaining two was retained, Hieronymus Froben – Beatus Rhenanus was replaced by the partner of Froben, Nicholas Episcopius.[8] Two legatees named in 1527 are not found in 1536: Botzheim (who had died), and Glareanus (perhaps because he remained in Freiburg, not because he did not continue to be a devoted friend and admirer of Erasmus). Nine persons not named in 1527 were to receive bequests according to the 1536 will: Viterius, Montanus, Lambert Coomans, John Brisgoicus (Erasmus' confessor), Paul Volz, Johann Erasmius Froben, Hieronymus Froben's wife, and Episcopius and Justina his wife. There are changes too, as Allen notes, in the monetary bequests.

Immediately after the funeral in Basel cathedral on 18 July 1536, his will was opened and read by the Basel clerk and notary; several days later another notary made a complete inventory of his money and goods.[9] It is evident that Erasmus must be accounted a wealthy man at his death, and that he was generous to his friends and benefactors.

The greater part of the monies at the disposal of the Basel executors became a trust for the support of students in the University of Basel, a part earmarked for poor students. From Roth it can be seen that the University of Basel still has Erasmus scholarships.[10]

Notes

1) In 1518 he thought of making a will: 'Things came to such a pass that I considered making my will' (Ep. 860/11–12 to Antonio Pucci 26 Aug. 1518, *CWE* 6:96/11–12). At that time he was about 51, well into the time of life when men thought of old age and death.

2) The importance of the choice of Bonifacius Amerbach as trustee must

be recognised: he was an eminent Basel jurist and holder of one of the chairs of law at the University of Basel. See *BR* and P.P.J.L. van Peteghem, 'Erasmus' Last Will, the Holy Roman Empire and the Low Countries,' in *Erasmus of Rotterdam*, ed. Sperna Weiland and Frijhoff (1988) 89.

3) See L. Sieber, *Das Testament von Erasmus* (Basel 1889), and Smith 261–2, with the documentation there given. The text of Erasmus' first will is given in Appendix XIX of Allen (VI, 503–6) and in Sieber.

4) A complete list is given in Allen VI, 505.

5) See van Peteghem, 91: 'The Labyrinthine state of law and legislation had its institutional counterpart. The administration of justice was plagued by a bewildering array of competing jurisdictions. Such matters as judging testaments could be complicated by the fact that ecclesiastical courts, royal tribunals and municipal justices would increase their own prestige by claiming exclusive jurisdiction.'

6) See now B.R. Jenny, 'Erasmus' Rückkehr nach Basel, Lebensende, Grab und Testament,' in *Erasmus von Rotterdam, Vorkämpfer für Frieden und Toleranz. Ausstellung zum 450. Todestag des Erasmus von Rotterdam veranstaltet vom Historischen Museum Basel* (Basel, 1986) 63–5.

7) On Goclenius, see *BR*; and on the deeding of monies placed in trust with Goclenius, see van Peteghem, 92 ff.

8) After 1527 Beatus left Basel and settled in Sélestat, but the two close friends kept in touch through friends they had in common: see *BR*.

9) Carl Roth, *Das Legatum Erasmianum,* in *Gedenkschrift zum 400. Todestage des Erasmus von Rotterdam* (Basel, 1936); and Allen, app. xxv (XI, 362–3). The inventory is summarised by Smith, 262.

10) Goclenius and Schets were responsible for the handling and investment of Erasmus' monies before his death.

APPENDIX E

Portraits of Erasmus

Erasmus was singularly fortunate in his portraitists, who included the leading portrait-painter of the Low Countries, Quentin Metsys, and two of the leading painters of Germany, Albrecht Dürer and Hans Holbein the Younger. Portraits were still a new genre in the early sixteenth century, and it is not surprising that there are no portraits of Erasmus as a young man. Not until 1517, when Erasmus was about fifty and able to afford to commission a painter, did he sit for a portrait.[1]

Born 1465/6 in Louvain, Metsys (the name is variously spelled: Metsys, Metsijs, Massys) was the son of a blacksmith and may have begun in that trade. But he set up shop in Antwerp as a painter and metal engraver not later than 1491. He is the artist of two multiple altar-pieces in Brussels and Antwerp, works of the period 1508–1511. A friend of Pieter Gillis, Metsys was commissioned by Erasmus to execute the twin portraits of Gillis and himself as a gift to Thomas More (Eps 584, 616, 654, 669). More's letter to Erasmus (Ep. 684) speaks glowingly of the accuracy of detail, and it is suffused with his enthusiasm (see fig. 2 and Vol. 1 frontispiece). The double picture is well conceived, both in the individual portraits and in the composition that relates the two paintings. In the one on the left, the Dutch humanist is represented at a desk with an open book before him, pen in hand as he writes the *Paraphrase to the Epistle to the Romans*. On the forefinger of the delicately drawn right hand a seal ring is conspicuous. We are given the humanist at work, writing, a significant emphasis that distinguishes the subject from portraits of Jerome in the Renaissance. In the twin portrait on the right, Gillis holds a letter of More in his hand (More speaks of it in Eps 683 & 684, which enclosed verses on the painting). In 1519 Metsys executed bronze medallions with a head of Erasmus, one of the medallions being now in the museum at Basel and the other at the Luther-house in Wittenberg. In 1528 Henry Botteus told Erasmus that he thought the medallion was wonderfully lifelike (Smith, 150).[2]

Albrecht Dürer (1471–1528) was first trained as a goldsmith by his father, next apprenticed to the leading painter of Nürnberg, Michael Wolgemut (1486–89), and then travelled as a journeyman, mainly in the Upper Rhineland. He later visited Italy twice, and after 1507 resided mainly in Nürnberg, where he was given an imperial salary by Charles V. In 1520 Dürer and Erasmus met in Antwerp and Brussels, and a first portrait drawing was made at this time. In 1526 an engraved portrait of Erasmus was made. In 1523 Erasmus asked for a painted portrait, which was apparently done by 1526; but Erasmus was not satisfied with the likeness (Epistles 1729 & 1985). In 1528 Erasmus eulogised Dürer in *De pronuntiatione*, and as Dürer died shortly after publication this proved to be an epitaph on him (see *BR* I, 413–5). Dürer also showed the humanist seated at his desk – *humanista scribens* – and on the desk there is a vase of flowers, and he is surrounded by books. Erasmus' hands are now much older, and perhaps Dürer is deliberately representing their goutiness: one hand holds a quill, the other a narrow inkhorn. Smith suggests (262) that what we are given here is not the individual in a character study, but the archetypical scholar: again, *humanista scribens.*[3]

The son of the Augsburg painter Hans Holbein the Elder (1465–1524), Hans the Younger (1497/8–1543) was a painter, miniaturist, worker in glass, jewellery and metal, and designer of woodcuts and painted glass. Holbein came to Basel from Augsburg in 1515, and he executed his first portraits there in 1516. After brief visits to France (1524) and England (1526), and a long stay in England from 1532 to 1538, he lived mainly in Basel (*BR* II). His earliest known surviving work is the group of drawings in the margins of a copy of the second edition of Erasmus' *Moriae Encomium* (Basel, Froben, 1515), a copy that belonged to the humanist Myconius and which is now in Basel (figures 4 and 5).[4] In 1523 Holbein painted two portraits of Erasmus that were sent to England. The first presumably was sent to archbishop Warham and depicts Erasmus resting his hands on a book bearing the inscription in Greek 'The labours of Hercules' (now in the Radnor collection). The second, now in the Louvre, displays Erasmus writing (frontispiece), as does a third portrait of 1523, now in Basel, showing Erasmus writing his *Paraphrase on Mark* (published by Froben in 1523).[5] Later Holbein produced several versions of his device Terminus.[6]

There is an anonymous woodcut dated 1522, showing Erasmus in profile, and claiming to be done from life. It bears the Greek inscription, 'his writings will show his image more truly' – the inscription found on the medallion and in the Dürer woodcut. Smith notes (151) 'there are also extant a woodcut after Matsys ascribed to Cranach, a drawing by Jerome Hopfer probably after the medallion, but showing a more humorous expression, and a very poor drawing ascribed to Lucas van Leyden, dated 1521'. Other drawings, portraits, medallions and statues were done after his death and have much less claim to authenticity.[7]

Notes

1) For a fuller view of his three principal portraitists, see further Aloïs Gerlo, *Erasme et ses portraitistes – Metsijs, Dürer, Holbein.* 2nd ed. (Nieuwkoop, 1969).

2) See M.M. Phillips, 'The Mystery of the Metsys Portrait,' *Erasmus in English* 7 (1975) 18–21; J.B. Trapp, et al., 'Quentin Metsys, Erasmus, Pieter Gillis, and Thomas More,' *Burlington Magazine* 120 (1978) 716–25; and J.B. Trapp, 'A postscript to Matsys,' *Burlington Magazine* 121 (1979) 437–7, which adds detail on the provenance. On Metsys himself, see *BR* II, 438–9, L. Schmolderen, 'Quentin Metsys, medailleur d'Erasme,' in *Scrinium Erasmium* II, 513–25; and Larry Silver, *The paintings of Quinten Massys* (Montclair, N.J., 1984), as well as Gerlo, cited above.

3) See Gerlo, *Erasme et ses portraitistes,* 29–44; and E. Panofsky, *Albrecht Dürer* (Princeton, 1943) and 'Erasmus and the Visual Arts,' *JWCI* 32 (1969) 200–27.

4) For the relations between Erasmus and Holbein, see A.K. Bruce, *Erasmus and Holbein* (London, 1936); and Hans Reinhardt, 'Erasmus and Holbein,' *Basler Zeitschrift für Geschichte und Altertumskunde* 81 (1981) 41–70.

5) See P. Ganz, *The Paintings of Hans Holbein* (London, 1950) nos 34 & 36.

6) See J. K. McConica, 'The Riddle of the Terminus,' *Erasmus in English* 2 (1971) 2–7.

7) See Erwin Treu, *Die Bildnisse des Erasmus von Rotterdam* (Basel, 1959), which discusses the death-portraits (*Die Totenbildnisse*), and the statue of Erasmus in Rotterdam. In 1986 the exhibition commemorating the 450th anniversary of Erasmus' death at the Historisches Museum, Basel, issued a catalogue rich in illustrations: medallions, drawing of his death-mask, etc.

An Erasmian Chronology:
Life and Writings *

1467(?), 28 Oct.	Erasmus born at Rotterdam (Gouda?)
1471)?)	to school at Gouda
1475– 1484(?)	school at Deventer, with interruption to attend choirschool at Utrecht
1484– 1486/7(?)	at 's-Hertogenbosch, ill at Gouda during this period
1487(?)	enters Steyn as novice
1488(?)	makes profession as Augustinian canon
1492, 25 Apr.	ordained priest
1493(?)	enters service of Hendrik van Bergen, bishop of Cambrai
1495	begins studies in theology at Paris (Collège de Montaigu)
1496– 1498	travels in Holland
1499	first trip to England, meeting Colet and More

1480(?) meeting with Rudolf Agricola

---

*For the writings, it is the dates of printing, not of composition, that are given. Titles are given here in Latin, cross-references to English titles are provided in the Index. Only first editions of individual works are included, and separate printings of such works as letters, prayers, colloquies, apologiae, etc., are not given here. By far the larger part of Erasmus' editions of the Church Fathers and of the Bible are omitted. For the first 25 years of his life, until his ordination, the dates are problematical, and largely deduced from his later writings.

1500	*Adagiorum Collectanea*	return to Paris, study of Greek and Bible
1501	Cicero, *De Officiis*	living in Louvain (1502–4)
1503	*Enchiridion (Lucubratiunculae)*	
1504	*Panegyricus*	discovers ms. of Valla at Abbey du Parc (Louvain)
1505	ed. of Valla's *Adnotationes Nov. Test.*	return to Paris
1506	*Epigrammata,* trans. with More of Lucian	second trip to England (1505–6) partial dispensation from vows; doctorate in theology (Turin)
1508	*Adagiorum Chiliades*	Italian travels (1506–9) 9 months in house of Aldus Manutius
		third visit to England: 1509 in home of Thomas More, lecturing at Cambridge 1511–4
1511	*Moriae Encomium*	
1512	*De Ratione Studii* *De Copia*	
1513	*Julius Exclusus* *Cato* *Parabolae*	
1514	*De Constructione Orationis*	Basel, 1514–6
1515	*Epistolae*	
1516	*Institutio Principis Christiani* *Paraclesis* *Querela pacis* ed. *Nov. Test.* ed. *Hieronymus*	supervision of printing of More's *Utopia*
1517		in Antwerp, Brussels, Louvain, 1517–21, with visits to Aachen, Cologne, Anderlecht, Bruges Papal dispensation (1517)
1518	*Colloquia* *Declamationes (Encomium Matrimonii & Encomium Medicinae)*	

1519	*Ratio Verae Theologiae Progymnasmata*	
	Commentaries on Psalms	
1520	*Antibarbari*	
1521	*De Conscribendis Epistolis De Contemptu Mundi*	move to Basel, 1521–9
1523	*De Immensa Dei Misericordia*	
1524	*De Libero Arbitrio Exomologesis*	controversy with Luther
1525	*Lingua*	
1526	*De Civilitate Institutio Christiani Matrimonis*	
1527	Commentary on Origen	
1528	*Ciceronianus Dialogus de Recta Latini Graecique Sermonis Pronuntiatione*	
1529	*Paraphrasis in Elegantias L. Vallae De Pueris Statim ac Liberaliter Instituendis Vidua Christiana*	move to Freiburg i. Breisgau, 1529–35
1530	*Consultatio de Bello Turcico*	
1531	*Apophthegmata*	
1533	*Explanatio Symboli Apostolorum Liber de Sarcienda Ecclesiae Concordia*	
1534	*Praeparatione ad Mortem*	
1535	*Ecclesiastes Precationes*	return to Basel, 1535 death of Fisher and More
1536	ed. Origen, *Opera De Puritate Tabernaculi*	death of Erasmus, 12 July 1536

Opera Omnia, Basel, 1540

For a much-expanded chronology of these years, see Germain Marc'hadour, *L'Univers de Thomas More – Chronologie critique de More, Erasme, et leur époque (1477–1536)*, Paris: Vrin, 1963, 586 pp.

Bibliography

The selective bibliography that follows includes only those titles that are not listed in Volume 1.

Acta Conventus Neo-Latini Torontonensis, ed. A. Dalzell, C. Fantazzi, and R.J. Schoeck (Binghamton, N.Y., 1991).

Adams, George Burton. *Civilization during the Middle Ages* (New York, 1894; rptd. 1922).

Adams, Robert P. *The Better Part of Valor* (Seattle, 1962).

Aland, Kurt. *Die 95 Thesen Martin Luthers and die Anfänge der Reformation* (Gütersloh, 1983).

Alberigo, J., et al. *Conciliorum Oecumenicorum Decreta* (Freiburg, 1962).

Allan P.S. and H. M. Allen, eds. *Letters of Richard Fox, 1496–1527* (Oxford, 1929).

Allen, P.S., Letters of, ed H.M. Allen (Oxford, 1939).

Althaus, Paul. *Forschungen zur Evangelischen Gebetsliteratur* (1972; rptd. Hildesheim, 1966).

Anderson, M.D. *Drama and Imagery in British Churches* (Cambridge, 1963).

Antiqui und Moderni: Taditionsbewusstsein und Fortschrittsbewusstein im späten Mittelalter (Berlin, 1974).

Ascham, Roger. *The Scholemaster* (1570), ed. R.J. Schoeck (Toronto, 1966).

Augustin, C. 'Le dialogue Érasme-Luther dans l'*Hyperaspistes* II', *Actes du Colloque International Érasme, Tours 1986,* ed. J. Chomarat, et al. (Geneva, 1990), 171–83.

Bachrach, A.G.H. 'In Conclusion', in *Sir Thomas Browne, M.D. and the Anatomy of Man* (Leiden, 1982).

Bainton, Roland H. *Yale and the Ministry* (New York, 1957).

——'Biblical Scholarship in the Renaissance and Reformation', rptd. from *Church History* x (1941) in Bainton, *Collected Papers in Church History,* Ser. One (Boston, 1962), 210–16.

Baldwin, Charles Sears. *Ancient Rhetoric and Poetic* (New York, 1924).

Bardenhewer, O. *Patrology* (Freiburg, 1908).

Baumann, E.D. *Medisch-historische Studiën over Des. Erasmus* (Arnhem, c. 1953).

Beatus Rhenanus, Briefwechsel des. ed. A. Horawitz and K. Hartfelder (Leipzig, 1886; rptd. 1966).

Bede, *The Ecclesiastical History of the English People,* ed. Bertram Colgrave and R.A.B. Mynors (Oxford, 1969).

Béné, Charles. 'Le *De Puritate Tabernaculi*: Testament spirituel d'Érasme', *Actes du Colloque International Érasme, Tours 1986,* ed. J. Chomarat, A. Godin and J.–C. Margolin (Geneva, 1990), 199–212.

Bentley, Jerry H. 'Erasmus, Jean LeClerc and the Principle of the Harder Reading',
    RenQ 31 (1978), 309–21.
——*Humanists and Holy Writ – New Testament Scholarship in the Renaissance*
    (Princeton, 1983).
Bierlaire, Franz. *La 'Familia' d'Érasme* (Paris, 1968).
Bietenholz, Peter G. *Der italienische Humanismus und die Blütezeit des Buchdrucks in
    Basel* (Basel, 1959).
——*Basle and France in the Sixteenth Century* (Geneva, 1970).
Binns, J.W. *Intellectual Culture in Elizabethan and Jacobean England* (Leeds, 1991).
Blau, Herbert, *The Audience* (Baltimore, 1990).
Bloch, Eileen. 'Erasmus and the Froben Press: The Making of an Editor', *Library
    Quarterly* 35 (1965), 109–20.
Blickle, Peter. *The Revolution of 1525*, trans. T.A. Brady, Jr. and H.C. Erik
    Midelfort (Baltimore, Md., 1981; rptd. 1985).
Blom, N. van der. 'Erasmus en Terminus', *Hermeneus* 28 (1957), 153–58.
——'Die letzten Worte des Erasmus', *Basler Zeitschrift für Geschichte und
    Alterumskunde* 65 (1965), no. 2, 195–214.
Bonaventure, St. *Commentary on the Sentences of Peter Lombard*, in *Opera* (Quarachi ed.,
    1882), vol. I.
Bonner, S.F. *Roman Declamation in the Late Republic and Early Empire* (Liverpool,
    1949).
Born, L.K. *The Education of a Christian Prince by Desiderius Erasmus* (New York, 1936).
Bouyer, Louis. *The Meaning of Sacred Scripture* (Notre Dame, Ind., 1958).
——'Erasmus in Relation to the Medieval Biblical Tradition', *The Cambridge
    History of the Bible*, vol. II, ed. G.W.H. Lampe (Cambridge, 1969).
Boyle, Marjorie O'R. *Erasmus on Language and Method in Theology* (Toronto, 1986).
Brachin, Pierre. '"Vox clamantis in deserto" ... reflexions sur le pacifisme
    d'Érasme', in *Colloquia Erasmiana Turonensia,* ed. J.-C. Margolin (Toronto,
    1972).
Bradshaw, Brendan and Eamon Duffy, eds. *Humanism, Reform and the Reformation –
    The Career of Bishop John Fisher* (Cambridge 1989).
Brecht, Martin. *Martin Luther – Shaping and Defining the Reformation, 1521–1532*
    (Minneapolis, 1990).
Brown, Andrew. 'The date of Erasmus' Latin translations of the New Testament',
    Transactions of the Cambridge Bibliographical Society 8.4 (1984–5).
Brosse, O., J. LeCler, H. Hostein and Ch. Lefevre, eds. *Latran V et Trente* – vol. 10
    of *L'Histoire des conciles Oecuméniques* (Paris, 1975).
Bruce, A.K. *Erasmus and Holbein* (London, 1936).
Buck, August, ed. *Erasmus und Europa – Wolfenbütteler Abhandlungen zur
    Renaissanceforschung* (Wiesbaden, 1988).
Bullock, Alan. *The Humanist Tradition in the West* (New York, 1985).
Burke, Peter. 'The Spread of Italian Humanism', in *The Impact of Humanism on
    Western Europe,* ed. A. Goodman and Angus Mackay (London, 1990), 1–22.
Burrow, J.A. *Medieval Writers and Their Work* (Oxford, 1982).
Bywater, Ingram. *The Erasmian Pronunciation of Greek and Its Precursors* (Oxford,
    1908).
Callewaert, H. *Physiologie de l'écriture cursive* (Bruges, 1937).
Camporeale, S. *Lorenzo Valla – Umanesimo e teologia* (Florence, 1972).
Cantimori, D. 'Note su Erasmo e la vita morale e religiosa italiana nel secolo XVI',
    in *Gedenkschrift* (1936), 98–112.

Carrington, Laurel. 'Erasmus' *Lingua*: TheDouble-Edged Tongue', *ERSYB* 9 (1989), 106–18.

Chambers, R.W. *Thomas More* (London, 1935).

Chrisman, Miriam U. *Strasbourg and the Reform: A Study in the Process of Change* (New Haven, Conn., 1967).

——'Le métier et la main: Matthias Schürer, humaniste-imprimeur', in *Grandes Figures de l'humanisme alsacien* (Strasbourg, 1978), 159–72.

——*Lay Culture, Learned Culture: Books and Social Change in Strasbourg, 1480–1599* (New Haven, Conn., 1982).

Clough, Cecil H. 'The Cult of Antiquity: Letters and Letter Collections', in *Cultural Aspects of the Italian Renaissance: Essays in Honour of Paul Oskar Kristeller,* ed. C.H. Clough (Manchester, 1976).

——'Erasmus and the Pursuit of English Royal Patronage in 1517 and 1518', *ERSYB* 1 (1981), 126–40.

Collingwood, R.G. *Principles of Art* (Oxford, 1938).

Collinson, Patrick. 'The Late Medieval Church and the Reformation (1400–1600)', in *The Oxford Illustrated History of Christianity,* ed. John McManners (Oxford, 1990), 233–66.

Colloquia Erasmiana Turonensia, 2 vols., ed. J.-C. Margolin (Paris, 1972).

Coppens, J., ed. *Scrinium Erasmianum,* 2 vols. (Leiden, 1969).

Corsten, Severin. 'Universities and early printing', in *Bibliography and the Study of 15th-century Civilisation* – British Library Occasional Papers 5, ed. Lotte Hellinga and John Goldfinch (London, 1987).

Croke, Richard. *Introductiones in rudimenta Graeca* (Köln, 1520).

——*Orationes Ricardi Croci Duae* (Paris, 1520).

Cuming, G.J. and Derek Baker, eds. *Councils and Assemblies* (Cambridge, 1971).

Cytowska, Maria. 'Erasmian Studies in Poland 1969–70: the Erasmus Quincentenary', *Erasmus in English* 2 (1971), 13–14.

D'Amico, John F. *Theory and Practice in Renaissance Textual Criticism* (Berkeley/Los Angeles, 1988).

Danielou, Jean. *The Bible and the Liturgy* (Notre Dame, Ind., 1956).

Dean, Leonard F. '*The Praise of Folly* and Its Background', in *Twentieth-Century Interpretations of the Praise of Folly,* ed. Kathleen Williams (Englewood Cliffs, N.J., 1969), 40–60.

De Jonge, H.J. 'Erasmus und die Glossa ordinaria zum Neuen Testament', *Nederlands archief voor kerkgeschiedenis,* n.s. 56 (1975), 51–77.

——'Novum testamentum a nobis versum. De essentie van Erasmus' uitgave van het Nieuwe Testament', *Lampas* 15 (1982), 231–48.

——'Wenn ist Erasmus' Übersetzung des Neuen Testament Entstanden?' in *Erasmus of Rotterdam,* ed. Sperna Weiland and Frijhoff (Rotterdam, 1988), 151–57.

De Jongh, H. *L'ancienne faculté de théologie de Louvain au premier siècle de son existence, 1432–1540* (Louvain, 1911).

de Lubac, Henri. *Exégèse Médiévale: Les quatre sens de l'écriture,* 3 vols. (Paris, 1959).

Denis, V. *Catholic University of Louvain, 1425–1958* (Louvain, 1958).

De Smet, A. 'Erasme et la cartographie' in *Scrinium Erasmianum,* I, 277–92.

De Vocht, H. *Texts and Studies about Louvain Humanists of the first Half of the XVIth Century* (*HumLov,* 4 – Louvain, 1934).

——*History of the Foundation and the Rise of the Collegium Trilingue Lovaniense, 1517–1550* (*HumLov,* 10–13; Louvain, 1951–5).

Dillinger, John, ed. *Martin Luther, Selections* (New York, 1961).

Douglas, A.E. 'Erasmus as Satirist', in *Erasmus,* ed. T.A. Dorey (London, 1970).

Dresden, Sem. *Humanism in the Renaissance* (London, 1968).

Durandus, Gulielmus. *Rationale Divinorum Officiorum* (Paris, 1475) – the first book translated into English as *The Symbolism of Churches and Church Ornaments* by J.M. Neale and B. Webb (London, 1906).

Edward, William A. *The Suasoriae of the Elder Seneca* (Cambridge, 1927).

Ehrenberg, R. *Das Zeitalter der Fugger, Geldkapital und Creditverkehr im 16. Jahrhundert* (Jena, 1896).

Eliot, T.S. *Essays Ancient and Modern* (London, 1936).

Emery, Kent, Jr. *Renaissance Dialectic and Renaissance Piety* (Nieuwkoop, 1987).

Epistolae Obscurorum Virorum, ed. F.G. Stokes (New York, 1909), with introd. by Hajo Holborn (New York, 1964).

Febvre, Joel. *Les fols et la folie* (Paris, 1968).

Febvre, Lucien. Preface to the French translation of J. Huizinga, *Erasme* (Paris, 1955).

Flitner, A. *Erasmus im Urteil seiner Nachwelt: Das literarische Erasmus-bild von Beatus Rhenanus bis zu Jean Le Clerc* (Tübingen, 1952).

Ganz, P. *The Paintings of Hans Holbein* (London, 1950).

Gavin, J. Austin and T.M.Walsh. '*The Praise of Folly* in Context: The commentary of Girardus Listrius', *RenQ* xxiv (1971), 193 ff.

Geanakoplos, D.J. *Greek Scholars in Venice* (Cambridge, Mass., 1962).

Gebhardt, *Die Gravamina der deutschen Nation gegen den römischen Hof* (Breslau, 1895).

Gedenkschrift zum 400. todestage des Erasmus von Rotterdam (Basel, 1936).

Godin, André. *Spiritualité franciscaine en Flandre au XVIème siècle: l'Homéliaire de Jean Vitrier* (Geneva, 1971).

——*Erasme lecteur d'Origène* (Geneva, 1982).

Grafton, Anthony. *Joseph Scaliger: A Study in the History of Classical Scholarship,* I (Oxford, 1983).

Grane, Leif. *Contra Gabrielem – Luthers Auseinandersetzung mit Gabriel Biel in der Disputation Contra Scholasticam Theologiam 1517* (Gylendal, 1962).

Gregorovius, F. *Geschichte der Stadt Rom im Mittelalter,* ed. W. Kamp, 3 vols. (Basel, 1953–7).

Groote, Gerard. *Tractaat Contra Turrim Traiectensem Teruggevonden,* ed. R.R. Post (The Hague, 1966).

Guggisberg, Hans R. *Basel in the Sixteenth Century* (St. Louis, 1982).

Halkin, L.-E. *Érasme. Sa pensée et son comportement* (London, 1988).

Headley, John M. 'Gattinara, Erasmus, and the imperial configuration of humanism', *ARG* 71 (1980), 64–98.

Heckscher, William S. 'Reflections on Seeing Holbein's Portrait of Erasmus at Longford Castle', in *Essays in the History of Art Presented to Rudolf Wittkower* (London, 1967), 132 ff.

Hellinga, Lotte and John Goldfinch, eds. *Bibliography and the Study of 15th-Century Civilisation* – British Library Occasional Papers 5 (London, 1987).

Henderson, Judith Rice. 'Erasmus and the Art of Letter-Writing' in *Renaissance Eloquence,* ed. J.J. Murphy (1983), 331–55.

Hermanns, Marie. *Erasmus von Rotterdam und seine ärztliche Freunde* (Würzburg, 1937).

Hilgart, Earle. 'Johann Froben and the Basel University Scholars, 1513–1523', *Library Q* 41 (1971), 141–169.

Hiper, F. 'Die Vorläufer des N. Copernicus, inbesondere C. Calcagnini', *Mitteilungen des Copernicus-Vereins zu Thurn* 4 (1882), 51–80.

Holborn, Hajo. *On the Eve of the Reformation* (New York, 1964).

Hugenholtz, F.W.N. 'The Fame of a Masterwork', in *Johan Huizinga 1872–1972* (1973), 91–103.

Huizinga, Johan, 1872–1972, ed. W.R.H. Koops, E.H. Kossman and Gees van der Plaat (The Hague, 1973).

Hutten, Ulrich von. *Opera poetica* (Frankfort, 1538).

——*Opera Hutteni,* ed. E. Böcking (Leipzig, 1859–70).

Iserloh, Erwin, et al. *Wandlungen des Lutherbildes* (Würzburg, 1966).

Jacob, E.F. *Studies in the Conciliar Epoch* (Manchester, 1943).

Janson, Tore. *Latin Prose Prefaces – Studies in Literary Conventions* (Stockholm, 1964).

Jarrott, Catherine A.L. 'Erasmus' Biblical Humanism', *StRen* 17 (1970), 119–52.

Jenny, B.R. 'Erasmus' Rückkehr nach Basel, Lebensende, Grab und Testament', in *Erasmus von Rotterdam, Vorkämpfer für Frieden und Toleranz.* Ausstellung zum 450. Todestag des Erasmus von Rotterdam veranstaltet vom Historischen Museum Basel (Basel, 1986), 63–5.

Jeremias, A., ed. *Johann von Staupitz, Luthers Vater und Schüler* (Berlin, 1926).

Johnson, Paul. *Intellectuals* (London, 1988).

Jones, Rufus M. *Spiritual Reformers in the 16th and 17th Centuries* (Boston, 1914; rptd. 1959).

Kalkoff, P. *Die Anfänge der Gegenreformation in den Niederlanden,* 2 vols. (Halle, 1903).

Kendall, Calvin B. 'Bede's *Historia ecclesiastica',* in *Medieval Eloquence,* ed. J.J. Murphy (Berkeley/Los Angeles, 1978), 145–72.

Kennedy, George. *Classical Rhetoric and Its Christian and Secular Tradition from Ancient to Modern Times* (Chapel Hill, N.C., 1980).

Kerrigan, William and Gordon Braden. *The Idea of the Renaissance* (Baltimore, Md., 1989).

Kisch, Guido. *Bonifacius Amerbach* (Basel, 1962).

——'Vadians Valla-Ausgaben', in *Aus Vadians Freundes- und Schülerkreis in Wien,* ed. Conradin Bonorand (St. Gallen, 1965).

——*Erasmus' Stellung zu Juden und Judentum* (Tübingen, 1969).

——*Claudius Cantiuncula: Ein Basler Jurist und Humanist des 16. Jahrhunderts* (Basel, 1970).

Kittelson, J.M. *Wolfgang Capito: From Humanist to Reformer* (Leiden, 1975).

Klacko, J. *Rome and the Renaissance,* trans. J. Dennie (New York, 1903).

Klawitter, R.J. *The Polemics of Erasmus of Rotterdam and Ulrich von Hutten* (Notre Dame, Ind., 1977).

Klein, Robert. 'Le thème du fou et l'ironie humaniste', *Archivio de Filosofia,* no. 3 (Padua, 1963), 11–25, rptd. in *La Forme et l'intelligible* (Paris, 1970), 433–50.

Kluge, O. 'Die Neulateinische Kunstprosa', *Glotta* xiii (1964), 67–8.

Koehler, Walter, ed. *Dokumente zum Ablass Streit von 1517,* 2d ed. (Tübingen, 1924).

Kohls, E.-W. 'Martin Bucer: Érasmien et Martien', in *Strasbourg au coeur religieux du XVIe siècle* (Strasbourg, 1977), 167–83.

——'The Principal Theological Thoughts in the *Enchiridion Militis Christiani',* in *Essays on the Works of Erasmus,* ed. R.L. DeMolen (New Haven, Conn., 1978).

——'La position théologique d'Erasme et la tradition dans le *De Libero Arbitrio',* in *Colloq. Erasm.,* 82–5.

Könneker, Barbara. *Wesen und Wandlung der Narrenidee im Zeitalter des Humanismus: Brant-Murner-Erasmus* (Wiesbaden, 1966).

Krivatsy, Peter. 'Erasmus' Medical Milieu', *Bulletin of the History of Medicine* xlvii (1973), 113–54.

Kuiper, G.C. '"Oleum in Auricula ferre" (Adagium 463)', *Humanistica Lovaniensia* xxxix (1990).

Kukenheim, Louis. *Contributions à l'histoire de la grammaire grecque, latine et hébraïque à l'epoque de la Renaissance* (Leiden, 1951).

Kytzler, Bernhard, ed. *Roma Aeterna – Lateinische und Griechische Romdichtung von der Antike bis in die Gegenwart* (Zürich, 1972).

Lebel, Maurice, ed. *Josse Bade, dit Badius (1462–1535)* (Louvain, 1988).

Lederer, J. *Der Dispensbegriff des kanon. Rechtes* (Mainz, 1957).

Lytle, Guy F., Jr., ed. *Reform and Authority in the Medieval and Reformation Church* (Washington, D.C., 1981).

McConica, J.K. 'The Riddle of "Terminus"', in *Erasmus in English* 2 (1971), 2.

——'Erasmus and the *Julius*: A Humanist Reflects on the Church', in *The Pursuit of Holiness in Late Medieval and Renaissance Religion*, ed. C. Trinkaus with H.O. Oberman (Leiden, 1974), 444–71.

——*Erasmus* (Oxford, 1991).

McDonough, T.M.. *The Law and the Gospel in Luther* (Oxford, 1963).

McGrath, Alister E. *Reformation Thought* (Oxford, 1988).

——*The Intellectual Origins of the European Reformation* (Oxford, 1987).

McSorley, Harry. *Luther, Right or Wrong* (New York, 1968).

Maddison, F., M. Pelling and C. Webster, eds. *Linacre Studies: Essays on the Life and Work of Thomas Linacre* (Oxford, 1977).

Maguire, John B. 'Erasmus' Biographical Masterpiece: *Hieronymi Stridonensis Vita*', *RenQ* xxvi (1973), 265–73.

Manschreck, C.L. *Melanchthon the Quiet Reformer* (New York-Nashville, 1958).

Margolin, J.-C. *Érasme par lui-même* (Paris, 1965).

Markish, Shimon. *Erasmus and the Jews*, trans. by A. Olcott (Chicago, 1986).

Martz, Louis L. *Thomas More* (New Haven, Conn., 1990).

Massaut, J.-P. *Critique et Tradition à la Veille de la Réforme en France* (Paris, 1974).

Maurer, Wilhelm. 'Melanchthons Anteil am Streit zwischen Luther und Erasmus', *ARG* 49 (1959), 89–114; rptd. in Maurer, *Melanchthon-Studien* (Gütersloh, 1964), 137–62.

Mayer, Hermann. *Die Matrikeln der Universität Freiburg-im-Breisgau, 1460–1656*. 2 vols (Freiburg, 1907–10).

Melanchthon on Christian Doctrine – Loci Communes 1555, ed. C.L. Manschreck (1965; rptd. Grand Rapids, Mich., 1982).

Mesnard, Pierre. *L'Essor de la Philosophie politique au XVIe siècle* (Paris, 1936; 2d ed., 1952).

——*Érasme: La philosophie chrétienne* (Paris, 1970).

Metzger, Bruce. *The Text of the New Testament*, 2d ed. (New York, 1968).

Meylan, M. 'Érasme et Pellican', in *Colloq. Érasm.* (1968), 244–54.

Miller, Clarence H., ed. *De Tristia* – vol. 14 in The Yale Edition of the Complete Works of St Thomas More (New Haven, Conn., 1976).

Miller, Clarence H. 'The Logic and Rhetoric of Proverbs in Erasmus' *Praise of Folly*', in *Essays on the Works of Erasmus*, ed. R.L. DeMolen (1978), 83–98.

Moss, Ann. 'Printed Commonplace Books in the Renaissance' in *Acta Neo-Latini Torontonensis* (1991), 509–18.

Oberman, Heiko O. *The Roots of Anti-Semitism in the Age of Renaissance and Reformation,* trans. by J.I. Porter (Philadelphia, 1984).

——*Forerunners of the Reformation* (Philadelphia, 1966; rptd. 1981).

Olney, James. *Metaphors of Self* (Princeton, 1972).

Owst, G.R. *Literature and Pulpit in Medieval England,* 2d ed. (Oxford, 1961).

Panofsky, Erwin. *Albrecht Dürer* (Princeton, 1943).

Parry, J.H. *Establishment of European Hegemony, 1415–1715,* 3rd ed. (New York, 1966; first publ. as *Europe and a Wider World,* London, 1953).

Partner, Peter. *The Pope's Men: The Papal Civil Service in the Renaissance* (Oxford, 1991).

Pelikan, Jarislav. *The Melody of Theology* (Cambridge, Mass., 1988).

Peteghem, P.P.J.L. van. 'Erasmus' Last Will', in *Erasmus of Rotterdam,* ed. Weiland and Frijhoff (1988), 88–97.

Phillips, M.M. 'The Mystery of the Metsys Portrait', *Erasmus in English* 7 (1975), 18–21.

——'Erasmus on the Tongue', *ERSYB* 1 (1981), 113–25.

Picotti, G.B. *La politica italiana sotto il pontificato di Giulio II* (Pisa, 1949).

Pijper, F. *Erasmus en de Nederlandsche Reformatie* (Leiden, 1907).

Poel, Marc van der. *De Declamatio bij de Humanisten* (Nieuwkoop, 1987).

Porter, H.D. and D.F.S Thomson, *Erasmus at Cambridge* (Toronto, 1963).

Quasten, Johannes. *Patrology,* vol. II (Utrecht, 1953); vol. III (Utrecht, 1960).

Rabil, Albert, Jr. *Erasmus and the New Testament* (San Antonio, Texas, 1972).

Raitt, J., et al., eds. *Christian Spirituality: High Middle Ages and Reformation* (London, 1988).

Reedijk, Cornelis. 'Das Lebensende des Erasmus', *Basler Zeitschrift für Geschichte und Altertumskunde* VII (1958), 23–66.

Reeve, Anne, ed. *Erasmus' Annotations on the Gospels,* with introd. by M.A. Screech (London, 1986).

Reilly, E. *The General Norms of Dispensation* (Washington, D.C., 1939).

Reinhardt, Hans. 'Erasmus und Holbein', *Basler Zeitschrift für Geschichte und Altertumskunde* 81 (1981), 41–70.

Renaudet, A. *Le Concile Gallican de Pise-Milan* (Paris, 1922).

Reuchlin, Jakob. *Clarorum virorum epistolae, latinae, graecae, et hebraicae* (Tübingen, 1514).

Reynolds, L.D. *The Medieval Tradition of Seneca's Letters* (Oxford, 1965).

——and N.G. Wilson. *Scribes and Scholars,* 2nd ed. (Oxford, 1974).

Rice, Eugene F., Jr. *Saint Jerome in the Renaissance* (Baltimore, 1985).

Roth, Carl. 'Das Legatum Erasmianum', in *Gedenkschrift* (1936), 282–98.

Ruderman, David B. 'The Italian Renaissance and Jewish Thought', in *Renaissance Humanism,* ed. A. Rabil (1988), I, 382–433.

Rüegg, Walter. *Die beiden Blütezeiten des Basler Humanismus – Eine Gedenkschrift zur Fünfjahrhundertfeier der Basler Universität* (Basel, 1960).

Rüsch, Ernst Gerhard. 'Erasmus in St. Gallen', in *Vom Heiligen in der Welt* (Biel, 1959).

Rummel, Erika. 'A Reader's Guide to Erasmus' Controversies', *Erasmus in English* 12 (1983), 16–19.

——*Erasmus' Annotations on the New Testament* (Toronto, 1986).

——*Erasmus and His Catholic Critics, I, 1515–1522* (Nieuwkoop, 1989).

——*Erasmus and His Catholic Critics, II, 1523–1536* (Nieuwkoop, 1989).

——'Erasmus' Conflict with Latomus: Round Two', *ARG* 80 (1989), 5–23.

Ryan, Lawrence V. 'Art and Artifice in Erasmus' *Convivium Profanum'*, *RenQ* xxxi (1978), 1–16.

Santayana, George. *Persons and Places* (New York, 1944).

Schäffer, Peter. 'Letters of Obscure Men', in *The Renaissance and Reformation in Germany*, ed. Gerhart Hoffmeister (New York, 1977), 129–140.

Schenk, Wilhelm. 'Erasmus and Melanchthon', *The Heythrop Journal* VIII (1967), 249–59.

Schmolderen, L. 'Quentin Metsys médailleur d'Erasme', in *Scrinium Erasm.* II, 513–25.

Schoeck, R.J. 'The Intellectual Milieu of More's *Utopia*', *Moreana* I (1963), 40–6.

——'The Affair of Richard Hunne', in *Proceedings of the Third International Congress of Medieval Canon Law, Strasbourg 1968*, ed. S. Kuttner (Rome, 1971), 237–54.

——'More, Sallust and Fortune', *Moreana* xvii (June, 1980), 107–10.

——'"In loco intertexantur": Erasmus as Master of Intertextuality', in *Intertextuality*, ed. H.F. Plett (Berlin, 1991), 181–91.

——and John Meagher. 'On Erasmus' "The Godly Feast"', in *Erasmus in English* 3 (1971), 10–12.

Schottenloher, Karl. *Die Widmungsrede im Buch des 16. Jahrhunderts* – Reformationsgeschichtliche Studien und Texte 76–7 (Münster, 1953).

Schroeder, H.J. *Disciplinary Decrees of the General Councils*, Text, Translation and Commentary (St. Louis, 1937).

Schulte Herbrüggen, Hubertus. 'Erasmus und England: Erasmus und Morus', *Erasmus und Europa*, ed. August Buck – Wolfenbütteler Abhandlungen zur Renaissanceforschung, Band 7 (Wiesbaden, 1988).

Schulze, M. *Calvins Jenseits-Christentum im Seinem Verhältnisse zu den religiösen Schriften des Erasmus* (Göritz, 1902).

Screech, M.A., ed. *Le tiers livre* (Geneva, 1964).

——'Folie érasmienne et folie rabelaisienne – Comment Rabelais a exploité les travaux d'Érasme', *Colloquia Erasmiana Turonensia* (1972), I, 441–52, 453–61.

——'Rabelais, Erasmus, Gilbertus Cognatus and Boniface Amerbach...' *Études Rabelaisiennes* 14 (1977), 43–6.

Scrinium Erasmianum. Actes du colloque international, ed. J. Coppens, 2 vols. (Leiden, 1969).

Shaw, S. Diane. 'A Study of the Collaboration between Erasmus of Rotterdam and His Printer Johann Froben at Basel during the Years 1514 to 1527', *ERSYB* 6 (1986), 31–124.

Sieber, *Das Testament von Erasmus* (Basel, 1889).

Silver, Larry. *The Paintings of Quinten Massys* (Montclair, N.J., 1984).

Simpson, Percy. *Proof-reading in the sixteenth, seventeenth and eighteenth centuries* (Oxford, 1935; rptd. 1970).

Spicq, C. *Esquisse d'une histoire de l'exégèse Latine au Moyen Âge* (Paris, 1944).

Steiner, George. *On Difficulty and Other Essays* (New York, 1978).

Stern, Leo, et al. *Philipp Melanchthon, Humanist, Reformer, Praeceptor Germaniae* (Berlin, 1960).

Strauss, Gerald. *Nuremberg in the Sixteenth Century* (New York, 1966).

Strieder, J. *Jakob Fugger der Reich* (Leipzig, 1926).

Suchet, J.-M. 'Jean Carondelet, grand chancelier de Flandre et de Bourgogne, 1428–1501 [sic]', *Mémoires de l'Academie des sciences, belles-lettres et arts de Besançon* (1898), 280–99.

Surtz, E., S.J. *The Works and Days of John Fisher, 1469–1535* (Cambridge, Mass., 1967).

Tentler, Thomas. 'Forgiveness and Consolation in the Religious Thought of Erasmus', *StRen* 12 (1965), 22.

Tilley, A. 'Greek Studies in England in the early 16th century', *EHR* 53 (1938), 228.

Thompson, Craig R., ed. *Translations of Lucian* – vol. 3 Part I in *The Complete Works of St Thomas More* (New Haven, Conn., 1974).

Thomson, D.F.S. 'Erasmus and Textual Scholarship in the Light of Sixteenth-Century Practice', in *Erasmus of Rotterdam,* ed. Weiland and Frijhoff (1988), 158–71.

Tierney, Brian. *Foundations of Conciliar Theory* (Cambridge, 1955).

Tracy, James D. 'Erasmus becomes a German', *RenQ* 21 (1968), 281–88.

——'Ad Fontes: The Humanist Understanding of Scripture as Nourishment for the Soul', in *Christian Spirituality: High Middle Ages and Reformation*, ed. J. Raitt et al. (London, 1988), 252 ff.

Trapman, J. 'Erasmus' *Precationes',* in *Acta Conventus Neo-Latini Torontonensis* (1991), 769–79.

Trapp, J.B. 'Notes on Manuscripts Written by Pieter Mieghen', *The Book Collector* 24 (1975), 80–96.

——'A Postscript to Matsys', *Burlington Magazine* 121 (1979), 435–37.

——et al. 'Quentin Matsys, Erasmus, Pieter Gillis, and Thomas More', *Burlington Magazine* 120 (1978), 716–25.

——*Essays on the Renaissance and the Classical Tradition* (London, 1990).

Treu, Erwin. *Die Bildnisse des Erasmus von Rotterdam* (Basel, 1959).

Trillitzsch, W. 'Erasmus und Seneca', *Philologus* 109 (1965), 270–92.

Trinkaus, Charles and H.O. Oberman, eds. *The Pursuit of Holiness in Late Medieval and Renaissance Religion* (Leiden, 1974).

Troeltsch, E. *Protestantism and Progress* (London, 1912).

——*The Social Teaching of the Christian Churches*, 2 vols (London, 1931).

Valéry, Paul. *Dialogues.* Bollingen Series XLV.4 (New York, 1956).

——*Monsieur Teste.* Bollingen Series XLV. 6 (New York, 1973).

Vida, Istvan. 'Erasmus in Eastern Europe Today', *Erasmus in English* 2 (1971), 14.

Wackernagel, R. *Geschichte der Stadt Basel* (1924), vol. III.

Walter, Robert. 'Une amitié humaniste: Erasme et Beatus Rhenanus', *Annuaire de la Socieété des Amis de la Bibliothéque Humaniste de Sélestat* 36 (1986), 13–23.

Waszink, J.H. 'Erasmus and His Influence on Anglo-Dutch Philology', in *The Anglo-Dutch Contribution to the Civilization of Early Modern Society. An Anglo-Netherlands Symposium 1974* (Oxford, 1976), 60–72.

Wimpheling, Jakob. *De vita et miraculis Joannis Gerson. Defensio wymphellingii...* (Strasburg, 1506?).

Wind, Edgar. '"Aenigma Termini": The Emblem of Erasmus', *JWCI* I (1937–8), 66–9.

Index of Subjects, Places and Books

Index of Names of Persons

The entry for Erasmus contains personal and biographical details only. His writings are entered in the Subject Index under their Latin titles. Only the more substantive references in footnotes are included.

Schürer, Matthias 30, 86, 116, 151, 153, 204
Scipio 151
Scott, Sir Walter 240
Scotus, Duns 302
Screech, M. A. 96, 100, 105, 186–7, 203, 357
Secundus, Johannes 63
Seidensticker 153
Semler, Johann 365
Seneca the Elder 101
Seneca, Lucius Annaeus 114, 152, 157–8, 247, 254, 329
Sepulveda, Juan Gines de 183, 258
Servatius *see* Rogers, Servatius
Seyssel, Claude de 166
Shakespeare, William 81–2, 240, 365, 372
Sichen (van der Rivieren), Eustachius 17
Simon of Aschaffenburg 149
Singer, Isaac Bashevis 306
Skelton, John 102
Šlechta, Jan 274
Smalley, Beryl 109, 175, 177, 202
Smith, Preserved 77, 128, 149, 226, 247, 270, 344
Snoy, Reyner 165
Socrates 78, 114, 239, 242, 245n, 356
Sophocles 79
Sowards, J. Kelly 88–9, 91
Spalatin, Georg 225, 234n, 269
Spitz, Lewis W. 298
Standish, Henry 187, 219–20
Standonck, Jan 18, 52
Staupitz, Johann von 268, 280n
Steiner, George 256
Sterne, Lawrence 240
Stewart, Alexander 68, 70, 292
Storck, Johann 153
Strauss, Gerald 273
Sturm, Johannes 150, 153, 324, 365
Suetonius 101, 201, 204, 342
Surgant, Johann Ulrich 321
Surtz, Edward 170
Sylvester, Richard S. 100
Symons, Jan 336n
Synesius 98
Szydłowiecki, Krzstof 311, 317n

Terence 6, 79
Tertullian 302
Tetzel, Johann 217, 267n
Theodore of Mopsuestia 22
Theophylactus 302
Thomas à Kempis 1, 46, 144, 178, 217, 354, 360n, 369, 375

Imitation of Christ ix, 1, 30, 110, 144, 241, 259n, 264, 297n
Thomas Aquinas, St 6, 28, 45, 188, 249, 300, 302
Thompson, Craig R. 237–42, 287, 290–1, 331, 362, 365
Thomson, D. F. S. 329
Thucydides 79
Tournoy, Gilbert 221, 225
Tracy, James D. 3, 5, 21–2, 28, 48, 63, 131, 167, 205, 225, 303, 353–4
Trapp, J. B. 55, 61n, 117
Trithemius of Sponheim, Abbot 154
Tudor, Lady Margaret 53
Tunstall, Cuthbert, Bishop 55, 57, 59, 61n, 209, 249, 339, 384
Tyndale, William 30, 122, 219, 221, 230, 365

Urswick, Christopher 55, 58–9, 197, 257
Utenheim, Christoph von, Bishop 322, 325, 332
Utenhove, Charles 321

Vadianus, Joachim 324–6
Valéry, Paul 245n, 364
Valla, Lorenzo x, 6, 158, 175, 179, 240–1, 266, 302, 357
  Adnotationes x, 44–6, 48, 51, 54, 113, 175, 178–9, 181; *Elegantiae* 46, 180, 316
Varro 6
Veere *see* Adolph van Borssele, Anna van Borssele
Vesalius 17
Villa Dei, Alexander de 18
Virgil 98
Virgil, Polydore 55
Vitrier, Jean x, 29, 39, 180, 274, 358
Vitrier, Pierre (Petrus Viterius) 385
Vives, Juan Luis 16–17, 221, 304, 342
Vlatten, Johann von 14
Voecht, Jacob de 3, 7
Volz, Paul, Abbot 28, 33, 87, 119, 202, 385

Walter, Robert 152, 253–4
Warburg, Aby 364
Warham, William, Archbishop 54, 67, 88–9, 120, 146, 158, 197, 257, 384
Waszink, J. H. 80
Watson, John 122
Webster, John 240
Weiss, Roberto 111
Wentford, Roger 110